SOFTWARE STATE-OF-THE-ART:
SELECTED PAPERS

SOFTWARE STATE-OF-THE-ART:
SELECTED PAPERS

edited by
Tom DeMarco
and Timothy Lister

DH

DORSET HOUSE PUBLISHING
353 West 12th Street
New York, NY 10014

Library of Congress Cataloging-in-Publication Data

Software state-of-the-art : selected papers / edited by Tom DeMarco
   and Timothy Lister.
     p.cm.
     Includes bibliographical references and index.
     ISBN 0-932633-14-5 : $45.00
     1. Computer software.   I. DeMarco, Tom.   II. Lister, Timothy R.
QA76.756.S64   1990
005.3--dc20   89-83372
                                                            CIP

For the cover, we gratefully acknowledge John Canemaker, John Canemaker Productions, Inc., for reproduction of "Wheels and Cogs" by Winsor McCay (October 3, 1920; collection of Ray Winsor Moniz). From *Winsor McCay: His Life and Art,* by John Canemaker (New York: Abbeville Press, 1987), pp. 168-69.

Additional cover design: Jeff Faville, Faville Graphics

Copyright © 1990 by Tom DeMarco and Timothy Lister. Published by Dorset House Publishing Co., Inc., 353 West 12th Street, New York, NY 10014.

Distributed in the United Kingdom, Ireland, Europe, and Africa by John Wiley & Sons Ltd., Chichester, Sussex, England

Printed in the United States of America

Library of Congress Catalog Number 89-83372
ISBN: 0-932633-14-5   10 9 8 7 6 5 4 3 2

Acknowledgments

We gratefully acknowledge the following organizations for their permission to reprint the articles in this volume:

1. "Overstructured Management of Software Engineering," by Gerald M. Weinberg, originally appeared as course notes in *Problem Solving Leadership Workshop.* It is reprinted from *Proceedings of the Sixth International Conference on Software Engineering,* September 13-16, 1982, Tokyo, Japan, pp. 2-8. Copyright © 1982 by Gerald M. Weinberg. Reprinted by permission.

2. "No Silver Bullet: Essence and Accidents of Software Engineering," by Frederick P. Brooks, Jr., originally appeared in *Information Processing '86* (North Holland: Elsevier Science Publishers B.V.). It is reprinted from *Computer,* Vol. 20, No. 4 (April 1987), pp. 10-19. Copyright © 1986 by IFIP. Reprinted by permission.

3. "Understanding and Controlling Software Costs," by Barry W. Boehm and Philip N. Papaccio. Copyright © 1988 by the Institute of Electrical and Electronics Engineers, Inc. Reprinted, with permission, from *IEEE Transactions on Software Engineering,* Vol. 4, No. 10 (October 1988), pp. 1462-77.

4. "Characterizing the Software Process: A Maturity Framework," by Watts S. Humphrey. Copyright © 1988 by the Institute of Electrical and Electronics Engineers, Inc. Reprinted, with permis-

sion, from *IEEE Software,* Vol. 5, No. 2 (March 1988), pp. 73-79.

5. "The Computer Software Industry in Japan," by Denji Tajima and Tomoo Matsubara. Copyright © 1981 by the Institute of Electrical and Electronics Engineers, Inc. Reprinted, with permission, from *Computer,* Vol. 14, No. 5 (May 1981), pp. 89-96.

6. "Inside the Japanese Software Industry," by Denji Tajima and Tomoo Matsubara. Copyright © 1984 by the Institute of Electrical and Electronics Engineers, Inc. Reprinted, with permission, from *Computer,* Vol. 17, No. 3 (March 1984), pp. 34-43.

7. "The Information Archipelago—Maps and Bridges," by James L. McKenney and F. Warren McFarlan. Reprinted by permission of *Harvard Business Review,* Vol. 60, No. 5 (September-October 1982), pp. 109-19. Copyright © 1982 by the President and Fellows of Harvard College; all rights reserved.

8. "The Dynamics of Software Project Staffing: A System Dynamics Based Simulation Approach," by Tarek K. Abdel-Hamid. Copyright © 1989 by the Institute of Electrical and Electronics Engineers, Inc. Reprinted, with permission, from *IEEE Transactions on Soft-*

ware Engineering, Vol. 15, No. 2 (February 1989), pp. 109-19.

9. "Reflections on Software Research," by Dennis M. Ritchie. Copyright © 1984 by the Association for Computing Machinery, Inc. Reprinted, with permission, from *Communications of the ACM,* Vol. 27, No. 8 (August 1984), pp. 758-60.

10. "A Meta-Model for Software Development Resource Expenditures," by John W. Bailey and Victor R. Basili. Copyright © 1981 by the Institute of Electrical and Electronics Engineers, Inc. Reprinted, with permission, from *Proceedings of the Fifth International Conference on Software Engineering,* March 9-12, 1981, San Diego, Calif., pp. 107-16.

11. "Function Point Analysis: Difficulties and Improvements," by Charles R. Symons. Copyright © 1988 by the Institute of Electrical and Electronics Engineers, Inc. Reprinted, with permission, from *IEEE Transactions on Software Engineering,* Vol. 14, No. 1 (January 1988), pp. 2-11.

12. "A Model for Estimating Program Size and Its Evaluation," by Minoru Itakura and Akio Takayanagi. Copyright © 1982 by the Institute of Electrical and Electronics Engineers, Inc. Reprinted, with permission, from *Proceedings of the Sixth International Conference on Software Engineering,* September 13-16, 1982, Tokyo, Japan, pp. 104-109.

13. "Demographic and Technical Trends in the Computing Industry," by T. Capers Jones. Copyright © 1983 by Ken Orr and Associates, Inc. Reprinted, with permission, from *Proceedings of the Eighth Data Structured Systems Development Conference,* 1983, Topeka, Kan., pp. 1-17.

14. "A Software Development Environment for Improving Productivity," by Barry W. Boehm, Maria H. Penedo, E. Don Stuckle, Robert D. Williams, and Arthur B. Pyster. Copyright © 1984 by the Institute of Electrical and Electronics Engineers, Inc. Reprinted, with permission, from *Computer,* Vol. 17, No. 6 (June 1984), pp. 30-42. An earlier version entitled "The TRW Software Productivity System" was presented at the *Proceedings of the Sixth International Conference on Software Engineering,* September 13-16, 1982, Tokyo, Japan, pp. 148-56.

15. "Box Structured Information Systems," by H.D. Mills, R.C. Linger, and A.R. Hevner. Copyright © 1987 by International Business Machines Corporation. Reprinted with permission, from *IBM Systems Journal,* Vol. 26, No. 4 (1987), pp. 395-413.

16. "Cleanroom Software Development: An Empirical Evaluation," by Richard W. Selby, Victor R. Basili, and F. Terry Baker. Copyright © 1987 by the Institute of Electrical and Electronics Engineers, Inc. Reprinted, with permission, from *IEEE Transactions on Software Engineering,* Vol. SE-13, No. 9 (September 1987), pp. 1027-37.

17. "Practical Priorities in System Testing," by Nathan H. Petschenik. Copyright © 1985 by the Institute of Electrical and Electronics Engineers, Inc. Reprinted, with permission, from *IEEE Software,* Vol. 2, No. 5 (September 1985), pp. 18-23.

18. "Software-ICs: A Plan for Building Reusable Software Components," by Lamar Ledbetter and Brad Cox. Reprinted, with permission, from *Byte* magazine, Vol. 10, No. 6 (June 1985), pp. 307-16. Copyright © 1985 by McGraw-Hill, Inc., New York 10020. All rights reserved.

Editors' Preface

On April 8, 1947, Americans awoke to be confronted by a gruesome story in their morning newspapers: Two elderly New Yorkers, Homer and Langley Collyer, had been found starved to death in their elegant uptown brownstone. The story was presented as a reflection on the isolation that even the rich are subject to in modern society: The brothers had had no friend or neighbor to look in on them to be sure they were coping with their advanced age.

As upsetting as their tragedy of aloneness was, it was not the plight of the brothers but the state of their townhouse that most captured readers' interest. The place was chock full of newspapers. There were papers everywhere, stacks of yellowing and brittle newsprint, mostly back copies of the *New York Times*. The only living space left in the house were the few narrow aisles separating the ceiling-high stacks of papers.

Anyone who has heard their story, from the forties down to modern times, can guess readily why the brothers had not thrown out those newspapers: *They hadn't finished reading them yet.* They died hoping for a little bit of idle time to catch up on their back reading.

It may be a particularly modern trait to be behind in one's reading, and anxious about it. We are all Collyer brothers to some extent. (What stack of unread journals are you pushing aside at this moment to make room for this book?) And if it's true of modern men and women in general, how much more true it is of those who practice the information trades, particularly software. For, to paraphrase a quip by Jim Highsmith: "More has been written about software . . . than is known."

Being of a metric bent, we set out to quantify for this Preface the amount written so far about computer software. (All the following data are courtesy of the National Bureau of Facts.) So far there have been 10 to the 51st power words written on the subject. The total of all copies distributed of this material is nearly 10 to the 70th words for a total information content of 10 followed by 83 zeroes of bits. The weight of this material is 4,850,625,000,000 metric tons. So far, 99.999999972 percent is still unread and sitting in someone's office. A good deal of it is in yours. Each unread word is a guilt-inducing accusation of how far behind you are.

Into the midst of this depressing situation come two intrepid editors, DeMarco and Lister by name (that's us). Concerned as we are about information anxiety and about possible deformation of tectonic plates due to the accumulation of unread *Datamation*s and *Computerworld*s, we decided to search through the tons of software literature published over the last ten years and select the good stuff. Hence this collection. We can't guarantee that it includes every single paper worth reading from the eighties, but we claim it is close. Close enough. Do yourself a huge favor: Read these thirty-one papers and throw out all the stacks of unread material dating back as far as 1980. You'll feel better immediately.

The selected papers have been grouped into four subsets, represented by Parts I through IV of the book. The four parts are entitled:

I.   Management
II.   Measurement
III. Methods
IV.   News from Left Field

(For those of our readers unfamiliar with the American idiom, Left Field is where weird and unclassifiable things come from.) The papers are drawn from seventeen different journals and proceedings. A becoming modesty has prohibited us from including any of our own stunning articles.

All of the papers are readable. We declined to include material that we simply couldn't wade through ourselves. You should be able to digest all of what follows without struggling to remember what those little upside-down triangles mean and without working any tensors. You can forget for the moment the sixteen basic lemmas of graph theory.

We think you'll encounter in each of the thirty-one papers at least one important insight. In fact, it was such a fresh, new insight that served as our main selection criterion. There are a lot of ahas in this book. We hope you'll find the papers as compelling and valuable as we have.

Good reading!

Tom DeMarco
Camden, Maine
Timothy Lister
New York, New York

Contents

Part I
Management

1

Editors' Note
Weinberg: "Overstructured Management of Software Engineering"

Insight: Programmers who become software managers are prone to a particularly unfortunate failing—they try to treat people like program components.

An important standard of our industry is that people are promoted into management because they have done well at non-management. A second industry standard is that they are rarely trained for the responsibilities of their new position. So young managers, at their worst, tend to manage based exclusively on lessons learned from wallowing around in programs: "Let's see here, programs are a lot easier to keep track of when each of the modules is treated as a black box. So that will probably work well with my staff, too. . . ."

People, however, find it distasteful to be managed this way. Consciously or unconsciously, they begin to exact a substantial price for such treatment. Weinberg makes the case for managing people as people, not modules.

This paper was presented as the Keynote address to the Sixth International Conference on Software Engineering. The site of the conference was Tokyo, where the conference hall was wired for sound, for simultaneous translation from Japanese into English and English to Japanese. We often hear that simultaneous translation is used (with at least some success, one presumes) at the United Nations and other international bodies.

But the evidence of the Sixth ICSE was not supportive of this general thesis: When the speakers were Japanese, the English-speaking part of the audience went immediately to sleep, and when the speakers spoke in English, the Japanese went to sleep. Listening in on the translation was painful. By the end of the conference, most attendees were talking about the dubious achievement of simultaneous translation.

We might have concluded that the quality of the translation was poor except for one counterexample that virtually everyone noticed: Jerry Weinberg's presentation had survived translation brilliantly; he kept both halves of the audience awake and following closely. Afterward he commented that he had taken particular pains to accommodate the translators by speaking slowly and furnishing them in advance with a list of some of the technical terms he would be using. But he had something else working for him as well. His presentation (live, as well as in its written form) had a quality seldom encountered at such conferences: lucidity.

1

Overstructured Management of Software Engineering
by Gerald M. Weinberg

The Problem

In *The Book of Five Rings,* the samurai, Miyamoto Musashi, wrote:

> Large things are easy to observe. Small things are difficult to observe. That is to say, it is difficult to actuate one's will with speed with a large number of people; it is difficult to know what is going on with one individual since the spirit of that individual can change very quickly.

In *Software Engineering Economics,* the software researcher, Barry Boehm, wrote:

> Poor management can increase software costs more rapidly than any other factor.

Boehm's book is a milestone contribution to our field, but it does not pursue the question of poor management. It is a book about software engineering, not software *engineers.* Like almost all work in our young field, it is about projects, not people.

Some years ago, I decided to shift my attention from the technical problems of software engineering to the problems of people who lead software engineering projects. The shift has not been easy.

Projects are large things. Managers are small things. We observe projects, even though they will be difficult to change, be-cause they are easy to observe. We neglect managers, because they are hard to observe, even though they might be changed very quickly.

In shifting my work from technical issues to leadership issues, I had to give up easy technical success for practically insoluble problems with people. When I became frustrated, I started treating people like machines. It didn't work.

Is it possible that some of our software engineering failures result from *trying to manage people as if they were computers?* After all, isn't that what we know best?

The Approach

Where should one begin a study of software engineering managers? I would like to study bad management, but I'm afraid people will think me entirely negative. Therefore, let me rationalize that approach by appeal to some authorities.

One of the most remarkable books in my library is a volume published in England in 1975 by The Institution of Mechanical Engineers. It is called *Engineering Progress Through Trouble.*

Trouble, as I like to call it, begins by noticing that in 1856 (over 120 years ago) Robert Stephenson said:

> . . .he hoped that all the casualties and accidents, which had occurred during

4

their progress, would be noticed in revising the Paper; for nothing was so instructive to the younger Members of the Profession, as records of accidents in large works...

In our own field of software engineering, the mushroom growth of "structured programming" is generally traced back to Dijkstra's 1968 letter in the May 1968 *Communications of the ACM*. Let me paraphrase Dijkstra's short argument:

1. We've developed quite a few programs, some successful, some not so successful.

2. We decided to look at the two kinds and see what were the differences between them.

3. In the unsuccessful programs, we found things that were out of our mental control, things such as the Go-To.

In *The Psychology of Computer Programming* (Weinberg, 1971), I suggested several places we might look for the sources of our failures. Some of the places I suggested looking were:

1. code, as Dijkstra had done

2. programmers

3. managers

A good deal of work has now been done about looking at code (see, for example, Freedman and Weinberg, 1982), and at programmers (Shneiderman, 1980). In this paper, I would like to concentrate here on the third area, in much the way Dijkstra did:

1. I've watched the development of quite a few software systems, some successful, some not so successful.

2. I decided to look at the behavior of management in the two kinds of developments and see what were the differences between them.

3. In the unsuccessful systems, I found things that the managers couldn't keep under mental control. Most of these things had to do with the way people in a project behave, and these managers were trying to control by using overstructured models of human behavior.

Curiously, these overstructured models of human behavior turned out to be exactly those models of program control that had proved so successful in structuring computer programs. Could these managers have made the error of believing that people were like programs? Why else would they be so dedicated to structural fallacies based on sequence, choice, iteration, recursion, refinement, modularization, and data structures such as stacks?

The DEAL Model

When interviewing managers about their role in software projects, I find the DEAL model of Fritz Heider (1958) particularly useful. DEAL is an acronym for four kinds of reasons people give for success or failure:

D — Difficulty of the task

E — Effort put into doing the task

A — Ability relevant to the task

L — Luck

Successful managers always talk about the effort they put in and the ability they possess. Unsuccessful managers always talk about how hard the task was and what bad luck they had. They also talk about their poorly trained and unmotivated staff.

I believe that unsuccessful managers make as much effort as successful managers. I believe their projects are no more difficult—unless they themselves have made them so. Sometimes there is such a thing as bad luck, but successful managers were able to deal with bad luck and overcome it.

When I asked managers to explain what they meant by "bad luck" or "difficulty," they usually told me about unexpected events. But unexpected events can also arise because our expectations are incorrect—because our models of the world are too simple. And these managers did seem to have an overly structured view of system development. Perhaps they had spent too much time working with computers, where a highly structured view is quite appropriate.

I believe that these unsuccessful managers lack ability. Like me, they may have a record of great skill in manipulating computers, but they lack the ability to use more realistic models of human behavior. The simple control structures of structured programming may be adequate for writing code, but they fall rather short of what we need for successful project management.

Sequence

The most fundamental control structure in programming is, of course, *sequence*.

A sequence of actions is conceptually simple, and managers are quite correct to try to structure software projects so that important events take place in fixed, predetermined sequences.

But the development of *new* things is hardly that predictable. Idealized models of developmental sequences must be tempered with some hard realities. Consider, for instance, the "classical" sequence—specification, design, code, test.

Most system development models have several alternatives to this sequence, such as,

1. specification, kill

2. specification, design, kill

3. specification, design, code, kill

Yet the truly unsuccessful development projects I have observed never went through any of these alternatives. They were never killed by their own managers, but always went into prolonged and agonizing testing phases, regardless of any indications from early phases that the system was already a disaster.

The problem here is that the alternative sequences in the development model do not have sufficient reality to the managers who must implement them. As one manager said to me, "Those development models are too academic. It's not realistic to kill a project after we have spent so much effort writing specifications. I would have to answer to my own management why I was so lax as to initiate a project if my people couldn't do it."

To make such alternatives realistic, upper management must be given an *expectation* that a certain number of projects will be killed in each stage of the life cycle. Natural systems—plants and animals —have evolved so that deaths of unfit individuals occur as early as possible. It's estimated that in human beings, one-third of all pregnancies end in spontaneous abortions within the first month, and are ordinarily not even recognized as pregnancies.

One image my clients have used successfully is that of *measures of balanced risk.* The concept is based on two types of errors (see Weinberg and Weinberg, 1979):

I.   attempting to build a system that should not be attempted

II.   failing to attempt a system that should be attempted

Managers tend to get punished for Type I errors because these errors are conspicuous, so they prefer to make Type II errors. To create a more balanced strategy, we have to make Type II errors equally conspicuous, but how can we measure what isn't attempted?

Physicians have a similar problem when deciding whether to operate for cancer. Every tumor that is removed is sent to the pathology lab to determine if it was indeed cancerous. The ratio of benign to malignant tumors is a measure of unnecessary surgery—if it gets too high, doctors are warned to be more careful in their diagnosis. But if it gets *too low,* they are also warned—because that means that they are probably allowing some cancers to remain!

To make development managers more balanced, we must measure the number of systems that are killed in the various stages of development. If the number killed in early stages is too small, that means either that they are not attempting

enough risky projects or that they are being too rigidly sequential. If they were called to account for these ratios, they might alter their overly structured models.

Choice

The second fundamental control structure in well-structured programs is *choice*— the selection of one of two alternatives. Although a simple choice structure is well suited to the binary nature of computers, it often fails in the fuzzier situations more typical of human activities.

Managers with overly structured choice models have difficulty making sensible tradeoff decisions. For instance, one of the most common tradeoff possibilities in system development is quality versus efficiency (Weinberg, 1982a, p. 117ff.). Figure 1 is a tradeoff chart relating quality and efficiency, with the curve representing the *best* we can do with a given technology. To be concrete, imagine that:

1.   Quality here means absence of bugs in a delivered system.

2.   Cost here means the development cost to deliver that system.

The curve indicates that the tradeoffs available to the development manager are not of the "either-or" variety. Indeed, there is a whole range of ways of doing "the best we can do"—anywhere on the curve, in fact. Figure 2 shows three of these choices—the different operating points with different choices between quality and efficiency. The movement from P to R to S might represent increasing emphasis on error-detection and error-prevention activities such as testing or structured design.

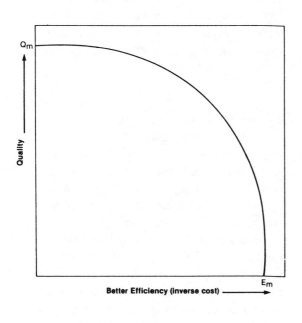

Figure 1.

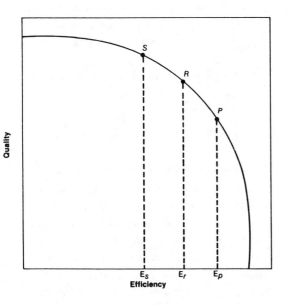

Figure 2.

The tradeoff curve represents one particular style or level of development technol-

ogy. A different development approach would be characterized by a different curve, as suggested in Figure 3. The existence of another approach gives the manager still more choices, such as moving from P to Q or E.

When a new technology comes along—the new curve—the overstructured manager tends to see only the choices Q or E:

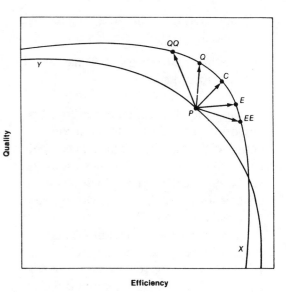

Figure 3.

Q. Raising the quality, holding the cost constant.

E. Lowering the cost, holding the quality constant.

Quite frequently, this perceived lack of choices leads to the decision to avoid the new technology altogether because "it doesn't address our problems."

Can managers learn to enrich their choice models? A few years ago, I would have said NO, because of my observations of managers on the job. But now I believe that pressures on the job are too great to allow the necessary experimenting. But in our workshops on problem-solving leadership, we've been able to create environments that encourage experimenting with new models. And many of our graduates have brought their new flexibility back to the office.

Modularization

Another concept from structured programming is the idea of the *functional module*—one module, one function. This idea is particularly appealing to the over-structured manager because it allows the substitution of *labelling* for thinking.

I most frequently run into modular thinkers when trying to introduce a system of technical reviews. These managers seem unable to understand that a technical review is a unit of work that does *several* functions (Freedman and Weinberg, 3rd edition, 1982):

1. testing of the reviewed material

2. technical training of the participants

3. communicating and enforcing standards

4. leadership training of the participants

5. developing a project's community spirit

Although one function per module certainly simplifies thought, it throws away one of the major advantages people have over machines—the ability to do several things at once, selecting what's most appropriate from the environment at the mo-

ment, without being programmed to do it. In a properly conducted technical review, everyone gains not one but several things, though we can't always predict in advance *which* things.

Modular thinkers tend to lack faith in people and their ability to find a way to get their jobs done. Modular thinkers place more faith in labels—if the chart says Jack is in training today, then Jack must be learning something today. Modular thinkers easily fall victim to the lure of the "magic box"—buy this package and things will get better.

When I suggested to one manager that productivity might be increased through increased use of software tools, he replied, "I bought $40,000 worth of software tools last year, though I didn't see any increase in productivity." When I went down into his shop, I found what I expected—$40,000 worth of software tools not being used by anybody. Modular thinkers seem to believe that buying the tool is the only step, rather than the *first* step, to *using* software tools.

What is the cure for modular thinking? Here there seems no substitute for experience with real human beings in all their lumpy glory. Sometimes this experience can be gained in workshops, though it may take many repetitions before the idea takes hold. I've noticed that volunteer community work, like working with handicapped children, seems to encourage remarkably fast erasure of modular thinking.

Iteration

Iteration, the third of the "big three" control structures, is also heavily favored by overstructured managers. One form of iteration is related to labelling. A manager simply repeats the same cliche over and over, as if it is a magical incantation that will solve problems.

Take the statement:

> Programmer productivity has grown at only 3% per year.

Over the past 15 years, I have heard this statement repeated to me by managers at least fifty times. None of these managers has been able to supply a reference to the source of this figure, or tell how it was computed. There are studies that estimate this figure, but there are also studies that estimate 25% or more annual increase.

But worse than the omission of sources is the commission of a classical "Composition Fallacy." This simplistic statement substitutes the individual worker, "programmer productivity," for the system under which the work is done, "software development productivity."

The net effect of this kind of mechanical repetition of cliches is some form of endless loop, such as,

1.   The manager believes that programmer productivity has grown only 3% per year.

2.   If the problem is programmers, then if we want to increase productivity, we must get rid of programmers.

3.   But much of the loss of productivity is precisely because experienced programmers are constantly being lost to the profession, which tends to keep down average productivity, even though individual productivity is increasing each year.

I've explored this particular cycle elsewhere (Weinberg, 1982b), so let me relate another one that parallels it. I recently suggested to a manager that if he wanted more productivity from his experienced programmers, he should spend more time, attention, and money on training. He replied, "Why bother sending them to expensive classes? The experienced ones just leave here for other shops, so I'd just be training them for other people."

When I interviewed two of his top programmers, they confided that they were seriously considering leaving, which tended to confirm the manager's pessimistic view. But when I asked *why* they were leaving, they independently said that "management doesn't value our work." What evidence did they have? Both told me that they had repeatedly been turned down on requests to attend courses!

Recursion

I could go on relating examples of over-structured management, such as,

1.   *refinement*—working out ever more precise details of the development process, when the overall approach is misguided.

2.   *data structures*—pushing problems into a stack, under the rigid belief that an organization can deal with only one problem at a time

3.   *top down design*—spending all the time and attention on the management levels, as if the people at the bottom were willing to wait passively for the management to get around to considering their level.

Instead, I'd like to confine myself to one more management control structure that may account in good measure for all of the others. I'm speaking of *recursion*— the technique of a system containing itself.

I often question development managers about their sources of information. Here are some things I've discovered:

1. Most managers attend seminars or conferences, but all were technical and all were *within data processing.*

2. All read books and magazines, but only a handful read anything significant outside of data processing—and these are mostly about hobbies.

They all seemed a bit apologetic about their reading tastes, but most explained that their work "didn't leave time for things outside their field." And so our leaders grind on endlessly taking their own output as input. Could that have anything to do with the way they endlessly repeat the same mistakes?

What Is to Be Done?

The structured programming strategies are designed to simplify the intellectual task of programming. Managers who come up through the ranks of programming have had many successes applying such strategies—that's why they became managers. So these overstructured strategies are not *bad* strategies, they are *good strategies misapplied.*

What is to be done? Try harder? People under pressure tend to revert to problem-solving strategies that worked for them in the past. If we tell managers to "try harder," it will only make the problem worse. If we are to achieve better

software engineering management, we must *alleviate* the pressure, not increase it. An overloaded manager is usually a bad manager.

If a manager has no time for "outside" interests, then the danger point is well past. If a manager says, "I can't afford the time to attend a seminar that isn't directly relevant to my work," then that manager's career is just about over.

If software engineering truly *is* engineering, then it ought to be able to learn from the evolution of other engineering disciplines. If mechanical engineers could increase the reliability of steam boilers by a factor of around 1,000,000,000,000 over a century, then perhaps software engineers would benefit from stepping back as they did and dispassionately examining their blunders.

Whenever I suggest stepping back, easing up, laughing a little at ourselves, and going outside our own field, somebody objects, saying, "But software is different. We have to work harder, concentrate more, because nothing is as complex as software." Well, of course software is different, and more complex than anything people have ever before attempted to engineer. But that's why we have to loosen our structures, not tighten them. That's why we must learn from any place we can, any way we can.

Perhaps this is only a prejudice of mine. Perhaps nobody else learns, as I do, from sticking my nose into other areas where people have struggled with complex systems. If that idea worries you, try a simple test of that notion by using this article. In the article, I've used insights I gained from:

1. mechanical engineering

2. social psychology

3. biology

4. medicine

5. literature

Did you notice? Did you lose patience? Did it make it harder for you to understand? Do you think any of the insights were relevant to the problems that plague software engineering? That plague your own work?

Only you can answer for yourself. Only you can step back from yourself, ease up on yourself. Only if you can stop overmanaging yourself can you stop overmanaging others.

REFERENCES

Boehm, Barry. *Software Engineering Economics*. Englewood Cliffs: Prentice-Hall, 1981.

Dijkstra, E.W. "Go-To Statement Considered Harmful," Letter to the Editor, *Communications of the ACM,* March 1968.

Freedman, Daniel, and Gerald M. Weinberg. *Handbook of Walkthroughs, Inspections and Technical Reviews, 3rd ed.* Boston: Little, Brown, 1982. (Also, New York: Dorset House Publishing, 1990.)

Heider, Fritz. *The Psychology of Interpersonal Relations.* New York: Wiley, 1958.

Musashi, Miyamoto. *The Book of Five Rings* (Gorin No Sho). New York: Bantam Books, 1982.

Shneiderman, Ben. *Software Psychology.* Boston: Little-Brown (Winthrop), 1980.

Weinberg, Gerald M., and Daniela Weinberg. *On the Design of Stable Systems.* New York: Wiley, 1979. (Retitled *General Principles of Systems Design.* New York: Dorset House Publishing, 1988.)

Weinberg, Gerald M. *Rethinking Systems Analysis and Design.* Boston: Little, Brown, 1982a. (Also, New York: Dorset House Publishing, 1988.)

Weinberg, Gerald M. *Understanding the Professional Programmer.* Boston: Little, Brown, 1982b. (Also, New York: Dorset House Publishing, 1988.)

Weinberg, Gerald M. *The Psychology of Computer Programming.* New York: Van Nostrand-Reinhold, 1971.

Whyte, R.R., ed. *Engineering Progress Through Trouble.* London: The Institution of Mechanical Engineers, 1975.

2

Editors' Note
Brooks: "No Silver Bullet: Essence and Accidents of Software Engineering"

Insight: Don't expect some new product or trick to come along and send your productivity soaring. It's not going to happen; and here is why.

Fred Brooks is the author of *The Mythical Man-Month*. It is fascinating to read his thoughts fifteen years after the publication of that classic. If you have a copy of his book handy, go back and breeze through his essays "The Surgical Team," "Sharp Tools," and "Plan to Throw One Away." Now read this article and see how the man's thinking has evolved.

The author leads us to and then rubs our noses in some of the realities of "fixing" the software process. If you *need* to believe that order-of-magnitude improvements in productivity, reliability, and simplicity are waiting just around the corner, well, maybe you'd better skip "No Silver Bullet."

2

No Silver Bullet:
Essence and Accidents of Software Engineering
by Frederick P. Brooks, Jr.

Of all the monsters that fill the nightmares of our folklore, none terrify more than werewolves, because they transform unexpectedly from the familiar into horrors. For these, one seeks bullets of silver that can magically lay them to rest.

The familiar software project, at least as seen by the nontechnical manager, has something of this character; it is usually innocent and straightforward, but is capable of becoming a monster of missed schedules, blown budgets, and flawed products. So we hear desperate cries for a silver bullet—something to make software costs drop as rapidly as computer hardware costs do.

But, as we look to the horizon of a decade hence, we see no silver bullet. There is no single development, in either technology or in management technique, that by itself promises even one order-of-magnitude improvement in productivity, in reliability, in simplicity. In this article, I shall try to show why, by examining both the nature of the software problem and the properties of the bullets proposed.

Skepticism is not pessimism, however. Although we see no startling breakthroughs—and indeed, I believe such to be inconsistent with the nature of software—many encouraging innovations are under way. A disciplined, consistent effort to develop, propagate, and exploit these innovations should indeed yield an order-of-magnitude improvement. There is no royal road, but there is a road.

The first step toward the management of disease was replacement of demon theories and humours theories by the germ theory. That very step, the beginning of hope, in itself dashed all hopes of magical solutions. It told workers that progress would be made stepwise, at great effort, and that a persistent, unremitting care would have to be paid to a discipline of cleanliness. So it is with software engineering today.

Does It Have to Be Hard?
—Essential Difficulties

Not only are there no silver bullets now in view, the very nature of software makes it unlikely that there will be any—no inventions that will do for software productivity, reliability, and simplicity what electronics, transistors, and large-scale integration did for computer hardware. We cannot expect ever to see twofold gains every two years.

First, one must observe that the anomaly is not that software progress is so slow, but that computer hardware progress is so fast. No other technology since civilization began has seen six orders of magnitude in performance-price gain in 30 years. In no other technology can one choose to take the gain in *either* improved performance *or* in reduced costs. These gains flow from the transformation of computer manufacture from an assembly industry into a process industry.

Second, to see what rate of progress one can expect in software technology, let us examine the difficulties of that technology. Following Aristotle, I divide them into *essence,* the difficulties inherent in the nature of software, and *accidents,* those difficulties that today attend its production but are not inherent.

The essence of a software entity is a construct of interlocking concepts: data sets, relationships among data items, algorithms, and invocations of functions. This essence is abstract in that such a conceptual construct is the same under many different representations. It is nonetheless highly precise and richly detailed.

I believe the hard part of building software to be the specification, design, and testing of this conceptual construct, not the labor of representing it and testing the fidelity of the representation. We still make syntax errors, to be sure; but they are fuzz compared with the conceptual errors in most systems.

If this is true, building software will always be hard. There is inherently no silver bullet.

Let us consider the inherent properties of this irreducible essence of modern software systems: complexity, conformity, changeability, and invisibility.

Complexity. Software entities are more complex for their size than perhaps any other human construct because no two parts are alike (at least above the statement level). If they are, we make the two similar parts into a subroutine—open or closed. In this respect, software systems differ profoundly from computers, buildings, or automobiles, where repeated elements abound.

Digital computers are themselves more complex than most things people build: They have very large numbers of states. This makes conceiving, describing, and testing them hard. Software systems have orders-of-magnitude more states than computers do.

Likewise, a scaling-up of a software entity is not merely a repetition of the same elements in larger sizes, it is necessarily an increase in the number of different elements. In most cases, the elements interact with each other in some nonlinear fashion, and the complexity of the whole increases much more than linearly.

The complexity of software is an essential property, not an accidental one. Hence, descriptions of a software entity that abstract away its complexity often abstract away its essence. For three centuries, mathematics and the physical sciences made great strides by constructing simplified models of complex phenomena, deriving properties from the models, and verifying those properties by experiment. This paradigm worked because the complexities ignored in the models were not the essential properties of the phenomena. It does not work when the complexities are the essence.

Many of the classic problems of developing software products derive from this essential complexity and its nonlinear increases with size. From the complexity comes the difficulty of communication among team members, which leads to product flaws, cost overruns, schedule delays. From the complexity comes the difficulty of enumerating, much less understanding, all the possible states of the program, and from that comes the unreliability. From complexity of function comes the difficulty of invoking function, which makes programs hard to use. From complexity of structure comes the difficulty of extending programs to new functions without creating side effects. From complexity of structure come the unvisualized states that constitute security trapdoors.

Not only technical problems, but management problems as well come from the complexity. It makes overview hard, thus impeding conceptual integrity. It makes it hard to find and control all the loose ends. It creates the tremendous learning and understanding burden that makes personnel turnover a disaster.

Conformity. Software people are not alone in facing complexity. Physics deals with terribly complex objects even at the "fundamental" particle level. The physicist labors on, however, in a firm faith that there are unifying principles to be found, whether in quarks or in unified-field theories. Einstein argued that there must be simplified explanations of nature, because God is not capricious or arbitrary.

No such faith comforts the software engineer. Much of the complexity that he must master is arbitrary complexity, forced without rhyme or reason by the many human institutions and systems to which his interfaces must conform. These differ from interface to interface, and from time to time, not because of necessity but only because they were designed by different people, rather than by God.

In many cases, the software must conform because it is the most recent arrival on the scene. In others, it must conform because it is perceived as the most conformable. But in all cases, much complexity comes from conformation to other interfaces; this complexity cannot be simplified out by any redesign of the software alone.

Changeability. The software entity is constantly subject to pressures for change. Of course, so are buildings, cars, computers. But manufactured things are infrequently changed after manufacture; they are superseded by later models, or essential changes are incorporated into later-serial-number copies of the same basic design. Call-backs of automobiles are really quite infrequent; field changes of computers somewhat less so. Both are much less frequent than modifications to fielded software.

In part, this is so because the software of a system embodies its function, and the function is the part that most feels the pressures of change. In part it is because software can be changed more easily—it is pure thought-stuff, infinitely malleable. Buildings do in fact get changed, but the high costs of change, understood by all, serve to dampen the whims of the changers.

All successful software gets changed. Two processes are at work. First, as a software product is found to be useful, people try it in new cases at the edge of or beyond the original domain. The pressures for extended function come chiefly from users who like the basic function and invent new uses for it.

Second, successful software survives beyond the normal life of the machine vehicle for which it is first written. If not new computers, then at least new disks, new displays, new printers come along; and the software must be conformed to its new vehicles of opportunity.

In short, the software product is embedded in a cultural matrix of applications, users, laws, and machine vehicles. These all change continually, and their changes inexorably force change upon the software product.

Invisibility. Software is invisible and unvisualizable. Geometric abstractions are powerful tools. The floor plan of a building helps both architect and client evaluate spaces, traffic flows, views. Contradictions and omissions become obvious. Scale drawings of mechanical parts and stick-figure models of molecules, although abstractions, serve the same purpose. A geometric reality is captured in a geometric abstraction.

The reality of software is not inherently embedded in space. Hence, it has no ready geometric representation in the way that land has maps, silicon chips have diagrams, computers have connectivity schematics. As soon as we attempt to diagram software structure, we find it to constitute not one, but several, general directed graphs superimposed one upon another. The several graphs may represent the flow of control, the flow of data, patterns of dependency, time sequence, name-space relationships. These graphs are usually not even planar, much less hierarchical. Indeed, one of the ways of establishing conceptual control over such structure is to enforce link cutting until one or more of the graphs becomes hierarchical. [1]

In spite of progress in restricting and simplifying the structures of software, they remain inherently unvisualizable, and thus do not permit the mind to use some of its most powerful conceptual tools. This lack not only impedes the process of design within one mind, it severely hinders communication among minds.

Past Breakthroughs Solved Accidental Difficulties

If we examine the three steps in software-technology development that have been most fruitful in the past, we discover that each attacked a different major difficulty in building software, but that those difficulties have been accidental, not essential, difficulties. We cán also see the natural limits to the extrapolation of each such attack.

High-level languages. Surely the most powerful stroke for software productivity, reliability, and simplicity has been the progressive use of high-level languages for programming. Most observers credit that development with at least a factor of five in productivity, and with concomitant gains in reliability, simplicity, and comprehensibility.

What does a high-level language accomplish? It frees a program from much of its accidental complexity. An abstract program consists of conceptual constructs: operations, data types, sequences, and communication. The concrete machine program is concerned with bits, registers, conditions, branches, channels, disks, and such. To the extent that the high-level language embodies the constructs one wants in the abstract program and avoids all lower ones, it eliminates a whole level of complexity that was never inherent in the program at all.

The most a high-level language can do is to furnish all the constructs that the programmer imagines in the abstract program. To be sure, the level of our thinking about data structures, data types, and operations is steadily rising, but at an ever-decreasing rate. And language development approaches closer and closer to the sophistication of users.

Moreover, at some point the elaboration of a high-level language creates a tool-mastery burden that increases, not reduces, the intellectual task of the user who rarely uses the esoteric constructs.

Time-sharing. Time-sharing brought a major improvement in the productivity of programmers and in the quality of their product, although not so large as that brought by high-level languages.

Time-sharing attacks a quite different difficulty. Time-sharing preserves immediacy, and hence enables one to maintain an overview of complexity. The slow turnaround of batch programming means that one inevitably forgets the minutiae, if not the very thrust, of what one was thinking when he stopped programming and called for compilation and execution. This interruption is costly in time, for one must refresh one's memory. The most serious effect may well be the decay of the grasp of all that is going on in a complex system.

Slow turnaround, like machine-language complexities, is an accidental rather than an essential difficulty of the software process. The limits of the potential contribution of time-sharing derive directly. The principal effect of time-sharing is to shorten system response time. As this response time goes to zero, at some point it passes the human threshold of noticeability, about 100 milliseconds. Beyond that threshold, no benefits are to be expected.

Unified programming environments. Unix and Interlisp, the first integrated programming environments to come into widespread use, seem to have improved productivity by integral factors. Why?

They attack the accidental difficulties that result from using individual programs *together,* by providing integrated libraries, unified file formats, and pipes and filters. As a result, conceptual structures that in principle could always call, feed, and use one another can indeed easily do so in practice.

This breakthrough in turn stimulated the development of whole toolbenches, since each new tool could be applied to any programs that used the standard formats.

Because of these successes, environments are the subject of much of today's software-engineering research. We look at their promise and limitations in the next section.

Hopes for the Silver

Now let us consider the technical developments that are most often advanced as potential silver bullets. What problems do they address—the problems of essence, or the remaining accidental difficulties? Do they offer revolutionary advances, or incremental ones?

Ada and other high-level language advances. One of the most touted recent developments is Ada, a general-purpose high-level language of the 1980's. Ada not only reflects evolutionary improvements in language concepts, but indeed embodies features to encourage modern design and modularization. Perhaps the Ada philosophy is more of an advance than the Ada language, for it is the philosophy of modularization, of abstract data types, of hierarchical structuring. Ada is over-rich, a natural result of the process by which requirements were laid on its design. That is not fatal, for subsetted working vocabularies can solve the learning problem, and hardware advances will give us the cheap MIPS to pay for the compiling costs. Advancing the structuring of software systems is indeed a very good use for the increased MIPS our dollars will buy. Operating systems, loudly decried in the 1960's for their memory and cycle costs, have proved to be an excellent form in which to use some of the MIPS and cheap memory bytes of the past hardware surge.

Nevertheless, Ada will not prove to be the silver bullet that slays the software productivity monster. It is, after all, just another high-level language, and the biggest payoff from such languages came from the first transition—the transition up from the accidental complexities of the machine into the more abstract statement of step-by-step solutions. Once those accidents have been removed, the remaining ones will be smaller, and the payoff from their removal will surely be less.

I predict that a decade from now, when the effectiveness of Ada is assessed, it will be seen to have made a substantial difference, but not because of any particular language feature, nor indeed because of all of them combined. Neither will the new Ada environments prove to be the cause of the improvements. Ada's greatest contribution will be that switching to it occasioned training programmers in modern software-design techniques.

Object-oriented programming. Many students of the art hold out more hope for object-oriented programming than for any of the other technical fads of the day. [2] I am among them. Mark Sherman of Dartmouth notes on CSnet News that one must be careful to distinguish two separate ideas that go under that name: *abstract data types* and *hierarchical types*. The concept of the abstract data type is that an object's type should be defined by a name, a set of proper values, and a set of proper operations rather than by its storage structure, which should be hidden. Examples are Ada packages (with private types) and Modula's modules.

Hierarchical types, such as Simula-67's classes, allow one to define general interfaces that can be further refined by providing subordinate types. The two concepts are orthogonal—one may have hierarchies without hiding and hiding without hierarchies. Both concepts represent real advances in the art of building software.

Each removes yet another accidental difficulty from the process, allowing the designer to express the essence of the design without having to express large amounts of syntactic material that add no information content. For both abstract types and hierarchical types, the result is to remove a higher-order kind of accidental difficulty and allow a higher-order expression of design.

Nevertheless, such advances can do no more than to remove all the accidental difficulties from the expression of the design. The complexity of the design itself is essential, and such attacks make no change whatever in that. An order-of-magnitude gain can be made by object-oriented programming only if the unnecessary type-specification underbrush still in our programming language is itself nine-tenths of the work involved in designing a program product. I doubt it.

Artificial intelligence. Many people expect advances in artificial intelligence to provide the revolutionary breakthrough that will give order-of-magnitude gains in software productivity and quality. [3] I do not. To see why, we must dissect what is meant by "artificial intelligence."

D.L. Parnas has clarified the terminological chaos: [4]

> Two quite different definitions of AI are in common use today. AI-1: The use of computers to solve problems that previously could only be solved by applying human intelligence. AI-2: The use of a specific set of programming techniques known as heuristic or rule-based programming. In this approach human experts are studied to determine what heuristics or rules of thumb they use in solving problems.... The program is designed to solve a problem the way that humans seem to solve it.
>
> The first definition has a sliding meaning.... Something can fit the definition of AI-1 today but, once we see how the program works and understand the problem, we will not think of it as AI any more.... Unfortunately I cannot identify a body of technology that is unique to this field.... Most of the work is problem-specific, and some abstraction or creativity is required to see how to transfer it.

I agree completely with this critique. The techniques used for speech recognition seem to have little in common with those used for image recognition, and both are different from those used in expert systems. I have a hard time seeing how image recognition, for example, will make any appreciable difference in programming practice. The same problem is true of speech recognition. The hard thing about building software is deciding what one wants to say, not saying it. No facilitation of expression can give more than marginal gains.

Expert-systems technology, AI-2, deserves a section of its own.

Expert systems. The most advanced part of the artificial intelligence art, and the most widely applied, is the technology for building expert systems. Many software scientists are hard at work applying this technology to the software-building environment. [3, 5] What is the concept, and what are the prospects?

An *expert system* is a program that contains a generalized inference engine and a rule base, takes input data and assumptions, explores the inferences derivable from the rule base, yields conclusions and advice, and offers to explain its results by retracing its reasoning for the user. The inference engines typically can deal with fuzzy or probabilistic data and rules, in addition to purely deterministic logic.

Such systems offer some clear advantages over programmed algorithms designed for arriving at the same solutions to the same problems:

- Inference-engine technology is developed in an application-independent way, and then applied to many uses. One can justify much effort on the inference engines. Indeed, that technology is well advanced.

- The changeable parts of the application-peculiar materials are encoded in the rule base in a uniform fashion, and tools are provided for developing, changing, testing, and documenting the rule base. This regularizes much of the complexity of the application itself.

The power of such systems does not come from ever-fancier inference mechanisms, but rather from ever-richer knowledge bases that reflect the real world more accurately. I believe that the most important advance offered by the technology is the separation of the application complexity from the program itself.

How can this technology be applied to the software-engineering task? In many ways: Such systems can suggest interface rules, advise on testing strategies, remember bug-type frequencies, and offer optimization hints.

Consider an imaginary testing advisor, for example. In its most rudimentary form, the diagnostic expert system is very like a pilot's checklist, just enumerating suggestions as to possible causes of difficulty. As more and more system structure is embodied in the rule base, and as the rule base takes more sophisticated account of the trouble symptoms reported, the testing advisor becomes more and more particular in the hypotheses it generates and the tests it recommends. Such an expert system may depart most radically from the conventional ones in that its rule base should probably be hierarchically modularized in the same way the corresponding software product is, so that as the product is modularly modified, the diagnostic rule base can be modularly modified as well.

The work required to generate the diagnostic rules is work that would have to be done anyway in generating the set of test cases for the modules and for the system. If it is done in a suitably general manner, with both a uniform structure for rules and a good inference engine available, it may actually reduce the total labor of generating bring-up test cases, and help as well with lifelong maintenance and modification testing. In the same way, one can postulate other advisors, probably many and probably simple, for the other parts of the software-construction task.

Many difficulties stand in the way of the early realization of useful expert-system advisors to the program developer. A crucial part of our imaginary scenario is the development of easy ways to get from program-structure specification to the automatic or semiautomatic generation of diagnostic rules. Even more difficult and important is the twofold task of knowledge acquisition: finding articulate, self-analytical experts who know *why* they do things, and developing efficient techniques for extracting what they know and distilling it into rule bases. The essential prerequisite for building an expert system is to have an expert.

The most powerful contribution by expert systems will surely be to put at the service of the inexperienced programmer the experience and accumulated wisdom of the best programmers. This is no small contribution. The gap between the best software engineering practice and the average practice is very wide—perhaps wider than in any other engineering discipline. A tool that disseminates good practice would be important.

''Automatic'' programming. For almost 40 years, people have been anticipating and writing about "automatic programming," or the generation of a program for solving a problem from a statement of the problem specifications. Some today write as if they expect this technology to provide the next breakthrough. [5]

Parnas [4] implies that the term is used for glamour, not for semantic content, asserting,

> In short, automatic programming always has been a euphemism for programming with a higher-level language than was presently available to the programmer.

He argues, in essence, that in most cases it is the solution method, not the problem, whose specification has to be given.

One can find exceptions. The technique of building generators is very powerful, and it is routinely used to good advantage in programs for sorting. Some systems for integrating differential equations have also permitted direct specification of the problem, and the systems have assessed the parameters, chosen from a library of methods of solution, and generated the programs.

These applications have very favorable properties:

- The problems are readily characterized by relatively few parameters.

- There are many known methods of solution to provide a library of alternatives.

- Extensive analysis has led to explicit rules for selecting solution techniques, given problem parameters.

It is hard to see how such techniques generalize to the wider world of the ordinary software system, where cases with such neat properties are the exception. It is hard even to imagine how this breakthrough in generalization could occur.

Graphical programming. A favorite subject for PhD dissertations in software engineering is graphical, or visual, programming—the application of computer graphics to software design. [6, 7] Sometimes the promise held out by such an approach is postulated by analogy with VLSI chip design, in which computer graphics plays so fruitful a role. Sometimes the theorist justifies the approach by considering flowcharts as the ideal program-design medium and by providing powerful facilities for constructing them.

Nothing even convincing, much less exciting, has yet emerged from such efforts. I am persuaded that nothing will.

In the first place, as I have argued elsewhere [8], the flowchart is a very poor abstraction of software structure. Indeed, it is best viewed as Burks, von Neumann, and Goldstine's attempt to provide a desperately needed high-level control language for their proposed computer. In the pitiful, multipage, connection-boxed form to which the flowchart has today been elaborated, it has proved to be useless as a design tool—programmers draw flowcharts after, not before, writing the programs they describe.

Second, the screens of today are too small, in pixels, to show both the scope and the resolution of any seriously detailed software diagram. The so-called "desktop metaphor" of today's workstation is instead an "airplane-seat" metaphor. Anyone who has shuffled a lap full of papers while seated between two portly passengers will recognize the difference—one can see only a very few things at once. The true desktop provides overview of, and random access to, a score of pages. Moreover, when fits of creativity run strong, more than one programmer or writer has been known to abandon the desktop for the more spacious floor. The hardware technology will have to advance quite substantially before the scope of our scopes is sufficient for the software-design task.

More fundamentally, as I have argued above, software is very difficult to visualize. Whether one diagrams control flow, variable-scope nesting, variable cross-references, dataflow, hierarchical data structures, or whatever, one feels only one dimension of the intricately interlocked software elephant. If one superimposes all the diagrams generated by the many relevant views, it is difficult to extract any global overview. The VLSI analogy is fundamentally misleading—a chip design is a layered two-dimensional description whose geometry reflects its realization in 3-space. A software system is not.

Program verification. Much of the effort in modern programming goes into testing and the repair of bugs. Is there perhaps a silver bullet to be found by eliminating the errors at the source, in the system-design phase? Can both productivity and product reliability be radically enhanced by following the profoundly different strategy of proving designs correct before the immense effort is poured into implementing and testing them?

I do not believe we will find productivity magic here. Program verification is a very powerful concept, and it will be very important for such things as secure operating-system kernels. The technology does not promise, however, to save labor. Verifications are so much work that only a few substantial programs have ever been verified.

Program verification does not mean error-proof programs. There is no magic here, either. Mathematical proofs also can be faulty. So whereas verification might reduce the program-testing load, it cannot eliminate it.

More seriously, even perfect program verification can only establish that a program meets its specification. The hardest part of the software task is arriving at a complete and consistent specification, and much of the essence of building a program is in fact the debugging of the specification.

Environments and tools. How much more gain can be expected from the exploding researches into better programming environments? One's instinctive reaction is that the big-payoff problems—hierarchical file systems, uniform file formats to make possible uniform program interfaces, and generalized tools—were the first attacked, and have been solved. Language-specific smart editors are developments not yet widely used in practice, but the most they promise is freedom from syntactic errors and simple semantic errors.

Perhaps the biggest gain yet to be realized from programming environments is the use of integrated database systems to keep track of the myriad details that must be recalled accurately by the individual programmer and kept current for a group of collaborators on a single system.

Surely this work is worthwhile, and surely it will bear some fruit in both productivity and reliability. But by its very nature, the return from now on must be marginal.

Workstations. What gains are to be expected for the software art from the certain and rapid increase in the power and memory capacity of the individual workstation? Well, how many MIPS can one use fruitfully? The composition and editing of programs and documents is fully supported by today's speeds. Compiling could stand a boost, but a factor of 10 in machine speed would surely leave think-time the dominant activity in the programmer's day. Indeed, it appears to be so now.

More powerful workstations we surely welcome. Magical enhancements from them we cannot expect.

Promising Attacks on the Conceptual Essence

Even though no technological breakthrough promises to give the sort of magical results with which we are so familiar in the hardware area, there is both an abundance of good work going on now, and the promise of steady, if unspectacular progress.

All of the technological attacks on the accidents of the software process are fundamentally limited by the productivity equation:

$$time\ of\ task\ =\ \sum_{i}(frequency)_i \times (time)_i$$

If, as I believe, the conceptual components of the task are now taking most of the time, then no amount of activity on the task components that are merely the expression of the concepts can give large productivity gains.

Hence we must consider those attacks that address the essence of the software problem, the formulation of these complex conceptual structures. Fortunately, some of these attacks are very promising.

Buy versus build. The most radical possible solution for constructing software is not to construct it at all.

Every day this becomes easier, as more and more vendors offer more and better software products for a dizzying variety of applications. While we software engineers have labored on production methodology, the personal-computer revolution has created not one, but many, mass markets for software. Every newsstand carries monthly magazines, which sorted by machine type, advertise and review dozens of products at prices from a few dollars to a few hundred dollars. More specialized sources offer very powerful products for the workstation and other Unix markets. Even software tools and environments can be bought off-the-shelf. I have elsewhere proposed a marketplace for individual modules. [9]

Any such product is cheaper to buy than to build afresh. Even at a cost of one hundred thousand dollars, a purchased piece of software is costing only about as much as one programmer-year. And delivery is immediate! Immediate at least for products that really exist, products whose developer can refer products to a happy user. Moreover, such products tend to be much better documented and somewhat better maintained than home-grown software.

The development of the mass market is, I believe, the most profound long-run trend in software engineering. The cost of software has always been development cost, not replication cost. Sharing that cost among even a few users radically cuts the per-user cost. Another way of looking at it is that the use of n copies of a software system effectively multiplies the productivity of its developers by n. That is an enhancement of the productivity of the discipline and of the nation.

The key issue, of course, is applicability. Can I use an available off-the-shelf package to perform my task? A surprising thing has happened here. During the 1950's and 1960's, study after study showed that users would not use off-the-shelf packages for payroll, inventory control, accounts receivable, and so on. The requirements were too specialized, the case-to-case variation too high. During the 1980's, we find such packages in high demand and widespread use. What has changed?

Not the packages, really. They may be somewhat more generalized and somewhat more customizable than formerly, but not much. Not the applications, either. If anything, the business and scientific needs of today are more diverse and complicated than those of 20 years ago.

The big change has been in the hardware/software cost ratio. In 1960, the buyer of a two-million dollar machine felt that he could afford $250,000 more for a customized payroll program, one that slipped easily and nondisruptively into the computer-hostile social environment. Today, the buyer of a $50,000 office machine cannot conceivably afford a customized payroll program, so he adapts the payroll procedure to the packages available. Computers are now so commonplace, if not yet so beloved, that the adaptations are accepted as a matter of course.

There are dramatic exceptions to my argument that the generalization of software packages has changed little over the years: electronic spreadsheets and simple database systems. These powerful tools, so obvious in retrospect and yet so late in appearing, lend themselves to myriad uses, some quite unorthodox. Articles and even books now abound on how to tackle unexpected tasks with the spreadsheet. Large numbers of applications that would formerly have been written as custom programs in Cobol or Report Program Generator are now routinely done with these tools.

Many users now operate their own computers day in and day out on various applications without ever writing a program. Indeed, many of these users can-

not write new programs for their machines, but they are nevertheless adept at solving new problems with them.

I believe the single most powerful software-productivity strategy for many organizations today is to equip the computer-naive intellectual workers who are on the firing line with personal computers and good generalized writing, drawing, file, and spreadsheet programs and then to turn them loose. The same strategy, carried out with generalized mathematical and statistical packages and some simple programming capabilities, will also work for hundreds of laboratory scientists.

Requirements refinement and rapid prototyping. The hardest single part of building a software system is deciding precisely what to build. No other part of the conceptual work is as difficult as establishing the detailed technical requirements, including all the interfaces to people, to machines, and to other software systems. No other part of the work so cripples the resulting system if done wrong. No other part is more difficult to rectify later.

Therefore, the most important function that the software builder performs for the client is the iterative extraction and refinement of the product requirements. For the truth is, the client does not know what he wants. The client usually does not know what questions must be answered, and he has almost never thought of the problem in the detail necessary for specification. Even the simple answer—"Make the new software system work like our old manual information-processing system"—is in fact too simple. One never wants exactly that. Complex software systems are, moreover, things that act, that move, that work. The dynamics of that action are hard to imagine. So in planning any software-design activity, it is necessary to allow for an extensive iteration between the client and the designer as part of the system definition.

I would go a step further and assert that it is really impossible for a client, even working with a software engineer, to specify completely, precisely, and correctly the exact requirements of a modern software product before trying some versions of the product.

Therefore, one of the most promising of the current technological efforts, and one that attacks the essence, not the accidents, of the software problem, is the development of approaches and tools for rapid prototyping of systems as prototyping is part of the iterative specification of requirements.

A *prototype software system* is one that simulates the important interfaces and performs the main functions of the intended system, while not necessarily being bound by the same hardware speed, size, or cost constraints. Prototypes typically perform the mainline tasks of the application, but make no attempt to handle the exceptional tasks, respond correctly to invalid inputs, or abort cleanly. The purpose of the prototype is to make real the conceptual structure specified, so that the client can test it for consistency and usability.

Much of present-day software-acquisition procedure rests upon the assumption that one can specify a satisfactory system in advance, get bids for its construction, have it built, and install it. I think this assumption is fundamentally wrong, and that many software-acquisition problems spring from that fallacy. Hence, they cannot be fixed without fundamental revision—revision that provides for iter-

ative development and specification of prototypes and products.

Incremental development—grow, don't build, software. I still remember the jolt I felt in 1958 when I first heard a friend talk about *building* a program, as opposed to *writing* one. In a flash he broadened my whole view of the software process. The metaphor shift was powerful, and accurate. Today we understand how like other building processes the construction of software is, and we freely use other elements of the metaphor, such as *specifications, assembly of components,* and *scaffolding.*

The building metaphor has outlived its usefulness. It is time to change again. If, as I believe, the conceptual structures we construct today are too complicated to be specified accurately in advance, and too complex to be built faultlessly, then we must take a radically different approach.

Let us turn nature and study complexity in living things, instead of just the dead works of man. Here we find constructs whose complexities thrill us with awe. The brain alone is intricate beyond mapping, powerful beyond imitation, rich in diversity, self-protecting, and self-renewing. The secret is that it is grown, not built.

So it must be with our software systems. Some years ago Harlan Mills proposed that any software system should be grown by incremental development. [10] That is, the system should first be made to run, even if it does nothing useful except call the proper set of dummy subprograms. Then, bit by bit, it should be fleshed out, with the subprograms in turn being developed—into actions or calls to empty stubs in the level below.

I have seen most dramatic results since I began urging this technique on the project builders in my Software Engineering Laboratory class. Nothing in the past decade has so radically changed my own practice, or its effectiveness. The approach necessitates top-down design, for it is a top-down growing of the software. It allows easy backtracking. It lends itself to early prototypes. Each added function and new provision for more complex data or circumstances grows organically out of what is already there.

The morale effects are startling. Enthusiasm jumps when there is a running system, even a simple one. Efforts redouble when the first picture from a new graphics software system appears on the screen, even if it is only a rectangle. One always has, at every stage in the process, a working system. I find that teams can *grow* much more complex entities in four months than they can *build*.

The same benefits can be realized on large projects as on my small ones. [11]

Great designers. The central question in how to improve the software art centers, as it always has, on people.

We can get good designs by following good practices instead of poor ones. Good design practices can be taught. Programmers are among the most intelligent part of the population, so they can learn good practice. Hence, a major thrust in the United States is to promulgate good modern practice. New curricula, new literature, new organizations such as the Software Engineering Institute, all have come into being in order to raise the level of our practice from poor to good. This is entirely proper.

Nevertheless, I do not believe we can make the next step upward in the same way. Whereas the difference between poor conceptual designs and good ones may lie in the soundness of design method, the difference between good designs and great ones surely does not. Great designs come from great designers. Software construction is a *creative* process. Sound methodology can empower and liberate the creative mind; it cannot inflame or inspire the drudge.

The differences are not minor—they are rather like the differences between Salieri and Mozart. Study after study shows that the very best designers produce structures that are faster, smaller, simpler, cleaner, and produced with less effort. [12] The differences between the great and the average approach an order of magnitude.

A little retrospection shows that although many fine, useful software systems have been designed by committees and built as part of multipart projects, those software systems that have excited passionate fans are those that are the products of one or a few designing minds, great designers. Consider Unix, APL, Pascal, Modula, the Smalltalk interface, even Fortran; and contrast them with Cobol, PL/I, Algol, MVS/370, and MS-DOS. (See Table 1.)

Hence, although I strongly support the technology-transfer and curriculum-development efforts now under way, I think the most important single effort we can mount is to develop ways to grow great designers.

No software organization can ignore this challenge. Good managers, scarce though they be, are no scarcer than good designers. Great designers and great managers are both very rare. Most organizations spend considerable effort in finding and cultivating the management prospects; I know of none that spends equal effort in finding and developing the great designers upon whom the technical excellence of the products will ultimately depend.

Table 1.
Exciting Vs. Useful But Unexciting Software Products.

Exciting Products	
Yes	No
Unix	Cobol
APL	PL/I
Pascal	Algol
Modula	MVS/370
Smalltalk	MS-DOS
Fortran	

My first proposal is that each software organization must determine and proclaim that great designers are as important to its success as great managers are, and that they can be expected to be similarly nurtured and rewarded. Not only salary, but the perquisites of recognition—office size, furnishings, personal technical equipment, travel funds, staff support—must be fully equivalent.

How to grow great designers? Space does not permit a lengthy discussion, but some steps are obvious:

- Systematically identify top designers as early as possible. The best are often not the most experienced.

- Assign a career mentor to be responsible for the development of the prospect, and carefully keep a career file.

- Devise and maintain a career-development plan for each prospect, including carefully selected apprenticeships with top designers, epi-

sodes of advanced formal education, and short courses, all interspersed with solo-design and technical-leadership assignments.

- Provide opportunities for growing designers to interact with and stimulate each other.

Acknowledgments

I thank Gordon Bell, Bruce Buchanan, Rick Hayes-Roth, Robert Patrick, and, most especially, David Parnas for their insights and stimulating ideas, and Rebekah Bierly for the technical production of this article.

REFERENCES

[1] D.L. Parnas, "Designing Software for Ease of Extension and Contraction," *IEEE Transactions on Software Engineering,* Vol. 5, No. 2, March 1979, pp. 128-38.

[2] G. Booch, "Object-Oriented Design," *Software Engineering with Ada,* 1983, Menlo Park, Calif.: Benjamin/ Cummings.

[3] *IEEE Transactions on Software Engineering* (special issue on artificial intelligence and software engineering), J. Mostow, guest ed., Vol. 11, No. 11, November 1985.

[4] D.L. Parnas, "Software Aspects of Strategic Defense Systems," *American Scientist,* November 1985.

[5] R. Balzer, "A 15-year Perspective on Automatic Programming," *IEEE Transactions on Software Engineering* (special issue on artificial intelligence and software engineering), J. Mostow, guest ed., Vol. 11, No. 11 (November 1985), pp. 1257-67.

[6] *Computer* (special issue on visual programming), R.B. Graphton and T. Ichikawa, guest eds., Vol. 18, No. 8, August 1985.

[7] G. Raeder, "A Survey of Current Graphical Programming Techniques," *Computer* (special issue on visual programming), R.B. Graphton and T. Ichikawa, guest eds., Vol. 18, No. 8, August 1985, pp. 11-25.

[8] F.P. Brooks, *The Mythical Man-Month*, Reading, Mass.: Addison-Wesley, 1975, Chapter 14.

[9] Defense Science Board, *Report of the Task Force on Military Software*, in press.

[10] H.D. Mills, "Top-Down Programming in Large Systems," in *Debugging Techniques in Large Systems*, R. Ruskin, ed., Englewood Cliffs, N.J.: Prentice-Hall, 1971.

[11] B.W. Boehm, "A Spiral Model of Software Development and Enhancement," 1985, TRW Technical Report 21-371-85, TRW, Inc., 1 Space Park, Redondo Beach, Calif. 90278.

[12] H. Sackman, W.J. Erikson, and E.E. Grant, "Exploratory Experimental Studies Comparing Online and Offline Programming Performance," *Communications of the ACM*, Vol. 11, No. 1 (January 1968), pp. 3-11.

3

Editors' Note
Boehm and Papaccio: "Understanding and Controlling Software Costs"

Insight: Software qualities and costs must be understood—and measured—if we are ever to increase our productivity.

In his classic 1976 paper "Software Engineering,"* Barry Boehm gave a report on the state of software practice at the time and his own metric assessment of what it all meant. Here, with co-author Philip Papaccio, he offers us an update. The paper provides an empirical view of where our effort and money go when we build large software systems. It suggests ways to reduce and control software costs.

Boehm and Papaccio point out that building software on the cheap will always result in a more expensive product than doing it right initially. They show that throwing warm bodies at a project is a disaster if we don't also invest in support tools and a good work environment. Their recommendations include minimizing the amount of code written (by using high-level languages and reusable software components), and avoiding rework (by opting for prototyping, good programming methods, and incremental development). Some of the strongest material here is the indictment of the software process as a documentation construction exercise.

The authors end with a plea for sensible risk analysis: identification right at the beginning of the project of the most likely causes of failure.

---

*B. Boehm, "Software Engineering," *IEEE Transactions on Computers,* December 1976, pp. 1226-41.

3

Understanding and Controlling Software Costs
by Barry W. Boehm and Philip N. Papaccio

I. THE NEED TO UNDERSTAND AND CONTROL SOFTWARE COSTS

In this section, we will explore three main reasons why it is important to understand and control software costs:

1) *Software costs are big and growing.* Thus, any percentage cost savings will be big and growing, also.

2) *Many useful software products are not getting developed.* Helping good software people work more efficiently will provide time for them to attack this backlog of needed software.

3) *Understanding and controlling software costs can get us better software, not just more software.* As our lives and lifestyles continue to depend more and more on software, this factor becomes the most important of all.

A. Software Cost Trends

A number of studies have indicated that software costs are large and rapidly increasing. For the United States in 1980, using two separate approaches and relatively conservative assumptions, Reference [24] derived a total of 900,000-1,000,000 software personnel, with a resulting annual cost of $40 billion, or roughly 2 percent of the U.S. Gross National Product. Reference [69] derived a comparable figure of 900,000 professional programmers in the U.S., and a total world programmer population of 3,250,000 (another 900,000 in Western Europe, 500,000 in the Far East, and about 950,000 elsewhere).

Reference [69] estimated the rate of growth of programming personnel at roughly 7 percent per year, which would yield a U.S. professional programmer population of roughly 3,000,000 people by the year 2000, and a world programmer population in the year 2000 of roughly 10,000,000 people. Recent estimates of the dollar growth in U.S. software costs have typically indicated around a 12 percent per year increase (indicating a 5 percent annual increase in personnel cost plus the 7 percent increase in number of personnel). This is consistent with the trends in U.S. Defense Department costs, which went from roughly $3.3 billion in 1974 [46] to roughly $10 billion in 1984 [78]. The recent Electronic Industries Association study of U.S. Defense Department mission critical software costs also predicted a 12 percent annual growth rate from $11.4 billion in 1985 to $36 billion in 1995 [42].

Using a 12 percent annual growth rate, the annual U.S. software cost would be roughly $70 billion in 1985 and $125 billion in 1990. Comparable world software costs are difficult to calculate due to differing salary scales, but they would be at least twice this high: over $140 billion in 1985 and over $250 billion in 1990. Clearly, these costs are sufficiently large to merit serious efforts to understand and control them.

B. The Software Backlog

Several studies (e.g., [23, 82]) have indicated that the demand for new software is increasing faster than our ability to develop it. For example, the U.S. Air Force Data Systems Design Office has identified a four-year backlog of important business data processing software functions which cannot be implemented because of a limited supply of personnel and funding, much of which must currently be devoted to supporting the evolution of existing software (often misleadingly called "software maintenance"). A number of other government and commercial organizations have identified similar backlogs.

This software backlog exacerbates two serious problems. First, it acts as a brake on our ability to achieve productivity gains in other sectors of the economy. It has been estimated that roughly 20 percent of the productivity gains in the U.S. are achieved via automation and data processing. The software backlog means that many non-software people's jobs still have a great deal of tedious, repetitive, and unsatisfying content, because the software to eliminate those parts of the job cannot be developed.

Second, and more serious, the software backlog creates a situation which yields a great deal of bad software, with repercussions on our safety and quality of life. Specifically, the backlog creates a personnel market in which *just about anybody can get a job to work off this software backlog, whether they are capable or not.*

Several studies have shown that, as with productivity, differences between people account for the largest source of variation in software quality. For example, the comparative experiment in Reference [30] showed a 10:1 difference in error rates between personnel. The numerous instances of risks to the public summarized by Neumann in *ACM Software Engineering Notes* provide graphic examples of how serious a problem we have created by unleashing unqualified software personnel onto projects producing critical applications software. This leads us to two primary conclusions:

- We need to understand and control software costs as a way of reducing software backlog, and thus of reducing the chances that bad programmers will continue to provide us with more and more bad software to live with.

- We need to understand and control software qualities as well as software costs.

C.   Understanding and Controlling Software Costs and Qualities

The interactions between software cost and the various software qualities (reliability, ease of use, ease of modification, portability, efficiency, etc.) are quite complex— as are the interactions between the various qualities themselves. Overall, though, there are two primary situations which create significant interactions between software costs and qualities:

a) A project which tries to reduce software development costs at the expense of quality can do so, but only in ways which increase operational and life cycle costs.

b) A project which tries to simultaneously reduce software costs and improve software quality can do so, by intelligent and cost-effective use of modern software techniques.

Going for Low-Cost, Low-Quality Software: One example of situation a) is provided by the Weinberg-Schulman [121] experiment, in which several teams were asked to develop a program to perform the same function, but each team was asked to optimize a different objective. Almost uniformly, each team finished first on the objective they were asked to optimize, and fell behind on the other objectives. In particular, the team asked to minimize effort finished with the smallest effort to complete the program, but also finished last in program clarity, second to last on program size and required storage, and third to last in output clarity.

Another example is provided by the COCOMO data base of 63 development projects and 25 evolution or maintenance projects [23]. This analysis showed that if the effects of other factors such as personnel, use of tools, and modern programming practices were held constant, then the cost to develop reliability-critical software was almost twice the cost of developing minimally reliable software. However, the trend was reversed in the maintenance projects; low-reliability software required considerably more budget to maintain than high-reliability software. Thus, there is a "value of quality" which makes it generally undesirable to reduce development cost at the expense of quality.

Achieving Low-Cost, High-Quality Software: Certainly, though, if we want better software quality at a reasonable cost, we are not going to hold constant our use of tools, modern programming practices,

and better people. This leads to situation b), in which many organizations have been able to achieve simultaneous improvements in both software quality and productivity. For example, the extensive survey in Reference [50] of about 800 user installations found that the four most strongly experienced effects of using modern programming practices were "code quality," "early error detection," "programmer productivity," and "maintenance time or cost." Thus, attempts to build quality into a software product will also lead to gains in productivity as well.

However, getting the right mix of the various qualities (reliability, efficiency, ease of use, ease of change) can be a very complex job. Several studies have explored these qualities and their interactions, e.g. [19] and [85]. Also, some initial approaches have had some success in providing methods for reconciling and managing to multiple quality objectives, such as Design by Objectives [51] and the GOALS approach [23, ch. 3]. An excellent review of the state of the art in software quality metrics is [49].

II. UNDERSTANDING SOFTWARE COSTS

We can consider two primary ways of understanding software costs:

A) The "black-box" or *influence-function* approach, which performs comparative analyses on the overall results of a number of entire software projects, and which tries to characterize the overall effect on software costs of such factors as team objectives, methodological approach, hardware constraints, turnaround time, or personnel experience and capability.

B) The "glass-box" or *cost-distribution*

approach, which analyzes one or more software projects to characterize their internal distribution of costs among such sources as labor versus capital costs, code versus documentation costs, development versus maintenance costs, or other distribution of costs by phase or activity.

These two primary perspectives complement each other, and certainly both are needed to achieve a thorough understanding of software costs. The two parts of this section will explore each of these perspectives in greater detail.

A.   Software Cost Influence Functions

The study of software cost influence functions similarly branches in two main directions: controlled experimentation and observational analysis. We shall discuss the results of each approach in turn below.

1) *Experimental Results:* Some of the earliest experimental results on software cost influence functions were the studies in Reference [54] comparing the effects of batch versus time-sharing computer operation on programming productivity. The experiments typically indicated a 20 percent productivity gain due to time shared interactive operation, but a much more remarkable variation in productivity (up to 26:1) due to differences in programming personnel.

Another set of significant insights resulted from the experiments in Reference [121] discussed earlier, showing the striking effect to team objectives on project productivity and product quality.

During the late 1970's, a number of experiments helped to illuminate the programming process, investigating the effects of code structuring, programming language constructs, code formatting,

commentary, and mnemonic variable names on programming productivity, program comprehensibility, and error rates. A good summary of these experiments is given in [104].

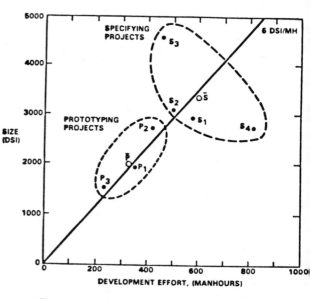

Figure 1.   Prototyping versus specifying size and effort comparisons.

Some initial experiments have explored the effects on productivity of prototyping and fourth-generation languages. A seven-project experiment comparing a specification-oriented versus a prototyping-oriented approach to the development of small, user-intensive application software products [28] found primarily that (see Fig. 1):

- Both approaches resulted in roughly equivalent "productivity" in delivered source instructions per man-hour (DSI/MH).

- The prototyping projects developed products with roughly equivalent performance, but requiring roughly 40 percent fewer DSI and 40 percent fewer manhours than the specifying projects ($\bar{P}$ versus $\bar{S}$ in Fig. 1).

- The specifying projects had less difficulty in debugging and integration due to their development of good interface specifications.

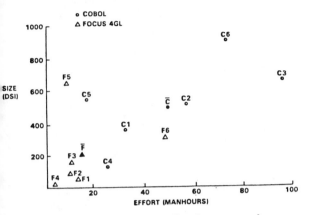

Figure 2. Fourth-generation language size and effort comparisons.

A six-project experiment comparing the use of a third-generation programming language (COBOL) and a fourth-generation language (FOCUS) on a mix of small business-application projects involving both experts and beginners developing both simple and complex applications [59] found primarily that (see Fig. 2):

- On an overall average ($\bar{F}$ versus $\bar{C}$ in Fig. 2), the fourth-generation approach produced equivalent products to the third-generation approach, with about 60 percent fewer DSI and 60 percent fewer manhours (again with roughly equivalent "Productivity" in DSI/MH).

- From project to project, there was a significant variation in the ratio of third generation:fourth generation

DSI (O.9:1 to 27:1), manhours (1.5:1 to 8:1) and DSI/MH (0.5:1 to 5:1).

Implications for Software Productivity Metrics: These two experiments and the earlier Weinberg experiments make it clear that we need better metrics for software productivity than DSI/MH. A number of alternative metrics have been suggested, such as:

- "Software science" or program information-content metrics [58].

- Program control-flow complexity metrics [84].

- Design complexity metrics [36].

- Program-external metrics, such as number of inputs, outputs, files, inquiries interfaces, or function points (a linear combination of those five quantities) [2, 70].

- Work-transaction metrics [38, 114].

In comparing the relative effectiveness of these productivity metrics to a DSI/MH metric, the following conclusions to date can be advanced:

- Each has advantages over DSI/MH in some situations.

- Each has more difficulties than DSI/MH in some situations.

- Each has equivalent difficulties to DSI/MH in relating software achievement units to measures of the software's value added to the user organization.

Thus, the area of software productivity metrics remains in need of further research and experimentation in search of more robust and broadly relevant metrics.

2) *Observational Analyses:* Having

summarized the major *experimental* investigation of software cost drivers, let us look at the related *observational* studies.

A major early observational analysis of software productivity factors was the study done by SDC for the U.S. Air Force in the mid-1960's [91]. This study collected over 100 attributes of 169 software projects. Although the study was not successful in establishing a definitive set of software cost influence functions robust enough for accurate cost estimation, it did identify some of the more significant candidate influence functions for further investigation, such as requirements and design volatility and concurrent hardware development.

Similar early studies which helped to identify significant candidate software cost influence factors were those of [7] and [124]. As an example, the analysis in [124] yielded a set of quantitative software cost influence factors (number of object instructions, type of application, novelty of application, and degree of difficulty) and relationships which were able to support practical software cost estimates across a range of command-control type applications. Some concurrent studies [123], [21] established a reasonably definitive relationship showing the asymptotic increase in software cost as hardware speed and storage constraints approached 100 percent.

A landmark study in analyzing the effect of modern programming practices on software costs was the IBM [115] study of over 50 software projects. It provided conclusive evidence that the use of such practices as structured code, top-down design, structured walkthroughs, and chief programmer teams correlated with software productivity increases on the order

of 50 percent. The study also confirmed the significant impact of such factors as personnel capability and hardware constraints on software productivity, as well as such additional factors as personnel experience and database size.

In the late 1970's a number of software cost models were developed, representing a further level of predictive understanding of the factors influencing software costs. Besides the IBM model based on the results in Reference [115], these included the Doty model [61], the Boeing model [11], the SLIM model [96], the RCA PRICE S model [48], and the COCOMO model [23]. More recently, some further software cost estimation models have been developed such as the Jensen model [68], the Estimacs model [103] and the SPQR model [70]. A comparison of these models (except the two most recent models) in terms of their primary cost driver factors, has been provided in [25].

Software Productivity Ranges: In the context of understanding and controlling software costs, a significant feature of some of these models is the *productivity range* for a software cost driver: the relative multiplicative amount by which that cost driver can influence the software project cost estimated by the model. An example of a set of recently updated *productivity ranges* for the COCOMO model is shown in Fig. 3.[1]

---

[1]The differences between Fig. 3 and its counterpart in [23] are the inclusion of the Requirements Volatility factor, the extension of the Modern Programming Practices range to cover lifecycle costs (using a 30:70 development-maintenance lifecycle cost ratio, this ranges from 1.57 for 2 KDSI products to 1.92 for 512 KDSI products), a widening of the software tools and turnaround time ranges to reflect recent experience with advanced software support environments [20, 26], and the addition of the open-ended range representing the number of software source instructions developed by the project.

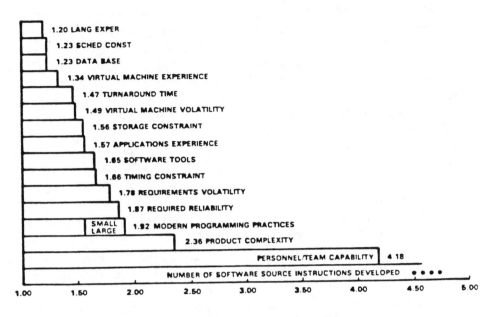

Figure 3. COCOMO software lifecycle productivity ranges, 1985.

Similar productivity ranges have been provided for some other cost models, e.g., [68].

The primary conclusions that can be drawn from the productivity ranges in Fig. 3 are as follows.

- The most significant influence on software costs is the number of source instructions one chooses to program. This leads to cost-reduction strategies involving the use of fourth-generation languages or reusable components to reduce the number of source instructions developed; the use of prototyping and other requirements analysis techniques to ensure that unnecessary functions are not developed, and the use of already-developed software products.

- The next most significant influence by far is that of the selection, moti-vation, and management of the people involved in the software process. In particular, employing the best people possible is usually a bargain, because the productivity range for people usually is much wider than the range of people's salaries. An overall discussion of the concerns involved here is provided in [23, ch. 33]. More extensive treatments of personnel and management considerations are provided in [120, 33, 88], and [98].

- Some of the factors, such as product complexity, required reliability, and database size, are largely fixed features of the software product and not management controllables. Even here, though, appreciable savings can be achieved by reducing unnecessary complexity, and by focusing on appropriate cost-quality tradeoffs as discussed in Section I.

- Requirements volatility is an important and neglected source of cost savings and control. A great deal can be done in particular in using incremental development to control requirements volatility. Frequently, users request (or demand, or require) new features while a software product is under development. In a single-shot full-product development, it is very hard to refuse these requests; as a result, the developers are continually thrashing as the ripple effects of the changes are propagated through the product (and through the project's highly interlocked schedules). With incremental development, on the other hand, it is relatively easy to say, "Fine, that's a good feature. We will schedule it for Increment 4." This allows each increment to operate to a stable plan, thus significantly decreasing the requirements volatility cost escalation factor.

- The other cost driver variables in Fig. 3 are also quite significant particularly if they are addressed in an integrated manner. For more details, see [23, ch. 33] for a discussion of potential productivity strategies for their successful application to an integrated software productivity improvement program.

- The productivity ranges can also be used to assess the impact of other proposed software strategy changes, such as a transition to Ada (and its associated support-environment and modern programming practices). Two such studies have been done for Ada to date. Reference [39], using the COCOMO framework and an expert-consensus approach, estimated a typical 30 percent cost penalty for using Ada in the near term and a cost reduction of at least 40 percent for using Ada in the long term. Reference [61], using the Jensen-model framework, estimated a significantly larger cost penalty for using Ada in the near term, and a typical 25 percent cost reduction for using Ada in the long term.

B.   Software Cost Distribution Insights

Having looked at the experimental and observational "black-box" approaches to understanding software costs, let us now look within the software-production "glass box" for further insight.

There are several approaches to analyzing the distribution of software costs which have provided valuable insights on software cost control. In this section, we will summarize some of the insights gained from analyzing the distribution of:

1)   development and rework costs;

2)   code and documentation costs;

3)   labor and capital costs;

4)   software costs by phase and activity.

We will conclude by presenting a particular type of phase and activity distribution called the *value chain,* and show how it leads to a useful characterization of productivity improvement avenues called here the *software productivity opportunity tree.*

1) *Development Versus Rework Costs:* One of the key insights in improving software productivity is that a large fraction of the effort on a software project is

devoted to rework. This rework effort is needed either to compensate for inappropriately-defined requirements, or to fix errors in the specifications, code or documentation. For example, Reference [70] provides data indicating that the cost of rework is typically over 50 percent on very large projects.

A significant related insight is that the cost of fixing or reworking software is much smaller (by factors of 50 to 200) in the earlier phases of the software life cycle than in the later phases [22, 44, 35]. This has put a high premium on early error detection and correction techniques for software requirements and design specification and verification such as the Software Requirements Engineering Methodology, or SREM [3, 4] and the Problem Statement Language/Problem Statement Analyzer [111]. More recently, it has focused attention on such techniques as rapid prototyping [126, 28, 118] and rapid simulation [125, 109], which focuses on getting the right user requirements early and ensuring that their performance is supportable, thus eliminating a great deal of expensive downstream rework.

Another important point is that rework instances tend to follow a Pareto distribution: 80 percent of the rework costs typically result from 20 percent of the problems. Figure 4 shows some typical distributions of this nature from recent TRW software projects; similar trends have been indicated in [102, 47], and [13]. The major implication of this distribution is that software verification and validation activities should focus on identifying and eliminating the specific *high-risk* problems to be encountered by a software project, rather than spreading their available early-problem-elimination effort uniformly

across trivial and severe problems. Even more strongly, this implies that a risk-driven approach to the software lifecycle such as the spiral model [27] is preferable to a more *document-driven* model such as the traditional waterfall model.

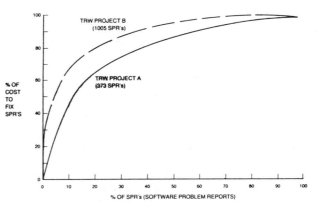

Figure 4. **Rework costs are concentrated in few high-risk items.**

The Spiral Model: The spiral model is illustrated in Fig. 5. The radial dimension in Fig. 5 represents the cumulative cost incurred in accomplishing the steps to date; the angular dimension represents the progress made in completing each cycle of the spiral. The model holds that each cycle involves a progression through the same sequence of steps, for each portion of the products and for each of its levels of elaboration, from an overall concept-of-operation document down to the coding of each individual program.

Each cycle of the spiral begins with the identification of:

•   The *objectives* of the portion of the product being elaborated (performance, functionality, ability to accommodate change, etc.).

•   The *alternative* means of imple-

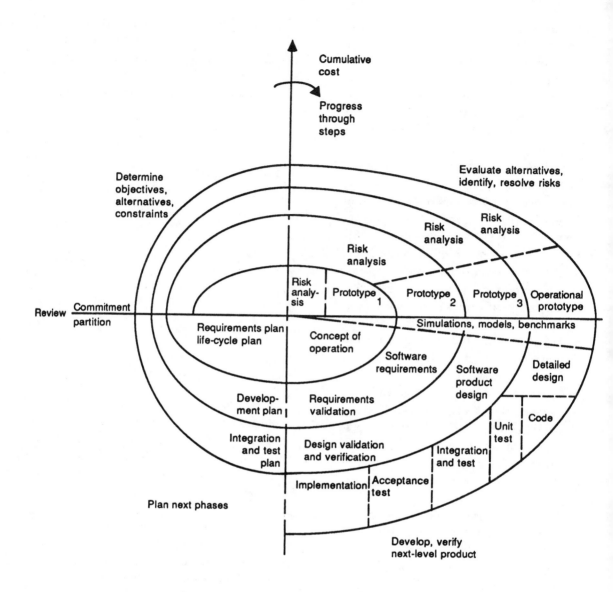

Figure 5. Spiral model of the software process (not to scale).

menting this portion of the product (design A, design B, reuse, buy, etc.).

- The *constraints* imposed on the application of the alternatives (cost, schedule, interface, etc.).

The next step is to *evaluate* the alternatives with respect to the objectives and constraints. Frequently, this process will identify areas of uncertainty which are significant sources of project risk. If so, the next step should involve the *formulation* of a cost-effective strategy for *resolving the sources of risk.* This may involve prototyping, simulation, administering user questionnaires, analytic modeling, or combinations of these and other risk-resolution techniques.

Once the risks are evaluated, the next step is determined by the relative risks remaining. If performance or user-interface risks strongly dominate program development or internal interface-control risks, the next step may be an evolutionary development step: a minimal effort to specify the overall nature of the product, a plan for the next level of prototyping, and the development of a more detailed prototype to continue to resolve the major risk issues. On the other hand, if previous prototyping efforts have already resolved all of the performance or user-interface risks, and program development or interface-control risks dominate, the next step follows the basic waterfall approach, modified as appropriate to incorporate incremental development.

The spiral model also accommodates any appropriate mixture of specification oriented, prototype-oriented, simulation-oriented, automatic transformation oriented, or other approaches to software development, where the appropriate mixed strategy is chosen by considering the relative magnitude of the program risks, and the relative effectiveness of the various techniques in resolving the risks. (In a similar way, risk-management considerations determine the amount of time and effort which should be devoted to such other project activities as planning, configuration management, quality assurance, formal verification, or testing.)

An important feature of the spiral model is that each cycle is completed by a review involving the primary people or organizations concerned with the products. This review covers all of the products developed during the previous cycle, including the *plans for the next cycle* and the resources required to carry them out. The major objective of the review is to ensure that all concerned parties are mutually committed to the approach to be taken for the next phase.

The plans for succeeding phases may also include a *partition* of the product into increments for successive development, or components to be developed by individual organizations or persons. Thus, the *review and commitment* step may range from an individual walkthrough of the design of a single programmer component, to a major requirements review involving developer, customer, user, and maintenance organizations.

2) *Code Versus Documentation Costs:* Most of the efforts to date in developing software support environments have been focused on capabilities to improve people's productivity in developing code. However, recent analyses have shown that most projects to develop production-engineered software products spend more of the project's effort in activities leading to a document as their immediate end product, as compared to activities whose immediate end product is code. These documents include not only specifications and manuals, but also plans, studies, reports, memoranda, letters and a wide variety of forms. The volume of documentation with respect to lines of code tends to vary by application; Reference [70] reports a typical 28 pages of documentation per thousand instructions (pp/KDSI) for internal commercial programs and a typical 66 pp/KDSI for commercial software products of the same size (50 KDSI).

The proportion of documentation-related to code-related effort averaged about 60:40 over the COCOMO data base of projects [23] and about 67:33 for large TRW projects [20]. These proportions have caused some recent software development environments such as the Xerox Cedar system [112] and the TRW Software Productivity System [20] to focus on the provision of extensive documentation and office-automation aids, and on the close integration of these functions with code-oriented functions.

3) *Labor Versus Capital Costs:* It is generally recognized that software development and evolution are extremely labor-intensive activities, and that a great deal of productivity leverage can be gained by making software production a more capital-intensive activity. Typically, capital investment per software worker has been little different from the $2000–3000 per person typical of office workers in general. However, a number of organizations such as Xerox, TRW, IBM, and Bell Laboratories have indicated that significantly higher investments per person have more than recaptured the investment via improved software productivity. Similar results on the payoffs of capital investments in better facilities and support capabilities have been reported in [81] and [37]. An excellent overall survey of software capitalization strategies is provided in [119].

4) *Software Costs by Phase and Activity:* A great deal of insight into controlling software costs has come from analyses of the distribution of costs by phase and activity. Some of the earliest results, such as [16], indicated the high proportion of project effort devoted to integration and test, and the importance of good test planning, test support, and interface specification. (Another early paper [63] stated that "a good software interface specification was quite literally worth its weight in gold.")

Subsequent analysis of software development effort distribution such as [124] indicated the significant fraction of project effort devoted to nonprogramming activities (configuration management, quality assurance, planning and control, etc.), and the high potential leverage involved in making these activities more productive.

Another major insight has been the recognition that most of the cost of a software product is incurred after its initial development is complete [43, 22, 35]. Subsequent analyses of the sources and distribution of these software life-cycle evolution costs (often misleadingly called maintenance costs) such as [14] and [79], provided a number of insights on how to reduce software evolution costs. Several recent sources such as [2] and [6] have provided more specific detail on software evolution cost reduction activities.

5) *The Software Product Value Chain:* The value chain, developed by Porter and his associates at the Harvard Business School [94, 95], is a useful method of understanding and controlling the costs involved in a wide variety of organizational enterprises. It identifies a canonical set of cost sources or value activities, representing the basic activities an organization can choose from to create added value for its products. Figure 6 shows a value chain for software development representative of experiment at TRW. Definitions and explanations of the component value activities are given below. These are divided into what Reference [95]

calls primary activities (inbound logistics, outbound logistics, marketing and sales, service, and operations) and support activities (infrastructure, human resource management, technology development, and procurement).

Primary Activities: Inbound logistics covers activities associated with receiving, storing, and disseminating inputs to the products. This can be quite large for a manufacturer of, say, automobiles; for software it consumes less than 1 percent of the development outlay. (For software, the related support activity of *procurement* is also included here.)

Outbound logistics covers activities concerned with collecting, storing, and physically distributing the product to buyers. Again, for software, this consumes less than 1 percent of the total.

Marketing and sales covers activities associated with providing a means by which buyers can purchase the product and inducing them to do so. A 5 percent figure is typical of government contract software organizations. Software product houses would typically have a higher figure; internal applications-programming shops would typically have a lower figure.

Service covers activities associated with providing service to enhance or maintain the value of the product. For software, this comprises the activities generally called software maintenance or evolution.

Operations covers activities associated with transforming inputs into the final product form. For software, operations typically involves roughly four-fifths of the total development outlay.

In such a case, the value-chain analysis involves breaking up a large component into constituent activities. Fig. 6 shows such a breakup into management

(7 percent), quality assurance and configuration management (5 percent), and the distribution of technical effort among the various development phases. This phase breakdown also covers the cost sources due to rework. Thus, for, example, of the 20 percent overall cost of the technical effort during the integration and test phase, 13 percent is devoted to activities required to rework deficiencies in or reorientations of the requirements, design, code, or documentation; the other 7 percent represents the amount of effort required to run tests, perform integration functions, and complete documentation even if no problems were detected in the process.

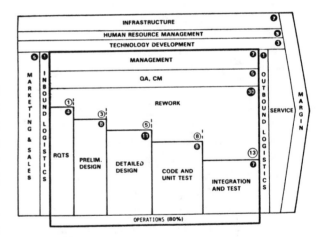

Figure 6. Software development value chain.

Support Activities: Infrastructure covers such activities as the organization's general management planning, finance, accounting, legal, and government affairs of the organization. The 8 percent figure is typical of most organizations.

Human resource management covers activities involved in recruiting, hiring, training, development, and compensation of all types of personnel. Given the labor-intensive and technology-intensive nature of software development, the 3 percent figure indicated here is a less-than-optimal investment.

Technology development covers activities devoted to creating or tailoring new technology to improve the organization's products or processes. The 3 percent investment figure here is higher than many software organizations, but still less than optimal as an investment to improve software productivity and quality.

Margin and Service: Margin in the value chain is the difference between the value of the resulting product and the collective costs of performing the value activities. As this difference varies widely among software products, it is not quantitatively defined in Fig. 6. Similarly, "service" or "evolution" costs have not been assigned a value in Fig. 6. Evolution costs are typically 70 percent of software lifecycle costs, but since some initial analyses have indicated that the detailed value chain distribution of software costs is not markedly different from the distribution of development costs in Fig. 6, we will use Fig. 6 to represent the distribution of lifecycle costs.

Software Development Value Chain Implications: The primary implication of the software development value chain is that the "Operations" component is the key to significant improvements. Not only is it the major source of software costs, but also most of the remaining components such as "Human Resources" will scale down in a manner proportional to the scaling down of Operations costs.

Another major characteristic of the value chain is that virtually all of the components are still highly labor-intensive.

Thus, as discussed in Section II-B-3, there are significant opportunities in providing automated aids to make these activities more efficient and capital-investive.

Further, it implies that human-resource and management activities have much higher leverage than their 3 percent and 7 percent investment levels indicate.

The breakdown of the Operations component indicates that the leading strategies for cost savings in software development involve:

- *Making individual steps more efficient,* via such capabilities as automated aids to software requirements analysis or testing.

- *Eliminating steps,* via such capabilities as automatic programming or automatic quality assurance.

- *Eliminating rework,* via early error detection or via such capabilities as rapid prototyping to avoid later requirements rework.

In addition, further major cost savings can be achieved by reducing the total number of elementary Operations steps, by developing products requiring the creation of fewer lines of code. This has the effect of reducing the overall size of the Value Chain itself. This source of savings breaks down into two primary options:

- *Building simpler products,* via more insightful front-end activities such as prototyping or risk management.

- *Reusing software components,* via such capabilities as fourth-generation languages or component libraries.

6) *The Software Productivity Improvement Opportunity Tree:* This breakdown of the major sources of software cost savings leads to the *Software Productivity Improvement Opportunity Tree* shown in Fig. 7. This hierarchical breakdown helps us to understand how to fit the various attractive productivity options into an overall integrated software productivity improvement strategy.

Most of the individual productivity options have been discussed in earlier sections of this paper. Here, we will provide a recap of the previous options, and further discussion of the additional options identified in the Opportunity Tree.

Making People More Effective: The major sources of opportunity in dealing with people were covered in discussing the large productivity range due to personnel capability in Section II-A-2, and the labor versus capital costs discussion in Section II-B-3. Additional facilities-oriented gains were covered in the discussions of interactive software development in Section II-A-1, and of avoiding hardware constraints in Section II-A-1. Providing software personnel with private offices is another cost-effective facilities opportunity, leading to productivity gains of roughly 11 percent at IBM-Santa Teresa [70] and 8 percent at TRW [20]. In addition, the productivity leverage of *creative incentive structures* can be quite striking. For example, a program to provide extra bonuses for people who reuse rather

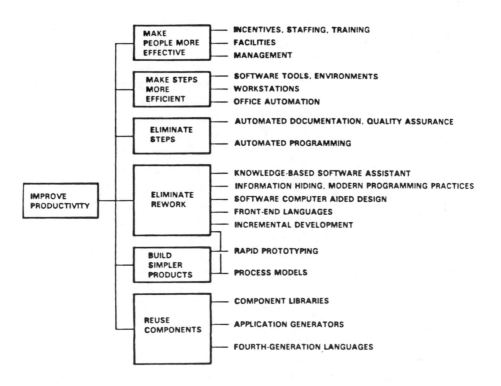

Figure 7. Productivity improvement opportunity tree.

than rebuild software has led to significant increases in the amount of software reused from previous applications.

Making Steps More Efficient: The primary leverage factor in making the existing software process steps more efficient is the use of software tools to automate the current repetitive and labor-intensive portions of each step. Such tools have a long history of development; some good surveys of various classes of tools are given in [74] and [99].

More recently, it has become clear that such tools are much more effective if they are part of an *Integrated Project Support Environment* (IPSE). The primary features which distinguish an IPSE from an ad hoc collection of tools are as follows:

- A *set of common assumptions* about the software process model being supported by the tools (or, more strongly, a particular software development method being supported by the tools).

- An integrated *Project Master Database* or *Persistent Object Base* serving as a unified repository of the entities created during the software process, along with their various versions, attributes, and relationships.

- *Support of the entire range of users and activities* involved in the software project, not just of programmers developing code.

- A *unified user interface* providing easy and natural ways for various classes of project personnel (expert programmers, novice librarians, secretaries, managers, planning and control personnel, etc.) to draw on the tools in the IPSE.

- A *critical-mass ensemble of tools,* covering significant portions of software project activities.

- A *computer-communication architecture* facilitating user access to data and resources in the IPSE.

Some good references describing the nature and functions of IPSE's are [32, 117, 64, 90] and [110]. Some good examples of IPSE's with extensive usage experience include CADES [87], Interlisp [113], the AT&T Unix environment [73], the U.S. Navy FASP system [108], the TRW Software Productivity System [20], and the Xerox Cedar System [112]. Some early examples of advanced concepts and prototype environments are found in [117]. Later examples are so abundant that it is virtually impossible to summarize them concisely; a good recent source is [12].

Eliminating Steps: A good many automated aids go beyond simply making steps more efficient, to the point of fully eliminating previous manual steps. If we compare software development today with its counterpart in the 1950's, we see that *assemblers and compilers* are excellent examples of ways of vastly improving productivity by eliminating steps. More recent examples of eliminating steps are process construction systems [122, 45], software standards checkers and other quality assurance functions [19, 106]; and requirements and design consistency checkers [3, 15, 111].

More ambitious efforts to eliminate steps involve the automation of the entire programming process, by providing capabilities which operate directly on a set of software specifications to automatically generate computer programs. There are two major branches to this approach:

domain-specific and *domain-independent* automatic programming.

The domain-specific approach gains advantages by capitalizing on domain knowledge in transforming specifications into programs, and in constraining the universe of programming discourse to a relatively smaller domain. In the limit, one reaches the boundary with fourth-generation languages such as Visicalc, which are excellent automatic programming systems within a very narrow domain, and relatively ineffective outside that domain. A good example and survey of more general approaches to domain-specific automatic programming is given in [11].

The domain-independent approach offers much broader payoff in the long run, but has more difficulty in achieving efficient implementations of larger-scale programs. Some good progress is being made in this direction, such as the USC-ISI work culminating in the FSD system [9], the Kestrel Institute work on the PSI and CHI systems [56, 105], and the MIT Programmer's Apprentice project [101, 118]. An excellent summary of automatic programming approaches can be obtained from the November 1985 issue of the *IEEE Transactions on Software Engineering.*

Eliminating Rework: One can also extend automatic programming in a direction which provides expert assistance to programmers (and more generally, to all software project members) to aid them in making the right decisions in algorithm selection, data structuring, choice of reusable components, change control, test planning, and overall software project planning and control. This concept of a *knowledge based software assistant* (KBSA) has been thoroughly described in

[55]. The primary benefit of a KBSA will be the elimination of much of the rework currently experienced on software projects due to the belated appreciation that a previous programming or project decision was inappropriate, resulting in work that needs to be redone. A number of prototype KBSA's are currently under development.

If we specialize the KBSA concept of the area of software design, we find the rich area of *software computer aided design* (CAD). In the hardware area, CAD has been a major source of improving productivity by eliminating rework via automated design checking and simulation, and also of promoting better designs via better visualization of a design and its effects. Recent examples of software CAD capabilities include *interactive graphics support systems* such as the Xerox CEDAR system [112], the Brown PECAN system [100], the Carleton CAEDE system [31], and such commercial systems as Excelerator, Teamwork, ProMod, Software Through Pictures, CASE, Ada Graph, and PRISM; *rapid simulation capabilities* such as RSA [109]; and executable specification capabilities such as PAISLEY [125].

A short step from software CAD systems are the *requirements and design language-oriented systems,* which eliminate a great deal of rework through more formal and unambiguous specifications, automated consistency and completeness checking and automated traceability of requirements to design. Probably the most extensive of these systems is the distributed Computing Design System [4], which includes a system specification language (SSL), a software requirements specification language (RSL), a distributed-system design language (DDL), and a module description language (MDL).

One of the main difficulties in developing good software CAD systems is our incomplete understanding of the software design process. Examples of recent progress in this direction can be found in [34, 1], and [71].

A most powerful technique for eliminating rework is the *information-hiding* approach developed by Parnas [92] and applied in the U.S. Navy A-7 project [93]. This approach minimizes rework by hiding implementation decisions within modules; thus minimizing the ripple effects usually encountered when software implementation decisions need to be changed. The information hiding approach can be particularly effective in eliminating rework during software evolution, by *identifying the portions of the software most likely to undergo change* (characteristics of workstations, input data formats, etc.) and hiding these sources of evolutionary change within modules.

Some other sources for eliminating rework have been discussed earlier, such as the use of *modern programming practices* in Section II-C and II-A-2, the use of *incremental development* to reduce requirements volatility in Section II-A-2, and the use of *rapid prototyping* and risk-driven *software process models* in the discussion of development versus rework costs in Section II-B-1.

Building Simpler Products: The last two approaches associated with eliminating rework in the Opportunity Tree in Fig. 7, rapid prototyping and improved software process models, can also be very effective in improving bottom-line productivity by building simple products. This is done largely by eliminating software gold-

plating: extra software which not only consumes extra effort, but also reduces the conceptual integrity of the product. The [28] prototyping versus specifying experiment discussed in Section II-A-1 indicated that prototyping resulted in an average of 40 percent less code, 40 percent less effort, and a set of products that were easier to use and learn. One of the telling insights in this experiment was the comment of one of the participants using the specification approach: "Words are cheap." During the specification phase, it is all too easy to add gold-plating functions to the product specification, without a good understanding of their effect on the product's conceptual integrity or the project's required effort. As expressed in the excellent book, *The Elements of Friendly Software Design* [60]:

> Most programmers. . .defined their use of a software feature by saying, "You don't have to use it if you don't want to, so what harm can it do?" It can do a great deal of harm. The user might spend time trying to understand the feature, only to decide it isn't needed, or he may accidentally use the feature and not know what has happened or how to get out of the mistake. If a feature is inconsistent with the rest of the user interface, the user might draw false conclusions about the other commands. The feature must be documented, which makes the user's manual thicker. The cumulative effect of such features is to overwhelm the user and obscure communication with your program. . .

A further discussion of typical sources of software gold-plating, and an approach for evaluating potential gold-plating features, is provided in [23]. A related phenomenon to avoid is the "second system syndrome" discussed in [29]. A recent useful technique for product feature prioritization called the request-success grid is provided in [107]. Further useful principles of good user-interface design are provided in [41] and [53].

Some of the newer *software process models* stimulate the development of simpler products. One of the difficulties of the traditional waterfall model is that its specification-driven approach can frequently lead one along the "words are cheap" road toward gold-plated products, as discussed above. The evolutionary development model [86] emphasizes the use of prototyping capabilities to converge on the necessary or high-leverage software product features essential to the user's mission. The related transformational model [10] shortcuts the problem by providing (where available) a direct transformation from specification to executing code, thus supporting both a specification-based and an evolutionary-development approach. The spiral model [27] focuses on a continuing determination of user's mission objectives, and a continuing cost-benefit analysis of candidate software product features in terms of their contribution to mission objectives. Further information on recent progress in software process models can be found in [77] and [40].

Reusing Components: Another key to improving productivity by writing less code involves the reuse of existing software components. The simplest approach in this direction involves the development and use of *libraries of software components*. A great deal of progress has been made in this direction, particularly in such areas as mathematical and statistical routines and operating system related utilities. A great deal of further progress is

possible via similar capabilities in user-application areas. For example, Raytheon's library and system of reusable business-application components has achieved typical figures of 60 percent reusable code for new applications [75] and typical cost savings of 10 percent in the design phase, 50 percent in the code and test phase, and 60 percent in the maintenance phase [97]. Toshiba's system of reusable components for industrial process control [83] has resulted in typical productivity rates of over 2000 source instructions per man-month for high-quality industrial software products.

At this level of sophistication, such systems should better be called *application generators,* rather than component libraries, because they have addressed several system-oriented component-compatibility issues such as component interface conventions, data structuring, and program control and error handling conventions. Similar characteristics have made Unix a particularly strong foundation for developing *application generators* [72, 116].

One can proceed even further in this direction to create a *very high level language or fourth generation language* (4GL) by adding a language for specifying desired applications and a set of capabilities for interpreting user specifications, configuring the appropriate set of components, and executing the resulting program. Currently, the most fertile areas for 4GL's are in the areas of spreadsheet calculators (Visicalc, Multiplan, 1-2-3, etc.), and small-business systems typically featuring a DBMS, report generator, database query language, and graphics package (NOMAD, RAMIS, FOCUS, ADF,

DBase II, etc). A good survey of these latter 4GL's is [62].

As discussed in Section II-A-1, the most definitive experiment to date comparing a 3GL (COBOL) and a 4GL (FOCUS) found an average reduction of about 60 percent in both lines of code developed and in man-hours expended to develop a sample of six applications. Reference [57] provides further evidence from a survey of 43 organizations that such 4GL's reduce personnel costs, reduce user frustrations, and more quickly satisfy user information needs within their domain of applicability. On the other hand, the survey found 4GL's extremely inefficient of computer resources and difficult to interface with conventional applications programs. Some major disasters have occurred in attempting to apply 4GL's to large, high-performance applications such as the New Jersey motor vehicle registration system [8].

Overall, though, 4GL's offer an extremely attractive option for significantly improving software productivity, and attempts are underway to create 4GL capabilities for other application areas. Short of a 4GL capability, the other more limited approaches to reusability such as component libraries and application generators can both generate near-term cost savings and serve as a foundation of more ambitious 4GL capabilities in the long run. A very good collection of articles on reusability in software development is the September 1984 issue of the *IEEE Transactions on Software Engineering*.

III. CONTROLLING SOFTWARE COSTS

Now that we have a better understanding of the primary sources of software costs and of the ways of reducing them, how can we use this understanding to improve our ability to control software costs? There are two primary avenues for doing this, as discussed below:

1) Building our understanding into a framework of objectives, which serve as a basis for a set of management-by-objectives (MBO) control loops.

2) Optimizing our software development and evolution strategy around predictability and control.

A.   Management By Objectives (MBO)

The simplest sort of MBO for software project predictability and control is exemplified by the earned-value framework discussed in [23, ch. 32], and illustrated in Fig. 8. In this framework, a set of cost and schedule estimates by phase, activity, and product components are used to generate a set of PERT charts, work breakdown structures, personnel plans, summary task planning sheets, and other scarce-resource allocations which determine a set of "should-cost" targets for each job. As the project progresses, various instruments such as unit development folders and earned value systems are used to compare actual progress and expenditure of time, cost, personnel, or other scarce resources versus the plans. Then, comparing the actual progress and expenditure versus the plans can generate a set of exception reports which flag key areas for MBO attention.

This generic approach has been highly successful in many situations, but it frequently needs extension to balance cost, schedule, and functionality objectives with other important quality-oriented objectives. The best approach to date in han-

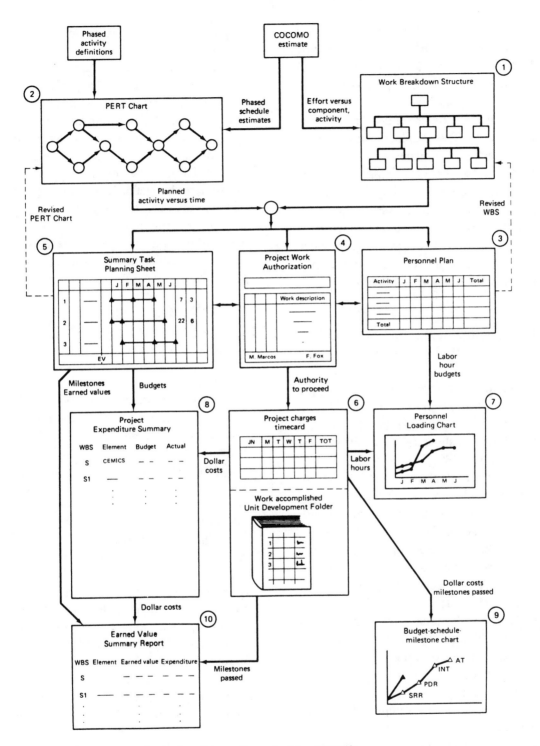

Figure 8. Software project planning and control framework.

dling these additional objectives has been to incorporate them as additional specific MBO targets, as in Design by Objectives [51] and the GOALS approach [23].

Actually, it is even better to do this in terms of the software end-user's mission objectives. This implies that the users must perform an analysis of the relative costs and benefits of alternative software product functions and features, to relate these to incremental gains in mission cost-effectiveness, and to use this information in an overall MBO control loop in which the software is only a part. For examples of this type of approach, see [80, 5, 65] and [76].

B.   Optimizing Around Software Predictability and Control

Frequently, software customers are more concerned about predictability and control of software cost and schedule than they are about the absolute values of the cost and schedule [89]. Such customers prefer a project which may cost a bit more, but which allows them to confidently synchronize their software development with other critical developments such as a satellite launch, a factory opening, or a major service cutover. In such situations, customers will generally prefer a risk-driven development approach which invests some additional early time and effort into identifying and eliminating the primary sources of project risk—as contrasted with a "success-oriented" approach which will be very efficient if all the project's optimistic assumptions are true, but very costly if reality runs out otherwise (as it frequently does). The spiral model discussed in Section II-B-1 is an ex-

ample of such a risk-driven development approach.

Another option which can be derived from the risk-driven spiral approach is the option to trade marginal product functionality for project predictability and control, using a design-to-cost or design-to-schedule approach. Thus, if the highest project risk is associated with exceeding the available budget or with missing a crucial delivery date, the project can reduce risk by designating borderline product capabilities as a management reserve to be traded against budget and schedule pressures as necessary.

IV.   CONCLUSIONS

The information and discussions above support the following primary conclusions:

1) Understanding and controlling software costs is extremely important, not just from an economic standpoint, but also in terms of our future quality of life.

2) Understanding and controlling software costs inevitably requires us to understand and control the various aspects of software quality as well.

3) There are two primary ways of understanding software costs. The "black box" or influence function approach provides useful insights on the relative productivity and quality leverage of various management, technical, environment, and personnel options. The "glass box" or cost distribution approach helps identify strategies for integrated software productivity and quality improvement programs, via such structures as the *value chain* and the *software productivity opportunity tree*.

4) The most attractive individual strate-

gies for improving software productivity are:

- *writing less code,* by reusing software components, developing and using very high level languages, and avoiding software gold-plating;

- *getting the best from people,* via better management, staffing, incentives, and work environments;

- *avoiding rework,* via better risk management, prototyping, incremental development, software computer aided design, and modern programming practices, particularly information hiding;

- *developing and using integrated project support environments.*

5) Good frameworks of techniques exist for controlling software budgets, schedules, and work completed. There have been some initial attempts to extend these to support control with respect to software quality objectives and end-user system objectives, but a great deal more progress is needed in these directions.

6) The better we are able to understand software cost and qualities, the better we are able to control them—and vice versa.

REFERENCES

[1] B. Adelson and E. Soloway, "The Role of Domain Experience in Software Design," *IEEE Transactions on Software Engineering,* Vol. SE-11, pp. 1351-60, November 1985.

[2] A.J. Albrecht, "Measuring Application Development Productivity," in *Proceedings of the SHARE-GUIDE Applications Development Symposium,* October 1979, pp. 83-92.

[3] M.W. Alford, "A Requirements Engineering Methodology for Real-Time Processing Requirements," *IEEE Transactions on Software Engineering,* Vol. SE-3, pp. 60-68, January 1977.

[4] _____ , "SREM at the Age of Eight: The Distributed Computing Design System," *Computer,* Vol. 18, April 1985.

[5] J. Allen and B.P. Lientz, *Systems in Action: A Managerial and Social Approach,* Goodyear, 1978.

[6] R.S. Arnold, ed., *Software Maintenance Workshop Record,* IEEE, December 1983.

[7] J.D. Aron, "Estimating Resources for Large Programming Systems," NATO Science Committee, Rome, Italy, October 1969; in *Software Engineering Techniques,* Buxton and Randell, eds.

[8] C. Babcock, "New Jersey Motorists in Software Jam," *Computerworld,* pp. 1, 6, September 30, 1985.

[9] R.M. Balzer, "A 15 Year Perspective on Automatic Programming," *IEEE Transactions on Software Engineering,* Vol. SE-11, November 1985.

[10] _____ , T.E. Cheatham, and C. Green, "Software Technology in the 1990's: Using a New Paradigm," *Computer,* Vol. 16, pp. 39-45, November 1983.

[11] D.R. Barstow, "Domain-Specific Automatic Programming," *IEEE Transactions on Software Engineering,* Vol. SE-11, pp. 1321-36, November 1985.

[12] _____ , H. Shrobe, and E. Sandewall, *Interactive Programming*

Environments. New York: McGraw-Hill, 1984.

[13] V.R. Basili and D.M. Weiss, "Evaluation of a Software Requirements Document by Means of Change Data," in *Proceedings of the Fifth International Conference on Software Engineering,* IEEE, March 1981, pp. 314-323.

[14] L.A. Belady and M.M. Lehman, "Characteristics of Large Systems," *Research Directions in Software Technology,* P. Wegner, ed. Cambridge, Mass.: MIT Press, 1979.

[15] T.E. Bell, D.C. Bixler, and M.E. Dyer, "An Extendible Approach to Computer-Aided Software Requirements Engineering," *IEEE Transactions on Software Engineering,* pp. 49-59, January 1977.

[16] H.D. Benington, "Production of Large Computer Programs," in *Proceedings of the ONR Symposium on Advanced Programming Methods for Digital Computers,* June 1956, pp. 15-27; also in *Proceedings of the Ninth International Conference on Software Engineering,* IEEE, March 1987.

[17] R.K.D. Black, R.P. Curnow, R. Katz, and M.D. Gray, "BCS Software Production Data," Boeing Computer Services, Inc., *Final Technical Report RADC-TR-77-116,* NTIS No. AD-A039852, March 1977.

[18] B.H. Boar, *Application Prototyping.* New York: Wiley, 1984.

[19] B.W. Boehm, J.R. Brown, H. Kaspar, M. Lipow, E.J. MacLeod, and M.J. Merritt, *Characteristics of Software Quality.* Amsterdam, The Netherlands: North-Holland, 1978.

[20] B.W. Boehm, M.H. Penedo, E.D. Stuckle, R.D. Williams, and A.H. Pyster, "A Software Development Environment for Improving Productivity," *Computer,* Vol. 17, pp. 30-44, June 1984.

[21] B.W. Boehm, "Software and Its Impact: A Quantitative Assessment," *Datamation,* pp. 48-59, May 1973.

[22] _____ , "Software Engineering," *IEEE Transactions on Computing,* Vol. C-25, pp. 1226-41, December 1976.

[23] _____ , *Software Engineering Economics.* Englewood Cliffs, N.J.: Prentice-Hall, 1981.

[24] _____ , "The Hardware/Software Cost Ratio: Is It a Myth?" *Computer,* Vol. 16, pp. 78-80, March 1983.

[25] _____ , "Software Engineering Economics," *IEEE Transactions on Software Engineering,* Vol. SE-10, pp. 4-21, January 1984.

[26] _____ ,"COCOMO: Answering the Most Frequent Questions," in *Proceedings of the COCOMO Users' Group,* Wang Institute, May 1985.

[27] _____ , "A Spiral Model of Software Development and Enhancement," *Computer,* Vol. 21, pp. 61-72, May 1988.

[28] _____ , T.E. Gray, and T. Seewaldt, "Prototyping vs. Specifying: A Multi-Project Experiment," *IEEE Transactions on Software Engineering,* Vol. SE-10, pp. 133-45, May 1984.

[29] F.P. Brooks, Jr., *The Mythical Man-Month.* Reading, Mass.: Addison-Wesley, 1975.

[30] J.R. Brown and M. Lipow, "The Quantitative Measurement of Software Safety and Reliability," TRW Report QR 1776, August 1973.

[31] R.J.A. Buhr, C.M. Woodside, G.M. Karam, K. Van Der Loo, and G.D. Lewis, "Experiments with Prolog Design Descriptions and Tools in CAEDE: An Iconic Design Environment for Multitasking, Embedded Systems," in *Proceedings of the Eighth International Conference on Software Engineering*, August 1985, pp. 62-67.

[32] J. Buxton, "Requirements for Ada Programming Support Environments: 'Stoneman,' " U.S. Dept. of Defense, OSD/R&E, Washington, DC, February 1980.

[33] J.D. Couger and R.A. Zawacki, *Motivating and Managing Computer Personnel.* New York: Wiley, 1980.

[34] B. Curtis, "Fifteen Years of Psychology in Software Engineering: Individual Differences and Cognitive Science," in *Proceedings of the Seventh International Conference on Software Engineering*, March 1984, pp. 97-106.

[35] E.B. Daly, "Management of Software Engineering," *IEEE Transactions on Software Engineering*, Vol. SE-3, pp. 229-42, May 1977.

[36] T. De Marco, *Controlling Software Projects.* New York: Yourdon, 1982.

[37] _____ and T. Lister, "Programmer Performance and the Effects of the Workplace," in *Proceedings of the Eighth International Conference on Software Engineering*, August 1985, pp. 268-72.

[38] W.J. Doherty and R.P. Kelisky, "Managing VM/CMS for User Effectiveness," *IBM Systems Journal*, Vol. 18, No. 1, pp. 143-63, 1979.

[39] A. Douville, J. Salasin, and T.H. Probert, "Ada Impact on COCOMO Workshop Report," *Inst. Defense Analysis*, May 1985.

[40] M. Dowson and J.C. Wileden, eds., *Proceedings of the Second Software Process Workshop (ACM Software Engineering Notes)*, August 1986.

[41] S.W. Draper and D.A. Norman, "Software Engineering for User Interfaces," *IEEE Transactions on Software Engineering*, Vol. SE-11, March 1985.

[42] Electronic Industries Association, "DoD Computing Activities and Programs: Ten Year Market Forecast Issues, 1985-1995," Oct. 1985.

[43] J.L. Elshoff, "An Analysis of Some Commercial PL/I programs," *IEEE Transactions on Software Engineering*, Vol. SE-2, pp. 113-20, June 1976.

[44] M.R. Fagan, "Design and Code Inspections to Reduce Errors in Program Development," *IBM Systems Journal*, Vol. 15, No. 3, pp. 182-211, 1976.

[45] S.I. Feldman, "MAKE—A Program for Maintaining Computer Programs," *Unix Programmers' Manual*, Vol. 9, pp. 255-65, April 1979.

[46] D. Fisher, "Software Costs in the Department of Defense," IDA Report R-1079, 1974.

[47] G. Formica, "Software Management by the European Space Agency: Lessons Learned and Future Plans," in *Proceedings of the Third International Software Management Con-*

ference, AIAA/RAeS, London, October 1978, pp. 15-35.

[48]   F.R. Freiman and R.E. Park, "PRICE Software Model Version 3: An Overview," in *Proceedings of the IEEE-PINY Workshop Quantitative Software Models,* IEEE Catalog No. TH0067-9, October 1979, pp. 32-41.

[49]   E. Frewin, P. Hamer, B. Kitchenham, N. Ross, and L. Wood, "Quality Measurement and Modeling—State of the Art Report," ESPRIT Report REQUEST/STC-gdf/001/51/QL-RP/00.7, July 1985.

[50]   "GUIDE Survey of New Programming Technologies," *Guide Proceedings,* GUIDE, Inc., Chicago, Ill., pp. 306-308, 1979.

[51]   T. Gilb, *Design by Objectives.* Amsterdam, The Netherlands: North-Holland, 1985.

[52]   R.L. Glass and R.A. Noiseux, *Software Maintenance Guidebook.* Englewood Cliffs, N.J.: Prentice-Hall, 1981.

[53]   J.D. Gould and C. Lewis, "Designing for Usability: Key Principles and What Designers Think," *Communications of the ACM,* pp. 300-11, March 1985.

[54]   E. Grant and H. Sackman, "An Exploratory Investigation of Programmer Performance Under On-Line and Off-Line Conditions," System Development Corp., Report SP-2581, September 1966.

[55]   C.C. Green, D. Luckham, R. Balzer, T. Cheatham, and C. Rich, "Report on a Knowledge-Based Software Assistant," USAF/RADC Report RADC-TR-195, August 1983.

[56]   C.C. Green, "The Design of the PSI Program Synthesis System," in *Proceedings of the Second International Conference on Software Engineering,* October 1976, pp. 4-18.

[57]   T. Guimaraes, "A Study of Application Program Development Techniques," *Communications of the ACM,* pp. 494-99, May 1985.

[58]   M.H. Halstead, *Elements of Software Science.* New York: Elsevier, 1977.

[59]   E. Harel and E.R. McLean, "The Effects of Using a Nonprocedural Language on Programmer Productivity," UCLA Graduate School of Management, Information Systems Working Paper 3-83, November 1982.

[60]   P. Heckel, *The Elements of Friendly Software Design.* Warner Books, 1984.

[61]   J.R. Herd, J.N. Postak, W.E. Russel, and K.R. Stewart, "Software Cost Estimation Study—Study Results," Doty Associates, Inc., Rockville, Md., Final Technical Report RADC-TR-77-220, Vol. I (of two), June 1977.

[62]   E. Horowitz, A. Kemper, and B. Narasimhan, "A Survey of Application Generators," *IEEE Software,* Vol. 2, pp. 40-54, January 1985.

[63]   W.A. Hosier, "Pitfalls and Safeguards in Real-Time Digital Systems with Emphasis on Programming," *IRE Transactions on Engineering Management,* pp. 99-115, June 1961; in *Proceedings of the Ninth International Conference on Software Engineering,* IEEE, March 1987.

[64]   H. Hunke, ed., *Software Engineer-*

ing Environments. Amsterdam, The Netherlands: North-Holland, 1981.

[65] M.A. Jackson, *System Development.* Englewood Cliffs, N.J.: Prentice-Hall, 1983.

[66] R.W. Jensen, "An Improved Macro-level Software Development Resource Estimation Model," in *Proceedings of the Fifth ISPA Conference,* pp. 88-92, April 1983.

[67] _____ , "Projected Productivity Impact of Near-Term Ada Use in Software System Development," in *Proceedings of the Seventh ISPA Conference,* May 1985.

[68] _____ and S. Lucas, "Sensitivity Analysis of the Jensen Software Model," in *Proceedings of the Fifth ISPA Conference,* April 1983, pp. 384-89.

[69] T.C. Jones, "Demographic and Technical Trends in the Computing Industry," Software Productivity Research, Inc., July 1983.

[70] _____ , *Programming Productivity.* New York: McGraw-Hill, 1986.

[71] E. Kant, "Understanding and Automating Algorithm Design," *IEEE Transactions on Software Engineering,* Vol. SE-11, pp. 1361-74, November 1985.

[72] B.W. Kernighan, "The Unix System and Software Reusability," *IEEE Transactions on Software Engineering,* Vol. SE-10, pp. 513-18, September 1984.

[73] _____ and J.R. Mashey, "The Unix Programming Environment," *Computer,* Vol. 14, pp. 12-24, April 1981.

[74] B.W. Kernighan and P.J. Plauger, *Software Tools.* Reading, Mass.: Addison-Wesley, 1976.

[75] R.G. Lanergan and C.A. Grasso, "Software Engineering with Reusable Designs and Code," *IEEE Transactions on Software Engineering,* Vol. SE-10, pp. 498-501, September 1984.

[76] J.Z. Lavi, "A Systems Engineering Approach to Software Engineering," in *Proceedings of the IEEE Software Workshop,* pp. 49-57, February 1984.

[77] M.M. Lehman, V. Stenning, and C. Potts, eds., *Proceedings of the Software Process Workshop,* IEEE, February 1984.

[78] E. Lieblein, "STARS Program Overview," in *Proceedings of the DoD/Industry STARS Workshop,* EIA, May 1985.

[79] B.P. Lientz and E.B. Swanson, *Software Maintenance Management: A Study of the Maintenance of Computer Application Software in 487 Data Processing Organizations.* Reading, Mass.: Addison-Welsey, 1980.

[80] M. Lundeberg, G. Goldkuhl, and A. Nilsson, *Information Systems Development: A Systematic Approach.* Englewood Cliffs, N.J.: Prentice-Hall, 1981.

[81] J.H. Manley, "Software Engineering Provisioning Process," in *Proceedings of the Eighth International Conference on Software Engineering,* August 1985, pp. 273-84.

[82] E.W. Martin, "Strategy for a DoD Software Initiative," *Computer,* Vol. 16, pp. 52-59, March 1983.

[83] Y. Matsumoto, "Management of Industrial Software Production," *Computer,* Vol. 17, pp. 59-70, February 1984.

[84] T.J. McCabe, "A Complexity Measure," *IEEE Transactions on Software Engineering,* Vol. SE-2, pp. 308-20, December 1976.

[85] J.A. McCall, P.K. Richards, and G.F. Walters, "Factors in Software Quality," General Electric Co., Report GE-TIS-77 CIS 02, 1977.

[86] D.D. McCracken and M.A. Jackson, "Life Cycle Concept Considered Harmful," *ACM Software Engineering Notes,* pp. 29-32, April 1982.

[87] R.W. McGuffin, A.E. Elliston, B.R. Tranter, and P.N. Westmacott, "CADES—Software Engineering in Practices," in *Proceedings of the Fourth International Conference on Software Engineering.* 1979, pp. 136-44.

[88] P.J. Metzger, *Managing a Programming Project,* 2nd ed. Englewood Cliffs, N.J.: Prentice-Hall, 1981.

[89] J. Munson, "Report of the USAF Scientific Advisory Board Committee on the High Cost and Risk of Mission-Critical Software," December 1983.

[90] Naval Ocean Systems Center, "SEATECS: Software Engineering Automation for Tactical Embedded Computer Systems," August 31, 1982.

[91] E.A. Nelson, *Management Handbook for the Estimation of Computer Programming Costs,* Systems Development Corp., Ad-A648750, October 31, 1966.

[92] D.L. Parnas, "Designing Software for Ease of Extension and Contraction," *IEEE Transactions on Software Engineering,* Vol. SE-5, pp. 128-37, March 1979.

[93] D.L. Parnas, P.C. Clements, and D.M. Weiss, "The Modular Structure of Complex Systems," *IEEE Transactions on Software Engineering,* Vol. SE-11, pp. 259-66, March 1985.

[94] M.E. Porter, *Competitive Strategy: Techniques for Analyzing Industries and Competitors.* New York: Free Press, 1980.

[95] _____, *Competitive Advantage.* New York: Free Press, 1985.

[96] L.H. Putnam, "A General Empirical Solution to the Macro Software Sizing and Estimating Problem," *IEEE Transactions on Software Engineering,* Vol. SE-4, pp. 345-61, July 1978.

[97] Raytheon Computer Services, "Reusable Software: Theory and Implementation," Raytheon Co., 1983.

[98] D.J. Reifer, *Tutorial: Software Management.* Washington, DC: IEEE Computer Society, 1981.

[99] _____ and S. Trattner, "A Glossary of Software Tools and Techniques," *Computer,* Vol. 10, pp. 52-60, July 1977.

[100] S.P. Reiss, "PECAN: Program Development Systems That Support Multiple Views," *IEEE Transactions on Software Engineering,* Vol. SE-11, pp. 276-85, March 1985.

[101] C. Rich and H.E. Shrobe, "Initial

Report on a Programmer's Apprentice," *IEEE Transactions on Software Engineering,* pp. 456-67, November 1978.

[102] R.J. Rubey, J.A. Dana, and P.W. Biche, "Quantitative Aspects of Software Validation," *IEEE Transactions on Software Engineering,* Vol. SE-1, pp. 150-55, June 1975.

[103] H.A. Rubin, "A Comparison of Cost Estimation Tools," in *Proceedings of the Eighth International Conference on Software Engineering,* August 1985, pp. 174-80.

[104] B. Shneiderman, *Software Psychology: Human Factors in Computer and Information Systems.* Cambridge, Mass.: Winthrop, 1980.

[105] D.R. Smith, G.B. Kotik, and S.J. Westfold, "Research on Knowledge-Based Software Environments at Kestrel Institute," *IEEE Transactions on Software Engineering,* Vol. SE-11, pp. 1278-95, November 1985.

[106] H.M. Sneed and A. Marey, "Automated Software Quality Assurance," *IEEE Transactions on Software Engineering,* Vol. SE-11, pp. 909-16, September 1985.

[107] D. Spadaro, "Project Evaluation Made Simple," *Datamation,* pp. 121-24, November 1985.

[108] H.G. Steubing, "A Software Engineering Environment (SEE) for Weapon System Software," *IEEE Transactions on Software Engineering,* Vol. SE-10, pp. 384-97, July 1984.

[109] G.E. Swinson, "Workstation-Based Rapid Simulation Aids for Distributed Processing Networks," in *Proceedings of the IEEE Simulation Conference,* 1984.

[110] STARS Joint Program Office, "STARS-SEE Operational Concept Document," October 2, 1985.

[111] D. Teichroew and E.A. Hershey III, "PSL/PSA: A Computer-Aided Technique for Structured Documentation and Analysis of Information Processing Systems," *IEEE Transactions on Software Engineering,* Vol. SE-3, pp. 41-48, January 1977.

[112] W. Teitelman, "A Tour Through Cedar," *IEEE Transactions on Software Engineering,* Vol. SE-11, pp. 285-302, March 1985.

[113] _____ and L. Masinter, "The Interlisp Programming Environment," *Computer,* Vol. 4, pp. 25-33, April 1981.

[114] A.J. Thadhani, "Factors Affecting Programmer Productivity During Application Development," *IBM Systems Journal,* Vol. 23, pp. 19-35, November 1984.

[115] C.E. Walston and C.P. Felix, "A Method of Programming Measurement and Estimation," *IBM Systems Journal,* Vol. 16, No. 1, pp. 54-73, 1977.

[116] S.P. Wartik and M.H. Penedo, "Fillin: A Reusable Tool for Form-Oriented Software," *IEEE Software,* Vol. 3, pp. 61-69, March 1986.

[117] A.I. Wasserman, *Tutorial: Software Development Environments.* Washington, DC: Computer Society, 1981.

[118] R.G. Waters, "The Programmer's

Apprentice: A Session with KBE-Macs," *IEEE Transactions on Software Engineering,* Vol. SE-11, pp. 1296-1320, November 1985.

[119]   P. Wegner, "Capital-Intensive Software Technology," *IEEE Software,* Vol. 1, pp. 7-45, July 1984.

[120]   G.M. Weinberg, *The Psychology of Computer Programming.* New York: Van Nostrand Reinhold, 1971.

[121]   _____ and E.L. Schulman, "Goals and Performance in Computer Programming," *Human Factors,* Vol. 16, No. 1, pp. 70-77, 1974.

[122]   R.D. Williams, "Managing the Development of Reliable Software," in *Proceedings of the 1975 International Conference on Relia-*

ble Software, IEEE/ACM, April 1975, pp. 3-8.

[123]   A.O. Williman and C. O'Donnell, "Through the Central 'Multiprocessor' Avionics Enters the Computer Era," *Astronautics and Aeronautics,* July 1970.

[124]   R.W. Wolverton, "The Cost of Developing Large-Scale Software," *IEEE Transactions on Computing,* Vol. C-24, pp. 615-36, June 1975.

[125]   P. Zave, "The Operational Versus the Conventional Approach to Software Development," *Communications of the ACM,* pp. 104-118, February 1984.

[126]   M. Zelkowitz and S. Squires, eds., *Proceedings of the ACM Rapid Prototyping Symposium,* ACM, October 1982.

4

Editors' Note
Humphrey: "Characterizing the Software Process: A Maturity Framework"

Insight: Software development organizations tend to mature in a very predictable way; they pass through five necessary and easily recognizable phases.

Watts Humphrey is a program director at the Software Engineering Institute. Since its formation in 1985, the SEI has focused on improvement of the software development process, particularly within the DoD and DoD-funded projects. One way to accomplish this is to help the entire software industry mature, and this has always been a broad goal of the SEI. But, since most DoD work is contracted to outside development organizations, SEI personnel made the astute observation that learning to pick vendors more cleverly could give the DoD a quick and relatively inexpensive productivity boost. The very first program set up within the Institute was therefore Software Productivity Assessment, managed by Watts Humphrey.

Near the end of 1987, the project issued its major report, "A Method for Assessing the Software Engineering Capability of Contractors" and an associated "Process Questionnaire." It is still early to judge the effect of this effort, but there is reason to hope that it will be the instrument of major progress in government contracting.

The following article presents the process model, used as part of the assessment of DoD vendors. It also presents the results of calibrating several dozen organizations against the model. And it gives enough detail for your organization to begin to calibrate itself. Once you have determined your stage of maturity, the model gives you specific directions to help advance to the next stage.

Most organizations are obliged to place themselves in the very first maturity level. And most of them are striving to get to maturity level 5 on Humphrey's scale. But the author makes the rather upsetting point that it is impossible to skip a stage, that arriving at 5 must necessarily involve passing through levels 2, 3, and 4. The attempt to move directly from level 1 to 5 is doomed to failure. Take a look at the five stages, and figure out where you stand. Then evaluate your organization's Grand Plan for progress. If it involves skipping the intermediate stages, you'll know what to expect.

4

Characterizing the Software Process:
A Maturity Framework
by Watts S. Humphrey

The amount of money spent on software in the US grows approximately 12 percent each year, and the demand for added software functions grows even faster. Software is a major and increasing portion of US Defense Dept. procurement costs, and software often adversely affects the schedules and effectiveness of weapons systems.

In recognition of the need to improve the development of military software, the Defense Dept. has launched several initiatives on software reliability, maintainability, and testing, including the Ada Joint Program Office and the STARS program. The Defense Dept. formed the Software Engineering Institute at Carnegie Mellon University in 1984 to establish standards of excellence for software engineering and to accelerate the transition of advanced technology and methods into practice.

One SEI project is to provide the Defense Dept. with some way to characterize the capabilities of software-development organizations. The result is this software-process maturity framework, which can be used by any software organization to assess its own capabilities and identify the most important areas for improvement.

Ideal Software Process

It is worthwhile to examine the characteristics of a truly effective software process. First, it is predictable: Cost estimates and schedule commitments are met with reasonable consistency and the quality of the resulting products generally meet user needs.

Statistical control. The basic principle of software process management is that if the development process is under statistical control, a consistently better result can be achieved only by improving the process. If the process is not under statistical control, sustained progress is not possible until it is. [1]

When a process is under statistical control, repeating the work in roughly the same way will produce roughly the same result.

W.E. Deming, in his work with Japanese industry after World War II, applied the concepts of statistical process control to industry. [1] While there are important differences, these concepts are just as applicable to software as they are to automobiles, cameras, wristwatches, and steel. A software-development process that is under statistical control will produce the desired results within the anticipated limits of cost, schedule, and quality.

Measurement. The basic principle behind statistical control is measurement. As Lord Kelvin said a century ago, "... when you can measure what you are speaking about, and express it in numbers, you know something about it; but when you cannot measure it, when you cannot express it in numbers, your knowledge is of a meager and unsatisfactory kind; it may be the beginning of knowledge, but you have scarcely in your thoughts advanced to the stage of science. . . ." [2]

There are several factors to consider in measuring the programming process. Perhaps most important is that the mere act of measuring human processes changes them. Since people's fears and motivations are involved, the results must be viewed in a different light than data on natural phenomena.

It is also essential to limit the measurements to those few items that will really be used. Measurements are both expensive and disruptive; overzealous measuring can degrade the processes we are trying to improve.

Development-Process Improvement

An important first step in addressing software problems is to treat the entire development task as a process that can be controlled, measured, and improved. We define a process as a sequence of tasks that, when properly performed, produces the desired result. Clearly, a fully effective software process must consider the relationships of all the required tasks, the tools and methods used, and the skill, training, and motivation of the people involved.

To improve their software capabilities, organizations must take five steps:

(1) understand the current status of their development process or processes,

(2) develop a vision of the desired process,

(3) establish a list of required process improvement actions in order of priority,

(4) produce a plan to accomplish these actions, and

(5) commit the resources to execute the plan.

The maturity framework developed at the SEI addresses these five steps by characterizing a software process into one of five maturity levels. By establishing their organization's position in this maturity structure, software professionals and management can more readily identify those areas where improvement actions are most likely to produce results.

Process Maturity Levels

As Figure 1 shows, the five levels of process maturity are:

1. Initial. Until the process is under statistical control, no orderly progress in process improvement is possible.

2. Repeatable. The organization has achieved a stable process with a repeatable level of statistical control by initiating rigorous project management of commitments, cost, schedule, and changes.

3. Defined. The organization has defined the process, to ensure consistent implementation and provide a basis for better understanding of the process. At this point, advanced technology can usefully be introduced.

4. Managed. The organization has initiated comprehensive process measurements, beyond those of cost and schedule performance. This is when the most significant quality improvements begin.

5. Optimizing. The organization now has a foundation for continued improvement and optimization of the process.

These levels have been selected because they

- reasonably represent the actual historical phases of evolutionary improvement of real software organizations,

- represent a measure of improvement that is reasonable to achieve from the prior level,

- suggest interim improvement goals and progress measures, and

- make obvious a set of immediate improvement priorities, once an organization's status in this framework is known.

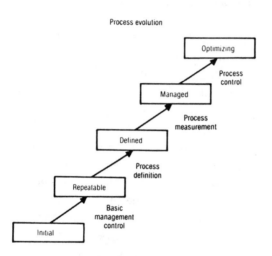

Figure 1. The five levels of process maturity.

While there are many other elements to these maturity-level transitions, the basic objective is to achieve a controlled and measured process as the scientific foundation for continuous improvement. This structure is intended to be used with an assessment and management methodology, as outlined in the box at the end of this article.

Initial Process

The Initial Process could properly be called ad hoc, and it is often even chaotic. Here, the organization typically operates without formalized procedures, cost estimates, and project plans. Tools are neither well integrated with the process nor uniformly applied. Change control is lax and there is little senior management exposure to or understanding of the problems and issues. Since problems are often deferred or even forgotten, software installation and maintenance often present serious problems.

While organizations at this level may have formal procedures for project control, there is no management mechanism to ensure they are used. The best test is to observe how such an organization behaves in a crisis. If it abandons established procedures and reverts to merely coding and testing, it is likely to be at the Initial Process level. After all, if the techniques and methods are appropriate, they must be used in a crisis and if they are not appropriate, they should not be used at all.

One reason organizations behave chaotically is that they have not gained sufficient experience to understand the consequences of such behavior. Because many effective software actions such as design and code reviews or test data analysis do not appear to directly support shipping the product, they seem expendable.

It is much like driving an automobile. Few drivers with any experience will continue driving for very long when the engine warning light comes on, regardless of their rush. Similarly, most drivers starting on a new journey will, regardless of their hurry, pause to consult a map.

They have learned the difference between speed and progress.

In software, coding and testing seem like progress, but they are often only wheel-spinning. While they must be done, there is always the danger of going in the wrong direction. Without a sound plan and a thoughtful analysis of the problems, there is no way to know.

Organizations at the Initial Process level can improve their performance by instituting basic project controls. The most important are:

- Project management. The fundamental role of a project-management system is to ensure effective control of commitments. This requires adequate preparation, clear responsibility, a public declaration, and a dedication to performance. [3]

  For software, this starts with an understanding of the job's magnitude. In any but the simplest projects, a plan must then be developed to determine the best schedule and the resources required. In the absence of such an orderly plan, no commitment can be better than an educated guess.

- Management oversight. A disciplined software-development organization must have senior management oversight. This includes review and approval of all major development plans before official commitment.

  Also, a quarterly review should be conducted of facility-wide process compliance, installed-quality performance, schedule tracking, cost trends, computing service, and qual-

ity and productivity goals by project. The lack of such reviews typically results in uneven and generally inadequate implementation of the process as well as in frequent over-commitments and cost surprises.

- Quality assurance. A quality-assurance group is charged with assuring management that the software-development work is actually done the way it is supposed to be done. To be effective, the assurance organization must have an independent reporting line to senior management and sufficient resources to monitor performance of all key planning, implementation, and verification activities. This generally requires an organization of about 5 to 6 percent the size of the development organization.

- Change control. Control of changes in software development is fundamental to business and financial control as well as to technical stability. To develop quality software on a predictable schedule, the requirements must be established and maintained with reasonable stability throughout the development cycle. Changes will have to be made, but they must be managed and introduced in an orderly way.

While occasional requirements changes are needed, historical evidence demonstrates that many of them can be deferred and phased in later. If all changes are not controlled, orderly design, implementation, and testing is impossible and no quality plan can be effective.

Repeatable Process

The Repeatable Process has one important strength over the Initial Process: It provides commitment control.

This is such an enormous advance over the Initial Process that the people in the organization tend to believe they have mastered the software problem. They do not realize that their strength stems from their prior experience at similar work. Organizations at the Repeatable Process level thus face major risks when they are presented with new challenges.

Examples of the changes that represent the highest risk at this level are:

• New tools and methods will likely affect how the process is performed, thus destroying the relevance of the intuitive historical base on which the organization relies. Without a defined process framework in which to address these risks, it is even possible for a new technology to do more harm than good.

• When the organization must develop a new kind of product, it is entering new territory. For example, a software group that has experience developing compilers will likely have design, scheduling, and estimating problems if assigned to write a control program. Similarly, a group that has developed small, self-contained programs will not understand the interface and integration issues involved in large-scale projects. These changes again destroy the relevance of the intuitive historical basis for the organization's work.

• Major organization changes can be highly disruptive. In the Repeatable Process organization, a new manager has no orderly basis for understanding what is going on and new team members must learn the ropes through word of mouth.

The key actions required to advance from the Repeatable Process to the Defined Process are:

1. Establish a process group. A process group is a technical group that focuses exclusively on improving the software-development process. In most software organizations, people are entirely devoted to product work. Until someone is given a full-time assignment to work on the process, little orderly progress can be made in improving it.

The responsibilities of process groups include defining the development process, identifying technology needs and opportunities, advising the projects, and conducting quarterly management reviews of process status and performance. Typically, the process group should be about 1 to 3 percent the size of the development organization. Because of the need for a nucleus of skills, groups smaller than about four are unlikely to be fully effective. Small organizations that lack the experience base to form a process group should address these issues through specially formed committees of experienced professionals or by retaining consultants.

2. Establish a software-development process architecture that describes the technical and management activities required for proper execution of the development process. [4] The architecture is a structural decomposition of the development cycle into tasks, each of which has entry criteria, functional descriptions,

verification procedures, and exit criteria. The decomposition continues until each defined task is performed by an individual or single management unit.

3. If they are not already in place, introduce a family of software engineering methods and technologies. These include design and code inspections, formal design methods, library control systems, and comprehensive testing methods. Prototyping should also be considered, along with the adoption of modern implementation languages.

Defined Process

With the Defined Process, the organization has achieved the foundation for major and continuing progress. For example, the development group, when faced with a crisis, will likely continue to use the Defined Process. The foundation has now been established for examining the process and deciding how to improve it.

As powerful as the Defined Process is, it is still only qualitative: There is little data to indicate what is going on or how effective the process really is. There is considerable debate about the value of software-process measurements and the best ones to use. This uncertainty generally stems from a lack of process definition and the consequent confusion about the specific items to be measured. With a defined process, we can focus the measurements on specific tasks. The process architecture is thus an essential prerequisite to effective measurement. The key steps [3, 4] to advance to the Managed Process are:

1. Establish a minimum, basic set of process measurements to identify the quality and cost parameters of each process step. The objective is to quantify the relative costs and benefits of each major process activity, such as the cost and yield of error detection and correction methods.

2. Establish a process database with the resources to manage and maintain it. Cost and yield data should be maintained centrally to guard against loss, to make it available for all projects, and to facilitate process quality and productivity analysis.

3. Provide sufficient process resources to gather and maintain this data and to advise project members on its use. Assign skilled professionals to monitor the quality of the data before entry in the database and to provide guidance on analysis methods and interpretation.

4. Assess the relative quality of each product and inform management where quality targets are not being met. An independent quality-assurance group should assess the quality actions of each project and track its progress against its quality plan. When this progress is compared with the historical experience on similar projects, an informed assessment generally can be made.

Managed Process

In advancing from the Initial Process via the Repeatable and Defined Processes to the Managed Process, software organizations typically will experience substantial quality improvements. The greatest potential problem with the Managed Process is the cost of gathering data. There are an enormous number of potentially valuable measures of software development and support, but such data is expensive to gather and maintain.

Therefore, approach data gathering with care and precisely define each piece of data in advance. Productivity data is generally meaningless unless explicitly defined. For example, the simple measure of lines of source code per development month can vary by 100 times or more, depending on the interpretation of the parameters. The code count could include only new and changed code or all shipped instructions. For modified programs, this can cause a ten-times variation. Similarly, you can use noncomment, nonblank lines, executable instructions, or equivalent assembler instructions, with variations again of up to seven times. [5] Management, test, documentation, and support personnel may or may not be counted when calculating labor months expended. Again, the variations can run at least as high as seven times. [6]

When different groups gather data but do not use identical definitions, the results are not comparable, even if it made sense to compare them. The tendency with such data is to use it to compare several groups and put pressure on those with the lowest ranking. This is a misapplication of process data.

First, it is rare that two projects are comparable by any simple measures. The variations in task complexity caused by different product types can exceed five to one. Similarly, the cost per line of code of small modifications is often two to three times that for new programs. The degree of requirements change can make an enormous difference, as can the design status of the base program in the case of enhancements.

Process data must not be used to compare projects or individuals. Its purpose is to illuminate the product being developed and to provide an informed basis for improving the process. When such data

is used by management to evaluate individuals or teams, the reliability of the data itself will deteriorate. The US Constitution's Fifth Amendment, which protects against self-incrimination, is based on sound principles: Few people can be counted on to provide reliable data on their own performance.

The two fundamental requirements to advance from the Managed Process to the Optimizing Process are:

1. Support automatic gathering of process data. Some data cannot be gathered by hand, and all manually gathered data is subject to error and omission.

2. Use this data to both analyze and modify the process to prevent problems and improve efficiency.

Optimizing Process

In varying degrees, process optimization goes on at all levels of process maturity. With the step from the Managed to the Optimizing Process, however, there is a paradigm shift. Up to this point, software-development managers have largely focused on their products and will typically only gather and analyze data that directly relates to product improvement. In the Optimizing Process, the data is available to actually tune the process itself. With a little experience, management will soon see that process optimization can produce major quality and productivity improvements.

For example, many errors can be identified and fixed far more economically by code inspections than through testing. Unfortunately, there is little published data on the costs of finding and fixing errors. [7] However, I have developed a useful rule of thumb from experience: It takes about one to four working hours to find and fix a bug through inspections and about 15 to 20 working hours to find and fix a bug in function or system test. It is thus clear that testing is not a cost-effective way to find and fix most bugs.

However, some kinds of errors are either uneconomical or almost impossible to find except by machine. Examples are errors involving spelling and syntax, interfaces, performance, human factors, and error recovery. It would thus be unwise to eliminate testing completely because it provides a useful check against human frailties.

The data that is available with the Optimizing Process gives us a new perspective on testing. For most projects, a little analysis shows that there are two distinct activities involved. The first is the removal of bugs. To reduce this cost, inspections should be emphasized together with any other cost-effective techniques. The role of functional and system testing should then be changed to one of finding symptoms that are further explored to see if the bug is an isolated problem or if it indicates design problems that require more comprehensive analysis.

In the Optimizing Process, the organization has the means to identify the weakest elements of the process and fix them. At this point in process improvement, data is available to justify the application of technology to various critical tasks and numerical evidence is available on the effectiveness with which the process has been applied to any given product. We no longer need reams of paper to describe what is happening because simple yield curves and statistical plots provide clear and concise indicators. It is now possible to assure the process and hence have confidence in the quality of the resulting products.

People in the process. Any software-development process is dependent on the quality of the people who implement it. Even with the best people, however, there is always a limit to what they can accomplish. When engineers are already working 50 to 60 hours a week, it is hard to see how they could handle the vastly greater challenges of the future.

The Optimizing Process helps in several ways:

- It helps managers understand where help is needed and how best to provide the people with the support they require.

- It lets professionals communicate in concise, quantitative terms. This facilitates the transfer of knowledge and minimizes the likelihood of their wasting time on problems that have already been solved.

- It provides the framework for the professionals to understand their work performance and to see how to improve it. This results in a highly professional environment and substantial productivity benefits, and it avoids the enormous amount of effort that is generally expended in fixing and patching other people's mistakes.

The Optimizing Process provides a disciplined environment for professional work. Process discipline must be handled with care, however, for it can easily become regimentation. The difference between a disciplined environment and a regimented one is that discipline controls the environment and methods to specific standards while regimentation defines the actual conduct of the work.

Discipline is required in large software projects to ensure, for example, that the people involved use the same conventions, don't damage each other's products, and properly synchronize their work. Discipline thus enables creativity by freeing the most talented software professionals from the many crises that others have created.

The need. There are many examples of disasters caused by software problems, ranging from expensive missile aborts to enormous financial losses. As the computerization of our society continues, the public risks due to poor-quality code will become untenable. Not only are our systems being used in increasingly sensitive applications, but they are also becoming much larger and more complex.

While proper questions can be raised about the size and complexity of current systems, they are human creations and they will, alas, continue to be produced by humans—with all their failings and creative talents. While many of the currently promising technologies will undoubtedly help, there is an enormous backlog of needed functions that will inevitably translate into vast amounts of code.

More code means increased risk of error and, when coupled with more complexity, these systems will become progressively less testable. The risks will thus increase astronomically as we become more efficient at producing prodigious amounts of new code.

As well as being a management issue, quality is an economic one. It is always possible to do more inspections or to run more tests, but it costs time and money

to do so. It is only with the Optimizing Process that the data is available to understand the costs and benefits of such work. The Optimizing Process thus provides the foundation for significant advances in software quality and simultaneous improvements in productivity.

There is little data on how long it takes for software organizations to advance through these maturity levels toward the Optimizing Process. Based on my experience, transition from level 1 to level 2 or from level 2 to level 3 takes from one to three years, even with a dedicated management commitment to process improvement. To date, no complete organizations have been observed at levels 4 or 5.

To meet society's needs for increased system functions while simultaneously addressing the problems of quality and productivity, software managers and professionals must establish the goal of moving to the Optimizing Process.

This software-development process-maturity model reasonably represents the actual ways in which software-development organizations improve. It provides a framework for assessing these organizations and identifying the priority areas for immediate improvement. It also helps identify those places where advanced technology can be most valuable in improving the software-development process.

The SEI is using this model as a foundation for a continuing program of assessments and software process development. These assessment methods have been made public [8, 9], and preliminary data is now available from several dozen software organizations.

Figure 2 shows the maturity distribution of these organizations and the three leading problems faced at each level. At level 1, the distribution is shown by quartile. There is not yet sufficient data to provide this detail for levels 2 or 3. As further data is gathered, additional reports will be published on the results obtained.

Acknowledgments

Much of the early work on software process maturity was suggested by my former colleagues at IBM. I am particularly indebted to Ron Radice and Jack Harding for their insights and support. In addition, William Sweet of the SEI and Martin Owens and Herman Schultz of Mitre Corp. have made valuable contributions to this work. I am also indebted to my colleagues at the SEI, particularly Rodger Blair, Larry Druffel, and Greg Hansen, for their helpful comments and suggestions. This work was supported by the Defense Dept.

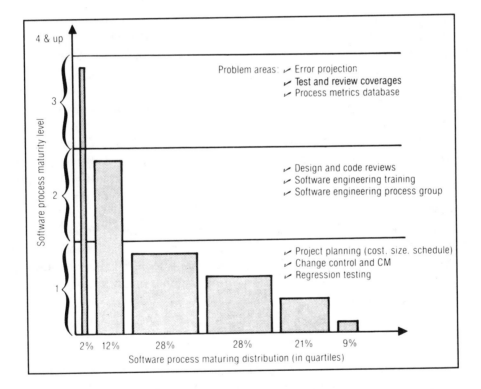

Figure 2. Early results from several dozen software organizations queried by the SEI shows the maturity distribution and the three leading problems faced at each level. At level 1, the distribution is shown by quartile. There is not yet sufficient data to provide this detail for levels 2 or 3. To date, no complete organizations have been observed at levels 4 or 5.

How to Use This Framework

This process-maturity structure is intended to be used with an assessment methodology and a management system. [1–3]

Assessment lets you identify the organization's specific maturity status. A management system establishes a structure for actually implementing the priority actions necessary to improve the organization. Once its position in this maturity structure is defined, the organization can concentrate on those items that will let it advance to the next level.

When, for example, a software organization does not have an effective project planning system, it may be difficult or even impossible to introduce advanced methods and technology. Poor project planning generally leads to unrealistic schedules, inadequate resources, and frequent crises. In such circumstances, new methods are usually ignored, and the focus is on coding and testing.

Using this maturity framework, the SEI has developed an assessment questionnaire and methodology, a portion of which is shown in Figure A. [4, 5] The questionnaire has been reviewed by more than 400 governmental and industrial organizations. Also, it has been completed by more than 50 programming professionals from nearly as many software organizations.

The SEI has also used the assessment methodology to conduct in-depth technical reviews of 25 programming projects in four large programming organizations.

Through this work, the assessment methodology and questionnaire have evolved, but the five-level maturity framework has remained essentially unchanged. We have found that it portrays, with reasonable accuracy, the status and problems as seen by the managers and professionals in the organizations reviewed.

These early results indicate that the model reasonably represents the state of such organizations and provides a mechanism to rapidly identify the key improvement issues they face. At this time, the data is too limited to provide any more detailed information as to maturity distribution by industry, organization size, or type of work.

References

[1] W.S. Humphrey, *Managing for Innovation: Leading Technical People,* Englewood Cliffs, N.J.: Prentice-Hall, 1987.

[2] R.A. Radice et al., "A Programming Process Study," *IBM Systems Journal,* Vol. 24, No. 2 (1985), pp. 91-101.

[3] _____ , "A Programming Process Architecture," *IBM Systems Journal,* Vol. 24, No. 2 (1985), pp. 79-90.

[4] W.S. Humphrey and D.H. Kitson, "Preliminary Report on Conducting SEI-Assisted Assessments of Software Engineering Capability," Technical Report SEI-87-TR-16, Pittsburgh: Software Engineering Institute, July 1987.

[5] W.S. Humphrey and W.L. Sweet, "A Method for Assessing the Software Engineering Capability of Contractors," Technical Report SEI-87-TR-23, Pittsburgh: Software Engineering Institute, September 1987.

2.3. Data Management and Analysis

Data management deals with the gathering and retention of process metrics. Data management requires standardized data definitions, data management facilities, and a staff to ensure that data is promptly obtained, properly checked, accurately entered into the data base, and effectively managed.

Analysis deals with the subsequent manipulation of the process data to answer questions such as, "Is there a relatively high correlation between error densities found in test and those found in use?" Other types of analyses can assist in determining the optimum use of reviews and resources, the tools most needed, testing priorities, and needed education.

2.3.1. Has a managed and controlled process database been established for process metrics data across all projects?

2.3.2. Are the review data gathered during design reviews analyzed?

2.3.3. Is the error data from code reviews and tests analyzed to determine the likely distribution and characteristics of the errors remaining in the product?

2.3.4. Are analyses of errors conducted to determine their process related causes?

2.3.5. Is a mechanism used for error cause analysis?

2.3.6. Are the errror causes reviewed to determine the process changes required to prevent them?

2.3.7. Is a mechanism used for initiating error prevention actions?

2.3.8. Is review efficiency analyzed for each project?

2.3.9. Is software productivity analyzed for major process steps?

Figure A. A portion of the SEI's assessment questionnaire.

REFERENCES

[1] W.E. Deming, "Quality, Productivity, and Competitive Position," Technical Report, Cambridge, Mass.: MIT Center for Advanced Engineering Study, 1982.

[2] J.R. Dunham and E. Kruesi, "The Measurement Task Area," *Computer*, November 1983, pp. 47-54.

[3] W.S. Humphrey, *Managing for Innovation: Leading Technical People*, Englewood Cliffs, N.J.: Prentice-Hall, 1987.

[4] R.A. Radice et al., "A Programming Process Architecture," *IBM Systems Journal*, Vol. 24, No. 2 (1985), pp. 79-90.

[5] M.L. Shooman, *Software Engineering: Design, Reliability, and Management*, New York: McGraw-Hill, 1983.

[6] R.W. Wolverton, "The Cost of Developing Large-Scale Software," *IEEE Transactions on Computers*, June 1974, pp. 615-36.

[7] M.L. Shooman and M.I. Bolsky, "Types, Distribution, and Test and Correction Times for Programming Errors," *Proceedings of the International Conference on Reliable Software*, New York: IEEE, 1975, pp. 347-57.

[8] W.S. Humphrey and D.H. Kitson, "Preliminary Report on Conducting SEI-Assisted Assessments of Software-Engineering Capability," Technical Report SEI-87-TR-16, Pittsburgh: Software Engineering Institute, July 1987.

[9] W.S. Humphrey and W.L. Sweet, "A Method for Assessing the Software Engineering Capability of Contractors," Technical Report SEI-87-TR-23, Pittsburgh: Software Engineering Institute, September 1987.

5

Editors' Note

Tajima and Matsubara: "The Computer Software Industry in Japan"

Insight: Some striking differences in the way that software is produced in Japan, compared to the West.

For years, we took comfort from conventional Western wisdom that "the Japanese are doing wonderful things in hardware, but their software is still primitive." Then, in the late sixties, there was that extraordinary Sumitomo Bank system. Those of us who got to see it in action were sobered. It was so huge and so fast and so functional. It was, in fact, the very on-line teller system that our largest banks were still trying and failing to build almost a full decade later. And it was built with Japanese software on American hardware. So much for our illusions.

Lately, we have begun to take it for granted that there is much to learn from Japan about software. But where to turn for the information? There is almost nothing published in English about Japanese software methodology. (It's not a plot to keep their best ideas under wraps; the Japanese don't write much in English for the same reason you probably don't read much in Japanese.) Now, at last, Tajima and Matsubara have come along with this fascinating peek into a truly different world.

5

The Computer Software Industry in Japan
by Denji Tajima and Tomoo Matsubara

Much has been written recently about Japanese industrial growth. Japan's successful penetration into world steel, shipbuilding, television, and automobile markets has stimulated widespread interest in that country's formula for productivity. Discussions have focused on Japanese manufacturing techniques, government-industry cooperation, and personnel practices. Relatively little, however, is known about Japan's computer industry, especially the computer software industry.

Mainframe Market

The software industry can hardly be discussed without mentioning the hardware mainframers. Figures 1 and 2 show the domestic Japanese mainframe market in installed dollar value and in installed number of sets. The total market shown (about one-fifth the size of the corresponding U.S. market) is dominated by the top five mainframers—IBM, Fujitsu, Hitachi, NEC, and Univac—who share 90 percent of it. As in the U.S. and some European countries, no single mainframer holds the majority of the market. The Japanese mainframers are not only competing with foreign mainframers, but with the other domestics as well. One of the ways to understand the result of this competition is to view the historical changes in the market share.

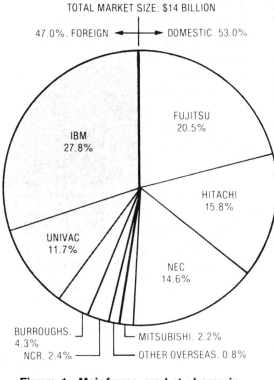

Figure 1. Mainframe market shares in Japan as of June 1979. (Source: *Computopia*, January 1980)

Figure 3 indicates that the American giants IBM and Univac have fallen back year by year while Japanese mainframers have continued to gain ground. Japanese domestics hold 53 percent in dollar value and 69 percent in installation numbers. This intense competition has a strong impact on the software industry.

76

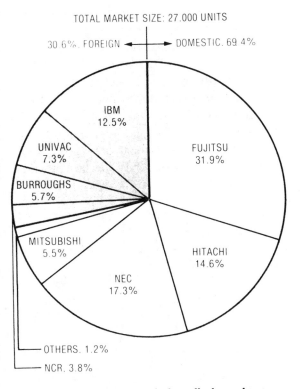

TOTAL MARKET SIZE: 27,000 UNITS

30 6%, FOREIGN ◄——————► DOMESTIC, 69.4%

IBM
12.5%

UNIVAC
7.3%

FUJITSU
31.9%

BURROUGHS
5.7%

MITSUBISHI
5.5%

HITACHI
14.6%

NEC
17.3%

OTHERS, 1.2%

NCR, 3.8%

Figure 2. Market share in installed number of sets, excluding micros, in June 1979.
(Source: *Computopia,* January 1980)

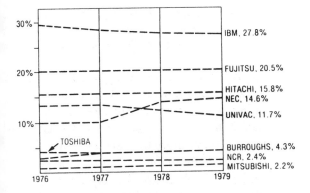

30%

20%

IBM, 27.8%

FUJITSU, 20.5%

HITACHI, 15.8%
NEC, 14.6%

UNIVAC, 11.7%

10%

TOSHIBA

BURROUGHS, 4.3%
NCR, 2.4%
MITSUBISHI, 2.2%

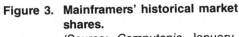
1976   1977   1978   1979

Figure 3. Mainframers' historical market shares.
(Source: *Computopia,* January 1980)

The shrinking market share of IBM and the expanding share of domestic mainframers may discourage overseas software vendors; a $14 billion hardware market split among five mainframers looks too crowded to penetrate. Actually, the opportunity is greater than meets the eye, for the hardware architectures and their operating systems are not very widely diversified. In fact, in 1974 traditional rivals Fujitsu and Hitachi carried their competition into the plug-compatible arena when they announced their IBM-compatible M-series. The combined market share of IBM, Fujitsu, and Hitachi is now 59 percent; hence the IBM family architecture can be seen to dominate the market. This fact makes the Japanese market very attractive to software houses selling computer software that runs under IBM operating systems.

Computer Users

The fact that the Japanese computer users need software to operate their mainframes suggests that a huge potential market exists for software houses. As shown in Fig. 4, however, the great preponderance of users opt for in-house implementation. Indeed, there has been a long-standing inclination among Japanese users to define their own systems. These systems are implemented by their own programmers—who like workers in other segments of Japanese industry are lifetime employees—as well as by programmers supplied from job shop-type software houses that specialize in meeting computer users' temporary programming needs.

Six percent of application program implementation is done by mainframers, who probably account for a far larger percentage of systems and utility software, though no statistics are available on this. In order to succeed in Japan's competitive market, the mainframers often offer not only systems and utility software, but also assistance in developing application programs—all free of charge.

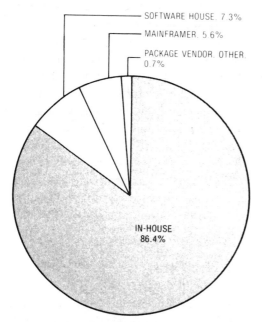

Figure 4. Implementor of user's application program, 1978.
(Source: Ministry of International Trade and Industry DP Survey)

Although competition continues to be severe, the "unbundling" concept of software separate from the mainframe will gradually become accepted, since users have begun to notice that software bundled with the mainframe is not necessarily cheap. Likewise, the amount of mainframe manufacturers' help in developing application programs will dwindle with time.

Only seven percent of the users' expenditures goes to outside software houses for application program implementation, and less than one percent is spent buying ready-made software packages.

Figure 5 breaks down the users' $240 million annual DP expenses: 42 percent for hardware, 30 percent for personnel, and four percent for manpower chartered from bodyshops. Only one percent of this amount, or $58 million, is spent for software developed on contract to agreed-upon specifications or for packaged software.

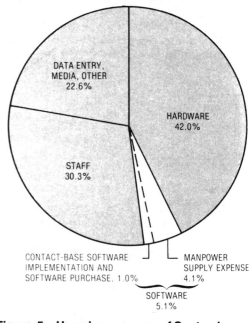

Figure 5. Users' expense as of September 1978.
(Source: MITI DP Survey)

Figure 6 compares the characteristics of DP expenditures in the U.S. with those in Japan. A remarkable difference can be seen in hardware and personnel expenses: the U.S. pays more for personnel and Japan spends more for hardware. The percentage of software looks very close, but there are significant differences. In the U.S. statistics, software means the expense for contract-base software implementation and for packaged software purchase.

In the Japanese statistics, software includes manpower expenditures, which amount to four-fifths of the total software expense. The packaged software expenditure is negligible in both cases.

The dollar amounts spent on software by the U.S. and Japan are compared in Fig. 7. The aggregate software expenditure of Japanese users is about $300 million, or roughly 15 percent of the U.S. total. Considering that the Japanese mainframe market size is one fifth that of the U.S., this percentage is considerable. But the component is the issue: $58 million out of $300 million can be truly compared to $1.945 billion dollars of U.S. expenditures, since those were the amounts spent on purchasing software in the two countries. Based on these figures, the Japanese computer software market can be considered as representing only three percent of the comparable U.S. market.

Software Houses

If we look at the aggregate revenue of software houses, we can see that the software market is far larger than the $297 million aggregate users' expense indicated in Fig. 7. In 1978, approximately 800 software houses employed some 30,000 programmers and earned no less than $710 million.

Figure 8 shows the structure of the software industry, highlighting the differences between the aggregate users' expense and the aggregate software houses' revenue. Part of the users' expenditure flows directly into the software houses, mostly for manpower supply. The majority of the software houses' revenue comes from the six Japanese mainframers, which independently develop their own operating systems, support their own customers, and sometimes help their customers to imple-

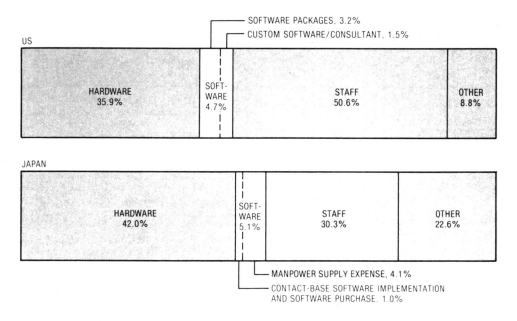

Figure 6. Comparison of DP expense structure.
(Sources: U.S., International Data Corporation 1978 Survey; Japan, MITI 1978 Survey)

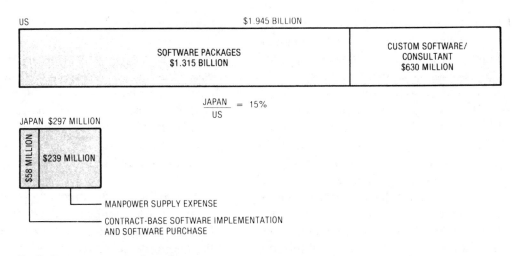

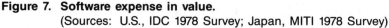

Figure 7. Software expense in value.
(Sources: U.S., IDC 1978 Survey; Japan, MITI 1978 Survey)

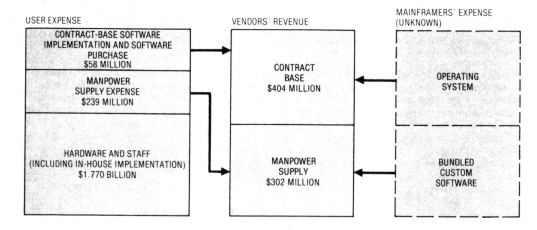

Figure 8. Cash flow in Japan's software industry.
(Source: MITI 1978 Survey)

ment applications. These tasks are partially done by the mainframers' own staff, but in most cases they need the outside software houses for contract-base implementation.

Figure 9 shows an average profile of the software houses. The revenue per programmer is $30 thousand, significantly lower than that of U.S. software houses. More than three-quarters of this amount

covers only wages, again showing that manpower occupies the major portion of the total revenue. In other words, per capita revenue of software houses is small since they serve mainly as programming labor pools, not as professionally skilled designers or systems engineers.

Most software houses work primarily for one mainframer, who on the average provides 60 percent of the revenue. The distribution of the software houses' annual revenue is shown in Fig. 10. Ninety percent of all software houses generate $10 million or less per year. These factors indicate that the mainframers have considerable power over the software houses.

tive. Among languages, Assembler and Fortran are more productive than Cobol and PL/I when measured by lines of code; however, this does not necessarily mean they are more productive in realizing a specific function.

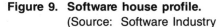

• AVERAGE ANNUAL REVENUE	$ 3,841,000
• AVERAGE NUMBER OF PROGRAMMERS	128,000
• PER CAPITA REVENUE	$ 30,000

| • PROPORTION OF REVENUE | MAINFRAMER | 60% |
| | USER | 40% |

• PROPORTION OF APPLICATION	BUSINESS APPLICATION	52%
	SYSTEM SOFTWARE	23%
	SCIENTIFIC APPLICATION	10%
	PROCESS CONTROL	10%
	OTHER	5%

Figure 9. Software house profile.
(Source: Software Industry Association Survey, March 1979)

PROGRAMMING PRODUCTIVITY	
APPLICATION	STEPS/MAN-MONTH
BUSINESS APPLICATION	737
SCIENTIFIC APPLICATION	439
PROCESS CONTROL	704
SYSTEMS SOFTWARE	792
MISCELLANEOUS	1077
AVERAGE	811

PROGRAMMING PRODUCTIVITY	
LANGUAGE	STEPS/MAN-MONTH
ASSEMBLER	1055
PL/I	541
COBOL	941
FORTRAN	1067

Figure 11. Software house productivity data.
(Source: SIA Survey, March 1979)

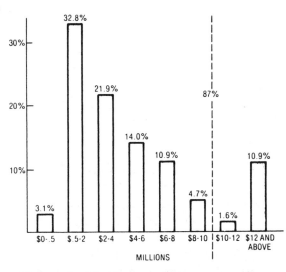

Figure 10. Distribution of software houses by annual revenue.
(Source: SIA Survey, March 1979)

Figure 11 indicates software house productivity by applications and languages. According to these statistics, scientific applications are the least produc-

The newness of the software industry and the nature of its products cause a certain degree of ambiguity in various statistics. The data shown here are not always consistent, but they do reveal some general characteristics of the Japanese software industry:

• Mainframers are in sharp competition, while software unbundling is not yet widespread.

• Software houses form a hierarchical structure, with software divisions of mainframers at the top. The mainframers control the market.

• Users are inclined to develop their own systems instead of buying from the outside. They implement their systems internally with the help of manpower supplied from the body-shop type of software house.

• Since manpower supply is the main

function of the software houses, they have a tough time concentrating their skills in a specific field.

In this rough sketch of the Japanese software industry, the lack of precise definitions of terms makes the structure of computer software and its management technologies, quality measurement, productivity measurement, and programmer ethics hard to discuss. In the following sections, we will explore several management aspects of one major software house.

A Japanese Software House: The Hitachi Software Engineering Company

In 1969 the Hitachi Software Engineering Company was established by Hitachi Ltd. as a wholly owned subsidiary to support that mainframer's software division. Within a decade, expanding demand caused HSE's revenue to grow sixteen-fold to $50 million and the number of employees to quadruple to 1500, making it the largest software house in Japan (see Figs. 12 and 13).

HSE originally provided basic software to Hitachi. During the late 1960's and early 1970's, prior to the establishment of the plug-compatible concept, HSE constructed operating systems, utilities, languages, and on-line communications from scratch. Even today, one of the company's major activities is in the mainframer's operating system development and maintenance.

Growing pressure on user ability to develop and implement systems created a market for HSE's expansion into application system consultation and implemen-

tation. Now, roughly 60 percent of its revenue is from the mainframer and 40 percent from end users.

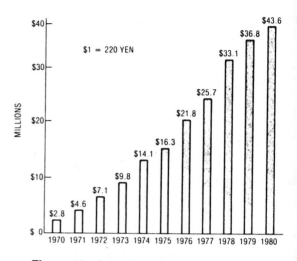

Figure 12. Annual revenue of Hitachi Software Engineering.

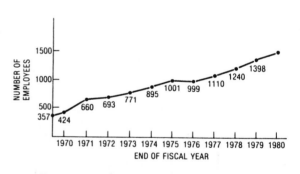

Figure 13. Number of employees at Hitachi Software Engineering.

The firm at first conducted business by dispatching programmers to its parent mainframer. With the understanding of the mainframer, the programmers did not work merely as temporary manpower support, but rather were assigned to specific tasks for which they were personally responsible. Thus the firm was able to respond to highly technical challenges and build up professional skills while minimizing business risks.

Now the house works mostly under a contract basis, except in cases where the requirements are not clear enough or the cost estimate is vague for both the house and the customer. In such cases, system engineers are paid hourly and work on a best-effort basis until specifications are fixed.

Presently active only in Japan's domestic software market, HSE is nevertheless studying and incorporating worldwide advanced technologies with firms and universities in the U.S. and hopes to expand its operations to the U.S. and Europe soon.

Education program. The house places a significant emphasis on employee education and training. New graduates are well grounded in theory but lack practical experience. On the other hand, employment tends to be a lifelong commitment. Hence, stable Japanese firms find it both essential and cost-effective to invest heavily in continuing education.

HSE recruits 100 to 200 new high school or college graduates annually; it seldom employs experienced people. Since computer science departments or courses are rare (and not very practical) in high schools and colleges, all newcomers receive two months' training in programming. Following that, they are assigned to relevant departments for four months of on-the-job training, after which they are ready to start working on actual jobs.

Employees periodically catch up on new technologies and broaden their knowledge in various internal courses, which they are encouraged—if not required—to attend. They may even get an opportunity to leave their jobs and study abroad for a year or two. The internal curriculum covers a wide range, from professional skill training programs in, for example, compiler structure, sorting, and relational data bases, to management training programs and even English conversation.

Cost and schedule control. Software is infamous for unpredictable costs and delivery dates. Months of delay and 300-percent cost overruns were not exceptional in the early days of HSE.

Trying various ways to manage software cost, schedule, and quality, HSE came to use several charts and diagrams. Figures 14 and 15 are diagrams that proved to be valuable management tools in this effort.

The most important thing is to detect problems at the earliest possible stage. Figure 14 depicts the progress of a project by showing the relation between man-hours and machine-hours. Using such a diagram, project leaders perform weekly updates of the project arrow diagrams they wrote at the start of the project, summarize the progress, and then plot it on the cost-progress diagram. Machine-time and man-hours are reported by the accounting department. Managers can easily point out a delay or overrun.

The cost and schedule control methods used by HSE today allow the house to complete 98 percent of its projects on time and 99 percent of its projects at an actual cost between 90 and 110 percent of the original estimate. The house is now focusing its efforts on raising programming productivity and improving quality.

Quality control. Japanese automobiles, televisions, semiconductors, and even computer mainframes are sought because of high reliability and good main-

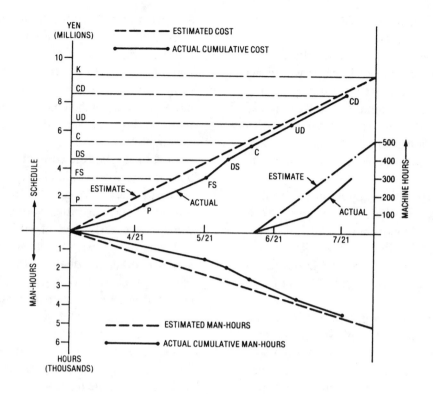

Figure 14. Cost-progress diagram.

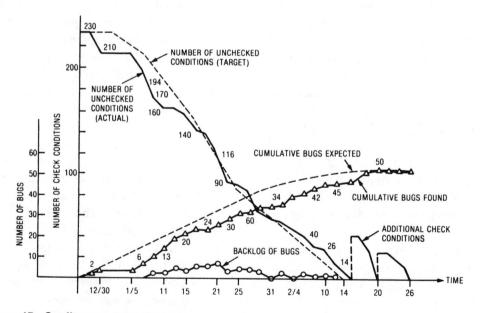

Figure 15. Quality-progress diagram.

tenance records. In Japan, most stable manufacturers consider quality improvement cost-effective in the long run, even though it incurs short-term out-of-pocket expenses.

Japanese users claim a high reliability in software as well as in hardware. The attitude in Japan is that software produced by professionals should have no bugs, since bugs are defects in the product; reliability of a product is considered equivalent to the reliability of the maker as a whole. Hence, a single bug may affect the credibility of a whole firm.

HSE, which produces only computer software, has an independent Quality Assurance Division, just as manufacturers of hard goods do. To assure software quality for the users, the division's engineers practice statistical testing during the debugging stage. Using empirical data and statistical analysis, they advise the implementation group to enrich their test conditions in certain areas. A software product is not approved by the division until its engineers are confident that the product is error free.

Figure 15 shows another way of illustrating the relation of progress to quality. Just before the coding starts, the number of check conditions is determined and the conditions are listed on a program checklist. Project leaders write a quality-progress diagram that includes the expected number of check conditions remaining and the number of bugs to be detected. As debugging goes on, the leaders check the outcome against the program checklist and plot the actual number on the quality-progress diagram.

The Accounting Division counts expenses to fix bugs after delivery as spoilage. The ratio of aggregate spoilage to aggregate project cost is a useful measure of software quality. This ratio, plotted in Fig. 16, improved considerably in the 1976-1979 period.

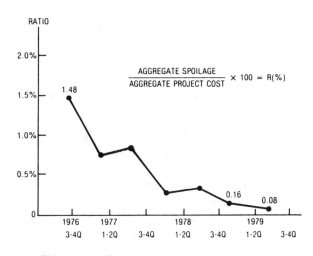

Figure 16. Quality improvement.

Employee participation. HSE encourages employee cooperation and participation as an important element in increasing productivity and improving quality. Ideas that emanate from "quality control circles" are rarely elegant, but they often provide practical ways of coping with actual circumstances.

The software industry depends largely upon individuals—a circumstance that may explain why product improvement is generally preceded by an improvement in the programming staff. Realizing the critical role that people play in the company's success, HSE makes a major educational investment that pays off in employee loyalty: The annual personnel turnover at HSE is 3.2 percent, significantly lower than the Japanese industrial average of 5.8 percent.

Projections

We have outlined the history, present condition, and some of the current techniques of the Japanese software industry as a whole and of a single software house. What does the industry face in the future?

- With the spread of computer usage, the demand for software development will continuously exceed the supply.

- The current software pricing schedule in Japan is almost totally on a cost or man-hour basis, with the exception of software packages. Thus, we are not selling technology or skill, but supplying manpower. The pricing mechanism will change so that the better the technology a firm has, the more profitable it will be.

- For both mainframers and users, the proportion of software expense to other expenses will become larger and larger. Software houses will have to develop a system to ease the cost of software development and maintenance.

- Software will become increasingly critical to the functions of society as computers become commonplace. Consequently, software reliability must be raised just as hardware reliability has been. Dependence on the individual programmer has to be overcome, and scientific proof of reliability has to be established.

The Japanese software industry has pluses and minuses. On one hand, Japanese workers are known for their loyalty, an important element in establishing stable organizations. On the other, the Japanese language is extremely difficult to handle by machine. If the difficulties can be overcome and the advantages exploited, the Japanese software industry will contribute significantly to the development of world software technology.

6

Editors' Note
Tajima and Matsubara: "Inside the Japanese Software Industry"

Insight: A glimpse into the uniquely Japanese approach to building and keeping professional software development staff.

In this second *Computer* magazine article, Tajima and Matsubara reveal some of the attitudes toward staff and professional growth that have set Japan apart. The people investment that they describe is virtually unheard of in the West. And yet it makes so much sense.

6

Inside the Japanese Software Industry
by Denji Tajima and Tomoo Matsubara

In 1966, when we came to America to visit the RCA computer division, Japan had just started to export automobiles to the U.S. We gazed into parking lots to catch a glimpse of Japanese automobiles, but we found scarcely any. At that time, we were excited by Japan's success in exporting automobiles to the U.S., although the market share was still small. We hoped that our computer industry might also catch up with U.S. technology and one day export our products to the U.S.

Initially, most Americans must have wondered, "What in the world would a Japanese car be like?" Later, they said, "Those Japanese cars are well-built." Yet, once the American market was flooded with Japanese automobiles, there was mounting concern in America, not only about the automobile, but also about the people who produced it—the Japanese, themselves. Today, it is time to end chauvinisms, recognize each other, and develop mutual understanding.

Until the mid-1970's, Japanese computer manufacturers had competed with each other in the closed, domestic market to stake out their market share. In 1981, the total dollar revenue of hardware exports from Japan to foreign OEMs had increased to $1.1 million. [1] However, all six major Japanese makers of large computers together have less than two percent of the U.S. business computer market [2], like

Japanese automobile exporters in 1966 except that hardware exports carrying the manufacturer's brand were rare, and likely for cultural reasons.

A computer system is influenced by the manufacturer's background. The cultural difference between the U.S. and Japan makes combining American systems with Japanese software more difficult than combining American drivers and Japanese automobiles. Still, in Japan, most machine-independent application packages—for which demand is high now—are imported from the U.S., and very few software packages are exported. As illustrated in Figure 1, 82 percent of the software packages on the Japanese market are imported. Also, among 14 types of packages that sold more than 50 units, 12 are foreign. In software, the Japanese trade balance is definitely at a deficit. For the time being, Japanese software, which is distributed independently or with Japanese hardware, is not exported in volumes that threaten the foreign software industry.

Nonetheless, many question whether Japan's software exports to the U.S. will ever equal its current imports. And as a result of the successful penetration of Japanese products into the U.S. automobile, steel, and semiconductor markets, the future threat of Japanese computers is being widely discussed. So far, the prevailing idea in the U.S. is, "The software gap is too big for Japan to catch up with the U.S. soon." [3]

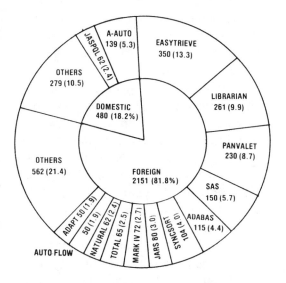

Figure 1. Japanese market share of general-purpose software packages, according to *Shukan Denpa Computer* (April 25, 1983).

In other words, the prevailing American attitude is that the Japanese growth in the worldwide computer market depends on its approach to manufacturing software. Therefore, identifying our current software methodology, understanding its background, and forecasting its future are the keys to resolving U.S. concerns about tomorrow's Japanese computer systems. This article describes the Japanese software industry from the inside, focusing on Hitachi Software Engineering (popularly known as HSK) and revealing a Japanese viewpoint affected by the philosophies, ways of living, and environments of both user and manufacturer. This focus should help the reader understand our software industry and its future.

Background

HSK's software sales in fiscal 1982 reached $62 million, and its total number of employees reached 1,900—1,450 working as programmers. In the 13 years since HSK was established, expanding demand spurred a fifty-fold increase in revenue from $1.2 million and a five-fold increase in employees from 420 (see Figure 2). Only three percent of its total revenue comes from sales in software products and stand-alone hardware equipment loaded with software; 13 percent comes from system analysis and consultation, and the remaining 84 percent from software development, which includes both system and application software. To satisfy Japan's expanding software demand, HSK seeks to improve its productivity and increase the number of employees. Therefore, software and system sales, which currently yield only three percent of the total revenue, are excepted to increase steadily.

Entrance ceremony and training for new employees. The Japanese business year (fiscal year of every government, company, institute and school) starts in April. In the first week of April, every company holds an entrance ceremony when new employees listen to the president's address. Then, they spend a few weeks in the classroom and start job-site training with the senior staff. In April 1983, HSK hired about 300 new graduates, 60 percent from college or junior college graduates, the rest senior high-school graduates. Most college and junior college graduates had majored in physics, mathematics, electric/electronic engineering, mechanical engineering, and computer science.

After the entrance ceremony, new em-

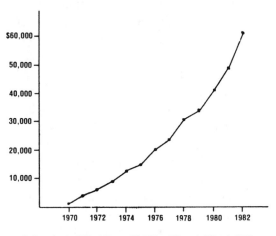

A. Net sales (×1000); 240 yen = US $1 (as of the end of March 1983)

B. Number of employees at the end of fiscal years

Figure 2. Hitachi net sales and number of employees.

ployees normally receive two months off-the-job training that provides them with a minimum knowledge of business regulations and rules and the prerequisites in programming other languages. At the end of the program, they express their preference for assignments. Then they are as-

signed to an appropriate section, where they receive job-site training. Generally, they are software trainees for the first six months while they learn their particular duties. Training is over after one year, but it is just an introductory step in a series of programs that make up Japan's lifetime educational system.

Recruitment. Japanese companies consider their new recruits to be a precious resource. Since World War II, the demand for qualified college graduates has consistently exceeded the supply, and every company has made great efforts to attract more highly qualified students. At HSK, for instance, no sooner has a flock of graduates been hired than recruitment starts for the coming year. After the year's employment policy is determined, representatives of the personnel department and management staff of technical departments visit most of the country's respected colleges and institutes. They meet influential professors and junior students to explain the HSK business and its features. It is an effective way to identify qualified students.

Six months before graduation, students start job-hunting officially. They visit the corporations in which they are interested. Students from leading universities or departments can choose from among the good offers they receive. Stability is a priority in selecting a company; they tend to avoid gambling with their future. Students in top-ranking universities with good grades can expect to be hired by major corporations. Then these new employees are expected to maintain a firm's image.

How are newly-hired employees, the source of vitality in Japanese business, cultivated in the Japanese education system? The structure of the Japanese education system is illustrated in Figures 3 and 4. In the middle of the recession of 1982, Japanese corporations absorbed 1,090,000 graduates from all types of schools. This is equivalent to two percent of the total number of employees, 55.8 million. [4] Forty percent of all graduates, 430,000, had received junior college or higher education. Japan's senior high schools, which furnished 603,000 employees (55 percent of the total), are more demanding than those in the U.S. or Europe. [5] Students with average grades are fully capable of becoming programmers. Therefore, most software houses are able to choose qualified employees from among the 1,050,000 applicants, who satisfy only one-third the demand for programmers.

pected to rise yearly. [6] By contrast, six percent of the American university students are in the physical sciences or engineering—and that percentage is falling. [7] And in 1983, 63,000 American students completed a BS degree. [8]

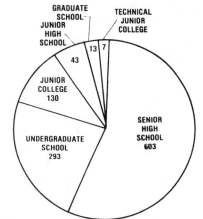

Figure 4. Number of graduates in Japanese education structure (by thousands) in 1982. From *Japanese Statistics in 1982*. [5]

Japanese universities and technical schools are the principal source of employees. In 1983, 80,700 new BSs and 6,300 technical junior college graduates were hired, mainly into high-tech industries.

It is rare for Japanese companies to hire experienced engineers away from other companies. In all Japanese software houses, only 3.9 percent of the junior programmers have changed companies. New graduates and other persons able to be trained as programmers are a company's major programming resource. [9]

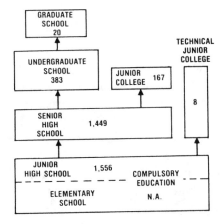

Figure 3. Number of new employees graduated from each academic level (by thousands) in 1982. From *Japanese Statistics in 1982*. [5]

Further comparisons between Japan and the U.S. are revealing. Twenty-one percent of the Japanese students major in physical sciences or engineering. In 1982, these curricula produced more than 100,000 graduates, and that number is ex-

Undertaking Large-Scale Projects

As the leading Japanese software house, HSK is widely reputed for its project management. Its average systems consist of 50,000 lines of code, and systems of more than 500,000 lines of code are not rare. Such large-scale projects require teams of scores, sometimes hundreds of persons.

It is, of course, more difficult to complete a large-scale system than a small one. First, careful cost analysis is necessary to prevent a flood of specification changes. Secondly, care must be taken to make a highly balanced, well-structured system, otherwise debugging may be delayed seriously by interface complexities. Finally, it is necessary to write interfaces between programs and modules.

Through continual refinement of our cost analysis process, we are able to reduce the difference between actual value and estimated value to less than 10 percent. As a result of thorough and early training in structured design, programmers can produce well-structured programs by top-to-bottom development and modules with as few as 100 lines of code. Structured programming has contributed to task subdivision and to home programming, allowing the Japanese software industry to raise the productivity of the individual programmer.

Productivity. From its experience in developing software bundled with hardware systems, HSK has come to regard software as an engineering product to which engineering production methods should be applied. In the early days, we developed a system that measured productivity and analyzed the difference between actual and target figures. Project leaders now use it to estimate the number of lines of code, required man-hours, and target costs for every project. Programmers record their hours under various account charge numbers and input them to summary files every week. Project leaders check the difference between the two values and, if necessary, modify the working procedures. When the project is completed, total costs are analyzed and reported to senior management, as illustrated in Table 1.

Table 1.
Factors Used to Assess
Software Production Costs.

1. Work efficiency = Lines of code/Hours worked
2. Reproduction efficiency = Lines of code produced/Hours worked
3. Cost efficiency = Total cost/Lines of code
4. Machine efficiency = Lines of code/Machine hours used

The preceding values are classified by the following factors:

1. Range on lines of code
2. Program category
3. Level of remodeling
4. Programming language used
5. Tool usability
6. Yearly trend
7. Programmer's class

HSK has used this system, with some enhancements, for 13 years. It provides a consistent system for measuring long-term trends, which we call "the standard value table." The standard value is revised upward when new tools and methodologies are adopted, for instance, when a new machine is installed in a hardware factory. Then, if actual costs coincide with projected standard values, we know we have production costs under control.

Our productivity improvement strategy has undergone four stages. Our approach up to 1975 was to implement a production audit system. We encouraged improvements in various individual projects, then applied them to other projects. A task force team specialized in various managerial operations observed the project team closely and suggested better procedures. In the second stage,

1976-1978, we applied a structured programming methodology, implementing time-sharing systems and software tools gradually. The third stage was the Skips I project directed at productivity improvement for the whole firm. Started in 1979, it became fully operational in November 1981. The concept behind Skips I was that all processes from system design to quality assurance should be interconnected in a continuous flow based on the same methodological tools. The fourth step, Skips II, started in 1982, brought modifications to Skips I, supplementing it with practical methods for generating programs from standard patterns (Fig. 5). [10]

In each stage, frequently used programming structures, including parametric parts, were standardized and cataloged in libraries as "reusable pattern modules." These structures can be recalled and combined with parametric variables and other pattern modules to generate new programs. Table 2 lists basic pattern modules.

We know that machines and tools are not enough to raise hardware production quality. Manufacturing processes, such as high-precision machining techniques, depend on individual expertise. HSK also uses a unique system called "technical discipline" to improve individual skill in the software field. Widely-used routines are collected and coded into elegant procedures for later use by programmers. Algorithms are expressed in an elegant, readable form that transcends differences among programming languages. The quality assurance division, or QAD, points out the modules for which technical discipline should be adopted. When this series was first completed, we referred to it manually, but now it is stored in the database for easy reference.

To improve programming discipline, programmers are assigned exercises every month, so they cannot avoid referring to the collection of algorithms. The exercises have the dual benefit of spreading good programming style and encouraging use of the library routines. The system is effective in preventing errors, such as miscalculation in the conversion between calendar dates.

Now, a major remaining problem is the standardization of Japanese documentation. Writing documents in Japanese is especially difficult and is one of the principal obstacles to improving software production. The recent price reduction and functional improvements in Japanese word processors is expected to solve this problem.

Table 2.
Basic Reusable Pattern Modules in Programming Library.

1. Main frame
2. Message reception
3. Message format and contents checking
4. DBMS processing
5. Message editing
6. Message switching
7. Initial screen mapping
8. Line overflow on screen
9. Error display on screen
10. PFK (Program Function Key) code analysis
11. Screen editing
12. Table lookup

To meet our production criteria, project procedures have been standardized and imposed on employees. If any modules deviate from the coding standard, they are returned to the production line. Our systematic policies have steadily increased HSK's software productivity, as shown in Fig. 5. Specific concepts for improving

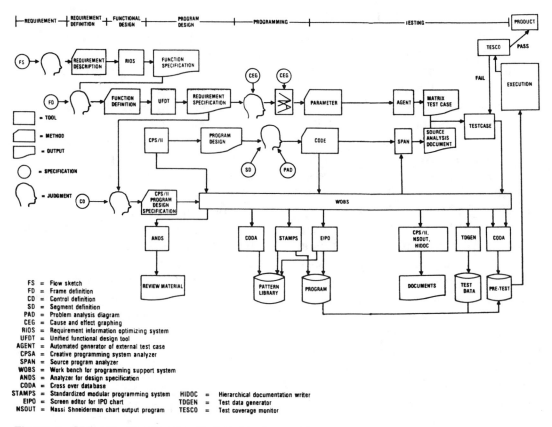

FS = Flow sketch
FD = Frame definition
CD = Control definition
SD = Segment definition
PAD = Problem analysis diagram
CEG = Cause and effect graphing
RIOS = Requirement information optimizing system
UFDT = Unified functional design tool
AGENT = Automated generator of external test case
CPSA = Creative programming system analyzer
SPAN = Source program analyzer
WOBS = Work bench for programming support system
ANDS = Analyzer for design specification
CODA = Cross over database
STAMPS = Standardized modular programming system   HIDOC = Hierarchical documentation writer
EIPO = Screen editor for IPO chart   TDGEN = Test data generator
NSOUT = Nassi Shneiderman chart output program   TESCO = Test coverage monitor

Figure 5. Skips II: Improved software development process.

productivity such as Skips are unique to HSK, but some Japanese software houses are extremely enthusiastic about research and development in software engineering. The problem is to realize the ideal software models with efficient operating procedures, developed methodologies, improved tools, and intensive training. Accordingly, our investment is divided between R&D and education.

Reliability. The Japanese demand for product reliability is uncompromising. The trade-off between price and quality does not exist in Japan. Rather, the idea that high quality brings on cost reduction is widely accepted. Japanese companies naturally accept what P.B. Crosby claims

in his book, *Quality Is Free* [11], and practice its concepts.

HSK is dedicated to strict, precise control of software quality. The QAD was established when HSK started business, and its manager has independent authority, surpassing the president's, to decide whether products pass or fail. One of the main QAD responsibilities is to monitor work in process, such as design specifications and program checklists, and warn production crews if standards are not being met. After the production process is completed, QAD conducts sample tests prior to delivery.

A program is tested with QAD's own test programs. If a program does not pass, it is returned to the production line, where the production crew is required to find a certain multiple number of bugs detected by QAD. The test process is then repeated, and only after a program earns an unconditional pass is it delivered to the user.

If users find a bug after delivery, the program must be fixed prior to any other work. If the bug induces troubles such as file contamination, destruction, or extensive system downtime, a special analysis and investigation is made. We analyze not only the errors in functional descriptions or position of branch statements in coding, but also why, by whom, when, where, and how the bug was caused. This quality and production management has enabled HSK to find designing or coding deficiencies and even to detect structural problems. And it enables us to build up a fundamental and consistent policy, in which production estimates are revised every six months to adjust the acceptable limits in such quality measurements as the number of field errors, defect rate, average number of returns to the production line, defect values per item, and the degree of degradation.

These rigorously controlled quality management and production standards have earned HSK a reputation for high quality. Currently, the firm is promoting projects to strengthen quality control. We recognize that the current policy of fixing problems after they are found is not enough. It is necessary to build in reliability so that we achieve the zero-defect goal [11], which means that no errors are allowed to leak into production anywhere during system design.

Group Dynamics and Originality

Japan has been absorbing foreign cultures for centuries, first from China, now from America. Software, an element of a foreign culture like Buddhist scripture or American realism, is viewed as the current object to absorb. Our well-studied—rather than well-trained—programmers are eager to learn new software methodologies and theories. They will put their knowledge to work in a team effort.

Although a well-organized team may remind us of military forces, its organization has another meaning. That is, the Japanese look for direction in the organization to which they belong. Organizational aims are supposed to take priority over the individuals who understand their roles and cooperate with each other to avoid conflict when involved in group projects to meet specific goals.

In Western countries, we often hear that a final product may not satisfy the user's requirements, but this objection is rare in Japan. Almost all large-scale systems are developed to satisfy accurate specifications. Misunderstandings between the clients and manufacturers are rare. A common cultural background and national character permits them to deal with computer systems in harmony with the human system, just as members of a village are in harmony with nature. This relation seems to be unique to Japan, where projects that seemed impossible a month before the due date are finished on schedule. Employees' willingness to work overtime to complete projects to satisfy a customer's needs is key to the success of new industry in Japan.

It is obvious that such a traditional society has some disadvantages. One often pointed out is a lack of originality. If there was a real disadvantage here, Japan would never catch up with the software technology in Western countries.

It is often said that not many theories and products were developed in Japanese universities or industries. And in the social system which is management-controlled and group-oriented, eccentric ideas may be suppressed. However, creativity exists in Japanese human nature as much as in European and American. Japanese originality infuses through its software systems and product lines. Furthermore, individual achievement is involved in the social or industrial organization. For instance, the Japanese National Railways' seat reservation system, the Magnetic Automated Reservation System [12] nicknamed "Green Window," is an excellent on-line, real-time system produced solely by Japanese originality. When MARS-1 and MARS-101 projects started in 1957, there was no model of a reservation system. The project started with requirement analysis. CPU, network control, hardware and peripheral equipment, and system operation were configured to be designed from scratch.

Methodologies adopted in MARS-101 involved control from real-time, front-end and on-line systems for multiprocessed multiprogramming with a back-end database management system. When this system was operated in the first computer generation, there was no concept of an operating system, multiprogram, multiprocess, or communication control. Today, despite the incredible number of transactions and the expanded system, sophisticated functions such as single-seat or group reservations are still operating without major changes. In the U.S., on the other hand, the Sabre airline seat reservation project also started in 1957 with a couple of general-purpose IBM 7090 computers. It was completed after MARS-101.

These applications are not very prominent in spite of their importance. Still, they are hardly comparable in their originality. And besides seat reservation systems, Japan's Comtrac train control system [13] for automatic control on JNR Shinkansen, the National Banking System, which links city banks and local banks, and the Stock Market System are among the most elaborate systems in the world. Still, other than customized computer systems, the Japanese are not producing innovative, general-use systems for the software market. This phenomenon is based more on economics than technology. Where many computer makers are competing heavily, applications are segmented by types of hardware and operating systems. Since normally there are only a dozen or so prospective clients for a single software product, a few hundred for the most general case, it is hardly worthwhile to risk significant losses for general applications products.

In recent years, however, the incredible expansion of personal computers has created a profitable, new market, and entrepreneurial spirits are moving in. Pan Information Processing System, a highly-regarded business-applied package, was made in Japan and spread to the world market. During next few years, similar PC products will be increasing. [14]

As long as the multidimensional aspects of software products—volumes, memory space, speed and so on—increase, the world-wide software demand will expand.

However, the marketing game will be played with different rules depending on whether the competitors are Japanese or Western. Japan's game is not always exciting, with players and tactics always changing. We hesitate to make drastic changes in personnel, staff, or R&D investment based on short-term results. Once our direction is set, we move forward step by step, keeping our sights on the goal. We try to move steadily, shifting our direction if necessary, but never stopping or back-tracking. The difference between management methods in Japan and Western countries reflects century-old cultural attitudes. Still the vast software market offers room for a variety of approaches. In order to meet the enormous demand for quality computer systems, the industry must exchange technologies across language barriers. We are ready to make our expertise available, particularly that of our software project management and production methods.

REFERENCES

[1]   "Trade Statistics," *JECC Note,* Printing Bureau in Ministry of Finance, Tokyo, 1983, p. 28.

[2]   "The Colossus That Works," *Time,* July 11, 1983, p. 46.

[3]   "A Worldwide Strategy for the Computer Market," *Business Week,* December 14, 1981, pp. 51-52.

[4]   "Educational Standards in Japan," *Japanese Statistics in 1982,* Prime Minister's Office, Printing Bureau in Ministry of Finance, Tokyo, 1981, pp. 277-78.

[5]   "How the Japanese Do It," *Newsweek,* May 9, 1983, p. 46.

[6]   "Fundamental Survey on Schools," *Educational Standards in Japan,* Ministry of Education, Printing Bureau in Ministry of Finance, Tokyo, 1981, p. 46.

[7]   "Low-Tech Education Threatens the High-Tech Future," *Business Week,* March 28, 1983, p. 59.

[8]   "Why Industry Must Step in to Train Engineers," *Business Week,* December 14, 1981, p. 78.

[9]   *Current Status in Japanese Information Processing,* Ministry of International Trade and Industry, Printing Bureau in Ministry of Finance, Tokyo, August 1982, p. 29.

[10] K.H. Kim, "A Look at Japan's Development of Software Engineering Technology," *Computer,* Vol. 16, No. 5 (May 1983), pp. 26-37.

[11] Y. Hayashi, S. Yokota, and T. Nauchi, "Train Operation Control System for High-Speed Railway," *AFIPS Conference Proceedings,* Vol. 47, 1978 NCC, Reston, Va.: AFIPS Press, pp. 1249-53.

[12] P.B. Crosby, *Quality Is Free,* New York: McGraw-Hill, 1979, p. 169.

[13] M. Hosaka, "On System Development of the Seat Reservation System of Japanese National Railways," *Johoshori,* Vol. 24, No. 3 (Mar. 1983), pp. 284-94 (in Japanese).

[14] W.L. Frank, "PIPS: A New Revolution in the Making?" *Computerworld,* Vol. 17, No. 15 (April 11, 1983), p. 49.

7

Editors' Note
McKenney and McFarlan: "The Information Archipelago— Maps and Bridges"

Insight: The concept of "stagnations," stable, no-exit states that organizations get themselves into due to excessive standardization or too much focus.

We humans are analogy-thinkers. When we discover good ones (atoms being like building blocks), we are better able to deal with complex realities and to make genuine progress. When we encounter flawed analogies (the falling dominoes of Southeast Asia), we are often seduced into error. A simple but accurate analogy can be a genuine contribution to understanding.

Harvard Professors McKenney and McFarlan have made such a contribution with their archipelago image. They portray the set of all information management schemes not as a continuum, but as a dotting of islands on a sea. Some of these islands lie close enough to other more desirable islands so that progress is possible in manageable hops. But others are just dead ends. And so a seemingly sensible approach to systems building and information management might suffer from the fatal flaw that it stops all future progress. Proceeding sensibly through the archipelago while avoiding dead ends is what information management is all about.

7

The Information Archipelago—Maps and Bridges
by James L. McKenney and F. Warren McFarlan

• The vice president of services of a large durables manufacturing company recently faced a dilemma. Her request for a stand-alone word processor to solve operating problems in her fastest-growing sales office had been denied. It had seemed a trivial request; yet having to do without the word processor would cause delays, and she thought that the decision set a dangerous precedent. The reason the accounting department gave for denying the machine was its incompatibility with the division's information services network. When she questioned this, an incomprehensible series of technical arguments ensued that appeared to have no relationship to her very real productivity problem. Should she fall in line, fight the decision, or resubmit the request as an operating expense instead of a capital expenditure?

• A major manufacturing company has reduced the processing capacity and staffing of its corporate data processing center by 60% over the past four years. The divisional data centers have grown to such an extent, however, that overall corporate data processing expenditures have risen more than 50% during the period.

• After careful analysis, the senior staff of a decentralized insurance company recommended an orderly dissolution of the company's $25 million data center and the creation of eight smaller diversified data centers over a 30-month period.

These actual incidents are not unusual. Repeatedly over the past ten years, technological change has made organization structures for information services obsolete in many companies and has forced, or will force, major reorganization. There are several reasons for this.

First, for reasons of both efficiency and effectiveness, in the 1980s information services must include office automation, telecommunications (data and voice communications), and data processing; and these must be managed in a coordinated and, in many companies, integrated manner. This coordination is not easy in many organizations, as each of these activities in the 1960s and 1970s not only had different technical bases but also was marketed to the company separately. In addition, the organization structures and practices that developed for handling the technologies are quite different from what are now needed. The different managerial histories and decision-making habits associated with each of these technologies make integration today exceptionally difficult.

Second, it has become increasingly clear that information services technologies that are new to the organization require different managerial approaches than do technologies with which the organization has had more experience. For example, the problems of implementing new office automation technology projects are quite different from those associated with more mature technologies.

Third, companies must rethink where data and computer hardware resources belong organizationally in the corporation. The dramatic improvements in hardware cost and performance for all three technologies in the past decade permit this issue to be addressed in the 1980s in a manner quite different from that of the early 1970s.

These improvements have occurred as computers have moved from vacuum tubes to very large scale integrated circuits. These technology changes continue to improve productivity as still smaller, more reliable, and more useful circuits are being developed. Exhibit I shows the cost trends per individual unit and circuit over the past 20 years, trends that will continue for the next decade. The cost reduction and capacity increases caused by these changes have reduced computer hardware cost as a fraction of total DP department cost to below 30% in most large data processing installations.

Today, computer cost often does not exceed corporate telecommunications (including telephone) expense and for many companies is much less than software development and maintenance charges. Equally significant, technology has permitted development of stand-alone minicomputer systems or office automation systems that companies can tailor to provide specific service for any desired location.

This improved technology has caused a dramatic shift in both the types of information services being delivered to users and the best organizational structure for delivering them. The most desirable structure has involved and will continue to involve not only the coordination of data processing, teleprocessing, and office automation but redeployment both physically and organizationally of the company's technical and staff resources that provide information services. By technical resources, we mean computers, word processors, private telephone exchanges, "intelligent" terminals, and so on. In staff resources, we include all the persons responsible either for operating these machines or for developing and maintaining new applications.

Exhibit I. Costs and performance of electronics.

Year	1958	1965	1972	1980
Technology	Vacuum tube	Transistor	Integrated circuit	Large-scale integrated circuit
Cost per unit	$8	$0.25	$0.2	$0.001
Cost per logic	$160	$12	$200	$.05
Operation time (in seconds)	16×10^{-3}	4×10^{-6}	40×10^{-9}	200×10^{-12}

Source: W.D. Fraser, "Potential Technology Implications for Computers and Telecommunications in the 1980s." *IBM Systems Journal,* Vol. 18, No. 2, 1979, p. 333.

MERGING ISLANDS OF IS TECHNOLOGY

The problems in speedily integrating the three technologies of data processing, telecommunications, and office automation are largely a result of their historically very different management (as shown in Exhibit II). Let us analyze these differences.

In 1920, in most organizations the manager and his secretary were supported by three forms of information services, each based on a different technology. For word processing, the typewriter was used to generate easily legible words. A file cabinet served as the main storage device for paper output, and the various organization units were linked by secretaries who moved paper from one unit to another.

Data processing, if automated at all, depended on card-sorting machines to develop sums and balances using punched cards as input. The cards served as memory for this system. The telecommunications system comprised wires and mes-

Exhibit II. Islands of technology.

Functions of technology	Islands of technology		
	Word processing	Data processing	Communication
1920			
Human-to-machine translation	Shorthand, dictaphone	Form, keypunch	Phone
Manipulation of data	Typewriter	Card sorting	Switch
Memory	File cabinet	Cards	None
Links	Secretary	Operator	Operator
1965			
Human-to-machine translation	Shorthand, dictaphone	Form, keypunch	Phone
Manipulation of data	Typewriter	Computer	Computer
Memory	File cabinet	Computer	None
Links	Secretary	Computer	Computer
1980			
Human-to-machine translation	Shorthand, dictaphone	Typewriter	Phone, typewriter
Manipulation of data	Computer	Computer	Computer
Memory	Computer	Computer	Computer
Links	Computer	Computer	Computer

sages that were manipulated by operator control of electromechanical switches. This telecommunications system had no storage capacity.

In 1920, the organizational designers of each of the three islands had significantly different roles, as shown in Exhibit III. For word processing, the office manager directed the design, heavily influenced by the desires of his or her manager. Although formal office systems were beginning to emerge, word processing remained primarily a means of facilitating secretarial

work. The chief means of obtaining new equipment was through purchasing agents and involved the selection of typewriters, dictaphones, and file cabinets from a wide variety of medium-sized companies. Standardization was not critical.

Data processing was the domain of the controller-accountant, and the systems design activity was carried out by either the chief accountant or a card systems manager, who set the protocols for the flow of information processing. The systems of machines for data processing were so

Exhibit III. Evolution of islands of technology.

Function	Islands of technology		
	Word processing	Data processing	Communication
	1920		
Design	Office manager	Card design	AT&T
Operation	Secretary	Machine operator	AT&T
Maintenance	Many companies	Single supplier	AT&T
User	Manager	Accountant	Manager
	1965		
Design	Office systems analyst	Systems analyst	AT&T
Operation	Secretary	Operator and analyst	AT&T
Maintenance	Many	Single supplier	AT&T
User	Manager	Manager and accountant	Everybody
	1980		
Design	Systems analyst	Systems analyst	Systems analyst
Operation	Manager, secretary, and editor	Manager and secretary	Manager and secretary
Maintenance	Many or single	IBM and other	AT&T and other
User	Everybody	Everybody	Everybody

complex and relatively expensive that managers had to develop a plan for their use. Telecommunications had neither design nor planning components, as these functions were performed by the telephone companies.

Starting in the 1920s, data processing services—that is, card-sorting machines —were normally purchased and maintained as a system from one supplier, so that from the beginning a systems relationship existed between buyer and seller. Teleprocessing (telephones), however, was a purchased service requiring no capital investment. All three islands, therefore, were served differently in 1920: one by many companies, one by a systems supplier, and one by a public utility.

In 1965, the servicing and management of the three islands still functioned in the 1920 pattern. Word processing was still largely influenced by the manager and centered around the secretary. Services such as typewriters and reproducing systems (mimeographs, for example) were purchased as independent units from a range of competitors offering similar technology. There was little long-term planning, and such systems as existed evolved in response to newly available machines.

Data processing, however, had emerged as an ever more complex process. In that area, systems and planning were dominated by the need for serious evaluation of major capital investments in computers and software, as well as for multiyear projects. In addition, so that companies could take advantage of the productivity of the new system, all employees and users had to undergo extensive training. At times, as in the insurance company example at the beginning of this article, even the corporate organization was changed to

accommodate the new potential and problems caused by computer technology. In regard to communications, however, in 1965 AT&T still completely dominated the supply of services; the equipment a company bought determined how the service was managed. In some organizations, managing communications implied placing three-minute hourglasses by phones so that employees would reduce the length of their calls.

By 1980, however, management's concerns for word processing and teleprocessing had become integrated with those for data processing for two important reasons. First, both areas now require large capital investments, large projects, large and complex implementation, and extensive user training. But the managers of these activities often lack the expertise to handle these types of problems.

For office automation, a special problem now is the move from multiple vendors and relatively small individual cost to, in many cases, one vendor that will provide integrated support to many units through a large capital purchase. The size of the purchase is several orders of magnitude larger and the applications are much more complex than those of a decade ago.

For telecommunications, now managers need to break the reliance on a service purchased from a public utility and to look at multiple sources for large capital investment for equipment. These developments in word processing and teleprocessing represent a sharp departure from past practices and create the need for new management skills, which were added to the data processing function years ago.

The second reason for linkage of word processing and teleprocessing to data processing is that key sectors of all three components—data processing, teleprocessing, and office automation—are increasingly physically linked in a network; consequently, managers cannot address the problems of one component independently of those of the other two. For example, in one manufacturing company over a 24-hour period the same WATS line is used for voice transmission, on-line data communications, and an electronic mail message-switching system.

The situation is complicated by the fact that in 1982 a dominant supplier in each of the three islands of technology is attempting to market its products as the technological base from which a company can develop its coordinated automation of the other islands. IBM, for example, is extending its data processing base to various products supporting office automation and communications. AT&T is extending its communications base to products supporting data processing and office automation, and Xerox is expanding its office automation effort to communications and DP.

Failure to address this issue of coalescing technologies poses great risk to an organization. Over the next few years, we believe most organizations will consolidate at least policy control, and perhaps management also, of the three islands into a single information services unit. The following are key reasons for such a move:

1. Decisions in each area now involve large amounts of money and complex technical and cost evaluations.

2. The types of analytic skills and project management skills and staff needed to plan and implement applications are similar for each of these technologies.

3. Many systems call for the combination of these technologies into networks that handle computing, telecommunications, and office automation in an integrated way.

A company can follow multiple paths in effecting the merger of the three islands of technologies as it moves toward a single information services function. We will discuss the three most common and most practical approaches.

DP & Telecommunications

In many larger organizations data processing and teleprocessing of data merged under DP leadership some years ago. In these cases, the DP staff had to become familiar with the technical aspects of data communication. In the early 1970s, the technical issues were formidable, and there was a clear separation technically between voice and data transmission. But in the mid-1970s technical changes in telecommunications systems permitted voice and data to be dealt with similarly so that the same line could be used for voice and data without the need for special equipment. On several nontechnical dimensions, however, initially voice and data communications continued to pose separate management problems: the telephone (voice) was still part of a carefully regulated utility and required little planning for purchase and use, while data communications, sold by many vendors, demanded increasingly sophisticated means for evaluating capital investments.

As the market for data communications has expanded, the economic advantages of merging voice and data communications, for example, in the WATS line, have become significant. In 1982, the trend is toward merging voice and data communications policy and operations in a single unit, usually located in the DP department. For example, a large bank recently installed an integrated network to replace the previously separate voice and data networks. The system reduced the bank's communication bill 35% and improved service to both the data processing installation and the telephone system.

Telecommunications & Office Automation

New technology has facilitated the joining of word processing and office automation to telecommunications. Designers of word processing equipment now include in their machines the ability to communicate both to other machines and to storage devices through telecommunications systems. With these features, word processors are no longer merely automated typewriters but links to word storage files, other employees, and data files. The communications process has been vastly accelerated by development of telecommunications storage capacity, which permits the sender to leave messages. In many offices, this capability has equaled or exceeded word processing use in importance, but the real potential of these linkages is only partially exploited today. Development of this potential is slowed when telecommunications and office automation report to widely separated parts of the corporation.

DP & Office Automation

In many companies today, technologically innovative DP managers are linking their data processing and their word processing by extending their DP terminals to remote sites. As these companies began to move words (as opposed to just numeric data) through computers from one site to another, demand arose for systems to store and forward large volumes of words to other sites.

Often, employees used the remote terminals more for word than for data communications. Soon DP assimilated all communications, voice and data, as well as word processing. The success of this arrangement depends on whether the mature DP organization can nurture the new technologies instead of smothering them with excessive controls.

In summary, at present a number of organization patterns are possible as companies move toward adopting and combining all information services. This heterogeneity is transitional, and most businesses will eventually merge management of these islands under one organization, certainly for policymaking, planning, and control—and in many settings for line control and execution. The timing of these moves in any organization depends on such factors as corporate structure and leadership style, the speed at which a company usually adopts new technologies, flexibility in staff assignments (for example, to remove deadwood), and current development priorities.

PHASES OF ASSIMILATION

The merger of the three technologies is complicated by managers' need for different approaches to a particular technology as their organization gains experience with it. For example, the approach to planning and using relatively mature DP technology, such as new batch systems, may be inappropriate for new office automation or new DP technologies. Failure to recognize this difference has led to mismanagement of major projects and missed opportunities for projects that should have been started but were not because no one knew enough about the technology to perceive the possibilities.

Organizations change much more slowly than technology. As Richard L. Nolan and Cyrus F. Gibson showed for data processing, an organization goes through stages in assimilating technology. [1] Recent work in office automation and data processing has revealed this model to be a special case of the situation of the learning cycle of adapting a technology to an organization's needs. [2] That companies have been surprisingly poor in transferring skills learned in managing the DP stages to office automation is shown in a recent study of 37 companies, of which 30 had not built on their DP technology experience when moving into word processing and office automation. [3] Of equal importance, more than two-thirds had not progressed beyond Nolan's stage 2 of office automation of tasks and experimentation with respect to word processing and were in a state of arrested development.

Another study tracing an organization's use of information services technologies in all three components found four phases of evolution that relate both to Nolan's original stages and to concepts of organizational change developed by Edgar H. Schein. [4] These phases can be characterized as (1) investment or project initiation, (2) technology learning and adaptation, (3) management control, and (4) widespread technology transfer (see Exhibit IV). Further, use of the technology must be managed or innovation will stagnate.

The first phase begins with a decision to invest in an information processing technology that is new to the organization and involves one or more complementary projects, as well as training users. The second phase usually follows, unless there is a disaster in phase 1, such as failure of the vendor or poor user involvement. Such a setback results in a delayed phase, which is shown as stagnation A in Exhibit IV.

Most companies in stagnation A decided to "disinvest" in the system because it increased work and provided few benefits. The causes were lack of management attention, incompetent project management, major unanticipated technical problems, or bad choice of hardware. Managers are usually slow to recognize problems leading to this type of stagnation.

The complexity and time requirements of implementing new information technology normally prevent discovery of the developing failure for 18 to 36 months. The project is usually not a clear technological disaster but rather an ambiguous situation that managers see as adding more work to the organization, with little measurable benefit. Hence, they reject the system.

All projects studied that were stalled in stagnation A had significant cost overruns. Each failure created anxieties and prevented any coordinated momentum. Organizations frozen in this state usually end up purchasing more services based on a familiar technology and become adept at adapting it to their use; for example, they might try to work with batch sales

Exhibit IV. Use of technology in a corporation.

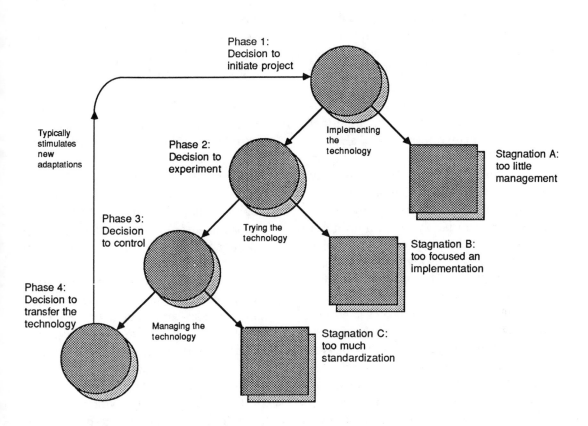

reports as opposed to learning how to use on-line sales updates. A two-year lag usually follows this stagnation state before new investments in this technology are tried again, often along with a complete change of personnel.

The second phase of adapting technology to an organization involves learning how to use it for tasks beyond those mentioned in the initial proposal. In none of the office automation sites studied was the technology implemented as originally planned. [5] In each case, managers learned a lot during implementation. If the second phase is managed so as to permit managers to develop and refine their new understanding of this technology, the organization moves to phase 3. Failure to learn from the first applications and to effectively disseminate this learning leads to stagnation B (see Exhibit IV).

A large manufacturing company experienced such an assimilation block during automation of clerical word processing activities that were under the control of a very cost-conscious accounting function. Highly conservative in its approach to technology in data processing, the company had introduced word processing to save clerical costs in mass mailings and customer billing.

Having developed this narrow word

processing application to reduce costs, the accounting department showed no interest in expanding its scope beyond simply automating the repetitive typing function of a typewriter. It made typing more capital-intensive and tapped only 2% to 5% of the possible productivity improvements. Focusing solely on clerical costs established a niche for office automation that was trivial relative to its potential.

Phase 3 typically involves a change in the organization (when one company reached this point, for example, it transferred projects using a technology from an entrepreneurial system group to a control-oriented group), continued evolution of the uses of technology, and, most important, development of precise controls to guide the design and implementation of systems using these technologies to ensure that later applications are made more cost efficient than the first. If, in this phase, control for efficiency is not all important and room is left for broader objectives, then the organization moves into phase 4, which involves broad-based communication and spread of technology to other groups in the organization.

Stagnation C comes when a company develops controls that are so onerous that they inhibit the legitimate profitable spread of the use of technology. An example of this block with respect to data processing is a manufacturing company that entered into large-scale centralization with distributed input systems. To justify the expense, it focused on gaining all the benefits of a standardized, highly efficient production shop. In this process, the organization lost its enthusiasm for innovation and change with respect to this technology and actively discouraged users. Further, the rigorous protocols of these standard pro-

grams irritated users and helped set the stage for local offices to experiment surreptitiously with automation—phase 1 in a different technology. The first incident we described at the beginning of this article was from that company.

As time passes, new technologies emerge that offer the opportunity either to move into new applications areas or to restructure old ones (see Exhibit IV). Each of the three components of information services thus involves waves of new technologies, and companies must continually adopt different approaches to managing and assimilating them, as each component of technology is in a different phase.

For example, in 1981 a manufacturing company was in phase 4 in terms of its ability to plan for and deal with enhancements to its batch systems over a period of years. At the same time, it was in phase 3 in terms of organizing protocols to solidify control over the efficiencies of its on-line inquiry and data systems, whose growth had exploded in the past several years. Finally, it had made an investment in several word processing systems and was clearly in phase 1 with respect to this technology.

Thus, as the islands of technology merge, managers must not try to use the same approach to technologies that are in different phases. A mismatch may be a reason to change the speed of reorganization.

The significant implications of these phases for organizations of IS technologies include the following:

1.   Where possible operationally, phase 1 and 2 technologies should be kept organizationally separate from phase

3 and 4 technologies so the efficiency goals of one do not blunt the effectiveness of the other.

2. The full operational integration of IS technologies will be a long time maturing; companies may have to tolerate a certain disorderliness during integration in order to gain technical experience.

3. Dispersion of technology into the hands of the users in phase 2 may be appropriate (although inefficient). However, managers may appropriately install tighter control after the original dispersion and make organizational shifts at a later phase.

PATTERNS OF DISTRIBUTION

As the three islands of technology coalesce and as structure and procedures emerge to manage the phases of technology assimilation, the question that remains is where the data and hardware elements should be located in the organization. At one extreme is the company that has a large centralized hub connected by telecommunications links to remote input-output devices. At the other is a small hub, or none at all, with most or all data and hardware distributed to users. Intermediate alternatives also exist.

In the past, hardware costs heavily influenced resolution of this organization problem. Because the cost per arithmetic operation was higher for small hardware (as opposed to large hardware) in the early 1960s, the first large investments in computing were consolidated into large data centers. In contrast, rapidly falling hardware costs and the introduction of the mini- and microcomputer in the early 1980s permit, but do not demand, cost-effective organizational alternatives.

To retain their market shares as the difference in efficiency between large and small computers erodes, vendors of large computers are suggesting that many members of an organization need access to the same large data files; hence, according to them, the ideal IS structure is a large central processing unit with massive data files connected by a telecommunications network to a wide array of intelligent devices (often at great distances). While this holds true in many situations, for some companies the problem is unfortunately more complex, as we will discuss later. The factors influencing the final decision on structure include management control, technology, data professional services, and organizational fit (see Exhibit V).

Pressures Toward a Central Hub

Multiple pressures, both real and illusory, can cause companies to use a large hub with a distributed network.

Need for management control. The ability to attract, develop, manage, and maintain staffs and controls to ensure high-quality, cost-effective operation of systems is a compelling reason for a strong central unit. A single large unit permits a more professional, cheaper, and higher-quality operation than would a series of much smaller units. These advantages caused the major decentralized company mentioned at the beginning of this article to retain its corporate data center rather than move to regional centers. The company was unconvinced that eight small data centers could be run as efficiently in

Exhibit V. Pressures on placement of the IS function.

Pressure	For centralization	For distribution
Management control	More professional operation	Better user control and response
	Flexible backup	Simpler control
	Efficient use of personnel	Improved local reliability
Technology	Large-scale capacity	Efficient size
	Efficient use of capacity	Reduced telecommunications costs
Data related	Multiple access to common data	Easier access
	Assurance of data standards	Better fit with field needs
	Better security	Data relevance
Professional service	Specialized staff	Stability of work force
	Reduced vulnerability to turnover	Better user career paths
	Richer DP career paths	
Organizational fit	Corporate style is central or functional	Decentralized corporate style
	History of IS	Meets business needs, e.g., for multinationals

aggregate and, even if they could, that it was worth the cost and trauma of making the transition.

Better backup is available through multiple central processing units in a single site. When hardware failure occurs in one CPU, pushing a button will switch the network from one machine to another. Obviously, this does not address the possibility that an environmental disaster could affect the entire center.

Available technology. The availability of large-scale processing capacity for users who need it only sometimes is another strong reason for a company to have a large hub. In a day when cheaper and more powerful computing has become available, it is easier for users to visualize doing some of their computing on their own personal computer, such as an Apple, or a stand-alone minicomputer. At the same time, however, some users have other problems, such as the need for large linear programming models and petroleum-reservoir-mapping programs, that require the largest available computing capacity. In such cases, the larger the computer capacity available, the more detail the company can profitably build into its computer programs.

Also, many companies see an opportunity to manage aggregate computing more efficiently, thereby reducing hardware expenditures. With many machines in the organization, and with each loaded to 70%, managers may feel that consolidation would make better use of the available processing power. Although it was clearly an important cost issue in the 1960s, it is largely irrelevant in the 1980s.

Control of data. Another argument for the large central hub is the ability it gives users to control access to common corporate data files on a need-to-know basis. This access, absolutely essential from the early days for organizations such as airlines and railroads, is now economically feasible in many other companies because of the sharp reductions in storage and processing costs.

Personnel services. The large staff that is necessary in a major IS data center provides an opportunity to attract a specialized technical staff and keep it challenged. The opportunity to work on a variety of problems and to share expertise with other professionals provides the requisite air of excitement. Having these skills in the organization also permits individual units to undertake complex tasks as needed without incurring risks of uncontrolled use. Further, since such skills are generally in short supply, consolidating them in a single unit permits better deployment from a corporate perspective. Finally, the large group's resources at a hub permit more comfortable adaptation to inevitable turnover problems; resignation of one person in a three-person group of a decentralized system is normally more disruptive than five persons leaving a group of a hundred professionals.

Organizational fit. In a centralized organization, the factors just mentioned take on particular weight since they lead to a good fit between IS structure and overall corporate structure and they help eliminate friction for organizations where IS hardware was introduced in a centralized fashion and whose management practices developed accordingly. Reversal of such a structure can be tumultuous.

Pressures Toward Distribution

In 1982, significant pressures argue for placing processing capacity and data in the hands of the users, with only limited or no processing power at a hub.

Management control. Most important among these factors is satisfaction of users' desire for control. Locally managed data files enable users to hear first about deviations from planned performance of their unit, giving them an opportunity to analyze and communicate their understanding of their operations on a regular basis.

Also, by being removed from the hourly fluctuations in demand on the corporate network, the user has a better chance of stability in response time. Most users find predictable response time very important in at least some of their applications.

The distribution of hardware to users helps them remove or insulate themselves from the more volatile elements of the corporate chargeout system. They can better predict their costs, thus avoiding the necessity of describing embarrassing variances. Often costs will actually be lower.

With distribution of processing power, the corporation is much less vulnerable to a massive failure in the corporate data center. Companies with very large IS budgets, by which computers support essential parts of the operations, have found it increasingly desirable to set up two or more large data centers and split the work between them so that if something happened to one data center, the core aspects of the company's operations could run at the other. These companies have in general been such large users of data processing services that arrangement of backup at some other neighboring site is impractical.

Medium-sized companies have had the practical option of making backup arrangements with other organizations (which often sound better in theory than they turn out to be) or of buying into something like the remote-site solution (where for about $6,000 per month they have emergency access to a fully equipped, unloaded data center). In case of less dramatic events causing a service interruption at the main location, a network of local minicomputers can keep crucial aspects of an operation going.

From the user's perspective, the distributed network simplifies operations both in the construction of the operating system and in feeding work into it. The red tape involved in routing work to a data entry department is eliminated and the procedures can be built right into the operations of the user department, although, surprisingly, some users regain this control with trepidation. Similarly, with the right type of software, the machines in the distributed network are user friendly.

Technology related. Although in the early days large central processing units were more efficient than smaller machines, in the 1980s several important changes make this no longer true:

- The size of CPUs and memories no longer governs their power [6], and their cost is a much smaller percentage of the total hardware expenditure in 1981 than in 1970.

- Grosch's Law (that computer processing power increases as the square of computer costs) was never intended to apply to peripheral units and other elements of a network.

- The percentage of hardware costs as a part of the total IS budget has dropped sharply over the past decade, as personnel, telecommunications, and other operating and de-

velopment costs have risen. Thus, efficiency of hardware use is not the burning issue it was ten years ago. These factors, in conjunction with the much slower improvement in telecommunications costs (falling 11% per year) and the explosion of user needs for on-line access to data files that can be generated and stored locally, often reverse the economic case for a large hub.

Data related. Because of telecommunications costs and the very occasional needs of access to some data files by users other than those originating the data, many companies will find it uneconomical or undesirable to manage all data by central access. Further, ability to access and relate data may not be necessary to corporate strategy.

A case in point is the large company we mentioned at the outset, which recently considered abandoning its corporate computing center. The center is a service bureau for its eight major divisions, where all development staff members reside. No common application or data file exists between even two of the divisions (not even for payroll). If its survival depended on it, the company could not identify in less than 24 hours its relationship with any customer.

In senior management's judgment, this organization of the development staff and the lack of data relationships among divisions reinforces the company's highly decentralized structure. Thus no pressure for change exists anywhere in the organization. The corporate computing center, an organizational anomaly, is considered simply a cost-efficient way of permitting each division to develop its own network of systems. Changing this approach would have had no practical use and could even threaten a soundly conceived organization structure.

Professional service. Moving functions away from the urban environment toward more rural settings can reduce employee turnover, which is the bane of metropolitan-area information service departments. While recruiting may be complicated and training facilities may not be available in such locations, once the employees are there, the lack of headhunters and attractive employers nearby can reduce turnover.

When the IS staff is closely linked to the user organization, it becomes easier to plan employee promotions that may move technical personnel out of the IS organization to other user departments. This is an important advantage for a department with low turnover, as technical staff members may develop burn-out symptoms. Such transfers also facilitate relations between users and IS.

Organizational fit. In many companies, the controls implicit in the distributed approach better fit the organization structure and general leadership style. This is particularly true for companies with highly decentralized structures (or organizations that wish to evolve in this fashion) and/or for those that are geographically very diverse.

Finally, highly distributed facilities fit the needs of many multinational structures. While airlines reservation data, shipping container operations, and certain banking transactions must flow through a central location, in many cases the overwhelming amount of work is more effectively managed in the local country. Communication to corporate headquarters can be handled by telex, mailing tapes, or a telecommunications link, depending on the organization's management style, the size of the unit, and so on.

Assessing the appropriateness of a particular kind or size of hardware and the data configuration for an organization is very challenging. All but the most decentralized of organizations have a strong need for central control over standards and operating procedures. The changes in technology, however, both permit and make desirable in some companies distribution of the *execution* of significant portions of hardware operations and data handling.

Reexamination of the deployment of hardware and software resources for the information services function has high priority in the 1980s. Changing technology economics, merging of formerly disparate technologies with different managerial traditions, and problems of administering each phase of IS technology assimilation in different ways have made the decisions appropriate to 1970 obsolete. The following steps can ensure appropriate handling of these issues:

1. Companies must make the development of a program to implement these decisions part of the mission of a permanent corporate policy group. This policy group must assess the current move toward merging the islands, ensure a balance of the desires for a central hub against the advantages of a distributed approach, and ensure appropriate guidance of different technologies.

2. The policy group must make sure that uniformity in management practice is not pushed too far and that diversity

exists where appropriate. Even within a company, it is fitting that different parts of the organization have different patterns of distributed support for hardware and data. Different phases of development, with respect to specific technologies, and geographical distance from central service support are among the valid reasons for approaches to differ.

3. The policy group must show particular sensitivity to the needs of the international activities. It may be inappropriate to enforce common approaches to these problems internationally, either for companies operating primarily in a single country or for the multinational that operates in many countries. Each country has a different cost and quality structure for telecommunications, a different level of IS achievement, different reservoirs of technical skills, and a different culture, at least. These differences are likely to endure. What works in the United States often will not work in, say, Thailand.

4. The policy group must address its issues in a strategic fashion. The arguments and reasoning leading to a set of solutions are more complex than simply the current economics of hardware or who should have access to what data files. Corporate organization structure, corporate strategy and direction, availability of human resources, and operating administrative processes are additional critical inputs. Both in practice and in writing, the technicians and information theorists oversimplify a very complex set of problems and options.

A critical function of the group is to ensure adequate R&D investment (phases 1 and 2). A special effort must be taken to make appropriate investments in experimental studies, pilot studies, and development of prototypes. Similarly, the group must ensure that proved expertise is being distributed appropriately within the company, especially to departments that may be unaware of IS potential.

5. The policy group must establish a proper balance between long- and short-term needs. A distributed structure optimally designed for the technology and economics of 1982 may fit the world of 1989 rather poorly. Often it makes sense to postpone feature development or to design a clumsy approach in today's technology in order to more easily and inexpensively adapt to the technologies of the late 1980s. As a practical matter, the group will work on these issues in a continuous, iterative fashion rather than implement a revolutionary change.

REFERENCES

[1] Richard L. Nolan and Cyrus F. Gibson, "Managing the Four Stages of EDP Growth," *Harvard Business Review,* January-February 1974, p. 76.

[2] James L. McKenney, "A Field Study on the Use of Computer-Based Technology to Improve Management Control," Harvard Business School Working Paper 7-46, December 1980.

[3] Kathleen Curley, "Word Processing: First Step to the Office of the Future? An Examination of the Evolving Technology and Its Use in Organiza-

tions," Harvard Business School un-published doctoral thesis, June 1981.

[4]   Edgar H. Schein, "Management Development as a Process of Influence," *Industrial Management Review,* Vol. 2, 1961, p. 59.

[5]   Kathleen Curley, "Word Processing."

[6]   Edward G. Cale, Lee L. Gremillion, and James L. McKenney, "Price/Performance Patterns of U.S. Computer Systems," *Proceedings of the ACM,* April 1979.

8

Editors' Note
Abdel-Hamid: "The Dynamics of Software Project Staffing: A System Dynamics Based Simulation Approach"

Insight: A simulation of project dynamics can guide the manager toward the most prudent estimation and staffing strategy.

Abdel-Hamid did his early work under Forrester at M.I.T., where the task at hand was the construction of monolithic models of the global economy. He has applied some of his modeling skills to the seemingly simpler matter of project dynamics. The result is a simulation.

With such a tool, the project manager has the luxury of tinkering with various project parameters and "re-running" the project to see what would have happened: Let's see, What would the effect have been if I had added two more people in January, instead of waiting till spring? And how might it have changed the outcome if I had goaded people with a tighter original schedule or eased up on them with a more realistic one? Of course, he/she can do this analysis before the project is ever run, and use the parameters of the best simulation to guide the real project.

This article is mostly concerned with one of the parameters that the simulation was used to study: staff size. And it is interesting for that alone. But the subtext of the article seems more valuable still. It describes the idea of a dynamic simu-

lation in broad terms. It provides enough of a hint so that you should be able to construct a simple model of your own. You write down the dozen or so parameters that seem likely to matter (these might be product size, staff levels, published deadlines, and so on) and then consider how results may depend on these inputs. You put this into the form of a spreadsheet with formulas relating project parameters to results. Now you test this out against a few past projects to see how well your model would have predicted their outcomes. You revise and refine till you have the best model you can come up with, and now you ask it to project the results for your next project.

Why would you want to burden yourself with so much extra work? Because the construction of your own model is exactly the process you have to go through anyway in order to come up with your best project strategy and estimated outcome. But typically you do this intuitively. By instead building an explict model, you expose your intuition to the light of day. You make it possible for others to critique and help you in a constructive way. Most of all, you establish a framework that will help you learn effectively as you gain more experience about project dynamics, and make you better able to pass what you've learned on to others.

116

8

The Dynamics of Software Project Staffing: A System Dynamics Based Simulation Approach
by Tarek K. Abdel-Hamid

Introduction

People issues have gained recognition, in recent years, as being at the core of effective software project management. [20] For several reasons:

> Personnel costs are skyrocketing relative to hardware costs. Chronic problems in software development and implementation are more frequently traced to personnel shortcomings. Information systems staff sizes have mushroomed with little time for adequate selection and training. It is little wonder, then, that software project managers find themselves focusing increasing amounts of attention on human resource issues. [36]

Along with this growing interest in human resource management there are, however, some serious and legitimate concerns. Chief among them is the belief that, as of yet, we still lack the fundamental understanding of the software development process, and that without such an understanding the likelihood of any significant improvements in this area are questionable. [37, 38]

This is no trivial impediment. But, if it is any solace, it is one that is not unique to this young field:

> Any worthwhile human endeavor emerges first as an art.... Over the centuries, management as an art has progressed by the acquisition and recording of human experience. But as long as there is no orderly underlying scientific base, the experiences remain as special cases. The lessons are poorly transferrable either in time or in space.... (And) in time (the art) ceases to grow because of the disorganized state of its knowledge....
>
> The management of the underlying science (is then) motivated by the need to understand better the foundation on which the art rested...
>
> When the need and necessary foundation coincide, a science develops to explain, organize, and distill experience into a more compact and usable form.... Such a base of applied science would permit experience to be translated into a common frame of reference from which they could be transferred from the past to the present or from one location to another, (and) to be effectively applied in new situations.... [15]

That we lack a scientific base is demonstrated by examining one example "lesson" in the "art" of managing the human resource in software development, namely, Brooks' Law. Brooks' Law states that adding manpower to a late software project makes it later. [6] Since its publication, Brooks' Law has been widely endorsed in the literature. This, in spite of the fact that it has *not* been formally tested. Furthermore, it has often been endorsed indiscriminately, e.g., for systems programming-type projects as well as applications-type projects, both large and small, [22] even though Brooks [6] was quite explicit in specifying the domain of applicability of his insights, i.e., to what he called "jumbo systems programming projects."

Later in the paper we will investigate the applicability of Brooks' Law to a real software project, namely, NASA's DE-A software development project. The project's uncharacteristic workforce staffing pattern is portrayed in Fig. 1. (Further details on the NASA DE-A project are provided in the Appendix.) The behavior indicates that management is (implicitly if not explicitly) oblivious to the lesson of Brooks' Law. Because NASA's launch of the DE-A satellite was tied to the completion of the DE-A software, serious schedule slippages could not be tolerated. Specifically, all software was required to be accepted and frozen 90 days before launch. As the project slipped and this date approached, management reacted (or overreacted) by adding new people to the project to meet the strict launch deadline, as evidenced by the rising workforce curve in the final stages of the project.

The lesson of Brooks' Law would, of course, suggest that by adding new people to the late DE-A project, management actually delayed it further. This raises the set of intriguing questions: *What if* new people were in fact not added at the later stages of the DE-A project? Would the DE-A project have completed earlier? And, why (or why not)?

The research vehicle we utilize to study the dynamics of the human resource management activity is a comprehensive system dynamics model of the software de-velopment process. The model was developed as part of an ongoing research effort for the purpose of studying, gaining insight into, and making predictions about the dynamics of the software development process. We begin our presentation, in the next section, with a discussion of the model's structure.

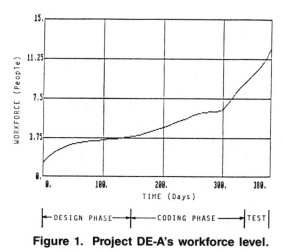

Figure 1. Project DE-A's workforce level.

An Integrative System Dynamics Model of Software Development

A major deficiency in much of the research to date on software project management has been its inability to integrate our knowledge of the microcomponents of the software development process such as scheduling, progress measurement, productivity, and staffing to derive implications about the behavior of the total sociotechnical system in which the micro components are embedded. [31] In the words of Jensen and Tonies [17]: "There is much attention on individual phases and functions of the software development sequence, but little on the whole lifecycle as an integral, continuous process—a process that can and should be optimized."

The model we are presenting in this paper provides such an integrative perspective. It integrates the multiple functions of the software development process, including both the management-type functions (e.g., planning, controlling, staffing) as well as the software production-type activities (e.g., designing, coding, reviewing, testing).

The model was developed on the basis of a battery of 27 field interviews of software project managers in five software producing organizations, supplemented by an extensive database of empirical findings from the literature. Figure 2 depicts the model's four subsystems, namely: 1) The Human Resource Management Subsystem; 2) The Software Production Subsystem; 3) The Control Subsystem; and 4) The Planning Subsystem. The figure also illustrates some of the interrelationships among the four subsystems.

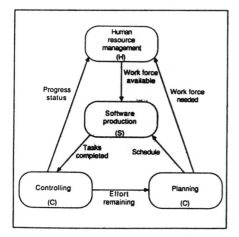

Figure 2. Overview of the model's four subsystems.

Because the model is quite comprehensive and highly detailed, it is infeasible to fully explain it in the limited space of this paper. We will, therefore, provide a detailed description for only the Human

Resource Management Subsystem (our focus in this discussion), while limiting our descriptions of the model's three remaining subsystems to high level overviews. The interested reader can refer to [1] or [2] for a full description of the model.

The Human Resource Management Subsystem

The Human Resource Management Subsystem, depicted in Fig. 3, captures the hiring, training, assimilation, and transfer of the project's human resource. (The schematic conventions used in Fig. 3 are the standard conventions used in System Dynamics models.) Such actions are not carried out in a vacuum, but, as Fig. 2 suggests, they are affected by the other subsystems. For example, the project's hiring rate is a function of the workforce level needed to complete the project on a certain *planned* completion data. Similarly, what workforce is available has direct bearing on the allocation of manpower among the different software *production* activities.

Returning back to Fig. 3, notice that the project's total workforce is comprised of two separate workforce levels, namely, "Newly Hired Workforce" and "Experienced Workforce." (In the model, workforce is actually more finely divided into four, not two, levels. However, for this presentation the simpler structure of Fig. 3 is quite sufficient to demonstrate the basic ideas.)

Segregating the workforce into these two categories of employees is needed for two reasons. First, newly hired project members pass through an "orientation phase" during which they are less than fully productive. The orientation process

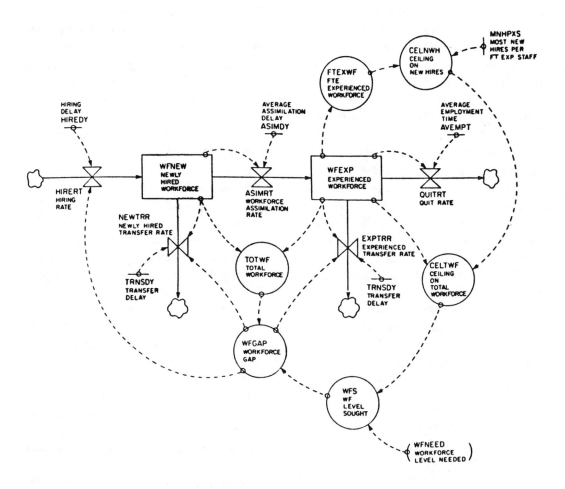

Figure 3. The human resource management subsystem.

has both technical as well as social dimensions. On the technical side,

> ...(newly hired) personnel often require considerable training to become familiar with an organization's unique mix of hardware, software packages, programming techniques, project methodologies and so on. [34]

As for "social orientation":

> ...(it) refers to the processes of teaching the new recruit how to get along in the or-

ganization, what the key norms and rules of conduct are, and how to behave with respect to others in the organization. The new recruit must learn where to be at specified times, what to wear, what to call the boss, whom to consult if he or she has a question, how carefully to do the job, and endless other things which insiders have learned over time. [25]

Of course, not all new project members are necessarily recruited from *outside* the organization; some might be recruited from within, e.g., transferred from other projects. For this type of employee, there will still be a project orientation period, e.g., to learn the project's ground rules, the goals of the effort, the plan of the work, and all the details of the system. [32] Although obviously less costly than the full orientation needed by an out-of-company recruit, such project orientation is still a significant drag on productivity.

Capturing the productivity differential that exists between the "Newly Hired Workforce" and the "Experienced Workforce" was, therefore, the first reason for disaggregating the workforce. The second reason arose from the need to capture the *training processes* involved in adding new members to the project. This training of newcomers, both technical and social, is usually carried out by the "oldtimers." [5, 10, 34] This is costly, because while the oldtimer is helping the new employee learn the job, his/her own productivity is reduced.

The determination of the amount of effort to commit to the training of new employees is typically based on organizational custom. There are no proposed formulas in the literature, nor did we find any in the organizations we studied. We did find, however, rules-of-thumb, and these ranged from committing 15 percent of an experienced employee's time (per new employee) to a 25 percent commitment.

The "Average Assimilation Delay" is the average time it takes a new recruit to be trained, i.e., to attain the "Experienced Employee" status. The assimilation delay is formulated in the model as a first-order exponential delay. Such delays are primary building-blocks of system dynamics models.

Besides the direct training overhead, adding people to a software project can di-lute overall project productivity in a perhaps less direct way, namely, by increasing the communication overhead. The nature of the relationship between communication overhead and team size has been investigated by several authors. It is widely held that communication overhead increases in proportion to n^2, where n is the size of the team. [6, 19, 26, 27, 35]

On deciding upon the "Total Workforce" level desired, project managers typically consider a number of factors. One important factor is the project's scheduled completion date. As part of the planning function (captured in the model's "Planning Subsystem"), management determines the workforce level that it believes is necessary to complete the project on schedule. This workforce level is referred to as the "Indicated Workforce Level" in the model. In addition to this factor, consideration is also given to the stability of the workforce. Thus, before adding new project members, management tries to contemplate the project employment time for the new members. Different organizations weigh this factor differently. In general, the relative weighing between the desire for workforce stability on the one hand and the desire to complete the project on time, on the other, is not static, but changes *dynamically* throughout the life of the project. For example, toward the end of the project there is typically considerable reluctance to bring in new people, even when the project is behind schedule. It would just take too much time and effort (relative to the time and effort that are remaining) to acquaint new people with the mechanics of the project, integrate them into the project team, and train them in the necessary technical areas.

These managerial considerations are operationalized in the model as follows:

Workforce Level Needed
    = (Indicated Workforce Level) * (WCWF)
    + (Current Workforce) * (1-WCWF).   (1)

The weight factor (WCWF) is termed "*Wi*llingness to *C*hange *W*ork*F*orce." It is a variable that assumes values between 0 and 1, inclusive. WCWF is itself comprised of two components, namely, WCWF-1 and WCWF-2. The first component, WCWF-1, captures the pressures for workforce stability (mentioned above) that develop as the project proceeds towards its final stages. Figure 4(a) depicts an example WCWF-1 policy curve.

To understand what Fig. 4(a) represents, assume for the moment that the "Willingness to Change Workforce" (WCWF) is only comprised of, and is therefore equal to, WCWF-1. In the early stages of the project when "Time Remaining" is generally much larger than the sum of the "Hiring Delay" and the "Average Assimilation Delay" (which for the DE-A project were 30 and 20 working days respectively), WCWF would be equal to 1. When WCWF = 1, the "Workforce Level Needed" in (1) would simply be equal to the "Indicated Workforce Level," i.e., management would be adjusting its workforce size to the level it feels is needed to finish on schedule. The "Indicated Workforce Level" can be determined by dividing the amount of effort that management perceives is still remaining (e.g., in man-days) by the time remaining to complete the project (e.g., in days).

When the "Time Remaining" drops below 0.3 * (Hiring Delay + Average Assimilation Delay), the particular policy curve of Fig. 4(a) suggests that no more

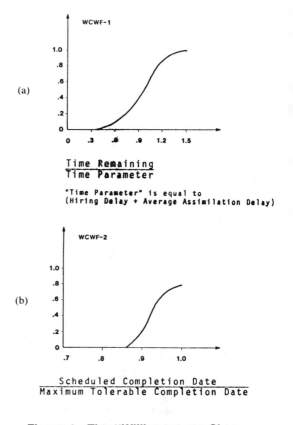

(a)

Time Remaining
―――――――――
Time Parameter

"Time Parameter" is equal to
(Hiring Delay + Average Assimilation Delay)

(b)

Scheduled Completion Date
―――――――――――――――――――
Maximum Tolerable Completion Date

Figure 4. The "Willingness to Change Workforce" policy curves.

additions would be made to the project's workforce. At that stage, WCWF equals exactly 0. The "Workforce Level Needed" in (1) would, thus, be equal to the "Current Workforce" i.e., management attempts to maintain the project's workforce at its current level. For example, for the case where the "Hiring Delay" is 30 working days and the "Average Assimilation Delay" is 20 working days, management refrains from adding new people as the "Time Remaining" drops below 15 working days (i.e., three calendar weeks). Schedule slippages at this late stage in the project would, thus, be handled through adjustments to the schedule completion date, and not through adjustments to the workforce level. (Other options might include trimming the project's deliverables, but this was infeasible in this particular case.)

When the "Time Remaining" on the project is between 0.3 and 1.5 times the sum (Hiring Delay + Average Assimilation Delay) the WCWF variable assumes values between 0 and 1. This represents a situation where management responds to schedule slippages by *partially* increasing the workforce level and partially extending the current schedule to a new date.

In our discussions at organizations such as NASA and MITRE, we learned that in projects involving embedded software (e.g., for weapon and space systems), serious schedule slippages could not be tolerated. In such projects software development is often on the critical path of a larger system development endeavor. Slippages in the software schedule can, thus, magnify into very costly overruns. Because of the software industry's less than impressive track record in delivering software projects on schedule, such imbedded software projects are often scheduled with some "safety factor" incorporated. For example, if some "Maximum Tolerable Completion Date" is say 100 months, and a 20 percent safety factor is used, then the project would be initially scheduled to complete in 0.80 * 100 = 80 months. If such a project, then, starts to fall behind schedule, management's reaction will depend on how close they are in violating the "Maximum Tolerable Completion Date." As long as the "Scheduled Completion Date" is comfortably below the "Maximum Tolerable Completion Date," decisions to adjust the schedule, add more people, or do a combination of both are

based on the balancing of scheduling and workforce stability considerations as captured by WCWF-1. *However,* if the "Scheduled Completion Date" starts approaching the "Maximum Tolerable Completion Date," pressures develop that override the workforce stability considerations. That is, management becomes increasingly willing to "pay any price" necessary to avoid overshooting the "Maximum Tolerable Completion Date." And this often translates into a management that is increasingly willing to keep on adding new people to the project.

The development of such overriding pressures is captured through the following formulation of the "Willingness to Change Workforce" (WCWF),

WCWF = MAXIMUM (WCWF-1, WCWF-2).

A WCWF-2 policy curve, the second component of WCWF, is depicted in Fig. 4(b). As long as "Scheduled Completion Date" is comfortably below the "Maximum Tolerable Completion Date," the value of WCWF-2 would be zero, i.e., it would have no bearing on the determination of WCWF, and consequently on the hiring decisions. When "Scheduled Completion Date" starts approaching the "Maximum Tolerable Completion Date," though, the value of WCWF-2 starts to gradually rise. Because such a situation typically develops towards the end of the project, it would be at a point where the value of WCWF-1 is close to zero and decreasing. If the value of WCWF-2 does surpass that of WCWF-1, the "Willingness to Change Workforce" (WCWF) will be dominated by WCWF-2 and, thus, the pressures not to overshoot the "Maximum Tolerable Completion Date."

Note that the above formulation of

WCWF allows us to easily simulate those environments in which there are no tight time commitments. In such cases we need only to set the value of the "Maximum Tolerable Completion Date" to some high value. This would keep WCWF-2 always at the zero level.

It is important to realize that the variable "Willingness to Change Workforce" (WCWF) is an expression of a *policy* for managing projects. For example, the curves of Fig. 4 characterize the particular staffing policy for the DE-A project. For any specific project environment, the shapes of the WCWF policy curves can be derived on the basis of interviews with project managers as well as reviews of historical project records.

Based on the above considerations, then, management can determine the value of the "Workforce Level Needed" to complete the project. This *needed* level does not necessarily translate into an *actual* hiring goal (which is referred to in the model as the "Workforce Level Sought"). A further consideration is given to the experienced staff's ability to absorb new employees. That is, the rate of adding new project members is often restricted to that level which management feels can be adequately handled (e.g., in terms of hand-holding, orienting, training, etc.) by its pool of experienced project members.

Such a restriction is formulated in the model through the variable we call "Ceiling on New Hires." It simply equals the full-time equivalent experienced workforce level multiplied by the limit on the number of new hires that a single full-time experienced staff member can be expected to effectively handle.

To recapitulate, the three factors: 1) schedule completion time; 2) workforce stability; and 3) training requirements, all affect management's determination of the "Workforce Level Sought." Once the determination is made, management could face one of three possible situations. First, the "Workforce Gap" between the "Workforce Level Sought" and the "Total Workforce Level" actually on hand could be zero. In this case no further staffing actions would be necessary.

A second, more common, situation is where the "Workforce Level Sought" is found to be larger than the current "Total Workforce Level." In this case, new staff will be added to the project. This, of course, takes time. While some recruits will generally be available within a short period of time from within the organization, others (especially when management is seeking special skills) will not be available for a much longer time. The delay in enlisting new software professionals is, on the average, several months long. [18]

The third possibility is where the "Workforce Level Sought" is less than the project's current "Total Workforce Level," e.g., if the project is perceived to be ahead of schedule. In this case, project members will be transferred out of the project. Again, this is not an instantaneous process. It takes time to transfer people, e.g., for paper work, making transfer arrangements, etc. Such delays are captured by the model's "Average Transfer Delay" variable.

Finally, there is the effect of turnover on the project's workforce. Turnover continues, of course, to be a chronic problem for software project managers. Studies of turnover place the annual turnover rate at 25.1 percent [29], 30 percent [23], and even as high as 34 percent. [5] In the DE-A project, for example, the turnover rate was 20 percent.

The Model's Other Subsystems

The four primary software production activities are: development, quality assurance, rework, and testing. The development activity comprises both the designing and coding of the software. As the software is developed, it is also reviewed (e.g., using structured walkthroughs) to detect any errors. Errors detected through such quality assurance activities are then reworked. Not all errors get detected and reworked, however. Some "escape" detection until the end of development, e.g., until the testing phase. A highly aggregated depiction of the Production Subsystem is provided in Fig. 5.

How is progress measured in a software project? Our own field study findings corroborate those reported in the literature, namely, that in the *earlier phases* of software development, progress is measured in most organizations by the rate of expenditure of resources rather than by some count of accomplishments. [13] For example, a project for which a total of 100 man-months is budgeted would be *perceived* as being 10 percent complete when 10 man-months are expended; and when 50 man-months are expended it would be perceived as 50 percent complete, etc.

This surrogate for measuring project progress has some interesting implications on how management assesses the project team's productivity. When progress in the earlier phases of software development (call it time period $t1$), is measured by the rate of expenditure of resources, status reporting ends up being nothing more than an echo of the original plan. That is, "Man-Days Perceived Still *Needed* for New Tasks (MDP/VNT) becomes, under such conditions, simply equal to the

"Man-Days Perceived *Remaining* for New Tasks" (MDPRNT):

$$MDPRNT_{t1} = MDPNNT_{t1}$$

But "Man-Days Perceived Still Needed for New Tasks" (MDPNNT) is (implicitly if not explicitly) equal to the value of "Tasks Perceived Remaining" (TSKPRM) divided by management's notion of the project team's productivity, i.e., by the value of "*Perceived* Development Productivity" (PRDPRD). That is,

$$MDPNNT_{t1} = TSKPRM_{t1}/PRDPRD_{t1}.$$

Substituting MDPRNT for MDPNNT, we get

$$MDPRNT_{t1} = TSKPRM_{t1}/PRDPRD_{t1}$$

which leads to,

$$PRDPRD_{t1} = TSKPRM_{t1}/MDPRNT_{t1}.$$

This is an interesting result. It suggests that as project members measure progress by the rate of expenditure of resources, they, by so doing, would be *implicitly* assuming that their productivity equals "Tasks Perceived Remaining" (TSKPRM) divided by the "Man-Days Perceived Remaining for New Tasks" (MDPRNT). Notice that such an assumed value of productivity is solely a function of *future* projections (i.e., remaining tasks and remaining man-days) as opposed to being a reflection of accomplishments (i.e., completed tasks and expended resources).

This implicit notion of productivity is captured in the model by the variable "*Projected* Development Productivity" (PJDPRD), defined as,

$$PJDPRD = TSKPRM/DMPRNT.$$

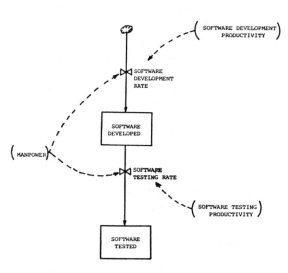

Figure 5. Overview of the software production subsystem.

As the project advances towards its final stages, however, and accomplishments become relatively more visible, project members become increasingly more able to perceive how productive the workforce has actually been. As a result, perceived productivity ceases to be a function of projected productivity and is determined instead on the basis of actual accomplishments. That is, "Perceived Development Productivity" approaches the value of the project team's "Actual Development Productivity" (ACTPRD), i.e., the value of "Cumulative Tasks Developed" (CUMTKD) divided by the value of "Cumulative Man-Days Expended" (CUMDMD).

In the model's Planning Subsystem, initial project estimates (e.g., for completion time, staffing load, man-days, etc.) are made at the initiation of the project. These estimates are then revised, as necessary, throughout the project's life. For example, to handle a project that is perceived to be behind schedule, plans can be re-

vised to (among other things) add more people, extend the schedule, or do a little of both. The Planning Subsystem is depicted in Fig. 6.

By dividing the value of "Man-Days Remaining" at any point in the project, by the "Time Remaining" a manager can determine the "Indicated Workforce Level." This represents the workforce size believed to be necessary and sufficient to complete the project on the currently scheduled completion date. However, as has been explained in the Human Resource Management Subsystem, hiring decisions are not determined solely on the basis of scheduling considerations. In addition, consideration is given to the training requirements and to the stability of the workforce.

By dividing the value of the "Workforce Level Sought" (that emerges after the above set of factors is contemplated) into the value of the "Man-Days Remaining," management can determine the time still required to complete the project. Once this, in turn, is known, it can be used to adjust the project's "Scheduled Completion Date," if necessary.

With this discussion of the model's Planning Subsystem we conclude our overview presentation of the model's structure. For the interested reader, a more detailed description of the model's structure and its mathematical formulation is provided in [1] and [2].

Model Experimentation

"In software engineering it is remarkably easy to propose hypotheses and remarkably difficult to test them." [33] Many authors have, thus, argued for the desirability of having a laboratory tool for test-

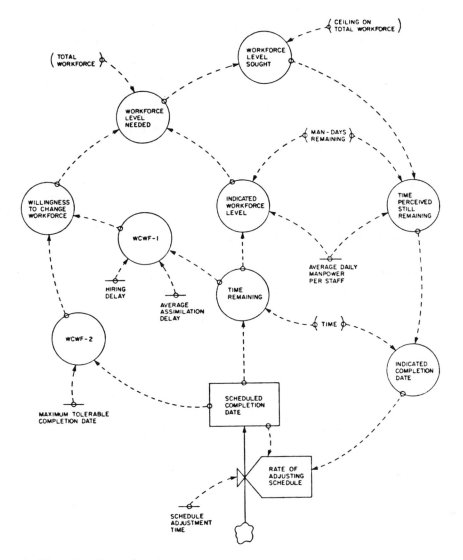

Figure 6. The planning subsystem.

ing ideas and hypotheses in software engineering. [31]

The computer simulation tools of system dynamics provide us with such an experimentation vehicle. Simulation's particular advantage is its greater fidelity in modeling processes, making possible both more complex models and models of more complex systems. It also allows for less time-consuming experimentation. According to Forrester: [15]

The effects of different assumptions and environmental factors can be tested. In the model system, unlike the real systems, the effect of changing one factor can be observed while all other factors are held unchanged. Such experimentation will yield new insights into the characteristics of the system that the model represents. By using a model of a complex system, more can be learned about internal interactions than would ever be possible through manipulation of the real system. Internally, the model provides complete control of the system's organizational structure, its policies, and its sensitivities to various events.

Fig. 7 demonstrates the kinds of dynamic behaviors reproduced by the model. It depicts the model's output that resulted from simulating the behavior of the DE-A software project. The model's results conformed quite accurately to the project's actual behavior (represented by the 0

points in the figure), as is documented in detail in [1].

One interesting dynamic captured in Fig. 7 concerns the inclination *not* to adjust the project's scheduled completion date during most of the development phase. This behavior is not atypical. It arises, according to DeMarco [13] because of political reasons:

Once an original estimate is made, it's all too tempting to pass up subsequent opportunities to estimate by simply sticking with your previous numbers. This often happens even when you know your old estimates are substantially off. There are a few different possible explanations for this effect: "It's too early to show slip" . . . "If I re-estimate now, I risk having to do it

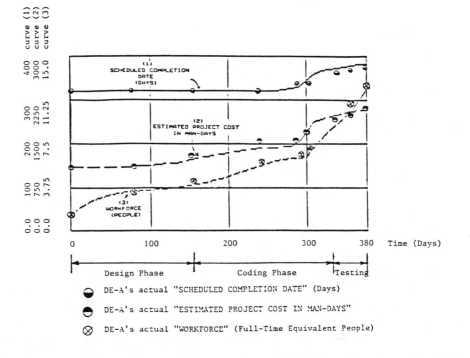

Figure 7. Model's simulation run of the NASA DE-A software project.

again later (and looking bad twice)" . . . As you can see, all such reasons are political in nature.

In the next section we will utilize the model to conduct a simulation experiment to investigate the interchangeability of people and months in the NASA DE-A software project.

Applicability of Brooks' Law to the DE-A Project

As noted in the presentation of the Human Resource Management Subsystem, several studies have demonstrated the negative impacts of communication and training overheads on software development productivity, the two insights upon which Brooks' Law is based. What has *not* yet been formally investigated though is what the *net* impact of adding new manpower to a late project is on productivity. That is, whether the productivity gained from adding new manpower is greater or smaller than the losses in productivity incurred as a result of increases in training and communication overheads. Brooks' Law, of course, implies that the *net* impact of adding more people to a late project is negative, and that as a result the already late project falls even more behind schedule. Our intent here is to test the validity of such an assumption.

As was explained in the previous section, management's policy on how to balance workforce and schedule adjustments is captured in the model through the formulation of the variable "Willingness to Change Workforce" (WCWF). By varying this variable we can, therefore, examine the impact of different manpower acquisition policies on the project's cost and duration.

Recall, WCWF-2 captures the impact of pressures to add new people towards the end of the project as a result of working under a "Maximum Tolerable Completion Date." Since we are attempting to test the applicability of Brooks' Law, we need to compare such a staffing practice to ones where management (in subscribing to the lessons of Brooks' Law) stubbornly refuses to add new people in the final stages of a late project, i.e., as is embodied by the WCWF-1 policy curve. By reformulating the "Willingness to Change Workforce" (WCWF) to be *solely* a function of WCWF-1, we can, therefore, simulate and test such policies.

Altering the value of the "Time Parameter" variable of Fig. 4(a) allows us to test a range of such policies. (Changing the "Time Parameter" is equivalent to shifting the WCWF-1 curve to the right or left along the X-axis.) For example, setting this time parameter to 100 working days instead of its base-case value of 50 represents a situation where management's reluctance to add to the workforce starts much earlier in the project. In Fig. 4(a), management starts becoming reluctant to increase the workforce level when the perceived number of days remaining to complete the project drops below $1.5 * (20 + 30) = 75$ days, and stops hiring completely when it drops below 15 working days. Under the above less aggressive policy, management starts becoming reluctant at 150 days and stops manpower additions completely at 30 working days. Simulating the DE-A project with this example staffing policy produces the workforce pattern depicted in Fig. 8.

The simulation result of Fig. 8 provides the first indication that perhaps Brooks'

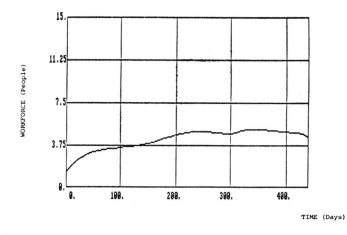

Figure 8. Simulating DE-A with the time parameter set to 100.

Law does not apply to the DE-A project environment. Notice that by refraining from adding people in the later stages of the lifecycle, the project required 440 days to complete. This is approximately three calendar months more than what was required in the base case of Fig. 1 (where more people were indeed added to the late project). By conducting further experimentation with different values of the "Time Parameter" variable we further examined the schedule consequences of a wide range of manpower acquisition policies. The results are depicted in Fig. 9.

As can be seen from the figure, the results for the DE-A project environment do not totally support Brooks' Law. What our results show is that adding more people to a late project always causes it to become more costly, but does not always cause it to complete later. The increase in the cost of the project is caused by the increased training and communication overheads, which in effect decrease the average productivity of the project team, and thus increase the project's man-day expenditures. For the project's schedule to

also suffer, the drop in productivity must be large enough to render an additional person's *net cumulative* contribution to the project to, in effect, be a *negative* contribution. We need to calculate the *net* contribution because an additional person's contribution to useful project work must be balanced against the losses incurred as a result of diverting available experienced man-days from direct project work to the training of and communicating with the new staff member. And we need to calculate the *cumulative* contribution because while a new hiree's net contribution might be negative initially, as training takes place and the new hiree's productivity increases, the net contribution becomes less and less negative, and eventually (given enough training on the project) the new person starts contributing positively to the project. Only when the cumulative impact is a negative one will the addition of the new staff member translate into a longer project completion time.

The results of Fig. 9 indicate that adding manpower to a late software project does not always cause a negative net cu-

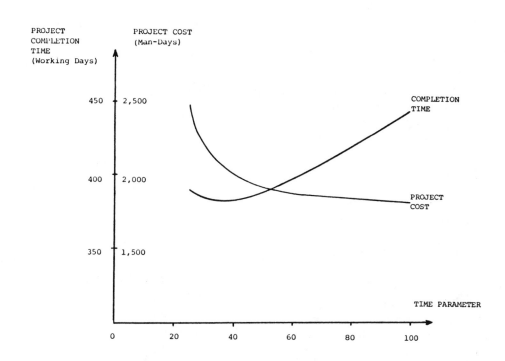

Figure 9. Impact of different staffing policies on cost and schedule.

mulative contribution to the project, and thus, does not always make the project later. The results indicate that Brooks' Law only holds when the time parameter is less than or equal to 30 working days. At that level, management would be willing to add more people up until the point where the time remaining to complete the project is less than 0.3 * 30 = 9 working days, i.e., approximately 2 weeks. That is, until the final stages of the testing phase of the project. It is at such extremely aggressive manpower acquisition policies that Brooks' Law holds in the DE-A project environment.

Summary

In this paper we reported on an ongoing research effort to study the dynamics of software project staffing. Our research vehicle is a comprehensive System Dynamics model of software project management. The model has two distinctive features. First, it is an integrative model that captures the multiple functions of software development, including both the management-type functions (e.g., planning, controlling, staffing) as well as the software projection-type functions (e.g., designing, coding, reviewing, testing). Second, we utilized the computer simulation tools of system dynamics to handle the high complexity of the resulting integrative feedback model.

Such a formal model of the software development process aids in the understanding of the process through both its formulation as well as the analysis of its behavior. The process of formulation forces explication, i.e., structural relations between variables must be explicitly and precisely defined. This, in Dubin's [14] view, is the "locus of understanding" of a theoretical model:

> A (theoretical model) tries to make sense out of the observable world by ordering the relationships among "things" that constitute the (modeler's) focus of attention in the world "out there" . . .What is gained in understanding. . . is achieved by comprehending the law or laws built into the model. The locus of understanding in a scientific model is to be found in its laws of interaction. (That is, the modes of interaction among the variables of the model.)

If understanding is the intellectual outcome of a theoretical model, then prediction is its practical outcome. The model was utilized as an experimentation vehicle to study/predict the dynamic implications of staffing policies and practices on project behavior. One example was provided in the paper in which the model was used to test for the degree of interchangeability of men and months in one particular software development environment.

APPENDIX

The DE-A Software Project

The DE-A software project was conducted at the Systems Development Section of NASA's Goddard Space Flight Center (GSFC) at Greenbelt, MD. The basic requirements for the project were to design, implement, and test a software system that would process telemetry data and would provide attitude determination and control for NASA's DE-A satellite.

The development and target operations machines were the IBM S/360-95 and -75.

The programming language was mostly Fortran. Other project statistics include:

- Project Size (in delivered source instructions): 24,000 DSI

- Cost (for design through system testing)
  Initial estimate: 1,100 man-days
  Actual: 2,220 man-days

- Completion Time (in working days)
  Initial estimate: 320 days
  Actual: 380 days

- Staffing-Type Parameters:
  Average productivity of experienced staff versus that for new hires: 2:1
  Hiring delay: 1.5 months
  Average assimilation delay: 1 month
  Average transfer delay: 2 weeks
  Turnover rate: 20 percent
  Average effort committed to train new hires: 25 percent

REFERENCES

[1] T.K. Abdel-Hamid, "The Dynamics of Software Development Project Management: An Integrative System Dynamics Perspective," Ph.D. dissertation, Sloan School of Management, MIT, January 1984.

[2] T.K. Abdel-Hamid and S.E. Madnick, *Software Project Management*. Englewood Cliffs, N.J.: Prentice-Hall, 1988.

[3] ———, "Software Productivity: Potential, Actual, and Perceived," *System Dynamics Review*, 1988, submitted for publication.

[4] B.W. Boehm, *Software Engineering Economics*. Englewood Cliffs, N.J.: Prentice-Hall, 1981.

[5]   H.S. Bott, "The Personnel Crunch," in *Perspectives on Information Management,* J.B. Rochester, ed. New York: Wiley, 1982.

[6]   F.P. Brooks, Jr., *The Mythical Man-Month.* Reading, Mass.: Addison-Wesley, 1975.

[7]   R. Burchett, "Avoiding Disaster in Project Control," *Data Processing Digest,* Vol. 28, No. 6, pp. 1-3, June 1982.

[8]   R.G. Canning, "Managing Staff Retention and Turnover," *EDP Analyzer,* pp. 1-13, August 1977.

[9]   E. Chrysler, "Some Basic Determinants of Computer Programming Productivity," *Communications of the ACM,* Vol. 21, No. 6, pp. 472-83, June 1978.

[10] F.J. Corbato and C.T. Clingen, "A Managerial View of the Multics Systems Development," in *Research Directions in Software Technology,* P. Wegner, ed. Cambridge, Mass.: MIT Press, 1979.

[11] J.D. Couger and R.A. Zawacki, *Motivating and Managing Computer Personnel.* New York: Wiley, 1980.

[12] E.B. Daly, "Management of Software Development," *IEEE Transactions on Software Engineering,* May 1977.

[13] T. DeMarco, *Controlling Software Projects.* New York: Yourdon Press, 1982.

[14] R. Dubin, *The Organization, Management, and Tactics of Social Research,* R. O'Toole, ed. Cambridge, Mass.: Schenkman, 1971.

[15] J.W. Forrester, *Industrial Dynamics.* Cambridge, Mass.: MIT Press, 1961.

[16] General Research Corp. (GRC), "Cost Reporting Elements and Activity Cost Tradeoffs for Defense System Software," Santa Clara, Calif., May 1977.

[17] R.W. Jensen and C.C. Tonies, *Software Engineering.* Englewood Cliffs, N.J.: Prentice-Hall, 1979.

[18] R.A. McLaughlin, "That Old Bugaboo, Turnover," *Datamation,* pp. 97-101, October 1979.

[19] H.D. Mills, "Software Development," *IEEE Transactions on Software Engineering,* Vol. SE-2, No. 4, December 1976.

[20] C.E. Oglesby and J.E. Urban, "The Human Resources Task Area," *Computer,* Vol. 16, pp. 65-70, November 1983.

[21] R.L. Paretta and S.A. Clark, "Management of Software Development," *Journal of Systems Management,* April 1976.

[22] R.S. Pressman, *Software Engineering: A Practitioner's Approach.* New York: McGraw-Hill, 1982.

[23] D. Richmond, "No Nonsense Recruitment," in *Perspectives on Information Management,* J.B. Rochester, ed. New York: Wiley, 1982.

[24] E.B. Roberts, ed., *Managerial Applications of System Dynamics.* Cambridge, Mass.: MIT Press, 1981.

[25] E.H. Schein, *Organizational Psychology,* 3rd ed. Englewood Cliffs, N.J.: Prentice-Hall, 1980.

[26] R.F. Scott and D.B. Simmons, "Predicting Programming Group Productivity—A Communications Model," *IEEE Transactions on Soft-*

ware Engineering, Vol. SE-1, No. 4, December 1975.

[27] M.L. Shooman, *Software Engineering—Design, Reliability, and Management.* New York: McGraw-Hill, 1983.

[28] W.R. Synnott and W.H. Gruber, *Information Resource Management.* New York: Wiley, 1981.

[29] M.R. Tanniru et al., "Causes of Turnover Among DP Professionals," in *Proceedings of the Eighth Annual Computer Personnel Research Conference,* Miami, June 1981.

[30] R.C. Tausworthe, *Standardized Development of Computer Science.* Englewood Cliffs, N.J.: Prentice-Hall, 1977.

[31] R.H. Thayer, "Modeling a Software Engineering Project Management System," Ph.D. dissertation, University of California, Santa Barbara, 1979.

[32] _____ and J.H. Lehman, *Software Engineering Project Management: A Survey Concerning U.S. Aerospace Industry Management of Software Development Projects,* Sacramento Air Logistics Center,

McClellan Air Force Base, Calif., November 1977.

[33] D.M. Weiss, "Evaluating Software Development by Error Analysis," *Journal of System Software,* Vol. 1, pp. 57-70, 1979.

[34] Winrow, "Acquiring Entry-Level Programmers," in *Computer Programming Management,* J. Hannan, ed. Pennsauken, N.J.: Auerbach, 1982.

[35] M.V. Zelkowitz, "Perspectives on Software Engineering," *Computing Surveys,* Vol. 10, No. 2, June 1978.

[36] K.M. Bartol and D.C. Martin, "Managing Information Systems Personnel: A Review of the Literature and Managerial Implications," *MIS Quarterly,* pp. 49-70, December 1982.

[37] V.R. Basili, "Improving Methodology and Productivity Through Practical Measurement," Lecture at Wang Institute of Graduate Studies, Lowell, Mass., November 1982.

[38] J.D. McKeen, "Successful Development Strategies for Business Application Systems," *MIS Quarterly,* September 1983.

9

Editors' Note
Ritchie: "Reflections on Software Research"

Insight: Innovative software takes time to work out, and an innovative software product takes time to find its market. (So much for the software revolution.)

This article is actually a transcript of Ritchie's Turing Award Lecture, given in October 1983. Dennis Ritchie and Ken Thompson won the 1983 Turing Award for the development and implementation of the UNIX* operating system. Here we learn part of the story of that project.

---

*UNIX is a trademark of AT&T Bell Laboratories.

9

Reflections on Software Research
by Dennis M. Ritchie

The UNIX* operating system has suddenly become news, but it is not new. It began in 1969 when Ken Thompson discovered a little-used PDP-7 computer and set out to fashion a computing environment that he liked. His work soon attracted me; I joined in the enterprise, though most of the ideas, and most of the work for that matter, were his. Before long, others from our group in the research area of AT&T Bell Laboratories were using the system; Joe Ossanna, Doug McIlroy, and Bob Morris were especially enthusiastic critics and contributors. In 1971, we acquired a PDP-11, and by the end of that year we were supporting our first real users: three typists entering patent applications. In 1973, the system was rewritten in the C language, and in that year, too, it was first described publicly at the Operating Systems Principles conference; the resulting paper [8] appeared in *Communications of the ACM* the next year.

Thereafter, its use grew steadily, both inside and outside of Bell Laboratories. A development group was established to support projects inside the company, and several research versions were licensed for outside use.

The last research distribution was the seventh edition system, which appeared in 1979; more recently, AT&T began to market System III, and now offers System V, both products of the development group. All research versions were "as is," unsupported software; System V is a supported product on several different hardware lines, most recently including the 3B systems designed and built by AT&T.

UNIX is in wide use, and is now even spoken of as a possible industry standard. How did it come to succeed?

There are, of course, its technical merits. Because the system and its history have been discussed at some length in the literature [6, 7, 11], I will not talk about these qualities except for one; despite its frequent surface inconsistency, so colorfully annotated by Don Norman in his *Datamation* article [4] and despite its richness, UNIX is a simple, coherent system that pushes a few good ideas and models to the limit. It is this aspect of the system, above all, that endears it to its adherents.

Beyond technical considerations, there were sociological forces that contributed to its success. First, it appeared at a time when alternatives to large, centrally administered computation centers were becoming possible; the 1970s were the decade of the minicomputer. Small groups could set up their own computation facilities. Because they were starting afresh, and because manufacturers' software was, at best, unimaginative and often horrible, some ad-

---

*UNIX is a trademark of AT&T Bell Laboratories.

venturesome people were willing to take a chance on a new and intriguing, even though unsupported, operating system.

Second, UNIX was first available on the PDP-11, one of the most successful of the new minicomputers that appeared in the 1970s, and soon its portability brought it to many new machines as they appeared. At the time that UNIX was created, we were pushing hard for a machine, either a DEC PDP-10 or SDS (later Xerox) Sigma 7. It is certain, in retrospect, that if we had succeeded in acquiring such a machine, UNIX might have been written but would have withered away. Similarly, UNIX owes much to Multics [5], as I have described [6, 7] it eclipsed its parent as much because it does not demand unusual hardware support as because of any other qualities.

Finally, UNIX enjoyed an unusually long gestation period. During much of this time (say 1969-1979), the system was effectively under the control of its designers and being used by them. It took time to develop all of the ideas and software, but even though the system was still being developed people were using it, both inside Bell Labs, and outside under license. Thus, we managed to keep the central ideas in hand, while accumulating a base of enthusiastic, technically competent users who contributed ideas and programs in a calm, communicative, and noncompetitive environment. Some outside contributions were substantial, for example those from the University of California at Berkeley. Our users were widely, though thinly, distributed within the company, at universities, and at some commercial and government organizations. The system became important in the intellectual, if not yet commercial, marketplace because of this network of early users.

What does industrial computer science research consist of? Some people have the impression that the original UNIX work was a bootleg project, a "skunk works." This is not so. Research workers are supposed to discover or invent new things, and although in the early days we subsisted on meager hardware, we always had management encouragement. At the same time, it was certainly nothing like a development project. Our intent was to create a pleasant computing environment for ourselves, and our hope was that others liked it. The Computing Science Research Center at Bell Laboratories to which Thompson and I belong studies three broad areas: theory; numerical analysis; and systems, languages, and software. Although work for its own sake resulting, for example, in a paper in a learned journal, is not only tolerated but welcomed, there is strong though wonderfully subtle pressure to think about problems somehow relevant to our corporation. This has been so since I joined Bell Labs around 15 years ago, and it should not be surprising; the old Bell System may have seemed a sheltered monopoly, but research has always had to pay its way. Indeed, researchers love to find problems to work on; one of the advantages of doing research in a large company is the enormous range of the puzzles that turn up. For example, theorists may contribute to compiler design, or to LSI algorithms; numerical analysts study charge and current distribution in semiconductors; and, of course, software types like to design systems and write programs that people use. Thus, computer research at Bell Labs has always had a considerable commitment to the world, and does not fear edicts commanding us to be practical.

For some of us, in fact, a principal frustration has been the inability to convince others that our research products can indeed be useful. Someone may invent a new application, write an illustrative program, and put it to use in our own lab. Many such demonstrations require further development and continuing support in order for the company to make best use of them. In the past, this use would have been exclusively inside the Bell System; more recently, there is the possibility of developing a product for direct sale.

For example, some years ago Mike Lesk developed an automated directory-assistance system. [3] The program had an online Bell Labs phone book, and was connected to a voice synthesizer on a telephone line with a tone decoder. One dialed the system, and keyed in a name and location code on the telephone's key pad; it spoke back the person's telephone number and office address (It didn't attempt to pronounce the name.). In spite of the hashing through twelve buttons (which, for example, squashed "A," "B," and "C" together), it was acceptably accurate: It had to give up on around 5 percent of the tries. The program was a local hit and well-used. Unfortunately, we couldn't find anyone to take it over, even as a supported service within the company, let alone a public offering, and it was an excessive drain on our resources, so it was finally scrapped. (I chose this example not only because it is old enough not to exacerbate any current squabbles, but also because it is timely: The organization that publishes the company telephone directory recently asked us whether the system could be revived.)

Of course not every idea is worth developing or supporting. In any event, the world is changing: Our ideas and advice are being sought much more avidly than before. This increase in influence has been going on for several years, partly because of the success of UNIX, but, more recently, because of the dramatic alteration of the structure of our company.

AT&T divested its telephone operating companies at the beginning of 1984. There has been considerable public speculation about what this will mean for fundamental research at Bell Laboratories; one report in *Science* [2] is typical. One fear sometimes expressed is that basic research, in general, may languish because it yields insufficient short-term gains to the new, smaller AT&T. The public position of the company is reassuring; moreover, research management at Bell Labs seems to believe deeply, and argues persuasively, that the commitment to support of basic research is deep and will continue. [1]

Fundamental research at Bell Labs in physics and chemistry and mathematics may, indeed, not be threatened; nevertheless, the danger it might face, and the case against which it must be prepared to argue, is that of irrelevance to the goals of the company. Computer science research is different from these more traditional disciplines. Philosophically it differs from the physical sciences because it seeks not to discover, explain, or exploit the natural world, but instead to study the properties of machines of human creation. In this it is analogous to mathematics, and indeed the "science" part of computer science is, for the most part, mathematical in spirit. But an inevitable aspect of computer science is the creation of computer programs: objects that, though intangible, are subject to commercial exchange.

More than anything else, the greatest danger to good computer science research today may be *excessive* relevance. Evidence for the worldwide fascination with computers is everywhere, from the articles on the financial, and even the front pages of the newspapers, to the difficulties that even the most prestigious universities experience in finding and keeping faculty in computer science. The best professors, instead of teaching bright students, join start-up companies, and often discover that their brightest students have preceded them. Computer science is in the limelight, especially those aspects, such as systems, languages, and machine architecture, that may have immediate commercial applications. The attention is flattering, but it can work to the detriment of good research.

As the intensity of research in a particular area increases, so does the impulse to keep its results secret. This is true even in the university (Watson's account [12] of the discovery of the structure of DNA provides a well-known example), although in academia there is a strong counterpressure: Unless one publishes, one never becomes known at all. In industry, a natural impulse of the establishment is to guard proprietary information. Researchers understand reasonable restrictions on what and when they publish, but many will become irritated and flee elsewhere, or start working in less delicate areas, if prevented from communicating their discoveries and inventions in suitable fashion. Research management at Bell Labs has traditionally been sensitive to maintaining a careful balance between company interests and the industrial equivalent of academic freedom. The entrance of AT&T into the computer industry will test, and perhaps strain, this balance.

Another danger is that commercial pressures of one sort or another will divert the attention of the best thinkers from real innovation to exploitation of the current fad, from prospecting to mining a known lode. These pressures manifest themselves not only in the disappearance of faculty into industry, but also in the conservatism that overtakes those with well-paying investments—intellectual or financial—in a given idea. Perhaps this effect explains why so few interesting software systems have come from the large computer companies; they are locked into the existing world. Even IBM, which supports a well-regarded and productive research establishment, has in recent years produced little to cause even a minor revolution in the way people think about computers. The working examples of important new systems seem to have come either from entrepreneurial efforts (Visicalc is a good example) or from large companies, like Bell Labs and most especially Xerox, that were much involved with computers and could afford research into them, but did not regard them as their primary business.

On the other hand, in smaller companies, even the most vigorous research support is highly dependent on market conditions. *The New York Times,* in an article describing Alan Kay's passage from Atari to Apple, notes the problem: "Mr. Kay . . . said that Atari's laboratories had lost some of the atmosphere of innovation that once attracted some of the finest talent in the industry. 'When I left last month it was clear that they would be putting their efforts in the short term,' he said. . . 'I guess the tree of research must from time to time be refreshed with the blood of bean counters.' " [9]

Partly because they are new and still immature, and partly because they are a creation of the intellect, the arts and sciences of software abridge the chain, usual in physics and engineering, between fundamental discoveries, advanced development, and application. The inventors of ideas about how software should work usually find it necessary to build demonstration systems. For large systems, and for revolutionary ideas, much time is required: It can be said that UNIX was written in the 70s to distill the best systems ideas of the 60s, and became the commonplace of the 80s. The work at Xerox PARC on personal computers, bit-map graphics, and programming environments [10] shows a similar progression, starting, and coming to fruition a few years later. Time, and a commitment to the long-term value of the research, are needed on the part of both the researchers and their management.

Bell Labs has provided this commitment and more: a rare and uniquely stimulating research environment for my colleagues and me. As it enters what company publications call "the new competitive era," its managers and workers will do well to keep in mind how, and under what conditions, the UNIX system succeeded. If we can keep alive enough openness to new ideas, enough freedom of communication, enough patience to allow the novel to prosper, it will remain possible for a future Ken Thompson to find a little-used CRAY/I computer and fashion a system as creative, and as influential, as UNIX.

REFERENCES

[1]   "Bell Labs: New Order Augurs Well," *Nature*, Vol. 305 (September 29, 1983), p. 5933.

[2]   "Bell Labs on the Brink," *Science,* Vol. 221 (September 23, 1983).

[3]   Lesk, M.E. "User-Activated BTL Directory Assistance," Bell Laboratories internal memorandum (1972).

[4]   Norman, D.A. "The Truth About UNIX," *Datamation,* Vol. 27, No. 12 (1981).

[5]   Organick, E.I. *The Multics System.* Cambridge, Mass.: MIT Press, 1972.

[6]   Ritchie, D.M. "UNIX Time-Sharing System: A Retrospective," *Bell Systems Technical Journal,* Vol. 57, No. 6 (1978), pp. 1947-69.

[7]   _____ . "The Evolution of the UNIX Time-Sharing System," in *Language Design and Programming Methodology,* Jeffrey M. Tobias, ed. New York: Springer-Verlag, 1980.

[8]   _____ , and K. Thompson. "The UNIX Time-Sharing System," *Communications of the ACM,* Vol. 17, No. 7 (July 1974), pp. 365-75.

[9]   Sanger, D.E. "Key Atari Scientist Switches to Apple," *The New York Times,* Vol. 133, No. 46, 033 (May 3, 1984).

[10] Thacker, C.P., et al. *Alto, a Personal Computer.* Xerox PARC Technical Report CSL-79-11.

[11] Thompson, K. "UNIX Time-Sharing System: UNIX Implementation," *Bell Systems Technical Journal,* Vol. 57, No. 6 (1978), pp. 1931-46.

[12] Watson, J.D. *The Double Helix: A Personal Account of the Discovery of the Structure of DNA.* New York: Atheneum Publishers, 1968.

Part II
Measurement

10

Editors' Note
Bailey and Basili: "A Meta-Model for Software Development Resource Expenditures"

Insight: Cost models do work, but they have to be made local to the environment in order to provide useful forecasts of development time and effort.

A *cost model* is a simple relationship between development effort and some early metric of software size. It can be used to forecast project costs with greater accuracy and precision than traditional seat-of-the-pants guestimates. At least, that's the theory. The problem is that there have been so many such models proposed in the past, and there is little or no similarity among them. Each one appears to have worked well for some organization, but don't get your hopes up much that it will work for you.

Bailey and Basili provide an obvious explanation for this phenomenon: The differences from one environment to another are much too significant to ignore—there will never be a global cost model, one that works well outside its own environment. Their solution is to encourage each organization to do some rudimentary cost modeling of its own. In order to facilitate such effort, they have invented a "meta-model," a kind of kit from which you can begin to build your own local cost model without incurring huge expense.

143

10

A Meta-Model for Software Development Resource Expenditures
by John W. Bailey and Victor R. Basili

INTRODUCTION

Several resource estimation models for a software-producing environment have been reported in the literature [1, 2, 3, 4, 5, 6, 7, 8, 9], each having been developed in a different environment, each having its particular strengths and weaknesses but with most showing fairly poor characteristics concerning portability to other environments. It is becoming apparent that it is not generally possible for one software development environment to use the algorithms developed at another environment to predict resource consumption. It is necessary for each environment to consider its own past productivity in order to estimate its future productivities. Traditionally, a good manager can estimate resource consumption for a programming project based on his past experience with that particular environment. A model should be able to do the same, and can serve as a useful aid to the manager in this estimating task.

However, if a manager uses a model developed at another environment to help him in his estimations, he will usually find that his intuitive estimates are better than any from the model. It would be advantageous for his software-development organization to generate a model of its own by duplicating the basic steps taken in the development of some outside environment's estimation model. The organization could parallel its own model's development with the development of the existing model, making decisions along the way with respect to which factors have an effect on its software environment, and could mold the newly emerging model to its specific environment. This is seen as an additional advantage over those models which are only "tuned" to the user's environment via a set of specified parameters, since in the latter case there may be no way to express certain peculiarities of the new environment in terms which the model can handle. When one considers in general how poorly a model from one environment fits another environment, it seems that such peculiarities are the rule rather than the exception. Unfortunately, there have been few attempts to reveal the steps taken in generating a resource estimation model which would be helpful to any organization wishing to establish a model for its own use.

This paper is a first attempt by the Software Engineering Laboratory of the University of Maryland at College Park to outline the initial procedures which we have used to establish this type of model for our environment. It is hoped that the framework for the model presented here is general enough to help another software development organization produce a model of its own by following a similar procedure while making decisions which mold the model to its own environment.

One basic approach will be outlined and developed here, but several variations will be discussed. The type of model used is based on earlier work of Walston and Felix at IBM Federal Systems Division and Barry Boehm at TRW in that it attempts to relate project size to effort. Some reasonable measure is used to express the size of a project, such as lines of source code, executable statements, machine instructions or number of modules, and, a base-line equation is used to relate this size to effort. Then, the deviations of the actual projects from this prediction line are explained by some set of factors which attempt to describe the difference among projects in the environment. These factors may include measures of skill and experience of the programming team, use of good programming practices and difficulty of the project.

Several of the alternatives became apparent during our study and these are mentioned when appropriate even if they are not examined further here. Although some of the details and ideas used in this study may not pertain to other environments, it is hoped that enough possibilities are given to show the general idea of how the technique we used can be applied. The study now involves complete data on eighteen projects and sub-projects but was begun when we had complete data on only five projects. It is hoped that the presentation of our work will save other investigators who are developing a model some time or at least provide a point of departure for their own study.

Background

There exist many cost estimation models ranging from highly theoretical ones, such as Putnam's model [1], to empirical ones, such as the Walston and Felix [2] and the Boehm model [3]. An empirical model uses data from previous projects to evaluate the current project and derives the basic formulae from analysis of the particular data base available. A theoretical model, on the other hand, uses formulae based upon global assumptions, such as the rate at which people solve problems, the number of problems available for solution at a given point in time, etc. The work in this paper is empirical and is based predominantly on the work of Walston and Felix, and Barry Boehm.

The Software Engineering Laboratory (SEL) has worked to validate some of the basic relationships proposed by Walston and Felix which dealt with the factors that affect the software development process. One result of their study was an index computed with twenty-nine factors they judged to have a significant effect on their software development environment. As part of their study, they proposed an effort equation which was of the form $E = 5.2 * L^{.91}$ where E is the total effort in man-months and L is the size in thousands of lines of delivered source code. Data from SEL was used to show that although the exact equation proposed by Walston and Felix could not be derived, the basic relationship between lines of code and effort could be substantiated by an equation which lay within one standard error of estimate for the IBM equation, and in a justifiable direction. [10] Barry Boehm has proposed a model that uses a similar standard effort equation and adjusts the initial estimates by a set of sixteen multipliers which are selected according to values assigned to their corresponding attributes. In attempting to fit an early version of this model, but with the SEL data, it was found that because of differing environments, a different base-line equation was needed, as well as a different set of environmental parameters or attributes. Many of the attributes found in the TRW environment are already accounted for in the SEL base-line equations, and several of the attributes in the SEL model which accounted for changes in productivity were not accounted for in the Boehm model, presumably because they had little effect in the TRW environment. Based upon this assumption and our experience with the IBM and TRW models, the meta model proposed in this paper was devised.

The SEL Environment

The Software Engineering Laboratory was organized in August, 1976. Beginning in November, 1976, most new software tasks that were assigned by the System Development Section of NASA/Goddard Space Flight Center began submitting data on development progress to our data base. These programs are mostly ground support routines for various spacecraft projects. This usually consists of attitude orbit determinations, telemetry decommutation and other control functions. The software that is produced generally takes from six months to two years to produce, is written by two to ten programmers most of whom are working on several such projects simultaneously, and requires from six man-months to ten man-years of effort. Projects are supervised by NASA/

GSFC employees and personnel are either NASA personnel or outside contractors (Computer Sciences Corporation).

The development facility consists of two primary hardware systems: a pair of S/360's and a PDP-11/70. During development of software systems users can expect turn-around time to vary from one or two hours for small, half-minute jobs, to one day for medium jobs (3 to 5 minutes, less than 600K), to several days for longer and larger jobs. The primary language used is FORTRAN although there is some application of assembler language.

THE META-MODEL

The meta-model described here is of the adjusted base-line type such as those proposed by Walston and Felix and Barry Boehm. Therefore, the basic approach is a two-step process. First, the effort expended for the average project is expressed as a function of some measure of size and, second, each project's deviation from this average is explained through the systematic use of a set of environmental attributes known for each project. The remainder of this paper will describe this process and will follow the format:

1) Compute the background equation

2) Analyze the factors available to explain the difference between actual effort and effort as predicted by the background equation

3) Use this model to predict the effort for the new project

The Background Equation

The background or base-line relationship between effort and size forms the basis for the local model. It is found by fitting some choice of curve through the scatter plot of effort versus size data. By definition, then, it should be able to predict the effort required to complete an average project, given its size. This average effort value as a function of size alone has been termed the "standard effort" throughout this paper. This section deals with:

1.1) Picking and defining measures of size and effort

1.2) Selecting the form of the base-line equation

1.3) Calculating an initial base-line for use in the model

In any given environment the decision of what size measure to use would have to depend initially upon what data is available. In our case, it was decided that size could be measured easily by lines of source code or by modules and that effort could be expressed in man-months. Consideration should also be given to the ease with which each measure can be estimated when the model is used to predict the effort required for future projects. The upper management in our programming environment was of the opinion that source lines with comments was the easier of the two readily available measures to predict. Also, it was decided that, based upon the data available and the ultimate use of the model, project effort would be defined to be measured from the beginning of the design phase through acceptance testing and to include programming, management and support hours.

In our data base, the total number of lines and modules as well as the number of new lines and new modules were avail-

able for the 18 projects and sub-projects. Initially, we expressed effort in terms of each of the four size measures mentioned above. To do this, we used three forms of equations to fit the data, using both the raw data and logarithms of the data, which provided functions we hoped would express the basic relationship between size and effort that exists in our environment. The forms of the three types of equations were:

$$E = \text{effort} \qquad S = \text{size}$$
$$E = a * S + b \tag{1}$$
$$E = a * S^b \tag{2}$$
$$E = a * S^b + c \tag{3}$$

Some difficulties were encountered when attempting to fit a conventional least-squares regression line through the raw data. One probable reason for this is that a correlation between the deviations from the prediction line and the size of the project could not easily be eliminated (heteroscedasticity). Rather than using a least-squares line with a single, arithmetic standard error of estimate which would be consistently large with respect to small projects and often too small when applying the equation to large projects, we opted for a prediction line which minimized the ratio between the predicted values for effort and each actual data point. In this way, the standard error is multiplicative and can be thought of as a percent error whose absolute magnitude increases as the project size increases. If, however, equations of the second or third form are derived by fitting a least-squares line through the logarithms of the data, the standard error automatically becomes multiplicative when converted back to linear coordinates.

The third form shown above was the

most successful for us. It was in the form of an exponential fit but included a constant which removed the constraint that the prediction line pass through the origin. This line was not found by converting to logarithms but by an algorithm that selected the values which minimized the standard error of estimate when expressed as a ratio. The theory behind the implementation of this multiplicative standard error of estimate is described later. Although the size of our data base was not large enough to firmly support using this fit rather than a straight line, we are using it here primarily as an illustration, and therefore felt justified in retaining it.

Turning back to the measurement of size, it was noted that neither the equations based upon size in terms of new lines of code or new modules nor those based upon total lines of code or total modules captured the intuitive sense of the amount of work required for each project. It was felt that although using previously-written code was easier than generating new code, the integration effort was still significant and should be accounted for. After examining the background relationships discussed above, another more satisfying measurement for size was derived. Instead of considering only the total lines or only the new lines to determine the size of a project, an algorithm to combine these sizes into one measure was selected. It was found that by computing the effective size in lines to be equal to the total number of new lines written plus 20% of any old lines used in the project, a base-line relationship of lower standard error could be derived. This new size measure will be called "developed lines" in this paper. The same technique was applied to numbers of modules and resulted in a measure of "developed modules." Other proportions of new and old sizes were tried as well as an algorithm which computed developed size based on a graduated mixture of new and old code where larger projects counted a higher percentage of their re-used code in the developed size. Often, these equations did produce slightly better background relationships, but the improvement in standard error was judged not to be worth the added complexity. It was hoped that as long as some reasonable algorithm was selected which captured the size as measured by both the amount of new product as well as old product, most of the remaining differences among the projects should be explainable by the varying environmental attributes.

At this point, the three base-line equations, based on the computed sizes of developed lines only, were:

E = effort in man-months of programming and management time

DL = number of developed lines of source code with comments (new lines with comments plus 20% of re-used lines)

Equation: *Standard error of estimate:

$$E = 1.36 * DL + 1.62 \qquad 1.269 \qquad (4)$$
$$E = 1.86 * DL^{.93} \qquad\qquad 1.297 \qquad (5)$$
$$E = 0.73 * DL^{1.16} + 3.5 \quad 1.250 \qquad (6)$$

Figure 1 shows how the exponential fit with constant for developed lines falls between those for new lines and total lines, hopefully doing a better job than either of the other two in relating a project's size

---

*Note that these are multiplicative factors. The predicted value given by the equation is multiplied and divided by this factor to get the range for one standard error of estimate. All standard errors of estimate (s.e.e.) in this paper are of this type.

to the resources consumed during its development. The remainder of this paper will deal entirely with this computed measure of size since it was our most successful expression for work output for a given project.

Figure 2 shows these three background prediction equations superimposed on the data points. It was decided to use equation 3, above, as the base-line throughout the remainder of the model generation since it achieved the best fit to the data points and suggested the intuitively satisfying fact that a project requires a minimum overhead effort (the Y-intercept of the function). Equation one, a straight line, does as well statistically, and could

well have been adopted for simplicity. Since this is meant to be an illustration, however, and it was felt that the non-linear relationship between size and effort was more common outside of our environment, equation three was adopted for use in this study. The remaining errors of estimation appear as the vertical distances between each point and the line. It is these distances in the form of ratios which we would like to explain in terms of the environmental attributes.

Project Factors

The next step in determining a model is to collect data about the programming en-

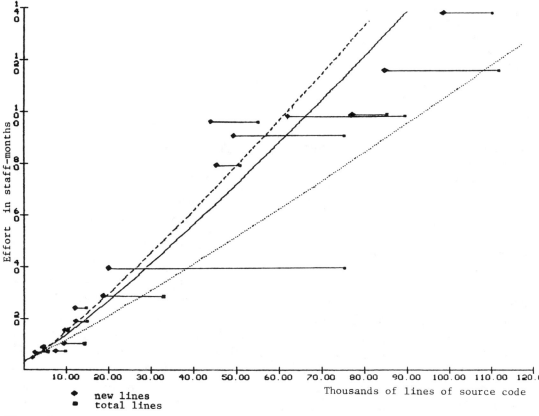

new lines ◆
total lines ■

Figure 1.

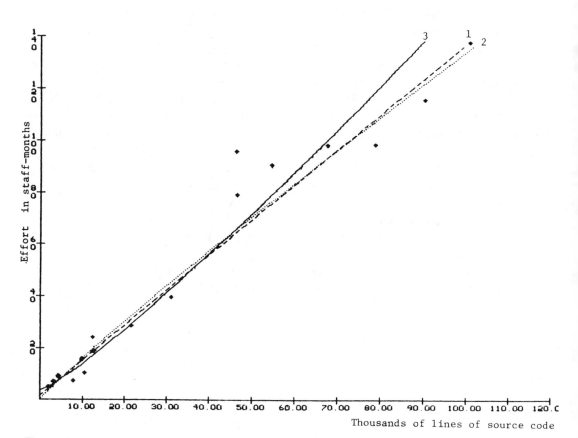

Figure 2.

vironment of each project which captures the probable reasons why some projects took more effort and thereby consumed more resources than others when normalized for size. This data could include such factors as methodologies used during design and development, experience of the customer and of the programmers, managerial control during development, number of changes imposed during the development and type and complexity of the project. It is assumed that the correct application of information such as this can assist in explaining the variations observed among projects in terms of their productivities. The steps described in this section include:

2.1) Choosing a set of factors

2.2) Grouping and compressing this data

2.3) Isolating the important factors and groups

2.4) Incorporating the factors by performing a multiple regression to predict the deviations of the points from the computed base-line

In all, close to one hundred environmental attributes were examined as possible contributors to the variations among the productivities of the projects. Table 1 shows a list of these factors as well as some others which we did not use.

Thirty-six of the factors were those used by Walston and Felix, sixteen were used by Boehm and 30 others were suggested by our environment. Although we did not use all these factors, they are included to provide additional ideas for other investigators. It should be noted that it is not necessary to consider any factors which are constant for the set of projects currently in the data base since the influence of this factor will already be contained in the base-line relationship. If, however, a future project is rated differently in one of these categories, it may be necessary to reinstate it into the model.

The process of selecting attributes to use is largely a matter of what information is available. Since many of the projects we studied were completed when this investigation began, it was necessary to rely on project management for the information required. The inclusion of past projects was justified in order to establish as large a data base as possible, however, it made it necessary to be particularly careful about the consistency between the ratings for current projects and those for projects already completed. To maintain the integrity of the values of these attributes, all ratings produced by the vendor's management were examined by the customer's management and also by us. In this way we hoped to avoid the temptation to adjust ratings to reflect the known ultimate success of past projects.

Many of the attributes required no special work to assign a value, such as "Team Size" or "Percent Code: I/O," but most required imposing a scale of some kind. We decided that an exact scale was not possible or even necessary so a six-point subjective rating was used. This format was chosen by the managers who would be making the ratings since it conformed well with the information they had already collected about many of the attributes. Most of the factors, then, are rated on a scale from 0 to 5 with 5 being the most of that particular attribute (whether it is "good" or "bad"). The most important point is that we tried to remain consistent in our ratings from project to project. The need for this was particularly noticeable when rating earlier projects in terms of development methodology. For instance, what may have been thought of as a "4" rating in "Formal Training" for a project which began coding over a year ago may actually be a "3" or even a "2" when compared with the increased sophistication of more recent projects. We found it necessary to re-scale a few of the attributes because of this consideration.

After a set of environmental factors is selected and the data collected, it is necessary to consider the number of these attributes versus the number of projects in the data base. It is not statistically sound to use a large group of factors to predict a variable with relatively few data points. Unless a very large number of projects is being used, it will probably be necessary to condense the information contained in the whole set of factors into just a few new factors. This can be accomplished entirely intuitively, based on experience, or with the help of a correlation matrix or factor analysis routines. Although there is no absolute rule as to how many factors should be used to predict a given number of points, a rule of thumb might be to allow up to ten or fifteen percent of the number of data points. Strictly speaking, the adjusted r-squared values or the F-values should be observed

Table I.

Walston and Felix:	Boehm:
Customer experience	Required fault freedom
Customer participation in definition	Data base size
Customer interface complexity	Product complexity
Development location	Adaptation from existing software
Percent programmers in design	Execution time constraint
Programmer qualifications	Main storage constraint
Programmer experience with machine	Virtual machine volatility
Programmer experience with language	Computer response time
Programmer experience with application	Analyst capability
Worked together on same type of problem	Applications experience
Customer originated program design changes	Programmer capabililty
	Virtual machine experience
Hardware under development	Programming language experience
Development environment closed	Modern programming practices
Development environment open with request	Use of software tools
Development environment open	Required development schedule
Development environment RJE	
Development environment TSO	**SEL:**
Percent code structured	Program design language (development and design)
Percent code used code review	Formal design review
Percent code used top-down	Tree charts
Percent code by chief-programmer teams	Design formalisms
Complexity of application processing	Design/decision notes
Complexity of program flow	Walk-through: design
Complexity of internal communication	Walk-through: code
Complexity of external communication	Code reading
Complexity of data-base structure	Top-down design
Percent code non-math I/O	Top-down code
Percent code math and computational	Structured code
Percent code CPU and I/O control	Librarian
Percent code fallback and recovery	Chief programmer teams
Percent code other	Formal training
Proportion code real time of interactive	Formal test plans
Design constraints: main storage	Unit development folders
Design constraints: timing	Formal documentation
Design constraints: I/O capability	Heavy management involvement and control
Unclassified	Iterative enhancement
	Individual decisions
	Timely specs and no changes
	Team size
	On schedule
	TSO development
	Overall
	Reusable code
	Percent programmer effort
	Percent management effort
	Amount documentation
	Staff size

as factors are added to the prediction equation via a multiple regression routine (described below) to avoid the mistake of using too many factors.

In our environment, we had data on 71 attributes which we suspected could affect the ultimate productivity of a project, but only 18 projects for which to see the results. We found it necessary, therefore, to perform such a compression of the data. Our next step, then, was to examine the attributes and group into categories those which we felt would have a similar effect on the project. As an aid to selecting potential groupings for analysis, a correlation matrix for all the attributes was studied. It was hoped that meaningful groups could be formed which would retain an intuitive sense of positive or negative contribution to the project's productivity. By studying the potential categorizations of the factors, and how they performed in potential models to predict developed lines, we settled upon three groups using 21 of the original attributes. The groups and their constituent attributes were:

Total Methodology
  Tree Charts
  Top Down Design
  Design Formalisms
  Formal Documentation
  Code Reading
  Chief Programmer Teams
  Formal Test Plans
  Unit Development Folders
  Formal Training

Cumulative Complexity
  Customer Interface Complexity
  Customer-Initiated Design Changes
  Application Process Complexity

Program Flow Complexity
Internal Communication Complexity
External Communication Complexity
Data Base Complexity

Cumulative Experience
  Programmer Qualifications
  Programmer Experience with Machine
  Programmer Experience with
    Language
  Programmer Experience with
    Application
  Team Previously Worked Together

We were particularly interested in using a methodology category due to the findings of Basili and Reiter [11] which implied improvement in the development process due to the use of a specific discipline. The methodology category was selected to closely coincide with the principles of the methodology used in the experiment. The complexity category was included to account for some of the known negative influences on productivity. The cumulative rating for each of these categories was merely a sum of the ratings of its constituents (each adjusted to a 0 to 5 scale). Although it was necessary to reduce the number of attributes used in the statistical investigation in this manner in order to give more meaningful results, the simple summing of various attributes loses some of the information which could be reflected in these categories. This is because even though one of the constituent attributes may be much more important than another, an unweighted sum will destroy this difference. One solution to this type of dilemma is to have many more data points, as mentioned before, and to use the attributes independently. Another would be to determine the relative effects of each attribute and to weight them accordingly. Without the necessary criteria for either of these solutions, however, we are forced to continue in this direction and to accept this trade-off.

Incorporating the Factors

The purpose of the attribute analysis is to explain the deviations displayed by each project from the derived background equation and, ultimately, to yield a prediction process where the attributes can be used to determine how far a project will "miss" the background equation, if at all.

The next step, then, is to compute these differences which must be predicted. A quantity based on the ratio between the actual effort expended and the amount predicted by the background equation was used as a target for the prediction. In this way, when the model is in use, the background equation can be applied to determine the standard effort (the amount needed if the project behaved as an average of the previous projects in the data base). Then, the attributes will be used to yield a ratio between this rough estimate and a hopefully more accurate expected value of the effort required.

The SPSS [12] forward multiple regression routine was used to generate an equation which could best predict each of the project's ratio of error. The actual ratio was converted to a linear scale with zero meaning the actual data point fell on the base-line. This was accomplished by subtracting one from all ratios greater than one and adding one to the negative reciprocals of those ratios which were less than one. For instance, if a project's standard effort was predicted to be 100 man-months and it actually re-quired 150 man-months, this ratio would be 1.5. Subtracting one makes this project's target value 0.5. If however it had needed only 66.7 man-months, its ratio would be .667 which is less than one. Adding one to the negative reciprocal of this number gives a target value of –0.5. The assumption is that this scale tends to be symmetrical in that the first project had as many negative factors impact its productivity as the second project had positive.

In the first pass at using the multiple regression routine, we were using five attribute groups. Since the data base was not very large, we were cautious about assigning any useful significance to the results. We therefore recondensed the attribute data into the three groups shown above. The results of this attempt are described in a later section.

Variations on the Model

We noticed that it was possible to combine the two processes of first isolating a background equation and then applying the environmental attributes to explain deviations from that equation into a single procedure. To do this, a measure of size was included as a factor with the set of environmental attributes and the whole group was used to predict effort. As expected, size was always chosen first by the forward routine, since it correlated the best with effort for each project. This single process lacked the intuitively satisfying intermediate stage which related to a base-line relationship as a half-way point in the model's results, but it streamlined the model somewhat.

In order to preserve the possibility of an exponential relationship between size and effort, this method was used with the logarithms of the size and effort values. The output of the regression analysis would be of the form,

$$\log(Effort) = A * \log(Size) + B * attr1 + C * attr2 + \ldots + K \quad (7)$$

This would convert to,

$$Effort = Size^A * 10^{(B * attr1 + C * attr2 + \ldots + K)} \quad (8)$$

assuming, here, that log base 10 was used in the conversion.

A third template for a model was tried which attempted to eliminate nearly all of the reliance on the actual numerical values of our attribute ratings in order to legitimize some of our statistical analyzes. Only two of the attribute groups mentioned before were considered, "Complexity" and "Methodology." Each of these two ratings were transformed into two new ratings of binary values resulting in four new attributes, "High Methodology," "Low Methodology," "High Complexity," and "Low Complexity." The transformation was accomplished as follows: if a project's rating fell in the upper third of all projects, the value of the "High" binary attribute of that type was assigned a 1 while the value of the "Low" attribute for that type was assigned a 0. If the value fell in the middle third, both binary values were assigned a 0. If the value fell in the low third, the "Low" attribute was assigned a 1 while the "High" was assigned a 0. This reduced our assumptions about the data to the lowest level for statistical analysis. For illustration, call the four new binary attributes HM, LM, HC, LC for high and low methodology and high and low complexity. The result of the multiple regression analysis, then, would be in the form,

$$Effort = Size^A * 10^{(B * HM + C * LM + D * HC + E * LC + K)} \quad (9)$$

Since the chance that any chosen attribute value will be 0 for a particular project is about $\frac{2}{3}$, most of those terms on the right will drop out when the model is actually applied to a given project. Although we did not expect to achieve the same accuracy from this method, the simplicity of it was appealing.

APPLYING THE MODEL

As an illustration of the results obtained thus far for our environment, this section deals with the actual values of the data we used and the models we generated. It should serve as a useful guide and a summary of the steps we chose to follow. In order to include an illustration of the functioning of the completed model, one project, the most recently completed project, will be removed from the analysis while a new model is developed. This project will then be treated as a new data point in order to test and illustrate the performance of the model. Typically, the use of the model will involve the following steps:

3.1) Estimate size of new project

3.2) Use base-line to get standard effort

3.3) Estimate necessary factor values

3.4) Compute difference this project should exhibit

3.5) Apply that difference to standard effort

Appendix 1 shows the eighteen projects and sub-projects currently in our data base with the measures of size previously discussed. As stated above, developed size is all of the newly written lines or modules plus 20% of the re-used lines or modules, depending on which size measure is being used. The developed size is what we chose to predict with the models generated. We also chose, as a base-line, the exponential equation with the constant term. The following illustration shows the development of the model with the first seventeen points in the data base. The base-line relationship between developed lines of code and effort was:

$$E = .72 * DL^{1.17} + 3.4 \text{ (s.e.e.} = 1.25) \quad (10)$$

The remaining information used about the projects is shown in the appendix. The remaining error ratios from this line to each project's actual effort were computed and listed. These are the values which should be explained by the multiple regression analysis. When the model is in use, then, an error ratio can be derived by using the multiple regression equation which can then be applied to the base-line equation to provide what should be an even better estimate of effort than the base-line alone. As discussed, the three main categories of environmental attributes shown are the result of distilling many attributes.

The equations computed by the SPSS forward multiple regression routine which

Appendix 1.

Project	Effort (man-months)	Total Lines	New Lines	Developed Lines	Predicted Standard Effort	Effort Ratio Standard/ Actual	Method-ology	Complex-ity	Exper-ience
1	115.8	111.9	84.7	90.2	138.7	.835	30	21	16
2	96.0	55.2	44.0	46.2	65.8	1.459	20	21	14
3	79.0	50.9	45.3	46.5	66.2	1.194	19	21	16
4	90.8	75.4	49.3	54.5	79.0	1.150	20	29	16
5	39.6	75.4	20.1	31.1	42.9	.924	35	21	18
6	98.4	89.5	62.0	97.5	100.1	.982	29	29	14
7	18.9	14.9	12.2	12.8	17.5	1.082	26	25	16
8	10.3	14.3	9.6	10.5	14.7	.704	34	19	21
9	28.5	32.8	18.7	21.5	29.2	.977	31	27	20
10	7.0	5.5	2.5	3.1	6.2	1.128	26	18	6
11	9.0	4.5	4.2	4.2	7.4	1.220	19	23	12
12	7.3	9.7	7.4	7.8	11.4	.640	31	18	16
13	5.0	2.1	2.1	2.1	5.2	.957	28	19	20
14	8.4	5.2	4.9	5.0	8.2	1.025	29	21	14
15	98.7	85.4	76.9	78.6	118.8	.831	35	33	16
16	15.6	10.2	9.6	9.7	13.7	1.138	27	21	16
17	23.9	14.8	11.9	12.5	17.1	1.398	27	23	18
18	138.3	110.3	98.4	100.8	157.4	.879	34	33	16

attempt to express the list of error ratios as functions of various of the attributes provided are:

ER   = Effort ratio (converted to linear scale)
METH = Methodology
CMPLX = Complexity

$$ER = -.036 * METH + 1.0 \qquad (11)$$

$$ER = -0.36 * METH + .006 * CMPLX + .86 \qquad (12)$$

To apply the model to the unused, eighteenth point, the base-line equation is first used to establish the standard effort. Since the estimated size of the project was 101,000 lines, this standard effort value was 163 man-months with a range for one standard error of from 130 to 204 man-months. When the additional attributes are used to compute the error ratio as given by the multiple regression equations, the results (for each of the above equations) are:

$$ER = -0.224 \quad \text{and} \quad ER = -0.166$$

Converting these numbers back to multiplicative factors means dividing the standard effort by 1.224 and by 1.166, respectively. When these ratios are applied to the standard effort value, the revised effort values are found to be 133 man-months with a range for one standard error from 115 to 154 man-months for the first equation, and 140 man-months with a range for one standard error of from 121 to 162 man-months for the second equation. The actual effort for the project is known to have been 138 man-months.

Once any new project is added to the data base, at least the generation of the base-line relationship and the multiple regression analysis of the error ratios should be repeated. It may also be necessary to examine the factor groupings to see if they could be modified to increase the accuracy

of the model or to include a previously unimportant attribute.

For our data, when this eighteenth point is added to the data base, the base-line equation becomes:

$$E = .73 * DL^{1.16} + 3.5 \ (\text{s.e.e.} = 1.25) \quad (13)$$

while the equations to predict the error ratio from the attributes become:

$$ER = -.035 * METH + .98$$
$$(\text{s.e.e.} = 1.16) \qquad (14)$$

$$ER = -.036 * METH + .009 * CMPLX + .80 \ (\text{s.e.e.} = 1.15) \quad (15)$$

It should be remembered that the original choice of factors from the entire set, and the groupings of these factors, was done with regard to predicting size as measured by developed lines and was not so specifically tuned to predicting developed modules. It is reasonable to expect, then, that the results of the models generated to predict effort from the number of developed modules using these attribute groupings will be less accurate than those using the number of developed lines. If the objective had been to generate a model specifically suited to predicting modules, various adjustments would have been made during the early part of the model's development. Also, it is advisable to review the model each time a new project is completed and its data is added to the data base. In this way the model can be refined and kept up-to-date, and will be able to take into account changes in the overall programming environment.

Although we are not reporting here the actual values and equations generated in the development of the other forms of this basic model (described under "Variations on the Model," above) it became apparent that none of the model types is by far better than the rest, especially considering the fact that they all have differing amounts of statistical significance. In terms of a purely investigative study, all of them should probably be examined further. As more environmental information is added to the data-base, it may be possible to reorganize the constituent groups involved in the environmental attributes and to produce better categories. Also, when several more projects are completed, it may be possible to justifiably expand the size of the set of variables used to predict the expected value in the multiple regression routine giving the potential for greater accuracy.

CONCLUSIONS

There is reason to believe that the techniques outlined here and used in our laboratory have potential in terms of producing a useful model which is specifically developed for use at any particular environment. The main difficulty seems to be in determining which environmental attributes really capture the reason for the differences in productivity among the projects. The use of too few of these attributes will mean less of the variation can possibly be explained, while the use of too many makes the analysis statistically meaningless. We found that it was necessary to stop including factors with the multiple regression analysis when the r-squared value indicated that we had explained no more than half of the variations among the error ratios. This would seem to indicate that there were considerably more influences upon the productivities of the projects than we managed to isolate. Simplifying the original idea for the model, however, which reduced the emphasis on the quality of the data did not weaken the accuracy of the model beyond

useful proportions. This is particularly important when so much of the data which is essential to build the model is subjective and consequently non-linear.

Acknowledgements: The authors would like to thank Dr. Jerry Page of Computer Sciences Corporation and Frank McGarry of NASA/Goddard Space Flight Center for their invaluable help in providing the data for this study.

Research for this study was supported in part by National Aeronautics and Space Administration grant NSG-5123 to the University of Maryland. Computer time supported in part through the facilities of the Computer Science Center of the University of Maryland.

REFERENCES

[1]   Putnam, L. "A General Empirical Solution to the Macro Software Sizing and Estimating Problem," *IEEE Transactions on Software Engineering,* Vol. 4, No. 4, 1978.

[2]   Walston, C., and C. Felix. "A Method of Programming Measurement and Estimation," *IBM Systems Journal,* Vol. 16, No. 1, 1977.

[3]   Boehm, Barry W. Draft of a book on Software Engineering Economics, to be published.

[4]   Lawrence, M.J., and D.R. Jeffery. "Interorganizational Comparison of Programming Productivity," Department of Information Systems, University of New South Wales, March 1979.

[5]   Doty Associates, Inc. Software Cost Estimates Study, Vol. 1, RADC TR 77-220, June 1977.

[6]   Wolverton, R. "The Cost of Developing Large Scale Software," *IEEE Trans-*

actions on Computers, Vol. 23, No. 6, 1974.

[7]   Aron, J. "Estimating Resources for Large Programming Systems," NATO Conference on Software Engineering Techniques, Mason Charter, N.Y., 1969.

[8]   Carriere, W.M., and R. Thibodeau. "Development of a Logistics Software Cost Estimating Technique for Foreign Military Sales," General Research Corp., Santa Barbara, Calif., June 1979.

[9]   Norden, Peter V. "Useful Tools for Project Management," *Management of Production,* M.K. Starr, ed. Baltimore: Penguin Books, 1970, pp. 77-101.

[10]   Basili, V.R., and K. Freburger. "Programming Measurement and Estimation in the Software Engineering Laboratory," *Journal of Systems and Software,* Vol. 2, No. 1, 1981.

[11]   Basili, V.R., and R.W. Reiter, Jr. "An Investigation of Human Factors in Software Development," *Computer,* December 1979, pp. 21-38.

[12]   Statistical Package for the Social Sciences, Univac 1100 series manual.

11

Editors' Note
Symons: "Function Point Analysis: Difficulties and Improvements"

Insight: Software metrics cannot be treated as off-the-shelf products. Organizations that adapt techniques and measures for their own use always seem to come out ahead.

Charles Symons offers a proposed variation on the widely used Function Points metric, as first defined by Allan Albrecht. He also includes data from some of his customers to show how his variation has been an improvement.

Your organization might profit from the Symons variation on the theme of function metrics. Better yet, you might use his thought process to come up with an additional adaptation of your own.

11

Function Point Analysis: Difficulties and Improvements
by Charles R. Symons

I. INTRODUCTION

The size of the task of designing and developing a business computerized information system is determined by the product of three factors (see Fig. 1).

- The *information processing size,* that is, some measure of the information processed and provided by the system.

- A *technical complexity factor,* that is, a factor which takes into account the size of the various technical and other factors involved in developing and implementing the information processing requirements.

- *Environmental factors,* that is, the group of factors arising from the project environment (typically as-

sessed in project risk measures), from the skills, experience and motivation of the staff involved, and from the methods, languages, and tools used by the project team.

The first two of these factors are intrinsic to the size of the system in the sense that they result directly from the requirements for the system to be delivered to the user.

Allan Albrecht has described a method known as "Function Point Analysis" for determining the relative size of a system based on these first two factors. [1-4] The method has gained widespread acceptance in the business information systems community, for system size assessment as a component of productivity measurement, when system development or maintenance and enhancement activities are com-

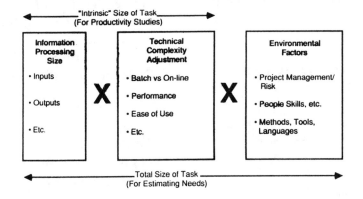

Figure 1. The three components of system size.

pleted. Where historic productivity data are available, the method can also be used as an aid in estimating man-hours, from the point where a functional requirements specification is reasonably complete. For estimating purposes, the third group of environmental factors clearly also has to be taken into account.

The aims of this paper are:

- to critically review function point analysis,
- to propose some ways of overcoming the weaknesses identified,
- to present some initial results of measurements designed to test the validity of the proposed improvements.

While the paper contains some criticisms of Albrecht's Function Point method, the author wishes to acknowledge the substantial contribution made by Albrecht in this difficult area. The ideas in this paper are an evolutionary step, only made possible by Albrecht's original lateral thinking.

However as Albrecht's method becomes ever more widely adopted, it will become a de facto industry standard. Before that happens it is important to examine the method for any weaknesses, and if possible to overcome them.

II. ALBRECHT'S FUNCTION POINT METHOD

In Albrecht's Function Point method, the two components of the intrinsic size of a system are computed as summarized in the following:

1) The Information Processing Size is determined by first identifying the system components as seen by the end-user, and classifying them as five types, namely the external (or "logical") inputs, outputs, inquiries, the external interfaces to other systems, and the logical internal files. The components are each further classified as "simple," "average," or "complex," depending on the number of data elements in each type, and other factors. Each component is then given a number of points depending on its type and complexity [see Fig. 2(a)] and the sum for all components is expressed in "Unadjusted Function Points" (or UFP's).

2) The Technical Complexity Factor is determined by estimating the "degree of influence" of some 14 component "General Application Characteristics" [see Fig. 2(b)]. The degree of influence scale ranges from zero (not present, or no influence) up to five (strong influence throughout). The sum of the scores of the 14 characteristics, that is the total degrees of influence (DI), is converted to the "Technical Complexity Factor" (TCF) using the formula

$$TCF = 0.65 + 0.01 \times DI.$$

Thus each degree of influence is worth 1 percent of a TCF which can range from 0.65 to 1.35.

3) The intrinsic relative system size in Function Points (FP's) is computed from

$$FP's = UFP's \times TCF.$$

Function Points are therefore dimensionless numbers on an arbitrary scale.

Albrecht's reasons for proposing Function Points as a measure of system size are stated (4) as:

- the measure isolates the intrinsic size of the system from the environmental factors, facilitating the study of factors that influence productivity,

- the measure is based on the user's external view of the system, and is technology-independent,

- the measure can be determined early in the development cycle, which enables Function Points to be used in the estimation process, and

- Function Points can be understood and evaluated by nontechnical users.

Another implied aim [2] is for a method which has an acceptably low measurement overhead.

III. FP ANALYSIS—A CRITICAL REVIEW

The following questions and difficulties have arisen in teaching and applying Albrecht's method.

A. Information Processing Size (Unadjusted FP's)

- Classification of all system component types (input, outputs, etc.) as simple, average, or complex, has the merit of being straightforward, but seems to be rather oversimplified. A system component containing, say, over 100 data elements is given at most twice the points of a component with one data element.

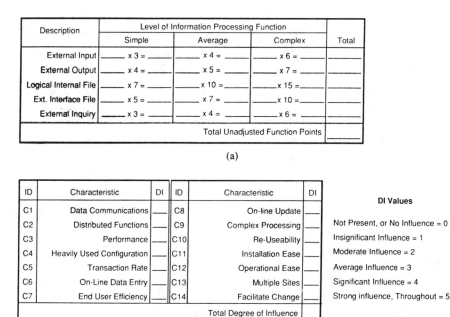

Description	Level of Information Processing Function			Total
	Simple	Average	Complex	
External Input	____ x 3 = ____	____ x 4 = ____	____ x 6 = ____	____
External Output	____ x 4 = ____	____ x 5 = ____	____ x 7 = ____	____
Logical Internal File	____ x 7 = ____	____ x 10 = ____	____ x 15 = ____	____
Ext. Interface File	____ x 5 = ____	____ x 7 = ____	____ x 10 = ____	____
External Inquiry	____ x 3 = ____	____ x 4 = ____	____ x 6 = ____	____
Total Unadjusted Function Points				____

(a)

ID	Characteristic	DI	ID	Characteristic	DI
C1	Data Communications	____	C8	On-line Update	____
C2	Distributed Functions	____	C9	Complex Processing	____
C3	Performance	____	C10	Re-Useability	____
C4	Heavily Used Configuration	____	C11	Installation Ease	____
C5	Transaction Rate	____	C12	Operational Ease	____
C6	On-Line Data Entry	____	C13	Multiple Sites	____
C7	End User Efficiency	____	C14	Facilitate Change	____
				Total Degree of Influence	

DI Values

Not Present, or No Influence = 0
Insignificant Influence = 1
Moderate Influence = 2
Average Influence = 3
Significant Influence = 4
Strong influence, Throughout = 5

TCF = 0.65 + 0.01 x (Total 'Degree of Influence')

(b)

Figure 2. (a) Unadjusted FP counting. (b) Technical Complexity Factor.

- The choice of "weights" [i.e., points per component type, see Fig. 2(a)] has been justified by Albrecht as reflecting "the relative value of the function to the user/customer" [3] and "was determined by debate and trial." It seems a reasonable question to ask if the weights obtained by Albrecht from his users in IBM will be valid in all circumstances, and useful for size measurement in both productivity assessment and estimating. Some more objective assessment of the weights seems advisable. The weights also give rise to some surprising effects. Why for example should an inquiry provided via a batch input/output combination gain more than twice as many points as the same inquiry provided on-line? Why should interfaces be of any more value to the user than any other input or output?

- Most of the UFP's for a system arise from its externally seen inputs, outputs, interfaces, and inquiries. Differences in *internal* processing complexity between systems are reflected in two ways. First, the classification of any input, output, inquiry, or interface as simple, average or complex depends in part on the number of logical file-types referenced from that component. As we shall see below, the latter is roughly related to internal processing complexity. (More recently guidelines have appeared [5] suggesting that "entities" should be counted rather than logical files.) Second, internal complexity appears as one of the 14 "General Application Characteristics," and can thus

contribute up to 5 percent to the Technical Complexity Factor. All in all, the way internal complexity is taken into account seems to be rather inadequate and confused. Systems of high internal complexity studied by the author do not appear to have had their size adequately reflected by the FP method in the opinion of the designers of those systems.

- Finally, Function Points do not appear to be "summable" in the way one would expect. For example, if three systems, discrete but linked by interfaces, are replaced by a single integrated system providing the same transactions against an integrated database, then the latter system will score less FP's than the three discrete systems. (Arguably the integrated system should score more FP's because it maintains data currency better.) This result arises partly because the FP counting rules credit an interface to both the issuing and receiving system, and partly because the integrated file will generally score less than the three discrete files.

One of Albrecht's findings from studies of productivity has been a falloff in productivity by a factor of roughly 3, as system size increases from 400 to 2000 FP's. [3] This is a very important result if true, but the finding depends on the accuracy with which FP's reflect relative system size. Most of the above criticisms of the FP method point toward the conclusion that the FP scale underweighs systems which are complex internally and have large numbers of data elements per component, relative to simpler and therefore "smaller" systems. If the criticisms are valid and significant, then the falloff in productivity with system size may not be as serious as apparently observed. Clearly it is an important issue to resolve.

B. The Technical Complexity Factor

- The restriction to 14 factors seems unlikely to be satisfactory for all time. Other factors may be suggested now, and others will surely arise in the future. A more open-ended approach seems desirable. Also some of the factors, as currently defined, appear to overlap (e.g., those concerned with application performance, a heavily used hardware configuration for processing, and a high transaction rate); some reshuffling of the factors appears desirable.

- The weights ("degree of influence") of each of the 14 factors are restricted to the 0-5 range, which is simple, but unlikely to be always valid. One obvious example is the factor which reflects whether the system is intended for multisite implementation. In practice, initial development of such a system can easily cost a great deal more than it would if intended only for a single site. A re-examination of the TCF weights is therefore also desirable.

In summary the Albrecht FP method and especially the weights, were developed in a particular environment. With the benefit of experience and hindsight various questions arise about the validity of the method for general application, especially for the information processing size com-

ponent. The GUIDE Project Team [5] has made steady progress in clarifying the detailed rules for FP counting to make them easier to apply, but has not questioned the underlying principles or weights. In the next section we will return to basic principles to develop an alternative approach for the information processing size component, and in Section V we will examine the calibration of the new UFP measure against practical data, and re-examine the calibration of Albrecht's Technical Complexity Factor. The resulting alternative approach will be referred to as the "Mark II" Function Point method, to distinguish it from Albrecht's method.

IV. A NEW MEASURE OF INFORMATION PROCESSING SIZE ("MARK II" FUNCTION POINTS)

Given that we want a measure of Information Processing Size which is independent of technology (if that is possible) and is in terms which the system user will easily recognize, we will start with certain basic assumptions, namely:

- We will regard a system as consisting of logical "transaction-types," that is, of logical input/process/output combinations.

- Interfaces at this logical level will be treated as any other input or output. (If an input or output happens to go to or come from another application, and that fact increases the size of the task, then it should be reflected in the Technical Complexity Factor.)

- Inquiries will be considered just as

any other input/process/output combination.

- The concept of a "logical file" is almost impossible to define unambiguously, particularly in a database environment, and at this level, the concept of "file" is not appropriate. The concept which correctly belongs at the logical transaction level is the "entity," that is anything (object, real, or abstract) in the real world *about which* the system provides information.

The other basic starting point is to establish the criterion which we will use to establish the size scale. As our aim is to obtain sizes which can be used for productivity measurement and estimating purposes, we will take the system size scale to be related explicitly to the *effort* to analyze, design, and develop the functions of the system. This is in contrast to Albrecht's aim of having a size which represents the *"value"* of function delivered to the user. The latter seems to be a more subjective criterion, and therefore less easy to verify or calibrate in practice.

The task then is to find properties of the input, process, and output components of each logical transaction-type which are easily identifiable at the stage of external design of the systems, are intelligible to the user, and can be calibrated so that the weights for each of the components are based on practical experience.

The most difficult component for which we need a size parameter is the process component. For this we rely on the work of McCabe [6] and others who have developed measures of software process complexity and shown for example that their measures correlate well with the frequency of errors found in the software. Such complexity measures are typically concerned with structural complexity, that is, they count and weight branches and loops. Sequential code between the branches and within loops does not add to complexity in this view. At the external design stage we do not know the processing structure of each logical transaction-type, and in any case this would be too complicated to assess and keep within the aims of method.

We do know however, from Jackson [7], that a well-structured function should match the logical data structure, which at this level is represented by the access path for the transaction through the system entity model. Since each step along the access-path through the entity model generally involves a selection or branch, or (if a one-to-many step) a loop, it seems a reasonable hypothesis that a measure of processing complexity is to count *the number of entity-types referenced by the transaction-type.* ("Referenced" means created, updated, read, or deleted.)

The above is a rather tenuous argument, and the result is a crude, first-order measure. Figure 3 shows an entity model for a simple order-processing system with a few logical transactions, and the number of entities referenced per transaction. Examples like this, and the experience of counting entity references per transaction in real systems, support this measure as a plausible hypothesis.

For the other (input and output) components of each logical transaction-type, we will take the number of data element types as being the measure of the size of the component. This is on the grounds that the effort to format and validate an input, and to format an output is in the first-order proportional to the number of data elements in each of those components, respectively. Figure 3 also shows illustrative numbers of input and output data element types for the order-processing transactions.

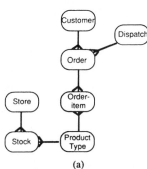

(a)

Transaction-Type	Input Data Elements	Entities Referenced		Output Data Elements
		Types	(Total)	
Add New Customer	53	Customer	1	3
Check Stock Availability	2	Product-Type Store, Stock	3	10
Process Order-Header	20	Customer Order, Dispatch	3	40
Process Order-Item	6	Order, Dispatch, Order-Item Product-Type, Store,Stock	6	14
Cancel Order-Item	2	Customer, Order, Order-Item Product-Type	4	15
Stock Report by Store & Product	1	Store, Product-Type Stock	3	21
Total	84		20	103

(b)

Figure 3. Example analysis of an order processing system for Mark II unadjusted function points. (a) Entity model. (b) Logical transaction analysis.

The net result of the above is that the Mark II formula for Information Processing Size expressed in Unadjusted Function Points becomes:

$$UFP's = N_I W_I + N_E W_E + N_O W_O$$

where

N_I = number of input data element types,
W_I = weight of an input data element type,
N_E = number of entity-type references,
W_E = weight of an entity-type reference,
N_O = number of output data element types,
W_O = weight of an output data element type,

and N_I, N_E, and N_O are each summed over all transaction-types.

(From now on whenever we refer to transactions, inputs, outputs, data elements, and entities, etc., it will be understood that we are referring to "types" unless it is necessary to distinguish between "types" and "occurrences.")

The next task is to attempt to determine the weights by calibrating this formula against practical data.

V. CALIBRATION OF MARK II FUNCTION POINTS

A first test and rough calibration of the Mark II Function Point method has been carried out using data collected from two Clients ("A" and "B") in consultancy studies. In each case the objective of the study was to explore the use of function point analysis for productivity measurement, and in particular the merits of the Mark II versus the Albrecht method.

Both Clients selected six systems for assessment, which were of varying size and technology. No constraint was placed on system selection, other than that the system should be of a size requiring at least 3-4 months to develop, and that an expert should be available to explain the system.

Collection of data for each system and its analysis fell into three categories, namely

- Unadjusted Function Point data
- Technical Complexity Factor data
- development effort data to calibrate the Mark II method

Since the last of these three categories has parts in common with each of the first two, it will be described first.

A. Analysis of Development Effort Data

Of the 12 systems, 9 had been developed recently, and adequate data were available about the development effort for further analysis.

For calibration purposes, the project representatives were asked to analyze the man-hours which had been used for development, and break them down as shown in Fig. 4. ("Development man-hours" were defined strictly according to Albrecht's rules.)

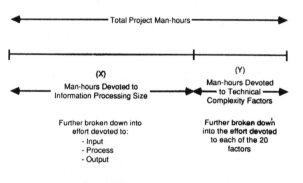

Figure 4. The analysis of project development time.

The first split required for each system is between the man-hours which had been devoted to the pure Information Processing Size, that is the effort devoted to analysis, design, and development purely to meet user requirements, and the man-

hours needed for the work on the various parts of the Technical Complexity Factor. The effort devoted to the Information Processing Size was further broken down into the effort required to handle input, processing, and output, defined as follows.

Input   Data entry, validation, error correction.

Processing   Performing the updates and calculations from availability of valid input until output data are ready for formatting.

Output   Formatting and transmission of output to the output device.

This required breakdown of development man-hours is unusual. No records were available, and therefore the breakdowns given are subjective. The project representatives did not demur from the task however; percentage breakdown splits between input, process, and output varied considerably, examples given including 35/10/55, 25/65/10, 40/40/20, etc. The validity of this approach can only lie in its statistical basis. Data from the nine systems analyzed so far appear to behave reasonably, as will be seen below. As data from more systems are collected so the quality and credibility of the derived weights will improve.

The man-hours apportioned to the Technical Complexity Factor were similarly further broken down by spreading them across the 14 Albrecht factors, and other factors proposed by the author (see below). This "top-down" split had the possibility of some "bottom-up" cross-checking by the project representatives, although still subjectively, as again no records were available. For example it might result from a first breakdown that two man-days were apportioned to a particular TCF factor. At this bottom level, project representatives could often recall how much effort really went into this particular factor. So with some iteration the size of the TCF component of development man-hours and its breakdown over the various factors was refined.

It should be emphasized that apart from prompting by the author on the required way of analysis, the development effort breakdown estimates are entirely those of the project representatives, working independently of each other, and without knowledge of the analysis which was to follow.

B. Collection and Analysis of UFP Data for Albrecht and Mark II Methods

All 12 systems were assessed according to the Albrecht and Mark II methods. First, for the Mark II method, an entity model of the system was derived, and at this point the "logical internal files" for Albrecht's method were identified and scored. Then each system was broken down into its logical transactions. The components of each transaction were classified for complexity and scored according to Albrecht's rules, and in parallel the counts of input and output data elements and entity references were collected for the Mark II method.

Early in the course of this work it became apparent that some counting conventions and definitions were needed for the Mark II method to ensure consistency and simplicity, such as have been developed

by GUIDE [5] and Albrecht [4] in their "Current Practice" chapters. Space does not permit a full account of these conventions, and they may well evolve further. An outline of the main types of conventions is given in the Appendix.

With the total counts of input and output data elements, and entity references for all transactions in each system, such as illustrated in Fig. 3, and the man-hours of development effort derived as in Section V-A above, it was possible to calculate the "man-hours per count" data shown for all nine systems in Fig. 5.

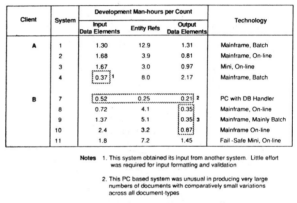

Client	System	Development Man-hours per Count			Technology
		Input Data Elements	Entity Refs	Output Data Elements	
A	1	1.30	12.9	1.31	Mainframe, Batch
	2	1.68	3.9	0.81	Mainframe, On-line
	3	1.67	3.0	0.97	Mini, On-line
	4	0.37 [1]	8.0	2.17	Mainframe, Batch
B	7	0.52	0.25	0.21 [2]	PC with DB Handler
	8	0.72	4.1	0.35	Mainframe, On-line
	9	1.37	5.1	0.35 [3]	Mainframe, Mainly Batch
	10	2.4	3.2	0.87	Mainframe On-line
	11	1.8	7.2	1.45	Fail-Safe Mini, On-line

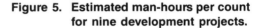

Notes
1. This system obtained its input from another system. Little effort was required for input formatting and validation.
2. This PC based system was unusual in producing very large numbers of documents with comparatively small variations across all document-types
3. This client had implemented special mainframe software to reduce the effort of preparing output

Figure 5. Estimated man-hours per count for nine development projects.

When examining Fig. 5, one must bear in mind the variety of system types, sizes and technologies, and of environments involved, and the crudity of the estimates of the breakdown of development effort over input, process and output. One should particularly note the sensitivity of some of the component man-hour estimates to a shift of a few percent between one category, e.g., input, and another, e.g., entity references.

In spite of these variations and uncertainties however, there is a clear pattern, and certain of the exceptionally high or low figures are explicable in terms of known project characteristics (the ringed figures in Fig. 5).

To get a "normative" set of weights for combined Client A and B data, averages were taken of all the nonringed figures in Fig. 5. These are

1.56   man-hours per input data element
5.9   man-hours per entity reference
1.36   man-hours per output data element.

These figures may be used directly as the weights in the Mark II UFP formula and could also have some value for future estimating purposes.

However, in order that the Mark II method produces UFP's comparable to Albrecht's, the Mark II scale was "pegged" to Albrecht's by scaling down the above weights so that the average system size in UFP's for all 8 systems under 500 UFP's came out to be identical on both scales.

The Mark II formula for Information Processing Size on the basis of this data therefore becomes

$$\text{UFP's} = 0.44N_I + 1.67N_E + 0.38N_O.$$

The UFP sizes for all 12 systems, calculated according to this formula, were then plotted against the corresponding Albrecht UFP's (see Fig. 6).

Two conclusions may be drawn in interpreting this graph. First, there is a general tendency for the Mark II method to give a larger information processing size relative to Albrecht's, as system size increases. More data are needed to confirm this trend, but the first results are in the direction expected from taking into account internal processing complexity in the Mark II method.

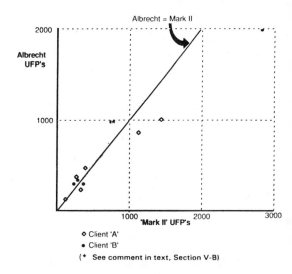

Figure 6.   Albrecht versus Mark II unadjusted function points comparison.

The second conclusion is that the Mark II method shows its sensitivity, especially in smaller systems, to relatively high or low average numbers of data elements per input or output component. The asterisked system in Fig. 6 (system 11 in Fig. 5) is unusual in having many transactions with exceptionally low counts of data elements per input and output relative to the amount of processing it carries out.

As to the Clients' interpretation of these data, Client A considered that the relative sizes of its systems and the derived productivity data were more plausible on the Mark II scale than on Albrecht's. Client B did not have sufficient feeling for the relative sizes to choose between the two methods. This Client did however prefer the Mark II method of analysis as giving more insight into the size measurement process.

C. Collection and Analysis of TCF Data According to Albrecht and Mark II Methods

The "Degree of Influence" of the 14 Albrecht Technical Complexity Factor components was scored for each system, using the scoring guidelines described by Albrecht [4] and Zwanzig. [5] A further five factors were proposed by the author, and project representatives were invited to nominate any other factors which they felt ought to be included in this category. The additional five factors are the needs

- to interface with other applications (project representatives suggested this should be broadened to include interfaces to technical software such as message switching),

- for special security features,

- to provide direct access for Third Parties,

- for documentation requirements, and

- for special user training facilities, e.g., the need for a training subsystem.

An additional factor suggested by project representatives was the need to define, select and install special hardware or software uniquely for the application.

Considerable debate took place about the criteria for what can be counted as a TCF component. The rule which evolved is that a TCF component *is a system requirement other than those concerned with information content, intrinsic to and af-* *fecting the size of the task, but not arising from the project environment.*

In total therefore 20 factors were scored on Albrecht's "Degree of Influence" scale, and in addition, for the 9 development systems, the actual effort devoted to each of these 20 factors was estimated by the project representatives (see Section V-A).

Two analyses were performed to calibrate Albrecht's Degree of Influence scale against estimates of actual effort.

For the first analysis, the actual TCF was computed for each system from the formula

$$\text{TCF (actual)} = 0.65 \, (1 + Y/X)$$

where (see Fig. 4)

$Y =$ man-hours devoted to Technical Complexity Factors

$X =$ man-hours devoted to the Information Processing Size as measured by Unadjusted Function Points.

Figure 7 shows the "TCF (actual)" plotted against the TCF derived from Albrecht's Degree of Influence scale for each of the 20 component factors. (Note the latter is not the pure Albrecht TCF, since Albrecht would only take 14 factors into account.)

In spite of the admitted roughness of the estimates going into the "TCF (actual)" figures, a clear pattern emerges from Fig. 7. First, Albrecht's method of assessing a TCF appears to work, but the weight of each Degree of Influence should vary with the technology. For the systems whose points lie close to the line labeled (2) in Fig. 7, a weight of 0.005 per Degree of Influence, or possibly less, is more appropriate than Albrecht's 0.01. In other words it seems to have taken less than half the effort to achieve these 20 technical complexity factors in practice than Albrecht's formula suggests. This correlates with the facts known about the systems lying along the line labeled (2). Client B has developed special software to simplify the development of on-line mainframe systems, while two of the other three systems along this line are personal computer based, and built with a fourth generation language ("Natural"), respectively. In contrast Albrecht's formula was derived from projects developed with technology available in the late 1970's.

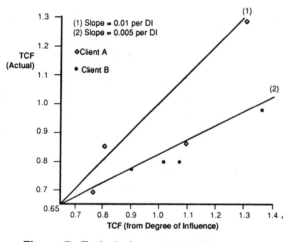

Figure 7. Technical complexity factor comparison (actual versus degree of influence of 20 factors).

The second more detailed analysis attempted to correlate the Degree of Influence scores of individual TCF components against the estimated actual percentage development effort. Owing to the small number (9) of projects, the 20 components, and the roughness of the estimates, no firm conclusions can be drawn about the relative weights of the individual

components. The following are first indications, but much more data will be needed to firm up these indications.

• Some grouping of Albrecht's components seems desirable; the distinctions made between his components 3, 4, and 5 concerned with performance, and 6, 7, and 8 concerned with on-line dialogs, were not completely clear to the project representatives.

• Components 11 (installation ease), 12 (operational ease), 14 (ease of changes) and 16 (security) seem to require less effort per Degree of Influence than the other components.

• Component 19 (documentation) requires maybe double the effort per Degree of Influence of the other components.

• Component 9 (complex internal processing) does not strictly fit into the criteria for TCF components as now defined above. If this component is to stay, the guidelines for its scoring need to be more sharply defined.

• Component 13 (multiple-site implementation), as already noted, needs to be much more open-ended in its scoring.

VI. CONCLUSIONS

The experience of applying Albrecht's Function Point method and the alternative Mark II approach to a variety of systems has led to three groups of conclusions:

1) Albrecht versus Mark II Function Points.

2) Use of function points for productivity measurement and estimating.

3) Limitations of function points.

A. Albrecht Versus Mark II Function Points

The criticisms of Albrecht's Function Point method were given in Section III of this paper. The aim of the Mark II approach has been to overcome these weaknesses, particularly in the area of reflecting the internal complexity of a system. There will never be any "proof" that the Mark II approach gives superior results to that of Albrecht. Only the plausibility of the underlying assumptions, and judgment of many users on the results provided by both methods over a long period, will support one approach or the other.

As practitioners have gained experience in Albrecht's method in the last few years, it has evolved in the direction of the Mark II approach. First, the count of data elements has been introduced to make the complexity classification of inputs, outputs, etc., more objective. More recently the concept of "entities" has begun to replace "logical files." The remaining essential difference between the two methods is the way of looking at *data*. Albrecht's criterion for attributing UFP's to data is simply that the data is seen to exist in the system, regardless of how much of it is used; the Mark II approach attributes UFP's to data depending on its *usage* (create, update, read, delete) transactions which form part of the system under study. Referring back to Albrecht's aims for Function Point Analysis, clearly it is the latter which is of "value" to the user. The *potential* value of stored data may be huge for a user, but it is only its actual

value, resulting from use by transactions provided in applications, which can be measured by function points.

Other differences or similarities in practice between the two methods which are worthy of note are as follows.

- The Mark II approach requires an understanding of entity analysis, and rules are emerging (see Appendix) for entity counting conventions. For the Albrecht approach a knowledge of entity analysis is advisable, but no entity counting conventions have yet been published.

- The simplicity of the Mark II approach in having fewer variables than Albrecht's method in the UFP component has a number of advantages, such as greater ease of calibration against measurements or estimates, as shown in this paper. Also, if another hypothesis is made in the future for one of the UFP components, e.g., that the "size" of an input is proportional to, say, the number of data elements plus a constant, then it is easy to recalibrate the weights and explore the sensitivity of relative system sizes to the new hypothesis.

- There is a potential in the Mark II method for refining the measurement of the work-output in maintenance and enhancement activities which has not been tested so far. With Albrecht's method it is only possible to measure the total size of the changed system components. No distinction is possible between small and large changes to any single component. With the Mark II method, by recording the numbers of data elements changed, and counting references to entities which have been changed (or whose attributes have been changed), it should be possible to produce a measure of the size of the changes themselves (made to the changed components), that is, a measure more directly related to the work-output of maintenance and enhancement activities.

• The effort of counting data elements for each input and output means that FP measurement following the Mark II method may require 10-20 percent more effort than with Albrecht's method (which typically imposes about a one quarter percent overhead for system size measurement on the man-hours for a development project). Also the latter method may be applicable slightly earlier in the project life-cycle than the Mark II method, although it should be possible to produce reasonably accurate estimates of numbers of data elements per transaction for early sizing purposes.

B. Use of Function Points for Productivity Measurement and Estimating

An important conclusion illustrated by results from this study is that *function points are not a technology-independent measure of system size*, which was one of Albrecht's stated claims. The technology dependence is implicit in the weights used for the UFP and TCF components. This conclusion applies equally to the Albrecht and Mark II approaches. The conclusion for the TCF component is clearly illustrated in the results shown in Fig. 7. In Fig. 8 a hypothetical example is given for

the size of error introduced into relative system size measurement by using an inappropriate set of weights, e.g., a set derived for a different technology from that actually being used.

Suppose we have two systems, A and B, with the following characteristics

	N_I	N_E	N_O
System A	100	20	100
System B	100	20	20
Weights (conventional technology)	0.5	2	0.4

Then   Size A   50 + 40 + 40 = 130

Size B   50 + 40 + 8 = 98

Ratio Sizes A/B = 1.33

But, if technology changes, such that weights should be

0.5   2   0.2

Then   Size A   50 + 40 + 20 = 110

Size B   50 + 40 + 4 = 94

Ratio Sizes A/B = 1.17

Conclusion: Use of the wrong set of weights may distort the ratio of sizes

Figure 8. Example of sensitivity of function points to weights.

A reasonable summary of the dependence of function points on technology is that the weights used by an organization in function point measurements imply a certain baseline or normative technology for that organization. If a system is built with a different technology, and its size is calculated with the organization's normative function point method, then the size calculated is the size the system would be if it were developed using the normative technology. This is clearly still very useful if the goal is to find out how productivity achieved with a new technology compares with that achieved with the normative technology. However

• if a new technology is introduced then sizes computed by function points cannot be reliably used for *estimating* unless a new set of weights is estimated or calibrated in line with the new technology, and

• if an organization changes its whole (normative) technology and it wants to continue to make fair size and productivity comparisons, then it must calibrate a new set of normative function point weights for the organization; clearly the latter will be necessary only at very infrequent intervals.

Generally for estimating purposes in an organization, a historical pool of information on actual productivity achieved using function point methods would be an invaluable asset. However, variations in environmental factors, especially project risk, the learning difficulties of new technologies and the performance of individuals can be extremely important considerations when estimating.

C. Limitations of Function Point Analysis

For completeness it is important to understand certain limitations of function point analysis.

• The method is not as easy to apply in practice as it first appears. In particular, working back from an installed physical system providing an interactive dialog to derive the logical transactions, requires some experience. Also cases sometimes arise where it becomes a matter of subjective judgment whether subtypes of a logical transaction (e.g., those which have slightly different processing paths depending on input values) are counted as separate logical transactions, or whether the differences can be ignored. For some time to come therefore it will be best in any one organization if all measurements are supervised by one objective, experienced function point analyst. Such an analyst should accumulate and document cases and derive general rules such as given in the Appendix, which will help ensure consistency and objectivity in function point analysis.

• The suggestion has been made that it should eventually be possible to compute Mark II unadjusted function points automatically from a functional model of a system stored for example in a data dictionary. The difficulty with this is not so much automating the counting but, bearing in mind the previous limitation, ensuring that the model is correct and in a form suitable for FP counting. (However the benefits of this effort may be much wider than just the benefit of being able to count function points!)

• FP analysis works for installed applications, not for tools, or languages, such as a general purpose retrieval language. The distinction between these two classes of systems is not always absolutely clear. Applications provide preprogrammed functions where the user is invited to enter data and receives output data. Tools provide commands with which the user can create his or her own functions. Business information systems are usually applications, but may sometimes incorporate tools, or features with tool-like characteristics as well. Tools have a practically infinite variety of uses. The productivity of a group which supports a series of tools for use by others, for example an Information Center, can only be measured indirectly by sampling the productivity achieved by the end-users who apply the tools.

• A further limitation is that although in general FP analysis works for business applications it may not work for other types of applications, such as scientific or technical. This arises from its limited ability to cope with internal complexity. Again there is no absolute distinction between these different categories but internal complexity in business applications arises mainly from the processes of validation, and from interactions with the stored data. The Mark II method has aimed at reflecting these processes in a simple way. But scientific and technical applications typically have to deal with complex mathematical algorithms; FP analysis as currently defined has no reliable way of coping with such processes.

VII. CONCLUDING REMARKS

The function point method as proposed by Albrecht has certain weaknesses, but it appears they can be overcome by adjustments to the counting method as outlined here in the Mark II approach. These methods still seem to offer one of the best lines of approach for an organization that wishes to study its trends in productivity and improve its estimating methods for the development and support of computerized business information systems.

APPENDIX: SUMMARY OF ENTITY AND DATA ELEMENT COUNTING RULES

The following is a brief outline of the rules which have evolved, and which will probably evolve further, to simplify entity and data element counting, and to introduce more objectivity into the counting.

A. Entities

A distinction is made between three types of entities.

First, we count those entities with which the system is primarily concerned. These are typically the subjects of the main files or database of the system.

Second, we distinguish those things which data analysts frequently and rightly consider as entities, but about which the system holds typically only at most an identifying code, or name, and/or a description, and which are stored only to validate input. There are many possible rules to help distinguish such entities; information about them is usually held in files referred to as "system master tables" or "parameter tables." These are not included in our count of entity-references per transaction, on the grounds that their contribution to system size will be taken into account in the count of input data elements (which is considered to account for validation).

Third, entities about which information is produced only on output, for example in summary data reports, are also not counted. Their contribution to system size is considered to be reflected in the count of output data elements per transaction.

B. Data Elements

Several data element counting conventions are required; examples include:

- Data element *types* are counted, not data element occurrences.

- Conventions are needed for counting of dates (which may be subdivided), address fields (which may be multi-line), and the like.

- Batch report jobs, whether initiated by an operator, or automatically at certain points in time, are considered to have always at least a one-data element input.

- Field labels, boxes, underlines, etc., should be ignored.

ACKNOWLEDGMENT

The author acknowledges with gratitude the permission of the two Clients A and B to use their data for this paper. He also wishes to thank Client staff for their patience, support, and enthusiasm in the collection and analysis of the data.

REFERENCES

[1] A.J. Albrecht, "Measuring Application Development Productivity," in *Proceedings of the IBM Applications Development Symposium,* GUIDE International and SHARE Inc., IBM Corp., Monterey, Calif., October 14-17, 1979, p. 83.

[2] _____ , "Function Points as a Measure of Productivity," in *Proceedings of GUIDE 53 Meeting,* Dallas, Tx., November 12, 1981.

[3] _____ and J.E. Gaffney, "Software Function, Source Lines of Code and Development Effort Prediction: A Software Science Validation," *IEEE Transactions on Software Engineering,* Vol. SE-9, No. 6, pp. 639-47, November 1983.

[4] A.J. Albrecht, "AD/M Productivity Measurement and Estimate Validation—Draft," IBM Corp. Information Systems and Administration, AD/M Improvement Program, Purchase, N.Y., May 1, 1984.

[5] K. Zwanzig, ed., *Handbook for Estimating Using Function Points,* GUIDE Project DP-1234, GUIDE International, November 1984.

[6] T.J. McCabe, "A Complexity Measure," *IEEE Transactions on Software Engineering,* Vol. SE-2, No. 4, pp. 308-20, 1976.

[7] M. Jackson, *Principles of Program Design.* London: Academic, 1975.

12

Editors' Note
Itakura and Takayanagi: "A Model for Estimating Program Size and Its Evaluation"

Insight: A repeatable and objective procedure for specification analysis can give a surprisingly accurate estimate of the size of the system to be constructed.

A small revolution in software metrics was caused by the publication of Albrecht's landmark Function Point paper in 1979. Since that time, metrics-conscious organizations have been experimenting with various *function metrics,* indicators of size and complexity derived from the problem specification. But in spite of nearly ten years of work on the subject, function metrics are still a bit esoteric for many practitioners.

Itakura and Takayanagi have come up with a charming way to give you the benefits of function metrics without all the hullabaloo. Their scheme is to use many of the same parameters that drive the function metrics, but to express the results in expected lines of code (LOC). Coupled with a LOC-based estimating tool, like COCOMO, the technique of this paper can help you move quickly toward a methodology of "guessless" estimating.

12

A Model for Estimating
Program Size and Its Evaluation
by Minoru Itakura and Akio Takayanagi

1. INTRODUCTION

Accurate estimation is a difficult aspect of software development because an inaccurate estimation causes losses due to cost overruns as well as losses in system reliability and project productivity. The losses are caused by having to increase the number of project members in the midst of development. New project personnel usually lack sufficient training and are not familiar with the project, reducing productivity and system reliability. Project success or failure depends on the degree of estimation accuracy.

To date, most estimates have been made by experts in the field. Usually these estimations have the following faults:

(1) Because, by definition, subjective estimates are not objective, they lack credibility.

(2) Subjective estimates follow no particular pattern that other people can learn, instead the estimators require experience in related projects.

(3) It is not easy to trace the effects of variable conditions on estimates.

To resolve these three problems, a technique for developing an objective estimation model is necessary. In the past ten years, several estimation models have been proposed. Typically, they are empirical models, derived statistically from data of previous projects.

Most of them are models which estimate manpower. These models usually contain program size as a variable. For example, Walston and Felix' model is presented as the following equation,

$$Y = 5.2 * X^{0.91} \qquad (1)$$

where Y is the total number of man-months and X is the total program size in thousands of lines of delivered source code. Basili et al. derived the following equation as their estimation model,

$$Y = 0.73 * X^{1.16} + 3.5 \qquad (2)$$

where Y is the total number of man-months and X is the number of source code with comments. Further, Basili et al. proposed a method to modify the estimated values from equation (2) based on project characteristics.

The principal problem with these formulas is that at the beginning of development actual program size are not yet determined but are also only estimates. Therefore, manpower estimated from the above equations will be inaccurate if the program sizes are inaccurately estimated. Models for estimating program size have not yet been proposed.

The authors attempted to develop a program size estimation model by looking at the program structure and logic, and determining the number of lines required for each type of process. Then we totaled these lines to estimate the total program size. Although we adapted the model for unknown data at the beginning of development, the results were no less accurate than subjective estimates made by experts.

We concluded that our model could resolve the three problems stated above. Therefore, we are introducing an outline of the model and discussion of the results obtained when we adapted the model to our project.

2. ESTIMATION MODEL

2.1 Development

We developed this model for batch programs in a banking system written in COBOL and Assembler.

2.2 Modeling Process

The modeling process is illustrated in Figure 1. Variables, structure, and coefficients were determined as follows:

(1)   Selection of variables
       We selected those variables that were obtained at the time of estimation and which affected program size.

(2)   Determination of structure
       We divided each program into several parts and derived equations for each part. In the procedure division, in particular, we derived equations for the various processes such as sorting, editing, calculating, and so on.

(3)   Values of coefficients
       We made assumptions about what the actual program codes would be and those who had experience in that field determined the values of coefficients.

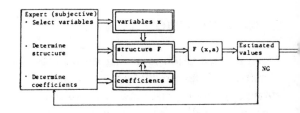

Figure 1. Process of modeling.

If the estimates derived from the models were inconsistent with the estimates made by the experts' subjective, we changed the variables, the structure, and the values of coefficients, and re-executed the modeling process.

2.3 Example of Modeling

We were unable to develop an all-encompassing model which could be adapted to all types of programs. For example, it is difficult to adapt the same model to both Assembler and COBOL programs. Therefore, we classified programs into three patterns: one model for COBOL programs and two models for Assembler programs. The two Assembler models are for ledger-files accessing programs and for merging programs. They are strongly dependent on our systems' characteristics, and lack the generality for adaptation to other systems. But the COBOL model is generally adaptable to other systems. Figure 2 illustrates the

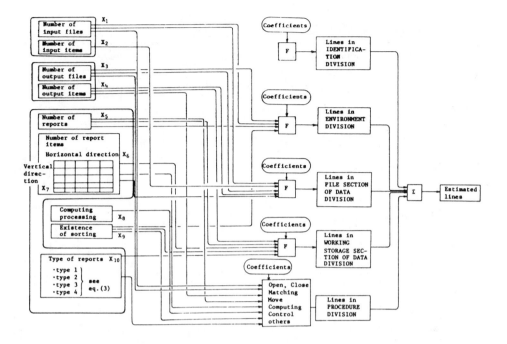

Figure 2. Example of modeling (COBOL report-writing programs).

outline of the modeling process for programs written in COBOL. We selected the following variables:

(1) Number of input files (X_1)

(2) Number of input items (X_2)

(3) Number of output files (X_3)

(4) Number of output items (X_4)

(5) Number of reports (X_5)

(6) Number of horizontal items in reports (X_6)

(7) Number of vertical items in reports (X_7)

(8) Number of calculating processes (X_8) (We counted the number as 80 steps per one calculating process.)

(9) Existence of sorting (X_9)

(10) Report type (X_{10})

- Transaction type (information about customer or account)
- Transaction, branch total, and bank total type
- Branch total and bank total type
- Bank total type

In Figure 2, the variables and the divisions for which the variables are used are connected by arrows. For example, input files are defined in the ENVIRONMENT DIVISION and the FILE SECTION of the DATA DIVISION.

OPEN/CLOSE processings of input files are written in the PROCEDURE DIVISION. Therefore, variable X_1 is con-

Table 1.
Values of Coefficients for Estimation Model.

Variables / DIVISION	Constant	Input file Number of files X_1	Input file Number of items X_2	Output file Number of files X_3	Output file Number of items X_4	Number of reports X_5	Each report Constant	Each report Number of horizontal items X_{61}	Each report Number of vertical items X_{71}	Computing X_{81}	Existence of sort X_{91}	Type of report X_{101}	Source lines in each DIVISION
ID.	10	-	-	-	-	-	-	-	-	-	-	-	10
ENV.	10	1	-	1	-	-	1	-	-	-	1	-	$10 + X_1 + X_3 + \sum_{i=1}^{X_5} (1 + X_{9i})$
DATA FILE	15	5	1.3	5	1.3	-	-	1.3	-	-	-	-	$15 + 5X_1 + 1.3X_2 + 5X_3 + X_5 + \sum_{i=1}^{X_5} 1.3X_{6i}$
DATA WORKING STORAGE	20	-	0	-	1	-	$10^{1)}$ $15^{2)}$ $40^{3)}$ $15^{4)}$	1.3 2.3 2.3 2.3	1	-	10	-	$20 + X_4 + 10X_5 + \sum_{i=1}^{X_5} (1.3X_{6i} + X_{7i} + 10X_{9i}) + \sum_{i=1}^{X_5} \left\{ \begin{matrix} 0 \\ X_{6i}+5 \\ X_{6i}+30 \\ X_{6i}+5 \end{matrix} \right.$
PROCEDURE	50	2	0	2	1	-	120	2 2 3 3	-	80	50	-	$50 + 2X_1 + 2X_3 + X_4 + 120X_5 + \sum_{i=1}^{X_5} (2X_{6i} + 80X_{8i} + 50X_{9i}) + \sum_{i=1}^{X_5} \left\{ \begin{matrix} 0 \\ 0 \\ X_{6i} \\ X_{6i} \end{matrix} \right.$
Total	105	8	1.3	8	3.3	-	$131 + \left\{ \begin{matrix} 0 \\ 5 \\ 30 \\ 5 \end{matrix} \right\}$	$4.6 + \left\{ \begin{matrix} 0 \\ 1 \\ 2 \\ 2 \end{matrix} \right\}$	1	80	61	-	$105 + 8X_1 + 1.3X_2 + 8X_3 + 131X_5 + \sum_{i=1}^{X_5} (4.6X_{6i} + X_{7i} + 80X_{8i} + 61X_{9i}) + \sum_{i=1}^{X_5} \left\{ \begin{matrix} 0 \\ X_{6i}+5 \\ 2X_{6i}+30 \\ 2X_{6i}+5 \end{matrix} \right.$

Note: 1) - 4) indicates the type of report. 1) type 1 2) type 2 3) type 3 4) type 4

nected with the ENVIRONMENT DIVISION, FILE SECTION of the DATA DIVISION, and the PROCEDURE DIVISION by three arrows.

The number of source codes which the above variables (X_1-X_{10}) require in each division (the values of the variable coefficients) are listed in Table 1. For example, input files (X_1) require one source code per file in the ENVIRONMENT DIVISION, five source codes in the FILE SECTION of the DATA DIVISION, and two source codes in the PROCEDURE DIVISION. So X_1 requires 8 source codes in all. The values of Table 1 were determined by experts who had written similar programs.

As indicated in Table 1, an equation is derived for each division and, by adding these together, the model equation is as follows:

$$Y = 105 + 8X_1 + 1.3X_2 + 8X_3 + 3.3X_4$$

$$+ 131X_5 + \sum_{i=1}^{X_5} (4.6X_{6i} + X_{7i} +$$

$$80X_{8i} + 61X_{9i}) + X_{10} \qquad (3)$$

where

$$X_{10} = \sum_{i=1}^{X_5} \begin{cases} 0: \text{ transaction type} \\ X_{6i} + 5: \text{ transaction, branch} \\ \qquad \text{total, and bank total} \\ \qquad \text{type} \\ 2X_{6i} + 30: \text{ branch total and} \\ \qquad \text{bank total type} \\ 2X_{6i} + 5: \text{ bank total type} \end{cases}$$

2.4 Estimation and Development Phase

Figure 3 illustrates the relation between model variables and development phases. The initial estimates are made at phase 0, where reports and process flows are tentative, and specifications and file formats do not yet exist. For example, estimation model (3) contains variables such as the number of input/output items (X_2/X_4), or the number of calculating processes (X_8). These values are not accurately determined until the design is complete. Therefore, initial estimates based on the model may be no more accurate than estimates made by experts. When the design is complete, detailed specifications and file formats are established as well as the values of the variables. The estimated results based on model (3) then increase in accuracy. It is important to look over previous estimation results based on model (3) before a new phase is started.

Further, model (3) can be used to estimate the amount of program source code variation when specifications are modified.

3. EVALUATION OF THE MODEL

3.1 Comparison Between Estimated and Actual Results

We compared the values estimated from equation (3) with the number of source lines of completed programs. Using estimated values from the following two phases (see Fig. 3), we measured the number of source lines for 38 unit-tested COBOL programs.

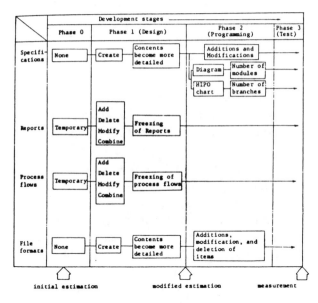

Figure 3. Estimation factors and development stages.

(1) Values at phase 0: These are initial estimation values. Because those values are estimated before any fundamental design work, only uncertain data obtained from temporary reports and process flows are used.

(2) Values at phase 2: These are modified estimation values. Because design work is complete, variable values for the model can be accurately determined.

Table 2 indicates the total source lines of the initial estimate, of the modified estimate, and of the actual results for the 38 COBOL programs.

Table 2.
Comparison Between Estimates and Actual Results.

	Source lines of initial estimate	Source lines of modified estimate	Source lines of actual program
Total * source lines	72600	77200	82615
Ratio to actual program	87.8	93.4	100

• Total source lines of 38 sample COBOL programs

It indicates that the values of the initial estimate are 13 percent less than the number of actual source lines. We conclude that these results are good, even though the estimation was done under poor initial conditions with potentially inaccurate data. The values of the modified estimate are only 7 percent less than the number of actual lines so that the modified estimate is better than the initial estimate, as might be expected.

Both Figures 4 and 5 illustrate the relation between the estimated and actual values for individual programs, and show the clear differences between the estimated and actual results. We defined these differences as errors in the model, and computed the root mean squares of these errors (σ). The obtained σ was 970 lines for the initial estimate and 690 lines for the modified one, showing that the modified estimate was better than the original.

The accuracy of estimations for any one of the 38 sample programs may be much worse than for all the programs combined (see Table 2). This is because the positive and negative errors cancel each other when added together.

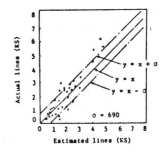

Figure 4. Relation between initial estimate and actual results.

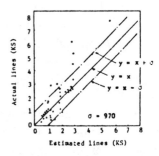

Figure 5. Relation between modified estimate and actual results.

We computed the regression equation (4) between the results of the modified estimates and the actual results.

$$y = 0.3666 \, x^{1.12797} \qquad (4)$$

In equation (4), y is the number of source lines and x is the number of source lines based on the modified estimate. As indicated in Figure 6, equation (4) and the straight line y = x crosses at x = 2500. In the region of x ≧ 2500, the straight line is less than equation (4), and in the region of x < 2500, the relation of the two lines is inverted. This means that there is a tendency to estimate less than the actual results for programs of more than 2500 source lines, while the reverse is true for programs of less than 2500 source lines.

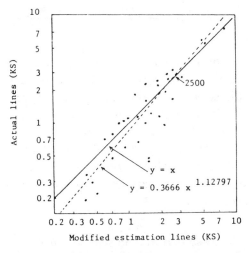

Figure 6. Regression curve between modified estimate and actual results.

3.2 Regression Analysis for Source Line Estimations

(1) Purpose

The initial estimation of the number of source lines of the sample programs erred by 13 percent. We conclude that this degree of accuracy is nearly the same as that achieved by estimates made by experts' subjective (Our past experience indicates that estimates by experts' subjective usually error by about 10 percent). Further, the modified estimates erred by only 7 percent. This indicates that our estimation model, equation (3), is very effective.

But, even with the modified estimates, σ values equal 690 lines (35 percent), although the average number of source lines of each sample program is only 2000 lines. It is important to accurately estimate the size of each program in order to smoothly manage the project's progress.

This leads us to conclude that more detailed discussions are necessary. Questions to be answered include:

(1) Is the structure of our estimation model correct?

(2) Is the selection of variables reasonable?

(3) Can we reduce the number of variables to derive a model simpler than model (3)?

To answer the above questions, we measured the values of variables contained in equation (3) from the sample source programs and performed a regression analysis.

(2) Regression model

We could not use equation (3) directly as a regression model because it contains the term $\sum_{i=0}^{X_5}$, where the number of variables vary according to the value of X_5.

Therefore, we changed the form of equation (3) and defined the regression model as follows:

$$Y = \beta_0 + \beta_1 X_1 + \beta_2 X_2 + \beta_3 X_3 + \beta_4 X_4 + \beta_5 X_5 + .. + \beta_{11} X_{11} \tag{5}$$

where, Y: the number of source lines of
an individual program without comments.

X_1 : the number of input files

X_2 : the number of input items

X_3 : the number of output files

X_4 : the number of output file items

X_5 : the number of items of transaction
type reports

X_6 : the number of vertical items in two-
dimensional table type reports

X_7 : the number of horizontal items in
two-dimensional table type reports

X_8 : the number of calculating processes

X_9 : the existence of sorting

X_{10}: the sum of output items in reports
$(X_5 + X_6 + X_7)$

X_{11}: the sum of output items in both files
and reports $(X_4 + X_5 + X_6 + X_7)$

β_0-β_{11}: constant and coefficients of variables $(X_1$-$X_{11})$

Equation (5) has the same terms as equation (3), though the forms of the two equations are different.

(3) Results of regression analysis

Table 3 indicates the correlation coefficients between X_i (i = 1-11) and Y. Variables X_1, X_2, X_3, X_8, and X_{10} are correlated to Y because their correlation
coefficients are more than 0.5. But, the
correlation coefficients for variables X_4,
X_5, X_6, X_7, and X_9 are less than 0.5 and
therefore we might consider program size
independent of these variables. Especially
in the correlation coefficient of X_9 (existence of sorting), where the value is negative (-0.37). In fact, because the number of codes required for sorting is nearly
constant in each program, variable X_9 is
not correlated to the program size.

The four variables, X_4-X_7, are all
related to output items. Although these

correlation coefficients are low, they are
not inherently so, for the following reasons. Because programs which contain
variables X_4, X_5, X_6, and X_7 differ in
their processing, regression analysis
should be done for each processing type.
But, we did not do this because of the few
programs involved.

Table 3.
Correlation Coefficients Between X and Y.

	X_1	X_2	X_3	X_4	X_5	X_6	X_7	X_8	X_9	X_{10}	X_{11}
Correlation coefficient	0.51	0.76	0.80	0.15	0.46	0.40	0.35	0.63	−0.37	0.64	0.45

The results of regression analysis are
shown in Table 4, where the standard deviations of the regression equation σ, and
the determination coefficients $\bar{R}^2$ are also
listed. Equation (6) contains all variables
of model (3). Equations (7) and (8) combine the variables. Equation (9) is the
equation which best fits the measured data
(see Figure 7).

Table 4.
Results of Regression Analysis.

$$Y = -843 + 248X_1 + 1.21X_2 + 566X_3 + 0.378X_4 + 5.82X_5 + 1.69X_6 + 1.92X_7 + 101X_8 + 136X_9 \quad (6)$$
$$\hat{\sigma} = 475, \bar{R}^2 = 0.928$$
$$Y = -842 + 267X_1 + 1.34X_2 + 518X_3 + 0.432X_4 + 87.9X_8 + 219X_9 + 3.45X_{10} \quad (7)$$
$$\hat{\sigma} = 561, \bar{R}^2 = 0.900$$
$$Y = -658 + 139X_1 + 1.45X_2 + 609X_3 + 128X_8 + 148X_9 + 0.924X_{11} \quad (8)$$
$$\hat{\sigma} = 621, \bar{R}^2 = 0.877$$
$$Y = -810 + 310X_1 + 1.12X_2 + 553X_3 + 5.91X_5 + 1.62X_7 + 99.7X_8 \quad (9)$$
$$\hat{\sigma} = 433, \bar{R}^2 = 0.940$$

We can conclude the following from the
results of regression analysis. The determination coefficient of equation (6), which
contains all the variables in model (3), is
0.93. This means that 93 percent of all

variations can be explained by regression equation (6). The values of σ and $\bar{R}^2$ of equations (7) and (8) (which combine the variables) show a degraded quality when compared with those of equation (6). These facts indicate that the selection of variables in model (3) is reasonable and that estimation accuracy is sacrificed if we try to simplify the model by reducing the number of variables.

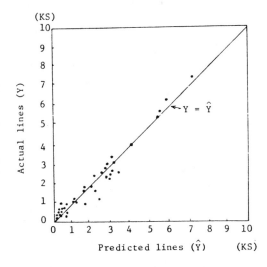

Figure 7. Relation between number of actual lines and the best prediction by regression analysis.

When we turn our attention to the coefficients of regression equations, the values for the constants (β_0) are negative, and the values for coefficients X_1, X_3 are noticeably high, when compared with the same items in model (3). It is especially curious that the value for the constants is negative. We believe the following to be the reason for this fact. X_1 and X_2, or X_3, X_4, X_5, and X_6 are not exactly independent. For example, X_2 depends on

X_1, because if the number of input files (X_1) increase, then the number of input items (X_2) also increases. Therefore we introduced a variable, Z_i, which combines the variables X_1, X_2, or X_3-X_6 by weighting. Further, we presume that program size, Y, is related to Z_i by equation (10).

$$Y = \alpha_0 + \alpha_1 Z_i^\gamma \qquad (10)$$

where α_0, α_1: constant and coefficient of Z_i, and $\gamma > 1$.

Because, in equation (5), we assume the linear relationship holds for data distributed about the curve as in equation (10), the value of constant β_0 becomes negative, and the value of coefficient β_i ($i = 1$–3) is noticeably high (see Figure 8). Therefore we might conclude that the linear structure considered in model (3) doesn't accurately reflect the actual program structure. But, when considering the usefulness of models, it is not practical to drive complex non-linear equations. Rather, it is more important to consider how corrections to linear models can be made.

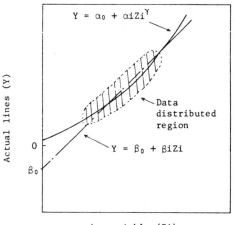

Figure 8. Illustration which indicates that constants are negative and coefficients are noticeably high.

4. CONCLUSIONS

Our model for estimating size proved to be nearly as accurate as estimates made by experts, indicating the model is sufficiently effective in objective estimation.

The results of regression analysis suggested the necessity of a non-linear model in spite of the correctness of variable selection. However, it is not practical to derive complex non-linear equations for models and it is necessary, instead, to correct values estimated from linear models. A discussion of these correction methods will be made in a later paper.

We conclude that our method sufficiently fulfilled our goal, the derivation of objective estimation methods. Although this estimation model is specifically for our projects and cannot directly be adapted to others, our modeling process is generally adaptable to any other project by the alternation and selection of variables and the values of coefficients.

REFERENCES

[1] Walston, C., and C. Felix. "A Method of Programming Measurement and Estimation," *IBM Systems Journal,* Vol. 16, No. 1, 1977.

[2] Bailey, John W., and Victor R. Basili. "A Meta-Model for Software Development Resource Expenditure," *Proceedings of the Fifth International Conference on Software Engineering,* IEEE Computer Society Press, March 1981.

13

Editors' Note
Jones: "Demographic and Technical Trends in the Computing Industry"

Insight: A quantitative portrait of our industry.

Capers Jones has spent nearly three decades studying the software industry. He has analyzed projects that together delivered some one hundred million lines of code, becoming in the process perhaps our most respected source for data on productivity, defect incidence, defect removal, and trends of all sorts.

As a by-product of this work, he has amassed facts and figures that are the envy of the Department of Commerce workers studying our industry. So, when he asserts that there are a million active programmers in the U.S., almost a factor of four more than Commerce had reported, most of us are inclined to believe Jones rather than the Department. He speaks with an authority that few can rival.

13

Demographic and Technical Trends in the Computing Industry
by T. Capers Jones

Introduction

The impact of computers on mankind is turning out to be one of the most significant events in human history, and in the future computers may well be ranked with the printing press, the internal combustion engine, the harnessing of electricity, and the airplane as a phenomenon that changed the way daily human activities are carried out.

The printing press was responsible for an enormous expansion in the amount of information available, and in the ability to share new discoveries widely and quickly. Computers are having the same general impact, and indeed are starting to open up several entirely new fields of research that were not possible before, since the volume of information and the quantity of calculations made manual or electromechanical techniques inadequate. For example, large-scale meteorological studies and long-range weather predictions could be carried out by hand calculations alone.

Thomas J. Watson, the former chairman of IBM, was recently quoted as saying that the computer industry would become the largest single industry in America. [1] John Marsiniak [2] observed at the recent NCC that there were already three times as many employees in the U.S. computing industry as in the automobile industry. My own demographic studies have led me to predict that if current trends continue, by the end of the 20th century the computing industry will become the fourth largest employer in all human history, outranked only by agriculture, government service, and military service in total numbers of workers on a global basis.

Demographic Trends

My demographic studies were begun when I noted that the U.S. Department of Commerce statistics [3] had not been updated with actual census data since 1978, and appeared to be significantly on the low side in reporting both the U.S. population of software personnel and of the rest of the computing industry (hardware, peripherals, marketing, research, and maintenance).

To form an independent view of the approximate numbers of U.S. and global computing employees, I took representative enterprises that had published data on the number of programming personnel, analysts, etc. (insurance companies, banks, several computer manufacturers, etc.) and extrapolated those counts to similar enterprises. This method has a high margin of error, but serves as a starting point until more detailed demographic studies take place.

My studies indicated that in 1983, the U.S. had about 900,000 professional programmers; Western Europe, another 900,000; Japan, Taiwan, and Hong Kong, about 500,000. The rest of the world totaled another 950,000, for a global total of programmers of about 3,250,000.

It might be of interest that the total working population of the U.S. was about 106,000,000 [4] when I did my study, so the approximate 900,000 total programmers represent about 0.85 percent of the working U.S. population.

I also did a 10 percent random sampling to the FORTUNE 500 companies [5], however, and noted that these large enterprises, which are heavily automated, seem to account for a very significant percentage of total programming skills. If my sampling is fairly representative, then the total employment of the FORTUNE 500 companies amounts to about 14,879,000 employees, with programmers totaling about 344,000. That would be 2.3 percent of the FORTUNE 500 employment: a very significant percentage for an occupation barely 30 years old.

In my demographic studies, I also tried to categorize programming populations both by the kinds of programming being done, and by the kinds of enterprise in which the programmers were employed, as shown in the following two figures:

Type	Number of Programmers
Applications Programmers	315,000
Data Base Programmers	180,000
Systems Programmers	180,000
Real-time Programmers	180,000
Scientific Programmers	45,000
Total	900,000

Figure 1. Estimated U.S. programming population by type.

Figure 1 is based on very limited sampling and is probably not reliable, but it is a starting point for more serious research in the future.

There are many ways of categorizing U.S. employment, but I selected ten overall categories: 1) Civilian Government from local through national; 2) Military; 3) Manufacturing; 4) Financial/Insurance; 5) Computing Industry; 6) Retailing; 7) Services; 8) Energy; 9) Education; and 10) Other. Figure 2 gives my demographic estimate by enterprise type:

Enterprise	Number of Programmers
Government	199,350
Military	74,250
Manufacturing	195,300
Financial/Insurance	76,950
Computing Industry	117,450
Services	43,200
Energy	63,900
Education	47,700
Other	28,800
Total	900,000

Figure 2. Estimated U.S. programming population by enterprise.

I also estimated the number of enterprises or government agencies that employed software personnel, and in 1983 the approximate number I came up with was about 32,000. Although this estimate was partly speculation, the International Data Corporation (IDC) published a fairly authoritative report on the number of computer installations in the 100 largest U.S. metropolitan areas [6]; the total number of sites having installed computers was 27,672.

The IDC study also had other interesting information: the total installed value of the computing equipment was reported to be $43,901,000,000, which averages to about $1,586,477 per site.

The IDC study brings up a point. For some classes of enterprise, such as large banks and insurance companies, large computer corporations, telecommunication corporations, and the like, there are many with more than 1,000 programmers working at a single location, where the total capital equipment in computing and peripherals would exceed $1,000,000,000 if it were purchased.

Figure 3 gives my rough breakdown of the size ranges of programming staffs within U.S. enterprises and government agencies:

Staff Sizes	Number of Enterprises	Average Staff Size	Total Programmers
More than 1,000	200	1,200	240,000
More than 100	1,800	200	360,000
More than 10	10,000	20	200,000
More than 1	20,000	5	100,000
Total	32,000	28	900,000

Figure 3. Estimated number of programmers per computer site for United States enterprises.

Here, too, the information is based on very limited sampling and is partly speculative, but the data will serve as a starting point for more serious research. The table in Figure 3 excludes private consultants and one-person companies, which I estimate at about 50,000 in 1983.

It is interesting that the programming industry is experiencing a fairly unusual trend currently. For the first 25 years of the approximate 30-year history of commercial software, the work and the programmers tended to be heavily concentrated in a small number of very large commercial and governmental enterprises, since computers were so expensive that only such enterprises could afford them. The enormous recent improvements in computer price/performance and the even more recent explosion of microcomputers are causing perhaps the largest number of startups and new small businesses in American history. As this is being written, there are over 3,000 new U.S. retail outlets for software and microcomputers, and probably more than 15,000 new U.S. corporations less than five years old that deal with computers, peripherals, software, consulting, and related services. Not since the Gold Rush in California has there been such a huge migration into a new area.

In 1982, the United States had almost 42,000,000 full-time students in primary and secondary schools, and about 6,000,000 in colleges and universities. [7] About 5,000,000 of the primary and secondary school children are taking some form of training in programming, and the number may be increasing by 2,000,000 per year. At the university level, some colleges such as Carnegie Mellon are actually requiring computer ownership on the part of all students, while a majority have at least courses in computer literacy, and many have full-fledged computer science schools. Perhaps 1,000,000 college students have or are taking at least introductory programming courses.

These figures appear likely to grow even larger with time, and it can be estimated that by the end of the 20th century, at least 50,000,000 U.S. citizens will have a working knowledge of computers and programming, while the number of U.S. professional programmers may grow to 3,000,000. The probable ownership of personal computers at the end of the century, assuming a total U.S. population of about 300,000,000 people, may exceed 25,000,000 units.

On a worldwide basis, the number of people who have had at least some training in programming and computers should exceed 200,000,000 by the end of the 20th century. The total of professional programmers may exceed 10,000,000 employees.

If the working population of the United States at the end of the 20th century is approximately 130,000,000 employees, of whom 3,000,000 are computer programmers, then the percentage would be 2.3 percent: a very significant number. In high-technology enterprises and large computer companies, as well as in software houses, the percentage of software employees will of course be much higher. If hardware, marketing, service, peripheral manufacturing, and computing research groups are considered, the total number of employees at the end of the century should exceed 10,000,000, or 7.69 percent of the U.S. work force.

The United States appears to be in transition from concentration in manufacturing to concentration in services, and the computing and software domain is likely to become one of the most significant industrial segments in all U.S. history.

It is widely stated that the output of computer science graduates in the U.S. has not kept pace with the demand for programmers, and that appears to be true. What is not widely realized, however, is that both private educational institutions and large corporations are adding to the total supply of programmers. Indeed, it is speculated that the FORTUNE 500 companies have in-house education staffs that may, collectively, exceed the total faculty size of all U.S. university computer science departments.

The demographic phenomena associated with computers and programming may turn out to be among the most significant in all human history. Even in 1983, computer technology has had a major impact on science, and widespread knowledge about and ownership of personal computers should introduce significant changes in our daily lives, about which we can only speculate today.

Technical Trends

Those of us who use computers for research and scientific purposes are aware that computers are starting to serve as tools for the human mind. That is, computers are extending the ranges of problems that humans can explore.

Some of the problem areas that computers are aiding include aeronautical design, astronomical research, chemical analysis, demographic analysis, economic modeling, energy optimization, linguistics, mathematics, medical analysis, physics, psychology, and many others. As a small experiment, I tried to enumerate the human occupations that had been impacted by computers, and my list contained over 300 entries.

For this paper, however, the subject under discussion will be the technical trends in the computing and software fields themselves, rather than the technical trends that computing and software are introducing into other disciplines.

Information Analysis

As all of you know, one of the origins of the modern computer industry was Herman Hollerith's work on punched card equipment to automate the calculations of the 1890 U.S. census. [8] From then until today, perhaps the most common application of computers in the world has been the manipulation of large volumes of data that go beyond the capacities of unaided human beings.

This need to manipulate data, and to convert raw data into useful information, has been partly responsible for two major fields of research. The first was the development of computers themselves, and the second is an emerging science that can provisionally be called "information analysis." The domain of information analysis includes all the ways to encode data, store it, search it out, modify it, and convert it into useful information. In other words, "information analysis" is a superset of the research going on in the fields of data base design, management information, decision support, and data communication.

Prior to the advent of computers and computer storage of data, enterprises used information without really thinking much about it. Because of the fairly expensive storage costs for data in the early days of the computer industry, enterprises and researchers started to think a great deal about data: What do we really need, how can we access it, and how do we keep it safe from damage and harm?

These considerations gave rise to the concepts of sequential files, random files, indexed sequential files, hierarchical file structures, network file structures, relational file structures, and many other concepts. They also gave rise to the fields of business information planning, management information, enterprise analysis, and most recently, decision support.

To convert these various concepts into a unified science, however, some form of global theoretical structure is needed. This structure is starting to take shape in the recognition that information is the driving force of enterprises, and the computing complex should be optimized to provide that information.

To optimize the use of computers to provide information, a new kind of software architecture has emerged in which the design of software systems begins by analyzing the data and information needs of the enterprise and its users. The functions of the software systems are then derived from analyzing the various data transformations that will take place. Also, since "information" is the output of a system while "data" is the input, this new architecture begins by exploring the output side of a system in terms of the information items that are to be delivered, rather than beginning at the input side or the raw data that will be collected.

The three names most widely associated with this new software architecture are Jean-Dominique Warnier [9, 10], Ken Orr [11, 12], and Michael Jackson [13]. The emerging science of information analysis is not yet a mature one, however, and many future extensions can be anticipated.

One of the more significant extensions will be widening the concepts of both data and information so they include visual information such as graphics, audible information such as voice, and some form of "information calculus" to deal with changes in the value of information over the passage of time.

As Kendall [14] and Copeland [15] have pointed out, the high costs of data storage until recently have caused some unfortunate limitations. One is the concept of having active files that contain only the current values of records, whereas past values are relegated to archive tapes, if they are saved at all. This makes an entire class of application difficult: the class that explores rates of change through time, or that seeks to examine prior values of important records.

Now that optical memory and perpendicular magnetic recording are about to reach the commercial marketplace, data storage should be reduced so much in cost as to become almost "free."

This is likely to result in two significant changes. One of them is that rather than updating a record when its value changes as is done today, a brand new date-stamped and time-stamped record will be created, and the prior value will remain in active storage for use if needed. The second change is that information about data, i.e., header records, can be enormously extended until this supplemental information actually takes more storage than the record values. The purpose of this second change is data reusability, to allow programs to access information without needing prior agreements between programmers and data administrators.

The end results of the emerging science of information analysis by the end of the decade should be these:

- New classes of application areas, such as those dealing with temporal and chronological variations, to which computing power may be applied.

- Data base systems and data dictionaries that are extended to include graphics and voice records, as well as conventional alphanumeric information.

- The ability to bring hundreds or thousands of separate information items to bear on key problems, such as those dealing with medical issues, epidemiology, meteorology, economic planning, and the like.

- Corporate information centers and decision support systems that go far beyond today's norms in the volume of data stored, the ability to search through the data and combine topics of interest, and the ability to access pertinent information with very little effort.

Conceptual Symbology

Once the importance of information analysis is realized, the next issue that presents itself is that of how human beings can make use of information in the most effective ways. It is obvious that ordinary reading will not be sufficient, because the amount of information that can now be applied to any significant technical problem would go beyond the lifetime reading speed of an average human, even if he or she read steadily for eight hours every day from the age of 21 until the age of 72.

Researchers from the domains of psychology, linguistics, education, and computer science have been relatively active in exploring this issue. It is turning out to be important enough that it may be the seed of an entirely new science, which might be called "conceptual symbology," the study of symbolizing and transmitting information in the most efficient way possible from human to human.

It has been known for many years that human memories have both a short-term and a long-term component. Short-term memory is used as a staging area for information that is symbolized by words, text, and characters. It is usually limited to about seven "chunks" of information, and requires frequent refreshment to keep information from being forgotten. This is why we spontaneously tend to repeat telephone numbers to ourselves: the purpose is to refresh short-term memory to keep the information available until we can write it down, or shift it into permanent memory.

Long-term memory is not fully understood even in 1983, but some current hypotheses are that long-term memories may be holographically distributed over much of the surface of the brain, and that long-term memories are not purely electrical phenomena, but also have a biochemical component.

What makes the distinction between long-term and short-term memory important in the context of computing is the observation that some kinds of information, such as pictures and graphical information, may go directly from the optical system into long-term memory without passing through short-term memory at all. Haber [16] performed an interesting set of experiments with textual passages and pictures, in which he noted that pictures could be recalled with very high accuracy after the subjects had seen them for only a short time, while to recall textual passages took effort and refreshment. Incidentally, this appears to be the reason why most of us can recall the faces of people we met only briefly, but have a terrible time remembering their names.

The science that may be on the verge of emerging from such findings is the exploration of what kinds of information hu-

mans can absorb most readily: from textual inputs, from verbal inputs, from graphic or pictorial inputs, or from hybrid combinations of various inputs.

A secondary exploration concerns human factors and the usability of computing systems. This study is starting to come to grips with the issues of what kinds of invocation and control methods are most comfortable and natural for human beings to use when interfacing with computers and on-line information systems.

Some findings of this emerging science are starting to show up in the "iconographic" interfaces of the Xerox STAR workstation, the new Apple Lisa computer, and the Visi-On general interface package that has been announced but is not yet available, where pictorial representations are augmenting and replacing textual menus as the primary means for invoking and controlling computer and software functions. It can be predicted, and should soon be confirmed or challenged by direct experience, that these new kinds of interfaces will make fewer demands on human temporary memories than menus, plus give the psychological impression of being much easier to use than the older menu-driven approach or direct-command approach.

Not only is it becoming possible to utilize computer and software functions via pictures or icons, but there are no intrinsic reasons why graphic programming languages are not possible. But to do meaningful editing or validation on a graphically based source language, the graphics elements have to have some kind of a regular "grammar." Jones [17] describes a class of graphics languages as "derived graphics," where the symbolic elements are derived from set theory, network theory, or the structured programming theorems.

This class of graphical languages is capable of being edited and even compiled, since the pictorial elements are regular and rule driven. Several languages are already in this class, including Warnier/Orr diagrams [11], which are derived from set theory; Nassi-Shneiderman charts [18], which are derived from the structured programming theorems; and the Galileo language [19] for real-time and telecommunications systems, which is derived from network theory.

Most of the experiments with graphics compilation use languages from the class of "derived graphics." If the current query languages and report generators are considered to be fourth-generation languages, then the new visual languages may perhaps be termed fifth-generation languages.

The science of conceptual symbology is very new, but it is already possible to predict that the coupling of psychology and linguistics that is starting to appear in the computing domain will lead to future systems of unparalleled ease of use.

Expert Systems

The term "expert system" means an automated system of some kind that can perform a task about as well as a human being might perform the same task. The task to be performed is assumed to require significant amounts of judgment and the analysis of many variables, such as medical diagnosis, trajectory predictions, navigation, weather prediction, and the like. A phrase similar in meaning to expert system is "knowledge-based system," which is defined as a system where the information that drives the system is embedded within it, rather than having to be supplied by a human user.

The concept of an expert system overlaps the concept of artificial intelligence, or developing a computer system that appears to be able to mimic some aspects of human thinking, such as the construction of general rules from the analysis of many individual phenomena.

When observed closely, human tasks can be divided into two major components: 1) the conscious or rational component; and 2) the intuitive or unconscious component. Most work in expert systems and artificial intelligence is only concerned with replication of the conscious and rational components of human problem solving.

Because of the natural limitations of human temporary memories, there is a human tendency when faced with large and complex problems to simplify them and break them down into a series of smaller and easier problems. This tendency is even more extreme when the problem requires numerous computations. For example, Diaconis and Efron [20] observed that most statistical methods were developed between 1800 and 1930 when computation was very slow and time consuming, and hence a set of assumptions grew up whose primary value was to ease computation, rather than to add statistical rigor. Now that computers are available, a new class of statistical techniques is emerging that may take millions of calculations, but that can greatly improve the accuracy of statistical analysis.

Essentially any human activity that requires more than a few dozen calculations, or the simultaneous evaluation of more than perhaps half a dozen variable items, is a candidate for a potential expert system. The more calculations and variable items involved, the greater the probable value of an expert system to aid human practitioners. As Feigenbaum and McCorduck [21] observe, the world is full of real problems where the complexity and information volume goes beyond convenient human processing, and knowledge-based systems would be useful aids to human practitioners.

In the computing, software, and information management domains, the potential value of expert systems is very great. For example, to estimate the schedules, resources, and costs of developing a new programming system requires the analysis of more than 75 variable items, and the performance of more than 1,000 calculations. Knowledge-based estimating systems are already being experimented with that can outperform most human managers.

It can be anticipated that by the end of the decade, it should be possible for software managers to simply "dial in" a description of the kinds of programs they have been asked to produce. In return, an expert system would point out the tools and methods that have given the best results for such programs, the schedules and costs that are likely to occur, a probable work-breakdown structure for the programs, the quality and reliability of the finished programs, and even the specific kinds of documents and user information that should be produced.

Two significant precursors leading to full-scale expert systems in the areas of software planning, management, and development will be advances in the emerging sciences of information analysis and conceptual symbology, with the first supplying much of the information on which

expert systems can be based, and the second supplying the mechanisms by which human users can most effectively employ the expert systems and interact with them.

Following are a few of the potential software-oriented expert system domains that show significant potentials.

Expert Planning and Estimating Systems

- Knowledge-based estimating tool for schedules, effort, costs, quality, and reliability that will project several hundred discrete activities with an overall accuracy of plus or minus 10 percent.

- Reverse estimating tool that accepts targets and constraints as inputs, and predicts the optimal set of tools and methods to maximize the probability of achieving the targets.

- Work-breakdown structure tool that will project the specific tasks and activities and the optimum department and team structures for any class of software project.

Expert Decision Support and Data Base Systems

- Knowledge-based data dictionary construction tool that is predefined with skeleton descriptors for specific enterprise classes (banks, insurance companies, state and local governments, etc.). This kind of expert system is prefaced on the emerging science of information analysis.

- Knowledge-based logical and physical data base design tool that will select optimal data configurations for major enterprise classes and application types.

- Knowledge-based bid and contract support tools for standard commercial contracts and government contracts.

Expert Requirements and Design Systems

- Knowledge-based requirements tool customized for major enterprise classes and application types, which would include skeleton outlines for requirements and in-depth knowledge of key areas such as security.

- Knowledge-based design tool that will describe optimal component and module structures for major application types such as accounting systems, insurance claims handling, check processing, etc. The tool would also describe the optimal output information, input data, query methods, etc.

- Knowledge-based tool that catalogs all existing reusable modules and code segments that can be utilized in the development of new programs.

Expert Documentation Systems

- Knowledge-based system with skeleton outlines and content guides for all standard document types supporting software project (User's Guides, Maintenance Manuals, etc.). Such a system would also support documentation types produced in accordance with military specifications.

- Knowledge-based system to aid in selecting menus, graphics, screen formats, etc. tailored to optimal human understanding when invoking and using interactive systems. This kind of system is prefaced on the emerging science of conceptual symbology.

- Knowledge-based spelling and syntax checkers with 100,000-word dictionaries in multiple languages, plus scientific and technical terms.

Expert Development Support Systems

- Knowledge-based system with optimal skeleton structures for major application types, and a linked catalog of reusable functional modules. The system would also be coupled to an optimal test library keyed to the specific attributes of major application types.

- Knowledge-based data definition tool keyed to the specific attributes of major application types, and suggesting appropriate data structures.

Expert Maintenance Support Systems

- Knowledge-based system that allows maintenance personnel to enter the symptoms that were noted when a fault occurred, will check to see if other users experienced the same fault, and if so, whether or not a fix is already available.

Although there are many other possibilities for expert systems in the field of software, the previous examples give the general flavor of the tools that are likely to appear before 1990, and that are almost certain to appear before the end of the 20th century.

Summary and Conclusions

The computing industry in all its forms— hardware, software, marketing, maintenance, and research—is already one of the largest and most significant business segments of the United States and other industrialized nations. If current trends continue, then by the end of the 20th century, the computing industry may become the fourth largest employer in all human history, only ranking behind agriculture, government service, and military service in total numbers of employees.

Not only is the computing industry large in economic terms, but its impact on both science and daily life has been one of the most significant in all of human history. Computers are starting to serve as tools for the human mind, and are allowing problems to be analyzed and solved that previously could not be dealt with because the volume of computations or the amount of data exceeded the capacities of unaided workers.

Because computers can deal with very large volumes of data, the appearance of computers in world industry may be on the verge of creating two new sciences: information analysis, or the study of optimal ways for encoding, storing, organizing, and searching large data collections; and conceptual symbology, or the study of the optimal methods for representing information so human beings can understand the meaning most easily.

Finally, these two emerging sciences may be recursively leading to new generations of expert systems that will aid programming practitioners in the requirements analysis, design, development, and maintenance of software systems.

REFERENCES

[1]   Watson, T.J. Interview in *Computerworld,* Vol. 17, No. 24, June 13, 1983.

[2]   Marsiniak, J. "Computing Industry." *Proceedings of the National Computer Conference,* Anaheim, Calif., May 1983.

[3]   1981 U.S. Industrial Outlook for 200 Industries with Projections for 1985. U.S. Department of Commerce, Bureau of Industrial Economics. U.S. Government Printing Office, Washington, D.C., 1981 (updated annually).

[4]   *The Hammond Almanac.* Hammond Almanac, 1982 ed., p. 204.

[5]   The *Fortune* Directory of the Largest U.S. Industrial Corporations. *Fortune,* May 2, 1983, pp. 226-47.

[6]   International Data Corporation, quoted in *Computer Careers.* New York: Fawcett Columbine, 1981, pp. 150-53.

[7]   *The World Almanac and Book of Facts 1982.* Newspaper Enterprise Association, 1981, pp. 165-92.

[8]   Goldstine, H.H. *The Computer from Pascal to Von Neumann.* Princeton, N.J.: Princeton University Press, 1972, pp. 65-70.

[9]   Warnier, J.-D. *Logical Construction of Programs.* New York: Van Nostrand Reinhold, 1976.

[10]   _____. *Logical Construction of Systems.* New York: Van Nostrand Reinhold, 1981.

[11] Orr, K.T. *Structured Systems Development*. New York: Yourdon Press, 1977.

[12] _____ . *Structured Requirements Definition*. Topeka, Kan.: Ken Orr & Associates, 1981.

[13] Jackson, M.A. *Principles of Program Design*. New York: Academic Press, 1965.

[14] Kendall, R.C. *An Architecture for Reusability in Programming*. Stratford, Conn.: ITT Programming, May 1983.

[15] Copeland, G. "What If Mass Storage Were Free?" *IEEE Computer Magazine,* July 1982, pp. 27-37.

[16] Haber, R.N. "How We Remember What We See," *Scientific American,* Vol. 222, No. 5, May 1970, pp. 104-12.

[17] Jones, C. "Programming Productivity: Issues for the Eighties." New York: IEEE Computer Society, Catalog No. 391, 1981, pp. 221-35.

[18] Yoder, C.M., and M.L. Schrag, "Nassi-Shneiderman Charts—An Alternative to Flowcharts," *Proceedings of SIGSOFT/SIGMETRICS Software and Assurance Workshop,* November 1978, pp. 386-93.

[19] Vidondo, F., I. Lopez, and J.J. Girod, "Galileo System Design Method." *ITT Electrical Communication,* Vol. 17, No. 1, November 1980.

[20] Diaconis, P., and B. Efron. "Computer-Intensive Methods in Statistics," *Scientific American,* Vol. 248, No. 5, May 1983.

[21] Feigenbaum, E.A., and P. McCorduck. *The Fifth Generation*. Reading, Mass.: Addison Wesley, 1983, pp. 61-94.

Part III
Methods

14

Editors' Note
Boehm et al.: "A Software Development Environment for Improving Productivity"

Insight: Significant productivity improvement is not likely to be brought about through any single measure. What is required is a coordinated and multi-faceted approach.

Chances are that you are as much bombarded as we are with claims of enormous productivity gains said to result from installing this package or that methodology or the other training sequence. They urge you to make a single change in your development approach and see productivity go through the roof. (Nobody talks about improvements of a mere twenty or thirty percent anymore, it's always hundreds or even thousands of percent.) If you were not born an eternal optimist, you're probably fast becoming a skeptic.

This paper from TRW presents a more considered view of productivity. It indicates that no single step you might take is going to reap much real improvement in productivity. Rather, it is the redesign of the entire working "environment" that is required. That means productivity improvement is going to be expensive in terms of initial investment in people, training, hardware, support tools, and the programmer workplace.

The paper is gently optimistic compared to the near hysteria of most articles about productivity. But it's *believable.*

14

A Software Development Environment for Improving Productivity
by Barry W. Boehm, Maria H. Penedo, E. Don Stuckle, Robert D. Williams, and Arthur B. Pyster

A major effort at improving productivity at TRW led to the creation of the software productivity project, or SPP, in 1981. The major thrust of this project is the establishment of a software development environment to support project activities; this environment is called the software productivity system, or SPS. It involves a set of strategies, including the work environment; the evaluation and procurement of hardware equipment; the provision for immediate access to computing resources through local area networks; the building of an integrated set of tools to support the software development life cycle and all project personnel; and a user support function to transfer new technology. All of these strategies are being accomplished incrementally. The current architecture is Vax-based and uses the Unix operating system, a wideband local network, and a set of software tools.

This article* describes the steps that led to the creation of the SPP, summarizes the requirements analyses on which the SPS is based, describes the components which make up the SPS, and presents our conclusions.

---

*An earlier version of this article, entitled "The TRW Software Productivity System," was presented at the Sixth International Conference on Software Engineering.

SPS REQUIREMENTS ANALYSIS

A software productivity study was performed at TRW during 1980. This study analyzed the requirements for a company-oriented software support environment, evaluated the technology base available for such a support environment and the likely trends in that base, and performed an economic analysis to determine whether a significant level of investment into software productivity aids would be justified. In the following paragraphs, each analysis is summarized, followed by the study's conclusions and recommendations.

Corporate Motivating Factors

Various factors have motivated a more substantial level of corporate investment for improving software productivity in recent years, including (1) increased demand for software, (2) limited supply of software engineers, (3) rising software engineer support expectations, and (4) reduced hardware costs.

Increased demand for software. Each successive generation of a data processing system experiences a significant increase in demand for software functionality. For example, manned spaceflight software support functions grew from 1.5 million object code instructions for the 1961 Mercury program to over 40 million object instructions for the 1980 space shuttle program. [1] The growth in corporate shipments of delivered software has experienced a similar increase and the rate of increase in demand appears to be growing rather than slackening.

Limited supply of software engineers. Several sources [2, 3] have indicated that the current U.S. shortage of software personnel is between 50,000 and 100,000 people and that the suppliers (primarily university computer science departments) do not have sufficient resources to meet the future demand.

Rising software engineer support expectations. Good software engineers are, in general, no longer satisfied to work with inadequate tools and a poor work environment. Successful hiring and retention of good software engineers requires an effective corporate software support environment.

Reduced hardware costs. The cost and performance improvements of supermini mainframes, powerful personal microcomputers, database machines, graphics devices, and broadband communication systems permit significantly more powerful and cost-effective software support systems.

The 1980 Software Productivity Study

Given the preceding motivating factors, an extensive study of corporate objectives, requirements, and alternatives was done in 1980. The study included an internal assessment, an external assessment, and a quantitative analysis, which led to recommended strategies for improving software productivity.

Internal assessment. Our internal assessment began with a series of interviews with representative high-level and intermediate-level managers and software performers. Each person interviewed was asked, "If there were only two or three things we could do to improve your software productivity, what would they be?"

In general, those interviewed were highly enthusiastic and provided a wide range of attractive suggestions for improving productivity. There was a general consensus that the primary avenues for improving software productivity were in the areas of management actions, work environment and compensation, education and training, and software tools. For example, Figure 1 shows the relative importance of these four areas from the standpoint of three classes of personnel: upper managers, middle managers, and performers.

It is evident from Figure 1, though, that the consensus was not universal. For example, the upper managers' worldview conditions them to see management actions as the high-leverage items, while the performers'—that is, nonmanagers such as engineers, analysts, and programmers— worldview conditions them to see software tools as providing the most leverage. The important point is not which group is more correct, but that each group brings a valid set of perceptions to bear on the problem. Furthermore, since motivation is such a key factor in software productivity, people's perceptions are an important consideration.

Software support environment requirements. Another portion of the internal assessment involved an analysis of our software support environment requirements. Since the DoD Ada Stoneman requirements document [4] had recently provided an excellent general definition of software

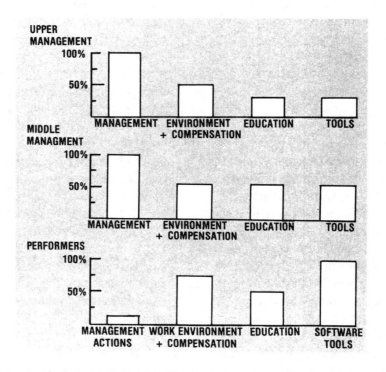

Figure 1. Responses or perceptions of major needs in software productivity. Upper managers, middle managers, and performers were asked "If there were only two or three things you could get TRW to do to improve software productivity, what would they be?"

support environment requirements for Ada, we used Stoneman as a baseline and focused on identifying the following additional company-specific environment requirements not included in Stoneman.

(1) *Support of multiple-programming languages.* The internal assessment included a forecast of the evolution of our government-systems business base, including its distribution by programming language. It showed that even though DoD is strongly committed to Ada for its new starts, there is likely to be a significant segment of software projects consisting of compatible developments and maintenance for existing Fortran and Jovial systems. Thus, a pure Ada-based environment would not support all of our needs even by the year 2000.

(2) *Support of mixed target-machine complexes.* A similar forecast of the hardware nature of our future business base indicated a strong trend towards distributed target-machine complexes with a wide range of computer types (micros, minis, and mainframes from different vendors). Although the concept of the Ada program support environment may provide a unified environment supported on each computer in such complexes, experience to date on such environments as the National Software Works indicates that a number of outstanding problems need to be resolved before this approach can be counted on.

(3) *Support of classified projects.* Much of our business involves classified projects for DoD. Such projects have severe access constraints and require extensive precautions to enforce those restrictions. Participation in a single corporate-wide network with shared data and programs would not be feasible for classified projects. The state of the art does not ensure such security in a wide-area network that would necessarily use insecure communications media. An alternative approach is to have a collection of local networks, each of which can individually impose tight security arrangements. A classified project could then use a single local network within a restricted area.

(4) *Integration with existing programs and data.* The company has a large collection of partially integrated programs and databases to support project activities, particularly in the areas of cost and schedule management. It is not practical to discard all of these at one time because of the large financial investment required to replace them. New tools must be integrated with this existing base of programs and data.

(5) *Support of nonprogramming activities.* Studies indicate that about two thirds of the time spent on a large software project results in documentation as its direct product, and only one third results in code as its direct product (see Figure 2). [1] For example, software requirements analysis and the preliminary design phases typically produce no code at all and may not even be performed by programmers. Even in the coding phase, peripheral activities—such as the generation of unit test plans, memos, and reports—consume a significant percentage of a programmer's

time. Since one of our goals is to support all efforts of all project personnel, the development and integration of word processing, calendar management, spreadsheet, and other office automation capabilities into the software development environment are required.

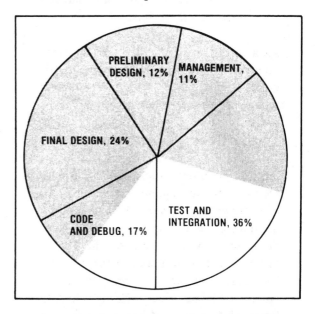

Figure 2. A breakdown of software development costs. The shaded area denotes the portion of project time used to produce documentation. The nonshaded area denotes the portion of project time used to produce code.

Uncertainty areas. In trying to determine the specific needs of project personnel, we encountered a wide variety of user opinions on such items as

• tool priorities (development, management, office support);

• attribute priorities (efficiency, extensibility, ease of use by experts versus novices);

• degree of methodology enforcement

(for example, do tools assume requirements are written in a specific requirements specification language or are they methodology independent?); and

- command language characteristics (such as menu versus command and terse versus verbose).

As a result, we concluded that it would be an extremely time-consuming, inefficient, and uncertain process to obtain universal concurrence on requirements for our software support environment. Thus, we decided to build the environment incrementally, using prototypes and incorporating both our experimental and user feedback in subsequent increments.

External assessment. The 1980 study included visits to a number of organizations with experience or active R&D programs on software support environments. The industrial organizations visited included IBM-Santa Teresa, Xerox Palo Alto Research Center, Bell Laboratories, and Fujitsu; the universities included Stanford, MIT, Harvard, and Carnegie-Mellon. The primary conclusions resulting from these visits were

(1)   Organizations investing in significant improvements in their software environments felt they were getting their money's worth. Some, such as IBM [5] and Bell Labs [6], were able to at least partially quantify their resulting benefits.

(2)   Organizations achieving some integration of software development support capabilities and office automation capabilities considered this a high-payoff step.

(3)   Organizations providing office facilities oriented towards the needs of software personnel (privacy; quiet; comfortable and functional furniture) such as IBM-Santa Teresa [7], felt the investment was highly worthwhile.

(4)   Significant progress was being made toward providing very high power personal workstation terminals (with high-resolution, bit-mapped displays supporting window editors, integrated text, and graphics and well-integrated screen-pointing devices) at a reasonable cost.

(5)   No system we saw provided all the capabilities required.

Quantitative assessment. Our quantitative assessment of alternative avenues for improving software productivity was based primarily on TRW's software cost estimation program, or SCEP. SCEP is similar in form to the *Cocomo* model described in detail elsewhere. [1] It estimates the cost of a software project as a function of program size in delivered source instructions, or DSI, and a number of other cost driver attributes summarized in Figure 3. Figure 3 shows the productivity range for each attribute. Thus, the 1.49 productivity range for the software tools attribute results from an analysis indicating that, all other factors being equal, a project with a very low level of tool support will require 1.49 times the effort required for a project with a very high level of tool support. The "very high" and "very low" ratings correspond to specific levels on a Cocomo rating scale for tool support. [1]

The software tools' rating scales and those of the other cost driver attributes

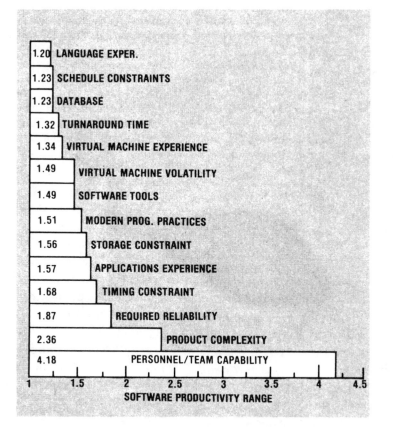

Figure 3.   Comparative software productivity ranges.   The overall impact of tools on software productivity can be determined, for example, in this way: If 1.24 = very low tool support and 0.83 = very high tool support, then the total impact is 1.24/0.83 = 1.49.

were used to conduct a "productivity audit" of our projects, to determine the weighted-average productivity multipliers characteristic of the overall distribution of software projects, both at present and for several future scenarios representing varying levels of company investment into productivity improvement programs. Table 1 summarizes a typical analysis of this nature. It shows that a productivity improvement program achieving several cost driver attribute improvements in parallel could improve productivity by a factor of 3.4 by 1985 and by a factor of 7.8 by 1990. Besides providing an estimated produc-

tivity gain, this analysis provided insights for determining which items (such as tools) to emphasize as part of a productivity improvement strategy. It also provides a valuable framework for tracking the actual progress of the productivity program and for determining whether its goals are actually being achieved.

Study conclusions. The 1980 productivity study reached some major conclusions. First, *significant productivity gains require an integrated program of initiatives in several areas.* These areas include improvements in tools, methodology, work environment, education, management, personal incentives, and software reuse. A fully effective software support environment requires integration of software tools and office automation capabilities. Second, *an integrated software productivity improvement program can have an extremely large payoff.* Productivity gains by factors of two in five years and factors of four in 10 years are generally achievable and are worth a good deal of planning and investment. Third, *improving software productivity involves a long, sustained effort.* The payoffs are large, but they require a long-range commitment. There are no easy, instant panaceas. Fourth, *in the very long run the biggest productivity gains will come from increasing use of existing software.* This requires building general tools and utilities suitable for reusability. Fifth and last, *software support environment requirements are still too incompletely understood to specify precisely.* In this respect, software support environments fall into an extensive category of man-machine systems whose user requirements are not completely understood.

Table 1.
Evaluation of Overall Productivity Strategy.

COCOMO ATTRIBUTE	WEIGHTED AVERAGE MULTIPLIER		
	1981	1985	1990
Use of Software Tools	1.05	0.94	0.88
Modern Programming Practices	1.07	0.89	0.83
Computer Response Time	1.02	0.91	0.89
Analyst Capability	1.00	0.88	0.80
Programmer Capability	1.05	0.90	0.80
Virtual Machine Volatility	1.06	0.95	0.90
Requirements Volatility	1.27	1.08	1.00
Use of Existing Software	0.90	0.70	0.50
Cumulative Multiplier	1.46	0.34	0.19
Productivity Gain		3.4	7.8

Study recommendations. Based on these conclusions, the 1980 study made several recommendations. First, *initiate a significant long-range effort to improve software productivity.* The recommended effort included initiatives in all areas of tools, methodology, work environment, education, management, personal incentives, and software reuse, and established goals of improving software productivity by (1) a factor of two by 1985, and (2) a factor of four by 1990. Although these goals are conservative with respect to the estimated productivity gains cited in the quantitative assessment, they are clearly large enough to justify a significant investment into a productivity improvement program. Second, *establish a software productivity project with responsibility for establishing a software development environment.* A single focal point is needed in order to be able to effectively produce the SPS environment. Third, *develop SPS incrementally.* Given that the SPS requirements and some of the technology issues were not completely understood, incremental development was the most effective strategy for proceeding. Fourth, *commit to using SPS on a large production software project.* This ensured that SPS would be realistic and that early feedback from its use could affect later increments. Fifth and last, *measure the impact of SPS on its users' productivity.* This helps determine whether the SPS is having the desired effect and helps shape requirements for future SPS increments.

SPS ARCHITECTURE AND COMPONENTS

On the basis of our preliminary conclusions, SPP was established in January 1981 to implement the SPS. This internally funded project's mission is to develop a fully integrated TRW software development environment. We recognize this goal is very ambitious, but we believe significant progress toward that goal will generate the desired productivity gains. The average number of people working on SPP over the last three years is 14, excluding personnel supporting the computing facilities.

The four major areas of the SPS environment are (1) *Work environment*—define better work environments, which includes providing private offices and immediate access to computing facilities; (2) *Hardware*—evaluate and procure new hardware equipment, including computers, printers, and local area networks; (3) *Master project database*—define and implement a master project database that contains all information relevant to project activities including budget, personnel, schedules, and other managerial data in addition to such technical information as software requirements, design, test procedures, and code; and (4) *Software*—provide an integrated tool set, supporting the entire software development life cycle with convenient access to the master project database.

Following the study recommendations, the work was to be done incrementally and a large production project was chosen to benefit from the improvements provided by SPS. These facts had an impact on the initial SPS requirements and implementation, since hardware decisions had to be made with current technology and availability and tool priorities were highly influenced by production project user needs. From 1981 to the present, progress has been made in all the preceding areas.

The most success achieved has been in the work environment; the most work remains to be done in producing an integrated master project database and a fully integrated set of tools. The remainder of this section describes the current state of each component, indicates the short-range compromises, and explains envisioned improvements.

Work Environment

SPS work in this area involved evaluating current office facilities and environmental conditions of project personnel, experimenting, and proposing a new environment. Typically, technical staff members work in relatively Spartan offices shared by two or sometimes three people. Large programming "bullpens" are a rarity; however, private offices are also a rarity and are provided on a space-available basis only. Standard functional business desks, filing cabinets, chairs, and bookcases adorn each office. Except in several leased buildings, there is typically no carpeting or wallpaper; however, each office usually has floor-to-ceiling walls with a closable door.

SPP proposed a *productivity environment* which includes (1) private offices of approximately 90 to 100 square feet with floor-to-ceiling walls, carpeting, soundproofing, an ergonomic chair, adequate work space, storage, and lighting; and (2) a terminal or personal workstation for each office, with a high-speed network connection to a number of computers, file servers, and printers. As part of the experiment, 39 productivity offices were constructed in one of our major facilities. A broadband coaxial cable was installed in this building and the office occupants had access to eight Vax computers through a local area network. These offices housed both SPP personnel and the supported project personnel. Two surveys of occupants conducted six months apart indicate that this productivity work environment had a real impact on their daily activities (see "Usage Measurement").

With the successful completion of the work environment experiment, the responsibility of building productivity facilities and cabling other buildings has been transferred to another organization. Currently, the lessons learned from this experiment are being incorporated into new company facilities and many other existing buildings are being cabled to provide LANs. Over the next several years, plans call for cabling virtually all major buildings within the TRW Redondo Beach complex.

Hardware

The current SPS architecture is shown in Figure 4. It supports a broadband local area network that has been operational since January 1982. Currently, approximately 200 users share this network. As more buildings are cabled, that number is expected to rise sharply. The network is used primarily for high-speed terminal-to-computer communications (up to 19.2K baud).

SPS is based on the source/target concept of operation; that is, the source development machine hosts the integrated

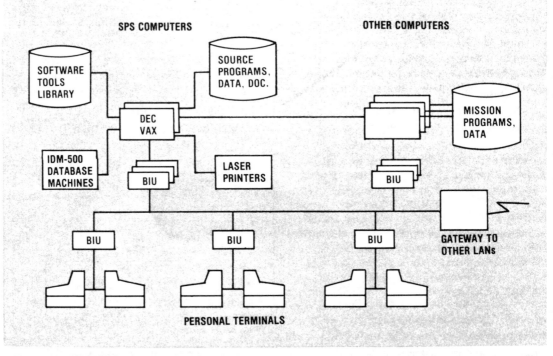

Figure 4. The SPS architecture. Two logically separate local area networks actually share the trunk cable: TRW's own network, supported by its standard bus interface units, or BIUs, and the Sytek Localnet 20.

tool set and the master project database. The source development machine can be reproduced from project to project providing the same source environment independent of the type of target machine. Currently, the configuration is centralized and the source machine is a Vax 11/780, which runs the Unix operating system as illustrated in Figure 4. An IDM-500 database machine and laser printers are attached to the source machine. In 1984, two more Vax machines will be added to the existing configuration, linked together through an Ethernet.

The LAN is a general utility that can be used by projects not using either Unix or SPS software. For example, one major project has eight Vax computers, all of which are attached to the LAN. Seven run VMS; one runs Unix with the full complement of SPP-developed software. Other large non-Unix machines, such as a large IBM mainframe used for business applications, will likely be connected to the LAN within the next year.

Several company computers running Unix are connected by way of a UUCP mail service and belong to the Usenet Unix network. Mail is exchanged daily with many sites around the country. Additionally, a Eunice Unix emulator furnished by the Wollengong Group permits electronic mail and file transfer service between the Unix and VMS machines.

It was realized early in the project that, as the SPS user community expanded, a centralized configuration using several Vax machines would rapidly become saturated. Thus, as early as 1981, personal workstations started being considered. Five Digital LSI-11/23-based semipersonal microcomputers (which supported Unix) were purchased for evaluation. However,

because Vax was available and the microcomputers' workstations had performance problems, the LSI-11/23-based microcomputers fell into general disuse. Because of the measurement data collected on SPS tool usage (see "Usage Measurement") we feel we are now in a better position to determine what equipment to purchase next to offload the Vax machines. SPP is currently investigating higher power workstations and microprocessors such as those available from Pyramid, Convergent Technologies, Sun Microsystems, and Apollo.

Master Project Database

As emphasized in the Ada Stoneman requirements document [4], the core of a software support environment is the project master database of software artifacts such as plans, specifications, standards, code, data, and manuals. Figure 5 shows a high level view of this project database. On the left are the various products generated by the project: specifications, code, manuals, and reports. On the right are the various classes or resources required to develop the products: capital dollars, labor dollars, personnel, and computer resources. In the center are the various plans that link the expenditure of resources to the creation of products: development plans, schedules, work breakdown structures, and unit development folders. The upper half of Figure 5 indicates the primary entities in the MPD, generally stored as hierarchical text files with change or version tracking. The lower half of the figure indicates the various attributes of the entities, such as architectural relationships (in the product portion) or traceability relationships (in the plans portion).

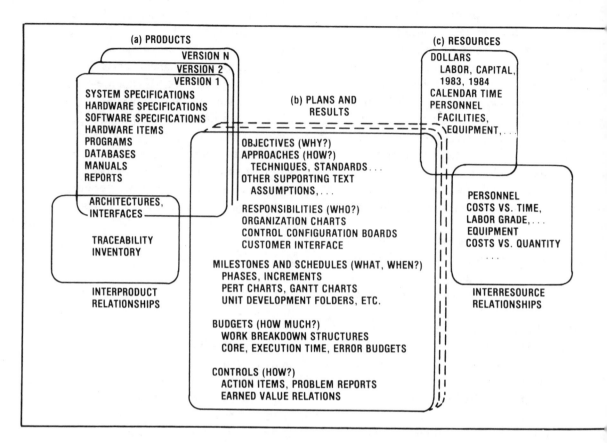

Figure 5. A high-level view of the project master database including (a) products—that is, what the project produces; (b) plans and results—that is, how resources are expended for such activities as product development, testing, maintenance, change control, and resource control; and (c) resources—that is, what the project consumes in developing products.

This master database must support efficient query and update of software artifacts; representation of relations between artifacts (such as requirements traceability), and effective configuration management (version control, change control, problem report tracking, and library management) of the various versions and updates of the software artifacts.

The definition of the contents of this MPS is an ongoing activity. The high-level structure defined is illustrated in Figure 5; the definition of the detailed entities, attributes, and relationships is being addressed as research projects. Some portions have been worked out in enough detail to support the development of key SPS tools such as the requirements traceability tool. Others, such as the entities, attributes, and relationships involved in software project planning and control, have been developed in some detail (see *Software Engineering Economics,* [1] chapter 32) but their implementation is still awaiting the complex job of integrating the SPS master project database with the corporate financial database.

On the basis of an analysis of our previous support environments, proposed Ada programming support environments, or APSEs, and others such as Unix/Programmer's Work Bench [8] and Gandalf [9], we determine that a single underlying database structure would be overly constrained to support a large software project. In the absence of a database management system to support this structure, we elected to use a multidatabase support structure for SPS's current MPD that includes

- *A hierarchical file system for the software artifacts.* This is provided by the Unix file system.

- *An update-tracking system for representing the successive updates of each artifact.* This is provided by the Unix source code control system, or SCCS. [10]

- *A relational database management system for representing the relations between artifacts.* This is currently provided by the Ingres relational DBMS [11, 12] and the IDM-500 database machine.

Integration of the various elements of this structure has been partially achieved; we envision doing much more work in this area in the near future. The MPD as currently organized has provided a solid, workable base for software configuration management for SPS. All baselined source code, manual pages, user's manuals, and other software artifacts are controlled through SCCS in what is called

an electronic maintenance folder, or EMF. All software produced by SPP is stored in a single Unix directory. Under this directory, there is a separate subdirectory for each package—that package's EMF. For example, there is a subdirectory *calendar,* a subdirectory *fillin,* and a subdirectory *menu* for three packages developed by SPP. Each EMF directory is further subdivided into separate subdirectories for source code, documentation, manual pages, test information, requirements, and design. Since the configuration for storing artifacts is uniform for all SPP software, it is a straightforward task to locate the artifacts relating to any version of SPP-developed code.

Using SCCS to guard the artifacts guarantees that no one except the SPP configuration manager may change any controlled document, that all changes are recorded, and that there is full opportunity to recover earlier versions. Through control procedures established by SPP and supported by SCCS, developers and managers have access to and can update a copy of a document without affecting the official baselined copy. In addition to using SCCS for documents controlled at the project level, many SPP members apply SCCS to other documents for subproject or personal use.

Until recently, almost no one outside SPP used SCCS for configuration control. That has been changing over the last few months as people in other projects have become aware of the power that SCCS offers. For example, one large project now baselines system engineering specifications using SCCS. It is expected that usage of SCCS will grow dramatically in the future.

Software

Internal projects develop software for a diverse array of target machines. The hardware requirements for these projects usually determine which operating system is used, and therefore, which software development tools are available. An unfortunate consequence of this diversity is the need to retrain developers when they change projects. One of the major focuses of SPS is to provide a portable software development environment that will operate on many hardware environments. The goal is to make it possible for a developer to change projects yet have a relatively constant software development environment. This would mitigate what is currently a large retraining problem.

Projects usually build a collection of software tools to support their software development. Unfortunately, the need to satisfy its own pressing project commitments typically makes it impractical for a project to design tools for reuse by other projects as a design goal. Such local optimization, while of advantage to the project that builds the tool, leads to considerable global duplication across many projects. SPP is chartered to address this problem by developing software tools useful across many projects. Its tools are crafted for flexibility; for example, SPP has constructed a forms management system in which the form and report formats and content are data driven. This allows different projects to easily create their own forms and reports.

An extensive study of candidate operating systems to support the SPS was performed in 1981. Because of the strong requirement for portability, the need to provide a sound basis for developing a powerful software development environment, and the need for immediate tool availability, SPP decided to use Unix to host its software development environment. SPP began with the large collection of tools offered in the UC Berkeley version of Unix. It has expanded that software base in three ways: building, buying, and porting.

In 1981, a group of software developers and managers identified a small set of software tools to be incorporated in the SPS to support our software development methodology. Since then, on a yearly basis, a new plan of expansion is prepared and coordinated with company management and existing or potential SPS users.

Whereas, the long-term goal is to build a fully integrated environment, short-term needs and limited resources influenced our decision of providing integration only at the level of the tools we build. Thus, tools that were bought and ported are not necessarily integrated with the existing ones. Examples of purchased tools are the Viewcomp spreadsheet calculator from Unicorp and the Ada compiler from the Irvine Computer Science Corporation. Examples of available tools that were obtained free or for a nominal fee from universities and research institutes are the Rand message handler, Wang Institute's Wicomo, Donald Knuth's text formatting language Tex, and Purdue University's revision control system. Occasionally a tool, such as the TRW Fortran 77 analyzer—which was written for another operating system in fairly portable Fortran 77 code—has been rehosted onto Unix by SPP.

The SPS tools built by the project are grouped in three general categories: (1) general utilities, (2) office automation and project support, and (3) software development.

General utilities. Reuse of existing software is being accepted as the most powerful way to improve productivity. Unix already provides a number of library packages that can be readily incorporated into new software—for such mundane tasks as mathematical computation to more interesting operations such as screen management. All software written by SPP takes as much advantage of these packages as possible. SPP has also spent much effort in building general tools and utilities that provide for reusability within the SPS environment. Written in the C programming language, these packages include

Menu, a menu user interface tool, available both at the command level and subroutine level, that (1) provides a simple menu language to allow format and contents of menus to be easily built, (2) supports convenient selection of menu choices, and (3) allows for prompts and help definition on each selection. The package is template-driven, and it handles all the user interaction with the menus. In this manner, any tool that provides menus uses this package, and user interface consistency is achieved across tools. A sample of a menu display is illustrated in Figure 6; this menu is the interface of a front end to the Rand mail system.

Software productivity editor, or Sped, a collection of subroutines that implement a simple screen-oriented editor, compatible with the Unix editor **vi.** It performs simple editing operations such as character insertion, deletion, replacement, and cursor movement operations. Tools can make use of this capability to permit the editing of windows without losing the context. Sped makes it possible for SPP-developed tools that require simple editors

to have a uniform interface.

Fillin, a fill-in-the-blank user interface tool, available both at the command level and subroutine level. It provides a simple form language that allows format and contents of forms to be easily built. The package is template driven, and it handles all the user interaction with the forms. It displays a form on the screen for editing or read-only access, and supports sophisticated editing within fields. Any tool that provides fill-in-the-blank interfaces makes use of this package, and thus user interface consistency is achieved across tools.

Date/time, a set of subroutines that does relatively sophisticated analysis of dates and times; expressions such as "three weeks from next Tuesday at noon" can be parsed, normalized, and displayed in a variety of output formats. Arithmetic operations on times and dates are defined.

Report writer, a set of subroutines to aid in report writing. It takes files containing data, header information, and formatting directions, and produces a new file suitable for processing by **tbl** and **troff**, two standard Unix programs for manipulating tables and performing text formatting. It supports the flexible generation and formatting of reports.

Every time a major application is developed by SPP, an analysis is performed to determine if a reusable library component can be constructed as a by-product of the implementation of that application. Further analysis determines whether already existing libraries can be used to minimize development effort.

Office automation and project support. A software environment must support all project personnel including secretaries, business managers, project managers, as well as technical staff. As illustrated in Figure 2, two thirds of the time spent on a large software project results in documentation (such as activity reports, memoranda, documents, and plans). Thus, SPS includes a large set of tools for office automation and project support, which constitute the automated office. Most of these tools provide both command-oriented and menu-driven access to a number of basic Unix tools relevant to office functions as well as to new tools developed by SPP. A user can choose which interface to use; thus, when a beginner becomes very familiar with a particular tool, going through the menu interface can be avoided. Because of their relative importance, word processing, forms management, electronic mail, and calendar management have received the greatest emphasis.

Large software projects must cope with a wide variety of forms such as software problem reports, change requests, expense reports, purchase requests, travel forms, and data entry forms. To accommodate these in an efficient and unified way, SPP has developed a forms management system, or FMS. With FMS a user can create, edit, summarize, copy, query, and perform a number of other operations on forms both individually and grouped into folders. For example, programmers can maintain a separate folder for each software unit they are developing; each folder containing the problem reports for that unit. Anyone with access to that folder can query on such attributes as whether a problem report is still open or when the problem is to be resolved. Summary reports can be produced on the form instances in the folder. About a third of the FMS consists of software components developed earlier by SPP. For example, the

FMS uses the *fillin* and *report writer* packages.

* <ELECTRONIC MAIL>*

Operation	Synopsis	Unix Command	
>>>co	: Compose a message	comp	
in	: Incorporate new mail	inc	[opts]
ch	: Change current message	folder	[opts]
sh	: Show text of message(s)	show	[opts]
lm	: List messages	scan	[opts]
fw	: Forward message(s)	forw	[opts]
rp	: Reply to message(s)	repl	[opts]
rm	: Remove message(s)	rmm	[opts]
fm	: File message(s)	filemsg	[opts]
pr	: Print text of message(s)	N/A	
rd	: Recover dead letter	N/A	
fd	: Display Folder Menu	N/A	
he	: Help for current menu	N/A	

^Nnext, ^Pprev, <CR>select, !shell, <pop, ?help, #top Mar 16 09:02

Figure 6. The menu for mail messages.

The SPS automated office differs from most of its commercial counterparts in that it is not a self-contained system complete with a menu-driven interface. The primary reason for this difference is to capitalize on the flexibility provided by Unix. One of the major strengths of Unix is the ready availability of large numbers of simple commands for a user to invoke at any time. Encased systems normally do not have full access to basic Unix services, such as pattern matching for file names. The user therefore loses much of the advantage of Unix or the tool builder is forced into duplicating services already on Unix but otherwise inaccessible to his system's users. All office functions in SPS are available as ordinary programs directly accessible from the Unix command interpreter.

In several instances, menus or on-line help capabilities have been added as front ends for what are otherwise independent programs. For example, a novice user can invoke a menu interface to the Rand message handler, the standard SPP mail system, as illustrated in Figure 6. Most experienced users prefer the raw command interpreter interface, but novices find the menus quite helpful.

Even though SPP has used most of the Unix tools as standards for tool integration, tools of similar functionality are made available upon user demand. For example, troff is the standard text formatter used by the project, but other formatters such as Scribe and Tex are also available.

The major automated office/project support components, other than those provided with the standard UC Berkeley Unix, are

SPS tool catalog, a catalog of the tools that are part of the SPS. This tool makes use of the menu utilities and the forms management system, where summaries of existing tools are built automatically. In this manner, the maintenance of this catalog as SPS grows is trivial.

Rand message handler, or MH, an electronic mail system from Rand.

Scribe, a text-formatting and document-preparation system that complements troff.

Tex, another text-formatting and document-preparation system that complements troff.

Author, a word processor built by SPP that closely approximates "what you see is what you get" text entry; actually a front end for the standard Unix text processor troff. The user is shielded from troff commands by seeing an approximation of their effects on the screen as he enters data. Author makes extensive use of keypad function keys; its back end produces a file compatible with troff so that the full power of that formatting program is retained.

Interoffice correspondence package, or ICP, a collection of commands created by SPP to manipulate TRW standard interoffice correspondences. ICP uses the fillin package.

Menu message handler, or MMH, a menu-driven variant of the Rand message handler that was created by SPP. MMH uses the SPP menu driver to provide menus complete with on-line help to aid the novice user of electronic mail.

Calendar management system, or CMS, a collection of programs created by SPP to manipulate personal calendars, including scheduling, summarizing, rescheduling, and canceling of appointments, travel, and daily notes.

Forms management system, or FMS, a system created by SPP that allows easy creation of new forms, a uniform way to manipulate electronic forms, management of forms in folders, easy report writing capability, and a version of query by example; and

Viewcomp, an electronic spreadsheet calculator.

Because the forms management system permits end users to define their own form formats and reports, SPS users have built additional tools as forms applications, including an inventory control system, a design problem report tracker, and the SPP automated library. New applications of FMS are being created by innovative users regularly. Of particular interest is that secretaries and administrative support personnel have created many of these applications, rather than technical staff.

Software development tools. TRW has iterated several times on a complete methodology for software development including the implementation of tools to automate and reinforce much of that methodology. [13, 14] Most of the currently available tools to support software development have been selected in part on their degree of support for that methodology.

The major software development components, other than those provided with standard UC Berkeley Unix, are

Requirements traceability tool, or RTT, a bookkeeping capability that allows the user to trace requirements through software design and test; it generates several reports including a test evaluation matrix and exception reports. The actual text of requirements is not stored as part of this tool, but it allows a user to specify the name of the file where it resides. This tool was built by SPP, and a user may choose to use either the Ingres database management system or the IDM-500 database machine.

Program design language 81, or PDL81, a well-known design tool that is available on Unix. It was purchased from Caine, Farber and Gordon, Inc.

Ada program design language, or Ada PDL, a tool supporting a program design language based on Ada. It supports Ada concepts such as packages, as well as providing such standard PDL capabilities as pretty-printing, and cross-referencing.

Fortran 77 analyzer, a code analyzer for ANSI Fortran 77 programs, originally developed by TRW for the National Bureau of Standards. It is useful as a static-code analyzer, test-effectiveness measurer, and

general software-development aid. This tool is widely used throughout the company, and it was ported to the SPS system.

Software requirements engineering methodology, or SREM, a methodology and a collection of tools, developed by TRW for the U.S. Army BMD-ATC, supporting the definition and analysis of software requirements. [14] A preliminary version of SREM was ported in 1982; an enhanced version including integration with the IDM-500 database machine is planned for 1984.

SPS Support Scenarios

All of the four major SPS components—hardware, software, office facilities, and master project database—are separable; that is, a project can use one or more of these components without the others (although effective use of the database without the accompanying software tools would be somewhat strained). Thus, projects using a non-Unix environment (such as the Sel MPX operating system, or DEC's VMS) have benefitted significantly from having a LAN and the specially furnished private offices. Conversely, projects whose current operating conditions have not permitted use of private offices have still benefitted by using SPS software and Unix to support their software development activities.

The simplest implementation scenario, of course, is for a project to have all SPS components, and to deliver software that is also SPS-based. However, it is often necessary to deliver software for target systems for which SPS-based software is not appropriate; for example, in many cases the target hardware is a network of small microcomputers with severe memory limitations intended for real-time applications. The source-target concept of operation offers an attractive approach that retains the advantages of an SPS-based software development environment, while satisfying customer requirements to deliver software on a non-SPS target system. If there is a large degree of support for source-target operations, including high-bandwidth communications and tools such as cross-compilers and remote testers, then a project can work almost exclusively from the SPS-based development system throughout the entire life cycle.

In the event that support for source-target operations is incomplete, an SPS-based system can still be used very effectively for the earlier life cycle when systems engineering, management planning, and design activities dominate, and in the later life cycle for such activities as documentation, configuration management, and project management, which do not rely on the particular target environment. This actually reflects the operating scenario for a major project which SPP is supporting. Development and maintenance of most documentation, design, and other activities that do not require actual use of the non-Unix-based target environment are done under Unix. Coding and testing are performed on the target machine.

PROJECT EXPERIENCE

SPP has learned many lessons during the last three years, including problems and benefits due to the incremental nature of SPS, the user support program, and some of the measurements to date.

Evolutionary Development

When developing a software environment, prototyping and evolutionary development is preferable to paper analysis and detailed requirements specifications. This has been especially true for SPP. The project has changed direction several times during the last two and one-half years as real user needs became better understood. For example, the earliest project plans did not call for the development of office automation software. However, the large production software project serving as the representative SPS user indicated that several office automation capabilities would be more valuable than some of the originally-planned SPS tools.

Two aspects of our evolutionary development have already returned benefits: the building of tools to provide for user interface consistency and the building of tools for reusability.

From the beginning of the project, special emphasis has been given to the uniformity of the user interface. Since most SPS tools are interactive, SPP developed a set of user interface standards that include syntax standards, a help language, interfacing, and documentation. Very soon we realized that reliance on tools to provide much of the user interface fosters more effective standardization than does the issuance of standards documents. Two examples of such tools are the *menu* and *fillin* subroutine libraries, the latter having been the most widely used SPP-developed tool. Thus, the commands to deal with menus or to fill forms on the screen are the same, independent of the tool being used. SPP needed to provide a friendly, uniform way for users to interact with the SPS, and these two libraries have been remarkably effective in doing just that.

Another advantage of these tools is the ease with which user interface protocols can be partially standardized for non-SPP-developed software. SPP recognizes that one role for SPS is to be a repository for useful programs such as the Rand message handler. Modifying the internals of that package so that it conforms to SPP user interface standards would be impractical because of the package's large size. However, placing menus or forms in front of package components to collect much of the information required to operate the package is relatively easy. Such efforts have the effect of providing high-level integration of otherwise independent tools.

In the early days of the project, we built a few tools that had hardwired information or hardwired attributes; these tools would suit one type of user, but not all. One example was the automated unit development folder, built in early 1982, which supports keeping a unit development folder for each software unit being developed. Every new user wanted one more attribute or one more report, which meant recoding parts of the tool. We realized that building general and flexible tools—that users could tailor to their own needs—was the only way to satisfy users within and across projects. This is not a trivial task, but we have been successful in building tools for that purpose; an example is the forms management system, where users can easily define the contents of forms and reports to be used by the system.

The building of reusable tools and libraries, some of which were previously described, have also increased SPP's productivity.

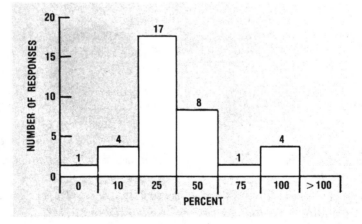

Figure 7. **Results of a June 1982 survey of productivity office occupants who were asked, "How much has your productivity improved?" Of the office occupants surveyed, an average of 39 percent noted productivity improvement.**

Training

SPP recognized early in the project that its best technical efforts could be thwarted by a lack of support for a large user community who would initially be unfamiliar with Unix and SPS. We have paid special attention to the beginner and the casual user. To ensure user satisfaction, SPP took a three-fold approach to meeting the general users' needs.

Documentation. User manuals are written and on-line help is provided for each locally developed tool. In addition, supplements to existing Unix documentation were written explaining, for example, the most commonly used system commands. Sections of existing Unix documents which were found lacking were re-written; for example, SPP wrote a tutorial introduction to the screen-editor **vi** more suitable for computer novices than the one distributed from UC Berkeley. This tutorial has proven instrumental in gaining acceptance for that editor.

A library has been established in a central location where a user can go to find a document about SPS. A reference copy of large manuals is available, as well as copies of smaller documents, which a user can take. Access to information in this paper library has also been automated as an application of the forms management system.

Consulting. A regular consulting service was established so that users outside SPP could obtain expert help on all aspects of SPS. Consultants are available daily.

Courses. Several in-house courses were developed and are offered regularly. Besides courses on introduction to Unix and specific Unix tools, specialty courses such as the forms management system,

Author, and the requirements traceability tool are offered.

Experience Supporting Other Projects

When SPP was formed, there was concern that the user community outside SPP would resist the different way of approaching software development that SPS and its accompanying methodology support. This skepticism was anticipated for several reasons. First, SPP proposed to automate many activities that had previously been done manually. Automation requires significant managerial and social adjustment. Second, Unix is different from what most TRW software developers are familiar with, and it takes a lot of work to learn another operating system and collection of tools; the users must be persuaded there is a large payoff in order to warrant such effort. Third, in some corners, Unix has the reputation of being too academic and therefore might not be appropriate for supporting large-scale real-time software development. Fourth and last, until the beginning of this year, Unix has not really been supported by AT&T or the major computer manufacturers in the sense that DEC supports VMS. This lack of visible support caused concern over operating system maintenance.

These concerns prompted SPP to pay extra attention to make sure that users were consulted on requirements, software worked well when released, users were trained on how to use it, user manuals were well written, the tools placed into SPS would offer valuable services not easily found elsewhere, and the released software baseline was placed under rigid software control. This strategy is paying off. Acceptance of Unix and SPS has been steadily increasing. SPP began supporting one project in 1982. It is now supporting several contract projects, several research and development projects, and non-project organizations. Use of Unix independent of SPP is also growing, providing an opportunity for SPS software to be disseminated. Some proposals are now being written specifically including the use of SPS for their software development.

Further enhancing the credibility of Unix are the many announcements of vendor support for Unix. Among these companies are AT&T, DEC, IBM, Gould, Hewlett-Packard, Intel, Motorola, Amdahl, Data General, and National Semiconductor. All these vendors have released or soon will release supported versions of Unix on their hardware. (In addition to providing support on their own computer systems, AT&T has entered into agreements with many vendors to support non-AT&T computers.)

Usage Measurement

To determine the effect of SPS on user productivity, and to identify areas most needing improvement, SPP is using a four-fold measurement and evaluation approach: (1) automatic instrumentation of system usage; (2) encouraging informal feedback from users; (3) questionnaires to assess system impact on software effort distribution, and to acquire subjective user inputs on SPS and its impact on productivity; and (4) long-range measurement of project size, attributes, and development effort to support a continuing productivity audit along the lines of the Cocomo model discussed earlier.

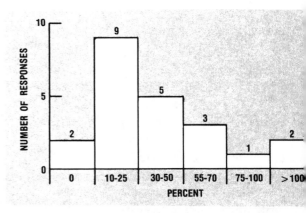

Figure 8. Results of a February 1983 survey of former productivity office occupants who were asked, "How much did your productivity improve while residing in the productivity bay?" Of the office occupants surveyed, an average of 47 percent noted productivity improvement.

SPP has started a system usage measurement activity, collecting data on tool usage and CPU utilization per user group. Tools have been categorized by their functionality and system users have been grouped by the type of job they perform (such as management, clerical, development, and engineering). Data is automatically collected and reports are generated weekly. Data is analyzed periodically, and some of our observations include: (1) word processing is the heaviest CPU-using application; (2) mail and network communications are not major CPU drains even though they are used heavily; and (3) the 80-percent-to-20-percent rule of program optimization seems to apply to computer usage; that is, 20 percent of the individual users consumed 76 percent of the CPU. The benefits of this measurement activity include a better understanding of which types of tools need to be added to the system, to pinpoint programs for which optimization would have a large payoff, to determine which user groups need better hardware support (for example, dumb terminals versus workstations).

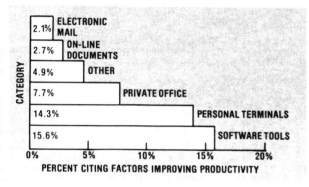

Figure 9. A breakdown of productivity improvements.

Unfortunately, it is still too early to be able to state productivity improvements for large software development projects in terms of lines of code per man-month. The initial project that SPP has been supporting is still early in its overall project life cycle. However, there are three significant measurements that can now be reported, two surveys and SPP's own productivity in developing software.

The surveys were conducted to obtain subjective feedback on the impact of being in a productivity office with access to the LAN through a personal terminal. The first survey of 37 people included 10 SPP personnel and 27 people from the project that SPP was supporting. That survey asked performers who had occupied the offices for approximately six months to estimate any changes in their productivity. The response, shown in Fig-

ure 7, indicates that on the average their estimated gain was 39 percent. In a second survey, people who had occupied a productivity office and subsequently moved to a new location were asked how their productivity was affected by that move. These people had the added perspective of moving out of the productivity environment into traditional TRW surroundings. Of the 23 possible respondents, 20 indicated that they felt their productivity in the SPP environment was 47 percent higher. Figure 8 shows by how much each respondent felt productivity was affected by occupying an SPP office. Figure 9 indicates how much each of five major factors contributed to the 47 percent productivity gain. The dominant features were the availability of software tools to support software development and office functions (15.6 percent), a personal terminal with high-speed access to the computers (14.3 percent) and a private office with modern office furniture (7.7 percent).

SPP recently completed the development of its own medium-size software package, the forms management system. This software, written in the C programming language, involved the writing of 11,995 lines of new code (excluding comments) and approximately 500 pages of documentation (including requirements, user interface specification, design, test information, and user manuals), plus the reuse of 4,974 lines of existing C code. The total effort for this development— where DSI is *delivered source instructions* —was 40 man-months, or MM, for a productivity of approximately

$$(11,995 + 4,974)DSI/40MM =$$
$$16,969 \ DSI/40MM = 424 \ DSI/MM$$

This productivity was analyzed using the

Cocomo model of software cost estimation. [1] Cocomo was supplied with parameters that represent the development environment that SPP would have had as a typical company project, without the benefit of the SPP environment and the SPP-developed software tool libraries. Under those conditions, Cocomo predicted an implementation effort of 83.7 MM, for a nominal productivity of 203 DSI/MM. SPP's actual productivity was 109 percent higher than that predicted for a typical company project. The dramatic difference between actual and estimated productivity is largely accounted for by the fact that 29.3 percent of the FMS is reused code. It justifies the direction that SPP has taken in building reusable components as its foundation for constructing application packages. Even without counting the reused code, the productivity gain on development of the 11,995 lines of new code was 42 percent over what Cocomo predicts a classical TRW project would have required.

The primary conclusions from the software productivity requirements analysis are (1) significant productivity gains require an integrated program of initiatives in several areas; (2) an integrated software productivity improvement program can have an extremely large payoff (a factor of four by 1990); (3) improving software productivity involves a long, sustained effort; (4) in the very long run, the biggest productivity gains will come from increased use of existing software; (5) software support environment requirements are still too incompletely understood to specify precisely.

The SPP development experience, to date, confirms the study conclusions. Additional conclusions are

Immediate access to a good set of software tools has the highest payoff. The key element noted has been the gradual change of daily habits, from preparing paper products manually to the automated way. This change is only made effective by providing immediate and easy access to computing facilities containing a good and integrated set of tools.

Office automation and project support capabilities are required for all project personnel. These are among the most often used programs on the system, crossing project assignments. However, in order to be fully effective, every member of the project must have a terminal on their desk.

There is a high payoff in placing all software development artifacts on-line and providing tools to support easy access to them. Developing a comprehensive master project database is extremely worthwhile, but costly. Developing the tools to take full advantage of the availability of the data is even more expensive, but can dramatically improve productivity.

User interface standards are essential for preserving the conceptual integrity of an evolving support system. An excellent way to implement such standards is to embed them into a family of toolbuilders' utilities supporting such functions as screen formatting, error processing, help messages, and data access.

User acceptance of novel development environments is a gradual process that requires careful nurturing by the sponsoring organization. Involvement of the user community in planning the growth and direction of the environment will help ensure their acceptance of it. Training and documentation writing efforts must be established early and be given strong support.

Local area networks strongly support distributed work environments. A LAN coupled with electronic mail allows a physically scattered group of individuals to work effectively as a team with excellent communications between project members.

Private offices improve productivity. Both surveys conducted by SPP indicated that privacy was a factor in improving productivity. Organizations should plan for enough space to ensure that each technical staff member has a private office.

The integrated approach produces a high payoff. The survey results of 39 percent and 47 percent productivity increases, and the 109 percent improvement on the forms management package indicate that the productivity results clearly justify the investment in the system.

The software productivity project is planning to continue its activities for many years. As mentioned, improving productivity involves a long, iterated, sustained effort. Main activities planned for 1984 include evaluation of workstations as part of the environment, enhancement of existing tools, evaluation of graphics hardware and software for use by tools with graphical applications, further database machine experimentation and expansion of the user community.

Acknowledgments

We thank all members of the software productivity project for their dedication, hard work, creative ideas, and enthusiastic support—which made this work possible.

REFERENCES

[1] B.W. Boehm, *Software Engineering Economics,* Englewood Cliffs, N.J.: Prentice-Hall, 1981.

[2] "Missing Computer Software," *Business Week,* September 1, 1980, pp. 46-53.

[3] "Science and Engineering Education in the 1980's and Beyond," *U.S. National Science Foundation and Department of Education,* Washington, D.C., October 1980.

[4] J. Buxton, *Requirements of Ada Programming Support Environments: Stoneman,* U.S. Department of Defense, OSD/R&E, Washington, D.C., February 1980.

[5] K. Christensen, "Programming Productivity and the Development Process," IBM-Santa Teresa Laboratory, Technical Report No. 03.083, January 1980.

[6] T.A. Dolotta, R.C. Haight, and J.R. Mashey, "The Programmer's Workbench," *Bell System Technical Journal,* July-August 1978, pp. 2177-200.

[7] G.M. McCue, "IBM's Santa Teresa Laboratory—Architectural Design for Program Development," *IBM Systems Journal,* Vol. 17, No. 1, January 1978.

[8] E.L. Ivie, "The Programmer's Workbench: A Machine for Software Development," *Communications of the ACM,* Vol. 20, No. 10, October 1977, pp. 746-53.

[9] A.N. Habermann, "An Overview of the Gandalf Project," *Carnegie-Mellon University Computer Science Research Review,* Pittsburgh, Penn., 1979.

[10] M.J. Rochkind, "The Source Code Control System," *IEEE Transactions on Software Engineering,* Vol. SE-1, No. 4, December 1975, pp. 364-69.

[11] G. Held, P. Kreps, M. Stonebraker, and E. Wong. "The Design and Implementation of Ingres," *ACM Transactions on Database Systems,* Vol. 1, No. 3, March 1976, pp. 189-222.

[12]   J. Woodfill et al., *Ingres Reference Manual, Version 7,* University of California, Berkeley, 1981.

[13]   E.A. Goldberg, "Applying Corporate Software Development Policies," *Proceedings of the AIAA Third Software Life-Cycle Management Conference,* 1978.

[14]   M.W. Alford, "Requirements Engineering Methodology for Real-time Processing Requirements," *IEEE Transactions on Software Engineering,* Vol. SE-3, No. 1, January 1977, pp. 60-68.

ADDITIONAL READING

Bell, T.E., D.C. Bixler, and M.E. Dyer, "An Extendable Approach to Computer-Aided Software Requirements Engineering," *IEEE Transactions on Software Engineering,* January 1977, pp. 49-59.

Boehm, B.W., "Structured Programming: A Quantitative Assessment," *Computer,* June 1975, pp. 38-54.

————, "Improving Software Productivity," *Proceedings of the IEEE COMPCON,* September 1981.

————, and R.W. Wolverton, "Software Cost Modeling: Some Lessons Learned," *Proceedings of the Second Software Life-Cycle Management Workshop,* U.S. Army Computer Systems Command, August 1978.

Penedo, M.H., and A.B. Pyster, "Software Engineering Standards for TRW's Software Productivity Project," *Proceedings of the Second Software Engineering Standards Application Workshop,* May 17-19, 1983.

15

Editors' Note
Mills, Linger, and Hevner: "Box Structured Information Systems"

Insight: The Box Structured method offers a systematic technique for designing and testing designs before coding begins. It also contains a method for verifying the accuracy of the design.

This article, which discusses a method for designing software called the Box Structured method, pairs nicely with the Selby, Basili, and Baker paper (No. 16) on cleanroom testing. Both emphasize debugging designs rather than coding them up to see if they are workable.

We can see the software development paradigm slowly but clearly shifting toward defect prevention and away from efficient defect removal. Wouldn't it be exciting to know that the software being written today could, at worst, contain coding defects, and not any design flaws?

15

Box Structured Information Systems
by H.D. Mills, R.C. Linger, and A.R. Hevner

Since their inception, information systems have been used in government and business, but research and development in information systems have increased dramatically since the advent of the computer some thirty years ago. As a result, a recognizable discipline of Information Systems is emerging in business and in university curricula. However, Information Systems is still a young field in terms of intellectual growth and development. Even with all the current excitement and progress, there is still a lot to discover. The search for fundamental ideas and deep simplicities takes time.

Structures and Data Flows

The revolution that changed trial-and-error computer programming into software engineering was triggered by Dijkstra's idea of structured programming. [1] Structured programming cleared a control flow jungle that had grown unchecked for twenty years in dealing with more and more complex software problems. It replaced that control flow jungle with the astonishing assertion that software of any complexity whatsoever could be designed with just three basic control structures—sequence (begin-end), alternation (if-then-else), and iteration (while-do)—which could be nested over and over in a hierarchical structure (the structure of structured

programming). The benefits of structured programming to the management of large projects are immediate. The work can be structured and progress measured in a top-down development in a direct way.

Even so, information systems development is much more than software development. The operations of a business involve all kinds of data that are transmitted, stored, and processed in all kinds of ways. The total data processing of a business is defined by the activities of all of its people and computers, as they interact with one other and with customer, vendor, and government personnel and computers outside the business. In a large company, it is a massively parallel operation with many thousands of interactions going on simultaneously. Information systems are called on to automate more and more of the information processing in business—in many cases these systems are required for survival in a competitive environment. And for these systems, a complete description of their data operations and uses leads to a data flow jungle that is even more tangled and arcane than the control flow jungle of software.

We will replace that data flow jungle with just three system structures that can be nested over and over in a hierarchical structure (the structure of box structures). Any information system—automatic, manual, or hybrid—can be described or designed in a hierarchy of these system structures step by step in a provable way. The benefits of box structures to the management of large projects are also immediate. The work can be structured and progress measured in top-down system development in a direct way.

State Machines and Data Abstractions

The origins of these system structures are in the hierarchical state machine methodology of software engineering found in References 2, 3, and 4 and taught at the IBM Software Engineering Institute. [5, 6] As discussed in the book by Mills, Linger, and Hevner [7], this methodology was used in the New York Times Information Bank, as reported by Baker [8, 9], with remarkable results in reliability. [9] A very large-scale use of this methodology in the modernization of U.S. Air Force satellite tracking and control systems has been reported by Jordano. [10]

The software counterparts of state machines have also been called data abstractions [11, 12], and more recently, software objects. [13] Their common feature is the presence of a state, represented in stored data, and accessed and altered by procedures that collectively define the state machine transition function. Since these data are accessed and altered by reusing the data abstraction or object, the hierarchy is a usage hierarchy, in the sense found in Parnas [14], rather than a parts hierarchy. That is, data abstractions appear in the hierarchy at each occasion of use in the design, rather than as a part in the design.

This usage hierarchy of data abstractions cuts a Gordian knot for the effective dual decomposition of data flows and processes in information systems. Data flows are convenient heuristic starting points in information systems analysis, as developed in References 15 through 18, but require a mental discontinuity to move to information systems design. The problem is that data flows describe all that can possibly happen, whereas processes must deal with one data instance at a time and prescribe precisely what will happen at each such instance. Each use of a data abstraction is an instance of data flow through a process, which provides for storage in its state as well. And the collective effects of the usage of the data abstraction throughout a hierarchy are summarized by a data flow through the process. Data abstractions have proved useful in software engineering in several specific languages and systems, as in CLU [19], VDM [20, 21], HDM [22], Larch [23], and object-oriented design [13].

Box Structures and Data Abstractions

The box structure methodology develops the usage hierarchy of data abstractions in a way especially suited for information systems development, in which the emphasis is jointly on mathematical rigor and management simplicity. [7] For this purpose, we not only need strong system development principles, but must also make these principles obvious in the methodology. We define three distinct forms for any data abstraction, namely, its *black box,* its *state machine,* and its *clear box.* A black box defines a data abstraction entirely in terms of external behavior, in transitions from stimuli to responses. A state machine defines a data abstraction in terms of transitions from a stimulus and internal state to a response and new internal state. A clear box defines a data abstraction in terms of a procedure that accesses the internal state and possibly calls on other black boxes. This recursion of black boxes with clear boxes that call on other black boxes defines a usage hierarchy that supports important principles for system development.

In the next section of this paper we summarize the principal concepts of the box structure methodology and explain their mathematical foundations. In the subsequent section, box structure hierarchies are defined, and the system development principles of referential transparency, state migration, transaction closure, and common services are described. Finally, we discuss the benefits of these structures in managing a spiral system development process.

BOX STRUCTURES

The behavior of any information system (or subsystem) can be rigorously described in three distinct box structure forms previously mentioned—the black box, state machine, and clear box of the system. We first define each of these structures and then show relationships among them.

Black Box Behavior

The *black box* gives an external view of a system or subsystem that accepts stimuli, and for each stimulus, *S,* produces a response, *R* (which may be null), before accepting the next stimulus. A diagram of a black box is shown in Figure 1. The system of the diagram could be a hand calculator, a personal computer, an accounts receivable system, or even a manual work procedure that accepts stimuli from the environment and produces responses one by

one. As the name implies, a black box description of a system omits all details of internal structure and operations and deals solely with the behavior that is visible to its user in terms of stimuli and responses. Any black box response is uniquely determined by its stimulus history.

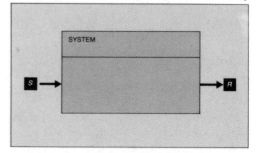

Figure 1. A black box diagram.

For example, an interactive workstation is a computer system that accepts keystrokes, one by one, and returns a new screen with each keystroke. Most keystrokes change the screen in small ways, say, by adding or deleting a character, but some keystrokes bring up entirely new screens, say, by an enter key or a menu choice. Each such keystroke is a stimulus for the black box. The user need have no idea of the internal structure—that some screens are created locally, some indirectly by remote computers, etc. The workstation behaves as a black box for the user.

The idea of describing a system as a black box is useful for analyzing the system from the user's point of view. Only system externals are visible; no system state or procedure is described. The mathematical semantics of black box behavior is a function from system stimulus histories to system responses. A black box is specified by its traces. [24, 25] In fact, Parnas uses the term *black box* to motivate the study of traces. [24]

State Machine Behavior

The *state machine* gives an intermediate system view that defines an internal system state, namely an abstraction of the data stored from stimulus to stimulus. It can be established mathematically that every system described by a black box has a state machine description. (Consider each stimulus history to be a state.) A state machine diagram is shown in Figure 2. The state machine part called Machine is a black box that accepts as its stimulus both the external stimulus and the internal state and produces as a response both the external response and a new internal state which replaces the old state. The role of the state machine is to open up the black box description of a system one step by making its state visible. State machine behavior can be described in the transition formula

(Stimulus, Old State) → (Response, New State)

Much of the work in formal specification methods for software applies directly to specification of the state machine system view. These methods, such as those presented in the literature [11, 12, 26, 27], specify the required properties of programs and abstract data types in axiomatic and algebraic models. The models represent behavior without presenting implementation details.

For information systems, however, we believe that direct descriptions are often sufficient—that indirect axiomatic and algebraic methods of describing data abstractions tend to obscure the essential simplicity of state machines. Also, the conceptual work required to derive axioms or algebras for a complete system state can

require deep research itself. (For an example of problems associated with the axiomatization of even a simple data abstraction, see Ferrentino and Mills. [2])

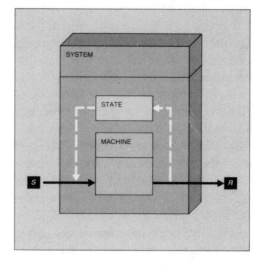

Figure 2. A state machine diagram.

Clear Box Behavior

The *clear box,* as the name suggests, opens up the state machine description of a system one more step in an internal view that describes the system processing of the stimulus and state. The processing is described in terms of three possible sequential structures, namely sequence, alternation, and iteration, and a concurrent structure. Figure 3 shows a clear box sequence structure with two internal subsystems represented as black boxes; each accepts both a stimulus and a state and produces both a response and a new state. In the sequence structure, the clear box stimulus is the stimulus to black box M1, whose response becomes the stimulus to M2, whose response is the response of the clear box. At this point, a hierarchical, top-down description can be repeated for each of the embedded black boxes at the next lower level of description. Each black box is described by a state machine, then by a clear box containing even smaller black boxes, and so on.

Figures 4, 5, and 6 show, respectively, the alternation, iteration, and concurrent clear box structures. The internal machines, Mi, can be expanded at lower levels of description in a box structure hierarchy. In alternation and iteration clear boxes, the condition C (denoted by a diamond) is a special black box that accesses the stimulus and old state to return responses T or F (True or False). The function of C is to direct the stimulus to the proper black box.

The clear box is an essential step of system description that is lacking in many information systems development methods. It specifies the procedurality that connects the usage of subsystems to be described at the next lower level in the box structure hierarchy. This explicit connection supports the principle of referential transparency, to be discussed in the next section.

Box Structure Derivation and Expansion

The relationships among the black box, state machine, and clear box views of a system or subsystem precisely define the tasks of *derivation* and *expansion*. As shown in Figure 7, it is a derivation task to deduce a black box from a state machine or to deduce a state machine from a clear box, whereas it is an expansion task to induce a state machine from a black box or to induce a clear box from a state machine. That is, a black box derivation from a state machine produces a *state-free* description, and a state machine derivation from a clear box produces a *procedure-free* description. Conversely, a state machine expansion of a black box produces a *state-defined* description, and a clear box expansion of a state machine produces a *procedure-defined* description. The expansion step does not produce a unique product because there are many state machines that behave like a given black box and many clear boxes that

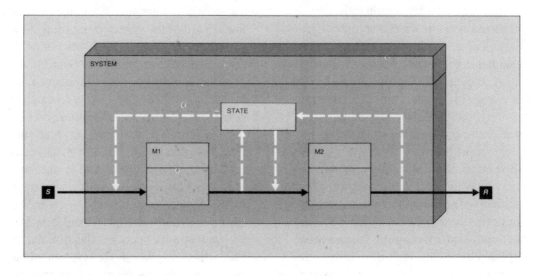

Figure 3. The clear box sequence structure.

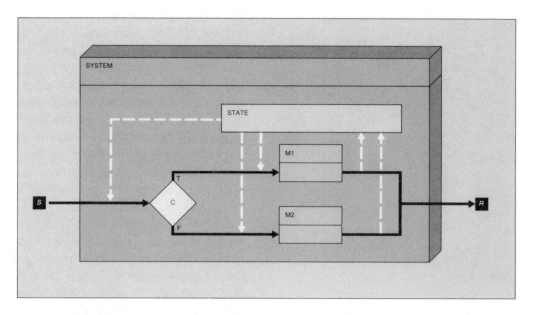

Figure 4. The clear box alternation structure.

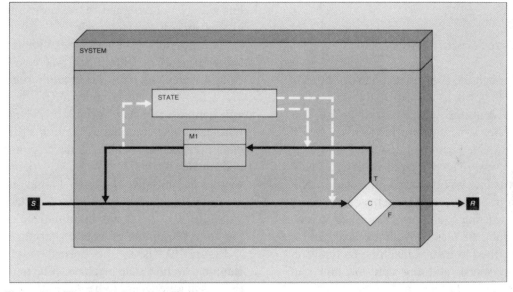

Figure 5. The clear box iteration structure.

behave like a given state machine. The derivation step does produce a unique product because there is only one black box that behaves like a given state machine and only one state machine that behaves like a given clear box.

In summary, black box, state machine, and clear box expansions provide behaviorally equivalent views of an information system or subsystem at increasing levels of internal visibility. This equivalence relationship is depicted in Figure 8.

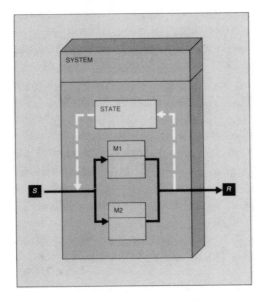

Figure 6. The clear box concurrent structure (shown with two machines).

A Box Structure Illustration

Although the concept of box structures is easy to grasp, its use in actual business systems requires business knowledge. In fact, box structures provide forms in which to describe business knowledge in a standard way. The principal value of a black box is that any business information system or subsystem will behave as a black box whether consciously described as such or not. In turn, any black box can be described as a state machine (actually in many ways), and any state machine can be described as a clear box (also in many ways), possibly using other black boxes. In practice, information systems or subsystems often have their own natural descriptions that can be reformulated as box structures.

As an illustration, a 12-month running average defines a simple, low-level black box that might be used in sales forecasting, for example, for a variety store with 10,000 items. A stimulus of last month's sales of an item produces a response of the past year's average monthly sales of the item. Each month a new sales amount produces a new average of the past 12 months. In the case of new items with less than 12 months of sales history, the response can be the average of sales to date. If i is the age of an item in months, then the number of months to average is $min(i,12)$, the minimum of i and 12, no matter how long the sales history is.

Figure 9 shows the Running Average black box where for an item of age i, $S.1 = S$ is last month's sales, $S.2$ is the next previous month's sales, and so on. The symbol ": = " means that the term on the left side (R) is assigned the value of the expression on the right side.

One possible state machine with the same behavior as this black box would store the previous $min(i,12)$ monthly sales $S.1, S.2, \ldots$ in state variables $S1, S2, \ldots$, and item age i in state variable I. Then, with each new stimulus S, there is sufficient information to calculate the response and update the state. The state variable I must be initialized, say to 1, and incremented with each stimulus. The state variables $S1, S2, \ldots$ will be initialized as the first 12 months of sales materialize.

Figure 10 shows the corresponding Running Average state machine. The multiple assignments are to be understood as concurrent. That is, all expressions on the right sides use the data available at the beginning of the transition, not data computed in assignments above them.

Note a distinction between $S.1, S.2, \ldots$, which are monthly sales, and $S1, S2, \ldots$, which are state variables. The values are

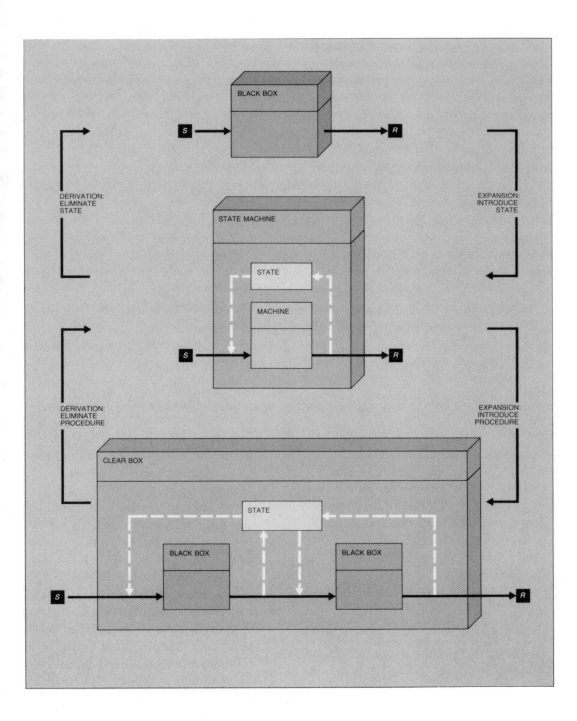

Figure 7. Box structure derivation and expansion (shown with sequence clear box).

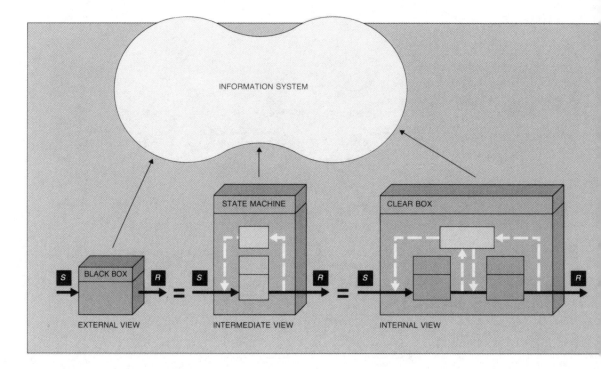

Figure 8. Three behaviorally equivalent views of an information system or subsystem.

the same (at the end of each transition), but unless $S.1, S.2 \ldots$ are recorded in $S1, S2, \ldots$, they will be lost to the state machine because it does not access stimulus history, as does the black box. The assignments made to $S2, S3, \ldots$ before $S1, S2, \ldots$ are initialized reference undefined values, but do no harm because they are not used in R.

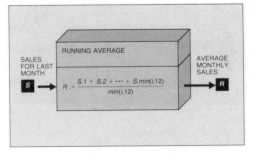

Figure 9. Running average black box.

A clear box will describe how the response and new state are computed in a sequential or concurrent structure of other black box uses. One possible design is to first update the sales data, then compute the running average from the new state data and increment the age of the item, as shown in Figure 11. In this case, no further black box expansion will be needed because both black boxes, Update Sales and Find Average, require no more than their last stimuli to compute their response [they can be defined as mathematical functions from stimuli (not stimulus histories) to responses]. Of course, the stimuli on which they operate include the state variables of Running Average.

Note that many other state machine and clear box designs could have been chosen to implement the Running Average black box. For example, after the value of *I* exceeds 11, the state data could be stored as monthly sales values divided by 12. The running average would then be found by adding all the state data.

A Running Average black box is a simple sales forecaster. However, if sales are

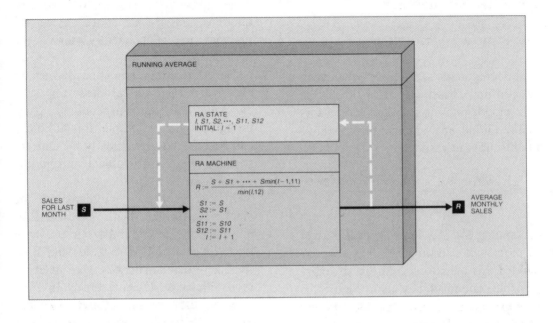

Figure 10. Running average state machine.

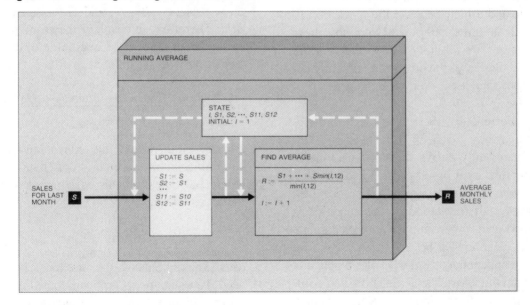

Figure 11. Running average clear box.

seasonal or have definite trends, a more suitable black box may be required. Such a forecaster will differ in details, but can still be described in a black box/state machine/clear box structure.

Box Structure Verifications

In the foregoing example, we began with an informal description of a black box ("12-month running average"), then formalized it into an assignment from stimulus histories to responses,

$$R := \frac{S.1 + S.2 + \ldots + S.min(i,12)}{min\ (i,12)},$$

accounting for new items with less than 12 months of sales history. Next, we expanded this black box into one of many possible state machines, as in Figure 10, then expanded the state machine into one of many possible clear boxes, as in Figure 11. These two expansions were simple and direct, because the black box itself is quite simple. Even so, these designs are possibly faulty, and in more complex cases the probability of faulty designs increases, even with the greatest of care.

Fortunately, there is a direct and rigorous way to check these designs: Independently derive the state machine of the final clear box expansion and compare it with the intended state machine designed above. If the intended state machine is recovered by derivation, the expansion into the clear box has been verified. Next, we can independently derive the black box from the verified state machine and compare it with the intended black box formulated initially.

We call this rederivation and comparison process a *box structure verification*. It works on the same principle used in division to check that the division has been done correctly, that is, a multiplication of quotient and divisor added to the remainder to independently derive the dividend.

Box structure verification defines an objective, rigorous process for self-checking and peer inspections. Even though people are fallible, this fallibility can be reduced dramatically by such inspections based on an objective, rigorous foundation.

In this example, beginning with the clear box of Figure 11, the first task is to eliminate the procedurality—in this case the sequence of Update Sales and Find Average—to obtain the black box machine of the derived state machine. In Find Average, the expression for R references $S1, \ldots, Smin(I,12)$, which were updated in Update Sales, where $S1$ was assigned S, $S2$ assigned $S1, \ldots$, and $S12$ assigned $S11$. Therefore, in terms of the stimulus and original state at the beginning of the transition, the assignment to R is

$$R := \frac{S + S1 + \ldots + Smin\ (I - 1,11)}{min(I,12)}$$

Also, in Find Average, the expression for I references only I which is not changed in Update Sales, so this assignment remains as before,

$$I := I + 1$$

Since Update Sales is the first black box used, its assignments are from the stimulus and original state, so those assignments remain the same. The result of collecting all these assignments into a single black box machine results in the derived state machine shown in Figure 12.

Now we can compare the derived state machine of Figure 12 with the Running Average state machine as shown in Figure 10. They are not identical, line by line, but they differ only in the placement of the line $I := I + 1$ in the multiple assignments. But since these multiple assignments are concurrent, the order of placement of $I := I + 1$ has no effect on the responses of these two machines. So they are identical in effect in returning a response and updating the state of the state machines. With this derivation and comparison, the Running Average clear box of Figure 11 has been verified to be a correct (and complete) expansion of the Running Average state machine of Figure 10.

Now that the Running Average clear box has been verified, we can turn our at-

tention to the verification of the Running Average state machine, by the independent derivation of its black box, to be compared with the original Running Average black box of Figure 9.

Each value in the state of the Running Average state machine is the cumulative result of its initial value and all subsequent transitions to date. Our objective is to determine the value assigned to R, which is

$$R := \frac{S + S1 + \ldots + Smin (I - 1,11)}{min(I,12)}$$

not in terms of stimulus and state data, but in terms of stimulus history data instead.

First, at age i of the item, we observe that $I = i$ at the beginning of the transition, because at age 1, $I = 1$ by initialization, and I is incremented by 1 at each transition. Therefore, at age i, by direct

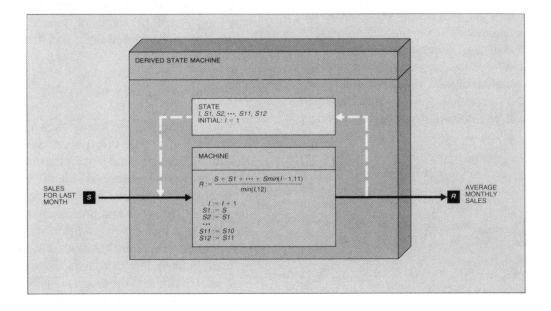

Figure 12. Derived state machine.

substitution of i for I in the assignment above,

$$R := \frac{S + S1 + \ldots + Smin(i - 1,11)}{min(i,12)}$$

Furthermore, at the beginning of the transition at age i, the state variables $S1$, $S2$, $\ldots$, $Smin(i{-}1,11)$ will contain the sales values $S.2$, $S.3$, $\ldots$, $S.min(i,12)$ for the following reason.

At age 1 of the item, all values of $S1$, $S2$, $\ldots$, $S12$ are uninitialized, but $S1 = S.1$ after the transition at age 1. At age 2, $S2$ is assigned the value of $S1$, which is the value of $S.1$ at age 1, but is renamed $S.2$ at age 2, so $S2 = S.2$, and $S1$ is assigned $S.1$. Continuing, at age i, $S1$, $S2$, $\ldots$, $Smin(i{-}1,11)$ are assigned $S.1$, $S.2$, $\ldots$, $S.min(i{-}1,11)$ after the transition. But at the beginning of the next transition, these sales values will have all aged one month. So, in fact, at the beginning of the transition at age i, the state variables $S1$, $S2$, $\ldots$, $Smin(i{-}1,11)$ will contain the sales values $S.2$, $S.3$, $\ldots$, $S.min(i,12)$.

Finally, we observe that $S = S.1$, the last sales value, so we can complete the substitution of sales values for state values in the calculations for R in the assignment above, to get the derived black box shown in Figure 13.

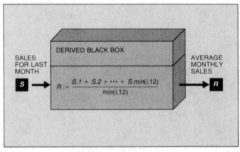

Figure 13. Derived black box.

The derived black box of Figure 13 is iden-

tical to the Running Average black box of Figure 9. With this derivation and comparison, the Running Average state machine of Figure 10 has been shown to be a correct (and complete) expansion of the Running Average black box of Figure 9.

The joint result of these two verifications is the verification that the Running Average clear box of Figure 11 is a correct (and complete) expansion of the Running Average black box of Figure 9.

INFORMATION SYSTEMS DEVELOPMENT WITH BOX STRUCTURES

The box structure concepts presented in the previous section can be expanded into a complete methodology for information systems development. The first step is to describe an information system as a multilevel usage hierarchy wherein each node is a box structure expansion of an independent system part. We then demonstrate how fundamental principles of system development can be applied in the box structure hierarchy.

Box Structure Hierarchies

A box structure hierarchy, as shown in Figure 14, provides an effective means of control for managing and developing complex information systems. By identifying black box subsystems in higher levels of the system, state data and processing are decentralized into lower-level box structures. Each subsystem becomes a well-defined, independent module in the overall system. Although the progression from black box to state machine to clear box at any point in the hierarchy may appear to be a triplication of effort, this is not the case. Each subsystem can be initially described in its most natural form, with the other forms determined as necessary for analysis and design.

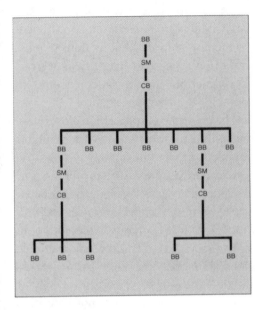

Figure 14. A box structure hierarchy.

The concept of hierarchies is crucial in system and program development. Top-down programming is based on the principle of stepwise refinement of program modules in a hierarchy. Similarly, usage hierarchies of system modules allow a top-down discipline of system specification and implementation.

The box structure hierarchy, in particular, provides for the systematic application of four essential principles of system development. These principles, called referential transparency, transaction closure, state migration, and common services, are discussed next.

Referential Transparency

The box structure hierarchy provides a formal method for defining system modules while preserving referential transparency between levels. Referential transparency is a guiding principle for forming system hierarchies.

Principle of Referential Transparency —In the delegation of any system part for design and implementation, all requirements should be specified explicitly and independently, so that no further communication or coordination is logically required to complete the system part.

The principle of referential transparency provides a crisp discipline for management delegation and assignment of responsibility. The lack of referential transparency can lead to management nightmares where nothing works and no one is to blame.

The kinds of system parts required to make the principle possible are data abstractions. The specification of such a part must be defined at the stimulus/response level (i.e., black box) for each access to the part, and account for the effect of any previous access to the part. Popularized system development methods that use plausible ideas such as HIPO charts [28], structure charts [15], or data flow diagrams [16] can still lose vital information and thus make referential transparency impossible. It takes the right kinds of system parts to defer details without losing them.

The clear box view of a system provides the key abstraction that ensures referential transparency in a box structure hierarchy. The procedurality of the clear box makes precise the control flow and data flow into and out of all embedded black boxes. At the next level of the system hierarchy, each black box can be designed and implemented independently of its surroundings in a system, so accountability is achieved in the delegation. Flexibility is achieved in the delegation because a black box can be redesigned with different state machines and clear boxes as required. As long as the new black box behavior is identical to that of the original, the rest of the system will operate exactly as before. Such black box replacement may be required or desirable for purposes of better performance, changing hardware, or even changing from manual to automatic operations.

When designers and implementers are required to discuss and coordinate details of separate parts after their assignment of responsibilities, gamesmanship becomes an important part of a day's work, in addition to system development. It's only sensible, with ill-defined responsibilities, to cover one's bets and tracks with activities and documents designed as much to protect as to illuminate.

Even with the best of intentions, extensive communication and coordination with respect to design and implementation details opens up many more opportunities for misunderstandings and errors. Such errors are always written off as human fallibilities (nobody is perfect), but errors of unnecessary communication and coordination should be charged to the methodologies that require them, not to the people forced to do the unnecessary communication and coordination.

Transaction Closure

Principle of Transaction Closure—The transactions (transitions) of a system or system part should be sufficient for the acquisition and preservation of all its state data, and its state data should be sufficient for the completion of all its transactions. In particular, system integrity as well as user function should be considered in achieving transaction closure.

The principle of transaction closure can forestall many surprises and afterthoughts in specifying and designing systems. A common mistake for amateur (and not so amateur) analysts and designers is concentrating so much on primary user transactions that the secondary transactions to make primary user transactions available and reliable become awkward or impossible. For example, if system security or recovery requirements are not identified up front, an ideal user system (imagined in a perfect world of hardware and people) may end up with data structures that make security or recovery difficult or impossible. Therefore, transactions provided for security and recovery need to be defined as early as user transactions, and as carefully.

The principle of transaction closure defines a systematic, iterative specification process, in ensuring that a sufficient set of transactions is identified to acquire and preserve a sufficient set of state data. The iteration begins with the transactions for the primary users, and the state data needed for those transactions, then considers the transactions required for the acquisition and preservation of those state data, then identifies the state data needed for those transactions, and so on. Eventually, no more transactions will be required in an iteration, and transaction closure will have been achieved.

The concept of system integrity plays a special role in transaction closure. Transaction closure assuming perfect hardware and people is not enough; many transactions can only be defined once specific hardware and people are identified for system use. For example, an information system using an operating system with automatic checkpoint and restart facilities will not need checkpoint and restart transactions, but one without them will. The problem of system security provides a classic example. Many operating systems and database systems in wide use today cannot be retrofitted for high-level multilevel security because they were conceived and specified before such security requirements were identified.

In simplest terms, information systems integrity is the property of the system fulfilling its function while handling all of the system issues inherent in its implementation. For example, systems are expected to be correct, secure, reliable, and capable of handling their applications. These requirements may not be explicitly stated by managers, users, or operators, but it is clear that the designed system must have provisions for such properties. Questions of system integrity are largely independent of the function of the system, but are dependent on its means of implementation, manual or automatic. Manual implementations must deal with the fallibilities of people, beginning with their very absence or presence (so backup personnel may be required), that include limited ability and

speed in doing arithmetic, limited memory capability for detailed facts, lapses in performance from fatigue or boredom, and so on. Automatic implementation must deal with the fallibilities of computer hardware and software, beginning with their total lack of common sense, that include limited processing and storage capabilities (much larger than for people, but still limited), hardware and software errors, security weaknesses, and so on.

The process of transaction closure is essential in the development of a top-level black box for any system. A useful beginning of this search for a top-level black box begins with the most obvious users of the system but seldom ends there. These most obvious users often interact with the system daily, even minute by minute, in entering and accessing data (for example, a clerk in an airline reservations system). Usually, however, the data they use are provided in part by other users who enter and access data less frequently, such as those entering flight availability information. And other users even more distant from the obvious users enter and access data even less frequently (for example, users who add route schedule information). All the while, an entirely different group, the operators of the system, is entering and accessing system control data that affect the users in terms of more or less access to the system because of limited capacity or availability.

The top-level black box must accommodate the transactions of all these users and operators, not just the most obvious ones. A cross-check can be made between the top-level black box and its top-level state machine. Every item of data in the top-level state must have been loaded with the original system or acquired by previous black box transactions. Are there any items not so loaded or acquired? It is easy, in concentrating on one set of transactions, to assume the existence of data to carry them out. A comprehensive scrutiny of these needed data items can discover such unwarranted assumptions early.

State Migration

Principle of State Migration—System data should be decentralized to the smallest system parts that do not require duplicating data updates. If, for geographic or security reasons, system data should be decentralized to smaller system parts, the system should be designed to ensure correctly duplicated data updates.

The principle of state migration eliminates the need for instant decisions (often faulty) about how data should be structured and how the data should be stored in a system. Instead, it permits the definition of system data at a conceptual level, and permits the concrete form and location of the data to be worked out interactively with the system design and decomposition into system parts. As better design ideas emerge, system data can be relocated effectively to accommodate such ideas, all the while maintaining correct function as required in the system transactions.

When system data need to be decentralized to smaller system parts than allowed by the principle of state migration, the smallest system defined by this part must be redesigned to accommodate correct duplicate updating. In this case, it is a different system and should be recognized as such from the outset. The problem of incorrect updating of duplicated data is a

well-known burden of faulty system designs.

System data in a box structure hierarchy are distributed into the states of their component box structures. State migration through the box structure hierarchy is a powerful tool in managing system development. It permits the placement of state data at the most effective level for its use. Downward migration may be possible when black boxes are identified in a clear box; state data used solely within the state machine expansion of one black box can be migrated to that state machine at the next lower level of the hierarchy. The isolation of state data at proper levels in the system hierarchy provides important criteria for the design of database and file systems. Upward migration is possible when duplicate state data are updated in identical ways in several places in the hierarchy. These data can be migrated up to the common parent state machine for consistent update at one location.

Common Services

Principle of Common Services—System parts with multiple uses should be considered for definition as common services. A corollary principle is to create as many opportunities as possible for reusability within and between system parts.

Operating systems, data management and database systems, network and terminal control systems are all illustrations of common services between systems. It is axiomatic in today's technology to seek as much reuse of common services as possible to multiply productivity and increase reliability. These common services must satisfy the principle of referential transparency in their use, so their specifications are as important as their implementations. On a smaller scale, effective system design seeks and creates commonality of services and identifies system parts for widespread multiple uses within a system.

When several black boxes of a clear box expansion access or alter a common state part, it is generally inadvisable to migrate the state part to those lower levels. But it may be advisable to define a new box structure hierarchy to provide access to or to alter this common state part for these several black boxes. Such a new box structure must be invoked in the clear box expansions of these black boxes. This new box structure thereby provides a common service to these several black boxes. Such a common service structure in effect encapsulates a state part, by providing the only means for accessing or altering it in the box structure hierarchy.

State encapsulation requires a new box structure whose state will contain the common state part and whose transactions will provide common access to that state part for multiple users. In essence, state encapsulation permits state migration to be carried out in another form, with the provision that the only possible access to the migrated state is by invoking transactions of the new box structure that encapsulates it.

Common service box structures are ubiquitous in information systems. For example, any database system behaves as a common service box structure to the people and programs that use it. As a simple illustration, consider a clear box expansion of a master file update state machine. Such a clear box would contain a number of black boxes which operate on the master file, for example, to open, close, read, and write the file, as well as

black boxes to access transaction files, directory and authorization information, etc. The master file of the clear box state cannot be migrated to these lower-level black boxes without duplication. However, the master file can be encapsulated, without duplication, in a new box structure that provides the required transactions to open, close, read, and write the file. These transactions can then be invoked from the original box structure hierarchy as required. The new box structure can be designed to ensure the integrity of the master file and all access directed to it. In fact, when the master file is migrated to this common service, it is protected from faulty access by the box structure in an effective way.

The Spiral Development Process

In information systems development, the box structure methodology defines a set of limited, time-phased *activities* to decompose and manage the work required. A formal *development plan* defines and schedules the specific activities required to address a specific problem. The development plan represents long-range planning for information system development; the activity plans represent short-range planning. As each activity is completed, the entire development plan is updated to account for the current situation.

Although the activities of a development plan are always specific to a particular system development problem, they can be categorized into three general classes: *investigation, specification,* and *implementation.* An investigation is a fact-finding, exploratory study, usually to assess the feasibility of an information system. For example, such a study may define the black box behavior of a projected information system. A specification is more focused to define a specific information system and its benefits to the business. For example, a specification activity may result in definition of state data and high-level clear boxes of a projected information system. An implementation converts a specification into an operational system. For example, implementation may elaborate the black boxes of high-level clear boxes into box structure hierarchies of their own, eventually arriving at human and computer procedures in user guides and software, respectively.

The System Development Spiral

Many current methods of information systems development reflect appearances rather than principles. One of the obvious appearances in information systems is the system development life cycle. It is certainly apparent that information systems go through various stages of conception, specification, design, implementation, operation, maintenance, modification, and so on. But although these terms are suggestive, real information systems do not pass through these stages in any simple or straightforward way.

In contrast to a fixed life cycle, the box structured system development process is defined by a set of time-phased activities that are initiated and managed dynamically on the basis of the outcome of previous activities in the development. This progression of activities is conveniently represented in a flexible *system development spiral* that reflects the actual progress of a development effort in terms of box structure analysis and design tasks.

The time-phased set of activities in a spiral can be strictly sequential or may have concurrent parts. If a development is sequential, it can be pictured, in prospect or retrospect, as shown in Figure 15. In this example, the activity sequence is a straightforward progression of

- Investigation
- Specification
- Implementation

with a management approval to enter each activity and to end the entire development. Such a progression for developing a system is ideal, but is not necessarily possible or even desirable.

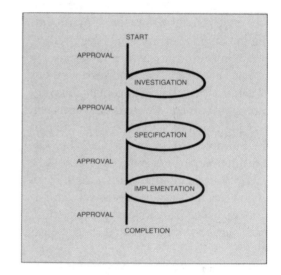

Figure 15. A system development spiral.

It may not be possible because the business problem is too complex and needs several investigation activities to arrive at a solution. It may not be possible because the system development problem is too complex and needs several specification/implementation activities in an incremental development. It may not be desirable because the business problem is too acute and a less-than-best implementation is called for as soon as possible. It may not be desirable because the happy outcome of the first investigation activity is the discovery of an existing implementation to meet the business need.

If a development is concurrent, it can be pictured in a network of spirals, as in the example of Figure 16. In this network, activity dependencies are shown by the approval lines ("A" lines here). For example, Investigation 1 enables both Specification 1 and Investigation 2, whereas both Implementation 1 and Specification 2 must be completed before Implementation 2 can be started. The specific network pictured might, for example, represent the concurrent development of a database system (Implementation 1) and an application system (Implementation 2) that uses it.

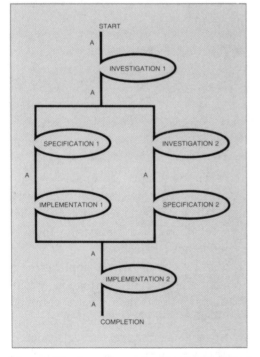

Figure 16. A system development spiral with concurrent activities.

Managing Spiral Development

The system development process generates limited, time-phased activities of investigation, specification, and implementation that must be managed. Formal stages of *planning, performance,* and *evaluation* in each activity define an orderly process for this management. The box structure methodology provides a great deal of commonality across these activities for the analysis and design work that is required. The management problems are also very similar. As the names imply, the most challenging stages for management are planning and evaluation, whereas the performance stage is the most challenging for technical professionals.

Planning. There are three basic results from the planning stage of any activity:

1. *Activity objective.* A statement of what the activity is to produce.

2. *Activity statement of work.* A statement of how the activity will achieve its objective.

3. *Activity schedule.* An assignment of work items in the Statement of Work to professionals together with agreed-on completion dates.

With such a plan, each member of the entire development team understands the objectives, Statement of Work, and the individual responsibilities for making good on the work objectives and schedule. Such a plan not only requires the agreement of the professionals, but also requires their direct participation in the planning process. But the planning process must be led by managers to address the proper questions and problems for the activity in the overall development plan.

Performance. If plans are well made, performance is focused and predictable. The management job in performance is to assess and track progress against the Statement of Work and schedules. Management must identify unexpected problems and help professionals decide how to meet them, and must identify unexpected windfalls in solutions that can free up people and resources. It is here that good understandings and agreements on assignments and schedules pay off.

Evaluation. Evaluation is both a closing out of one activity and a basis for selecting and commencing one or more following activities. The objectives and results of performance can be compared and related to the business and its situation. Even if objectives are not met, the lessons learned may be useful. If the objectives are met, so much the better, and the expected next activities can be initiated. In particular, the evaluation stage is the point where the development plan for future activities can be assessed and modified.

These activities and stages can be organized in tabular form, as shown in Table 1, which indicates typical tasks in systems development. A detailed discussion of these tasks is found in Mills et al. [7]

Concluding Remarks

The box structure methodology provides a rigorous approach for information systems analysis and design. The black box, state machine, and clear box present three different, yet complementary, views of an information system and any of its subsystems. The methodology provides for-

mal techniques for relating these structures and constructing box structure hierarchies.

Table 1.
Stages in Activities: Typical Tasks.

Activities	Stages		
	Planning	Performance	Evaluation
Investigation	Activity objective	Business process and objectives	Feasibility assessment
	Statement of work	Requirements analysis	Review and acceptance
	Scheduling	System prototype	Development plan update
Specification	Activity objective	Systems analysis and design	Design verification
	Statement of work	Operations analysis and design	Review and acceptance
	Scheduling		Development plan update
Implementation	Activity objective	Resource acquisition	System testing
	Statement of work	Systems integration	Review and acceptance
	Scheduling	Operations education	Development plan update

The correctness of box structure designs can be verified in stepwise fashion from clear boxes by systematically deriving their actual state machine and black box behaviors, and comparing them to their intended behaviors.

Box structures permit application of specific principles of information systems development that help ensure complete and well-structured designs. Referential transparency permits precise delegation of black box expansions once their clear box connections have been designed. Transaction closure ensures complete system behavior for users and complete state definitions for developers. State migration avoids data flow jungles in systems by decentralizing data storage and access into box structure subsystems. Common service design permits migration of widely used data into new box structure hierarchies that provide all required data access.

Box structures permit a flexible management process of spiral development, in contrast to a fixed life cycle. Spiral development is characterized by steps of investigation, specification, and implementation of box structures that can be dynamically sequenced and managed to best capitalize on the current progress and remaining resources of a development effort.

CITED REFERENCES

[1] O. Dahl, E. Dijkstra, and C.A.R. Hoare, *Structured Programming.* New York: Academic Press, 1972.

[2] A.B. Ferrentino and H.D. Mills, "State Machines and Their Semantics in Software Engineering," *Proceedings of COMPSAC 1977,* Chicago (November 1977), pp. 242-51.

[3] R.C. Linger, H.D. Mills, and B.I. Witt, *Structured Programming: Theory and Practice.* Reading, Mass.: Addison-Wesley, 1979.

[4] H.D. Mills, D. O'Neill, R.C. Linger, M. Dyer, and R.E. Quinnan, "The Management of Software Engineering," *IBM Systems Journal,* Vol. 19, No. 4, pp. 414-77 (1980).

[5] M.B. Carpenter and H.K. Hallman, "Quality Emphasis at IBM's Software Engineering Institute," *IBM Systems Journal,* Vol. 24, No. 2, pp. 121-33 (1985).

[6] M. Schaul, "Designing Using Software Engineering Principles: Overview of an Educational Program," *Proceedings of the Eighth International Conference on Software Engineering,* London (1985), pp. 201-208.

[7] H.D. Mills, R.C. Linger, and A. Hevner, *Principles of Information Systems Analysis and Design.* New York: Academic Press, 1986.

[8] F.T. Baker, "Chief Programmer Team Management of Production Programming," *IBM Systems Journal,* Vol. 11, No. 1, pp. 56-73 (1972).

[9] F.T. Baker, "System Quality Through Structured Programming," *AFIPS Conference Proceedings Fall Joint Computer Conference* Vol. 41, pp. 339-43 (1972).

[10] A.J. Jordano, "DSM Software Architecture and Development," *IBM Technical Directions,* Vol. 10, No. 3, pp. 17-28 (1984).

[11] D. Parnas, "A Technique for Software Module Specification with Examples," *Communications of the ACM,* Vol. 15, No. 5, pp. 330-36 (May 1972).

[12] J. Guttag and J. Horning, "The Algebraic Specification of Abstract Data Types," *Acta Informatica,* Vol. 10 (1978).

[13] G. Booch, "Object-Oriented Development," *IEEE Transactions on Software Engineering,* Vol. SE-12, No. 2, pp. 211-21 (February 1986).

[14] D.L. Parnas, "Designing Software for Ease of Extension and Contraction," *IEEE Transactions on Software*

Engineering, Vol. SE-5, No. 3, pp. 128-38 (March 1979).

[15] E. Yourdon and L. Constantine, *Structured Design: Fundamentals of a Discipline of Computer Program and System Design,* 2nd ed. New York: Yourdon Press, 1978.

[16] T. DeMarco, *Structured Analysis and System Specification.* New York: Yourdon Press, 1979.

[17] W.P. Stevens, *Using Structured Design.* New York: John Wiley & Sons, 1981.

[18] _____ , "How Data Flow Can Improve Application Development Productivity," *IBM Systems Journal,* Vol. 21, No. 2, pp. 162-78 (1982).

[19] B. Liskov, A. Snyder, R. Atkinson, and C. Schaffert, "Abstraction Mechanisms in CLU," *Communications of the ACM,* Vol. 20, No. 8, pp. 564-76 (August 1977).

[20] D. Bjorner and C. Jones, "The Vienna Development Method: The Meta-Language," *Springer-Verlag Lecture Notes in Computer Science,* Vol. 61, New York: Springer-Verlag, 1978.

[21] D. Bjorner, "On the Use of Formal Methods in Software Development," *Proceedings of the Ninth International Conference on Software Engineering* (1987), pp. 17-29.

[22] K. Levitt, P. Neumann, and L. Robinson, "The SRI Hierarchical Development Methodology and Its Application to the Development of Secure Software," *Proceedings of Software Engineering Applications,* Capri (1980).

[23] J. Guttag, J. Horning, and J. Wing, *Larch in Five Easy Pieces,* Technical Report, Digital Equipment Corporation Systems Research Center, Maynard, Mass. (1985).

[24] D.L. Parnas and W. Bartussek, *Using Traces to Write Abstract Specifications for Software Modules,* UNC Report TR 77-012, University of North Carolina, Chapel Hill, N.C. 27514 (1977).

[25] C.A.R. Hoare, "Some Properties of Predicate Transformers," *Journal of the ACM,* Vol. 25, No. 3, pp. 461-80 (July 1978).

[26] B. Liskov and S. Zilles, "Specification Techniques for Data Abstraction," *IEEE Transactions on Software Engineering,* Vol. SE-1, No. 3, pp. 114-26 (March 1975).

[27] M. Shaw, "Abstraction Techniques in Modern Programming Languages," *IEEE Software,* Vol. 1, No. 4 (October 1984).

[28] H. Katzen, *Systems Design and Documentation: An Introduction to the HIPO Method.* New York: Van Nostrand Reinhold, 1976.

GENERAL REFERENCES

R. Burstall and J. Goguen, "An Informal Introduction to Specifications Using CLEAR," in Boyer and Moore, eds., *The Correctness Problem in Computer Science.* New York: Academic Press, 1981.

L. Robinson and O. Roubine, *SPECIAL—A Specification and Assertion Language,* Technical Report CSL-46, Stanford Research Institute, Stanford, Calif. (1977).

16

Editors' Note
Selby, Basili, and Baker: "Cleanroom Software Development: An Empirical Evaluation"

Insight: It may cost less to leave the bugs out of the code entirely instead of paying to put them in and then paying again to take them out.

The term *cleanroom software engineering* was originally coined by IBM Fellow Harlan Mills. It refers to a software development technique that emphasizes building the product right the first time rather than the more common build-and-fix cycle. The most visible element of Mills's scheme is the complete separation of software construction from testing. In this approach you may participate as a builder or as a tester, but not both. If you produce any code, you do not test at all. And if you test, you do not design and write code.

Imagine yourself for a moment working in cleanroom mode. If you're not going to be allowed to test your own code (or anybody else's either), how might you go about building it in the first place so as not to look like an idiot when the testers get hold of it? Well, first of all, you would put a lot more emphasis on the design step. You would act to incorporate serious reviews and inspections. You might consider certain reuse schemes more favorably, because they let you incorporate known-quantity components. And you might even flirt with the notions of proof of correctness and formal specification. The cleanroom method is important, because the changes you make to accommodate it are long overdue.

By considering a test-free development process for even one paragraph, you have probably come up with a few questions: Is it possible at all? Could I stand it? Could it conceivably achieve its goal of improved product quality? The Selby-Basili-Baker study set out to answer these questions with a series of experiments. They formed five three-person teams and gave them identical systems to develop, some in cleanroom mode and others in a more conventional approach. The results speak for themselves.

16

Cleanroom Software Development:
An Empirical Evaluation
by Richard W. Selby, Victor R. Basili, and F. Terry Baker

I. INTRODUCTION

The need for discipline in the software development process and for high quality software motivates the Cleanroom software development approach. In addition to improving the control during development, this approach is intended to deliver a product that meets several quality aspects: a system that conforms with the requirements, a system with high operational reliability, and source code that is easily readable.

Section II describes the Cleanroom approach and Section III presents a framework of goals for characterizing its effect. Section IV describes an empirical study using the approach. Section V gives the results of the analysis comparing projects developed using Cleanroom with those of a control group. The overall conclusions appear in Section VI.

II. CLEANROOM DEVELOPMENT

The following sections describe the Cleanroom software development approach, discuss its introduction to an environment, describe the relationship of Cleanroom to software prototyping, and explain the role of software tools in Cleanroom development.

A. Cleanroom Software Development

The IBM Federal Systems Division (FSD) [23, 19, 24, 21, 16] presents the Cleanroom software development method as a technical and organizational approach to developing software with certifiable reliability. The idea is to deny the entry of defects during the development of software, hence the term "Cleanroom." The focus of the method, which is an extension of the FSD software engineering program [22], is imposing discipline on the development process by integrating formal methods for specification and design, nonexecution-based program development, and statistically based independent testing. These components are intended to contribute to a software product that has a high probability of zero defects and consequently a high measure of operational reliability.

1) *Software Life Cycle of Executable Increments:* In the Cleanroom approach, software development is organized around the incremental development of the software product. [16] Instead of considering software design, implementation, and testing as sequential stages in a software life cycle, software development is considered as a sequence of executable product increments. The increments accumulate over the development life cycle and result in a final product with full functionality.

2) *Formal Methods for Specification and Design:* In order to support the life cycle of executable increments, Cleanroom developers utilize "structured specifications" to divide the product functionality into deeply nested subsets that can be developed incrementally. The mathematically based design methodology in Cleanroom [22] incorporates the use of both structured specifications and state machine models. [26] A systems engineer introduces the structured specifications to restate the system requirements precisely and organize the complex problems into manageable parts. [41] The specifications determine the "system architecture" of the interconnections and groupings of capabilities to which state machine design practices can be applied. System implementation and test data formulation can then proceed from the structured specifications independently.

3) *Development without Program Execution:* The right-the-first-time programming methods used in Cleanroom are the ideas of functionally based programming in [38, 32]. The testing process is completely separated from the development process by not allowing the developers to test and debug their programs. The developers focus on the techniques of code reading by stepwise abstraction [32], code inspections [25], group walkthroughs [40], and formal verification [29, 32, 44, 20] to assert the correctness of their implementation. These nonexecution-based methods are referred to as "off-line software review techniques" in this paper. These constructive techniques apply throughout all phases of development, and condense the activities of defect detection and isolation into one operation. Empirical evaluations have suggested that the software review method of code reading by stepwise abstraction is at least as effective in detecting faults as execution-based methods [7, 43]. The intention in Cleanroom is to impose discipline on software development so that system correctness results from a coherent, readable design rather than from a reliance on execution-based testing. The notion that "Well, the software should always be tested to find the faults" is eliminated.

4) *Statistically Based, Independent Testing:* In the statistically based testing strategy of Cleanroom, independent testers simulate the operational environment of the system with random testing. This testing process includes defining the frequency distribution of inputs to the system, the frequency distribution of different system states, and the expanding range of developed system capabilities. Test cases then are chosen randomly and presented to the series of product increments, while concentrating on functions most recently delivered and maintaining the overall composite distribution of inputs. The independent testers then record observed failures and determine an objective measure of product reliability. Since software errors tend to vary widely in how frequently they are manifested as failures [1], operational testing is especially useful to assess the impact of software errors on product reliability. In addition to the statistical testing approach, the independent testers submit a limited number of test cases to ensure correct system operation for situations in which a software failure would be catastrophic. It is believed that the prior knowledge that a system will be evaluated by random testing will affect system reliability by enforcing a new discipline into the system developers.

The independent testing group operationally tests the software product increments from a perspective of reliability assessment, rather than a perspective of error detection. The responsibility of the test group is, therefore, to certify the reliability of the increments and final product rather than assist the development group in getting the product to an acceptable level of quality. One approach for measuring the reliability of the increments is through the use of a projected mean-time-between-failure (MTBF). MTBF estimations, based on user representative testing, provide both development managers and users with a useful, readily interpretable product reliability measure. Statistical models for calculating MTBF's projections include [34, 39, 33, 45, 15, 27, 16].

B. Introducing Cleanroom into a Development Environment

Before introducing the Cleanroom methodology into a software production environment, the developers need to be educated in the supporting technology areas. The technology areas consist of the development techniques and methods outlined in the above sections describing the components of Cleanroom. Potential Cleanroom users should also understand the goals of the development approach and be motivated to deliver high quality software products. One fundamental aspect of motivating the developers is to convince them that they can incorporate error prevention into the software process and actually produce error-free software. This "error-free perspective" is a departure from a current view that software errors are always present and error detection is the critical consideration.

C. Cleanroom versus Prototyping

The Cleanroom methodology and software prototyping are not mutually exclusive methods for developing software—the two approaches may be used together. The starting point for Cleanroom development is a document that states the user requirements. The production of that requirement document is an important portion of the software development process. Software prototyping is one approach that may be used to determine or refine the user requirements, and hence, produce the system requirements document [31, 47]. After the production of the requirements document, the prototype would be discarded and the Cleanroom methodology could be applied.

D. Tool Use in Cleanroom

Since Cleanroom developers do not execute their source code, does that mean that Cleanroom prohibits the use of tools during development? No—software tools can play an important role in the Cleanroom development approach. Various software tools can be used to help construct and manipulate the system design and source code. These tools can also be used to detect several types of errors that commonly occur in the system design and source code. The use of such tools facilitates the process of reviewing the system design and source code prior to submission for testing by the independent group. Some of the tools that may assist Cleanroom developers include various static analyzers, data flow analyzers, syntax checkers, type checkers, formal verification checkers, concurrency analyzers, and modeling tools.

III. INVESTIGATION GOALS

Some intriguing aspects of the Cleanroom approach include 1) development without testing and debugging of programs, 2) independent program testing for quality assurance (rather than to find faults or to prove "correctness" [30]), and 3) certification of system reliability before product delivery. In order to understand the effects of using Cleanroom, we proposed the following three goals: 1) characterize the effect of Cleanroom on the delivered product, 2) characterize the effect of Cleanroom on the software development process, and 3) characterize the effect of

Cleanroom on the developers. An application of the goal/question/metric paradigm [6, 10] lead to the framework of goals and questions for this study which appears in Fig. 1. The empirical study executed to pursue these goals is described in the following section.

IV. EMPIRICAL STUDY USING CLEANROOM

This section describes an empirical study comparing team projects developed using Cleanroom with those using a more conventional approach.

I. Characterize the effect of Cleanroom on the delivered product.
    A. For intermediate and novice programmers building a small system, what were the operational properties of the product?
        1. Did the product meet the system requirements?
        2. How did the operational testing results compare with those of a control group?
    B. What were the static properties of the product?
        1. Were the size properties of the product any different from what would be observed in a traditional development?
        2. Were the readability properties of the product any different?
        3. Was the control complexity any different?
        4. Was the data usage any different?
        5. Was the implementation language used differently?
    C. What contribution did programmer background have on the final product quality?
II. Characterize the effect of Cleanroom on the software development process.
    A. For intermediate and novice programmers building a small system, what techniques were used to prepare the developing system for testing submissions?
    B. What role did the computer play in development?
    C. Did the developers meet their delivery schedule?
III. Characterize the effect of Cleanroom on the developers.
    A. When intermediate and novice programmers built a small system, did the developers miss the satisfaction of executing their own programs?
        1. Did the missing of program execution have any relationship to programmer background or to aspects of the delivered product?
    B. How was the design and coding style of the developers affected by not being able to test and debug?
    C. Would the developers use Cleanroom again?

Figure 1. Framework of goals and questions for Cleanroom development approach analysis.

A. Subjects

Subjects for the empirical study came from the "Software Design and Development" course taught by F.T. Baker and V.R. Basili at the University of Maryland in the Falls of 1982 and 1983. The initial segment of the course was devoted to the presentation of several software development methodologies, including top-down design, modular specification and design, PDL, chief programmer teams, program correctness, code reading, walkthroughs, and functional and structural testing strategies. For the latter part of the course, the individuals were divided into three-person chief programmer teams for a group project [2, 37, 3]. We attempted to divide the teams equally according to professional experience, academic performance, and implementation language experience. The subjects had an average of 1.6 years professional experience and were university computer science students with graduate, senior, or junior standing. The subjects' professional experience predominantly came from government organizations and private software contractors in the Washington, DC area. Figure 2 displays the distribution of the subjects' professional experience.

B. Project Developed

A requirements document for an electronic message system (read, send, mailing lists, authorized capabilities, etc.) was distributed to each of the teams. The project was to be completed in six weeks and was expected to be about 1,500 lines of Simpl-T source code. [9]* The development machine was a Univac 1100/82 running EXEC VIII, with 1,200 baud interactive and remote access available.

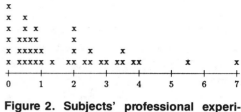

Figure 2. Subjects' professional experience in years.

C. Cleanroom Development Approach versus Traditional Approach

The ten teams in the Fall 1982 course applied the Cleanroom software development approach, while the five teams in the Fall 1983 course served as a control group (non-Cleanroom). All other aspects of the developments were the same. The two groups of teams were not statistically different in terms of professional experience, academic performance, or implementation language experience. If there were any bias between the two times the course was taught, it would be in favor of the 1983 (non-Cleanroom) group because the modular design portion of the course was presented earlier. It was also the second time F.T. Baker had taught the course.

The Cleanroom teams entered their source code on-line, used a syntax-checker (but did not do automated typechecking across modules), and were not able to execute their programs. The Cleanroom teams relied on the techniques of code

---

*Simpl-T is a structured language that supports several string and file handling primitives, in addition to the usual control flow constructs available, for example, in Pascal. If Pascal or Fortran had been chosen, it would have been very likely that some individuals would have had extensive experience with the language, and this would have biased the comparison. Also, restricting access to a compiler that produced executable code would have been very difficult.

reading, structured walkthroughs, and inspections to prepare their evolving systems before submission for independent testing. The non-Cleanroom teams were able to execute and debug their programs and applied several modern programming practices: modular design, top-down development, data abstraction, PDL, functional testing, design reviews, etc. The non-Cleanroom method was intended to reflect a software development approach that is currently in use in several software development organizations. Note that the non-Cleanroom method was roughly similar to the "disciplined team" development methodology examined in an earlier study. [5]

One issue to consider when comparing a "newer" approach with an existing one is whether one group will try harder just because they are using the newer approach. This effect is referred to as the Hawthorne effect. In order to combat this potential effect, we decided to have all the members of one course apply the same development approach.* In order to diffuse any of the Cleanroom developers from thinking that they were being compared relative to a previously applied approach, we decided that Cleanroom would be used in the earlier (1982) course. Therefore, there was no obvious competing arrangement in terms of approaches that were newer versus controlled.

D. Project Milestones

The objective for all teams from both groups was to develop the full system described in the requirements document.

---

*This decision also happened to result in the two groups not being as close in terms of size as they could have been.

The first document every team in either group turned in contained a system specification, composite design diagram, and implementation plan. The implementation plan was a series of milestones chosen by the individual teams which described when the various functions within the system would be available. At these various dates—minimum one week apart, maximum two—teams from the groups would then submit their systems for independent testing. Note that both the Cleanroom and non-Cleanroom teams had the benefit of the independent testing throughout development. An independent party would apply statistically based testing to each of the deliveries and report to the team members both the successful and unsuccessful test cases. The unsuccessful test cases would be included in a team's next test session for verification. The following section briefly describes the operationally based testing process applied to all projects by the independent tester.

E. Operational Testing of Projects

The testing approach used in Cleanroom is to simulate the developing system's environment by randomly selecting test data from an "operational profile," a frequency distribution of inputs to the system. [46, 18] The projects from both groups were tested interactively by an independent party (i.e., R.W. Selby) at the milestones chosen by each team. A distribution of inputs to the system was obtained by identifying the logical functions in the system and assigning each a frequency. This frequency assignment was accomplished by polling eleven well-seasoned users of a University of Maryland Vax 11/780 mailing system. Then test data were generated randomly from this profile and presented to the system. Recording of failure severity and times between failure took place during the testing process. The operational statistics referred to later were calculated from 50 user-session test cases run on the final system release of each team. For a complete explanation of the operationally based testing process applied to the projects, including test data selection, testing procedure, and failure observation, see [42].

F. Project Evaluation

All team projects were evaluated on their use of the particular software development techniques, the independent testing results, and a final oral interview. Both groups of subjects were judged to be highly motivated during the development of their systems. One reason for their motivation was their being graded based on the evaluation of their team projects. Information on the team projects was also collected from a background questionnaire, a post-development attitude survey, static source code analysis, and operating system statistics.

V. DATA ANALYSIS AND INTERPRETATION

The analysis and interpretation of the data collected from the study appear in the following sections, organized by the goal areas outlined earlier. In order to address the various questions posed under each of the goals, some raw data usually will be presented and then interpreted. Figure 3 presents the number of sources lines, executable statements, and procedures and functions to give a rough view of the systems developed.

Team	Classroom	Source Lines	Executable Statements	Procedures & Functions
A	yes	1681	813	55
B	yes	1626	717	42
C	yes	1118	573	42
D	yes	1046	477	30
E	yes	1087	624	32
F	yes	1213	440	35
G	yes	1196	581	31
H	yes	1876	550	51
I	yes	1305	608	23
J	yes	1052	658	24
a	no	824	410	26
b	no	1429	633	18
c	no	2264	999	46
d	no	1629	626	67
e	no	1310	459	43

Figure 3. System statistics.

A. Characterization of Effect on the Product Developed

This section characterizes the differences between the products delivered by the two development groups. Researchers have delineated numerous perspectives of software product quality [36, 14, 13], and the following sections examine aspects of several of these perspectives. Initially we examine some operational properties of the products, followed by a comparison of some of their static properties.

1) *Operational System Properties:* In order to contrast the operational properties of the systems delivered by the two groups, both completeness of implementation and operational testing results were examined. A measure of implementation completeness was calculated by partitioning the required system into 16 logical functions (e.g., send mail to an individual, read a piece of mail, respond, add yourself to a mailing list, . . .). Each function in an implementation was then assigned

a value of two if it completely met its requirements, a value of one if it partially met them, or zero if it was inoperable. The total for each system was calculated; a maximum score of 32 was possible. Figure 4 displays this subjective measure of requirement conformance for the systems. Note that in all figures presented, the ten teams using Cleanroom are in upper case and the five teams using a more conventional approach are in lower case. A first observation is that six of the ten Cleanroom teams built very close to the entire system. While not all of the Cleanroom teams performed equally well, a majority of them applied the approach effectively enough to develop nearly the whole product. More importantly, the Cleanroom teams met the requirements of the system more completely than did the non-Cleanroom teams.

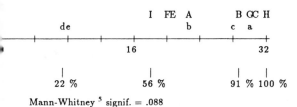

Mann-Whitney [5] signif. = .088

Figure 4. Requirement conformance of the systems.*

To compare testing results among the systems developed in the two groups, 50 random user-session test cases were executed on the final release of each system to simulate its operational environment. If the final release of a system performed to expectations on a test case, the outcome

was called a "success;" if not, the outcome was a "failure." If the outcome was a "failure" but the same failure was observed on an earlier test case run on the final release, the outcome was termed a "duplicate failure." Figure 5 shows the percentage of successful test cases when duplicate failures are not included. The figure displays that Cleanroom projects had a higher percentage of successful test cases at system delivery.[†] When duplicate failures are included, however, the better performance of the Cleanroom systems is not nearly as significant (MW = 0.134).[‡] This is caused by the Cleanroom projects having a relatively higher proportion of duplicate failures, even though they did better overall. This demonstrates that while reviewing the code, the Cleanroom developers focused less than the other group on certain parts of the system. The more uniform review of the whole system makes the performance of the system less sensitive to its operational profile. Note that operational environments of systems are usually difficult to define *a priori* and are subject to change.

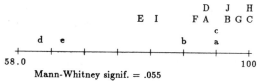

Mann-Whitney signif. = .055

Figure 5. Percentage of successful test cases during operational testing (without duplicate failures).

---

*The significance levels for the Mann-Whitney statistics reported are the probability of Type I error in a one-tailed test.

[†]Although not considered here, various software reliability models have been proposed to forecast system reliability based on failure data (see Section II-A-4).

[‡]To be more succinct, MW will sometimes be used to abbreviate the significance level of the Mann-Whitney statistic.

In both of the product quality measures of implementation completeness and operational testing results, there was quite a variation in performance.* A wide variation may have been expected with an unfamiliar development technique, but the developers using a more traditional approach had a wider range of performance than did those using Cleanroom in both of the measures—even with there being twice as many Cleanroom teams. All of the above differences are magnified by recalling that the non-Cleanroom teams did not develop their systems in one monolithic step, they (also) had the benefit of periodic operational testing by independent testers. Since both groups of teams had independent testing of all their deliveries, the early testing of deliveries must have revealed most faults overlooked by the Cleanroom developers.

These comparisons suggest that the non-Cleanroom developers focused on a "perspective of the tester," sometimes leaving out classes of functions and causing a less completely implemented product and more (especially unique) failures. Off-line software review techniques, however, are more general and their use contributed to more complete requirement conformance and fewer failures in the Cleanroom products. In addition to examining the operational properties of the

---

*An alternate perspective includes only the more successful projects from each group in the comparison of operational product quality. When the best 60 percent from each approach are examined (i. e., removing teams "d," "e," "A," "E," "F," and "I"), the Mann-Whitney significance level for comparing implementation completeness becomes 0.045 and the significance level for comparing successful test cases (without duplicate failures) becomes 0.034. Thus, comparing the best teams from each approach increases the evidence in favor of Cleanroom in both of these product quality measures.

product, various static properties were compared.

2) *Static System Properties:* The first question in this goal area concerns the size of the final systems. Figure 3 showed the number of source lines, executable statements, and procedures and functions for the various systems. The projects from the two groups were not statistically different (MW > 0.10) in any of these three size attributes. Another question in this goal area concerns the readability of the delivered source code. Although readability is not equivalent to maintainability, modifiability, or reusability, it is a central component of each of these software quality aspects. Two aspects of reading and altering source code are the number of comments present and the density of the "complexity." In an attempt to capture the complexity density, syntactic complexity [4] was calculated and normalized by the number of executable statements. In addition to control-flow complexity, the syntactic complexity metric considers nesting depth and prime program decomposition. [32] The developers using Cleanroom wrote code that was more highly commented (MW = 0.089) and had a lower complexity density (MW = 0.079) than did those using the traditional approach. A calculation of either software science effort [28], cyclomatic complexity [35], or syntactic complexity without any size normalization, however, produced no significant differences (MW > 0.10). This seems as expected because all the systems were built to meet the same requirements.

Comparing the data usage in the systems, Cleanroom developers used a greater number of nonlocal data items (MW = 0.071). Also, Cleanroom projects possessed a higher percentage of assignment statements (MW = 0.056). These last two observations could be a manifestation of teaching the Cleanroom subjects modular design later in the course (see Section IV-C), or possibly an indication of using the approach. One interpretation of the Cleanroom developers' use of more nonlocal data could be that the resulting software would be less reusable and less portable. In fact, however, the increased use of nonlocal data by some Cleanroom developers was because of their use of data abstraction. In order to incorporate data abstraction into a system implemented in the Simpl-T programming language, developers may create independently compilable program units that have retained, nonlocal data and associated accessing routines.

Some interesting observations surface when the operational quality measures of just the Cleanroom products are correlated with the usage of the implementation language. Both percentage of successful test cases (without duplicate failures) and implementation completeness correlated with percentage of procedure calls (Spearman $R = 0.65$, signif. $= 0.044$, and $R = 0.57$, signif. $= 0.08$, respectively) and with percentage of IF statements ($R = 0.62$, signif. $= 0.058$, and $R = 0.55$, signif. $= 0.10$, respectively). However, both of these two product quality measures correlated negatively with percentage of CASE statements ($R = -0.86$, signif. $= 0.001$, and $R = -0.69$, signif. $= 0.027$, respectively) and with percentage of WHILE statements ($R = -0.65$, signif. $= 0.044$, and $R = -0.49$, signif. $= 0.15$, respectively). There were also some negative correlations between the product quality measures and the aver-

age software science effort per subroutine ($R = -0.52$, signif. $= 0.12$, and $R = -0.74$, signif. $= 0.013$, respectively) and the average number of occurrences of a variable ($R = -0.54$, signif. $= 0.11$, and $R = -0.56$, signif. $= 0.09$, respectively). Considering the products from all teams, both percentage of successful test cases (without duplicate failures) and implementation completeness had some correlation with percentage of IF statements ($R = 0.48$, signif. $= 0.07$, and $R = 0.45$, signif. $= 0.09$, respectively) and some negative correlation with percentage of CASE statements ($R = -0.48$, signif. $= 0.07$, and $R = -0.42$, signif. $= 0.12$, respectively). Neither of the operational product quality measures correlated with percentage of assignment statements when either all products or just Cleanroom products were considered. These observations suggest that the more successful Cleanroom developers simplified their use of the implementation language; i.e., they used more procedure calls and IF statements, used fewer CASE and WHILE statements, had a lower frequency of variable reuse, and wrote subroutines requiring less software science effort to comprehend.

3) Contribution of Programmer Background: When examining the contribution of the Cleanroom programmers' background to the quality of their final products, general programming language experience correlated with percentage of successful operational tests (without duplicate failures: Spearman $R = 0.66$, signif. $= 0.04$; with duplicates: $R = 0.70$, signif. $= 0.03$) and with implementation completeness ($R = 0.55$; signif. $= 0.10$). No relationship appears between either operational testing results or implementation completeness and either professional* or testing experience. These background/quality relations seem consistent with other studies. [17]

4) *Summary of the Effect on the Product Developed:* In summary, Cleanroom developers delivered a product that 1) met system requirements more completely, 2) had a higher percentage of successful test cases, 3) had more comments and less dense control-flow complexity, and 4) used more nonlocal data items and a higher percentage of assignment statements. The more successful Cleanroom developers 1) used more procedure calls and IF statements, 2) used fewer CASE and WHILE statements, 3) reused variables less frequently, 4) developed subroutines requiring less software science effort to comprehend, and 5) had more general programming language experience.

B. Characterization of the Effect on the Development Process

In a postdevelopment attitude survey, the developers were asked how effectively they felt they applied off-line software review techniques in testing their projects (see Fig. 6). This was an attempt to capture some of the information necessary to answer the first question under this goal (question II-A). In order to make comparisons at the team level, the responses from the members of a team are composed into an average for the team. The responses to the question appear on a team

basis in a histogram in the second part of the figure. Of the Cleanroom developers, teams "A," "D," "E," "F," and "I" were the least confident in their use of the off-line review techniques and these teams also performed the worst in terms of operational testing results; four of these five teams performed the worst in terms of implementation completeness. Off-line review effectiveness correlated with percentage of successful operational tests (without duplicate failures) for the Cleanroom teams (Spearman $R = 0.74$; signif. $= 0.014$) and for all the teams ($R = 0.76$; signif. $= 0.001$); it correlated with implementation completeness for all the teams ($R = 0.58$; signif. $= 0.023$). Neither professional nor testing experience correlated with off-line review effectiveness when either all teams or just Cleanroom teams were considered.

The histogram in Fig. 6 shows that the Cleanroom developers felt they applied the off-line review techniques more effectively than did the non-Cleanroom teams. The non-Cleanroom developers were asked to give a relative breakdown of the amount of time spent applying testing and off-line review techniques. Their aggregate response was 39 percent off-line review, 52 percent functional testing, and 9 percent structural testing. From this breakdown, we observe that the non-Cleanroom teams primarily relied on functional testing to prepare their systems for independent testing. Since the Cleanroom teams were unable to rely on testing methods, they may have (felt they had) applied the off-line review techniques more effectively.

Since the role of the computer is more controlled when using Cleanroom, one would expect a difference in on-line ac-

---

*In fact, there are very slight negative correlations between years of professional experience and both percentage of successful tests (without duplicate failures: $R = -0.46$, signif. $= 0.18$) and implementation completeness ($R = -0.47$, signif. $= 0.17$).

tivity between the two groups. Figure 7 displays the amount of connect time that each of the teams cumulatively used. A comparison of the CPU-time used by the teams was less statistically significant (MW = 0.110). Neither of these measures of on-line activity related to how effectively a team felt they had used the off-line review techniques when either all teams or just Cleanroom teams were considered. Although non-Cleanroom team ''d'' did a lot of on-line testing and non-Cleanroom team ''e'' did little, both teams performed poorly in the measures of operational product quality discussed earlier.

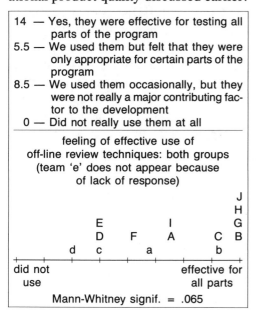

14 —	Yes, they were effective for testing all parts of the program
5.5 —	We used them but felt that they were only appropriate for certain parts of the program
8.5 —	We used them occasionally, but they were not really a major contributing factor to the development
0 —	Did not really use them at all

feeling of effective use of
off-line review techniques: both groups
(team 'e' does not appear because
of lack of response)

Mann-Whitney signif. = .065

Figure 6. Breakdown of responses to the attitude survey question, ''Did you feel that you and your team members effectively used off-line review techniques in testing your project?'' (Responses are from Cleanroom teams.)*

The operating system of the development machine captured these system usage statistics. Note that the time the independent party spent testing is included.†

These observations exhibit that Cleanroom developers spent less time on-line and used fewer computer resources. These results empirically support the reduced role of the computer in Cleanroom development.

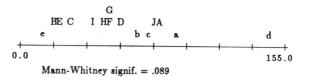

Mann-Whitney signif. = .089

Figure 7. Connect time in hours during project development.‡

Schedule slippage continues to be a problem in software development. It would be interesting to see whether the Cleanroom teams demonstrated any more discipline by maintaining their original schedules. All of the teams from both groups planned four releases of their evolving system, except for team ''G'' which planned five. Recall that at each delivery an independent party would operationally test the functions currently available in the system, according to the team's implementation plan. In Fig. 8, we observe that all the teams using Cleanroom kept to their original schedules by making all planned deliveries; only two non-Cleanroom teams made all their scheduled deliveries.

---

*There are half-responses because an individual checked both the second and third choices. The responses total to 28, not 30, because two separate teams lost a member late in the project. (See Section V-D.)

†When the time the independent tester spent is not included, the significance levels for the nonparametric statistics do not change.

‡Non-Cleanroom team ''e'' entered a substantial portion of its system on a remote machine, only using the Univac computer mainly for compilation and execution. Team ''e'' was the only team that used any machine other than the Univac. (See Section V-D.)

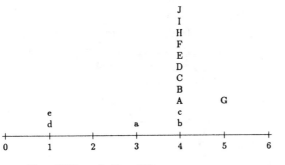

Mann-Whitney signif. = .006

Figure 8. Number of system releases.

1) *Summary of the Effect on the Development Process:* Summarizing the effect on the development process, Cleanroom developers 1) felt they applied off-line review techniques more effectively, while non-Cleanroom teams focused on functional testing; 2) spent less time on-line and used fewer computer resources; and 3) made all their scheduled deliveries.

13 — Yes, I missed the satisfaction of program execution.
11 — I somewhat missed the satisfaction of program execution.
4 — No, I did not miss the satisfaction of program execution.

Figure 9. Breakdown of responses to the attitude survey question, "Did you miss the satisfaction of executing your own programs?"

C. Characterization of the Effect on the Developers

The first question posed in this goal area is whether the individuals using Cleanroom missed the satisfaction of executing their own programs. Figure 9 presents the responses to a question included in the postdevelopment attitude survey on this issue. As might be expected, almost all the individuals missed some aspect of program execution. As might not be expected, however, this missing of program

Spearman correlations: −.85 (signif. = .002) with source lines; −.70 (signif. = .03) with number separately compilable modules; −.57 (signif. = .09) with number procedures and functions.

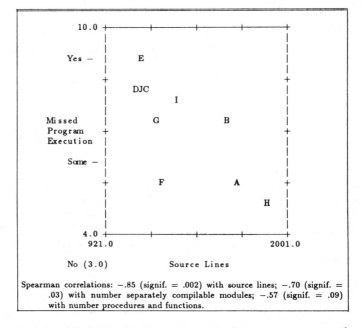

Figure 10. Relationship of program size versus missing program execution.

execution had no relation to either the product quality measures mentioned earlier or the teams' professional or testing experience. Also, missing program execution did not increase with respect to program size (see Fig. 10).

Figure 11 displays the replies of the developers when they were asked how their design and coding style was affected by not being able to test and debug. At first it would seem surprising that more people did not modify their development style when applying the techniques of Cleanroom. Several persons mentioned, however, that they already utilized some of the ideas in Cleanroom. Keeping a simple design supports readability of the product and facilitates the processes of modification and verification. Although some of the objective product measures presented earlier showed differences in development style, these subjective ones are interesting and lend insight into actual programmer behavior.

---

2 — Yes, my style was substantially revised.
15 — I modified some of my tendencies.
11 — It did not affect my style at all.

Frequently mentioned responses include

— kept design simple, attempted nothing fancy
— kept readability of code in mind
— already was a user of off-line review techniques
— very careful scrutiny of code for potential mistakes
— prepared for a larger range of inputs

Figure 11. Breakdown of responses to the attitude survey question, "How was your design and coding style affected by not being able to test and debug?"

One indicator of the impression that something new leaves on people is whether they would do it again. Figure 12 presents the responses of the individuals when they were asked whether they would choose to use Cleanroom again as either a software development manager or as a programmer. Even though these responses were gathered (immediately) after course completion, subjects desiring to "please the instructor" may have responded favorably to this type of question regardless of their true feelings. Practically everyone indicated a willingness to apply the approach again. It is interesting to note that a greater number of persons in a managerial role would choose to always use it. Of the persons that ranked the reuse of Cleanroom fairly low in each category, four of the five were the same people. Of the six people that ranked reuse low, four were from less successful projects (one from team "A," one from team "E" and two from team "I"), but the other two came from reasonably successful developments (one from team "C" and one from team "J"). The particular individuals on teams "E," "I," and "J" were the four that rated reuse fairly low in both categories.

As a software manager?
   8 —Yes, at all times
  14 —Yes, but only for certain projects
   5 —Not at all

As a programmer?
   4 —Yes, for all projects
  18 —Yes, but not all the time
   5 —Only if I had to
   0 —I would leave if I had to

Figure 12. Breakdown of responses to the attitude survey question, "Would you use Cleanroom again?" (One person did not respond to this question.)

1) *Summary of the Effect on the Developers:* In summary of the effect on the developers, most Cleanroom developers 1) partially modified their development style, 2) missed program execution, and 3) indicated that they would use the approach again.

D. Distinction Among Teams

In spite of efforts to balance the teams according to various factors (see Section IV-A), a few differences among the teams were apparent. Two separate Cleanroom teams, "H" and "I," each lost a member late in the project. Thus at project completion, there were eight three-person and two two-person Cleanroom teams. Recall that team "H" performed quite well according to requirement conformance and testing results, while team "I" did poorly. Also, the second group of subjects did not divide evenly into three-person teams. Since one of those individuals had extensive professional experience, non-Cleanroom team "e" consisted of that one highly experienced person. Thus at project completion, there were four three-person and one one-person non-Cleanroom teams. Although team "e" wrote over 1,300 source lines, this highly experienced person did not do as well as the other teams in some respects. This is consistent with another study in which teams applying a "disciplined methodology" in development outperformed individuals. [5] Appendix A contains the significance levels for the results of the analysis presented when team "e," when teams "H" and "I," and when teams "e," "H," and "I" are removed from the analysis. Removing teams "H" and "I" has little effect on the significance levels, while the removal of team "e" causes a decrease in all of the significance levels except for executable statements, software science effort, cyclomatic complexity, syntactic complexity, connect-time, and CPU-time.

VI. CONCLUSIONS

This paper describes "Cleanroom" software development—an approach intended to produce highly reliable software by integrating formal methods for specification and design, nonexecution-based program development, and statistically based independent testing. The goal structure, experimental approach, data analysis, and conclusions are presented for a replicated-project study examining the Cleanroom approach. This is the first investigation known to the authors that applied Cleanroom and characterized its effect relative to a more traditional development approach.

The data analysis presented and the testimony provided by the developers suggest that the major results of this study are the following. 1) Most of the developers were able to apply the techniques of Cleanroom effectively (six of the ten Cleanroom teams delivered at least 91 percent of the required system functions). 2) The Cleanroom teams' products met system requirements more completely and had a higher percentage of successful operationally generated test cases. 3) The source code developed using Cleanroom had more comments and less dense control-flow complexity. 4) The more successful Cleanroom developers modified their use of the implementation language; they used more procedure calls and IF statements, used fewer CASE and WHILE statements, and had a lower frequency of variable reuse (average number of occurrences per variable). 5) All ten Cleanroom teams made all of their scheduled intermediate product deliveries, while only two of the five non-Cleanroom teams did. 6) Although 86 percent of the Cleanroom developers indicated that they missed the satisfaction of program execution to some extent, this had no relation to the product quality measures of implementation completeness and successful operational tests. 7) Eighty-one percent of the Cleanroom developers said that they would use the approach again.

Based on the experience of applying Cleanroom in this study, some potential areas for improving the methodology are as follows. 1) As mentioned above, several Cleanroom developers tended to miss the satisfaction of program execution. In order to circumvent a potential long-term psychological effect, a method for providing such satisfaction to the developers would be useful. One suggestion would be for developers to witness, but not influence, program execution by the independent testers. 2) Several of the persons applying the Cleanroom approach mentioned that they had some difficulty visualizing the user interface, and hence, felt that the systems suffered in terms of "user-friendliness." One suggestion would be to prototype the user interfaces as part of the requirement determination phase, and then describe the interfaces in the requirements document, possibly using an interactive display specification language [11]. 3) A few of the Cleanroom developers said that they did not feel subjected to a "full test." Recall that the reliability certification component of the Cleanroom approach stands on the premise that operationally-based testing is sufficient to assess system reliability. One suggestion may be to augment the testing process with methods that enforce increased coverage of the system requirements, design, and implementation and/or methods that utilize frequent error profiles.

Overall, it seems that the ideas in Cleanroom help attain the goals of producing high quality software and increasing the discipline in the software development process. The complete separation of development from testing appears to cause a modification in the developers' behavior, resulting in increased process control and in more effective use of methods for software specification, design, off-line review, and verification. It seems that system modification and maintenance would be more easily done on a product developed in the Cleanroom method, because of the product's thoroughly conceived design and higher readability. Facilitating the software modification and maintenance tasks results in a corresponding reduction in associated costs to users. The amount of development effort required by the Cleanroom approach was not gathered in this study because its purpose was to examine the feasibility of Cleanroom and to characterize its effect. However, even if using Cleanroom required additional development effort, it seems that the potential reduction in maintenance and enhancement costs may result in an overall decrease in software life cycle cost. Thus, achieving high requirement conformance and high operational reliability coupled with low maintenance costs would help reduce overall costs, satisfy the user community, and support a long product lifetime.

Other studies which have compared

software development methodologies include [5] and [12].* In [5] three software development approaches were compared: a disciplined-methodology team approach, an ad hoc team approach, and an ad hoc individual approach. The development approaches were applied by advanced university students comprising seven three-person teams, six three-person teams, and six individuals, respectively. They separately built a small (600-2,200 line) compiler. The disciplined-methodology team approach significantly reduced the development costs as reflected in program changes and runs. The resulting designs from the disciplined-methodology teams and the ad hoc individuals were more coherent than the disjointed designs developed by the ad hoc teams. In [12] two software development approaches were compared: prototyping and specifying. Seven two- and three-person teams, consisting of university graduate students, developed separate versions of the same (2,000-4,000 line) application program. The systems developed by prototyping were smaller, required less development effort, and were easier to use. The systems developed by specifying had more coherent designs, more complete functionality, and software that was easier to integrate.

Future possible research directions include 1) assessment of the applicability of Cleanroom to larger software developments (note that aspects of the Cleanroom approach are being used in a 30,000 source line project [21, 16]); 2) empirical evaluation of the effect of Cleanroom from additional software quality perspectives, including reusability and modifiability; and 3) further characterization of the number and types of errors that occur when Cleanroom is or is not used.

This empirical study is intended to advance the understanding of the relationship between introducing discipline into the development process, as in Cleanroom, and several aspects of product quality: conformance with requirements, high operational reliability, and easily readable source code. The results given were calculated from a set of teams applying Cleanroom development on a relatively small project—the direct extrapolation of the findings to other projects and development environments is not implied.

---

*For a survey of controlled, empirical studies that have been conducted in software engineering, see [8].

APPENDIX A

Figure 13 presents the measure averages and the significance levels for the above comparisons when team "e," when teams "H" and "I," and when teams "e," "H," and "I" are removed. The significance levels for the Mann-Whitney statistics reported are the probability of Type I error in a one-tailed test.

ACKNOWLEDGMENT

The authors are grateful to D.H. Hutchens and R.W. Reiter for the use of their static analysis program in this study.

Measure	Average		Mann-Whitney significance levels			
	Clean-room Teams	Non-Clean-room Teams	All Teams	With-out Team e	With-out Teams H,I	With-out Teams e,H,I
Source lines	1320.0	1491.2	.196	.240	.153	.198
Executable stmts	604.1	625.4	.500	.286	.442	.367
Procedures & functions	36.5	40.0	.357	.500	.330	.500
%Implementation completeness	82.5	60.0	.088	.197	.093	.196
%Successful tests (w/o duplicate failures)	92.5	80.8	.055	.128	.053	.116
%Successful tests (w/ duplicate failures)	78.7	59.2	.134	.285	.151	.304
Comments	194.9	122.2	.089	.102	.190	.198
Syntactic complexity/ executable stmts	1.5	1.6	.079	.179	.082	.175
Software Science E	6728.6e3	7355.4e3	.451	.240	.442	.248
Cyclomatic complexity	196.8	212.2	.250	.198	.255	.248
Syntactic complexity	917.5	1017.0	.500	.286	.500	.305
Non-local data items	37.6	24.2	.071	.129	.053	.117
%Assignment stmts	34.2	26.6	.056	.129	.040	.087
Off-line effectiveness	3.2	2.5	.065	.065	.098	.098
Connect-time (hr.)	41.0	71.3	.089	.012	.121	.021
Cpu-time (min.)	71.7	136.1	.110	.017	.072	.009
Deliveries	4.1	2.6	.006	.015	.010	.022

Figure 13. Summary of measure averages and significance levels.

REFERENCES

[1] E.N. Adams, "Optimizing Preventive Service of Software Products," *IBM Journal of Research & Development,* Vol. 28, No. 1, pp. 2-14, January 1984.

[2] F.T. Baker, "Chief Programmer Team Management of Production Programming," *IBM Systems Journal,* Vol. 11, No. 1, pp. 131-49, 1972.

[3] ———, "Chief Programmer Teams," in *Tutorial on Structured Programming: Integrated Practices,* V.R. Basili and F.T. Baker, eds. New York: IEEE, 1981.

[4] V.R. Basili and D.H. Hutchens, "An Empirical Study of a Syntactic Metric Family," *IEEE Transactions on Software Engineering,* Vol. SE-9, pp. 664-72, November 1983.

[5] V.R. Basili and R.W. Reiter, "A Controlled Experiment Quantitatively Comparing Software Development Approaches," *IEEE Transactions on Software Engineering,* Vol. SE-7, May 1981.

[6] V.R. Basili and R.W. Selby, "Data Collection and Analysis in Software Research and Management," in *Proceedings of the American Statistical Association and Biometric Soviet Joint Statistical Meetings,* Philadelphia, Penn., August 13-16, 1984.

[7] ———, "Comparing the Effectiveness of Software Testing Strategies," Dept. of Computer Science, University of Maryland, College Park, Technical Report TR-1501, May 1985; to appear in *IEEE Transactions on Software Engineering.*

[8] V.R. Basili, R.W. Selby, and D.H. Hutchens, "Experimentation in Software Engineering," *IEEE Transactions on Software Engineering,* Vol. SE-12, pp. 733-43, July 1986.

[9] V.R. Basili and A.J. Turner, *SIMPL-T: A Structured Programming Language.* Geneva, Ill.: Paladin House, 1976.

[10] V.R. Basili and D.M. Weiss, "A Methodology for Collecting Valid Software Engineering Data," *IEEE Transactions on Software Engineering,* Vol. SE-10, pp. 728-38, November 1984.

[11] L.J. Bass, "An Approach to User Specification of Interactive Display Interfaces," *IEEE Transactions on Software Engineering,* Vol. SE-11, pp. 686-98, August 1985.

[12] B.W. Boehm, T.E. Gray, and T. Seewaldt, "Prototyping versus Specifying: A Multiproject Experiment," *IEEE Transactions on Software Engineering,* Vol. SE-10, pp. 290-303, May 1984.

[13] T.P. Bowen, G.B. Wigle, and J.T. Tsai, "Specification of Software Quality Attributes," Rome Air Development Center, Griffiss Air Force Base, N.Y., Technical Report RADC-TR-85-37 (3 volumes), February 1985.

[14] J.P. Cavano and J.A. McCall, "A Framework for the Measurement of Software Quality," in *Proceedings of the Software Quality and Assurance Workshop,* San Diego, Calif., November 1978, pp. 133-39.

[15] P.A. Currit, "Cleanroom Certification Model," in *Proceedings of the 8th Annual Software Engineering Workshop,* NASA/GSFC, Greenbelt, Md., November 1983.

[16] ———, M. Dyer, and H.D.

Mills, "Certifying the Reliability of Software," *IEEE Transactions on Software Engineering,* Vol. SE-12, pp. 3-11, January 1986.

[17]   B. Curtis, "Cognitive Science of Programming," in *Sixth Minnowbrook Workshop Software Performance Evaluation,* Blue Mountain Lake, N.Y., July 19-22, 1983.

[18]   J.W. Duran and S. Ntafos, "A Report on Random Testing," in *Proceedings of the Fifth International Conference on Software Engineering,* San Diego, Calif., March 9-12, 1981, pp. 179-83.

[19]   M. Dyer, "Cleanroom Software Development Method," IBM Federal Systems Division, Bethesda, Md., October 14, 1982.

[20]   _____ , "Software Validation in the Cleanroom Development Method," IBM-FSD Technical Report 86.0003, August 19, 1983.

[21]   _____ , "Software Development Under Statistical Quality Control," in *Proceedings of the NATO Advanced Study Institute: The Challenge of Advanced Computing Technology to System Design Methods,* Durham, UK, July 29-August 10, 1985.

[22]   M. Dyer, R.C. Linger, H.D. Mills, D. O'Neil, and R.E. Quinnan, "The Management of Software Engineering," *IBM Systems Journal,* Vol. 19, No. 4, 1980.

[23]   M. Dyer and H.D. Mills, "The Cleanroom Approach to Reliable Software Development," in *Proceedings of the Validation Methods Research for Fault-Tolerant Avionics and Control Systems Sub-Working-Group Meeting: Production of*

Reliable Flight-Crucial Software, Research Triangle Institute, N.C., November 2-4, 1981.

[24]   _____ , "Developing Electronic Systems with Certifiable Reliability," in *Proceedings of the NATO Conference,* Summer 1982.

[25]   M.E. Fagan, "Design and Code Inspections to Reduce Errors in Program Development," *IBM Systems Journal,* Vol. 15, No. 3, pp. 182-211, 1976.

[26]   A.B. Ferrentino and H.D. Mills, "State Machines and Their Semantics in Software Engineering," in *Proceedings of the IEEE COMPSAC,* 1977.

[27]   A.L. Goel, "A Guidebook for Software Reliability Assessment," Dept. of Industrial Engineering and Operations Research, Syracuse University, N.Y., Technical Report 83-11, April 1983.

[28]   M.H. Halstead, *Elements of Software Science.* New York: North-Holland, 1977.

[29]   C.A.R. Hoare, "An Axiomatic Basis for Computer Programming," *Communications of the ACM,* Vol. 12, No. 10, pp. 576-83, October 1969.

[30]   W.E. Howden, "Reliability of the Path Analysis Testing Strategy," *IEEE Transactions on Software Engineering,* Vol. SE-2, No. 3, September 1976.

[31]   P. Kerola and P. Freeman, "A Comparison of Lifecycle Models," in *Proceedings of the Fifth International Conference on Software Engineering,* March 1981, pp. 90-99.

[32]   R.C. Linger, H.D. Mills, and B.I.

Witt, *Structured Programming: Theory and Practice.* Reading, Mass.: Addison-Wesley, 1979.

[33] B. Littlewood, "Stochastic Reliability Growth: A Model for Fault Renovation Computer Programs and Hardware Designs," *IEEE Transactions on Reliability,* Vol. R-30, October 1981.

[34] B. Littlewood and J.L. Verrall, "A Bayesian Reliability Growth Model for Computer Software," *Applied Statistics,* Vol. 22, No. 3, 1973.

[35] T.J. McCabe, "A Complexity Measure," *IEEE Transactions on Software Engineering,* Vol. SE-2, pp. 308-20, December 1976.

[36] J.A. McCall, P. Richards, and G. Walters, "Factors in Software Quality," Rome Air Development Center, Griffiss Air Force Base, N.Y., Technical Report RADC-TR-77-369, November 1977.

[37] H.D. Mills, "Chief Programmer Teams: Principles and Procedures," IBM Corp., Gaithersburg, Md., Report FSC 71-6012, 1972.

[38] _____ , "Mathematical Foundations for Structural Programming," IBM Report FSL 72-6021, 1972.

[39] J.D. Musa, "A Theory of Software Reliability and Its Application," *IEEE Transactions on Software Engineering,* Vol. SE-1, No. 3, pp. 312-27, 1975.

[40] G.J. Myers, *Software Reliability: Principles & Practices.* New York: Wiley, 1976.

[41] D.L. Parnas, "On the Criteria to Be Used in Decomposing Systems into Modules," *Communications of the ACM,* Vol. 15, No. 12, pp. 1053-58, 1972.

[42] R.W. Selby, "Evaluations of Software Technologies: Testing, CLEANROOM, and Metrics," Ph.D. dissertation, Dept. of Computer Science, University of Maryland, College Park, Technical Report TR-1500, 1985.

[43] _____ , "Combining Software Testing Strategies: An Empirical Evaluation," in *Proceedings of the Workshop on Software Testing,* Banff, Alta., Canada, July 15-17, 1986, pp. 82-91.

[44] K.S. Shankar, "A Functional Approach to Module Verification," *IEEE Transactions on Software Engineering,* Vol. SE-8, March 1982.

[45] J.G. Shanthikumar, "A Statistical Time Dependent Error Occurrence Rate Software Reliability Model with Imperfect Debugging," in *Proceedings of the 1981 National Computer Conference,* June 1981.

[46] R.A. Thayer, M. Lipow, and E.C. Nelson, *Software Reliability.* Amsterdam, The Netherlands: North-Holland, 1978.

[47] M.V. Zelkowitz and M. Branstad, in *Proceedings of the ACM SIGSOFT Rapid Prototyping Symposium,* April 1982.

17

Editors' Note
Petschenik: "Practical Priorities in System Testing"

Insight: In order to boldly go where no one has gone before and come back alive, at least in the universe of large software system testing, you had better prioritize what you wish to accomplish, and measure what results you get.

This article is all about the early stages of transition from Art to Science. Today, most organizations treat software testing either as a mystic art or as a political ritual.

Testing as mystic art: The code is left in front of the testers' caves. It disappears, then reappears with red ink. What goes on in the cave is unknown, but often strange chanting can be heard from within the cave's dark recesses.

Testing as political ritual: The software must be delivered to the field by September 1 at 0900 hours. It is now July 29, 1700 hours. Guess how long the testing process will take? Hint: What testing uncovers is irrelevant to the answer.

Petschenik led a system test organization that avoided falling into either of the two categories. This was accomplished even though the methods of present-day software testing are demonstrably inadequate for a system as large as the one described.

Leading the way from Art, Petschenik's group used two weapons: measurement and rational decision making. The group measured most everything its members did. (Can your testers give you comparable information for your systems?) Second, the group had a rational decision making process in place because the testers never expected to complete their job. (What would happen in your organization if a system had to go out the door, but the testers could show that the product was still unstable?)

Testing is so hard that we tend to talk about only those testing problems that we can solve. This article provides a reasonable response to a problem that has no known solution.

17

Practical Priorities in System Testing
by Nathan H. Petschenik

Selecting test cases for system testing of the PICS/DCPR database application poses a fundamental problem. Due to the size of the system, methodologies described in the literature do not apply. Their formulations of "thorough testing" require so many test cases that they are not practical for system testing.

To deal with this problem, we have adopted an approach to test case selection that uses a simple set of priority rules to judge which test cases are more important than others. These priority rules derive from the charter of the system test group in the PICS/DCPR project, observations about developer testing, and the consequences of different types of software defects on users.

These practical priority rules are believed to constitute a more realistic approach to system-testing large database applications than current theory does. System testers of other large systems probably select test cases by approaches that are, in effect, similar. However, little information has been published.

In our project, PICS/DCPR, a system test group is positioned between the developers and the users. Our job is to uncover problems that should be dealt with before a release is transmitted to the field. [1]

Due to practical constraints stemming from the size of our system, it is not pos-

sible for our system tests to satisfy any of the coverage criteria considered "thorough" in the literature. [2, 3, 4] Yet we judge our system to be successful; our users seem pleased with it; and the quality of the product that reaches the field seems favorable when measured with the few unpublished industrial software quality standards we have encountered.

To judge the quality of our system test work internally, we conduct annual effectiveness studies. By system test effectiveness we mean specifically:

$$\frac{\text{defects avoided} \times 100}{\text{defects avoided} + \text{defects missed}}$$

where "defects avoided" refers to unique problems found during system testing that never reach users, and "defects missed" refers to unique problems reported by users that could have been found during system testing.

Our most recent study shows us operating with about 75 percent effectiveness. These studies also show that without our work, our users would be disrupted by two to three times the number of unique defects than they currently encounter—and we believe that this would *not* be acceptable.

More significant than the number of defects we avoid is the seriousness of the defects. Our testing is consistently fruitful in revealing a high concentration of problems that would receive emergency treatment if reported by the field. A problem is given emergency status if it disrupts a core capability of the system and no user bypass is available. Our effectiveness is 90 percent for these types of problems.

PICS/DCPR users report emergency problems at a remarkably low rate (for example, during 1981-82 the total user community reported only nine problems that temporarily prevented use of a major system capability). This rate would increase by an order of magnitude without our work.

So, our test case selection approach seems to work for us. The essence of the approach is this: We use a set of priority rules to judge which test cases are more important than others.

PICS/DCPR Background

PICS/DCPR (Plug-In Inventory Control System/Detailed Continuing Property Records) is a large, successful database application. It helps Bell operating companies (known as BOCs) manage their inventory of electronic plug-in equipment and maintain a detailed continuing property record of their investment in central office equipment. [5]

The system provides on-line and batch facilities to access and update a large database containing inventory and investment data, along with reference data and information associated with such processes as the acquisition, use, movement, repair, and retirement of central office equipment.

PICS/DCPR currently has about 280 on-line formats, and about 300 batch runs each producing three to four user reports. The system is implemented using IBM's Information Management System (IMS)

with 60 databases. The implementation involves approximately 1.8 million lines of assembler language, Cobol, and PL/I source code, plus about 200,000 lines of specialized IBM/IMS code for job control, database specification, and screen design. About 750 deliverable documents (19,000 pages) describe the capabilities of the system from the user's point of view.

There are currently 22 installations of PICS/DCPR across the country. The system is directly involved in the jobs of several thousand people. PICS/DCPR users control about $40 billion worth of plug-in and central office equipment property records. We estimate that the system saves about $250 million in capital expenditures each year as compared to decentralized, manual inventory control techniques.

PICS/DCPR is being vigorously enhanced and maintained by Bell Communications Research. This work involves 15 groups organized into three divisions. The enhancements and nearly all of the maintenance changes are provided to our users in three scheduled releases per year.

System Test Group Charter

During the development phase of a release, developers are expected to do all testing necessary to convince themselves that the release will operate in BOC environments exactly as they intend it to operate. At the end of the development interval the release is expected to be ready to be shipped to our users.

However, instead of sending the release to our users on that date, the release is given to the system test group, and thus we become the first user to receive it. For about two months, our charter is to find as many problems with the release as we can. By "problem" we mean a discrepancy between what the developers intended the system to do and what the system actually does.

For each problem we find, we document the problem and indicate whether we believe it is serious enough that it must be fixed before the release is transmitted. Each such problem is routed to the responsible developer, who is encouraged to solve the higher priority problems immediately.

The changes to the release necessary to fix the higher priority problems are then routed back to the system test group. We continue to look for more problems on the modified release. This iterative testing process continues until the scheduled end of the system test interval. At that time, the problems still open are evaluated by representatives of the system test group, the development groups, the field support group, and the project management, who collectively decide how to handle these problems. These decisions generally result in shipping the release on schedule but informing the users about open problems and when they will be resolved.

In summary, the charter of the PICS/DCPR system test group is to provide an extra level of testing on our releases beyond developer testing, to advise management of the quality of the release, and, after management decides how to handle any outstanding problems, to give our customers an accurate truth-in-packaging statement.

There is no specific type of testing allocated to the system test group that developers are not also expected to do. We do not see our role as a functional part of the development process; for example,

our charter does not include "integrating" the system. Our job is to point out important problems that were missed during development testing and to see that these problems are dealt with so that a better product goes out to our users than came to us.

Stated another way, our charter is to reduce the number of unpleasant surprises our users encounter with our product as compared to what they would have encountered if there were no system test group.

Existing Methodologies Do Not Apply

All testing theoreticians agree that exhaustive testing is impossible. [2, 3, 6] Instead, they seek "thorough" testing methodologies that satisfy one of two types of coverage criteria.

The white-box criteria are based on the system's source code. Exercising all possible outcomes of every decision statement at least once is considered a thorough criterion that is feasible to attain.

The black-box criteria are based on the system's functional specifications. If a natural language specification of the system's input/output relationships is transformed into a formal language known as a cause-effect graph [2], a thorough set of tests can be generated systematically.

In both the white-box and black-box methodologies, data for realizing the test conditions need to be selected once the test conditions have been determined. In applicable problem domains, boundary value analysis is usually the suggested technique. [2] Boundary value conditions are data situations directly at, above, or below the extremes of a set of equivalent inputs or outputs.

Neither of these methodologies applies to our system testing job because of the size of our system. Extrapolating from examples in the literature,* 1.8 million lines of source code or 19,000 pages of external specifications require more than 250,000 test cases to satisfy the coverage criteria. Coding these test cases (including analysis of results) in our test automation language would result in about as much test source code as there is source code in PICS/DCPR itself.

In addition to the problems of producing and maintaining so much test code, practical problems would arise when we tried to repeatedly execute so many test cases during the system test interval. It takes about four on-line IMS transactions to implement the average PICS/DCPR test case. Thus, 250,000 test cases would require executing about one million on-line IMS transactions. Since our objective is to repeat all our test cases approximately once per week as we iteratively improve a release, we would need to execute about 10 million transactions during the system test interval for a major release.

Such a load is impractically large. It is about five times more than our biggest production user would execute in an equivalent period and an order of magnitude more than we have achieved so far. Further, we believe our results indicate that there is no need to execute such a load to achieve effective system testing.

We are currently doing effective system testing with about 40,000 test cases derived almost entirely through the black-box priority rules described below. We are able to run the corresponding 160,000 on-line IMS transactions frequently during the system test interval, but not once per week. The most important tests, about 15 percent of the total, are run every week or two; the rest less frequently.

Whether you compare test cases or transaction throughput, our practical experience says we can do well with less than 15 percent of what existing test methodologies suggest is necessary.

So, the test cases we select only represent a proper subset of what test theoreticians consider thorough. In practice, it's a rather small subset. With the possibility of a theory-based solution ruled out, system testers are faced with an engineering problem† of how to choose test cases effectively given practical limitations on the number of test cases that can be selected.

Practical Priorities

Our approach to selecting test cases makes use of two factors not considered in the methodologies we have just discussed. These derive directly from the charter of our system test group, our understanding of the priorities of PICS/DCPR users, and the roles we have established for testers and developers in our project.

The first factor is that we are specifically looking for "important" problems in system testing. The only way we can fulfill our charter to reduce the number

---

*For example, Myers [2] derives 37 test cases from a one-page specification. We estimate that Myers' specification is about twice as dense as an average page of PICS/DCPR user documentation. Miller [7] suggests that you need about one test case per four or five lines of source code. Based on these examples and our estimates of equivalence, our extrapolation is conservative.

†Redwine [8] recognizes the engineering nature of test case selection as the title of the referenced paper indicates. However, the program testing methodology he proposes (a combination of white box and black box) is still too "thorough" to be practical for system testing.

of field defects is by finding problems that are worth the risk of fixing (that is, the risk of introducing new problems) before the release is transmitted—problems that would clearly disrupt our customers' operations. The methodologies described above strive to find all or nearly all the problems, regardless of their relative importance. Neither source code nor cause-effect graphs contain information about the potential consequences of a defect to the user or the type of inputs users are more or less likely to make. But this must be taken into account if we are going to maximize our chances of finding important problems with a less-than-thorough set of test cases.

The second factor in our test case selection is that, by the time PICS/DCPR software reaches the system test group, it has already been tested by our software developers. As is described below, our test case selection approach is based on observations and reasonable assumptions about the types of testing developers do.* By emphasizing the types of test cases least likely to draw the attention of our developers, we stand the best chance of finding residual problems.

Priority rules. With these two factors as motivation, the essence of our approach to system test case selection is a set of three priority rules that provide a criterion for selecting some test cases over others. These are:

- *Rule A:* Testing the system's capabilities is more important than testing its components.

- *Rule B:* Testing old capabilities is more important than testing new capabilities.
- *Rule C:* Testing typical situations is more important than testing boundary value cases.

Rule A seeks out important defects by emphasizing that, to users, PICS/DCPR is a tool for getting a job done, not an end in itself. While a defect in a particular on-line screen or batch run may be annoying to them, they will be less upset if they can still accomplish the job they set out to do. Choosing test cases that relate the input of a total process with its final end result focuses our attention on testing the system the way it is used.

For example, in testing the plug-in repair process our test cases illustrate a "test story" that begins when a plug-in at a field office fails and ends when that plug-in is fixed by a repair center and returned to service. Testing a particular on-line format that updates the repair log database is an important byproduct of our work but is not the main thrust of the test. The main thrust is to verify that BOCs can use PICS/DCPR capabilities to manage the plug-in repair process.

Rule A is also based on our perception that regardless of the feature development methodology being used, developers will tend to check out individual system components more carefully than they will check out how these components are supposed to work together. We perceive this to be especially the case where the testing would have required close coordination between developers in different supervisory groups.

In our system test of a new feature we assume that each developer's individual

---

*Thus far, we have found it impractical to capture the specific cases that developers actually used in their testing. However, our project is pursuing software engineering techniques that will make those test cases more visible.

contribution (perhaps one new on-line transaction and one changed batch run) will have been carefully verified. But we understand the difficult scheduling and coordination problems our developers face in producing new features for such a large system. We are skeptical that the interfaces between components were verified under realistic situations (as opposed to being simulated using utilities and debugging tools).

Natural vs. simulated interfaces. We believe the system test group should concentrate on test cases that will reveal problems that might have been missed because of the possible lack of coordinated testing during development testing. So, in the PICS/DCPR system test group, we string user-level components into complete and meaningful flows, causing interfaces to occur naturally (rather than simulating them), and ignoring any intermediate results that are not visible to the user. [9]

Our concentration on integrated testing is not meant to relieve the developers from their responsibility of integrating the system before it reaches the system test phase. It just means that we have more confidence in the effectiveness of developer component testing than in developer integration testing.

New vs. old capabilities. The main justification for Rule B is that the old capabilities of a PICS/DCPR release are of more immediate importance to our users than the new capabilities. BOCs are currently operating on a PICS/DCPR release that has a set of features they rely on to do their work.

When they install a new release, they expect to continue to rely on the features they had before the new release was installed. The new capabilities of the system may involve significant procedural changes and in some cases additional hardware. Users may not attempt to exercise the new features until many months after the relevant release is installed. The problems they may encounter when they do use them could certainly represent inconvenience; but they will be far less disruptive than a problem that impacts the existing features which are already in production operation.

Rule B is also based on our belief that developers' test cases will tend to be more thorough in verifying the new capabilities than in assuring the old capabilities still work. This is consistent with the psychological thrust of the developers' job: to produce change.

Our perception is that the developers' motivation toward getting a new capability or maintenance fix out to the users is considerably stronger than their fear of introducing an unexpected result. With this mental set, it seems likely to us that their zeal to prove their changes were constructive may overshadow their efforts in trying to reveal that their change inadvertently destroyed an old capability.

When a new feature needs to be tested, PICS/DCPR system testers apply Rule B by first insuring that we have test cases that would represent a BOC who does *not* want to make use of the new feature. Since many of our new features represent optional improved ways of doing things that are already getting done, these test cases protect us against the worst type of defects —the type that break old, existing system capabilities.

Should we find problems in testing the old capabilities, we will try to get our developers to give them more urgency than problems with new capabilities that may come up. As the system test interval progresses, we are reluctant to accept fixes for new capabilities while problems with old capabilities remain open. If necessary, we lobby to delete new capabilities from the advertised content of the release to avoid jeopardizing the resources required to do a good job of testing the old capabilities.

Data typical to the real world. Rule C is not meant to dispute the merits of boundary value testing. To the contrary, we believe boundary value testing is a reliable way to reveal problems in programs, and we assume our developers use it conscientiously. The reason that we believe that boundary value testing is less valuable to a system test group like ours than the conventional wisdom would have it is strictly due to priorities.

Since our charter is to reveal problems that would disrupt our users, we must always give priority in our system testing to problems that have a relatively high probability of occurring in the real world, as opposed to those that require less typical stimuli or which only could occur under rare, degenerate situations.

This is not to say that boundary values cannot represent typical inputs; such inputs belong in the system test group's test cases. The point is that systematic boundary value testing does not distinguish the typical from the unusual or extreme. As long as practical considerations force us to limit our selection of test cases, we must always give priority to testing typical inputs, whether or not they are boundary values.

Rule C is the most difficult of the three priority rules to apply. It is not easy for system testers to become experts, down to the detailed data situations, in the typical

BOC use of PICS/DCPR. We are experimenting with ways to build such expertise by providing more and better opportunities for contact between system testers and users.

Analysis of user problems encouraged. One of the most effective ways we have devised thus far involves analysis of the problems that get past our testing. We encourage test developers to use the problems reported by our users as a very important source of test cases. While this may seem like closing the barn door after the horse is gone, there are several reasons why this is productive.

In the first place, every system change to resolve BOC-reported problems will ultimately have to be tested by the group anyway; by getting the stimuli to produce the symptoms of the problem into an automated test, the testing of that problem resolution is taken care of, regardless of when the corresponding system change is later made.

Secondly, including field-reported problems in our regression tests protects against the embarrassing possibility of the problem reappearing in a future release due to, for example, the wrong version of a module getting released.

Finally, we consider the user stimuli that demonstrate field problems to be excellent examples of real BOC situations. By studying such situations and adding them to tests, our tests and our testers become more attuned to the environment our software encounters in the field. Uncovering related problems often occurs as a side benefit. For these reasons, we encourage testers to include important BOC-reported problems in their tests as soon as the problems come in from the field.

Testing methodologies described in the

literature do not apply to the job of system testing in the PICS/DCPR project because our system is so large. While that means that our testing cannot be thorough in the theoretical sense, our approach to test case selection is nonetheless methodical and effective.

The PICS/DCPR approach to system test case selection uses information that is not contained in the source code or in the specifications. It uses observations about the testing performed by developers and experience with judging the penalty of defects to our users to establish a set of priority rules. These rules are used to judge which test cases are more important than others. Our effectiveness data indicates that our approach works.

This article has presented our engineering priorities so other test practitioners can compare them with their own. In addition, I urge test theoreticians and software quality researchers to study and understand practical constraints of large, real projects. Accommodation of these constraints should generate a whole range of new, important questions to be answered.

REFERENCES

[1]   N.H. Petschenik, "System Testing a Large Database Application," Bell Laboratories, June 9, 1982; software engineering paper available from the author at Bell Communications Research, Livingston, N.J. 07039.

[2]   Glenford J. Myers, *The Art of Software Testing*. New York: John Wiley and Sons, 1979, pp. 37-87.

[3]   W.E. Howden, "Reliability of the Path Analysis Testing Strategy," *IEEE Transactions on Software Engineering*, September 1976, pp. 208-15.

[4]   E.J. Weyuker and T.J. Ostrand, "Theories of Program Testing and the Applications of Revealing Subdomains," *IEEE Transactions on Software Engineering*, May 1980, pp. 236-46.

[5]   H.O. Burton, "PICS: A Computerized Inventory Control System for Plug-In Equipment," *Compcon 75 Digest of Papers*, February 1975, pp. 277-80.

[6]   H. Kopetz, *Software Reliability.* New York: Springer-Verlag, 1979, pp. 54-62.

[7]   Edward F. Miller, Jr., *Software Quality Assurance—A Professional Development Seminar*, Software Research, San Francisco, 1982.

[8]   S.T. Redwine, Jr., "An Engineering Approach to Software Test Case Design," *IEEE Transactions on Software Engineering*, Vol. SE-9, March 1983, pp. 191-200.

[9]   L.W. Smith, "Solving Test Automation Problems in a Large Software System with Integrated On-Line and Batch Processes," Bell Laboratories, September 16, 1982; software engineering paper available from the author at Bell Communications Research, Livingston, N.J. 07039.

18

Editors' Note
Ledbetter and Cox: "Software-ICs"

Insight: The so-called object paradigm can be described in a way that normal human beings can understand.

In spite of all the excitement about O.O.W. (Object-Oriented Whatever), there has been precious little written on the subject that is comprehensible. Ledbetter and Cox, in this admirable piece, set out to describe the three Ahahs of the object paradigm: encapsulation, dynamic binding, and inheritance. And they succeed. You find yourself practically sighing your Ahahs as you read. If you've never understood what all the fuss was about, give Ledbetter and Cox a chance to make it clear.

While this is the most readable description we know of the object paradigm, it is also an important statement about software reuse. Object methods make sense even if you're not trying to improve software reusability. But the authors make the point here that the real payback of object methods is that they open wonderful possibilities for utilizing pre-made software components, almost the way that hardware developers use ICs.

18

Software-ICs:
A Plan for Building Reusable Software Components
By Lamar Ledbetter and Brad Cox

The software world has run headlong into the Software Crisis—ambitious software projects are hard to manage, too expensive, of mediocre quality, and hard to schedule reliably. Moreover, all too often, software delivers a solution that doesn't meet the customers' needs. After delivery, if not before, changing requirements mean that systems must be modified.

We must build systems in a radically different way if we are going to satisfy tomorrow's quantity and quality demands. We must learn to build systems that can withstand change.

Some system developers are already building software much faster and of better quality than last year. Not only that, the systems are much more tolerant of change than ever before, as a result of an old technology called message/object programming. This technology, made commercially viable because of the cost/performance trends in hardware, holds the key to a long-awaited dream—software reusability. A new industry is developing to support the design, development, distribution, and support of reusable Software-ICs (integrated circuits). A forthcoming series in *UNIX/World* will address message/object programming.

Message/Object Programming and Software-ICs

In this article we'll look at the concepts of message/object programming and how they support the building of "Software-ICs," as we call them, by satisfying the requirements for reusability.

A Software-IC is a reusable software component. It is a software packaging concept that combines aspects of subroutine libraries and UNIX filter programs. A Software-IC is a standard binary file produced by compiling a C program generated by Objective-C.

The notion of *objects* that communicate by *messages* is the foundation of message/object programming and fundamental to Software-ICs. An object includes data, a collection of procedures (*methods*) that can access that data directly, and a selection mechanism whereby a message is translated into a call to one of these procedures. You can request objects to do things by sending them a message.

Sending a message to an object is exactly like calling a function to operate on a data structure, with one crucial difference: Function calls specify not *what* should be accomplished but *how*. The function name identifies specific code to

287

be executed. Messages, by contrast, specify what you want an object to do and leave it up to the object to decide how.

Requirements for Reusability

Only a few years ago, hardware designers built hardware much as we build software today. They assembled custom circuits from individual electrical components (transistors, resistors, capacitors, and so on), just as we build functions out of low-level components of programming languages (assignment statements, conditional statements, function calls, and so on). Massive reusability of hardware designs wasn't possible until a packaging technology evolved that could make the hardware environment of a chip (the circuit board and adjoining electrical components) relatively independent of the detailed workings of that chip. The IC quickly developed to the point that multiple chip vendors now vie to sell their hardware design effort in a market for reusable hardware designs.

One concept that stands out in hardware systems is that many of the components perform unique services. Services are provided upon request and the requester need not be concerned with the internal methods or data used, only the result. The equivalent software concept, *encapsulation,* is fundamental to success in software reusability. Encapsulation defines a data structure and a group of procedures for accessing it. Users access the data structure only through a set of carefully documented, controlled, and standardized interfaces.

The concept of *messaging* is also prevalent in the hardware world. It is through messaging that the loose coupling of components is achieved and the division of responsibility between the user and the supplier is defined and enforced.

The hardware industry has also achieved a high degree of reusability through the development of standards. There are standards for interconnection, power, and processing, for example. In contrast, in the software world standards for the syntax and semantics of only a few languages have been defined and adhered to across a range of hardware. There have also been many unsuccessful attempts to define standards for the implementation of software algorithms and applications (such as GOTO-less programming, no global data, loose coupling, tight binding, and data hiding, among others). Stressing strict static "type checking" as a standard helps solve the problems of integration and debugging but does not change the basic operator/operand concept embodied in most languages; it only moves it to a higher level of abstraction. To reuse modules developed using the operator/operand concept you have to hope that the output of one module is compatible with the "type" of the input of the receiver, redefine the type of the operands in either the receiver or sender, or transform the operands. Because of the complexity, there has been little progress in the definition of standards for reusability in the operator/operand model. In contrast, useful standards for reusability are in use or being developed in organizations that have embraced the message/object paradigm.

In the hardware world, the functions of standard components are well defined and identifiable. Given a knowledge of the functions available and a high level of standardization, hardware designers routinely integrate reusable hardware components into new systems. Standard functions are easy to identify because they map into the real-world model of hardware systems. In the software world, the definition of standard, identifiable functions is still a dream, even with our "standard" utility libraries. If software reusability is to become a reality, languages must support a more direct mapping from the model of the real-world functions to the implementation.

Hardware components are delivered in an unmodifiable form. That means that standard functions are protected. If Software-ICs are to become a reality, the languages and standards must support the delivery of components that operate as advertised and are immune to modification by the system builder. If the system builder wants different functions, he must go back to a Software-IC "foundry" for a new component.

Reusability can have several meanings in both the hardware and software worlds. A hardware designer would never think (as we do in software) of starting the design of a modification with a blank piece of paper or by looking at the design of all of the connecting components. A designer also doesn't worry about needing to modify the interfaces or components not affected by the change. Modified components "inherit" most of the previous implementation and contain only the changes necessary to provide the required new behavior. The inheritance of already-working methods by a new Software-IC has tremendous productivity implications.

Why Didn't Software-ICs Exist Before?

One of the main reasons Software-ICs didn't exist before is that the cost performance of hardware did not support the requirement that computer cycles must be used ("wasted") to enhance software reusability. The cycles were too expensive, and performance optimization was necessarily a primary goal. Strict implementations such as Smalltalk-80 consume orders of magnitude in performance. Less revolutionary implementations of the message/object paradigm, such as Objective-C, while paying some performance price, are viable for commercial systems and are in use today in companies building major software systems.

Most of us have been taught to think within the conceptual framework of operators and operands. That framework has led many to conclude that the complexity involved in reusing a software component far exceeds the possible benefits.

In order for Software-ICs to work, the manner in which systems evolve has to be fundamentally different. The concept of *inheritance,* discussed in detail later, is that fundamental difference. The concept of Software-ICs also demands a level of standardization in system implementation that has not been feasible until recently. Finally, the market for Software-ICs is a recent reality created by the recognition that what I call the Software Crisis can be solved only by fundamental changes in the way we build systems. It is no longer competitively viable to ignore the products of previous development efforts if there is any way to reuse or reapply those products.

Objects, Messages, and Encapsulation

The distinction between specifying what should be done as opposed to how it should be done is subtle and often misunderstood. It is, however, a crucial one because, as has been demonstrated in the hardware world, it is central to reusability.

By way of example, imagine a programmer building an electronic mailbox in an electronic office system, and focus on the mailbox developer's role as a user of services provided by his supplier, the developer of the forms being mailed. The mailbox developer must provide a way to

implement the intention to display the selected item. If he does this using the conventional operator/operand model and specifying how, not what, as depicted in Fig. 1, the code given in Listing 1(a) results.

Notice the separation of responsibilities. Because the mailbox developer is responsible for deciding how to implement the function that is called selectItemFor-

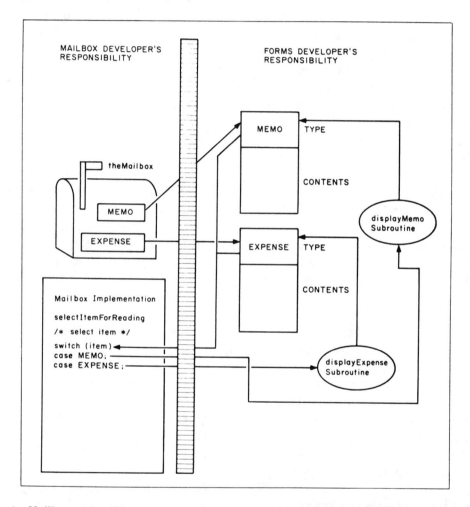

Figure 1. Mailbox using the operator/operand model. The Mailbox developer must specify *how* to display the form by checking the form type and calling the correct subroutine. As a result, every form type must be enumerated and the implementation changed as form types are added or deleted.

Reading, the code must enumerate every data type the forms developers might provide. This results in code that is inherently nonreusable; the case labels explicitly state that this mailbox is useless except for memo and expense contents.

Now notice what happens in the rewritten code [Listing 1(b)] using messages and objects as depicted in Fig. 2. The message expression, item display, commands the object, item, to display itself, thus specifying only what the object is to do. How the object is to do it is decided by the forms developers so the mailbox code becomes independent of its contents.

The technical term for this is *dynamic binding*. Dynamic binding and encapsulation are at the root of the reusability provided by this variety of message/object programming.

Some modern programming languages (Ada, Modula-2, and CLU, for example) provide a different form of encapsulation by binding statically at compile time. While this certainly is an improvement over traditional languages like C and Pascal, it provides no new help in solving the reusability problem. The mailbox example coded in any of these languages would still need the switch statement.

The notion of a Software-IC, in which reusable code is built and tested by a supplier and then delivered to consumers in binary form, is not possible without dynamic binding.

Using Software-ICs

We will demonstrate the use of Software-ICs by building a simple program that counts the unique words in a file. For the sake of comparison, we will discuss two different solutions based on reuse of ex-

isting software and then turn our attention to the Software-IC solution.

The subroutine-library solution would reuse library functions for managing files, printing results, and comparing strings. Custom software would be required for the word parser, hash function, hash table/collision handling, counting words in the hash table, and printing the formatted results. Much of the significant new development and debugging effort concerns algorithms that have been implemented in many previous applications. Once working, however, the implementation should be fairly efficient.

A UNIX-style solution would consist of small "tools" connected by pipes. The off-the-shelf utilities that could be reused include tr (translate characters), sort (sorting utility), and wc (word-count utility). The programmer would have to custombuild a script for assembling the utilities. This particular problem requires a good working knowledge of applicable UNIX utilities but no custom software. The implementation would be noticeably slower than both the subroutine library and Software-IC solutions.

The Software-IC solution involves assembling two prefabricated Software-ICs from a library of components. A String is used to hold words, and a Set can be used to hold the unique words. Both are standard components in the library released with Objective-C. The performance of the Software-IC solution would not be as good as the first solution, but it would certainly be acceptable and could be optimized by tuning. The full text for this solution, except for the small function nextWord( ), which parses words from the input stream, is presented in Listing 2.

The two external symbols Set and

Listing 1: *Operator/operand versus message/object implementations. Listings 1a and 1b are, respectively, examples of portions of code that create an electronic Mailbox using conventional (operator/operand) and message/object models. Comparing the two illustrates the difference between the Mailbox developer specifying "how" versus "what."*

(1a)

```
selectItemForReading(theMailbox) {
   .
   .
     .
   /* Select an item in theMailbox and. . . */
/* check the item type flag */
   switch(item->type)
/* Now call the appropriate display subroutine */
{
  case MEMO:            displayMemo(item); break;
  case EXPENSE:         displayExpense(item); break;
  .
  .
  .
  default; error("unknown contents"); break;
  }
  .
  .
}
```

(1b)

```
selectitemForReading(theMailbox) {
   . . .
   /* Select an item in theMailbox and. . . */
   [item display];      /* Send item a message to display itself */
   .
   .
}
```

Listing 2: *Using Software-ICs. This message/object program counts the unique words in a file using preexisting Software-ICs from the Objective-C library:* Set *and* String.

```
// Reads words from stdin and counts unique ones main( ) {
   extern id String, Set;     // Specify object (instance) factory ids

   id uniqueWords, currentWord;      // Local object (instance) ids
   char buf(MAXBUF);      // Word buffer

   uniqueWords = [Set new];     // Create a new empty set instance
   while (nextWord(buf) I = EOF) {     // forEachWord. . .
     currentWord = [String str:buf];   // Create a string instance for each word
     [uniqueWords filter:currentWord];// Store unique ones in set
   }
   printf("The number of unique words is %d \n", [uniqueWords size]);
}
```

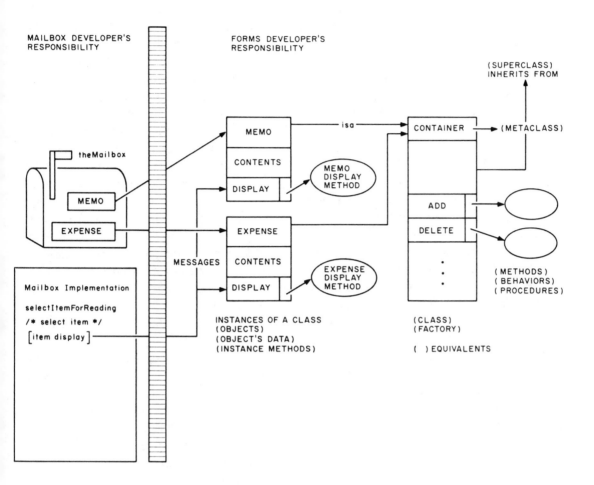

**Figure 2. Mailbox using the message/object model. The Mailbox developer specifies *what*
the form should do by sending it a message to display itself. As a result, form types
can be added or deleted without changing the Mailbox implementation.**

String identify a pair of *factory objects* whose function is to produce instances of their *classes* (Software-ICs). Each class defines behaviors and declares data for (a) its factory object and (b) its instances. The two local symbols uniqueWords and currentWord identify instances, which will be manufactured by Set and String at run time.

In this example, String responds to a str: message by allocating enough space to hold the characters in the message argument buf. The next statement commands the set uniqueWords to perform the filter: function on currentWord.

How are reusable sets possible, since they must work properly with many different kinds of contents? For example, the same Set code may need to compare strings, points, symbols, and so on, often within the same application. The answer is that dynamic binding allows the Set to legitimately consider equality testing, for example, none of its business. Instead, it pushes that decision back onto its contents. When it needs to test the equality of two items, it merely commands one of them to report whether it isEqual: to the other.

Classes, Methods, and Inheritance

So far we have focused primarily on encapsulation. This technology should be thought of as an aid to using the services in a system. It also provides some advantages for the suppliers (builders) of message/object systems as well. Consider the job facing the builders of three familiar components of an office-automation system: Mailbox, Envelope, and FileFolder.

At one level a Mailbox is very different from a FileFolder, but they are similar in that they are kinds of containers. Each will have some amount of code involved in managing collections of other objects.

Inheritance allows containment code to be built, stockpiled, and thereafter reused as often as needed. This is done by building a class named Container, whose methods support the operations we expect of containers: adding elements, removing them, expanding and shrinking their internal capacity as needed. Thereafter, specialized container classes like Mailbox, Envelope, and FileFolder are built by describing only how each subclass differs. They may differ by having additional private data fields or by having additional (or modified) behaviors. Figure 3 depicts a typical inheritance hierarchy.

To design a new capability, the pro-grammer's thoughts turn immediately to "What do I already have that is most like the thing I need?" (see Fig. 4). For example, to develop an Envelope the programmer focuses on describing how Envelopes should differ from Containers. Envelopes differ from Containers by, for example, having additional data variables such as returnAddress, targetAddress, and stamp. Envelopes also differ by exhibiting additional behaviors (or methods), for example, mailTo:, open, and discard. Note that no methods need be defined for adding and removing contents from envelopes because they, and the data variables that support them, are acquired automatically, or *inherited,* from Container.

FileFolders and Mailboxes will have their own distinctive implementations. However, only their differences from a Container need to be designed, coded, tested, documented, delivered, and maintained. Their containment abilities were developed once and thereafter reused. Containment is defined consistently, systemwide. You add a letter to a Mailbox in precisely the same manner as you add a letter to a FileFolder.

System Building with Software-ICs

System requirements normally model data, data flow, and actions on data. In traditional system building, the system requirements must then be mapped into the operator/operand model in order to optimize the implementation on a computer. Message/object programming allows a more direct representation of the real-world model in the code. The result is that the normal radical transformation from system requirements (defined in users' terms) to system specifications (de-

(3a)

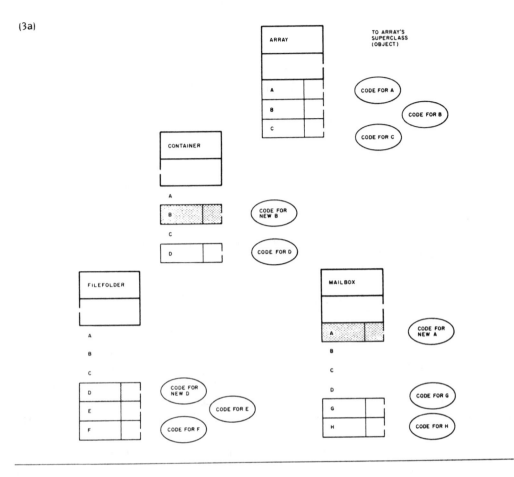

(3b)

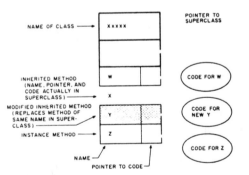

Figure 3. Inheritance. New specialized classes can be, and almost always are, defined by inheriting the data and behaviors of older generic classes, then specifying only how the new ones differ. Figure 3a shows how the classes Container, FileFolder, and Mailbox are created; 3b explains the notation used. Note that, for example, the definition of Container includes only definitions for methods B and D. It inherits definitions for methods A and C from Array; these definitions do not need to be explicitly specified by the programmer, nor do they take any room in the definition of Container.

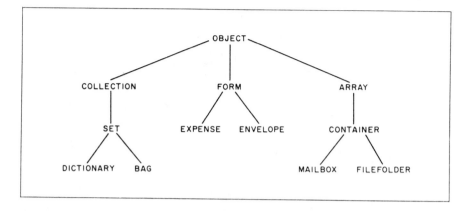

Figure 4. Opportunities to reuse work emerge. As the design proceeds, similarities to previously developed Software-ICs become apparent, and a large degree of reuse results.

fined in computer terms) is greatly reduced.

Software-ICs directly support the concept of rapid prototyping (or, in hardware terms, *breadboarding*). The ability to demonstrate a subset of a system's final functionality (particularly the human interface) in a rapid prototype helps ensure that the system built is the system needed.

No matter how well the delivered system satisfies the requirements, people usually have an immediate desire to change/evolve the system. Fortunately, as we have seen, it is possible to build changeable systems.

System builders using Objective-C employ a combination of aids to enhance the reusability of their Software-ICs. The standard libraries, for example, are documented using a catalog composed of Software-IC specification sheets. Table 1 summarizes the specification sheet for a Software-IC called Point.

Conclusions

The tools exist today in the software world to build Software-ICs. They are in use in a number of major companies and have demonstrated (see Fig. 5) code bulk reductions of between 2.5-1 and 5-1.

As the use of Software-ICs spreads productivity in the software world should improve much as hardware ICs improved productivity in the hardware world. The use of Software-ICs also will promote the evolution of optimized system-building methodologies and tools. Just as semiconductor foundries produce both standard and custom ICs, Software-IC foundries will do exactly the same in the software industry.

Table 1.
Software-IC specification sheets. This is a condensed version of the specification sheet for the *Point* Software-IC. The complete version contains 21 methods (versus the 9 shown).

Point

Instance variables: { short xLoc, yLoc; }

Inherits: Object
Inherited by:
Referenced by: Point Rectangle
Refers to: Geometry Point Primitive_Object_Object_csav msg fprintf lmul sqrt

Discussion

Points are vectors (i.e., coordinates) on a two-dimensional plane. When displayed on a graphics terminal, the origin is at the top left; the horizontal axis increases to the right. . .

Instance Variables

xLoc   A short integer specifying the value for the horizontal axis (e.g., column).
yLoc   A short integer specifying the value for the vertical axis (e.g., row).

Instance Creation

+x:(int)xy=(int)y
   Replies a new point at coordinates (x@y).
+fromUser
   Prompts the user to specify the coordinates for a new point. The default implementation is. . .

Instance Variable Access

Unless otherwise specified, these methods reply to the receiver.
−(int)x Replies the x-coordinate of the receiver.
−(int)y Replies the y-coordinate of the receiver.
−X:(int)xy;(int)y
   Sets the coordinates of the receiver to (x@y).

Conditionals

In the following, words like "isAbove" or "isLeft" are with respect to a screen-oriented point of reference, not the numerical magnitudes of the coordinates. For example, the point (0, 0) is above and to the left of all other positive coordinates.
-(BOOL)isBelow:aPoint
      Replies YES of receiver is below aPoint

Equality Testing

−(int)hash
   Replies xLoc * yLoc.
−(BOOL)isEqual:aPoint
   The receiver and someObject are equal if and only if they are both points and have equal coordinates.

Printing

−printOn:(IOD)anIOD
   Prints the receiver as: fprintf(anIOD,'')%d@%d)'', xLoc, yLoc);

Declarations:Points.m

==Point:Object (Geometry, Primitive){
   short xLoc, yLoc;
}
+x:(int)xy:(int)y
+fromUser

−(int)x

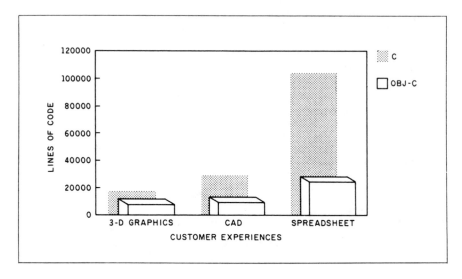

Figure 5. Productivity experiences. Actual decreases in lines of code experienced by PPI customers using Objective-C in three different application areas.

REFERENCES

[1]   Love, T., "Application Development in Smalltalk-80," Arlington, Va.: *Proceedings of Softfair-83.*

[2]   *Objective-C Reference Manual,* Version 3.0, Sandy Hook, Conn. Productivity Products International, December 1984.

19

Editors' Note
Bassett: "Frame-Based Software Engineering"

Insight: The reusable unit of choice may not be the subroutine after all. Paul Bassett tells of some exciting results in the reuse of what he calls "frames."

This paper provides a brief glimpse into the future world of software engineering. (Have you noticed that during the '70s, we all changed from being simply "programmers" to "software developers," and that in the '80s we changed again, this time to "software engineers," yet most of us have never changed anything else about our work?)

In the article are the ultimate engineers: builders who create product components (frames) independent of any given instantiation of a product. The system builders then use these standard components in such a way as to only have to describe what is *unique* about their particular products.

19

Frame-Based Software Engineering
by Paul G. Bassett

It is ironic that software—the very engine of our high-tech, automated society—is such a low-tech cottage industry. While no civil engineer would dream of designing a bridge from scratch (and few would cross the bridge if it were), software is routinely designed that way.

Craftsman programmers still build programs character by character, obliviously reinventing similar wheels over and over again. When they do notice, it often takes more work to separate and recustomize the common parts than to rewrite them from scratch. And, although less than 10 percent of a typical Cobol program is nonreusable or worth maintaining [1], 100 percent of the program's code is maintained.

Reuse concepts play a key role in several issues: productivity, maintainability, portability, quality, and standards. Reusability can be applied to each major stage of the software life cycle: analysis and design, construction and testing, maintenance, and new releases.

The simplest possible notion of reusability is use-as-is. Obviously, if the shoe fits, wear it. Beneath most software problems, however, are too many ill-fitting shoes. Such problems are manifest in the use of subroutines, structured programming, programming languages, and code generators. [2, 3]

The notion of same-as-except ("*A* is the same as *B* except. . . .") is a needed generalization of use-as-is.

In design, the more we can take for granted about the basic features and functions of a system, the more we can concentrate on its unique aspects. Unfortunately, use-as-is is impossible at the system-design level or we would have nothing to design. Nor can we simply add and subtract components. Too many things must be modified in unforeseen ways.

Program construction can benefit from fixed, use-as-is text components. But again, people must be able at construction time to tailor the original component to their needs. These modifications are made at construction time so we do not pay unnecessary overhead in time or space at runtime. Moreover, programs often can be generated largely from declarative specifications (such as screen and report definitions).

But patching generated code prevents reuse of the generator (within the same program) on pain of destroying the patches already made. (Many commercial generators, recognizing this problem, attempt to overcome it by providing user exits; but this approach is also fraught with use-as-is difficulties.)

At execution time, use-as-is is both trivial and vital. Programs and subroutines get reused by simply invoking them as is. The less we need to vary things at runtime, the faster and simpler our code will run because runtime variables and parameters create complexity and overheads. Minimizing such complexities and overheads is why we need variability during design, construction, and maintenance.

Maintenance is by far the most expensive part of the life cycle, yet it too is a process of reusing modules (across time rather than across applications). Changing circumstances force software to be modified in unforeseen ways, much as happens during design. Same-as-except can close the loop, making maintenance a process of design refinement and giving real meaning to the word "cycle" in the software life cycle.

Frames usefully formalize same-as-except and provide a basis for a rigorous software-engineering discipline. Generally speaking, a frame is any fixed theme plus the means to accommodate unforeseen variations on that theme.

For example, how many seconds of unique melody are contained in a typical song? Composers have fixed, frame-like patterns for repeating the themes with variations in words, harmonies, instruments, and the like.

Also consider manufacturing: In about 20 minutes you can order a new car that is as unique as your fingerprints. In principle, every car on the assembly line can be one of a kind. How can they be made in high volume and quality at reasonable cost? When you tour an automobile plant, the first thing you notice is that every car on the line looks the same. Of course, you are looking at the frames. The unique results are obtained from the combinatorial explosion of options that can be bolted, sprayed, and welded onto the frame. And because the frame is engineered for such options, hundreds of millions of dollars can be invested in automatic assembly equipment such as robot welders.

Programs are variations on themes that recur again and again. A software-engineering frame is a model solution to a class of related programming problems containing predefined engineering change points.

What are model solutions to related programming problems? When we speak informally about data entry or spectral analysis or matrix inversion, we are not referring to specific programs; we are referring to infinite classes of programs, each class sharing common properties among its members. Frames let you formalize what you mean by those properties so the computer can create custom program instances automatically. Where does the custom code come from? Other frames.

A COBOL IMPLEMENTATION

The definition of frame makes no reference to any language. Frames can apply the same-as-except notion to any language (including documentation). While the language places no intrinsic constraints on frame engineering, the types of applications written in that language induce characteristic frame sets. Over the past 10 years, extensive Cobol frame experience has been accumulated (as have some with Lisp [4] and Ada [5]). Cobol applications are an excellent source of potential gains because the scope for reusability is immense.

For example, Noma Industries, Ltd.,

a Toronto-based diversified group of manufacturing concerns and Netron's parent company, has developed and installed more than 20 million lines of custom Cobol in thousands of programs, forming scores of different applications. We accomplished this over the past five years with a staff that has grown from six to 15 people. Moreover, some four million lines are being added or replaced each year.

The programs are composed from 30 input/output frames, 38 application-oriented frames, about 400 data-view frames (defining more than 10,000 data fields), screen and report frame generators, and one custom specification frame per program. The specification frames contain less than four percent of the total Cobol.

Of pivotal importance are the specification frames. Each program corresponds to one specification frame, which is the root of a frame hierarchy. The specification frame controls the hierarchy's composition of the program and stores all its custom aspects.

Specification frames typically contain less than 10 percent of a program's source code—and specification frames are the only Cobol frames for which application developers are ever responsible.

Specification frames are created from template specification frames. A template defines a default frame composition for an application domain and provides all the important options, with explanations to guide the choices. The two-dimensional hierarchy of options is flattened into a linear list. The application engineer, unaware of the underlying tree structure, customizes a renamed copy of the template. The resulting specification frame, with the underlying frames, is processed automatically (including a compile and link) to produce an executable load module.

While the specification frame is unique to a single program (not reused), more than 90 percent of the program is constructed from frames that are reused or generic. A frame tree stratifies contexts, with generic or context-free frames (such as I/O) at or near the leaves and with custom or context-sensitive frames at or near the root.

One type of engineering change point in the frames is Break. Breaks are slots that can receive frame text from any parent frame in the hierarchy, including the specification frame. (When several parent frames try to fill the same Break, the one in the hierarchy that is at or closest to the specification frame takes precedence.)

Breaks can be located anywhere that code changes are anticipated but not specifically known in advance. Breaks are also associated with defaults, which will be used as part of the resulting program unless overridden by some parent frame.

A good technique to engineer code for such changes is to let the structured programming code units be the defaults. A good structured decomposition yields the appropriate graininess levels where change is possible.

Another type of predefined engineering change point is Select: It stores predefined variations on an algorithmic theme. For example, a date-conversion frame might map dates from one format to another. By setting the appropriate Select parameter in the specification frame (or some other parent frame), any map can be selected and constructed using a mixture of code common to every map and code unique to each format.

Select is also used to protect programs against incompatible upgrades to generic frames: Frame version symbols are used to control frame upgrades and rewrites. Select chooses the correct version according to the one locked into the specification frame at creation (when its template was copied). Any obsolete frame code that predates the frame's use of a version symbol is put into Otherwise clauses of the Selects. (The Otherwise clause is exercised when no other Select clauses are selected.)

Obsolete frame parts can also be split into a separate file. While logically still part of the frame, they are effectively archived, so programmers don't have to wade through them when reading the frame. The archived parts are still dependent on those parts.

Text symbols, such as file names, record names, and picture-clause elements, that tend to change from program to program can be defined generically. The Replace command will instantiate a specific value for the symbol wherever it occurs within the subtree rooted in the frame containing the Replace.

Because Cobol is not block-structured (so code must be separated into its various divisions and sections), the Group command is used to logically tag the code in each frame. After the frames have been spliced together, there is an automatic sort that satisfies the divisional needs of the Cobol compiler.

Frames are also handy for defining generic record structures and user data views. A typical Cobol program may deal with several files having similar but different structures. By defining record structures generically, it becomes easy to create multiple instances of such structures in one program, avoiding name clashes and the like.

Another important engineering issue is fine-tuning and optimizing code that was generated from declarative notations, such as screen and report definitions. By generating frames, rather than raw source code, such generators can now be reused throughout the program's life cycle without fear of destroying previous customizations. The specification frame keeps the custom code permanently factored for easy maintenance and retuning. [2]

Frames embody an interesting notion of "standard": You should always apply a standard whenever appropriate and never when inappropriate. But if a standard can be applied automatically on a same-as-except basis, it becomes the path of least resistance in getting the job done. Frames provide an engineering basis for this. By storing exceptions in custom frames that are separated from the standard frames, you can concentrate on needed exceptions while taking for granted the great bulk of details that are still standard.

Hence, frames do more than reuse code. They facilitate the design, manufacture, and maintenance of software. In design, a generic frame is a rigorous, parameterized analysis of a problem domain. A library of such frames constitutes an inventory of standard designs, a same-as-except basis for defining new applications.

Construction is an automated manufacturing process where frames play the role of standard subassemblies. Engineering specifications—in the form of screen and report definitions, relational data frames, and fine-tuning specification frames—are *translated* into executable code. (Conventional manufacturing requires specifications to be *transduced* from abstract to physical form, an intrinsically more complex problem.)

Rapid prototyping [6] also plays a new and important role because prototypes can be evolved into production-quality versions rather than being scrapped. There are more engineering degrees of freedom available to a software frame than to physical frames; for example, it is just as easy to subtract software functionality as it is to add it. (Try subtracting the back seat from an automobile frame.)

Debugging and maintenance efforts are reduced tenfold because there is a tenth of the usual source code to maintain. Also, rather than tracing a bug from its symptoms through a tortuous inference chain to its diagnosis, you simply read the specification frame with the symptoms in mind. The robustness of the underlying frames makes it very likely that the bug is localized to the one-shot, custom code. Moreover, all and nothing but the one-shot code is in the specification frame rather than being scattered in the nooks and crannies of the whole program.

Maintenance always takes place on the specifications, never on the resulting source code, so effort becomes proportional to the novelty of the application, not to the number of lines of source code. Logically, maintenance disappears as an activity distinct from the refinement process that produced the software in the first place.

Portability is a special case of same-as-except reusability. We handled portability this way in our software-engineering system partly by writing system tools with the system itself. The tools operate in a variety of computer hardware (IBM, Dig-

ital Equipment Corp., and Wang) and operating system environments. One set of specifications is enough to manufacture application software that will run with equivalent functionality on any of these machines.

FRAME FORMALIZATION

When implementing an actual frame system to be used with a particular language, you may want to change the details of the frame syntax to suit that language's style.

General frame semantics

Figure 1 shows the frame syntax. To be understood, the syntax should be read in the context of the frame semantics.

In the artificial intelligence literature [7, 8] the word "frame" is associated with decomposition of wholes into parts. Here, frames are applied to the inverse problem: composition of parts into wholes. As an operator, a frame contains the glue necessary to compose and adapt the information in frames below it in a hierarchy. As an operand, it contains information to be adapted by frames above it in the hierarchy. The result is text in some target language not described here. Typically, the text is a compilable program, but could just as well be documentation or another frame. Frames are a form of macros. [9, 10]

Starting with some root frame, its Text is evaluated from left to right. All Texts are a mixture of Commands embedded in some target text, such text being simply output as is. Commands handle the variations and exceptions and are always delimited by a pair of braces ({ }). The root frame is always the most specific

```
Frame_Set     :: =  + (Frame)
Frame         :: =  { Name Text }
Text          :: =  + [Commands, $]
Commands      :: =  { + [Frame_Call, Parm_Name, ( (Expr, + ({, })) ),
                      Assign, Group Select, Loop, Comments] }
Frame_Call    :: =  Name_Ref [$] { + [Assign] }
Parm_Name     :: =  (;, ;) Name_Ref
Name_Ref      :: =  + (Name, ( Expr ))
Name          :: =  + (letter, digit, underscore)

Expr          :: =  Term + [(+ , -) Term]
Term          :: =  Factor + [(*, /) Factor]
Factor        :: =  (Parm_Name, + (digit), ( Expr ))

Assign        :: =  Parm_Name = + [( (Expr, + ({, })) ), { Text }] !
Group         :: =  @ ;Name_Ref
Select        :: =  ? ;Name_Ref + (Bool_Expr { Text }) .
Loop          :: =  # ( + (Name_Ref), = ;Name_Ref Expr) { Text }
Comments      :: =  % + ($) %

Bool_Expr     :: =  Bool_Term + [| Bool_Term]
Bool_Term     :: =  Bool_Fac + [& Bool_Fac]
Bool_Fac      :: =  (Reln (Expr, { Text }), [~] ( Bool_Expr ))
Reln          :: =  (<, >, =, < >, < =, = >)
```

Figure 1. **Frame syntax. The modified Backus-Naur form (, ,) means choose one syntax option from the list. [, ,] means the list is optional. + ( ) means choose one or more from the list. + [ ] means choose zero or more. $ means any literal text symbol. Terminal symbols are in reverse-video display. The delimiters { and } should be seldom used in the target language (because they are less easy to generate), and they must be distinct from the other symbols in the syntax of the commands.**

(context-sensitive) frame. Frames lower in the hierarchy are progressively more generic (context-free).

Vital to the frame concept are the scoping and evaluation properties of parameters. (To avoid confusion between variables used by frames during program construction and variables used by programs at runtime, I shall call frame variables parameters.)

An undefined parameter, V, becomes defined by executing an assignment to it.

If V is defined, no assignment to V in any direct or indirect descendant frame can be executed. In effect, *all assignments are defaults,* subject to overrides from more specific context frames. V becomes undefined by exiting the frame in which V is defined.

However, if frame A calls frame B with a list of executed assignments, parameters thus assigned become undefined on exit from B, rather than A, because each time A calls B a different subset of defaults may need to be executed in the tree of frames rooted in B.

These scoping rules allow the relatively context-sensitive frame A to directly modulate any relatively context-free frame in the subtree rooted in frame A—context optimizations can be factored (localized) to maximize reusability.

There are three ways to evaluate parameters. The : prefix means evaluate and convert into target-language text, and ; means do not evaluate. Thus, evaluation can take place at each assignment, at each reference, or at neither. Evaluation-at-assignment propagates target text to all frames in the subtree rooted in the first reference, while evaluation-at-reference propagates frame Text. Such Text is treated as part of the referencing frames. Text can be output completely unevaluated, when frames construct other frames (see Example 3).

Breaks as described in the Cobol implementation correspond to evaluate-at-reference parameters (these are also called slots in the AI literature on frames). Replaceable symbols correspond to evaluate-at-assignment parameters.

Because frames must often reference frames and parameters whose specific names are not known when the frame is written (for example, when a static or prewritten frame must reference generated frames), such names can themselves be constructed from parameters.

Detailed frame semantics

For each major syntactic construct, an explanation of the meaning is provided, followed by an instance of its use.

Frame_Call: Name_Ref { }

This command invokes the frame whose name is determined by evaluating Name_Ref. Name_Ref is an expression that must evaluate to the name of a frame in Frame_Set (see Name_Ref semantics below). Recursive calls, direct or indirect, are not permitted. Frames can have hundreds of parameters, even though very few are typically altered at each invocation. Thus values are passed by overriding assignments to defaulted parameters rather than by positional correspondences between actual and formal arguments. Intermediate context frames can be used to constrain highly parameterized (very generic) frames.

The list of assignments—if executed (if not overridden in some parent frame)—cause the assigned parameters to be undefined on exit from the called frame. $ lets frames containing independent information be linked together at the same context level. If $ is present, then the Text of the called frame is processed as if it were part of the calling frame (it is not treated as a descendant frame).

For example,

```
MERGE $ {;P1 = {a}. :P4 =
            (;Num + 1) {:A}.}
```

calls the Merge frame at the same level, passing values for parameters P1 and P4 (presumably P2 and P3 exist with default values).

Evaluate-on-assignment: :Name_Ref =

If Name_Ref has not been assigned in a parent frame, it is assigned a list of zero or more *evaluated* Expr expressions and

Texts, not including the delimiters (parentheses and braces). No text is output. (If Name_Ref has been assigned in a parent frame, this assignment is ignored.) By enclosing delimiters { and } in parentheses, these symbols are treated as ordinary symbols, not delimiters of Commands (see Example 3).

For example, in

```
:P4 = (;Num + 1) {:A}.
```

P4 is assigned a two-element list. The first element is the value of Num added to 1, and the second element is the evaluated value of A.

Reference-as-is Parm_Name: ;Name_Ref

This outputs Name_Ref's current list element for further use *as is*. If Name_Ref is not defined, or if Name_Ref is a zero-element list, its value is null and nothing is output. If Name_Ref is a one-element list, it is output as is. If it is a multielement list, ;Name_Ref must occur inside the scope of a loop command that declares it—otherwise it is an error.

For example,

```
;P4
```

Assuming P4 was assigned as :P4 above and that it is referenced in its declaring loop, the first time through the loop, the first element of P4 will be output for further use as is; the second time, the second value of P4 will be output as is.

Assignment-as-is: ;Name_Ref =

If Name_Ref has not been assigned in a parent frame, it is assigned a list of zero or more *un*evaluated Expr expressions and

Texts, not including the delimiters. No text is output. (If Name_Ref has been assigned in a parent frame, this assignment is ignored.) As with : assignments, { and } can be stored as ordinary symbols. But, so unevaluated expressions and texts can be scanned efficiently, the frame processor simply increments one for each { and decrements one for each } until the count equals zero.

For example, in

```
;P4 = (;Num + 1) {:A}.
```

P4 is assigned a two-element list. The first element is the expression ;Num + 1, and the second element is the text :A.

Evaluate-on-reference Parm_Name:
:Name_Ref

This *evaluates* Name_Ref's current list element and outputs the literal for further use. If the element has been evaluated at assignment, the literal is simply output because the combination is redundant. If Name_Ref is not defined, or if Name_Ref is a zero-element list, its value is null and nothing is output. If Name_Ref is a one-element list, its evaluated text is output. If it is a multielement list, Name_Ref must occur inside the scope of a Loop command that declares it—otherwise it is an error.

For example,

```
:P4
```

Assuming P4 was assigned as ;P4 was above and that it is referenced in its declaring loop, the first time through the loop, the expression ;Num + 1 will be evaluated and then output for further use; the

Examples

The following examples are meant only to illustrate the use of the commands. Realistic frames are usually larger than space permits here. Generic frames usually carry more functionality than is used in any particular instance. Thus it is possible for the resulting code to be smaller than the frames themselves.

Example 1. Two frames combine to generate a list of range checks.

A. Here is IF_STM, a generic or reusable frame:

```
{IF_STM { # VRBL MIN MAX     { :ERR = (;ERR+1).
   IF NAME_{VRBL} IS LESS THAN {;MIN} OR NAME_{;VRBL} IS GREATER THAN {;MAX}
      THEN PERFORM ERROR_{;ERR}.
                              }}}
```

B. SPECIFY_IFS is a custom frame that uses the IF_STM frame created above:

```
{SPECIFY_IFS {IF_STM {    ;VRBL = {A} {B} {C}.
                          ;MIN  = {15} {57} {1000}.
                          ;MAX  = {30} {60} {1500}.
                    }}}
```

Assuming a suitable implementation convention for breaking output text into lines, the result of invoking SPECIFY_IFS is

```
IF NAME_A IS LESS THAN 15 OR NAME_A IS GREATER THAN 30
   THEN PERFORM ERROR_1.
IF NAME_B IS LESS THAN 57 OR NAME_B IS GREATER THAN 60
   THEN PERFORM ERROR_2.
IF NAME_C IS LESS THAN 1000 OR NAME_C IS GREATER THAN 1500
   THEN PERFORM ERROR_3.
```

Example 2: This three-part example illustrates how a problem context can be stratified into three levels (generic, intermediate, and specific) to facilitate multiple contexts of use.

A. Shown below is a "toy" routine, RIGHT_TO_BLANK, for scanning text, followed by a generic frame, SCAN, whose frame parameters default to the RIGHT_TO_BLANK version. The target language is Pascal-like. Program comments are prefixed by dashes (—) and continue to the end of the line.

```
RIGHT_TO_BLANK(p: INTEGER) RETURN INTEGER:
— Scan TEXT to the RIGHT, starting at position p, until
— a BLANK is found. Return the first BLANK position found.
— Failure to find a BLANK is detected.

j: INTEGER;
BEGIN j := p;
    WHILE NOT (j GT 80 OR TEXT(j) EQ BLANK)
       DO j := j + 1;
    IF j GT 80 THEN
       RETURN p−1
    ELSE RETURN j;
END FUNCTION RIGHT_TO_BLANK
```

Notice in SCAN that PAST_LIMIT is evaluated on assignment and FAILURE is evaluated on reference (part C below explains why).

```
{SCAN   {;DIRECTION  = {RIGHT}.  ;NOT   = . ;CHAR = {BLANK}.
         ;VAR_NAME   = {TEXT}.    ;LGTH = {30}.
         :PAST_LIMIT = {{? ;DIRECTION   = {LEFT} {LT 1}
                                        = {RIGHT} {GT {;LGTH}}.}}.}
```

```
— Scan {;VAR_NAME} to the {;DIRECTION}, starting at position p, until
— a {;CHAR} is {;NOT} found. Return the first {;NOT;CHAR} position found.
— Failure to find a {;NOT;CHAR} is detected.
```

```
        j: INTEGER;
        BEGIN j := p;
            WHILE NOT (j {;PAST_LIMIT} OR {;VAR_NAME}(j) {;NOT} EQ {;CHAR})
                DO j := j {? ;DIRECTION = {LEFT} { − } = {RIGHT} { + }.} 1;
            IF j {;PAST_LIMIT} THEN
                {;FAILURE = {RETURN p − 1}. :FAILURE}
            ELSE RETURN j;
        END FUNCTION {;DIRECTION}_TO_{;NOT;CHAR}
}
```

B. Here we see an intermediate context frame that makes some assumptions about a class of usage for the SCAN frame.

```
{SCAN_FUNCTIONS {%Create four variations of scanning functions. User frames
    may assign VAR_NAME, LGTH, FAILURE, RIGHT-JUSTIFIED.%
    %Left-to-right until blank:%       SCAN{ }
    %Left-to-right until nonblank:%    SCAN{;NOT = {NOT}.}
    %Right-to-left until nonblank:%    SCAN{;DIRECTION = {LEFT}. ;NOT= {NOT}.}
    %Right-to-left until blank (this rare case is provided only when asked)%
    ? ;RIGHT-JUSTIFIED = {YES} {{SCAN{;DIRECTION = {LEFT}.}}}.} }
```

C. Now a context-specific frame, NAME_SWITCH, is provided that uses the frame tree developed in part B. You are left to determine that the resulting source code, when executed, will extract the surname from the beginning of the input and place it behind the given names.

Controlling when evaluation occurs is important:

• FAILURE is evaluated several times, a different variation produced each time because of parameters assigned *after* FAILURE is assigned as a default override. (This explains why evaluate-on-reference is important, as part A mentions.)

• LGTH modulates every context except the intermediate context frame, SCAN_FUNCTIONS.

• RIGHT-JUSTIFIED's null default modulates the intermediate context appropriately.

```
{NAME_SWITCH {;LGTH = {30}.}
DECLARE:
    SUR-NAME-FIRST, GIVEN-NAMES-FIRST: STRING(1..{;LGTH}) := {;LGTH}" ";
    LENGTH-SUR, LENGTH-GIVEN, START-OF-GIVEN: INTEGER;

BEGIN
    READ(SUR-NAME-FIRST);
    LENGTH-SUR      := RIGHT_TO_BLANK(1) − 1;   GET LENGTH OF SUR NAME
    START-OF-GIVEN := RIGHT_TO_NONBLANK(LENGTH-SUR + 1);
    LENGTH-GIVEN   := LEFT_TO_NONBLANK({;LGTH}) − START-OF-GIVEN + 1;

    GIVEN-NAMES-FIRST(1, LENGTH-GIVEN)
                    := SUR-NAME-FIRST(START-OF-GIVEN, LENGTH-GIVEN);
    GIVEN-NAMES-FIRST(LENGTH-GIVEN +)
                    := SUR-NAME-FIRST(1, LENGTH-SUR);

    WRITE(GIVEN-NAMES-FIRST);
END

{SCAN_FUNCTIONS{   ;VAR_NAME    = {SUR-NAME-FIRST}.
              {    ;FAILURE     = GIVEN-NAMES-FIRST(1,{;LGTH}) := "BAD
                                  {;DIRECTION}-TO-{;NOT.CHAR} SCAN.";}. }}}
```

Example 3. As an interesting stunt, CLONE is a self-reproducing frame (the format highlights the self-encoding, not a desire to reproduce the blanks). To appreciate this solution, try solving it in other languages!

```
{    CLONE  {      ;DNA =      {
{({ )}} CLONE {({ )}   ;DNA =   {({ )  ;DNA ( }}). :DNA {( }})}
                                    }  .  :DNA   }}
```

CLONE does two things: (1) It assigns an unevaluated string to the parameter DNA, then (2) it evaluates DNA: DNA's text is output as is except for what is inside the command delimiters. {({)} has the net effect of outputting a {. {({) ;DNA ()}} outputs a { followed by the value of DNA, *unevaluated*, followed by a }. In other words, the infinite regress of self-encodings is avoided.

second time through, the value of A will be evaluated and then output.

Constructing names: Name_Ref

Name_Ref is a rule for constructing a parameter name or frame name. The rule evaluates Expr expressions and concatenates the resulting character strings (not including the delimiting parentheses). The constructed name must be a letter followed by zero or more letters, numerals, and underscores, or else it is an error.

For example,

```
ABC (;Num + 1)_23
```

Assuming Num's value is -1, the name of the parameter or frame is ABC0_23.

Group: @;Name_Ref

The order in which the text is output may differ from the order required by whatever consumes the output text (such as a compiler). This command invisibly tags all subsequently output text with Name_Ref's value until another group command is executed. After the root frame exits, the entire output is sorted, using the tags as the sort key. (The tags are then discarded.)

For example,

```
@; Generics
```

tags all subsequently output text (until the next group command) with the value of the parameter called Generics. Presumably the sort code assigned to Generics will cause all generic functions in an Ada frame hierarchy to be brought together in

the required order for the resulting Ada program.

Select: ?

This operation assumes that ;Name_Ref is on the left of every relational operator in every Bool_Expr. The first (if any) true Bool_Expr selects the corresponding Text to be evaluated. If the last Bool_Expr is = ;Name_Ref, where both Name_Refs evaluate to the same parameter, it functions as an Otherwise clause.

For example,

```
?  ;Matrix    = {Regular} {text1}
              = {Sparse} {text2}.
```

will process text1 if the value of Matrix equals Regular; it will process text2 if the value of Matrix equals Sparse. If Matrix equals neither, nothing will be processed.

Loop: #

This operation is valuable when code generators and variably iterated texts are required. If a set of + (Name_Ref)s is declared, the loop is controlled by the Name_Ref with the most elements (this could change due to assignments in Text). Each time Text is iterated, each Name_Ref reference in Text accesses its next list element. The last element of each Name_Ref is reused, if necessary, until the loop terminates. Name_Refs with zero elements are permitted (implying zero iterations). The = ;Name_Ref option lets Name_Ref be assigned the loop counter value at the beginning of each iteration. The value is preserved on loop exit.

If = ;Name_Ref Expr is declared, the loop is iterated Expr times (Expr must evaluate to a nonnegative integer). Each time Text is iterated, Name_Ref is incremented, from 1 to Expr, and the value is preserved on loop exit. If Text contains loops, no declared Name_Ref can be declared for those loops.

For example,

```
# P1 P2 = ;TOT { Text }
```

Assume P1 has five elements and P2 has seven elements. The frame processor acts as if P1 is extended to seven elements with the last two elements having the same value as the fifth element. Text will be processed seven times, and during iteration i, the value of Tot will be i and each reference to P1 or P2 will cause element i to be processed (used as is if ; is prefixed or evaluated if : is prefixed).

Comments: % . . . %

These are delimited by a pair of percent symbols and can be placed anywhere a Command is permitted. They are ignored by the frame processor.

For example,

```
% This is a comment. %
```

Expressions

Bool_Expr is a Boolean combination of terms using, for the Or operator, & for the And operator, and –( ) for the Not operator. Similarly, Expr is an arithmetic combination of terms using +, −, *, and / as the usual operators. If these operators are present, both operands of each operator must evaluate to integers, or an error results.

For example,

```
:A & −(:B , :C)
```

If *A, B,* and *C* are true, false, and false, respectively, the value of the Boolean expression is true.

The operation

```
(35 + 7) * 2
```

results in 84.

———————

A function is a map from a domain to a range. Mathematics has traditionally focused on the properties of functions. As representations of functions, algorithms have additional properties—time and space—that are irrelevant to the study of functions. Recent work in mathematics, such as automata and complexity theory, is helping us understand these properties.

Programs are representations of algorithms that carry still more properties: ease of construction and modification. Studying these properties involves the formalization of software engineering.

We need a mathematics of software engineering. Because software is still new, mathematics has not yet gotten around to the formal study of program properties not found in algorithms and functions. The frame technique is an empirical example of a construction system that makes precise some fuzzy issues about ease of construction and modification. Frame hierarchies embody the notion of context stratification. They also provide a consistent way to reconcile inconsistent information structures: generic frames that must be blended but not at the expense of their reusability or the efficiency of the resulting program.

Can a calculus of frames be developed? How about correctness-preserving transformations? Can canonical or normal forms be found that minimize redundancy while maximizing reusability (the dual of relational database normal forms)?

Frame-based software engineering clearly works well. The bonus is that it provides grist for some interesting mills in both mathematics and computer science.

REFERENCES

[1] Judith Drake, "Software Manufacturing: A Case Study," Technical Report, Netron, Inc., Toronto, 1983.

[2] Paul G. Bassett, "Brittle Software: A Programming Paradox," *Journal of Information Systems Management,* July 1987.

[3] _____, "Design Principles for Software Manufacturing Tools," *Proceedings of the ACM Conference Fifth-Generation Challenge,* New York: ACM, 1984.

[4] Larry Jones, "A Frame-Based Regression Test Synthesizer for VAX/VMS," Technical Report, Dig-

ital Equipment Corp., Nashua, N.H., June 1985.

[5] Paul G. Bassett, "Frames and Ada: A Reusability Analysis," Technical Report, Netron, Inc., Toronto, 1985.

[6] *Proceedings of the Rapid Prototyping Workshop,* University of Maryland, Columbia, Md., 1982.

[7] Marvin Minsky, "A Framework for Representing Knowledge," in *Psychology of Computer Vision,* P. Winston, ed., New York: McGraw-Hill, 1975, pp. 211-77.

[8] Richard Fikes and T. Kehler, "The Role of Frame-Based Representation in Reasoning," *Communications of the ACM,* September 1985, pp. 904-41.

[9] *Cobol/MP Macro Facility Reference Manual Version 9,* Allied Data Research, Princeton, N.J., 1979.

[10] Calvin N. Mooers, quoted in *Computer Lib,* Theodor H. Nelson, Hugo's Book Service, Chicago, 1974, pp. 18-21.

20

Editors' Note
Lanergan and Grasso: "Software Engineering with Reusable Designs and Code"

Insight: Opportunities to take advantage of software reuse are everywhere. Witness the report in this paper of a sixty percent reuse factor in a data processing/COBOL environment.

Increasing the reuse factor is seen as a possible path to higher productivity and more reliable software. Typically, when you read about advances in reuse, you are reading about the reusability of software in Ada or Modula-2 environments, or about higher reuse factors attainable with object-oriented design and programming.

In this paper, however, the authors describe an environment that scores zero on the new-and-sexy scale: an environment in which programs are written in . . . COBOL! Lanergan and Grasso report that their organization has attained a sixty percent reuse factor, with an estimated fifty percent productivity increase for new software development.

20

Software Engineering with Reusable Designs and Code
by Robert G. Lanergan and Charles A. Grasso

INTRODUCTION

It is common practice when writing scientific programs to use prewritten subroutines or functions for common mathematical operations. Examples of these are logarithmic or trigonometric subroutines. The computer manufacturer usually writes, supplies, and documents these subroutines as part of his software. For instance, they usually come with the Fortran compiler. The functions are universal. Square root is square root regardless of the computer, company, or application.

In business programming it is common belief that each system application is so unique that it must be designed and coded from the beginning. For instance, it has been the belief that the coding scheme that our company, even our plants, use for material classification code, or make or buy code, or vendor code, or direct labor code, and the algorithms used for processing these data elements are unique to the company or plant. Therefore, prewritten reusable modules cannot be designed, coded, and reused.

A close examination of this reasoning has led us to believe that there are two fallacies in it. The first is that, contrary to common belief, there are at least a few business functions that are sufficiently universal to be supplied by the manufacturer of a Cobol compiler. There are many others applicable to a company, plant, functional area, or application area that could be prewritten.

How many manufacturers supply a Gregorian date edit routine with their compilers?

How many manufacturers supply a Gregorian to Julian date conversion routine or vice-versa, with their compiler?

How many manufacturers supply a date aging routine for such applications as accounts receivable?

In every one of the above cases the application is probably written and rewritten in every business shop in North America.

In addition to universal routines, there are company-wide applications. Examples in our company include:

- part number validation routines,
- manufacturing day conversion routines,
- edits for data fields used throughout the company, such as employee number.

Within a functional area in any company, such as manufacturing or accounting, there are routines that can be prewritten, tested, documented, and then copied into a program.

Within a system such as payroll there

are often routines that also can be prewritten, such as tax routines.

Yet we believe that the false notion of uniqueness still persists to such a degree that this approach is used at about one-tenth of its potential. We will discuss later the way we have used this concept to produce programs that have an average of 60 percent reusable code.

The second fallacy, in our opinion, involves the program as a whole. It is commonly believed that each business program (as well as each data field) is so unique that it must also be designed and developed from the start. In our opinion there are only six major functions you can perform in a business application program. You can sort data, edit or manipulate data, combine data, explode data, update data, or report on data. By identifying the common functions of these six types of programs, we have produced seven "logic structures." These logic structures give the programmer a head start and provide a uniform approach that is of value later in testing and maintenance.

REUSABLE MODULE DESIGN APPROACH

Our reusable module design approach strategy separates reusable modules into two distinct categories, functional modules and Cobol program logic structures.

Functional Modules

Functional modules are designed and coded for a specific purpose. Then they are reviewed, tested, documented, and stored on a standard copy library. As mentioned earlier, some of the business routines have universal application, such as date aging; tax routines and others have more limited application to a company, plant, functional area, or system application.

Within our company we classify these functional modules in several Cobol language categories. These categories are:

- file descriptions, i.e., FD's

- record descriptions, i.e., 01 levels in an FD or in working storage

- edit routines, i.e., the data area and procedure code to edit a specific data field

- functional routines, i.e., the data area and procedure code to perform some function, such as left justify and zero fill data elements

- database I/O areas

- database interface modules

- database search arguments

- database procedure division calls

As can be seen from the above list, we have some modules that are solely data related, such as 01 level record descriptions. The majority of the modules involve both data areas and procedure code. For instance, a database call paragraph, designed to retrieve a specific series of segments, works in conjunctin with a program control block module, a segment search argument module, and a database I/O module.

There are approximately 3,200 modules in the above categories, supporting over 50 system applications at three plants. By using these functional modules and logic structures, we have been producing programs that average 60 percent reusable code. This produces more reliable programs, with less testing and coding. The maintainability and documentation associated with these applications has also improved substantially because the code is not physically contained in each program.

Cobol Program Logic Structures

A Cobol program logic structure has a prewritten identification division, environment division, data division, and procedure division. It is not a complete program because some paragraphs contain no code, and some record descriptions are also empty, consisting only of the 01 level. It does not however, contain many complete 01 levels and procedure paragraphs.

To illustrate the concept behind logic structures we will describe three types.

The *update* is designed for the classical, sequential update. There is a version with an embedded sort and a version without. The update is designed for situations where the transaction record contains a transaction type field (add, change, or delete). The update logic structure is also designed to accommodate multiple transactions per master record. Error messages to a transaction register are provided for standard errors such as an attempt to add an already existing record. Final totals are also provided, as well as sequence checking.

The *report* logic structure is also written in two versions, one with and one without a sort of the input records prior to report preparation. Major, intermediate, and minor levels of totals are provided for, but more may be added if needed. If multiple sequences of reports are desired, the record can be released to the sort with

multiple control prefixes. Paragraphs are also provided for editing, reformatting, and sequence checking.

The *edit* logic structure is also written in two versions, with or without a sort of the input records. This logic structure was designed for two purposes. One is the editing of input records. In effect the input records are examined based on some criteria and written to the selected (good records) or nonselected (error) files. Another use for this logic structure is the selection of records from a file, based on some criteria, for later use in a report.

CONSTRUCTION OF LOGIC STRUCTURES

For each type of logic structure there is a central supporting paragraph.

- For the update program it is the high-low-equal comparison.
- For the report program it is the paragraph that determines which level of control break to take.
- For the selection program it is the select/nonselect paragraph.

Let us consider the report program as an example.

Prior to the control break paragraph we can identify support functions that must occur in order for the control break paragraph to function. Examples are: get-record, sequence-check-record, edit-record-prior-to-sort, and build-control-keys. These are supporting functions. Other functions such as major-break, intermediate-break, minor-break, roll-counters, build-detail-line, print-detail-line, page-headers, etc., are dependent on the control break or central paragraph.

Obviously many of these paragraphs (functions) can be either completely or partially prewritten.

Our report program logic structure procedure division contains 15 paragraphs in the version without a sort, and 20 paragraphs in the version with a sort.

To further clarify what we mean when we talk about logic structures, it might be helpful to specify some data and procedure division areas in a report logic structure, without an embedded sort.

```
Identification Division
Environment Division
Data Division
    File Section
    Working Storage Section
        01  AA1—CARRIAGE-CONTROL-
                SPACING
        01  BB1—CONSTANTS-AREA
        01  BB2—TRANSACTIONS-STATUS
        01  BB4—FILES-STATUS
        01  CC1—COUNT-AREA
        01  DD1—MESSAGE-AREA
        01  EE1—TRANSACTION-READ-AREA
        01  FF1—KEY-AREA
        01  GG1—HEAD-LINE1
        01  GG2—HEAD-LINE2
        01  GG3—HEAD-LINE3
        01  HH1—DETAIL-LINE
        01  LL1—TOTALS-AREA
        01  SS1—SUBSCRIPT-AREA
        01  TT1—TOTAL-LINE-MINOR
        01  TT2—TOTAL-LINE-INTER
        01  TT3—TOTAL-LINE-MAJOR
        01  TT4—TOTAL-LINE-FINAL

Procedure Division
    0010—INITIALIZE
    0020—MAIN-FLOW
    0030—WRAP-IT-UP
    0040—CHECK-CONTROLS
    0050—FINAL-BREAK
    0060—MAJOR-BREAK
    0070—INTER-BREAK
    0080—MINOR-BREAK
    0090—PRINT-TOTAL
    0100—ROLL-COUNTERS
    0110—FILL-DETAIL-LINE
    0120—WRITE-PRINT-LINE
    0130—NEW-PAGE-HEADING
    0140—GET-TRANSACTION-RECORD
    0150—TRANSACTION-FORMAT-OR-
            EDIT
    0160—SEQUENCE-CHECK
```

The above area, combined together as a program, provides the programmer with a modular functional structure on which to build a report program very easily.

For the update logic structure, the central paragraph is the hi-low-equal control paragraph. Prior to the central control paragraph there must be supporting functions such as get-transaction, sequence-check-transaction, edit-transaction, sort-transaction, get-master, sequence-check-master, build-keys, etc. As a result of this central paragraph you will have functions such as add-a-record, delete-a-record, change-a-record, print-activity-register, print-page-heading, print-control-totals, etc.

Our update logic structure procedure division contains 22 paragraphs in the nonsort version and 26 paragraphs in the version with an embedded sort.

BENEFITS OF LOGIC STRUCTURES

We believe that logic structures have many benefits.

- They help clarify the programmer's thinking in terms of what he is trying to accomplish.

- They make design and program reviews easier.

- They help analysts communicate with the programmer relative to the requirement of the system.

- They facilitate testing.

- They eliminate certain error-prone areas such as end of file conditions since the logic is already built and tested.

- They reduce program preparation time, since parts of the design and coding are already done.

However, we believe that the biggest benefit comes after the program is written, when the user requests modifications or enhancements to the program. Once the learning curve is overcome, and the programmers are familiar with the logic structure, the effect is similar to having team programming with everyone on the same team. When a programmer works with a program created by someone else, he finds very little that appears strange. He does not have to become familiar with another person's style because it is essentially his style.

RESEARCH STRATEGY USED TO TEST THE CONCEPT OF REUSABILITY

In August 1976 a study was performed at Raytheon Missile Systems Division to prove that the concept of logic structures was a valid one. Over 5,000 production Cobol source programs were examined and classified by type, using the following procedure.

Each supervisor was given a list of the programs that he was responsible for. This list included the name and a brief description of the program along with the number of lines of code.

The supervisor then classified and tabulated each program using the following categories:

edit or validation programs

update programs

report programs

If a program did not fall into the above three categories, then the supervisor assigned his own category name.

The result of classification analysis by program type was as follows:

1089 edit programs

1099 update programs

2433 report programs

247 extract programs

245 bridge programs

161 data fix programs

5274 total programs classified

It should be noted that the bridge programs were mostly select (edit and extract) types, and the data fix programs were all update programs. The adjusted counts were as follows as a result of this adjustment.

1581 edit programs

1260 update programs

2433 report programs

5,274 adjusted total programs classified

The average lines of code by program type for the 5,274 programs classified were as follows:

626 lines of code per edit program

798 lines of code per update program

507 lines of code per report program

The supervisors then selected over 50 programs that they felt would be good candidates for study. Working with the supervisors, the study team found that approximately 40-60 percent of the code in the programs examined was redundant and could be standardized. As a result of these promising findings, three prototype logic structures were developed (select, update, and report) and released to the programming community for selective testing and feedback. During this time a range of 15-85 percent reusable code was attained. As a result of this success, it was decided by management to make logic structures a standard for all new program development in three data processing installations. To date over 5,500 logic structures have been used for new program development, averaging 60 percent reusable code when combined with reusable functional modules. It is felt at this time that once a programmer uses each logic structure more than three times, that 60 percent reusable code can easily be attained for an average program. We believe this translates into a 50 percent increase in productivity in the development of new programs.

In addition, programmers modifying a logic structure written by someone else agree that, because of the consistent style, logic structure programs are easier to read and understand.

This is where the real benefit lies since most data processing installations are using 60-80 percent of their programming resource to support their maintenance requirements.

To summarize: the basic premise behind our reusability methodology is that a large percentage of program code for business data processing applications is redundant and can be replaced by standard program logic.

By supplying the programmer standard logic in the form of a logic structure we can eliminate 60 percent of the design, coding, testing, and documentation in most business programs. This allows the programmer to concentrate on the unique part of the program without having to code the same redundant logic time and time again.

The obvious benefit of this concept is that after a programmer uses a structure more than three times (learning curve time) a 50 percent increase in productivity occurs. The not so obvious benefit is that programmers recognize a consistent style when modifying a program that they themselves did not write. This eliminates 60-80 percent of the maintenance problem that is caused by each programmer using an individual style for redundant functions in business programs. This is one of the basic problems in maintenance programming today and is causing most programming shops to spend 60-80 percent of their time in the modification mode instead of addressing their new application development backlog.

CONCLUSION

After studying our business community for over six years, we have concluded that we do basically the same kind of programs year in and year out and that much of this work deals with redundant programming functions. By standardizing those functions in the form of reusable functional modules and logic structures, a 50 percent gain in productivity can be attained and programmers can concentrate on creative problems rather than on redundant ones.

In addition to the one time development benefit, the data processing organizations can redeploy 60-80 percent of their resources to work on new systems development applications.

REFERENCES

[1] R.M. Armstrong, *Modular Programming in COBOL*. New York: Wiley, 1973.

[2] R. Canning, "The Search for Reliability," *EDP Analyzer*, Vol. 12, May 1974.

[3] G. Kapur, "Toward Software Engineering," *Computerworld*, In-Depth Section, November 1979.

[4] R. Lanergan and B. Poynton, "Reusable Code—The Application Development Technique of the Future," in *Proceedings of the IBM GUIDE/SHARE Application Symposium*, October 1979, pp. 127-36.

[5] D. Leavit, "Reusable Code Chops 60% Off Creation of Business Programs," *Computerworld*, pp. 1-4, October 1979.

[6] D. Schechter, "The Skeleton Program Approach to Standard Implementation," in *Computer Programming Management*. Pennsauken, N.J.: Auerbach, 1983.

21

Editors' Note
Harel et al.: "STATEMATE: A Working Environment for the Development of Complex Reactive Systems"

Insight: The state behavior of a real-time system (or any complex system) can be described using a simple but elegant notation of leveled transition diagrams.

There is a mystique surrounding real-time systems such as the avionics applications Harel and his colleagues work with. Real-time system developers have previously claimed, with some justice, that present-day software engineering methods were insufficient to their needs. What this paper demonstrates is that the baby need not be thrown out with the bathwater—that a relatively small addition to the developers' current bag of tricks can make near-formal software engineering a real possibility, even for the developers of these highly complex systems.

21

STATEMATE:* A Working Environment for the Development of Complex Reactive Systems

by D. Harel, H. Lachover, A. Naamad, A. Pnueli, M. Politi,
R. Sherman, and A. Shtul-Trauring

1. INTRODUCTION

Reactive systems (see [5, 13]) are characterized as owing much of their complexity to the intricate nature of reactions to discrete occurrences. The computational and continuous parts of such systems are assumed to be dealt with using other means, and it is their reactive, control-driven parts that are considered here to be the most problematic. Examples of reactive systems include most kinds of real-time computer embedded systems, control plants, communication systems, interactive software of varying nature, and even VLSI circuits. Common to all of these is the notion of *reactive behavior,* whereby the system is not adequately described by a simple relationship that specifies outputs as a function of inputs, but, rather, requires relating outputs to inputs through their allowed combinations in time. Typically, such descriptions involve complex sequences of events, actions, conditions and information flow, often with explicit timing constraints, that combine to form the system's overall behavior.

It is fair to say that the problem of finding good methods to aid in the development of such systems has not been satisfactorily solved. Standard structured design methods do not adequately deal

---

*STATEMATE is a registered trademark of i-Logix, Inc.

with the dynamics of reactive systems, since they were proposed to deal primarily with nonreactive, data-driven applications, in which a good functional decomposition and data-flow description are sufficient. As to commercially available tools for real-time system design, most are, by and large, but sophisticated graphics editors, in which one can model certain aspects of reactive systems but in which a user can do little with the resulting descriptions beyond testing them for syntactic consistency and completeness and producing various kinds of output reports. These systems are often helpful in organizing a designer's thoughts and in communicating those thoughts to others, but they are vastly inadequate when it comes to the more difficult task of preparing reliable specifications and designs that satisfy the initial requirements, that behave over time as expected, and from which a reasonable final system can be constructed with relative ease.

If we were to draw an analogy with the discipline of conventional programming, there is an acute need for the reactive system's analog of a programming environment that comes complete, not only with a programming language, a useful program editor and a syntax checker, but also with a working compiler and/or interpreter with debugging facilities, so that programs can be not only written but also run, tested, debugged and analyzed. As it turns out, the problems confronting a team out to design a reactive system are far more difficult than those confronting a programmer out to write a conventional program. Typical reactive systems are highly concurrent and distributed; they fall quite naturally into multiple levels of detail, and usually display unpredictable, often catastrophic, behavior under unanticipated circumstances. More often than not, the development phases of such systems are laden with misunderstandings between customers, designers and users, as well as among the various members of the design team itself, and their life-cycle is replete with trouble-shooting, modifications and enhancements.

The languages in which reactive systems are specified ought to be clear and intuitive, and thus amenable to generation, inspection and modification by humans, as well as precise and rigorous, and thus amenable to maintenance, analysis and simulation by computers. Such languages ought to make it possible to move easily, and with sufficient semantic underpinnings, from the initial stages of requirements and specification to prototyping and design, and to form the basis for modifications and maintenance at later stages. One of the underlying principles adopted in this paper is such specifications, the behavioral aspects included, should be based to a large extent on *visual formalisms,* i.e., on languages that are highly visual in nature, depending on a small number of carefully chosen diagrammatic paradigms, yet which, at the same time, admit a formal semantics that provides each feature, graphical and nongraphical alike, with a precise and unambiguous meaning. For reactive systems this means that it should

be possible to prepare intuitive and comprehensible specifications that can be analyzed, simulated and debugged at any stage with the aid of a computerized support system.

This paper describes the ideas behind STATEMATE, a computerized working environment for the development of reactive systems, which adheres to these principles.

2. STATEMATE AT A GLANCE

The underlying premise of STATEMATE is the need to specify and analyze the system under development (SUD in the sequel) from three closely related points of view: structural, functional and behavioral. These are illustrated in Fig. 1.

In the *structural view* one provides a hierarchical decomposition of the SUD into its physical components, called *modules* here, and identifies the *information* that flows between them; that is, the "chunks" of data and control signals that flow through whatever physical links exist between the modules. The word "physical" should be taken as rather general, with a module being anything from an actual piece of hardware in some systems to the subroutines and blocks in the software parts of others.

The dominant conceptual decomposition of the SUD is carried out via the *functional view,* where one identifies a hierarchy of *activities,* complete with the details of the *data items* and *control signals* that flow between them. This is essentially what is often called the *functional decomposition* of the SUD. However, in the functional view we do not specify dynamics: we do not say when the activities will be activated, whether or not they

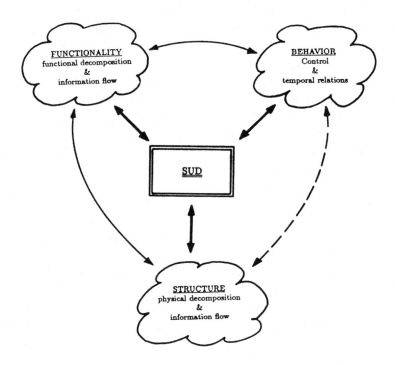

Figure 1. Three views of the system under description (SUD).

terminate on their own, and whether they can be carried out in parallel. The same is true of the data-flow: in the functional view we specify only that data *can* flow, and not whether and when it will. For example, if we have identified that two of the subactivities of an **Automatic Teller Machine** we are describing are **identify-customer** and **report-balance,** and that the data item **account-number** can flow from the former to the latter, then no more and no less than that is implied; we still have not specified when that item will flow, how often will it flow, and in response to what, and indeed whether the flow will be initiated by the former activity or requested by the latter. In other words, the functional view provides the decomposition into activities and the possible flow of information, but it says little about

how those activities and their associated inputs and outputs are controlled during the continued behavior of the SUD.

It is the *behavioral view,* our third, that is responsible for specifying control. This is achieved by allowing a *control activity* to be present on each level of the activity hierarchy, controlling that particular level. It is these controllers that are responsible for specifying when, how and why things happen as the SUD reacts over time. Among other things, a controlling statechart can start and stop activities, can generate new events, and can change the values of variables. It can also sense whether activities are active or data has flown, and it can respond to events and test the values of variables. These connections between activities and control will be seen in Section 3 to involve a rather elaborate set of events, conditions and actions, whereas the relationship between modules and activities is far simpler, and consists essentially of specifying which modules implement which activities. (Some of our ideas as to the way functionality and control are related, are similar to those appearing independently in [7, 11, 13].)

For each of these three views, the structural, functional and behavioral, STATEMATE provides a graphical, diagrammatic language, complete with a rule-based graphics editor that checks for syntactic validity as the appropriate specifications are developed. These languages, *module-charts, activity-charts*

and *statecharts,* respectively, are all based on a common set of simple graphical conventions (see [4]) and come complete with formal semantics that are embedded into STATEMATE. They are described in more detail in Section 3.

Figure 2 illustrates the overall structure of STATEMATE. The database is central, and obtains much of its input from the three graphics editors, and also from an editor for a *forms language,* in which the nongraphical information is specified.

Perhaps the most interesting parts of STATEMATE are the queries, testing and simulation (i.e., execution) packages, described in Section 4, and the code-generation and prototyping capabilities,

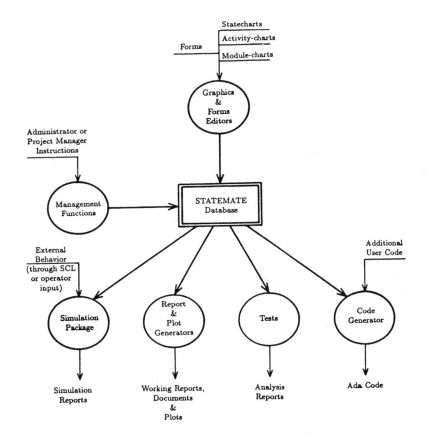

Figure 2. Overall structure of STATEMATE.

described in Section 5. As mentioned, the entire approach is governed by the desire to enable the user to run, debug and analyze the specifications and designs that result from the graphical languages. To this end, the database has been constructed to make it possible to rigorously execute the specification and to retrieve information of a variety of kinds from the overall three-sided description of the SUD provided by the user. Two of the special tools provided by STATEMATE for these purposes are the *object list generator* (OLG), a language for querying the database and retrieving information from it, and the *simulation control language* (SCL), which allows the user to emulate the SUD's environment, execute the specifications with animated response, and track errors and run-time problems. In addition, STATE-MATE provides a number of dynamic tests, such as reachability and the detection of deadlock and nondeterminism.

STATEMATE provides an automatic translation of the entire specification into Ada,* yielding code that can be linked to real or simulated environment modules, and enriched by additional code describing the bottom-level activities that were left unspecified in the specification itself. This results in a prototypical version of the final system that can be run much faster than the animated simulation.

STATEMATE was constructed by a team of around 25 people over a period of three years. The currently available version runs on a color† VaxStation (or a network of such) with a VMS operat-

ing system, and its database is DEC's Rdb. Unix‡ versions running on Sun and Apollo workstations will become available in the Summer of 1988.

We should note that most of the ideas and methods embodied in STATEMATE have been field-tested successfully in a number of large real-world development projects, among which is the mission-specific avionics system for the Lavi fighter aircraft designed by the Israel Aircraft Industries.

3. THE MODELLING LANGUAGES OF STATEMATE

In this section we present the highlights of the three graphical languages and the forms language that the user of STATE-MATE employs to specify the SUD. No formal syntax or semantics are given here, neither are all of the features presented. The reader is referred to [9] for a more comprehensive description, and to [3, 6] for a detailed treatment of the language of statecharts. The languages are described with the help of a simple example of an **Early Warning System** (EWS in the sequel), which has the ability to take measurements from an external sensor, compare them with some prespecified upper and lower limits and warn the user when the measured value exceeds these limits.

The structural view of the SUD is described using the language of *module-charts,* which describe SUD *modules* (i.e., its physical components), environment modules (i.e., those parts that for the purpose of specification are deemed to be external to the SUD), and the clusters of data and/or control signals that may flow

---

*Ada is a trademark of the U.S. Department of Defense.

†While color appears to significantly enhance the appeal of STATEMATE, a monochrome version of STATEMATE is also available.

---

‡Unix is a registered trademark of AT&T Bell Labs.

among them. Modules are depicted as rectilinear shapes, with storage modules having dashed sides and with encapsulation capturing the submodule relationship. Environment modules appear as dashed-line rectangles external to that of the SUD itself. Information flow is represented by labelled arrows or hyperarrows.* Various kinds of connectors can appear in these charts, both to abbreviate lengthy arrows and to denote compound chunks of data.

Figure 3 is (part of) the module-chart of our early warning system. It specifies in a self-explanatory fashion that the modules, or subsystems, of the EWS are a main component, a **man-machine-interface** (MMI) and a **signal-handler**, and that the **sensor**, **timer**, and **alarm** are considered to be external to the system. The MMI is further decomposed into submodules, as shown. The information

flowing between the modules is specified too.

The functional view of the SUD is captured by the language of *activity-charts.* Graphically, these are very similar to module-charts, but here the rectilinear shapes stand for the *activities,* or the functions, carried out by the system. Solid arrows represent the flow of data items and dashed arrows capture the flow of control items. †

A typical activity will accept input items and produce output items during its active time-spans, its inner workings being specified by its own lower level decomposition. Activities that are *basic* (i.e., on the lowest level) are assumed to be

---

*A hyperarrow has more than two endpoints.

†In displaying module-charts and activity-charts on the screen STATEMATE employs different conventions regarding color and arrow type, so that a user can distinguish between them quite easily. Thus, for example, the arrows in module-charts are drawn using rectilinear segments parallel to the axes, whereas in activity-charts they are drawn using smooth spline functions.

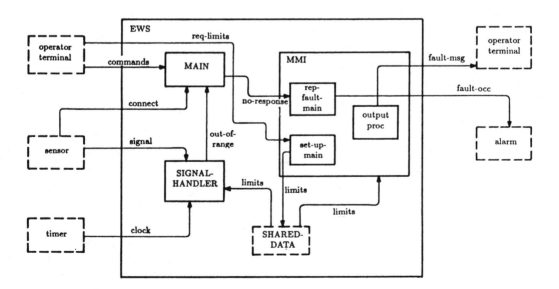

Figure 3. Module-chart of the early warning system.

described as simple input/output transformations using other means. More about this in Sections 4 and 5.

Activity-charts may contain two additional kinds of objects: *data-stores* and *control activities*. Data-stores can be thought of as representing databases, data structures, buffers of various kinds, or even physical containers or reservoirs, and typically correspond to the storage modules in the module-chart. They represent the ability to store the data items that flow into them and to produce those items as outputs upon request.

The control activities constitute the behavioral view of the system and they appear in the activity-chart as empty boxes only, one (at most) within each non-basic activity, as shown in Fig. 4. The contents of the control activities are described in the third of our graphical languages, *statecharts,* which are discussed below. In general, a control activity has the ability to control its sibling activities by essentially sensing their status' and issuing commands to them. Thus, for example, in Fig. 4 the control activity S_1 can, among other things, perform *actions* that cause subactivities *A, B* and *D* to start and stop, and can sense whether those subactivities have started or stopped by appropriate *events* and *conditions*. Various consequences of such occurrences are integrated into the semantics of the activity-charts language, such as the fact that all subactivities stop (respectively, suspend) upon the stopping (respectively, suspension) of the parent activity.

We now turn to the behavioral view. Statecharts, which were introduced in [3] (see also [4, 6]), are an extension of conventional finite-state machines (FSMs) and their visual counterpart, state-transition di-

agrams. Conventional state diagrams are inappropriate for the behavioral description of complex control, since they suffer from being flat and unstructured, are inherently sequential in nature, and give rise to an exponential blow-up in the number of states (i.e., small extensions of a system cause unacceptable growth in the number of states to be considered). These problems are overcome in statecharts by supporting decomposition of states in an AND/OR fashion, combined with an instantaneous broadcast communication mechanism. A rather important facet of these extensions is the ability to have transitions leave and enter states on any level.

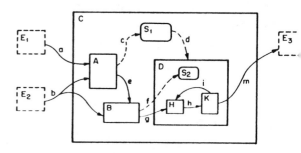

Figure 4. An activity-chart.

Consider Fig. 5, in which (a) and (b) are equivalent. In 5(b) states *S* and *T* have been clustered into a new state, *U,* so that to be in *U* is to be either in *S* or in *T.* The *f*-arrow leaving *U* denotes a high-level interrupt, and has the effect of prescribing an exit from *U,* i.e., from whichever of *S* or *T* the system happens to be in, to the new state *V.* The *h*-arrow entering *U* would appear to be underspecified, as it must cause entry to *S* or *T;* in fact, its meaning relies on the internal default arrow attached to *T* to indeed effect an entrance to *T.*

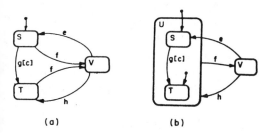

Figure 5. OR-decomposition in a state-chart.

Turning to AND decomposition, consider Fig. 6, in which, again, (a) and (b) are equivalent. Here, to be in state *U* the system must be in *both* *S* and *T.* An unspecified entrance to *U* relies on both default arrows to enter the pair {*V,W*}, from which an occurrence of *e,* for example, would lead to the new pair {*X,Y*}, and *k* would lead to {*V,Z*}. The meaning of the

other transitions appearing therein, including entrances and exits, can be deduced by comparing 6(a) and 6(b). It is worth mentioning that this AND decomposition, into what we call *orthogonal* state components, can be carried out on any level of states and is therefore more convenient than allowing only single-level sets of communicating FSMs. Orthogonality is the feature statecharts employ to solve the state blow-up problem; see [3, 4]. (Clearly, orthogonal state decomposition also replaces the need to allow multiple control activities within a single activity, as is done, e.g., in [13].)

The general syntax of an expression labelling a transition in a statechart is

$$\alpha[C] \;/\; \beta$$

where α is the event that triggers the transition, *C* is a condition that guards the transition from being taken unless it is true when α occurs, and β is an action that is carried out if, and precisely when, the

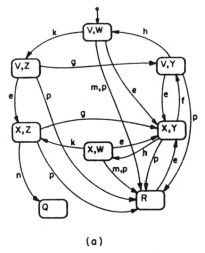

(a)

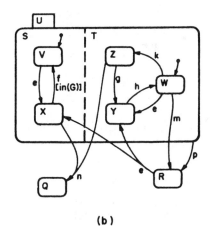

(b)

Figure 6. AND-decomposition in a statechart.

transition is taken. Any of these can be omitted. Events and conditions can be considered as inputs, and actions as outputs, except that here this correspondence is more subtle, due to the intricate nature of the statecharts themselves and their relationship with the activities. For example, if β appears as an action along one transition and also as a triggering event on a transition in an orthogonal component of the same statechart, then executing the action will immediately cause the transition to be taken simultaneously. Moreover, in the expression $\alpha \, / \, \beta$, rather than being simply a *primitive action* that might cause other transitions, β might be the special action start (A) that causes the activity A to start, and similarly, rather than being simply an external, primitive event, α might be the special event stopped (B) that occurs (and hence causes the transition to take place) when B stops or is stopped. Table 1 shows a selection of some of the special events, conditions and actions that can appear as part of the labels along a transition. It should be noted that the syntax is also closed under Boolean combinations, so that, for example, the following is a legal label:

entered(S) [in (T) and not active (C)] /
suspend(C); $X := Y + 7$

Notice that conventional variables can be used too, with changing values allowed as events, standard comparisons as conditions and assignment statements as actions.

Besides allowing actions to appear along transitions they can also appear associated with the entrance to or exit from a state (any state, of course, on any level).* This association is specified in a form in the forms language discussed below. Thus, if we associate the action **resume** (A) with the entrance to state S, activity A will be resumed whenever S is entered.

Some of the special constructs appearing in Table 1 thus serve to link the control activities with the other objects appearing in an activity-chart, and, as such, are part of the way behavior is associated with functionality and data-flow. There are other facets to this association, one of which is the ability to specify an activity A as taking place *throughout* a state S, which is the same as saying that A is started upon entering S and stopped upon leaving it. This connection is also stated via forms.

Table 1.
Some Special Events,
Conditions and Actions.

	EVENTS	CONDITIONS	ACTIONS
in statechart	entered(S) exited(S)	in(S)	
connecting statechart to activities	started(A) stopped(A)	active(A) hanging(A)	start(A) stop(A) suspend(A) resume(A)
information items	read(D) written(D) true(C) false(C)	D=exp D <exp D >exp ⋮	D:=exp made_true(C) make_false(C)
time	timeout(E,n)		schedule(Ac,n)

---

*In this way, statecharts can be seen to generalize both Mealy and Moore automata; see [8].

The power to control and sense the status of activities is limited by a scoping rule to the control activity appearing on the same level as the activities and flow in question. Thus, in Fig. 4, for example, some of the events and actions that can appear in the statechart S_1 are $st(A)$, $rs!(B)$ and $wr!(d)$, but ones referring to, say, H and K, such as $st!(H)$, cannot, and would appear only in S_2.* This scoping mechanism for hiding information is intended to help in making STATEMATE specifications modular and amenable to the kind of division of work that is required in large projects. There are ways of utilizing primitive events and actions to override this scoping rule, but we shall not describe them here.

Figure 7 shows the activity-chart of the early warning system. The user, via the operator terminal, can send **commands** to the control activity, a structured data item which, via a form, is specified to consist of **set-up**, **execute** and **reset** instructions. The operator can also send the upper and lower required limits to the **get&check** subactivity of **set-up**. These limits can be stored in the data-store **range**, to be sent upon request to the **compare** and **report-fault** activities. (The item **req-limits** is also structured, and stands for the pair containing the required upper and lower limits.) A special activity, **get-measure-**

---

*Here, and also in the Figure 8, we are using abbreviations of the elements appearing in Table 1, such as st instead of **started**, $rs!$ instead of **resume** and tm instead of **timeout**. STATEMATE recognizes these abbreviations too.

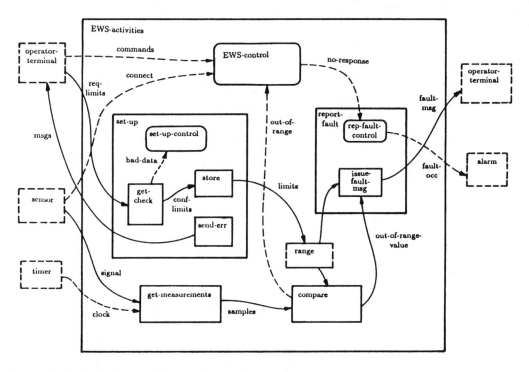

Figure 7. Activity-chart of the early warning system.

ments can receive the **signal** from the sensor and a **clock** reading from the timer, and translates these into a time-stamped digital value **sample**, which can be sent to the comparing activity. If out of range, a signal and value can be sent to the controller and the **report-fault** activity, respectively. The latter is responsible for sending out an alarm and formatting and sending the user an appropriate message. The second level of Fig. 7 is self-explanatory.

It is important to emphasize the recurring word "can" in the previous paragraph. Figure 7 is not required to provide dynamic, behavioral information about the EWS; that is the role of the controlling statecharts. Figure 8, for example, shows one possible statechart for the high-level control activity of Fig. 7, i.e.,

EWS-**control**, and the reader should be able to comprehend it quite easily.

While the connections between activity-charts and statecharts are rather intricate, those between module-charts and activity-charts are more straightforward. Using forms, one indicates the module that implements a given activity, and the storage module that implements a given data store. In our example, some of these associations are that MAIN module implements the EWS-**control** activity, SIGNAL-HANDLER implements **get-measurements** and **compare**, and MMI implements **set-up** and **report-fault**. Within the latter association the **send-err** subactivity is implemented by the **output-proc** submodule and the other three by **set-up-main**.

We now turn to the *forms language*.

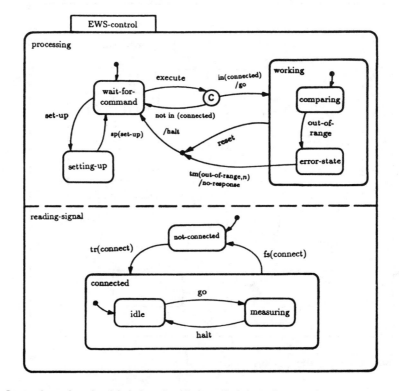

Figure 8. Statechart for the high-level activity of the early warning system.

It maintains a special form for each of the elements in the description, in which additional information can be input. This includes details that do not normally show up in the graphics, such as lengthy definitions of compound events and conditions, as well as elements that are nongraphical in nature, such as the type and structure of data items. Figure 9 shows an example of the form for a data item, in which most items are self-explanatory. The "Consists of" field therein makes it possible to structure data items into components, and the "Attribute" fields make it possible to associate attributes with the items (e.g., units and precision for certain kinds of data-items, or the names of the personnel responsible for the specification for certain high-level elements). The attributes are recognizable by the query language and therefore able to be part of the criteria for retrieving information about the SUD.

The color graphical editors for all three charts languages are rule-driven, continuously checking the input for syntactic soundness, and the database of STATE-MATE is updated as graphical elements are introduced. They are mouse- and menu-based, and support a wide range of possibilities, including move, copy, stretch, hide, reveal and zoom options, all applicable to single or multiple elements in the charts, that can be selected in a number of ways. The form for a selected element can be viewed and updated not only from STATEMATE's special forms editor but from the appropriate graphical editor too.

Extensive consistency and completeness tests, as well as more subtle *static logic* tests can be carried out during a STATE-MATE session. Examples include checking whether the hierarchy of modules is consistent with that of the activities, listing modules that have no outputs or activities that are never started, and identifying cyclic definitions of nongraphical elements (e.g., events and conditions).

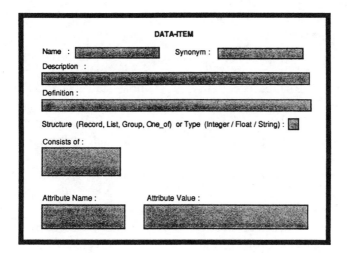

Figure 9. The form for a data item.

4. QUERIES, EXECUTIONS AND DYNAMIC TESTS

In this section we describe some of the tools that STATEMATE supplies for debugging and analyzing the specification of the SUD as provided by the user via the modelling languages.

STATEMATE provides a query language, the *object list generator* (OLG), with which the user can retrieve information from the database, effectively querying the model of the SUD as described in the modelling languages. The OLG works by generating lists of elements that satisfy certain criteria. At all times it keeps a *pending list* that gets modified as the user refines the criteria or asks for a list of elements of another type. For example, starting with an empty pending list, one can ask for all states in the controlling statechart of activity *A,* and the resulting list promptly becomes the new pending list. This list might then be refined by asking for those states therein that contain a substate named "**off**." Then one might ask for all activities that are started within any of those states, and so on. This query language, on the face of it, might appear to be bounded in its expressive power by that of the conjunctive queries of [2]. However, since the OLG supports certain kinds of transitive closures (such as the ancestor and descendent relationships between states or activities), it is not directly comparable with the conjunctive queries, and can be shown to be a subset of the more general fixpoint queries of [1].

Turning to the execution and simulation capabilities, the heart of these is STATEMATE's ability to carry out a *step* of the SUD's dynamic behavior, with all its consequences taken into account. Thus, the semantics of all of our modelling languages (in particular, that of the statecharts) are fully incorporated into STATEMATE's software. A step, briefly, is one unit of dynamic behavior, at the beginning and at the end of which the SUD is in some legal *status*. A status captures the system's currently active states and activities, the current values of variables and conditions, etc. During a step the environment activities can generate external events, change the truth values of conditions, and update variables and other data items. Given the potentially intricate form that STATEMATE's description of the SUD might take on, such changes can have a profound effect on the status, triggering transitions in statecharts, activating and deactivating activities, further updating data items, and so on. Clearly, each of these changes, in turn, can possibly cause many others. The portion of STATEMATE that is responsible for calculating the effect of a step contains involved algorithmic procedures, which, among many other things, implement a formal semantics of statecharts similar to that described, e.g., in [6].

STATEMATE supports two basic ways of "running" the SUD: *interactive* and *batch*. In the first, the user specifies some initial status of the SUD and thereafter proceeds to generate external events, change conditions and carry out other actions (such as changing the values of variables) at will, and STATEMATE considers all these to have occurred within a single step. When the user gives the GO command STATEMATE responds by transforming the SUD into the new resulting status. Typically, there will be a statechart on the screen while this is happening, and also an activity-chart, and the currently active states and activities will be highlighted with special coloring.* Batch simulation (or execution) can be described as the ability to carry out many steps in order, controlled by a *simulation control program* (SCP in the sequel) written in STATEMATE's specially tailored *simulation control language* (SCL). During a batch execution, the same color codes are used to continuously update the displayed charts. The result is a visually pleasing discrete animation of the behavior for the SUD.

The SCPs themselves look a little like conventional programs in a high-level language; they employ variables and support several control structures that can be nested and indented. They are used to control the simulation by reading events and changes from previously prepared files and/or generating them using, say, random sampling from a variety of probability distributions. Several kinds of *breakpoints* can be incorporated into the program, causing the execution to stop and take certain actions when particular situations come up. These actions can range from adding 1 to a counter (e.g., to accumulate statistics about performance), through switching to interactive mode (from which the user can return to batch mode by a simple command), and all the way to executing a lengthy calculation that might constitute the inners of a basic, unspecified, activity.

Executions can thus be stopped and restarted, and intervening changes can be made; the effects of events generated with prescribed probabilities can be checked, and the computational parts of the SUD

and its environment can be emulated. Moreover, during such simulated executions a *trace database* is maintained, which records all changes made in the status of the SUD. The trace database can later be reviewed, filed away, printed or discarded, and, of course, is an invaluable tool for analyzing the execution and its effects. A variety of *simulation reports* can be produced, in which parts of the information are gathered as the execution proceeds, via instructions in the SCP, and other parts are taken from the trace database after the execution ends.

The part of the SUD that is simulated in either interactive or batch modes can be restricted in scope. For example, one can simulate any part of the description that is identifiable by the name of some state or activity, and the rest of the STATEMATE specification is considered to be nonexistent for the duration of that simulation. Moreover, there is no need to wait until the entire SUD is specified before initiating executions and simulations; a user can start simulating, or running, a description from the moment the portion that is available is syntactically intact. In the simulation the user will typically provide those events and other items of information that are external to the specified portion, even though later they might become internal to the specification.

In general, then, a carefully prepared SCP can be used to test the specification of the SUD under a wide range of test data, to emulate both the environment and the as-of-yet unspecified parts of the SUD, to check the specification for time-critical performance and efficiency, and, in general, to debug it and identify subtle runtime errors. Needless to say, the kinds of errors and misconceptions that can be

---

*Actually, the system will highlight only those states and activities that are on the lowest level visible.

discovered in this way are quite different from the syntactic completeness and consistency checks that form the highlights of most of the other available tools for system design, and which STATEMATE carries out routinely.

Since STATEMATE can fully execute specifications, it becomes tempting to provide the ability to test, quite rigorously, for some of the crucial dynamic properties of the SUD—those we desire it to satisfy as well as those we want to make sure it does not. Accordingly, STATE-MATE has been programmed to provide several kinds of *dynamic tests,* essentially by carrying out exhaustive, brute-force, sets of executions. These include *reachability, nondeterminism, deadlock* and *usage of transitions.* For the first of these the user inputs final conditions and STATEMATE will seek sequences of external events and other occurrences that lead from an initial status to one that satisfies these conditions, producing them if they exist and stating that there are none otherwise. It is important to stress that this is run-time, dynamic, reachability, not merely a test for whether two boxes in a diagram are connected by arrows. The same applies to the other dynamic tests too.

5. CODE-GENERATION AND RAPID PROTOTYPING

An additional feature recently added to the basic STATEMATE system is the code-generation capability. The user can request that the specification of the SUD (or some portion thereof) be translated automatically into Ada. The system will apply a fixed translation scheme to convert the specified activity-chart and statecharts

into Ada. Moreover, code can be added by the user to emulate the environment and/or to supply meanings for the bottom-level basic activities. All of this results in a prototypical version of the final system, and will typically run much faster than the animated simulation. This Ada prototype has the ability to form the basis of a realistic simulation of the system itself, with simulated graphics representing the various physical interfaces with the user. STATEMATE might be extended in this direction in the future.

The rigid nature of the translation scheme prevents a user from incorporating his or her own design decisions into the code, except insofar as such decisions were incorporated already into the STATEMATE specification. For this reason the Ada code that STATEMATE produces is of prototype quality only and will not necessarily be as efficient or as fine-tuned as production code. Future plans call for enhancing the code generator with the ability to incorporate decisions made interactively by the human designer, as well as with various further optimization features.

6. REPORTS AND DOCUMENT GENERATION

STATEMATE can be asked to plot the charts that constitute the SUD's description. The user has control over the portion of the chart that will be plotted, as well as its size and depth. In addition, the user can ask for several kinds of fixed-format *reports* that are compiled directly from the description of the SUD in the database, and which can be displayed on the workstation screen or output to an alphanumeric terminal or printer. Each of these can be projected, so to speak, on any part of the description that is retrievable by the OLG. In other words, the user may first use the OLG to capture, say, a set of activities of particular interest, and then request the report; it will be applied only to the activities in the list. Among the reports currently implemented are *data dictionaries* of various kinds, textual *protocols* of states or activities containing all the information relevant to them, *interface diagrams,* tree versions of the various hierarchies, and the so-called *N^2-diagrams.* Using a number of parameters, the user can control various aspects of the reports produced, such as the depth of the trees in the tree reports, and the keys by which the dictionaries will be sorted.

In late 1988 STATEMATE will be able to generate documentation to comply with the requirements of the DoD Standard 2167. This will not be a stand-alone feature, but, rather, part of a more general approach that involves a language for user-specified document generation. In this language the user constructs his or her own document template, complete with the queries whose responses will serve to fill in the required information, and thereafter the document will be generated automatically, projected on any retrievable portion of the description of the SUD.

7. CONCLUSIONS

In conclusion we might say that the STATEMATE system combines two principles, or theses, which we feel should guide future attempts to design support tools for system development. The first is the long-advocated need for *executable specifications,* and the second is the advantage of using *visual formalisms.*

As far as the first of these goes, the development of complex systems must not allow for design and construction of the final product from untested requirements or specifications. Rather, ways should be found to model the SUD on any desired level of detail in a manner that is fully executable, or simulatable, and which allows for deep and comprehensive testing and debugging prior to building the system itself.

As to the second principle, we believe that visual formalism will turn out to be a crucial ingredient in the next stage of the continuous search for more natural and powerful ways to exploit computers. It is our feeling that the ever-falling prices and ever-rising quality of graphical computers and workstations, combined with the incredible capabilities of the human visual system, will result in a revolution in the way we carry out many of our conceptually complex engineering activities. The surviving approaches will be, to a very large extent, of diagrammatic nature, yet will be formal and rigorous, in both syntax and semantics.

Acknowledgments

We are grateful to all the staff members of Ad-Cad Ltd., the research and development branch of i-Logix Inc., who have been indispensable in turning the ideas described here into a real working system. Ido Lachover deserves special thanks for being the most pleasant manager imaginable, contributing his experience and expertise to all phases of the work. We would also like to thank Jonah Lavi and his group at the Israel Aircraft Industries for their constructive criticism during the period in which the system was developed.

REFERENCES

[1]   A.K. Chandra and D. Harel, "Structure and Complexity of Relational Queries," *Journal of Computer Systems Science,* Vol. 25 (1982), pp. 99-128.

[2]   A.K. Chandra and P. Merlin, "Optimal Implementation of Conjunctive Queries in Relational Databases," *Proceedings of the 9th ACM Symposium on Theory of Computing,* Boulder, Colo., 1977, pp. 77-90.

[3]   D. Harel, "Statecharts: A Visual Formalism for Complex Systems," *Science of Computer Programming,* Vol. 8 (1987), pp. 231-74.

[4]   _____ , "On Visual Formalisms," *Communications of the ACM,* June 1987.

[5]   D. Harel and A. Pnueli, "On the Development of Reactive Systems," in *Logics and Models of Concurrent Systems,* K.R. Apt, ed., New York: Springer-Verlag, 1985, pp. 477-98.

[6]   _____ , J.P. Schmidt, and R. Sherman, "On the Formal Semantics of Statecharts," in *Proceedings of the 2nd IEEE Symposium on Logic in Computer Science,* Ithaca, N.Y., 1987, pp. 54-64.

[7]   D.J. Hatley, "A Structured Analysis Method for Real-Time Systems," *Proceedings of the DECUS Symposium,* December 1985.

[8]   J.E. Hopcroft and J.D. Ullman, *Introduction to Automata Theory, Languages, and Computation,* Reading, Mass.: Addison-Wesley, 1979.

[9]   "The Languages of STATEMATE," Technical Report, i-Logix Inc., Burlington, Mass., 1987.

[10] "Methodologies of Building Specifications Using the STATEMATE System," Technical Report, i-Logix Inc., Burlington, Mass., 1987.

[11] J.Z. Lavi and E. Kessler, "An Embedded Computer Systems Analysis Method," Manuscript, Israel Aircraft Industries, November 1986.

[12] A. Pnueli, "Applications of Temporal Logic to the Specification and Verification of Reactive Systems: A Survey of Current Trends," in *Current Trends in Concurrency* (de Bakker, et al., eds.), Lecture Notes in Computer Science, Vol. 224, Berlin: Springer-Verlag, 1986, pp. 510-84.

[13] P. Ward, "The Transformation Schema: An Extension of the Data Flow Diagram to Represent Control and Timing," *IEEE Transactions on Software Engineering,* Vol. 12 (1986), pp. 198-210.

22

Editors' Note
Sumner and Gleaves: "Modula-2—A Solution to Pascal's Problems"

*Insight: **Some languages are better than others, and one is best. (Maybe it's Modula-2.)***

Niklaus Wirth's Pascal was probably the most significant language of the 1970s. It dominated the universities and its various dialects gained a real foothold in the microprocessor communities. When the Department of Defense began their huge effort to build the ultimate block structured language (the Ada Project), DoD decided to make it a Pascal-derivative. Ada was chartered to become a real-world Pascal.

Pascal did need to be enhanced to remain relevant. The language's elegant spareness made it a favorite of programming teachers, but the limitations were significant enough to matter. Serious implementors needed supersets of the language. Thus were born the dialects (UCSD Pascal is one example). They remained relatively spare, but they just were not Pascal. All hope of portability was lost when you coded in a dialect.

While the Ada Project ground on and Pascal dialects sprouted like weeds, Wirth himself was hard at work. With a tiny staff at the Swiss Federal Technical College (ETH), he designed and implemented the Modula-2 language. Sumner and Gleaves describe the result.

22

Modula-2—A Solution to Pascal's Problems
by Roger T. Sumner and R.E. Gleaves

INTRODUCTION

At the 1981 Software Engineering Conference in San Diego, Niklaus Wirth demonstrated the personal computer Lilith. Lilith contains a number of interesting features, including high resolution graphics, a "mouse" for cursor positioning, and a fast 2901 bit-slice processor. The most interesting feature, however, is that Lilith is programmed entirely in Modula-2, Wirth's latest programming language. [3]

At the time, our company was searching for a good systems programming language for use in various in-house projects, and—like so many others—we were leaning towards an extended version of Pascal. Our chance discovery of Modula-2 came as somewhat of a surprise! Now, after twelve months of experience in programming and implementing Modula-2, we are convinced of its superiority as a programming language.

Though Modula-2 is a general purpose language, it is designed primarily for systems implementation. It has inherited most of Pascal's features: data types include records, arrays, sets, and pointers, and statements include the familiar if, for, while, repeat, case, and with statements. The original Modula language [2] contributes the module concept, facilities for low-level machine access, and a more consistent syntax. Finally, the design of Modula-2 systematically addresses Pascal's problems.

PASCAL'S PROBLEMS

Our experiences with Pascal began as student members of the UCSD Pascal Project. As early users of Pascal, the Project quickly discovered its inherent limitations. These were solved by adding several extensions; unfortunately, in most cases extensions were added in an ad hoc (some might say "ad hack") manner. The UCSD Pascal* extensions were originally intended only for systems programming, but experience revealed their necessity in most programming tasks other than teaching.

The need for extensions did not escape the attention of other Pascal implementors; as a result, each pragmatic Pascal implementation provided its own peculiar set of extensions, resulting in a computerized Tower of Babel. This unfortunate situation defeated one of Pascal's original design goals: portability across implementations.

Meanwhile, back at UCSD, the ever-increasing number of extensions was creating a huge maintenance problem. Every extension consumed symbol table and ob-

---

*UCSD Pascal is a registered trademark of the Regents of the University of California.

ject code space, and a new version of the compiler was required for each new extension. To compound the problem, the compiler was intimately tied to the operating system's support routines. Eventually, it was realized that unacceptable amounts of compile-time storage were being sacrificed to parse the multitude of extensions. In a classic example of "tail wagging dog," heroic efforts were subsequently undertaken to regain the lost compile-time space: the compiler was restructured into a collection of swappable code segments, ruining its performance in the process.

All of this resulted from attempts to use Pascal in tasks beyond its intended scope. Pascal's problems have been described in several papers, usually by comparing Pascal with other languages. In one such paper, Kernighan [1] identifies Pascal's major problems:

1) Arrays are fixed in size. This makes string handling difficult and general purpose math routines impossible.

2) The lack of static (or "own") variables and their initialization. This forces the programmer to use global variables which have a larger scope than they ought to.

3) The lack of facilities for separate compilation hinders the development of large programs. It also makes the use of libraries impossible.

4) The required declaration order—constants, types, variables, procedures—prevents related declarations from being grouped together.

5) The order of Boolean expression evaluation is not specified, resulting in convoluted code and extraneous state variables.

6) The case statement is hampered by its lack of an "otherwise" clause.

7) The I/O facilities are severely limited. There is no sensible way of dealing with real-world files or program arguments as part of the language.

8) There is no escape from the limitations of the language. Type checking is always enforced, and I/O routines cannot be written in Pascal itself.

Many of these problems have been addressed by various Pascal implementations; however, each offers a different solution and none satisfactorily addresses all of these problems. Languages such as "C" offer workable solutions, but sacrifice readability and many of Pascal's obvious advantages (e.g., type checking). Modula-2 solves each of these problems without sacrificing Pascal's advantages (and does so with a language which is smaller than most Pascal dialects).

MODULA-2

In addition to Pascal's data types and statement structures, Modula-2 introduces a handful of new concepts. The most important of these is the module construct, which improves program organization and provides a foundation for separate compilation and libraries. Other new concepts include low-level machine access, coroutines (for constructing process schedulers), and procedure types (similar to Pascal's procedural parameters, but generalized to include variables).

Modula-2 defines no standard procedures for I/O, storage allocation, and process scheduling; instead, these facilities are programmed in Modula-2 and stored in library modules. The burden of providing extensions thus shifts from the language to the library, allowing the language (and compiler) to remain quite small.

Along with the new concepts, Modula-2 contains a number of minor improvements to Pascal, including the standard type CARDINAL (for unsigned integer operations), octal and hexadecimal constants, constant expressions, and the LOOP/EXIT statement.

Modula-2 addresses each of the problems identified by Kernighan. The solutions presented below correspond to the problems enumerated above. We have taken the liberty to present a few samples of the language in order to convey its flavor.

1) Modula-2 allows formal parameter types of the form "ARRAY OF <base type>." This type is compatible with all arrays declared with the same base type. The bounds of an actual parameter are mapped onto the range 0 . . HIGH (<formal param>): HIGH is a standard procedure which returns the upper bound of its array argument. Dynamic parameter types are useful for manipulating text strings and numeric vectors. Also, string constants are assignable into character arrays of greater length; such string values are terminated with a null character.

```
PROCEDURE Length (s: ARRAY OF CHAR):
        CARDINAL;
    VAR i: CARDINAL;
BEGIN
    i :  = 0;
    WHILE (i < = HIGH (s)) AND (s[i] < > OC)
        DO INC (i);
    END;
    RETURN i;
END Length;
```

2) Modules provide a nice abstraction for creating "own" variables. A module declaration restricts the visibility of its locally declared variables without restricting their existence. In the following example, the variable Seed serves as an "own" variable.

```
MODULE RandomNumberGenerator;
    IMPORT TimeOfDay;
    EXPORT Random;

    CONST Modulus   = 2345;
          Increment = 7227;

    VAR Seed:  CARDINAL;

    PROCEDURE Random ():  REAL;
    BEGIN
        Seed : = (Seed + Increment) MOD
            Modulus;
        RETURN FLOAT(Seed) /
            FLOAT(Modulus);
    END Random;

BEGIN
    Seed : = TimeOfDay ();
END RandomNumberGenerator;
```

3) Modula-2 defines three kinds of compilation units. Program modules constitute executable programs. A program module serves either as a "main" program or as a subprogram invoked by another module. Library modules consist of two separately compiled sections: the so-called definition module and its corresponding implementation module. Compilation units which import a library module access only its definition module; thus, the implementation module can be

recompiled without affecting the rest of the system.

```
DEFINITION MODULE M;
   EXPORT QUALIFIED p1;
   PROCEDURE p1 ( . . .);
END M.

IMPLEMENTATION MODULE M;
   FROM B IMPORT c,d;
   VAR y:  . . .;
   PROCEDURE p1 ( . . .);
   BEGIN . . . y . . . c . . . END p1;
BEGIN . . . y . . .
END M.
```

4) Constants, types, variables, procedures, and modules can be declared in any order within a block, allowing related declarations to be grouped together. Modules provide a more rigorous mechanism for grouping related objects.

5) The evaluation order of logical expressions is specifically defined as conditional "short-circuit" evaluation. The AND and OR operators are defined as

```
a AND b = "if a then b otherwise FALSE"
a OR b = "if a then TRUE otherwise b"

WHILE (p < > NIL) AND (p^.field < 0) DO
   p := p^ .next;
END;
```

6) Case statements (as well as record case variants) can have an ELSE clause. Subranges are allowed in the case constant lists.

```
CASE ch OF
    '0'..'9':     number;
                  nextch;

    'A'..'Z',
    'a'..'z':     letter;
                  nextch;
```

```
    '*', '/',
    '+', '-':     arithop;
ELSE
    otherchar;
END;
```

7) Modula-2 defines no facilities for input and output. I/O routines are provided by standard library modules; when the need arises, these can be supplemented with implementation-specific library modules. The following example presents a library module implementing part of UCSD Pascal's block I/O facilities.

```
DEFINITION MODULE UCSDBlockIO;
   FROM SYSTEM IMPORT WORD;
   EXPORT QUALIFIED FILE, Reset,
        BlockRead;

   TYPE FILE; (* Opaque type defined in
        impl.  module *)

   PROCEDURE Reset (Var f:  FILE;
        fileName:  ARRAY OF CHAR);

   PROCEDURE BlockRead (VAR f:  FILE;
        VAR buffer:  ARRAY OF WORD;
        blocks:  CARDINAL;
        blockNum:  CARDINAL):
                CARDINAL;
END UCSDBlockIO.
```

8) Modula-2's low-level programming facilities allow direct access to machine storage, enabling low-level system facilities to be expressed as library modules. The predefined module SYSTEM provides machine-dependent types and procedures. The type WORD is compatible with any object occupying one storage unit. The type ADDRESS is compatible with CARDINAL and all pointer types. The procedures ADR, SIZE, and TSIZE return the memory address and size of variables and types. The type PROCESS

and the procedures NEWPROCESS and TRANSFER implement coroutines.

Type compatibility rules are circumvented by using type identifiers as type transfer functions.

```
TYPE DL11Ptr = POINTER TO BITSET;
VAR ConsoleDLPtr: DL11Ptr;
    . . .
ConsoleDLPtr : = DL11Ptr (17756 0B);
        (* Convert octal constant *)
```

Variables can be declared to reside at fixed memory addresses.

```
VAR ConsoleDL [ 17756 0B ]:  BITSET;
```

CONCLUSIONS

Experience with programming in Pascal has revealed the many advantages of type checking, readability, and simplicity. These concepts reduce program development time and increase reliability. Unfortunately, Pascal suffers from its limited scope: no separate compilation, no machine access, and an inflexible I/O definition.

Modula-2 solves Pascal's problems with a handful of simple concepts (as opposed to a plethora of extensions). It is equally suited to programming high-level machine-independent applications and low-level embedded systems.

An obvious question arises at this point: who needs Modula-2 when we have Ada*? It is indeed interesting to note that Modula-2 satisfies most of the DoD STEELMAN requirements. Strong typ-

ing, separate compilation, machine access, and multitasking are well represented. Overloading, exceptions, and generics are conspicuously absent. Wirth's comments in [3] are telling: "An extended opportunity to use the sophisticated MESA system has taught me how to tackle problems on many occasions, and on a few that it is wiser to avoid them altogether." He further acknowledges his associates as having ". . . helped to keep the language designer's fancies on firm ground."

In short, Modula-2 offers Ada's functionality with a language the size of Pascal. The reference manual is small and comprehensible, compilers are small and efficient, and mastering the language does not require extensive training. Perhaps it is a solution to Ada's problems, too.

REFERENCES

[1]   Kernighan, B. *Why Pascal Is Not My Favorite Programming Language.* Computing Science Technical Report No. 100, Bell Laboratories, July 18, 1981.

[2]   Wirth, N. "Modula: A Language for Modular Multiprogramming." *Software—Practice and Experience,* Vol. 7 (1977), pp. 3-35.

[3]   Wirth, N. *Modula-2.* Report No. 36, Institut fur Informatik, ETH Zurich (1980).

---

*Ada is a registered trademark of the Department of Defense.

23

Editors' Note
Parnas and Clements: "A Rational Design Process: How and Why to Fake It"

Insight: We may yearn for the software design process to become a set of rational, deterministic procedures with a simple, linear path of progress from start to final product. The authors argue here that the software design process will never be entirely rational, but it behooves us to present our final designs as if it were.

The following article is the winner of the *Attention Grabbing Title of the 1980s* Award, and it is no surprise that David Parnas has something to do with it. This is the same David Parnas who brought us the "information hiding" strategy of software design, and who jarred the S.D.I. establishment with his remarkable speech entitled *The Technical Feasibility of Software for the Strategic Defense Initiatives* at the Eighth International Conference on Software Engineering in London in 1985.

In the following paper, Parnas and Clements describe why software design will always be iterative. They are the first writers we know of to state that software is not designed from a complete specification because designers simply cannot hope to deal with the "plethora of details."

Although many software engineers have great difficulty putting down anything that is less than perfect, they must learn to fit their designs to their maturing understanding of the problem.

23

A Rational Design Process: How and Why to Fake It
by David Lorge Parnas and Paul C. Clements

I. THE SEARCH FOR THE PHILOSOPHER'S STONE: WHY DO WE WANT A RATIONAL DESIGN PROCESS?

A perfectly rational person is one who always has a good reason for what he does. Each step taken can be shown to be the best way to get to a well defined goal. Most of us like to think of ourselves as rational professionals. However, to many observers, the usual process of designing software appears quite irrational. Programmers start without a clear statement of desired behavior and implementation constraints. They make a long sequence of design decisions with no clear statement of why they do things the way they do. Their rationale is rarely explained.

Many of us are not satisfied with such a design process. That is why there is research in software design, programming methods, structured programming, and related topics. Ideally, we would like to derive our programs from a statement of requirements in the same sense that theorems are derived from axioms in a published proof. All of the methodologies that can be considered "top down" are the result of our desire to have a rational, systematic way of designing software.

This paper brings a message with both bad news and good news. The bad news is that, in our opinion, we will never find the philosopher's stone. We will never find a process that allows us to design software in a perfectly rational way. The good news is that we can fake it. We can present our system to others as if we had been rational designers and it pays to pretend to do so during development and maintenance.

II. WHY WILL A SOFTWARE DESIGN "PROCESS" ALWAYS BE AN IDEALIZATION?

We will never see a software project that proceeds in the "rational" way. Some of the reasons are listed below:

1) In most cases the people who commission the building of a software system do not know exactly what they want and are unable to tell us all that they know.

2) Even if we knew the requirements, there are many other facts that we need to know to design the software. Many of the details only become known to us as we progress in the implementation. Some of the things that we learn invalidate our design and we must backtrack. Because we try to minimize lost work, the resulting design may be one that would not result from a rational design process.

3) Even if we knew all of the relevant facts before we started, experience shows that human beings are unable to compre-

hend fully the plethora of details that must be taken into account in order to design and build a correct system. The process of designing the software is one in which we attempt to separate concerns so that we are working with a manageable amount of information. However, until we have separated the concerns, we are bound to make errors.

4) Even if we could master all of the detail needed, all but the most trivial projects are subject to change for external reasons. Some of those changes may invalidate previous design decisions. The resulting design is not one that would have been produced by a rational design process.

5) Human errors can only be avoided if one can avoid the use of humans. Even after the concerns are separated, errors will be made.

6) We are often burdened by preconceived design ideas, ideas that we invented, acquired on related projects, or heard about in a class. Sometimes we undertake a project in order to try out or use a favorite idea. Such ideas may not be derived from our requirements by a rational process.

7) Often we are encouraged, for economic reasons, to use software that was developed for some other project. In other situations, we may be encouraged to share our software with another ongoing project. The resulting software may not be the ideal software for either project, i.e., not the software that we would develop based on its requirements alone, but it is good enough and will save effort.

For all of these reasons, the picture of the software designer deriving his design in a rational, error-free way from a statement of requirements is quite unrealistic.

No system has ever been developed in that way, and probably none ever will. Even the small program developments shown in textbooks and papers are unreal. They have been revised and polished until the author has shown us what he wishes he had done, not what actually did happen.

III. WHY IS A DESCRIPTION OF A RATIONAL IDEALIZED PROCESS USEFUL NONETHELESS?

What is said above is quite obvious, known to every careful thinker, and admitted by the honest ones. In spite of that we see conferences whose theme is the software design process, working groups on software design methods, and a lucrative market for courses purporting to describe logical ways to design software. What are these people trying to achieve?

If we have identified an ideal process, but cannot follow it completely, we can still follow it as closely as possible and we can write the documentation that we would have produced if we had followed the ideal process. This is what we mean by "faking a rational design process."

Below are some of the reasons for such a pretense:

1) Designers need guidance. When we undertake a large project we can easily be overwhelmed by the enormity of the task. We will be unsure about what to do first. A good understanding of the ideal process will help us to know how to proceed.

2) We will come closer to a rational design if we try to follow the process rather than proceed on an ad hoc basis. For example, even if we cannot know all of the facts necessary to design an ideal system, the effort to find those facts before we start

to code will help us to design better and backtrack less.

3) When an organization undertakes many software projects, there are advantages to having a standard procedure. It makes it easier to have good design reviews, to transfer people, ideas, and software from one project to another. If we are going to specify a standard process, it seems reasonable that it should be a rational one.

4) If we have agreed on an ideal process, it becomes much easier to measure the progress that a project is making. We can compare the project's achievements to those that the ideal process calls for. We can identify areas in which we are behind (or ahead).

5) Regular review of the project's progress by outsiders is essential to good management. If the project is attempting to follow a standard process, it will be easier to review.

IV. WHAT SHOULD THE DESCRIPTION OF THE DEVELOPMENT PROCESS TELL US?

The most useful form of a process description will be in terms of work products. For each stage of the process, this paper describes

1) What product we should work on next.

2) What criteria that product must satisfy.

3) What kind of persons should do the work.

4) What information they should use in their work.

Management of any process that is not described in terms of work products can only be done by mindreaders. Only if we know which work products are due and what criteria they must satisfy, can we review the project and measure progress.

V. WHAT IS THE RATIONAL DESIGN PROCESS?

This section describes the rational, ideal software design process that we should try to follow. Each step is accompanied by a detailed description of the work product associated with that step.

The description of the process that follows includes neither testing nor review. This is not to suggest that one should ignore either of those. When the authors apply the process described in this paper, we include extensive and systematic reviews of each work product as well as testing of the executable code that is produced. The review process is discussed in [1] and [17].

A. Establish and Document Requirements

If we are to be rational designers, we must begin knowing what we must do to succeed. That information should be recorded in a work product known as a requirements document. Completion of this document before we start would allow us to design with all the requirements in front of us.

1) Why do we need a requirements document?

1) We need a place to record the desired behavior of the system as described to us

by the user; we need a document that the user, or his representative, can review.

2) We want to avoid making requirements decisions accidentally while designing the program. Programmers working on a system are very often not familiar with the application. Having a complete reference on externally visible behavior relieves them of any need to decide what is best for the user.

3) We want to avoid duplication and inconsistency. Without a requirements document, many of the questions it answered would be asked repeatedly throughout the development by designers, programmers and reviewers. This would be expensive and would often result in inconsistent answers.

4) A complete requirements document is necessary (but not sufficient) for making good estimates of the amount of work and other resources that it will take to build the system.

5) A requirements document is valuable insurance against the costs of personnel turnover. The knowledge that we gain about the requirements will not be lost when someone leaves the project.

6) A requirements document provides a good basis for test plan development. Without it, we do not know what to test for.

7) A requirements document can be used, long after the system is in use, to define the constraints for future changes.

8) A requirements document can be used to settle arguments among the programmers; once we have a complete and accurate requirements document, we no longer need to be, or consult, requirements experts.

Determining the detailed requirements may well be the most difficult part of the software design process because there are usually no well-organized sources of information.

2) *What goes into the requirements document?*

The definition of the ideal requirements document is simple: it should contain everything you need to know to write software that is acceptable to the customer, and no more. Of course, we may use references to existing information, if that information is accurate and well organized. Acceptance criteria for an ideal requirements document include the following:

1) Every statement should be valid for all acceptable products; none should depend on implementation decisions.

2) The document should be complete in the sense that if a product satisfies every statement, it should be acceptable.

3) Where information is not available before development must begin, the areas of incompleteness should be explicitly indicated.

4) The product should be organized as a reference document rather than an introductory narrative about the system. Although it takes considerable effort to produce such a document, and a reference work is more difficult to browse than an introduction, it saves labor in the long run. The information that is obtained in this stage is recorded in a form that allows easy reference throughout the project.

3) *Who writes the requirements document?*

Ideally, the requirements documents would be written by the users or their representatives. In fact, users are rarely equipped to write such a document. Instead, the software developers must produce a draft document and get it reviewed and, eventually, approved by the user representatives.

4) What is the mathematical model behind the requirements specification?

To assure a consistent and complete document, there must be a simple mathematical model behind the organization. The model described here is motivated by work on real-time systems but, because of that, it is completely general. All systems can be described as real-time systems—even if the real-time requirements are weak.

The model assumes that the ideal product is not a pure digital computer, but a hybrid computer consisting of a digital computer that controls an analog computer. The analog computer transforms continuous values measured by the inputs into continuous outputs. The digital computer brings about discrete changes in the function computed by the analog computer. A purely digital or purely hybrid computer is a special case of this general module. The system that will be built is a digital approximation to this hybrid system. As in other areas of engineering, we can write our specification by first describing this "ideal" system and then specifying the allowable tolerances. The requirements document treats outputs as more important than inputs. If the value of the outputs is correct, nobody will mind if the inputs are not even read. Thus, the key step is identifying all of the outputs. The heart of the requirements document is a set of mathematical functions described in tabular form. Each table specifies the value of a single output as a function of external state variables.

5) How is the requirements document organized?

Completeness in the requirements document is obtained by using separation of concerns to obtain the following sections:

a) Computer Specification: A specification of the machines on which the software must run. The machine need not be hardware—for some software this section might simply be a pointer to a language reference manual.

b) Input/Output Interfaces: A specification of the interfaces that the software must use in order to communicate with the outside world.

c) Specification of Output Values: For each output, a specification of its value in terms of the state and history of the system's environment.

d) Timing Constraints: For each output, how often, or how quickly, the software is required to recompute it.

e) Accuracy Constraints: For each output, how accurate it is required to be.

f) Likely Changes: If the system is required to be easy to change, the requirements should contain a definition of the areas that are considered likely to change. You cannot design a system so that everything is equally easy to change. Programmers should not have to decide which changes are most likely.

g) Undesired Event Handling: The requirements should also contain a discussion of what the system should do when, because of undesired events, it cannot fulfill its full requirements. Most requirements documents ignore those situations;

they leave the decision about what to do in the event of partial failures to the programmer.

It is clear that good software cannot be written unless the above information is available. An example of a complete document produced in this way is given in [9] and discussed in [8].

B. Design and Document the Module Structure

Unless the product is small enough to be produced by a single programmer, one must give thought to how the work will be divided into work assignments, which we call modules. The document that should be produced at this stage is called a module guide. It defines the responsibilities of each of the modules by stating the design decisions that will be encapsulated by that module. A module may consist of submodules, or it may be considered to be a single work assignment. If a module contains submodules, a guide to its substructure is provided.

A module guide is needed to avoid duplication, to avoid gaps, to achieve separation of concerns, and most of all, to help an ignorant maintainer to find out which modules are affected by a problem report or change request. If it is kept up-to-date, this document, which records our initial design decisions, will be useful as long as the software is used.

If one diligently applies "information hiding" or "separation of concerns" to a large system, one is certain to end up with a great many modules. A guide that was simply a list of those modules, with no other structure, would help only those who are already familiar with the system. The module guide should have a tree structure,

dividing the system into a small number of modules and treating each such module in the same way until all of the modules are quite small. For a complete example of such a document, see [3]. For a discussion of this approach and its benefits, see [6, 15].

C. Design and Document the Module Interfaces

Efficient and rapid production of software requires that the programmers be able to work independently. The module guide defines responsibilities, but it does not provide enough information to permit independent implementation. A module interface specification must be written for each module. It must be formal and provide a black box picture of each module. Written by a senior designer, it is reviewed by both the future implementors and the programmers who will use the module. An interface specification for a module contains just enough information for the programmer of another module to use its facilities, and no more. The same information is needed by the implementor.

While there will be one person or small team responsible for each specification, the specifications are actually produced by a process of negotiation between implementors, those who will be required to use it, and others interested in the design, e.g., reviewers. The specifications include

1) a list of programs to be made invokable by the programs of other modules (called "access programs");

2) the parameters for the access programs;

3) the externally visible effects of the access programs;

4) timing constraints and accuracy constraints, where necessary;

5) definition of undesired events.

In many ways this module specification is analogous to the requirements document. However, the notation and organization used is more appropriate for the software-to-software interface than is the format that we use for the requirements.

Published examples and explanations include [1, 2, 5, 11].

D. Design and Document the Uses Hierarchy

The "uses" hierarchy [13] can be designed once we know all of the modules and their access programs. It is conveniently documented as a binary matrix where the entry in position (A, B) is true if and only if the correctness of program A depends on the presence in the system of a correct program B. The "uses" hierarchy defines the set of subsets that can be obtained by deleting whole programs without rewriting any programs. It is important for staged deliveries, fail soft systems, and the development of program families [12]. The "uses" hierarchy is determined by the software designers, but must allow the subsets specified in the requirements document.

E. Design and Document the Module Internal Structures

Once a module interface has been specified, its implementation can be carried out as an independent task except for reviews. However, before coding the major design decisions are recorded in a document called the module design document [16]. This document is designed to allow an ef-

ficient review of the design before the coding begins and to explain the intent behind the code to a future maintenance programmer.

In some cases, the module is divided into submodules and the design document is another module guide, in which case the design process for that module resumes at step B above. Otherwise, the internal data structures are described; in some cases, these data structures are implemented (and hidden) by submodules. For each of the access programs, a function [10] or LD-relation [14] describes its effect on the data structure. For each value returned by the module to its caller, another mathematical function, the abstraction function, is provided. This function maps the values of the data structure into the values that are returned. For each of the undesired events, we describe how we check for it. Finally, there is a "verification," an argument that programs with these properties would satisfy the module specification.

The decomposition into and design of submodules is continued until each work assignment is small enough that we could afford to discard it and begin again if the programmer assigned to do it left the project.

Each module may consist of one or more processes. The process structure of the system is distributed among the individual modules.

When one is unable to code in a readable high-level language, e.g., if no compiler is available, pseudocode must be part of the documentation. It is useful to have the pseudocode written by someone other than the final coder, and to make both programmers responsible for keeping the two versions of the program consistent [7].

F. Write Programs

After all of the design and documentation has been carried out, one is finally ready to write actual executable code. Because of the preparatory work, this goes quickly and smoothly. The code should not include comments that are redundant with the documentation that has already been written. It is unnecessary and makes maintenance of the system more expensive. Redundant comments increase the likelihood that the code will not be consistent with the documentation.

G. Maintain

Maintenance is just redesign and redevelopment. The policies recommended here for design must be continued after delivery or the "fake" rationality will disappear. If a change is made, all documentation that is invalidated must be changed. If a change invalidates a design document, it and all subsequent design documents must be faked to look as if the change had been the original design. If two or more versions are being maintained, the system should be redesigned so that the differences are confined to small modules. The short term costs of this may appear high, but the long term savings can be much higher.

VI. WHAT IS THE ROLE OF DOCUMENTATION IN THIS PROCESS?

A. What is wrong with most documentation today? Why is it hard to use? Why is it not read?

It should be clear that documentation plays a major role in the design process that we are describing. Most programmers regard documentation as a necessary evil, written as an afterthought only because some bureaucrat requires it. They do not expect it to be useful.

This is a self-fulfilling prophecy; documentation that has not been used before it is published, documentation that is not important to its author, will always be poor documentation.

Most of that documentation is incomplete and inaccurate, but those are not the main problems. If those were the main problems, the documents could be easily corrected by adding or correcting information. In fact, there are underlying organizational problems that lead to incompleteness and incorrectness and those problems, which are listed below, are not easily repaired.

1) Poor Organization: Most documentation today can be characterized as "stream of consciousness," and "stream of execution." "Stream of consciousness" writing puts information at the point in the text that the author was writing when the thought occurred to him. "Stream of execution" writing describes the system in the order that things will happen when it runs. The problem with both of these documentation styles is that subsequent readers cannot find the information that they seek. It will therefore not be easy to determine that facts are missing, or to correct them when they are wrong. It will not be easy to find all the parts of the document that should be changed when the software is changed. The documentation will be expensive to maintain and, in most cases, will not be maintained.

2) Boring Prose: Lots of words are used to say what could be said by a single programming language statement, a formula, or a diagram. Certain facts are repeated in many different sections. This increases the cost of the documentation and its maintenance. More importantly, it leads to inattentive reading and undiscovered errors.

3) Confusing and Inconsistent Terminology: Any complex system requires the invention and definition of new terminology. Without it the documentation would be far too long. However, the writers of software documentation often fail to provide precise definitions for the terms that they use. As a result, there are many terms used for the same concept and many similar but distinct concepts described by the same term.

4) Myopia: Documentation that is written when the project is nearing completion is written by people who have lived with the system for so long that they take the major decisions for granted. They document the small details that they think they will forget. Unfortunately, the result is a document useful to people who know the system well, but impenetrable for newcomers.

B. How can one avoid these problems?

Documentation in the ideal design process meets the needs of the initial developers as well as the needs of the programmers who come later. Each of the documents mentioned above records requirements or design decisions and is used as a reference document for the rest of the design. However, they also provide the information that the maintainers will need. Because the documents are used as reference manuals throughout the building of the software, they will be mature and ready for use in the later work. The documentation in this design process is not an afterthought; it is viewed as one of the primary products of the project. Some systematic checks can be applied to increase completeness and consistency.

One of the major advantages of this approach to documentation is the amelioration of the Mythical Man Month effect [4]. When new programmers join the project they do not have to depend completely on the old staff for their information. They will have an up-to-date and rational set of documents available.

"Stream of consciousness" and "stream of execution" documentation is avoided by designing the structure of each document. Each document is designed by stating the questions that it must answer and refining the questions until each defines the content of an individual section. There must be one, and only one, place for every fact that will be in the document. The questions are answered, i.e., the document is written, only after the structure of a document has been defined. When there are several documents of a certain kind, a standard organization is written for those documents [5]. Every document is designed in accordance with the same principle that guides our software design: separation of concerns. Each aspect of the system is described in exactly one section and nothing else is described in that section. When documents are reviewed, they are reviewed for adherence to the documentation rules as well as for accuracy.

The resulting documentation is not easy or relaxing reading, but it is not boring. It makes use of tables, formulas, and other formal notation to increase the density of information. The organizational rules prevent the duplication of information.

The result is documentation that must be read very attentively, but rewards its reader with detailed and precise information.

To avoid the confusing and inconsistent terminology that pervades conventional documentation, a system of special brackets and typed dictionaries is used. Each of the many terms that we must define is enclosed in a pair of bracketing symbols that reveals its type. There is a separate dictionary for each such type. Although beginning readers find the presence of !+terms+!, %terms%, #terms#, etc., disturbing, regular users of the documentation find that the type information implicit in the brackets makes the documents easier to read. The use of dictionaries that are structured by types makes it less likely that we will define two terms for the same concept or give two meanings to the same term. The special bracketing symbols make it easy to institute mechanical checks for terms that have been introduced but not defined or defined but never used.

VII. FAKING THE IDEAL PROCESS

The preceding describes the ideal process that we would like to follow and the documentation that would be produced during that process. The process is "faked" by producing the documents that we would have produced if we had done things the ideal way. One attempts to produce the documents in the order that we have described. If a piece of information is unavailable, that fact is noted in the part of the document where the information should go and the design proceeds as if that information were expected to change. If errors are found, they must be corrected

and the consequent changes in subsequent documents must be made. The documentation is our medium of design and no design decisions are considered to be made until their incorporation into the documents. No matter how often we stumble on our way, the final documentation will be rational and accurate.

Even mathematics, the discipline that many of us regard as the most rational of all, follows this procedure. Mathematicians diligently polish their proofs, usually presenting a proof very different from the first one that they discovered. A first proof is often the result of a tortured discovery process. As mathematicians work on proofs, understanding grows and simplifications are found. Eventually, some mathematician finds a simpler proof that makes the truth of the theorem more apparent. The simpler proofs are published because the readers are interested in the truth of the theorem, not the process of discovering it.

Analogous reasoning applies to software. Those who read the software documentation want to understand the programs, not to relive their discovery. By presenting rationalized documentation we provide what they need.

Our documentation differs from the ideal documentation in one important way. We make a policy of recording all of the design alternatives that we considered and rejected. For each, we explain why it was considered and why it was finally rejected. Months, weeks, or even hours later, when we wonder why we did what we did, we can find out. Years from now, the maintainer will have many of the same questions and will find his answers in our documents.

An illustration that this process pays off

is provided by a software requirements document written some years ago as part of a demonstration of the ideal process [9]. Usually, a requirements document is produced before coding starts and is never used again. However, that has not been the case for [9]. The currently operational version of the software, which satisfies the requirements document, is still undergoing revision. The organization that has to test the software uses our document extensively to choose the tests that they do. When new changes are needed, the requirements document is used in describing what must be changed and what cannot be changed. Here we see that a document produced at the start of the ideal process is still in use many years after the software went into service. The clear message is that if documentation is produced with care, it will be useful for a long time. Conversely, if it is going to be extensively used, it is worth doing right.

VIII. CONCLUSION

It is very hard to be a rational designer; even faking that process is quite difficult. However, the result is a product that can be understood, maintained, and reused. If the project is worth doing, the methods described here are worth using.

Acknowledgment

R. Faulk, J. Shore, D. Weiss, and S. Wilson of the Naval Research Laboratory provided thoughtful reviews of this paper. P. Zave and anonymous referees provided some helpful comments.

REFERENCES

[1] D.L. Parnas, D.M. Weiss, P.C. Clements, and K.H. Britton, "Interface Specifications for the SCR (A-7E) Extended Computer Module," NRL Memorandum Report 5502, December 31, 1984 (major revisions to NRL Report 4843).

[2] K.H. Britton, R.A. Parker, and D.L. Parnas, "A Procedure for Designing Abstract Interfaces for Device-Interface Modules," in *Proceedings of the Fifth International Conference on Software Engineering,* 1981.

[3] K.H. Britton and D.L. Parnas, "A-7E Software Module Guide," NRL Memorandum Report 4702, December 1981.

[4] F.P. Brooks, Jr., *The Mythical Man-Month: Essays on Software Engineering.* Reading, Mass.: Addison-Wesley, 1975.

[5] P. Clements, A. Parker, D.L. Parnas, J. Shore, and K. Britton, "A Standard Organization for Specifying Abstract Interfaces," NRL Report 8815, June 14, 1984.

[6] P. Clements, D. Parnas, and D. Weiss, "Enhancing Reusability with Information Hiding," in *Proceedings of the Workshop on Reusability in Programs,* September 1983, pp. 240-47.

[7] H.S. Elovitz, "An Experiment in Software Engineering: The Architecture Research Facility as a Case Study," in *Proceedings of the Fourth International Conference on Software Engineering,* September 1979.

[8] K.L. Heninger, "Specifying Software Requirements for Complex Systems: New Techniques and Their Applica-

tion," *IEEE Transactions on Software Engineering,* Vol. SE-6, January 1980, pp. 2-13.

[9] _____ , J. Kallander, D.L. Parnas, and J. Shore, "Software Requirements for the A-7E Aircraft," NRL Memorandum Report 3876, November 27, 1978.

[10] R.C. Linger, H.D. Mills, B.I. Witt, *Structured Programming: Theory and Practice.* Reading, Mass.: Addison-Wesley, 1979.

[11] A. Parker, K. Heninger, D. Parnas, and J. Shore, "Abstract Interface Specifications for the A-7E Device Interface Module," NRL Memorandum Report 4385, November 20, 1980.

[12] D.L. Parnas, "On the Design and Development of Program Families," *IEEE Transactions on Software Engineering,* Vol. SE-2, March 1976.

[13] _____ , "Designing Software for Ease of Extension and Contraction," in *Proceedings of the Third International Conference on Software Engineering,* May 10-12, 1978, pp. 264-77.

[14] _____ , "A Generalized Control Structure and Its Formal Definition," in *Communications of the ACM,* Vol. 26, No. 8, August 1983, pp. 572-81.

[15] _____ , P. Clements, and D. Weiss, "The Modular Structure of Complex Systems," in *Proceedings of the Seventh International Conference on Software Engineering,* March 1984, pp. 408-17.

[16] S. Faulk, B. Labaw, and D. Parnas, "SCR Module Implementation Document Guidelines," NRL Technical Memorandum 7590-072:SF:BL:DP, April 1, 1983.

[17] D.L. Parnas and D.M. Weiss, "Active Design Reviews: Principles and Practices," in *Proceedings of the Eighth International Conference on Software Engineering,* August 1985, pp. 132-36.

Part IV
News from Left Field

24

Editors' Note
Weiss and Parker: "Self-Assessment Procedure IX"

Insight: Ethical considerations can be not only important, but fascinating.

At least once a year, we come across indignant articles and lectures on the sad state of ethics in industry, perhaps even in our own industry. You may conclude from these that there is a distressingly common inclination to behave unethically, at least when there is some offsetting advantage in doing so. But there is something else at work here as well: Many cases of unethical behavior stem from a failure to consider actions in an ethical context, rather than from acting badly for advantage.

In "Self-Assessment Procedure IX," Weiss and Parker set out to raise your consciousness about ethical considerations. They do this by drawing you through a dozen scenarios in which people either did or did not act unethically. You be the judge. At the end, you compare your answers with those of a panel of participants.

For the most effective (and enjoyable) use of the scenarios, we suggest you go through them with some of your co-workers. Make copies of the scenarios and the response form—both Dorset House and the ACM grant you limited permission to make a copy of these pages for your own use—and draw your own conclusions about the ethics of each situation. Compare your findings to those of your colleagues. Discuss. Avoid physical violence.

When you're finished, you may not be more ethical; you will only be more inclined to look for ethical significance in your own and others' actions. And you'll have learned something valuable about yourself and about your co-workers.

24

Self-Assessment Procedure IX:
A Self-Assessment Procedure Dealing with Ethics in Computing
Edited by Eric A. Weiss from a book by Donn B. Parker *

What Is Self-Assessment Procedure IX?

This is the ninth self-assessment procedure. The earlier ones appeared in *Communications* in May 1976, May 1977, September 1977, February 1978, August 1978, August 1979, August 1980, and October 1981. The first seven are collected in a single volume available from ACM.†

This procedure deals with ethics, in particular with the special ethical considerations in the computer field that arise from the unique characteristics of computers and their use.

The earlier procedures dealt with technical subjects. This is the first to deal with a nontechnical subject, but it shares with the earlier procedures the basic educational aim of self-assessment. The procedure is short and is neither exhaustive nor balanced in its coverage. It merely provides a path to some self-assessment.

What Is Self-Assessment?

Self-assessment is based on the idea that a question and answer procedure can be devised that will help a person appraise

---

*From Donn B. Parker, *Ethical Conflicts in Computer Science and Technology*. Arlington, Va.: AFIPS Press, 1981.

†Available from the ACM Order Department, P.O. Box 64145, Baltimore, MD 21264, for $7 to members and $15 to nonmembers.

and develop his or her knowledge about a particular topic. In the case of ethics, the objective is understanding rather than knowledge. Thus, the objective of this procedure is to help the reader think about ethics and ethical behavior.

Self-assessment is intended to be an educational experience for a participant. In this case, the educational experience is to be that which will come about as a result of adult conscientious thought. The scenarios and the associated questions are only the beginning of the procedure. The scenarios were selected to help the participant think about the ethical concepts and to decide whether to pursue the matter further.

The primary motivation of self-assessment is *not* for an individual to satisfy *others;* rather it is for the participant to appraise and develop himself or herself. This means that there are several ways to use a self-assessment procedure. The only test of whether the use has been satisfactory is that if at the end of the procedure the participant can say, "Yes, this has been a worthwhile experience" or "I have gained some understanding."

How to Use This Self-Assessment Procedure

We suggest the following way of using the procedure, but, as noted earlier, there are others. This is not a timed exercise; therefore, plan to work with the procedure when you have an hour to spare, or you will be short-changing yourself on this educational experience.

First reproduce four copies of the page of the Reader Scenario Analysis Form in Part IV.

Next read Part I, the Introduction. It explains why there is a need for special ethical considerations in the computer field and lists computer-specific ethical issues.

Then read Part II, the ACM Code of Professional Conduct. This gives the ethical principles, ideals, and rules for behavior considered to be applicable to ACM members.

Now read the first scenario in Part III, pause, deliberate, reach your own conclusion and note your opinions on a copy of the Reader Scenario Analysis Form reproduced from the form provided in Part IV. The Committee thinks it would be particularly appropriate to add a note which would key your analysis to the ACM Code.

Consider the scenario in more detail and try to look at it from different points of view. See if your analysis leads you to any other thoughts. Revise your analysis form or fill out a new one.

No suggested responses are provided, but Part V of the procedure gives the votes, opinions, and suggested ethical principles applied to each scenario by the participants in a project described in Reference 1. You may compare your conclusion with theirs.

Now loop to the next scenario in Part III.

The Introduction, scenarios, and panel responses are reprinted from Reference 1, which gives the details of how the project was conducted and includes more extended remarks on ethics.

The Committee is particularly anxious to get responses concerning this new kind of self-assessment procedure. You may respond either by sending in copies of your Reader Scenario Analysis Forms or by letter commenting on any aspect of the matter.

The Committee will prepare a summary of the responses and submit it for publication in *Communications* and will refer appropriate responses to the ACM Committee on Professional Standards and Practices.

Self-Assessment Procedure IX*

Approved and submitted by the ACM Committee on Self-Assessment—a committee of the ACM Education Board.

Chairman

Robert I. Winner

Members

Neal S. Coulter
Howard Getz
Charles Gold
Edward G. Pekarek
Eric A. Weiss

---

*This self-assessment procedure is not sanctioned as a test nor endorsed in any way by the Association for Computing Machinery. Any person using any of the questions in this procedure for the testing or certification of anyone other than himself or herself is violating the spirit of this self-assessment procedure and the copyright on this material.

PART I. INTRODUCTION

The need for special ethical considerations in the computer field arises from several unique characteristics of computers and their use. Computers are rapidly becoming the primary repositories of negotiable assests and representations of many other assets in new forms consisting of electronic pulses and magnetic patterns. These assets are not directly subject to manual handling and observation; they can be obtained and used only through technical and automated means. The concentration in computer and data communications systems of vital business information, research and development data, marketing information, and personnel and other statistical data of organizations has created a power base in electronic data processing (EDP) departments. Because computer technology places a new power in the hands of the technologists who deal with data storage, processing, and dissemination, personal privacy and fair information practices have become major legislative issues. At the same time, however, the technology offers a practical means of constraining and regulating information usage.

Unlike the computer field, other sciences and professions have had hundreds of years in which to develop ethical concepts that form the basis for dealing with new issues. Biologists debate issues in genetic research, medical practitioners are concerned with definitions of death and abortion, engineers must cope with the safety of nuclear reactors and the handling of atomic waste materials, Congress debates its rules of ethics, lawyers evaluate the implications of Watergate, and auditors ponder their responsibilities to detect business fraud. The codes of ethics for these disciplines are enforced in varying degrees at various times. They are well-established codes; but perhaps more importantly, an ethical continuity is maintained in each discipline as these codes are transferred from professor to student in universities. In contrast, computer science and technology have been in existence for only 30 years. The need for ethical standards in computer science and technology is equally as critical as it is in other fields. It is little wonder, therefore, that serious problems arise in developing ethical concepts and practices in such a comparatively short period of time.

Computer-specific ethical issues arise as the result of the roles of computers such as

- Repositories and processors of information. Unauthorized use of otherwise unused computer services or of information stored in computers raises questions of appropriateness or fairness.

- Producers of new forms and types of assets. For example, computer programs are entirely new types of assets, possibly not subject to the same concepts of ownership as other assets.

- Instruments of acts. To what degree must computer services and users of computers, data, and programs be responsible for the integrity and appropriateness of computer output?

- Symbols of intimidation and deception. The images of computers as thinking machines, absolute truth producers—infallible, subject to blame—and as anthropomorphic replacements of humans who err should be carefully considered.

PART II. ACM CODE OF PROFESSIONAL CONDUCT

PREAMBLE

Recognition of professional status by the public depends not only on skill and dedication but also on adherence to a recognized Code of Professional Conduct. The following Code sets forth the general principles (Canons), professional ideals (Ethical Considerations), and mandatory rules (Disciplinary Rules) applicable to each ACM Member.

The verbs "shall" (imperative) and "should" (encouragement) are used purposefully in the Code. The Canons and Ethical Considerations are not, however, binding rules. Each Disciplinary Rule is binding on each individual Member of ACM. Failure to observe the Disciplinary Rules subjects the Member to admonition, suspension, or expulsion from the Association as provided by the Procedures for the Enforcement of the ACM Code of Professional Conduct, which are specified in the ACM Policy and Procedures Guidelines. The term "member(s)" is used in the Code. The Disciplinary Rules of the Code apply, however, only to the classes of membership specified in Article 3, Section 4, of the Constitution of the ACM.

CANON 1

An ACM member shall act at all times with integrity.

Ethical Considerations

EC1.1. An ACM member shall properly qualify himself when expressing an opinion outside his areas of competence. A member is encouraged to express his opinion on subjects within his area of competence.

EC1.2. An ACM member shall preface any partisan statements about information processing by indicating clearly on whose behalf they are made.

EC1.3. An ACM member shall act faithfully on behalf of his employers or clients.

Disciplinary Rules

DR1.1.1. An ACM member shall not intentionally misrepresent his qualifications or credentials to present or prospective employers or clients.

DR1.1.2. An ACM member shall not make deliberately false or deceptive statements as to the present or expected state of affairs in any aspect of the capability, delivery, or use of information processing systems.

DR1.2.1. An ACM member shall not intentionally conceal or misrepresent on whose behalf any partisan statements are made.

DR1.3.1. An ACM member acting or employed as a consultant shall, prior to accepting information from a prospective client, inform the client of all factors of which the member is aware which may affect the proper performance of the task.

DR1.3.2. An ACM member shall disclose any interest of which he is aware which does or may conflict with his duty to a present or prospective employer or client.

DR1.3.3. An ACM member shall not use any confidential information from any employer or client, past or present, without prior permission.

CANON 2

An ACM member should strive to increase his competence and the competence and prestige of the profession.

Ethical Considerations

EC2.1. An ACM member is encouraged to extend public knowledge, understanding, and appreciation of information processing, and to oppose any false or deceptive statements relating to information processing of which he is aware.

EC2.2. An ACM member shall not use his professional credentials to misrepresent his competence.

EC2.3. An ACM member shall undertake only those professional assignments and commitments for which he is qualified.

EC2.4. An ACM member shall strive to design and develop systems that adequately perform the intended functions and that satisfy his employer's or client's operational needs.

EC2.5. An ACM member should maintain and increase his competence through a program of continuing education encompassing the techniques, technical standards, and practices in his fields of professional activity.

EC2.6. An ACM member should provide opportunity and encouragement for professional development and advancement of both professionals and those aspiring to become professionals.

Disciplinary Rules

DR2.2.1. An ACM member shall not use his professional credentials to misrepresent his competence.

DR2.3.1. An ACM member shall not undertake professional assignments without adequate preparation in the circumstances.

DR2.3.2. An ACM member shall not undertake professional assignments for which he knows or should know he is not competent or cannot become adequately competent without acquiring the assistance of a professional who is competent to perform the assignment.

DR2.4.1. An ACM member shall not represent that a product of his work will perform its function adequately and will meet the receiver's operational needs when he knows or should know that the product is deficient.

CANON 3

An ACM member shall accept responsibility for his work.

Ethical Considerations

EC3.1. An ACM member shall accept only those assignments for which there is reasonable expectancy of meeting requirements or specifications, and shall perform his assignments in a professional manner.

Disciplinary Rules

DR3.1.1. An ACM member shall not neglect any professional assignment which has been accepted.

DR3.1.2. An ACM member shall keep his employer or client properly informed on the progress of his assignments.

DR3.1.3. An ACM member shall not attempt to exonerate himself from, or to limit his liability to clients for his personal malpractice.

DR3.1.4. An ACM member shall indicate to his employer or client the consequences to be expected if his professional judgment is overruled.

CANON 4

An ACM member shall act with professional responsibility.

Ethical Considerations

EC4.1. An ACM member shall not use his membership in ACM improperly for professional advantage or to misrepresent the authority of his statements.

EC4.2. An ACM member shall conduct professional activities on a high plane.

EC4.3. An ACM member is encouraged to uphold and improve the professional standards of the Association through participation in their formulation, establishment, and enforcement.

Disciplinary Rules

DR4.1.1. An ACM member shall not speak on behalf of the Association or any of its subgroups without proper authority.

DR4.1.2. An ACM member shall not knowingly misrepresent the policies and views of the Association or any of its subgroups.

DR4.1.3. An ACM member shall preface partisan statements about information

processing by indicating clearly on whose behalf they are made.

DR4.2.1. An ACM member shall not maliciously injure the professional reputation of any other person.

DR4.2.2. An ACM member shall not use the service of or his membership in the Association to gain unfair advantage.

DR4.2.3. An ACM member shall take care that credit for work is given to whom credit is properly due.

CANON 5

An ACM member should use his special knowledge and skills for the advancement of human welfare.

Ethical Considerations

EC5.1. An ACM member should consider the health, privacy, and general welfare of the public in the performance of his work.

EC5.2. An ACM member, whenever dealing with data concerning individuals, shall always consider the principle of the individual's privacy and seek the following:

—To minimize the data collected.
—To limit authorized access to the data.
—To provide proper security for the data.
—To determine the required retention period of the data.
—To ensure proper disposal of the data.

Disciplinary Rules

DR5.2.1. An ACM member shall express his professional opinion to his employers or clients regarding any adverse consequences to the public which might result from work proposed to him.

PART III. SCENARIOS

Scenario 1.8*

PROFESSOR, UNIVERSITY:
NOT GIVING CREDIT FOR ASSISTANCE

A professor of computer science at a university developed a new computer programming language for a range of computer applications. Two of his graduate students tested the language for consistency and completeness. They discovered and corrected several significant shortcomings and added several new features. A programmer on the staff of the university's computer center programmed the compiler for the language. He discovered flaws in the syntax and corrected them, with the permission of the professor. He also found ways to change the language that improved the compiler performance. The graduate students and programmer documented the language and the compiler, and they wrote a user's manual.

The professor compiled the writings into a scientific paper and published it under his own name alone, with no acknowledgment of the contributions of the graduate students or the programmer.

* * * * *

Pause, deliberate. Is there an ethics issue involved? Were the professor's actions unethical or not unethical? What general principles apply? Record your responses on the form in Part IV. (Panel responses are given in Part V.)

---

*Scenarios are numbered and identified as in Reference 1.

Scenario 1.9

PROGRAMMER, TIME-SHARING SERVICES:
INFILTRATING A RIVAL COMPANY'S COMPUTER SERVICE

A programmer employee of a time-sharing computer service company signed an agreement to purchase time-sharing services from a competing company. He used the services for over a year and promptly paid his bills. Nothing in the agreement he signed, messages to him from the system, nor the user's manual issued to him limited his actions in the computer as long as he paid for the time used.

He routinely attempted to obtain copies of the data and programs, i.e., other users' and the service company's files, to obtain copies of system and utility programs, to identify other customers and ascertain their billings, to test programs without charge for which there is normally a charge, and to gain privileged access available only to the service company employees. He also attempted to "crash" the system (cause loss of service to others).

He claimed there were no limitations placed on him to prohibit him from doing these things, and that he was simply engaged in accepted business intelligence activities and reverse engineering (General Motors buying a Ford to see how it was made and constructed).

* * * * *

Pause, deliberate. Is there an ethics issue involved? Was the programmer's action unethical or not unethical? What general principles apply? Record your responses on the form in Part IV. (Panel responses are given in Part V.)

Scenario 2.5

PROGRAMMER, BUSINESS ENTERPRISE:
SELLING A PROGRAM NO LONGER USED

A computer programmer works for a business enterprise. He participated, along with other programmers, in the development of a major application computer program. When the application was finished, the business changed its business activities, no longer needed the program, and never used it. The programmer discovered that there was a possible market for the program, with customers who would purchase licensed use of the program, along with the service of programmers who would adapt and service the program. He suggested to his employer the sale of the program in this fashion, but found there was no interest in marketing it.

The programmer decided that he would go into business for himself, marketing copies of the program and documentation, and providing services in conjunction with the sales. He had few personal resources to do this, so he started the business while he was still employed. He was fearful of telling his employer about his side business because he was sure he would be fired, and that attempts would be made to stop him. He was also not certain that the business would succeed and wanted to be sure he could retain his present job if it did not pan out.

* * * * *

Pause, deliberate. Is there an ethics issue involved? Were the programmer's actions (marketing the program, moonlighting to start a new business) unethical or not unethical? What general principles apply? Record your responses on the form in Part IV. (Panel responses are given in Part V.)

Scenario 2.7

PROGRAMMER, PERSONAL PROGRAM:
TAKING THE PROGRAM TO HIS NEW POSITION

A computer programmer worked for a business enterprise that was highly dependent on its own computer system. He was the sole author of a computer program he used as an aid in his programming work. Nobody else used the program, and his manager was only nominally aware of its existence. He had written it and debugged it on his own time on a weekend, but had used his employer's materials, facilities, and computer services.

The programmer terminated his employment, giving due notice, and with no malice on his or his manager's part. He immediately went to work for a competitor of his former employer.

Without his former employer's permission, he took the only copy of the program with him to his new employer and used it in his work. He did not share it with any others. The new employer was not aware of the program or its use, but it enhanced the programmer's performance.

* * * * *

Pause, deliberate. Is there an ethics issue involved? Was the programmer's action unethical or not unethical? What general principles apply? Record your responses on the form in Part IV. (Panel responses are given in Part V.)

Scenario 3.4

SCIENTIST, PROGRAMMER, FILES OF PERSONAL DATA: MAKING NEW USE OF DATA WITHOUT SUBJECTS' PERMISSION

A scientist employed as a researcher in a university learned that two different kinds of data on essentially the same subject pool were contained in two files stored in the university's computer. He believed that there would be significant scientific value in merging the files and reanalyzing the data.

Although the subjects' informed consent had been obtained for the earlier studies (they were students who had since graduated), their permission for this new use for the data had not been sought. Although the scientist was aware that it would have been desirable to seek permission of the subjects, he decided not to do so because it would have been time-consuming and would have added considerably to the cost of the study he was proposing.

He thus asked one of the university's programmers to access the data, merge the files on the same subjects, and analyze the data as he indicated. The programmer did as the scientist requested.

* * * * *

Pause, deliberate. Is there an ethics issue involved? Were the scientist's or the programmer's actions unethical or not unethical? What general principles apply? Record your responses on the form in Part IV. (Panel responses are given in Part V.)

Scenario 3.5

PROGRAMMER, EMPLOYER, GOVERNMENT, PERSONAL DATA: USING GOVERNMENT-OWNED PERSONAL DATA FOR BUSINESS PURPOSES

A marketing company's employee was doing piecework production data runs on company computers after hours under contract for a state government. Her moonlighting activity was performed with the knowledge and approval of her employer.

The data were questionnaire answers of 14,000 public school children. The questionnaire contained highly specific questions on the domestic life of the children and their parents. The government's purpose was to develop statistics for behavioral profiles, for use in public assistance programming. The data included the respondents' names, addresses, and so forth.

The employee's contract contained no divulgence restrictions, except a provision that statistical compilations and analyses were the property of the government.

The employer discovered the exact nature of the information in the tapes and its value in the business services his company supplied. He requested that the data be copied for subsequent use in his business. The employee decided the request did not violate the terms of the contract, and she complied.

* * * * *

Pause, deliberate. Is there an ethics issue involved? Were the actions of the programmer, the employer, or the state government unethical or not unethical? What general principles apply? Record your responses on the form in Part IV. (Panel responses are given in Part V.)

Scenario 4.3

SYSTEMS ANALYST, SOFTWARE COMPANY: DESIGNING A COMPUTER SYSTEM TO REPLACE A CUSTOMER'S EMPLOYEES

A systems analyst in a software development company was made leader of a project for a customer to develop a new computer application that was designed to replace as many production workers as possible in the customer's factory.

The systems analyst's brother-in-law was one of the workers to be replaced. He convinced the systems analyst that the workers would be laid off and would not be assisted in any way by their employer in finding new jobs. In keeping with the objectives and spirit of the contract between his employer's company and the customer, the systems analyst continued his design work maximizing as diligently as possible the number of production workers who could be replaced.

* * * * *

Pause, deliberate. Is there an ethics issue involved? Were the systems analyst's actions unethical or not unethical? What general principles apply? Record your responses on the form in Part IV. (Panel responses are given in Part V.)

Scenario 4.4

PROJECT LEADER, MANAGEMENT, RETAIL COMPANY: INSTALLING AN INADEQUATE SYSTEM

A programmer analyst was given project responsibility to develop a customer billing and credit system for his employer, a large retail business. He thought the budget and resources he was given were adequate. However, the budgeted amount was expended before completion of the system. He had continually warned management of impending problems, but was directed to finish the development as soon as possible and at lowest cost. He

was forced by management to do this foregoing many of the program functions, including audit controls, safeguards, flexibility, error detection and correction capabilities, automatic exception handling, and exception reporting. A "bare bones" system was installed. He was told that he could add all the omitted capabilities in subsequent versions, after production of the initial system.

A difficult, expensive, and extensive conversion to the new system occurred. After the new system was in production, great problems arose. Many customers received incorrect and incomprehensible billings and credit statements and became outraged. The retail company was unable to correct errors or explain confusing system output. Fraud increased. Business and profits declined, and customers suffered much anguish and personal expense. The project leader was blamed for the losses.

* * * * *

Pause, deliberate. Is there an ethics issue involved? Were the actions of the project leader or management unethical or not unethical? What general principles apply? Record your responses on the form in Part IV. (Panel responses are given in Part V.)

Scenario 5.4

PROGRAMMING MANAGER, COMPANY: DEVELOPING PROGRAMS WITHOUT ADEQUATE CONTROLS

A programming manager received a directive to develop a set of programs that would circumvent the normal accounting controls in his employer's business. It was explained to him that the purpose was only to test new business functions. He protested to his senior manager, but was told that the dangers of circumventing the controls had been assessed, and a decision had been made to proceed as planned. The manager implemented the programs.

* * * * *

Pause, deliberate. Is there an ethics issue involved? Were the programming manager's actions unethical or not unethical? What general principles apply? Record your responses on the form in Part IV. (Panel responses are given in Part V.)

Scenario 5.5

CONSULTANT, COMPUTERIZATION OF A GOVERNMENT DEPARTMENT: DISREGARDING IMPACT ON EMPLOYEES

A consultant has a government client which is embarked on a large scale computerization of one of its service departments. It is clear that a very large number of jobs will vanish, and the job content of many others will be changed.

The union of public employees is pressing to have a voice in the system design, but the government has taken the position that all aspects of the new system fall within the rights and responsibilities of management to conduct its operations in an efficient manner, and are therefore not subject to union negotiation. The consultant accepts the view of the management and refrains from any discussion of job levels, job content, or quality of working life in his design study.

* * * * *

Pause, deliberate. Is there an ethics is-

sue involved? Were the consultant's actions unethical or not unethical? What general principles apply? Record your responses on the form in Part IV. (Panel responses are given in Part V.)

Scenario 6.3

CONSULTANT, PROGRAMMER, A PROJECTED NUCLEAR ENERGY PLANT: SELECTING FAVORABLE COMPUTER OUTPUT IN A FEASIBILITY STUDY

A consultant specialized in feasibility studies for nuclear energy plants. He was under contract to a utility company to compare a new breeder type plant with fossil fuel alternatives. His computer projections showed the nuclear plant to be marginally feasible, perhaps dangerous, and far less efficient than a plant using fossil fuels. Because of his dependence on utility company business and his desire to protect his reputation, he decided to use only that part of the computer output that he regarded as most useful, and, in the process, made the projections look much more favorable for the nuclear plant. A programmer working for the consultant knew about the change and protested to him about "falsification of the results of the study." When the consultant defended the course of action taken, the programmer went to his congressman with the story.

* * * * *

Pause, deliberate. Is there an ethics issue involved? Were the actions of the consultant and the programmer unethical or not unethical? What general principles apply? Record your responses on the form in Part IV. (Panel responses are given in Part V.)

Scenario 6.5

RESEARCHER, PREDICTIONS BY COMPUTER
MODELING: SHAPING PUBLIC OPINION

At a time when experts were beginning to
question the merits of current agricultural
practices, a researcher used computer
modeling techniques to predict that a
global agricultural disaster would occur
in fifty years. To stimulate public concern
and debate about agricultural practices, he
published his prediction in a low-priced,
mass-market paperback. The book emphasized the role of the computer in making this prediction, for example, by including computer-generated graphs as
illustrations. But the book did not discuss
the fact that the prediction depended on
debatable assumptions and selection of
data, and could be radically different with
a slight change of assumptions. Being unaware of these facts, the general public accepted the dramatic prediction as in-
disputable and objective, in significant part
because it came from a computer, and the
public became deeply concerned with
agricultural practices.

* * * * *

Pause, deliberate. Is there an ethics issue involved? Were the researcher's actions unethical or not unethical? What
general principles apply? Record your
responses on the form in Part IV. (Panel
responses are given in Part V.)

Reader Scenario Analysis

Your participation is solicited. To save
space, only one page of the Reader Scenario Analysis Form is printed here.
Please complete and return a questionnaire
for each scenario. Use reproductions of
the form as necessary.

PART IV. READER SCENARIO ANALYSIS FORM

Please reproduce this form
as necesary

SCENARIO NO. _____

PARTY _____   ACT _____

unethical ☐   not unethical ☐   no ethics issue ☐

General Principle: _____

Canons, professional ideals, or mandatory rules influencing your judgment _____

Comments _____

SCENARIO NO. _____

PARTY _____   ACT _____

unethical ☐   not unethical ☐   no ethics issue ☐

General Principle: _____

Canons, professional ideals, or mandatory rules influencing your judgment _____

Comments _____

- -

SCENARIO NO. _____

PARTY _____   ACT _____

unethical ☐   not unethical ☐   no ethics issue ☐

General Principle: _____

Canons, professional ideals, or mandatory rules influencing your judgment _____

Comments _____

PART V. PANEL RESPONSES TO SCENARIO

Scenario 1.8

PROFESSOR, UNIVERSITY: NOT GIVING CREDIT FOR ASSISTANCE

Party, Professor: Producing a Scientific Paper Without Acknowledgments

Total	Unethical	Not Unethical	No Ethics Issue
30	28	2	0

Opinions

Although the professor had the original idea and wrote the final paper, his work could not have been acceptable from a scientific point of view without the work contributed by the students and the computer programmer. He violated principles of fairness and was unethical in taking full credit for the work. Those who make significant contributions to a project deserve credit, even though they may be working for the project leader.

While it is common practice for professors to use students' research in preparation of scientific papers, in this case the material contribution was sufficient to warrant explicit credit. However, a difficult problem is raised in applying the concept of property and associated ethics to ideas, theories, arguments, proofs, and computer programs.

The opinion was also advanced that the professor was not unethical. The three contributors were all working for him. However, he might find it difficult to get work done for him in the future.

General Principles

Plagiarism may be the highest form of flattery, but it is a low form of thievery. The difference between plagiarism and the scientific method is acknowledgment. A scientific worker should honestly acknowledge the work of others. It is the heart of the research payoff to encourage the good work of students by acknowledgment.

Scenario 1.9

PROGRAMMER, TIME-SHARING SERVICES: INFILTRATING A RIVAL COMPANY'S COMPUTER SERVICE

Party, Programmer: Compromising and Gathering Intelligence on a Competitor's Time-Sharing Service

Total	Unethical	Not Unethical	No Ethics Issue
28	26	2	0

Opinions

The programmer was not simply testing a competitor's product, but was gaining sensitive information, gaining services for which he was not paying, identifying other users, and generally trying to cause harm to the service, all of which actions are questionable on moral grounds. Even if they can be viewed as accepted business practices, they are not justified from a moral point of view, for there could be no credible explanation for this behavior except to wish to cause harm to a competitor and take advantage of his weaknesses. It is reasonable to believe that the company employing this programmer would not easily accept similar treatment from a competitor.

Testing programs for which there is a charge without paying the charge was nothing less than stealing. Gaining privileged access available only to company employees was another form of stealing. Attempting to identify customers and ascertain their billings was certainly an invasion of the company's privacy. The programmer's attempt to crash the system was clearly illegal. Paying airfare on an airplane does not authorize a person to rip the seats or tear up the navigational charts. Sabotage cannot be condoned.

In view of newspaper accounts of international business intrigue, it is understandable that a programmer might consider his actions as accepted business intelligence activities.

One participant reasoned that if "manufacturing" a system is like manufacturing a car, then the behavior of the programmer was morally acceptable. However, if the development and use of a system is like the development and use of one's own body, then access to the system could be morally warranted only with the owner's consent. The latter appears to be more the case than the former.

Other participants were more decided in their opinion that the reverse engineering analogy was fallacious, expressing views that overlapped and sometimes differed in emphasis.

Attempting to crash a system, unless authorized as a testing activity, is at least mischief, if not sabotage. The analogy is false. The equivalent would be to read a computer program without making a copy to see how it works, then to write one's own version. The car business equivalent of what the programmer did would be industrial spying, using such means as telephone bugs and infrared cameras to steal trade secrets without breaking into the plant. The argument by analogy is lame. The programmer did not buy the software from the service. He bought computer time and the right to use the system and utility programs. As for looking at users' files, that was clearly a violation of trust, and trying to crash the system is comparable to interfering with a vital business function, such as telephone operation.

If a trade secret law does not cover this kind of activity, it will. A person who exploits the slowness of the law in responding to new technology may stay out of jail, but his actions are unethical.

The programmer was trying to harm his company's competitor in ways which go well beyond accepted forms of competition. His attempted justification will not do: The fact that an activity is not explicitly forbidden does not justify nor permit that activity. Things which are obviously illegal or wrong do not need to be expressly prohibited. He could not be serious in thinking that as long as he paid his user charge he could do just anything to the computer. When GM buys a Ford to see how it is made, it does not at the same time attempt to crash Ford's assembly line. There is great difference between trying to find out what a competitor is doing, especially by such innocuous means as buying his product on the open market to evaluate it, and trying to disrupt his production. Perhaps this is the difference between intelligence gathering and sabotage.

The competing company should have stipulated allowable or prohibited uses of its services in the contract, and at least spot-checked on the actual use being made of its system. On the other hand, there is such a thing as generally accepted

probity. You do not have to promise to be honest in a contract. It is understood that you will be. This was a clear violation, or attempted violation, of trade secret principles.

The only opinion exonerating the programmer was this: If his place of work was clearly shown on the contract, there was no unethical action. If he hid crucial facts (e.g., used only his home address) his actions were unethical.

General Principles

Implicit in any contract are the ethical principles generally accepted in the community.

A computer time-sharing user should not maliciously or recklessly injure or attempt to injure, directly or indirectly, the professional reputation, prospects, or business of others.

You do not have to build a fence around your property to expect others to respect it.

Scenario 2.5

PROGRAMMER, BUSINESS ENTERPRISE: SELLING A PROGRAM NO LONGER USED

Party, Programmer: Selling the Use of His Employer's Computer Program

Total	Unethical	Not Unethical	No Ethics Issue
29	25	3	1

Opinions

There was unanimous agreement that the company's not wanting to market the program or any other product did not give the programmer the right to market it for his own benefit. Rationalizing that the program was no longer used did not change the ethics of his act. Under the circumstances, it would appear that the programmer could have negotiated some arrangement with the company that would have been ethical.

A majority agreed that since the scenario does not make clear the positions of the participants regarding ownership of the program, differing conclusions could be reached. If the programmer had been led to believe the program was available for his personal use, then his marketing action was not unethical. If there was any question about the employer's ownership of the program, then the ethical course for the programmer would be to explain his plans openly and settle the issue through negotiation.

If the programmer had permission to take the program or took only his knowledge and did not use company resources to develop his business, his actions were ethical, as well as common in the business world.

Discussion divided equally on the following opinion: If the program was not considered proprietary by the employer, then the programmer's not telling his employer of his activities was not unethical. One side mentioned that he perceived a use for the program which his employer did not express an interest in pursuing. There was nothing wrong with being prudent in trying to maintain his present employment while discovering whether or not marketing the program was profitable. He had no obligation to inform his employer of his activities. His actions could not directly harm his employer. The other side felt that, even though the program was scrapped and the employer did not want the business, the firm probably did not want him marketing on the side, especially

using the firm's name. He should have resigned and taken his chances.

Only one individual believed that the programmer was free to use the program as he saw fit.

Party, Programmer: Moonlighting to Start a New Business

Total	Unethical	Not Unethical	No Ethics Issue
7	2	2	3

Opinions

A majority agreed that if the programmer could perform his assigned duties competently and the employer had no expressed policy against moonlighting, he could do as he wished with his own time, assuming there was no agreement between him and his employer about side businesses. It might be different if he were in a managerial position. In contrast, there was mixed reaction to moonlighting in competition with his employer. Certainly such moonlighting without his employer's knowledge violated usual understandings about the nature of full time, salaried employment, and commitments by both the employer and employee.

General Principles

Programmers do not have a property right in programs written for others in the absence of any agreement otherwise.

An employer has a right to expect no conflict of interest in the outside activities of an employee.

An owner's dormancy of interest in his property does not justify appropriation of the property by another party.

Moonlighting is justified, but there

should be a primary loyalty to the employer in case of conflict.

It is not unethical to moonlight in absence of an agreement not to do so, and when the moonlighting does not detract from employment obligations.

Full time employment implies collateral commitments by both parties, including the employer's intention to provide continuing employment and intangible support, as well as each party's commitment to tangible support of the other. The obligation is implied rather than expressed.

In the absence of a clear idea about ownership of programs, it could at least be advocated that when a programmer takes a job, a written agreement be made between a programmer and his employer about program ownership.

The First Amendment of the Constitution and the spirit of free enterprise encourage employees in the use of their skills, so long as the fruits of another's efforts are not adversely affected.

Scenario 2.7

PROGRAMMER, PERSONAL PROGRAM: TAKING
THE PROGRAM TO HIS NEW POSITION

Party, Programmer: Taking the Only Copy of His Program with Him to a New Position

Total	Unethical	Not Unethical	No Ethics Issue
27	13	11	3

Opinions

Almost all agreed that the first employer acquired some interest in the program when his resources were used for its development. At least, the programmer should have obtained permission from the first employer and left a copy of the program behind.

Most participants argued that the program had value only when used by the programmer. The former employer received the benefit when the programmer worked for him. This was not a company program; the programmer wrote it for his own use. No one else used it and, in all probability, no one would want to use it or know how to. The program was an aid for this programmer alone. When he changed jobs, he took his tools with him.

Some participants thought that since the programmer used his own time to develop the program, and even though he used his employer's facilities, on balance the employer benefited. If it enhanced the programmer's performance at the new company, it did so at the old company as well. These participants felt the program could be seen as a material instance of the programmer's professional development. In working for his employer he gained personal experience and, if by reason of this experience, he could get and perform better jobs, then he had enhanced his development by this experience.

In determining that this was not an unethical act, some participants gave great weight to the fact that he developed a programming tool on his own time. His using the employer's facilities on a weekend might raise an ethical question. However, in this instance the employer benefited directly from the programmer's efforts. It was not incumbent upon the programmer to turn his efforts over to the company so that all programmers' work would be improved. Improving his own performance did not carry the responsibility or moral obligation to improve that of others in the company.

Some participants definitely concluded that the programmer was at fault in making unauthorized use of resources to develop the program. Since he was expected to use his best skills in performing his job, he had a duty to obtain his employer's support to develop the best tools for his work.

Some participants stated that the employer should have protected his programs more effectively. The new employer should not have hidden his head in the sand and should have questioned the source of the program.

Participants split evenly between agreement and disagreement with the statement that the program could be regarded as a tool developed in part with the employer's resources. If it is so regarded, in the absence of provisions in the employment contract governing such a situation, the program probably belonged to the employee.

Opinion also split evenly on whether the programmer should have obtained his old employer's consent to the intended use of the program in his new position. Use without knowledge of the true owner constitutes theft. Full disclosure and informed agreement should have preceded the use of the program anywhere except in the first employer's service.

The majority of participants took the position that nothing in the case altered the fact that a program, the property of one company, was taken and used to benefit a competitor.

Most disagreed with the observation that "as long as the programmer uses his program for his own work and does not sell it, there is nothing wrong with his action."

General Principles

Items developed with company resources belong, at least partly, to the company.

A programmer possesses the tools of his trade.

Current use of a product owned in whole or in part by one's employer should not be the sole criterion for determining who has the right to it.

Scenario 3.4

SCIENTIST, PROGRAMMER, FILES OF PERSONAL DATA: MAKING NEW USE OF DATA WITHOUT SUBJECTS' PERMISSION

First Party, Scientist: Merging Files Without Permission of Subjects

Total	Unethical	Not Unethical	No Ethics Issue
28	19	8	1

Second Party, Programmer: Performing Requested Merging of Files

Total	Unethical	Not Unethical	No Ethics Issue
25	14	5	6

Opinions

A majority of participants felt that the scientist's action was a borderline case in terms of ethics. It could be said dogmatically that he was unethical because he did not have informed consent of the subjects. Nor did he ascertain, by consulting researchers in charge of the original studies, whether the combining of the two subject populations would possibly render the new research invalid. On the other hand, while the principle of informed consent is important, there is a practical limit to its application, and it is doubtful that the scientist's action was unethical. There should be no restrictions on use and dissemination of data unless individuals can be identified. When data are collected about identifiable individuals, as in this case, questions of informed consent must be addressed, but they cannot be answered by any large generalizations. It would be a mistake to impose a general restriction on the use of personal information. A problem should be identified before restriction of use is imposed.

Informed consent is important, but where the expense of obtaining it was prohibitive, an independent committee should have been consulted to weigh the benefits of the research against the costs, i.e., the invasion of privacy which seems to be inherent. To take an independent action, presumably without even checking with those who collected the data, would appear to be unethical.

The participants were split over whether the programmer was unethical. Some felt that he should not have performed his services, using the files without the consent of the researchers who owned them, that is, those who obtained consent from the subjects for the original research.

General Principles

A programmer or systems analyst should always seek direct and positive authorization for the use of data fields from whomever he identifies, in his best effort, as the custodian of the files.

Scenario 3.5

PROGRAMMER, EMPLOYER, GOVERNMENT, PERSONAL DATA: USING GOVERNMENT-OWNED PERSONAL DATA FOR BUSINESS PURPOSES

First Party, Programmer: Complying with the Employer's Request to Supply Personal Data

Total	Unethical	Not Unethical	No Ethics Issue
31	31	0	0

Second Party, Employer: Requesting Personal Data from a Government Study

Total	Unethical	Not Unethical	No Ethics Issue
25	24	1	0

Third Party, State Government: Not Providing Sufficient Protection for Personal Data

Total	Unethical	Not Unethical	No Ethics Issue
13	13	0	0

Opinions

All participants agreed that, although using personal information without the consent of the subjects may be common practice, it is not, thereby, ethical.

All but one agreed that the employer was unethical to act coercively in requesting the data. The employee as a contractor had a duty to protect the data and was unethical. Most participants agreed that even though there was no explicit government restriction—in fact, even with the government's permission—it was unethical to comply, since the programmer should not have agreed to supply such personal information for business purposes without the informed consent of the individuals.

It was unanimously agreed that the government was unethical in not providing more adequate protection for the personal data.

General Principles

Common practice does not make an act ethical. Some kinds of personal information by their very nature must be handled confidentially, independent of specific confidentiality agreements or lack thereof.

Scenario 4.3

SYSTEMS ANALYST, SOFTWARE COMPANY: DESIGNING A COMPUTER SYSTEM TO REPLACE A CUSTOMER'S EMPLOYEES

Party, Systems Analyst: Developing a Computer System Application to Replace as Many Workers as Possible

Total	Unethical	Not Unethical	No Ethics Issue
27	4	21	2

Opinions

All agreed that the systems analyst was not unethical in fulfilling the contract. A purpose of computer technology in automation is to replace people, where replacement is practical and cost-effective. However, the systems analyst has a responsibility when opportunity arises to do what he can to assure fair treatment for people affected by his work.

The group also agreed that the brother-in-law was not unethical in bringing the situation to that analyst's attention.

Finally, all but one participant agreed that the customer company, when introducing productivity improvements, has a social responsibility to minimize the impact on the replaced employees.

General Principles

Employers introducing productivity improvements have a social responsibility to minimize the impact on replaced or displaced employees.

Scenario 4.4

PROJECT LEADER, MANAGEMENT, RETAIL COMPANY: INSTALLING AN INADEQUATE SYSTEM

First Party, Project Leader: Implementing and Putting into Production an Incomplete and Inadequate System

Total	Unethical	Not Unethical	No Ethics Issue
31	9	14	8

Opinions

The participants were split on all the opinions given. There was significant agreement on none of them. One participant stated that the scenario is not clear enough about the assignment of responsibility to permit a judgment on ethics.

Some participants saw this as a clear case of a professional computer person's allowing a bad system to be used. He continued development even though he knew the system would be inadequate.

Some thought that the project leader should not have been held responsible, because he did warn management of impending problems and was told they would be corrected later. Having warned management of the problems that might result from their decision, he acted ethically and had no further responsibility for that decision. He merely followed orders.

Some maintained that this was a matter of poor judgment in several respects. The project leader who developed the system with so few checks and so little flexibility was apparently not competent to judge what was minimally essential. He should have known enough, and documented his complaint. Finally, he should have resigned when no corrective action was taken. By not doing so, for whatever reasons, he was in part morally responsible for the damage that resulted. He deserved blame.

The project leader was not practicing in the best interest of his employer or the public. Every business student learns early how vital the billing process is to a company. As the expert, he was responsible for establishing the overall effectiveness of the system and should not have allowed himself to be compromised. Without error detection and audit controls, the system could not be said to be complete. By letting it go into production, he implied it was complete. He was not ethical, because he did not resign. Other participants, however, suggested that the project leader only allowed himself to be bullied into doing bad work. That was unwise and incompetent, but not unethical.

Second Party, Management: Ordering the System into Production Prematurely and Blaming the Project Leader

Total	Unethical	Not Unethical	No Ethics Issue
12	11	1	0

Opinions

It was almost unanimously agreed that management should have provided staff and funds for a sound and complete system. It should have taken the blame for failure, and it was unethical to make a scapegoat of the project leader.

At best, the managers were culpably ignorant of the possible consequences of an incomplete system. If they did not trust the judgment of their own expert, they should have asked for an outside consultant's advice. Managers learn early how susceptible a system is to negative factors, and how devastating even minor perturbations can be. Management's action was a dereliction of responsibility to the stockholders, customers, and employees by knowingly allowing bad work and blaming the project leader for the results. These actions were unethical.

General Principles

Persons in responsible positions, whose decisions affect other people in significant ways, have an obligation to base their decisions on all relevant, reasonably available information and are morally responsible for foreseeable consequences of their actions.

When a professional person is given only partial authority or inadequate resources to perform his work and bad consequences result, he cannot be held responsible for factors outside his control.

The accountability standards developed for accountants should be used as a model for certifying computer technologists.

Scenario 5.4

PROGRAMMING MANAGER, COMPANY: DEVELOPING PROGRAMS WITHOUT ADEQUATE CONTROLS

Party, Programming Manager: Implementing Programs That Circumvented Accounting Controls

Total	Unethical	Not Unethical	No Ethics Issue
30	6	19	5

Opinions

The participants unanimously agreed that the senior manager made a decision that involved no ethical issues, and the programming manager acted ethically in warning the senior manager. If the programming manager did not believe that his senior's judgment was correct and competent, then he should have taken positive action against the decision.

All but one participant agreed that if the programs were ultimately to be used for real business functions, then the manager was obligated to make sure there were adequate controls to protect the business against loss. Also, if the two managers could not agree, then it was necessary either that they call for independent arbitration, or that the programming manager resign to remain ethical.

General Principles

An individual responsible for business computer programs is also responsible for assuring there are adequate controls to protect the business against loss.

Scenario 5.5

CONSULTANT, COMPUTERIZATION OF A GOVERNMENT DEPARTMENT: DISREGARDING IMPACT ON EMPLOYEES

Party, Consultant: Accepting His Client's Views and Refraining from Considering Adverse Effects on Employees

Total	Unethical	Not Unethical	No Ethics Issue
25	16	8	1

Opinions

All but one participant agreed that, if the consultant disagreed with his client's position with respect to work force reduction, he should not accept the assignment and should attempt to advance his views through social and political processes.

A great majority supported the opinion that the consultant had an ethical responsibility to communicate to his client his concerns about wider implications, independent of union or government views. He could communicate his views in an attachment to the product, and he should not bill the client for the extra effort. The consultant was unethical to go along with management's views and limit his study.

A smaller majority agreed that the consultant's obligation was to design an efficient operation for the government department. It was not part of his professional obligation to give advice on whether there should be more or fewer government jobs. If the consultant had a personal opinion about job reduction and if he believed his professional advice would lead to consequences he would not approve of, he should not have accepted the job. By the same vote, an additional point was supported: The job levels, job content, and quality of working life have an impact on the degree to which his system will be accepted and successful. Therefore, the consultant would be unethical in not discussing these factors with management if he was aware of them.

Most agreed with, but a few rejected, the statement that this scenario required distinguishing between legal and ethical obligations in the following way. It is not expected that a consultant should be legally required to go beyond the terms of reference of scope of his study. But it is reasonable that ethical considerations will always make him take human factors into account, even at the expense of operating efficiency.

In the same statement, it was expressed that management had taken the position that it had unilateral responsibility for human factors. If the consultant viewed this as wrong because, among other reasons, the operation would be affected, he was ethically obligated to raise the larger issues. By not doing so, he was acting unethically.

The group was evenly split between rejecting and agreeing with the notion that management was at fault for ignoring important aspects of the problem and, especially, the impact of the reorganization on the working conditions of employees. In any case, union or management prerogatives are a legal, not a professional, matter and represent a "red herring" in this scenario. The social judgment with respect to the size of the government work force is not an ethical issue in the computer profession. Nevertheless, several participants pursued the issue of the government's policy in this instance saying that to refrain from taking job levels and content and quality of working life into account was to place a higher value on efficiency than on human needs. This sacrifices human values and violates the government's mandate and moral priorities to protect the interests of its citizens. In making no objections, the consultant helped promote and legitimize a morally untenable policy.

Finally, only a small minority supported a statement about the union and the consultant: The consultant would have been unethical to include any of the concerns of the union, because he should not use his special position to unduly influence socially derived policies. The employees make their bargain through the union in a socially approved and public process that best serves the public, and the consultant should not interfere or be involved with that process.

General Principles

All parties involved in design, assessment, and implementation of computer systems should always consider human consequences, not in the sense of serving special social or political interests in particular cases, but to develop habits of addressing classes of human problems that are exemplified in particular cases, e.g., job losses, dehumanization of work, or physical danger.

While it is agreed that an increased level of sensitivity to wider implications of technical endeavor is needed, it is also important to recognize the practical negative consequences of suppressing concern and of inaction.

Scenario 6.3

CONSULTANT, PROGRAMMER, A PROJECTED NUCLEAR ENERGY PLANT: SELECTING FAVORABLE COMPUTER OUTPUT IN A FEASIBILITY STUDY

First Party, Consultant: Selecting Computer Output to Bias the Study

Total	Unethical	Not Unethical	No Ethics Issue
32	32	0	0

Second Party, Programmer: Revealing Proprietary Information to His Congressman

Total	Unethical	Not Unethical	No Ethics Issue
31	6	25	0

Opinions

It was unanimously agreed that selecting data to achieve a predetermined conclusion is scientifically unethical. All but two participants agreed that the consultant should place the community ahead of his private interests, as should the programmer.

Most agreed that it seemed unlikely that the programmer would have been privy to all of the relevant factors, and therefore the programmer should not have gone outside his relationship with the consultant until all remedies within the relationship had been exhausted. While the vote was split on the ethics of revealing the fact to the congressman, most participants agreed that, generally speaking, it is unethical to reveal proprietary information even though there are more important considerations.

General Principles

A consultant must act with strict impartiality when purporting to give independent advice, and in doing so he must disclose all relevant information and interests.

Scenario 6.5

RESEARCHER, PREDICTIONS BY COMPUTER MODELING: SHAPING PUBLIC OPINION

Party, Researcher: Misrepresenting Facts

Total	Unethical	Not Unethical	No Ethics Issue
26	26	0	0

Opinions

There is no issue over the unethical acts of the researcher. It was unethical for him to use the public perception of the nature of a computer to increase the credibility of a computer-related work product and to present the computer as an active agent. It was also unethical not to make clear the basis and reliability of modeling results—prior to presenting conclusions. He should have stated confidence bounds and sufficient and relevant caveats.

The participants had mixed opinions concerning the publisher's role. One individual stated that he had an ethical obligation to distinguish opinion from fact and should not have published the book. Another said he had no ethical obligation to check the validity of the material. Several participants agreed that the publisher had an obligation not to publish knowingly fraudulent material.

General Principles

The computer should never be presented as an active agent.

The basis for credibility of a computer-related product should be validity of the data and methods used and the inclusion of data and methods, along with the results, in the publication.

Epilogue

Now that you have reviewed this self-assessment procedure, and have compared your responses to those of the panel, you should ask yourself whether this has been a successful educational experience. The Committee suggests that you conclude that it has only if you have

- discovered some concepts that you did not previously know about or understand,

or

- increased your understanding of those concepts which were relevant to your work or valuable to you,

or

- turned your mind to a consideration of ethics.

PART VI.   REFERENCE AND BIBLIOGRAPHY

REFERENCE

[1]   Parker, D.B. *Ethical Conflicts in Computer Science and Technology.* Arlington, Va.: AFIPS Press, 1981.

BIBLIOGRAPHY

Books, papers, and reports relating to professionalism and ethics in computing, technology, and engineering.

[1]   Barbour, I.G. *Technology, Environment, and Human Values.* New York: Praeger, 1980. (Paperback)

[2]   Baum, R.J. *Ethics and Engineering Curricula.* Monograph VII of the Teaching of Ethics Project. Hastings-on-Hudson, N.Y.: The Hasting Center, 1980.

[3]   _____, and A. Flores. *Ethical Problems in Engineering.* Troy, N.Y.: RPI Studies in the Human Dimensions of Science and Technology, 1978. (Paperback)

[4]   Bereano, P.L. *Technology as a Social and Political Phenomenon.* New York: John Wiley & Sons, 1976.

[5]   Fruchtbaum, H., ed. *The Social Responsibility of Engineers.* Proceedings of a conference sponsored by the New York Academy of Sciences. *Annals of the New York Academy,* Vol. 196, Article 10 (February 28, 1973), pp. 409-73.

[6]   Hughson, R.V., and P.M. Kohn. "Ethics." Two articles in *Chemical Engineering,* May 5 and September 22, 1980.

[7]   Ladenson, R.F., et al. *A Selected Annotated Bibliography of Professional Ethics and Social Responsibility in Engineering.* Chicago, Ill.: Center for the Study of Ethics in the Professions, Illinois Institute of Technology, 1980. (Paperback)

[8]   Layton, E. *The Revolt of the Engineers.* Cleveland: Case Western Reserve Press, 1971.

[9]   McCarter, P. *Background Papers Presented for AFIPS Study on Professionalism.* Summer 1969, 130 pp., multilith, Arlington, Va.: AFIPS Press.

[10]   Mowshowitz, A. "On Approaches to the Study of Social Issues in Computing." *Communications of the ACM,* Vol. 24, No. 3 (March 1981), pp. 146-55.

[11]   Oldenquist, A., and E.E. Slowter. "Proposed: A Single Code of Ethics for All Engineers." *Professional Engineer,* May 1979, pp. 8-11.

[12]   Parker, D.B. "Rules of Ethics in Information Processing," *Communications of the ACM,* Vol. 11, No. 3 (March 1968), pp. 198-201.

[13] "Code of Conduct." *The Computer Bulletin,* March 1970, British Computer Society, 23 Dorset Square, London N.W. 1, England.

[14] "Code of Ethics." American Documentation Institute (now American Society for Information Science, ASIS). *1967 Handbook and Directory,* ASIS, 1010 16th Street, N.W., Washington, D.C. 20036.

[15] *Code of Professional Ethics.* American Institute of Certified Public Accountants, Inc., 1211 Avenue of the Americas, New York, N.Y. 10036.

[16] *Code of Professional Responsibility.* Institute of Management Consultants, Inc., 19 West 44th Street, New York, N.Y. 10036, 6 pp.

[17] DPMA Code of Ethics (Imprinted on membership certificates). Data Processing Management Association, 505 Busse Highway, Park Ridge, Ill. 60068.

[18] "Professional Conduct in Information Processing," *Communications of the ACM,* Vol. 11, No. 3 (February 1968), p. 135.

[19] "Standards of Conduct," *1969 Data Processing Service Center Directory,* p. 14. Association of Data Processing Service Organizations (ADAPSO), 1300 North 17th Street, Arlington, Va. 22209.

[20] "The Question of Professionalism," *EDP Analyzer,* Vol. 6, No. 12 (December 1968), Canning Publications, Inc., Vista, Calif.

25

Editors' Note
McCue: "IBM's Santa Teresa Laboratory–
Architectural Design for Program Development"

Insight: There is at least one company that realizes programmers can't be expected to work efficiently in the cramped, noisy, unprivate workplace most organizations provide.

Near the end of his article, Gerald McCue refers to "the timeless tradition of man's careful attention to tools and habitation." There is a marvelous irony in this phrase, because the "timeless tradition" in the design of programmers' workspace has been to stuff them cheek by jowl into the cheapest, noisiest possible space. The noise level in a typical workplace is simply *appalling*. Programmers in all parts of the industry work without privacy and without protection from visual noise or in-terruption. It's a wonder they can work at all.

In contrast to this dismal picture, IBM took a refreshingly sane approach to the design of its then-new Santa Teresa Laboratory. They actually studied the problem. (The industry standard is to by-pass this step and let the entire office be designed by some partition-and-furniture vendor, a salesman who wouldn't know programmer productivity if it bit him.) They observed programmers at work and came to the conclusion that they needed at least one hundred square feet each in private offices with doors and windows and thirty square feet of work surface. Only a company that knows productivity really matters is willing to come face to face with these requirements.

25

IBM's Santa Teresa Laboratory– Architectural Design for Program Development
by Gerald M. McCue

Computer programming normally is performed in work areas intended for other uses—typically in offices designed for business. As a result, programmers have had to contend with a number of practical problems, such as the need to work with and store items of unusual dimensions. Program listings and punch cards, in particular, pose special problems in desks and cabinets and on shelves intended for the standard size documents of the business world. In addition, there have been significant changes in the way programming is practiced. More and more programs are developed on line at computer terminals, and concepts such as the chief programmer team have been introduced. These changes have altered the programmer's working environment, creating a need for ready access to terminals and conference rooms, for example.

Recognizing these requirements, IBM commissioned MBT Associates, a San Francisco architectural firm, to design a building and interiors intended specifically for program development. That facility, opened in 1977, is the Santa Teresa Laboratory of IBM's General Products Division. Located in San Jose, California, it provides the working environment for 2,000 people engaged in systems and applications programming. Although IBM has many programming facilities throughout the world, this is the first designed specifically for the activities involved in program development.

This essay is concerned mainly with the special needs of the computer programmer, how those needs were perceived, and the process by which they became generators of design concepts. The design challenge was to bring a large number of people together into a close-knit working community and at the same time create an environment conducive to enhanced programmer productivity through team interaction as well as individual concentration.

The work environment of the programmer is emphasized, although the requirements of the laboratory's computing center and of personnel working there also were important design considerations. The computing center supports the General Products Division's West Coast data processing network as well as all on-site processing. Other planning and design factors, such as energy conservation and seismic provisions, were major architectural considerations but are not discussed here in order to focus on the programmer's work environment.

The essay includes three sections, *Defining the Work Environment, Designing the Site and Building Complex,* and *Furnishing the Individual Work Area.* These sections are presented in approximately the order of the actual design steps

389

and are preceded by a description of the architectural design process.

Architectural Design

In many respects, architectural design follows a standard three-step problem solving model:

- identification of needs and objectives
- design concept (generation and evaluation of alternatives)
- design development (refinement of the selected solution)

These steps normally are taken in sequence, but in the designing of Santa Teresa, the identification of needs and the generation of alternatives were combined, permitting a better collaboration between programmers and designers and providing greater opportunity for innovation.

Innovative design is often derived from a careful analysis of the issues that influence the solution. Needs are identified, prototypical solutions evaluated, and new approaches considered. The design process is one of synthesis, where optimal designs for different issues are combined in an attempt to meet objectives.

The process is not linear, but proceeds in cycles, each cycle building upon knowledge gained from the previous one, so that successive design concepts can be responsive to a greater number of relevant issues. The designer is called upon to consider a large number of variables simultaneously, and complete synthesis is rarely possible because of the number of often conflicting requirements. Consequently, early design concepts usually are advanced to satisfy the most fundamental objectives, and these approaches are evaluated with respect to other requirements. In the designing of Santa Teresa, consideration of the work environment was perceived as the fundamental need, and it served to generate the form of the complex as a whole, as well as the individual work space.

The process does not proceed from major considerations, such as building form, toward details such as the form of individual rooms. Instead, initial studies attempt to identify both the detailed and the more general requirements for an ideal solution. The first studies for Santa Teresa, for example, concurrently explored the needs of the individual project work areas and the characteristics of the site environment, as well as the needs of the building complex as a whole.

Different issues often suggest conflicting spatial solutions, and resolution of conflict may offer the greatest opportunities for innovation. An apparent conflict between the need for interior planning flexibility and the desire for outside awareness (that is, visual contact with and proximity to the natural environment) brought forth the unusual design solution that gives Santa Teresa its distinctive character.

The design process is laden with value judgments, first as to which needs and preferences are considered, then as to the relative priority to be given different needs when conflicts arise. Attempts to make such judgments more explicit through cost benefit techniques usually are not credible for problems with so many variables. Similarly, decomposition methods, which build decision networks based on minute detail, are tedious, and the results rarely warrant the laborious process. Thus, in most cases, design is essentially the systemic revealing of relevant considerations and the formulating of design solutions that reflect the specific needs and relative values among the many objectives.

The personal values of those who participate have a critical influence on the solution. The Santa Teresa Laboratory is significant, in part, because of the active participation of user groups—programmers, program managers, and several levels of IBM management. Communication among these groups, IBM's Real Estate and Construction Division, and the designers of MBT Associates, achieved an iterative design process. Through continued dialog, needs were identified, compatible solutions sought, and different values respected. Alternatives were explored that otherwise might have been precluded. Interaction during the problem identification and design concept steps proved invaluable, permitting subtle qualities of the programmer's needs and preferences to be incorporated into the final design.

Defining the Work Environment

The first IBM statement of requirements for Santa Teresa was in two parts, a summary of building requirements, and a description of the programmer's activities and preferred amenities (see Appendix A). Both documents tended to be statements of objectives rather than prescriptive solutions. The programmer's activities are described as primarily "project work" in which system and application programs are designed, coded, documented, tested, and supported. Specific development projects range in length from one to three years. The typical development programmer performs in-

tensive and creative work as part of a project team of two to five persons. Two to four teams, with a secretary and manager, form the typical department of ten to fifteen persons.

According to information provided by an IBM User's Study Group, about 30 percent of the individual programmer's time is spent working alone, about 50 percent with groups of two or three, and the balance with larger groups, in travel, or handling other responsibilities. The programmer's role is dynamic, for programmers may be moved and regrouped as required for specific project teams. These activities are defined below in terms of functional requirements and qualitative preferences.

Functional Requirements

Consideration of the needs of both the programmer and the programming center resulted in a summary of specific requirements (see Appendices A and B). Programmers perceived the following as most essential for individual work areas:

- a private, personal work area that permits intense concentration, screens distractions, and discourages interruptions, with connections for a computer terminal and adequate space to lay out and store large quantities of paper goods;

- proximity to common terminal rooms for team programming work and small meetings, as well as for additional layout space and storage;

- proximity to conference rooms and classrooms;

- access to the computer room, library, and food service area, preferably under cover;

- furniture designed to reflect the programmer's special layout and storage needs (detailed requirements, prepared at a later stage in the project, are discussed in the last section of the essay).

Functional requirements for programming teams and for site support, reflecting management's concern for communal needs, were perceived as follows:

- encouragement of effective communication and interaction within teams and departments, and with other groups;
- flexibility of spatial arrangements to facilitate reorganization of teams and departments and adjustment to changes in technology;
- integration of the manager's office, secretarial area, and common terminal rooms with programmers' work areas;
- proximity of project work areas to the computing center, library, business center, and other support services;
- efficient paper handling techniques and adequate service access to all work areas;
- a high level of security.

Functional requirements expressed by IBM's Real Estate and Construction Division stressed issues affecting capital investment, operating costs, and long-range flexibility. They included:

- a modular building plan with mechanical services designed to accommodate either open-office planning or subdivision into separate offices;
- flexibility in office groupings so that programmers and departments can be regrouped without moving partitions and with minimal moving of furniture;
- full access for handicapped personnel;
- easy accommodation of service and materials handling;
- energy conservation and heat recovery from computers, with low operating and maintenance costs.

Qualitative Preferences

The designers of MBT Associates were charged by IBM to create an environment that would be "conducive to productive and creative work" (Appendix A). The programmers were characterized as being involved in imaginative synthesis and productive processes requiring personal privacy. The facility would have a large number of people, but a strong desire for a noninstitutional environment was stressed.

After privacy, the environmental amenity that seemed to be of most significance to the programmers was outside awareness. Stimulating interior and exterior spaces, with natural light and interesting colors and materials, were requested, and the ability to arrange and personalize office space was also considered highly important.

Apparent Contradictions

There were apparent contradictions in some of the expressed requirements and preferences:

- a desire for individual offices, and also a need to accommodate open planning;

- a desire for individually customized work spaces, and also a need for aggregate work areas and flexibility for future change;

- a requirement for closely grouped work areas near central services, also a desire for a sense of small scale and identity;

- a need to provide major centralized services for 2,000 people, and also a strong desire for an informal, noninstitutional setting.

Some of these contradictions could not be resolved, but the level of success in reconciling them was one guide in evaluating alternative design concepts.

One of the first design steps was evaluating alternative designs for the project work areas, where more than 1,900 people would be engaged in the primary site activity. After comparison of several configurations, the bay space labelled C in Fig. 1 was selected tentatively as the most desirable. In contrast with a single-office-depth bay along a corridor as shown in A, or a double office depth as shown in B, the type C bay could accommodate several arrangements of open space planning, or it could be efficiently subdivided into offices. Its size and shape also accommo-dated two exits, obviating the need for either a permanent fire-rated corridor or a separate fire-exit stair within the bay. The type C bay also had the significant advantages of bringing individuals working on the same team into close proximity, and if subdivided, provided access to offices and common rooms from a semiprivate aisle. This bay appeared to meet the functional requirements as well as the desire for a sense of privacy and personal territory.

Studies of the individual work spaces indicated that 10-by-10-foot space would be most versatile, so the type C bay was designed with a 5-by-5-foot grid, to accommodate 10-by-10-foot individual work areas and 10-by-15-foot or larger team rooms. It was determined that individual offices would be planned with the provision that programmers, senior programmers, and program managers all would occupy the same size offices. Thus the regrouping of teams and departments could be accomplished without having to move walls.

The C-type bay, measuring about 45 by 50 feet, was accepted tentatively as the basis for further planning because of its potential for optimal interior space planning. However, at this time there was no agreement about the manner in which the bays should by grouped into a building form, or which of the edges, if any, might be exterior walls. A major concern was that modules so closely tailored to the size of a typical department might not accommodate the balancing of teams and departments. These considerations were the subject of the next design studies, which explored alternate ways of organizing the individual modules into a building form.

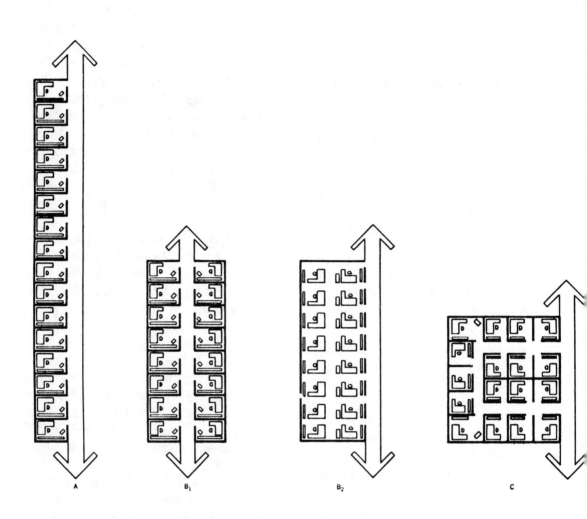

Figure 1. Office layouts considered for Santa Teresa.

Designing the Site and Building Complex

Conservation and ecological considerations were central themes in the site planning. Of the 1,180-acre property, all but 271 acres is to be preserved in its natural state. The portion of the site being utilized is a 90-acre planned-development parcel, and currently only a 50-acre area is actually developed. Of this area, only about 15 percent is devoted to buildings and about 30 percent to parking; the balance is open space.

Among the many considerations that influenced the design of the site, such as topography, expense, traffic, and drainage, a major factor was the providing of building service. A study of the service requirements for Santa Teresa indicated that over 200 boxes of computer output paper will be consumed each day, requiring delivery and pick-up in bulk. Almost all of this paper will be delivered through a central service area for transfer to the computing center. Most eventually will find its way to the various project work areas and then to a shredder and back to the service area for shipping to a recycling center. The paper handling requirement is massive, involving outside service access for trucks and semi-trailers. This requirement proved to be a critical consideration in the evaluation of site development concepts.

Building Design

Tentative acceptance of the type C bay for the project work areas, and approval of the site development concept, provided the basis for considering alternative ways of grouping spaces and organizing them on the site. Among the needs and preferences expressed by the programmers, the most influential in affecting spatial organization were aggregation of bays to achieve operating flexibility and arrangement of work areas to achieve maximal outside awareness. As a result, the design team proposed to isolate the outside awareness issue as a means of exploring organizational principles. For purposes of study, it was assumed that the generic difference between all building configurations was the extent of outside awareness that alternative grouping of the type C project work area would permit. Under this assumption, the amount of outside exposure would be the only variant, and overall building configuration, whether "lines," "ells," "U's," "O's," or other shapes, temporarily would be considered irrelevant. Though an oversimplification, this assumption permitted objective studies by which various degrees of outside aware-

ness might be compared directly with other sought-after planning objectives.

The selected C-type bay had several work spaces in the center, so it would not be possible to achieve 100-percent outside awareness. Therefore, preliminary studies examined levels of exposure ranging from zero to 70 percent. Three alternatives, as illustrated in Fig. 2, were selected for more detailed study:

- Alternative I—no project areas with outside awareness. This scheme was based on the assumption that if one person had to work in an inside space, everyone should. Type C bays would be grouped adjacent to one another in interior loft-type space, and outside awareness would be provided only from special spaces and circulation corridors located adjacent to the outside walls.

- Alternative II—30 percent of project work areas with outside awareness. In this scheme, only one edge of the type C bay would have outside exposure, and the bays would be grouped adjacent to each other along one outside wall.

- Alternative III—70 percent (the maximum) of project work areas with outside awareness. In this alternative, the type C bays would by grouped in cruciform pavilions so that three edges of each bay would have outside walls.

Each alternative was evaluated with respect to the following criteria:

Functional criteria—

- flexibility in the balancing of proj-

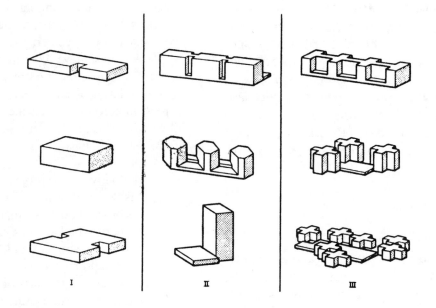

I   II   III

Figure 2. Building configurations considered for Santa Teresa.

ect teams and department sizes within a series of type C bays;

- adjacency of spaces such as conference rooms, classrooms, and service areas common to several project teams or departments;
- efficiency of mechanical and electrical service systems;
- effectiveness of communications among functions;
- sufficient building access and control for visitors, employees, and service personnel.

Qualitative criteria—

- extent of outside awareness and quality of view;
- coherence and visual quality of circulation systems;

- pedestrian rather than elevator circulation;
- sense of place and orientation within the building;
- accessibility, usability, and visual quality of exterior spaces.

Efficiency and value criteria—

- efficiency of space utilization (net assignable square feet divided by gross building area);
- efficiency of the structural system (in terms of cost per square foot of building area);
- efficiency of the mechanical system (in terms of cost per square foot of building area);
- efficiency of enclosure systems (in terms of cost per square foot of enclosed wall);

• cost of total development, operation, and energy consumption.

Note: It was assumed that the cost of interior finishes would be the same in all schemes.

Design Development

The Alternative III grouping, in which the type C bay has three outside walls, was selected as providing the best balance of expressed needs and preferences. Based on this grouping concept, several overall building organizations were explored. The approach that met most requirements for both internal arrangement and site development began as a set of separate programming buildings around a central, one-story service building. Through successive steps of refinement, it evolved to the present form—a series of pavilions integrated into a large, contiguous ground-floor area.

Two of the many objectives for Santa Teresa dominated the final solution: the preference for individual work areas with special qualities, and the need for centralized service and close communication with central facilities. In the final design, illustrated in Fig. 3, several four-story programming pavilions containing the project work areas are grouped around and joined to a large, one-story central area. At the ground floor, the central area contains the computing center and other facilities. At the second level, on the roof of the computing center, there is a garden quadrangle which is the focus of the scheme. Six smaller courtyards are formed by the groupings of the individual pavilions around the central quadrangle.

In its final form, the scheme provides multiple yet differentiated access with a two-level circulation system. Visitors enter the building complex through a central lobby at ground level. From there, they can be escorted into the building at ground level or through the courtyard behind the lobby and up to the garden quadrangle at the second level.

Service access is by way of a loop road to the rear of the developed portion of the site, where the service dock is located. From the service dock there is immediate vertical access to the food service area on the second level and direct horizontal access to the computing center. An extended service corridor at ground level also provides access to elevators serving all programming pavilions.

IBM personnel enter the building complex through the courtyards between the programming pavilions. From the courtyards they move up one level to the main circulation level in the garden quadrangle. All programming pavilions and the food service facility are accessible at the garden level. The pedestrian scale of the complex is enhanced by this arrangement, since other floors are only two stories up or one story down from the garden level.

Geometric ordering of the complex is achieved by a "tartan grid," the C-type bay being separated on all sides by a narrow band of space. Except at ground level, the narrow spaces are always open, either as exterior spaces or as interior corridors. Thus each pavilion presents the visual appearance of four separate project work areas. This coherent system of open spaces provides a sense of orientation and a close relationship with the exterior.

Figure 4 illustrates the spatial organization and suggests the sense of openness and contact with the outside as one moves

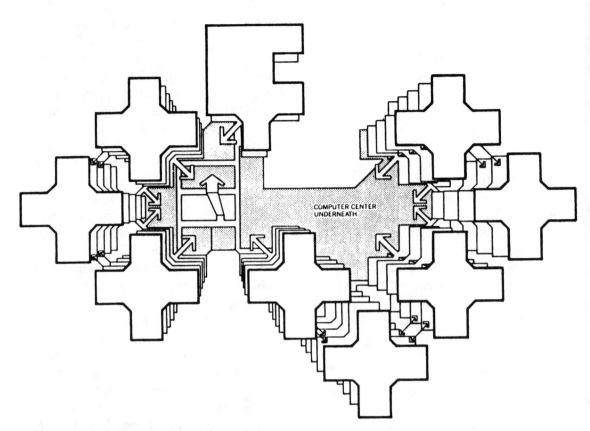

COMPUTER CENTER
UNDERNEATH

Figure 3. The final design of Santa Teresa.

through the buildings. On the second, third, and fourth levels this spatial system provides views from all corridors, not only into adjacent courtyards, but through and into the next pavilions and into the countryside beyond.

Furnishing the Individual Work Area

Two adjacent programming pavilions are linked to form a contiguous work area on each floor. A typical building module is shown in Fig. 5. One stair in each pavilion provides the two exits required by code for each floor, and one service elevator serves two pavilions. A pavilion of four

bays provides about 10,250 net assignable square feet in a gross building area of about 13,200 square feet per floor and will accommodate about 70 people. Figure 5 also illustrates a typical interior space planning layout, with individual offices for programmers and managers, common workrooms and terminal rooms, conference rooms and classrooms, and other jointly used services.

As a prelude to interior and furniture design, additional studies reconfirmed the principles established earlier—the need for private individual work areas, the desirability for the 10-by-10-foot enclosed office as the basic work area, and the adaptabil-

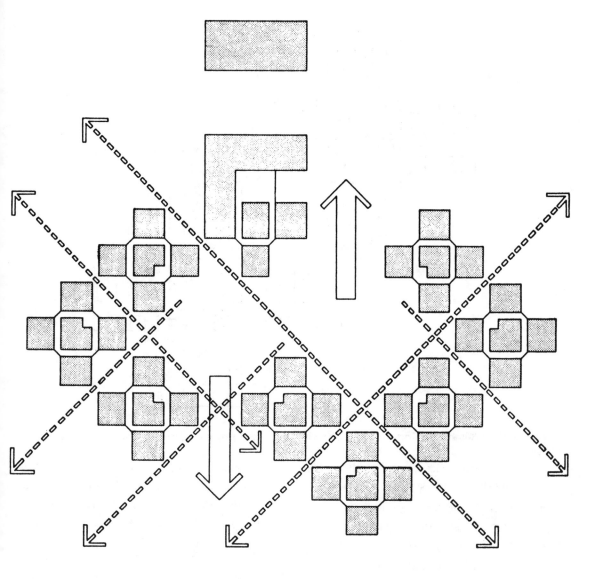

Figure 4. Plan diagram showing views from interior courtyards.

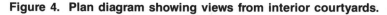

ity of the 45-by-50-foot bay. In addition, the following more detailed requirements were established for the individual work areas:

- a standard set of movable furniture components, intended to remain in an office when programmers or managers are transferred from one office to another;

- efficient work surfaces both for individuals and for programming teams;

- a flexible environment conducive to individual expression;

- furniture components that can be

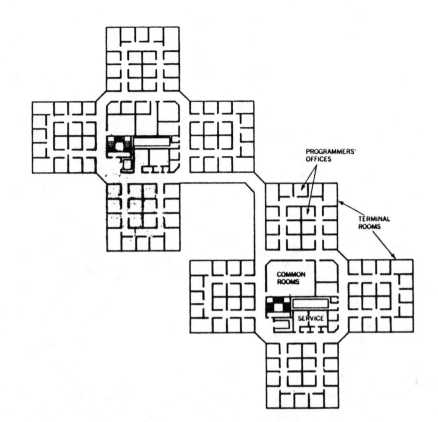

Figure 5. Typical building module, showing how two programming pavilions are linked.

rearranged to accommodate individual work styles;

- storage units for program listings and standard-size office paper;
- large quantities of lockable storage that can be expanded incrementally;
- generous work surfaces without leg obstructions and deep enough to accommodate program listings;
- comfortable seating.

The requirements for large storage units and generous work surfaces were the most critical for the programmer's daily efficiency. These requirements could not easily be met by existing office furniture, so users and designers collaborated to modify standard furniture and design some new items. Perhaps the most unusual aspect of this design effort was the testing and evaluation of prototypes, or mock-ups, under working conditions. At two programming locations not far from the Santa Teresa Laboratory, IBM prepared 12 offices to resemble those intended for the new laboratory. The prototype furniture was installed and used under a full range of working conditions for several months. The programmers using the offices were interviewed, and many of their suggestions were incorporated into the final furniture design (see Appendix C).

Final design options are illustrated in

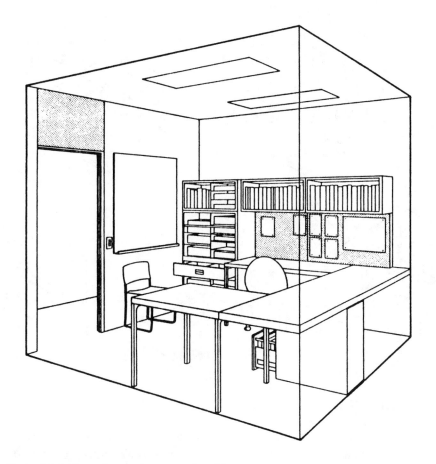

Figure 6. Typical interior of a programmer's office.

Figs. 6 and 7. The only fixed features of the furniture arrangement are wall-hung units and a 24-inch-deep counter under the window. The primary work surface, 30 inches deep, can be attached to the fixed counter in any of several places, yielding a number of possible furniture arrangements. Leg obstructions and left- or right-hand bias have been eliminated. Lockable storage units can be slipped under the work surface or stacked to form a storage wall. A pedestal unit with a lockable file drawer and box drawers is also provided. All storage units and work surfaces are dimensionally coordinated to permit a variety of arrangements.

Selection of colors and materials was central to the space planning and furniture design. Finish materials are related to both functional and aesthetic values. To add variety and aid orientation, the small courtyards and the walls of the central core of each pavilion are color coded. The doors and window blinds in the project work areas in each pavilion recall the same colors. The floors of the main corridors are hard surfaced to accommodate heavy paper carts, and the aisles and work

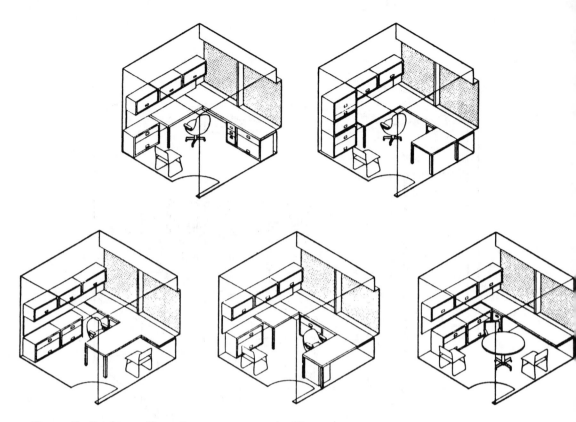

Figure 7. Design options for programmers' offices.

areas are carpeted. The change in floor material further enhances the sense of privacy in the work areas. To accommodate individual expression, fabrics, finishes, and colors are coordinated to provide variety within the context of a neutral background.

Summary

The design of the Santa Teresa Laboratory is derived from both the functional and qualitative needs of programmers. On the functional level, the building brings 2,000 people together in close working proximity. A number of design features have been combined to promote centralized convenience and easy communication. For example, interior circulation connects all central facilities at the ground level, and pedestrian access is encouraged from floor to floor and from building to building.

Qualitatively, the laboratory provides personal scale and outside awareness. The low-rise, four-story buildings, the identifiable programming pavilions, and the interior work bays all tend to provide a sense of personal space. The geometry of the formal organization provides a high degree of outside awareness. Above ground level, for example, no place is more than 25 feet from a window.

The Santa Teresa Laboratory is not designed merely to fulfill functional and qualitative needs. A building complex such as this, with small increments of highly flexible space, must have some fundamental elements that are strong and seem permanent. At Santa Teresa, a few such elements can be traced to historical images. Three may serve to illustrate this point. The first is the relationship between the complex as a whole and its setting; it has sharp, specific edges and is contained at the side of a valley. This relationship is almost monastic in concept, in that the buildings are sheltered and withdrawn from the surrounding countryside, yet they maintain a direct view toward the outside world.

The second element is the garden quadrangle, which, in the absence of a large interior space, becomes the focal point of the complex. This central plateau, though surrounded by buildings, provides a sheltered place with views of the distant hills. Third, the interior circulation system provides logic and organization for the interior spaces; it provides continuous orientation and visual links to the site and the central garden.

Fundamental elements such as these bind the Santa Teresa Laboratory to the timeless tradition of man's careful attention to tools and habitation. Although the design is derived from specific needs and objectives, it expresses spatial relationships that have always brought meaning and interest.

APPENDIX A

Adapted from IBM's *Statement of Requirements, Santa Teresa Laboratory,* July 16, 1974.

Building Requirements

A campus-like cluster of identifiable buildings is desired that blends with the natural environment in a pleasing and reserved fashion. The offices should be conducive to productive and creative work.

Programming project work is the major activity to be performed at the site. System and application programs will be designed, coded, documented, tested, and supported. Programming project areas will be used by functional and project teams to carry out these activities. Teams will consist of two to five individuals organized into departments of two to four teams, plus a manager and a secretary. Extensive computer services and flexible use of internal space will be required.

Primary considerations are as follows:

- Outside awareness is essential for as many offices as possible. Natural lighting is highly desirable for all work areas.

- Emphasis should be placed on soundproofing, particularly between adjacent offices.

- Maximum flexibility is desired for placement and use of computer terminals and associated work space.

Programmers' Requirements

The primary mission of personnel at the site will be programming. Several different programming projects will be active at any given time. A typical programming project goes through a sequence of phases, and many persons participate at various times. Effective interaction among these individuals is the most important ingredient in the success of a project.

Care must be taken in the design of the buildings and site to provide the environment and tools required for programmers to perform their tasks. Special consideration should be given to the following criteria:

- Communication. The primary consideration in designing the offices, buildings, and site must be ease of communication. Team members will have to communicate within programming teams, with other teams on the same project at the site, and with teams at other sites, worldwide.

- Privacy. Each individual will require a personal work area with an environment that supports the intensive concentration needed for high quality problem solving. Acoustical isolation, adequate ventilation, and individual control of the office environment are key design considerations.

- Furniture. The architect should make a special study and recommend office furniture and fixtures that will be effective for many different tasks. The programmer's basic document is a 15-by-11-inch fanfold program listing which opens to 15 by 22 inches. Work surfaces that can accommodate several listings simultaneously, and lockable storage that can accommodate these documents in hanging vertical files, are required.

- Computer connections. A most essential tool of the project programmer is computer time. Access to the

computer must be provided throughout the project areas for video, high-speed, and low-speed communication facilities. Remote job entry stations and printers should be provided, and every office should have terminal connections.

- Security. The site and, in particular, the data processing and project buildings must be secure.

- Technology. Design flexibility should be maintained with regard to current and future programming technology.

APPENDIX B

Adapted from IBM's *Santa Teresa Laboratory Interior Design—Programmer Function,* June 19, 1975.

Space Utilization

In programming areas, occupancy requirements per floor will be 60 people, four terminal rooms, four structured-programming-control rooms, one conference room, one remote-job-entry room, and support areas for mail, reproduction facilities, etc. A typical mix of employees on a floor will include 44 programmers, six senior programmers, six managers, and four secretaries.

Programmers' Requirements

Work Surfaces

The programmer's work area will include one 30-by-60-inch surface and one 24-by-60-inch surface. These surfaces are to be table-like, without leg-room obstructions, and they are to be movable. They should have a nonreflecting matt finish. Their height is to be standard, but one section of the 24-inch surface must be adjustable in height to accommodate a terminal. Surface arrangements should not exhibit left- or right-hand bias. These surfaces are intended to accommodate two open program listings, bound or loose, as well as bound reference material.

Storage Facilities

Type A storage (averaging 8 linear feet) is intended to accommodate loose-leaf binders containing IBM System Library publications, functional specifications, development guides, etc.

Type B storage (averaging 8 linear feet) is intended to accommodate bound computer printouts used for reference.

Type C storage (one drawer) is equivalent to the common desk file drawer. It is combined with two box drawers to form a mobile pedestal that can be located beneath the work surface.

Type D storage (four box drawers) is equivalent to storage in common desk drawers. Two drawers will be hanging file space (Type C), combined to form a mobile pedestal that can be located beneath the work surface. The remaining box drawers will be located within a storage unit.

Type E storage (adjustable pigeonholes averaging a total of 36 cubic feet) is intended to handle the programmer's working paper, including program listings, punch cards, magnetic tape, and miscellaneous notes and forms. The lack of this type of storage is a principal deficiency in the traditional programming environment.

Type F storage (ten drawers) is to be used for microfiche cards containing program listings or computer printout.

Approximately 100 cubic feet of storage space will adequately support programming, programming management, and staff assignments, but specific storage requirements vary greatly. Therefore it is essential to have basic storage areas with modular components designed specifically for each kind of material. These components will be combined according to each individual's requirements. In addition, chalkboards, tack-boards, and flip-chart holders will be available for each office.

Services

Each individual will have a telephone with a cord of sufficient length to reach his work surfaces.

At least three double-plug power outlets must be available to each individual. Some of these must be just above table height, and at least one must be next to a coaxial terminal cable outlet. Each programmer must be able to use a terminal in his office.

Additional terminal rooms will be located in each wing of each floor. Keypunch and computer services, as well as copying equipment, will be available on each floor.

APPENDIX C

Adapted from MBT Associates' *Mock-up Evaluation Report,* April 15, 1977.

Evaluation of Mock-up Offices

Twelve mock-up offices were constructed to simulate the office configurations and furniture components specified for the

Santa Teresa Laboratory. Eight mock-ups in IBM's Palo Alto facility and three in San Jose were in daily use for five months. The 12th mock-up was on display in the cafeteria at the Palo Alto facility during the same period. Key components of the mock-ups were the 10-by-10-foot office size, the office furniture, column locations, and power and terminal outlets.

Ten IBM programmers, involved in various phases of program development, were chosen to participate in evaluating the mock-up offices. Each selected the office arrangement he preferred, and the office components were installed according to individual preference.

MBT Associates interviewed the programmers shortly after they had occupied the mock-up offices, and further interviews were conducted during the following months. Based on the programmers' suggestions, a number of refinements were made in the design of the office components.

Work Environment

All programmers preferred the new office arrangements for a number of reasons. Most important, the large work area allowed them to lay out and maintain several tasks at once and to organize materials according to individual work styles. The lack of leg-room obstruction facilitated small group working sessions. In addition, the ample storage space permitted efficient organization of paper work.

Flexibility

The flexibility of being able to move personnel from one office to another was not tested with the mock-ups, but flexibility within individual offices was tested by most of the programmers. At least three tried more than one space plan arrangement, and most of them modified the storage arrangements within the components.

Incremental Growth

Most programmers required additional storage for 8½-by-11-inch paper, filing, and hanging program listings. This need was accommodated by redesigning one of the two-high lateral files to accept a hanging file drawer and a smaller bin unit. The space planning standard permits the installation of another unit, if needed, for heavy storage.

Summary

The reaction to the office environment was highly favorable. The increased work surface, the work surface arrangement, and flexibility in arranging the office components appeared to be key elements. The programmers' comments indicated that the space standards, as tested in the mock-ups, satisfied their operational criteria.

26

Editors' Note
Gould, Conti, and Hovanyecz: "Composing Letters with a Simulated Listening Typewriter"

*Insight: **Some significant testing of a system can be completed long before the system is built.***

Gould and his colleagues set out to discover certain human factors characteristics of a listening typewriter, a device that types a document onto a screen as the human operator speaks his or her text. (You know all about listening typewriters, since you've seen Captain Kirk make frequent use of such a device on *Star Trek.*) Of course, the "right" way to perform this study is to build a prototype listening typewriter and try it out in repeated trials by composing and dictating letters to it. However, the present technology for speech recognition is far from adequate for the construction of such a prototype. Lesser minds would have put the investigation on hold for a decade or two. But Gould, Conti, and Hovanyecz had a better idea....

26

Composing Letters with a Simulated Listening Typewriter
by John D. Gould, John Conti, and Todd Hovanyecz

INTRODUCTION

A "listening typewriter" is a potentially valuable aid in composing letters, memos, and documents. Indeed, it might be a revolutionary office tool, just as the typewriter, telephone, and computer have been. With a listening typewriter, an author could dictate a letter, memo, or report. What he or she says would be automatically recognized and displayed in front of him or her. A listening typewriter would combine the best features of dictating (e.g., rapid human output) and the best features of writing (e.g., visual record, easy editing). No human typist would be required, and no delay would occur between the time an author creates a letter and when he or she gets it back in typed form. This might lead to faster and better initial composition by the author, psychological closure because of no wait for (and uncertainty about) a typed copy, quicker and better communication, and displaceable typing and organizational costs.

The state of the art in automatic speech recognition today, however, is not advanced enough to make a reliable listening typewriter (see summaries in [9, 14]).

An increasingly important—and available—human factors tool is simulation of user interfaces before the interfaces are ever built. Such studies can guide and

impact the development of technology when the most flexibility for change and improvement exists. The present experiments make use of simulation in studying the value of composing letters with a listening typewriter (since a real listening typewriter does not exist today).

This study compared people's performance on and feelings about a listening typewriter with their performance on and feelings about traditional methods of composing (writing and dictating). Of particular interest was whether an imperfect listening typewriter would be useful in composing letters.

Perhaps the most difficult technical problem for automatic speech recognition today is the problem of word segmentation. The boundary cues marking the end of one word and the beginning of the next word, although good enough for human perception, are generally not clear enough for automatic speech recognition. That is why most speech recognition devices commercially available today require the user to speak in isolated words, that is, to put a clear pause of 100 msec. or longer between each word. Thus, one variable studied was speech mode. Participants composed some letters by speaking in isolated words and some letters with consecutive word speech. Would the necessity to pause between each word bother people, significantly interrupt their thought processes, or otherwise affect their composition behavior? If people compose letters with isolated words as well as they compose with consecutive word speech, then a useful listening typewriter would be much easier to make.

A second variable studied was the size of the vocabulary that the listening typewriter could recognize. Reviews of commercially available isolated word systems report that in actual applications they can recognize only about 10–30 words (at any word choice position) with an accuracy of 97–98 percent [2, 12]. Much better performance is reported in laboratory settings [14]; some of this gain in vocabulary size seems to be occurring now in applications. For example, Poock [13] recently showed (using a Threshold Technology T600 recognition system) that vocabularies of up to 240 words are recognized with 97–98 percent accuracy. Nippon Electric Company reports they are able to recognize a vocabulary size of 120 continuously spoken words, and estimates they can recognize 1,000 isolated words. [10] Thus, progress is being made toward successful recognition of larger vocabulary sizes. Clearly, the particular words that comprise the set of words to be recognized significantly affect recognition accuracy. In practice, speech recognition devices attempt to recognize whatever utterance is said within a time window of a second or two, regardless of whether the utterance is a single word or short phrase. Thus, single isolated words could be considered as a special case of isolated phrase recognition.

In the present study, vocabulary sizes of 1,000, 5,000, and an unlimited number of words were used. Again, if people perform as well with a relatively small vocabulary as with the (theoretically unrealizable) unlimited one, then a useful listening typewriter could probably be designed sooner and the resulting system would be less costly.

Two additional variables, composition strategy and whether participants had experience at dictating, were also studied. In Experiment 1 participants composed half their letters using a draft strategy (as explained below) and half their letters using a first time final strategy. Pilot data suggested these strategies interacted with the system parameters, and therefore needed to be studied separately. In Experiment 1 participants had no experience at dictating, whereas in Experiment 2 participants were experienced dictators.

We had several hypotheses:

1. Participants would compose written letters somewhat faster than they would compose letters with the listening typewriter because of their relative unfamiliarity with the latter and because of the lack of easy editing with the listening typewriter simulated here.

2. Participants would compose letters in consecutive word speech faster than in isolated words because of the required pauses in the latter.

3. Quality of letters would be the same with all methods, based upon earlier findings about lack of quality differences among methods of composing [5–7].

4. In the subsequent proofediting stage, there would be more changes made and more time spent on letters composed with the listening typewriter than on letters composed with writ-

ing because of the limited editing capability provided with the former. Also, in this proofediting stage, there would be more changes made and more time spent on letters composed with a first time final strategy because in the latter some of this work was done while composing. Finally, there would be more changes made and more time spent on letters composed with consecutive word speech than on letters composed with isolated words because in the latter the pauses would serve to allow the author to be more careful about sentence construction and word selection.

GENERAL METHOD

General Procedure

Participants learned to use a listening typewriter by watching a 20 minute videotape that showed another author using it. The videotape made reference to one page of editing instructions that participants had in front of them (Appendix A). Participants then practiced composing two to four letters with different versions of the listening typewriter. No mistakes in using the listening typewriter were ever made after two letters.

The formal experiment then started. Participants were given the description of a letter to compose and the method to use to compose it. In each letter, participants tried to convince a recipient of something. These included trying to win a bid for paper supplies and recommending a favorite teacher for an annual award. Participants were allowed to make written notes if they chose. While composing, they were allowed to make any changes they wanted. After composing a letter, participants were given a typed version of it about 20 minutes later and allowed to proofedit it. This was called the Proofediting stage. There was only one redo, or proofediting, of the printed version. While composing, participants were videotaped. The amount of time they actually talked was automatically recorded. [6] When participants finished, they were briefly interviewed about their feelings for that method and they formally rated it.

Simulation of Listening Typewriter

Figure 1 depicts the simulation method. A typist, located in another room, listened to a participant dictate via a closed-circuit TV system and typed what was said. The information typed was not only displayed on the typist's computer-controlled cathode-ray tube (CRT) display terminal (IBM 3277), but also appeared on the participant's terminal (IBM 3277), which was yoked to the typist's through the IBM full screen support system. Specifically, the typist heard a word, typed it, and then hit the "Enter" key on the terminal. The computer then checked whether the word was in the dictionary being simulated. The dictionaries were taken from Kucera and Francis' norms [11] of the most frequently used English words, and were stored in the computer (IBM 168V). If the word was not in the dictionary, XXXX's were displayed on the participant's screen. If it was in the dictionary, the computer then checked whether it was a homophone (or homonym, as such words are usually referred to in the literature). If it was, then the most frequent version of the homophone was displayed, regardless of the version that had been typed.

This was done because we wanted to simulate an "unintelligent" recognition system. These data could then be used as a baseline for comparison with recognition systems of various amounts of "intelligence."

Figure 1. Schematic of the experimental setup.

In simulation of isolated word versions of the listening typewriter, the typist hit the "Enter" key after each word. Participants were instructed not to say the next word until the previous word had been displayed to them. A beep sounded when the word was displayed, so that participants did not always have to look at the screen. There was almost a two-second delay from the time participants began to say a word until they could begin to say the next word. This estimated delay was the sum of the following approximate values: (a) 0.3 sec for a participant to say the word; (b) 1.0 sec for the typist to type the word and press the Enter key; (c) 0.1 sec for the computer to process and display the word; (d) 0.2 sec reaction time for the participant to say the next word. Thus this isolated

word simulator could achieve rates of about 30 wpm.

If a participant said the next word too quickly, an electronic monitoring device detected this and prevented the typist from hearing the next word. In practice this was not necessary, as it almost never happened.

In consecutive word speech, participants could talk as fast as they wanted. They did not have to wait between words. (One participant had to be told to slow down, however, because the typist could not keep up with him.) If a participant was speaking rapidly, the typist would type several words before hitting the Enter key. This had little or no effect on the computer processing time, allowed the typist to get up to speed, and thus allowed the simulator to keep up better with a participant. Presumably, the typist was typing these word strings at about 80 wpm. Thus, the consecutive word speech simulator could achieve rates of 50–60 wpm.

Participants' Editing Commands

Participants spoke each editing or formatting command. The typist typed an abbreviation of it, and its effect was shown on the participants' screen. Participants could use editing commands offering function equivalent to that contained in ordinary dictating equipment. We provided this limited function rather than a more elaborate facility because this was standard, easily describable, required less training of participants, less programming of the simulator, and did not force us to invent an editor for a composing method that did not exist anyway. In addition, the results could serve as a baseline against which to measure editors having more power.

The only way a participant could change what he or she had already said was, in effect, to record over the word. A participant would say "NUTS," which erased the last word shown, and say another word. If a participant wanted to change the fifth to last word, he would say "NUTS 5," which erased the last five words, and then say the new word and the last four words over. If the wrong homophone (e.g., "in" rather than "inn") was displayed, a participant could say "NUTS" and repeat the homophone, which caused a different version of it to appear (regardless of which version the typist typed).

Participants could spell unrecognized words by saying "SPELLMODE," spelling the word, and then saying "END-SPELLMODE." They could capitalize the first letter of a word ("CAPIT") or capitalize all letters of a word ("CAPALL"). They could cause numerals to be displayed ("NUMMODE". . ."END-NUMMODE") rather than the spelled out version of them. They could cause modifications in the formatting of a letter with four commands: "NEWPARA-GRAPH," "NEWLINE," "INDENT N(spaces)," and "SPACE N(spaces)." (The simulator automatically started a new line once the previous line was filled; the NEWLINE command started a new line without the previous line being filled.)

The inside address and return address were supplied for participants on their CRT prior to the beginning of each letter. The CRT could display 20 lines at one time. Once participants had composed a longer letter than this, they could scroll through parts of their letter not dis-played by saying "SCROLL-TOWARD-BEGINNING" and "SCROLL-TOWARD-END."

The Typist

The typist played a critical role in the success of these experiments. Our typist was selected because she typed 80 wpm, was excellent at following the rules of simulation, remained cool, did not provide a participant with any help, and was available for several months. In addition, she was a practicing stenotypist, which gave her experience with transcribing oral material in real time. She also knew shorthand, which was useful in Experiment 2. She practiced with the simulator for two to three weeks prior to the experiments. During this time, several human factors improvements were introduced to lighten her burden, speed overall performance, and make the simulation more compelling. She was particularly accurate at typing exactly what the participant said, including exclamations and parenthetical comments which a participant made to himself. She seemed effective in typing what she heard, even when context suggested that the participant had said a different word. However, she did misspell words occasionally.

EXPERIMENT 1

Method

Participants. Ten people with characteristics similar to many professional, managerial, and technical office workers, spent two days each composing letters. They ranged in age from about 25 to 70. Most had at least a bachelor's degree, four worked for IBM, four were female. The IBMers were volunteers, and the non-IBMers were obtained from a local temporary employment agency.

Letter-tasks. There were ten letter-tasks, or composing assignments. In each a participant composed a letter to convince a recipient of something. Tasks included applying for a job, applying for a grant of money for a favorite project, and recommending a relocation site for one's office.

Composing Methods and Design. Eight composing methods used the listening typewriter. These corresponded to the eight combinations of three variables: speech mode [isolated word *(I)* vs. consecutive word speech *(C)*], vocabulary size [1,000 words *(1)* vs. unlimited *(U)*)], and composing strategy [draft *(D)* vs. first time final *(F)*]. Sometimes a method will be referred to by its initials, for example, *CID* stands for a letter composed in consecutive word speech with the 1,000 word vocabulary with the author using a Draft strategy. With a Draft strategy, participants were instructed to make a quick draft. They were told they could leave unrecognized words on the screen, and make any changes they wished in the subsequent proofediting stage. With a Final strategy, participants were instructed to make the listening typewriter version of their letter as close as possible to the final version of their letter. They were told to remove all unrecognized words by spelling them. They were told they could, however, make any changes they wanted to in the subsequent proofediting stage.

For control or comparison purposes, participants wrote two letters, one when they arrived for the experiment and the other later on during the experiment. Each participant wrote his/her first letter on a different letter-task. The order of the remaining nine composing methods, the order of the letter-tasks, and the combination of the composing methods and letter-tasks were varied from participant to participant, with a 9 x 9 greco-latin square. The tenth participant received another row from a different 9 x 9 square. The use of ten participants let each letter-task be completely balanced with the two written letters and the other eight composing methods.

Performance Evaluation. Participants were told their performance would be evaluated on the time to compose their letters and the resulting effectiveness of them, and that these two factors would be weighted equally. Composition time was measured from when the participant began reading about a letter-task until he or she was finished composing. Effectiveness was rated by three judges (one experimenter and two English teachers) who compared all ten letters written on a particular topic and rank-ordered the best three. Since all letters were essentially requests or recommendations, a judge rated the letters' effectiveness according to how likely he or she would be to grant the request or follow the recommendation. The three judges worked independently.

A letter was assigned an effectiveness score of 10 if it received a first place vote from a judge (i.e., it was the best of 10 letters), 9 if it received a second place vote, and 8 if it received a third place vote. A score of 4 was assigned if it received no vote (4 is the average score if the remaining seven letters had been rank-ordered). The scores for each letter were summed over the three judges, and ranged from 30 for a letter with the three first place votes to 12 for a letter with no votes.

We attempted to weight effectiveness and time equally by transforming the effectiveness scores to have the same mean, same variance, and same range as the time scores, and to go in the same direction as the time scores (i.e., smaller values reflect better performance). We could not achieve all these goals with a single linear transformation. As a compromise, we transformed the effectiveness scores linearly to decrease with greater effectiveness, to have the same mean as the time scores, and to have the same interquartile range as the time scores. The effectiveness scores were calculated with (64 − .5R), where R is the sum of the ratings of the three judges, which varied from 12 to 30.

Preference Rating Scale. After using a version of the listening typewriter, each participant compared it to writing using a seven-point scale, where 1 = significantly worse than writing, 3 = a little worse than writing, 4 = same as writing, 5 = a little better than writing, and 7 = significantly better than writing.

Results

Time and Effectiveness of Letters. Table I shows detailed results for the eight versions of the listening typewriter studied. As shown by the standard errors of the means, composition times and total times were highly variable. Some of this was due to the letter-tasks themselves, which accounted for as much variance as did composition methods. Most individual time scores or effectiveness means in any one row in Table I were not significantly different from each other.

Figure 2 shows that composition times for letters composed with the listening

typewriter under Draft instructions tend to be faster than composition times for written letters, whereas letters composed with the listening typewriter under Final instructions were closer to the times for Written letters. This is consistent with the fact that participants were instructed to compose Written letters with a first time final strategy.

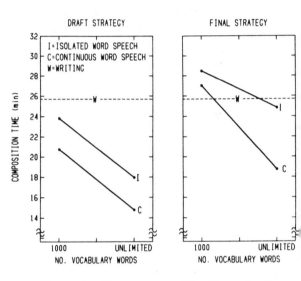

Figure 2. Mean composition times for the composing methods in Experiment 1.

With the listening typewriter, letters composed under Draft instructions were faster than letters composed under first time final instructions [analysis of variance; $F(1,9) = 9.28$; $p < .05$].* Letters composed in consecutive word speech were somewhat faster than letters com-

*For the reader unfamiliar with statistical tests of significance, the p values given following the result of an F-test or an R-analysis estimate the probability that the difference reported is due to chance. For example, a p < .05 provides an estimate that the difference among the scores tested could occur by chance less than 1 out of 20 times.

Table I.
Participants' Mean Composing Time (min.), Mean Effectiveness Arbitrary Units (with lower scores being more effective than higher scores), and Median Preferences (scale of 1–7) in Experiment 1. (W1 = first written letter; W2 = second written letter; I = isolated word speech; C = connected word speech; 1 = 1000 word vocabulary; U = unlimited word vocabulary; D = draft strategy; F = first time final strategy).

	W1	W2	I1D	I1F	IUD	IUF	C1D	C1F	CUD	CUF
Composition time	24.0	26.5	23.8	28.4	18.1	24.8	20.6	27.0	14.7	18.7
(St. Error)	(3.5)	(5.9)	(4.8)	(4.1)	(3.3)	(3.2)	(3.2)	(5.4)	(2.7)	(2.6)
Proofedit time	2.6	2.3	4.0	1.6	3.7	2.1	4.4	1.8	3.7	2.0
(St. Error)	(0.6)	(0.5)	(0.6)	(0.5)	(2.0)	(0.4)	(0.6)	(0.5)	(1.5)	(0.5)
TOTAL TIME	26.6	28.7	27.9	30.0	21.8	26.9	25.0	28.8	18.4	20.7
(St. Error)	(3.7)	(6.3)	(5.2)	(4.5)	(4.7)	(3.5)	(3.3)	(5.8)	(3.9)	(2.8)
Effectiveness	34.2	30.8	31.2	27.8	31.4	28.2	34.8	27.0	34.8	31.2
(St. Error)	(2.6)	(2.9)	(3.5)	(4.6)	(3.3)	(4.3)	(3.5)	(3.8)	(1.8)	(2.4)
Composition time + Effectiveness	29.1	28.6	27.5	28.1	24.7	26.5	27.7	27.0	24.8	25.0
(St. Error)	(2.0)	(2.2)	(2.4)	(2.3)	(1.5)	(2.0)	(2.6)	(2.6)	(1.6)	(1.1)
Total time + Effectiveness	30.4	29.8	29.5	28.9	26.6	27.5	29.9	27.9	26.6	26.0
(St. Error)	(1.9)	(2.4)	(2.5)	(2.3)	(2.1)	(2.0)	(2.6)	(2.7)	(2.1)	(1.1)
Preference Rating re Writing (on 7-pt scale)	—	—	5	6	5	6	5	4	6	6

posed in isolated word speech [$F(1,9)$ = 3.99; p < .10]. Letters composed with an unlimited vocabulary were somewhat faster than letters composed with the 1,000 word vocabulary [$F(1,9)$ = 4.69; p < .10]. When proofediting time was added to composition time, these trends remained about the same (Figure 3).

As shown in Table I, letters composed with a Final strategy were more effective (28.6) than letters composed with a Draft strategy [33.1; $F(1,9)$ = 5.23; p < .05]. Effectiveness was not influenced by speech mode or vocabulary size [analyses of variances; p > .10]. Interjudge reliability on effectiveness of these letters was low.

Figure 4 shows combined performance scores, based upon equal weighting of effectiveness and total time. Combining time scores and effectiveness measures

may seem curious since this is a little like mixing apples and oranges and secondly, they have the opposite polarity (until effectiveness scores are transformed, as explained in the Methods section). However, their combination gives a more complete picture of composing efficiency, and that is why we report the combined scores. Lower scores mean better performance. Although the trends are similar to those for time scores alone, none of the differences shown in Fig. 4 are significant [analyses of variance; all p > .10]. The rank-order correlation, grouped across participants, between the effectiveness of a method and total time spent with that method was not significant (R = −.54; p > .10). (There was a significant negative rank-order correlation between effectiveness and composition time, however; R = −.81; p < .01, that is, methods which led to faster composition times also led to less effective letters.)

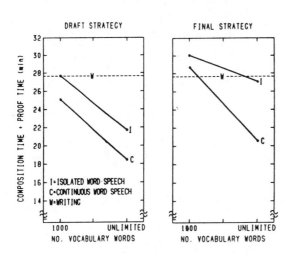

Figure 3. Mean total time (composition time plus proofediting time) for the composing methods in Experiment 1.

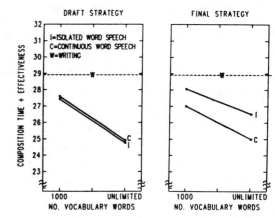

Figure 4. Mean performance scores, based upon equal weighting of composition time and effectiveness for each letter, for the composing methods of Experiment 1. The effectiveness scores have been transformed so that, like the time scores, smaller values are better.

Composition Rate. The mean number of words in a letter did not differ significantly from method to method (Table II; mean = 179 words; analysis of variance; p > .10). (These word counts do not include the 30-word return address and inside address which were supplied to participants.) This implies that differences in composition rate (words/composition time) are mainly due to differences in composition time only. Composition rate was faster for unlimited vocabulary than for limited vocabulary (11.5 vs. 7.1 wpm; $F(1,9) = 46.0$; p < .001). Composition rate was also faster for Draft strategy than for Final strategy (10.6 vs. 8.0 wpm; $F(1,9) = 5.13$; p < .05), but was only somewhat faster for consecutive word speech than for isolated word speech (10.3 vs. 8.3 wpm; $F(1,9) = 4.49$; p < .10).

Differences Among Participants. The range of participants' composition time scores was 10.8–39.8 min. After adding proofediting times to these, the range was 12.2–44.2 min. The variance among participants' total time scores was about seven times greater than the variance among the ten composition methods. There was a significant negative rank-order correlation between the time a participant spent composing letters and the resulting effectiveness of them ($R = -.79$; p < .01), and between a participant's total time and the resulting effectiveness of his or her letters ($R = -.75$; p < .01). Participants, for example, who took relatively long to compose letters had more effective letters than did participants who were faster.

Proofediting. In the proofediting stage, participants were given a printout of their letter about 20 minutes after they had composed it. They spent 2.8 min. proofediting. The quality of their proofediting was poor. Forty-five of 100 letters were left with at least one spelling error. The average was about two spelling errors in these 45 letters. In addition, participants left homophone spelling errors that would rarely occur in more traditional forms of composition (e.g., ". . . body and sole"). Almost no major changes were made. As shown in Table III, only a few changes were made in each letter, except in I1D and C1D where participants spelled out over 20 XXXX's per letter. Most changes were minor rewordings, punctuation, and capitalization.

We expected that there would be more changes to Draft letters than to Final letters. This was not the case, however, as there were fewer changes made in each of nine categories in Table III with the Draft strategy! This may explain why Final letters were judged more effective than *D* letters. Letters composed with *C1D* and *CUD* were proofread especially poorly,

and letters composed with these two methods were rated as least effective. In Written letters, participants made fewer punctuation and capitalization changes, and more minor rewordings, than with the listening typewriter.

Participants' Opinions. Participants compared each method with Writing, on a seven-point scale. Participants varied considerably among themselves on how well they liked individual versions of the listening typewriter. Four participants gave (almost) all versions a rating of 6 ("Better than writing") or 7 ("Significantly better than writing"). Two participants rated most versions less favorably than writing. The remaining participants differentiated more broadly among the methods. As shown in Table I, the median rating of all versions was either 4 ("Same as writing"), 5 ("A little better than writing"), or 6 ("Better than writing").

General Observations. Participants made few notes. They easily learned how to use the listening typewriter. None of

Table II.

Word Analyses Based upon Means of Each Method in Experiment 1. (*W1* = first written letter; *W2* = second written letter; *I* = isolated word speech; *C* = connected word speech; *1* = 1000 word vocabulary; *U* = unlimited word vocabulary; *D* = draft strategy; *F* = first time final strategy).

	W1	W2	I1D	I1F	IUD	IUF	C1D	C1F	CUD	CUF
Number of words in letter	155	200	162	152	174	198	157	186	204	201
Number unrecognized words	(41)	(54)	39	39	(44)	(54)	32	43	(51)	(48)
Number XXXX's left for proofediting	. . .	. . .	22.2	. . .	. . .	. . .	25.7	. . .	. . .	. . .
Percent words in 1000 vocabulary	(74)	(73)	76	74	(75)	(73)	80	77	(75)	(76)
Percent words if 5000 vocabulary	(91)	(91)	(90)	(91)	(92)	(89)	(93)	(91)	(91)	(92)
Composition rate (words per min.)	7.2	8.5	7.2	5.6	12.2	8.4	9.3	6.5	13.9	11.5

Note. The numbers in parentheses in lines 2 and 4 indicate the words that would have been affected if the 1,000 word vocabulary limitation had been applied to those composition methods. The numbers in parentheses in line 5 indicate the percent of words that would have been affected if the 5,000 word vocabulary limitation used in Experiment 2 had been applied to all these composition methods.

them quit the experiment. They had no difficulty giving verbal commands to the simulator while composing. They made almost no mistakes in using it after their first practice letter. They reported feeling no pressure to talk—unlike novices upon first learning to use traditional dictating equipment (see [3]). They did not view this as dictating. Rather they said they could "see their writing." No one reported being frightened of the microphone.

Observations on Methods of Composition

Writing. Participants volunteered that editing, or making changes, was much easier with writing than with a listening typewriter.

Isolated Word Speech/1,000 Word Vocabulary. Behaviorally, participants had little trouble speaking in isolated words. Typically, they would say a word while looking at the screen, wait for it to be displayed, and then say another word. They almost never spoke the next word too soon. Indeed, there often was a pause between when a participant could speak the next word and when he or she actually did speak it. Participants usually looked at the screen while composing, although they could look away and listen for a beep that signalled when they could say the next word.

Participants' comments were mainly negative, with more centering on the limited vocabulary size than on the restriction to speak in isolated words. Twenty-four percent of the words participants used were not recognized (Table II), and XXXX's were therefore displayed. When using a Final strategy, participants became

aggravated at having to spell out about one of every four words. Use of SPELL-MODE "...adds time," "...requires more concentration," and "...is distracting." The limited vocabulary required spelling the more difficult words, and "I'm a poor speller," said one participant. With a Draft strategy, participants were often uncertain about how to handle XXXX's. They could either spell them or leave them to the proofediting stage. Some participants found that if they waited they forgot what a particular XXXX stood for. This was frustrating, as much of the meaning was in these words ("meat words," said one participant). On the average, 22.2 XXXX's were left in these Draft letters, which was about half of the 40 unrecognized words per letter with this version (Table II).

Isolated Word/Unlimited Vocabulary. Participants preferred this method to the 1,000 word vocabulary because there were no XXXX's to handle. Some participants criticized the isolated word restriction, saying that it was "...hard to wait for the beep," it "...interrupts flow," "...interrupts plans," "...doesn't allow cohesive thought." Others said it provided a "nice pace." I "...can choose my words," and "...don't have to think as fast."

The simulator, displaying one word at a time, could handle dictating rates of about 30 wpm. Participants dictated much slower than this (Table II) and did not complain about delays (although, as will be seen, participants in Experiment 2 did complain).

Consecutive Word Speech/1,000 Word Vocabulary. A significant finding was that participants were, in effect, compelled to dictate in isolated words when using this consecutive speech method with a Final strategy. In order to change a word participants had to erase all words said after the one to be changed. Thus, they typically would say a word, wait to see whether it was recognized, and go on to say the next word if it was. If it was not, they would spell the word before saying the next word.

Participants commented mainly on the disadvantages of the 1,000 word vocabulary. With a Draft strategy, they left 25.7 XXXX's, or 70 percent of the words that were not recognized (Table II). "XXXX's are more annoying in consecutive speech," said one participant. "You get ahead," said another, "then you must go back and spell." "I forgot a lot of phrases because of the need to spell," said another. "It's disconcerting not to know the 1,000 words." "It's no good with adjectives," and ". . .anything technical." "I have to look at the screen constantly to fill in words."

Consecutive Word Speech/Unlimited Vocabulary. This is the unachievable ultimate in speech recognition. Typically a participant said a phrase, read it, possibly edited it, paused, said another phrase, etc. Editing was very local, probably influenced by the primitive editing facilities. Participants dictated substantially faster with this version of the listening typewriter than with the others (Table II, mean = 12.7 wpm). They did not, however, dictate as fast as the simulator could go with this method (about 50–60 wpm), or as fast as the rates of 17–25 wpm found with standard dictating equipment. [4]

Unlike with the other three versions, participants' comments centered on composing, not on the listening typewriter itself. "Final strategy is hard work," and "I must think more." "With Draft (as opposed to Final) I get my thoughts down quickly," ". . .could concentrate on content," and ". . .can talk without looking at screen." On the other hand, one participant said, "I didn't notice much difference between Draft and first time Final strategies." Participants mentioned that spelling out XXXX's was compelling even with Draft, that waiting for the machine was disconcerting, and that the conversational tone was more human than they imagined working with computers would be. They said that they were able to visualize their work better than with traditional Writing.

Table III.
Total Number of Changes Made in the Proofediting Stage of the Ten Letters Composed with Each Method in Experiment 1. (*W1* = first written letter; *W2* = second written letter; *I* = isolated word speech; *C* = connected word speech; *1* = 1000 word vocabulary; *U* = unlimited word vocabulary; *D* = draft strategy; *F* = first time final strategy).

	W1	W2	I1D	IUD	I1F	IUF	C1D	CUD	C1F	CUF
Formatting; spacing	6	4	3	1	5	2	4	1	7	2
Spelling	1	4	4	0	0	3	2	1	7	0
Punctuation	2	4	3	3	6	1	2	5	10	6
Minor rewording	29	24	14	6	17	15	19	15	41	11
Major rewording	1	0	2	0	6	1	1	0	4	2
Defining XXXX's	0	0	196	0	0	0	249	0	0	0
Capitalizing	0	4	8	7	36	8	19	0	11	7
Homophones	2	1	4	0	2	1	4	2	7	3
Typos made by the simulator	3	4	1	0	2	1	0	1	1	0
System problems	0	1	2	0	0	2	0	3	6	1

EXPERIMENT 2

This experiment evaluated the use of a listening typewriter by experienced dictators. It compared their performance and attitudes on listening typewriters with their performance and attitudes on dictating to a machine (*DMACH*) and dictating to a secretary taking shorthand (*DSEC*).

We hypothesized that their performance would be at least as good with the more efficient versions of the listening typewriter as with *DMACH*. This was based upon the finding that experienced dictators are 25 percent faster at dictating than at writing [4], and the finding that letters composed with several of the listening typewriters studied in Experiment 1 were composed more than 25 percent faster than were Written letters. We also hypothesized that they would like at least some listening typewriters better than *DMACH* and *DSEC* because they could see what they had said.

The importance of studying experienced dictators was to learn whether they displayed differential performance and attitudes, compared to nondictators, on various versions of the listening typewriter. For example, experience at dictating might enhance performance with a listening typewriter. Also, dictation experience might lead to more positive attitudes about using listening typewriters.

We were particularly interested in carefully assessing the opinions of these participants about different versions of the listening typewriter. We did this in three ways. Participants compared each version of the listening typewriter, just after using it, with their favorite method of composition. Second, after having used all versions of the listening typewriter, participants rank-ordered each version according to which one they would most likely use in real life. Third, at the end of the experiment, participants composed a letter of their own and had to choose a method of composition with which to do it.

We reduced the number of conditions studied because we thought that this might have contributed to the large variance in Experiment 1. Five listening typewriter versions were studied. Four of these were the same as in Experiment 1. Isolated word speech/1,000 word vocabulary (*I1000*) was chosen because it was a minimal version, and consecutive word speech/unlimited word vocabulary (*CU*) was chosen as the ultimate, although unachievable, speech recognition system. The trade-off between vocabulary size and speech mode was assessed by studying *C1000*, *I5000*, and *IU*. Had a 5,000 word vocabulary been used in Experiment 1, about 91 percent of words would have been recognized (Table II), which is what the Kucera and Francis [11] norms predict also.

Method

Participants. Eight IBM executives, all with considerable experience with dictation, spent one day composing eight letters. Most participants were in their thirties, and they ranged in age from 33-52. All had at least a bachelor's degree. They were professionals in marketing requirements for office products.

Composing Methods. Each participant composed a different letter with seven different methods: *I1000*, *I5000*, *IU*, *C1000*, *CU*, dictating to an IBM 6:5 dictating machine (*DMACH*), and dictating to a secretary taking shorthand (*DSEC*). Participants were allowed to use either a Draft or first time Final strategy.

Letter-tasks. Seven of the ten letter-tasks used in Experiment 1 were used here.

Design. The order of the seven composing methods, the order of the seven letter-tasks, and the combination of the composing methods and letter-tasks were varied, from participant to participant, with a *7 x 7* greco-latin square. We were able to obtain an eighth participant, and he received a row from a different *7 x 7* square.

Performance Evaluation. Performance was evaluated just as in Experiment 1.

Preference Rating Scale. Prior to the experiment participants told us their favorite method of composing. Five preferred *DMACH* (oftentimes after writing an outline) and three preferred Writing. After using a version of the listening typewriter, each participant compared it to his or her favorite method of composing on a seven-point scale, where 1 = significantly worse than my favorite method, 3 = a little worse than my favorite method, 4 = same as my favorite method, 5 = a little better than my favorite method, and 7 = significantly better than my favorite method.

Results

Time and Effectiveness of Letters. Figure 5 shows that time scores for *DMACH* and *DSEC* were faster than several versions of the listening typewriter. They were significantly faster than all three isolated word versions [Table IV; $F(6,42) = 19.34$; $p < .001$; Duncan range test; $p < .05$].

I1000 was significantly slower than all methods (Duncan range test; $p < .05$).

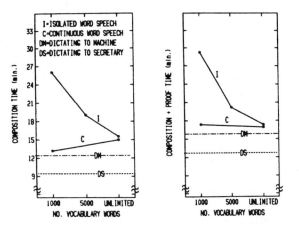

Figure 5. Mean composition times (left panel) and mean total time (composition time plus proofediting time) for the composing methods in Experiment 2.

Figure 5 shows that *C1000* was relatively faster in this experiment than in the previous one. This was due, at least in part, to participants speaking fast, not spelling a large proportion of XXXX's (Table VI), and leaving them until the proofediting stage (see Table IX). Also, letters composed with *C1000* were the least effective (Table IV).

As shown in the right panel of Fig. 5, proofediting time partially compensated for some of the differences in composition times among the methods. The result was that total times (composition time plus proof time) were about the same on four of the listening typewriter versions as on *DMACH* (Table IV). Only *I1000* differed significantly from both controls, as well as from all listening typewriter versions.

Table IV.
Participants' Mean Composing Times (min.) and Mean Effectiveness (arbitrary units) in Experiment 2. (*I* = isolated word speech; *C* = connected word speech; *1* = 1000 word vocabulary; *5* = 5000 word vocabulary; *U* = unlimited word vocabulary; *DMACH* = dictated with dictating equipment; *DSEC* = dictated to a secretary).

	I1000	I5000	C1000	CU	IU	DMACH	DSEC
Composition time	26.0	18.8	13.3	15.2	15.7	12.2	9.2
(St. Error)	(5.2)	(2.6)	(2.9)	(4.6)	(2.6)	(2.7)	(2.5)
Proofedit time	2.9	1.9	4.4	2.5	1.8	3.8	3.0
(St. Error)	(0.9)	(0.7)	(0.7)	(0.4)	(0.4)	(1.0)	(0.7)
TOTAL TIME	28.9	20.7	17.7	17.7	17.5	16.0	12.2
(St. Error)	(4.8)	(2.7)	(2.5)	(5.2)	(2.9)	(3.2)	(3.1)
Effectiveness	14.8	16.1	16.7	13.6	13.1	10.2	11.7
(St. Error)	(1.9)	(2.0)	(1.4)	(2.2)	(2.9)	(2.2)	(2.4)
Composition time +							
Effectiveness	20.4	17.5	15.0	14.4	14.4	11.2	10.4
(St. Error)	(2.0)	(0.9)	(1.6)	(2.1)	(1.2)	(1.3)	(1.0)
Total time +							
Effectiveness	21.8	18.4	17.2	15.7	15.3	13.0	11.9
(St. Error)	(1.9)	(0.9)	(1.5)	(2.3)	(1.3)	(1.4)	(1.2)

Note. Means underlined by the same line in the same row are not significantly different from each other. Means not underlined by the same line in the same row are significantly different from each other at the 0.05 significance level, as measured with Duncan's range test.

There were no significant differences in the effectiveness of the letters composed with different methods of composition (Table IV), and (unlike in Experiment 1) there was no significant rank-order correlation between composition time and effectiveness (Table IV; p > .10). Figure 6 shows the combined score for the total time and effectiveness. Effectiveness was calculated by $(34.4 - 1.5R)$, where R varied from 12 for letters receiving no votes to 23 for a letter receiving two first place votes and one second place vote. The trends in Fig. 6 for the various listening typewriter versions are similar to those of Experiment 1. *I1000, I5000,* and *C1000* all had significantly poorer scores than did *DMACH* and *DSEC* (see Table IV for Duncan range results). *I5000* was not sig-

nificantly different from any listening typewriter version.

Composing with the Listening Typewriter. Table V shows how participants spent their time while composing with the listening typewriter. Two-thirds of their time was spent planning (range = 58 to 78 percent, depending upon method). Planning time was divided into three subtimes (Table V). Prior to actually dictating a letter, participants typically spent about three minutes reading over the description of the letter to be composed, thinking about what they would say, and making notes. While composing, the four participants who made notes spent at least one minute referring to them. The third subtime, other pauses, accounted for the majority of planning time (Table V).

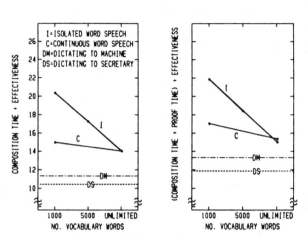

Figure 6. **Mean performance scores, based upon equal weighting of time and effectiveness for each letter, for the composing methods of Experiment 2. The effectiveness scores have been transformed so that, like the time scores, smaller values are better.**

Participants spent 10–18 percent of their composition times actually generating (dictating) their letters. This is a slight overestimate because it includes key words for the editor, for example, "PERIOD," "COMMA." Participants did not appear in the videotapes to spend much time reviewing what they had already said (i.e., reading the screen). These review times may be an underestimate, as we did not include times in this category unless we were certain about them.

The remaining component time identified in Table V is editing or revising time. Editing time is the time taken to revise what has already been said. It is the time from when a participant began saying an editing command until the ef-

fect of that command was displayed, for example, "NUTS"; or until the participant was done with that command, for example, "SPELLMODE . . . END-SPELLMODE." About 21–28 percent of the time was spent editing with the limited vocabulary methods, and about half that was spent editing with the unlimited vocabulary. Editing, as measured here, is a behavioral activity and does not include the time for much of the cognitive activity (presumably included in planning time) during which a decision is reached whether and how to revise.

Table V.
Mean Component Times (min.) in Experiment 2. (*I* = isolated word speech; *C* = connected word speech; *1* = 1000 word vocabulary; *5* = 5000 word vocabulary; *U* = unlimited word vocabulary).

	I1000	I5000	IU	C1000	CU
Planning					
Getting started	3.1	3.7	3.1	2.1	2.4
Looking at notes	1.0	0.9	1.1	0.8	0.8
Pausing	12.0	6.4	8.0	4.1	7.7
Generating	3.3	3.4	1.6	2.1	1.5
Reviewing	0.8	0.4	0.4	0.4	0.4
Editing					
Looking at editing instr.	0.1	0.1	0.1	0.1	0.1
Modifying	5.7	3.9	1.4	3.7	2.3
COMPOSITION TIME	26.0	18.8	15.7	13.3	15.2

The most frequent editing command was "NUTS," as shown in Table VI. More editing was done with limited vocabulary letters than with unlimited vocabulary letters (Table VI), which is consistent with the fact that about twice as much time was spent in editing limited vocabulary letters as unlimited vocabulary letters. Most of the "NUTS" commands were used to erase XXXX's, so that a participant could then spell an unrecognized word. The remainder were used prior to making word substitutions. Most often participants erased just one previous word, but occasionally they erased two or more previous words with a single NUTS command (Table VI). There was more erasing with the limited vocabulary methods than with the unlimited methods because participants would erase XXXX's and then spell the word.

Table VI.
Total Frequency of Use of Editing Commands in the 8 Letters Composed with Each Method in Experiment 2. (*I* = isolated word speech; *C* = connected word speech; *1* = 1000 word vocabulary; *5* = 5000 word vocabulary; *U* = unlimited word vocabulary).

	I1000	I5000	IU	C1000	CU
NUTS	289	87	77	144	54
NUTS 2	9	3	7	13	11
NUTS 3 +	10	6	5	22	16
SPELLMODE	194	69	17	108	16
NUMMODE	8	2	3	4	1
CAPIT	8	1	5	1	—

When participants used SPELLMODE to spell a word, they usually did so after that word was not recognized and they had erased it with the NUTS command. Sometimes, however, they anticipated that a word would not be recognized, and spelled it in advance. Besides the editing commands shown in Table VI, participants also used the punctuation commands (period, comma, etc.) and formatting commands (INDENT, NEWLINE, NEWPARAGRAPH, etc.).

Composition Rate. As shown in Table VII, letters composed with the listening typewriter tended to have fewer words in them than letters composed with traditional dictation methods, particularly with *DMACH* [$F(6,42) = 3.84$; $p < .01$; Duncan range test, $p < .05$]. The difference between *DSEC* and listening typewriters was not statistically significant. Composition rates with *DMACH* and *DSEC* were two to four times faster than composition rates with the listening typewriter [Table VII; $F(6,42) = 16.4$; $p < .001$]. As shown in Table VII, the 15 wpm composition rates for *CU* and *C1000* were about twice as fast as the 8 wpm composition

Table VII.
Word Analyses Based upon Means of Each Method in Experiment 2. (*I* = isolated word speech; *C* = connected word speech; *1* = 1000 word vocabulary; *5* = 5000 word vocabulary; *U* = unlimited word vocabulary; *DMACH* = dictated with dictating equipment; *DSEC* = dictated to a secretary).

	I1000	I5000	C1000	CU	IU	DMACH	DSEC
Number of words in letter	155	146	143	168	152	250	206
Number unrecognized words	39	34	32	(41)	(38)	(63)	(52)
Number XXXX's left for proofediting	15.8	4.8	4.8	. . .	. . .	. . .	. . .
Percent words in 1000 vocabulary	74	(76)	77	(75)	(75)	(75)	(75)
Percent words in 5000 vocabulary	90	91	(92)	(90)	(92)	(91)	(91)
Composition rate (words per min.)	7.5	8.4	14.1	15.8	10.2	24.8	30.1

Note. The numbers in parentheses in lines 2 and 4 indicate the words that would have been affected if the 1,000 word vocabulary limitation had been applied to those composition methods. The numbers in parentheses in line 5 indicate the percent of words that would have been affected if the 5,000 word vocabulary limitation had been applied to all those composition methods.

rates for *I1000* and *I5000*. Composition rate for *DMACH* was about that found in earlier experiments on dictation (25.2 wpm) [4].

Participants' Opinions. After using each method, participants compared that method with their favorite method of composition (specified before the experiment). Table VIII shows that *CU* was rated higher than participants' favorite method, whereas *I1000* and *C1000* were rated lower. Participants said they did not like these two methods because they were slow and distracting. *IU* and *I5000* were rated equivalent to their favorite method.

Although these ratings were favorable for three of the five listening typewriter versions, participants' remarks after rating each one were generally not enthusiastic—even for *CU* which received a rating of 6. The gist of most remarks was to point out weaknesses. Their views seemed stronger, more assured, and more authoritative than did those of the participants in Experiment 1. Two negative opinions were voiced strongly by nearly every participant: the discomfort in dealing with XXXX's and the perceived slowness of composing with listening typewriters, compared to *DMACH*. This apparent slowness was perceived to be affected by both (a) speaking in isolated words and (b) use of a limited vocabulary, which introduced uncertainty about whether a word would be recognized and sometimes required spelling it out. Participants reported that these problems sometimes led to losing their train of thought. Thus, these experienced dictators were more critical of the listening typewriters than were the inexperienced dictators.

The most frequently cited advantages of the listening typewriter were seeing what one said and lack of need to spell (recognized words) as one must with traditional handwriting. Some participants volunteered that they had for years secretly worried about spelling words correctly and a listening typewriter relieved them of this concern.

No mention was made about any lack of realism in the experimental environment, simulation, or letters. Although no reference was made directly to a slow response time computer, participants did say that the listening typewriters themselves were slow.

Table VIII.

Participants' Mean Opinions About Different Versions of the Listening Typewriter Used in Experiment 2. (*I* = isolated word speech; *C* = connected word speech; *1* = 1000 word vocabulary; *5* = 5000 word vocabulary; *U* = unlimited word vocabulary; *DMACH* = dictated with dictating equipment; *DSEC* = dictated to a secretary).

	I1000	I5000	C1000	CU	IU	DMACH	DSEC
Rating re previous favorite method	2.0	3.5	2.5	6.0	4.0	4.0	3.5
Median rank	5th	3rd	4th	1st	2nd	. . .	. . .
No. participants choosing this method	. . .	. . .	. . .	5	1	1	. . .

Note. Preference rating is based upon participants comparing each method with their previous favorite composing method on a 7-point scale, where 1 = significantly worse than my favorite method and 7 = significantly better than my favorite method. Seven participants composed a letter with a method of their own choice, whereas one did not have time to do this. She indicated that she would have written her letter, however.

After the experiment, participants rank-ordered the five listening typewriter versions with respect to which "one you would most often use if it were conveniently available to you." Table VIII shows that, based upon the median ranks, the methods were ordered, from most likely to be used to least likely, *CU, IU, I5000, C1000,* and *I1000.* Four participants gave exactly this ranking, and three of the other four ranked the first three exactly this way.

Afterwards, when asked to compose a letter that they needed in their business or personal life, five participants chose to compose with *CU,* one chose *IU,* one chose *DMACH,* and the remaining participant did not have time to do this task. She indicated she would have chosen *W,* however.

Differences Among Participants. The variance among individual participants' time scores was about half that of Experiment 1. It was 2.5 times the variance among the seven methods of composition. The range of composition time scores was 6.6 to 34.1 min., and the range of the total time scores was 9.6 to 38.0 min. As in Experiment 1, participants who took longer to compose their letters had more effective letters (Spearman rho rank-order correlation = $-.90$; p < .01). There was a similar negative rank-order correlation (rho = $-.86$; p < .01) between total time and effectiveness.

Proofediting. Participants spent 2.9 min. proofediting. They made few major changes. They detected fewer than half of the misspellings, leaving spelling errors in 22 of the 56 letters. In letters composed with the limited vocabulary listening typewriters, they had to define 24 XXXX's in *C1000,* 16 in *I1000,* and 5 in *I5000* (Table IX) in the Proofediting stage. Aside from this, they made about seven minor changes (punctuation, capitalization, formatting, homophones, minor rewordings) per letter composed with the listening typewriter, and about 10 per letter composed with *DMACH* and *DSEC* (Table IX).

DISCUSSION

In Experiment 1 participants' performance (combined time and effectiveness) with all

Table IX.
Total Number of Changes Made During Proofediting Stage in Experiment 2 to the 8 Letters Composed with Each Method. (*I* = isolated word speech; *C* = connected word speech; *1* = 1000 word vocabulary; *5* = 5000 word vocabulary; *U* = unlimited word vocabulary; *DMACH* = dictated with dictating equipment; *DSEC* = dictated to a secretary).

	I1000	I5000	C1000	CU	IU	DMACH	DSEC
Formatting: spacing	0	1	1	4	0	6	3
Spelling	2	0	0	2	1	1	0
Punctuation	4	5	5	8	9	22	13
Minor rewording	17	7	28	18	17	44	33
Major rewording	0	1	1	2	1	2	5
Defining XXXX's	127	39	180	0	0	0	0
Capitalizing	2	8	19	31	22	12	9
Homophones	2	0	1	9	4	1	0
Typos made by the simulator	0	0	0	7	1	0	0
System problems	0	0	0	0	0	0	0

versions of the listening typewriter was at least as good as with Writing (Fig. 4). This was true even though participants (a) had no experience at using the listening typewriter; (b) had only primitive editing tools; and (c) had never dictated a letter before. In Experiment 2, the performance of experienced dictators was better (but not significantly so) than the performance of the inexperienced dictators in Experiment 1. The experienced dictators performed as well with some versions of the listening typewriter as with traditional dictation methods. The picture that emerges, then, is that all versions of the listening typewriter tested lie, for first time users, somewhere between the traditional methods of writing and dictating.

Why was this so? A main reason that several versions of the listening typewriter were faster than Written letters was because participants used a Draft strategy with them and used a Final strategy with Written letters (Fig. 2). Two reasons why some versions of the listening typewriter were slower than *DMACH* and *DSEC* was because participants often waited with the slower versions of the listening typewriter and spent more time changing what they had already said. Measured in several different ways, participants preferred most versions of the listening typewriter, particularly those with unlimited vocabulary, to traditional methods of composing.

The gap between Written letter times in Experiment 1 (25.3 min.) and *DMACH* times in Experiment 2 (12.2 min.) was greater than expected on the basis of earlier work [4]. That study showed, for experienced dictators, that *DMACH* required about 80 percent of the time that Written letters did (rather than 50 percent as found here).

Why this larger than expected gap? One possibility is that the present study is correct in showing that *DMACH* is twice as fast as *W*—at least for letters of this type. This is certainly understandable given the 500 percent difference in potential output rates (see [4]). Consistent with this notion is that *DMACH* letters were even longer than Written letters.

A second possibility is that the gap between Written and *DMACH* letters is narrower than what the present experiments showed. Perhaps participants in Experiment 1 were simply slower composers than participants in Experiment 2. Consistent with this is that participants in Experiment 1 (mean = 22.0 min.) were somewhat slower, on the average, at composing than were participants in Experiment 2 (mean = 17.6 min.) on the four versions of the listening typewriter that both groups used in common, although this difference was not significant [$F(1,16)$ = 1.02; p < .10]. A similar difference was found for wpm (Tables II and IV). In the earlier work a "within subject" design was used which prevented intergroup differences from arising. If the gap is, in fact, narrower, then either Written letter composition time is overestimated, *DMACH* time is underestimated, or both. Written letter times may be overestimated here since wpm for Written letters (7.9) were less than those found previously for written letters of this type (12.8 wpm in [6]; and 13.0 wpm in [7]). It is also possible, but less likely, that *DMACH* composition time is underestimated here. Participants in the earlier experiment [4] used a Final strategy with both Written and *DMACH* letters. Here they used a Final strategy with Written letters (as instructed), but apparently used a Draft strategy with *DMACH* (where they had a choice of strategies). This is supported from their comments and from the fact that they made about 10 changes per letter in the Proofediting stage with *DMACH* letters (Table IX), which is more than in the earlier experiments on *DMACH* letters. [4] However, this argument of explaining some of the gap between Written and *DMACH* letters in terms of different strategies is weakened by the fact that the composition rate for *DMACH* letters (24.8 wpm) is not much higher than that found previously for *DMACH* letters when participants were using a Final strategy. [4]

At any rate, these speculations are somewhat idle because we are talking about composition method means that have large standard errors—much greater than in our previous studies of writing, dictating, speaking, and textediting.

Knowing how to dictate did not enhance performance with the listening typewriter. We found no qualitative differences in the performances of the two groups of participants on the versions of the listening typewriter which they used in common, and their composing times did not differ significantly [$F(1,16) = 1.02$; p > .10]. The experienced dictators were much more aware of and concerned about sometimes being slowed down, however.

Wpm composition rate was affected by all three variables studied. Summed over results in both experiments, composition rate was 40 percent faster for unlimited vocabulary than for limited vocabularies (12.0 vs. 8.4 wpm) primarily because participants had to spell 25 percent of the words in the former. It was also faster for consecutive word speech than for isolated word speech (11.8 vs. 8.5 wpm) primarily because participants had to wait between

words with the latter. It was also faster for Draft than for Final (Experiment 1; 10.7 vs. 8.0 wpm) because participants could leave unspelled words in Draft letters and because they spent less time planning (presumably) their word selection.

The finding that letters composed with a Final strategy take more time than letters composed with a Draft strategy suggests that more time is spent planning them, which is exactly what occurred in Experiment 1. Further, participants spelled all unrecognized words when composing letters with a Final strategy but spelled only some of them when composing letters with a Draft strategy. In addition, the proofedited versions of the letters composed with a Final strategy were judged to be more effective than the proofediting versions of letters composed with a Draft strategy.

The lack of differences in the percent of recognized words with the limited vocabulary listening typewriter, compared to *W, DMACH, DSEC,* and the unlimited vocabulary listening typewriters (Tables II, V), suggests participants did not (successfully) use a different vocabulary to avoid XXXX's—even though some suggested they were trying to do so.

One might think that people's performance would improve with additional experience in using the listening typewriter and with additional editing capability. Perhaps the limited editing capability had more serious consequences for the versions of the listening typewriter which fared relatively poorly than for those which fared better, since the letters composed with the latter probably required less editing.

Of theoretical interest, this experiment demonstrates what we found in earlier studies of dictation, namely, that people can rapidly learn to use oral language (required in using a listening typewriter) to mimic their written language (produced to be read). This finding shows the adaptability of human language, and indicates that differences between written and oral language are differences in practice and not in principle.

Differences Between the Two Groups of Participants

The experienced dictators, who in real life have responsibility for recommending the characteristics that office products should have, were more critical of the listening typewriter than were the other participants. They felt strongly about the need for a faster system, whereas participants in Experiment 2 said little about this. Both groups disliked the XXXX's. In addition, the experienced dictators viewed using a listening typewriter as dictating, whereas the nondictators of Experiment 1 thought of it as being able to see their writing.

Observations About This Simulation Technique

This simulation was extremely compelling. Once participants began the experiment, they seemed to think about and refer to what they were working with as a real system. No references were ever made to a typist, but rather to "it," or "the system," or "the computer." Midway through the experiment we reminded participants about the simulation and, in case they had not already surmised, revealed the facts about a human typist being involved. Most were surprised; some even

tried to explain why this could not be the case. The fact that the typist and the computer program followed consistent rules, especially with the use of homophones, contributed to this feeling. We have simulated user interfaces prior to their being built before (e.g., [8, 15]). When done while a language or technology is still evolving, such human factors efforts can be supportive to and guide the direction of development. They can provide critical contributions, perhaps gained no other way, to the design of tools for people that will be useful and usable.

Implications for Speech Recognition Systems

The present simulation serves to organize and structure the human factors issues for speech recognition research aimed at developing a listening typewriter. People will probably be able to compose letters with listening typewriters at least as efficiently as with traditional methods. Even with the little editing capability used here, they are preferred to traditional methods. A listening typewriter can lead to productivity increases in the office with a clear displaceable cost because no typing may be required. In addition, it would lead to productivity increases in the organization because faster distribution of documents is possible, due to the document being in machine readable form immediately upon creation. Further, there is undoubtedly some value to an author in having a final typed version as soon as he or she is done composing.

Participants felt *CU* and *IU* were the versions they would most like to have themselves. But unlimited vocabulary is theoretically impossible in a real system.

Participants were clear in their dislike for *I1000* and *C1000* for composing letters. Participants felt vocabulary size was more important than speech mode. They felt that *I5000* would be a better system to compose with than *C1000*. The implications of the present experiments, in the absence of data on *C5000,* is that an *I5000* listening typewriter, which participants rate as almost equivalent to their favorite composing method today, would be a good target system to try to build. However, as participants clearly stated, they should be able to dictate more rapidly than they could with the isolated word speech system stimulated in this study.

A note of caution is necessary here. There was a lack of enthusiasm in participants' comments in Experiment 2 about using a listening typewriter. Similarly, while the experiments were going on, no one familiar with them tried to convince us to let them use the system to compose letters of their own. Thus, the evidence presented here should not be taken as convincing that an *I5000* system would be in high demand if it were available. Work needs to be done to determine if a faster *I5000* system would be more in demand.

It appeared from experienced dictators' comments that they saw a major difference between a hit rate of 91 percent and a hit rate of 100 percent. An increase in system speed might reduce some of this attitudinal difference, since speed was a big concern of these experienced dictators. Perhaps the vocabulary could be customized to reduce unrecognized words. Or, perhaps an author's spoken version of each unrecognized word could be stored and replayed upon demand, which would eliminate participants concern about not remembering what they had said. Welch

(as cited by [1]) is evaluating image interpreters using a combination of speech recognition and typing (unrecognized words) for vocabularies of up to 1,000 words. We suspect that an improved editing system would not have helped participants' performance much, but would have made them feel even more positive toward a listening typewriter.

Some limitations of these experiments are that it was possibly a slow system, had limited editing capability, and studied only one type of letter. Participants did not compose letters in the course of their own work, and we were unable to assess the value to them of having a typed (or final) copy when they completed composing.

This simulation differed in several ways from what a potential listening typewriter might likely be. The required pauses in isolated word speech were longer, by perhaps a factor of 5 or 10, than what they may have to be. In isolated word speech, each word was displayed just after it was said, whereas some possible language models might want to postpone deciding upon what the word just said is until the speaker says a few more words. There were no "false recognitions" (except for typos and for homophones). A word was either "recognized" and printed correctly or XXXXs were displayed. The "processing delay" (the typing time in this simulation) might be different. Editing capability will almost certainly be more powerful with an actual listening typewriter.

CONCLUSIONS

Isolated word speech with large vocabularies may be nearly as good as connected speech systems for a listening typewriter.

An imperfect listening typewriter is a potentially useful composition tool. With respect to the hypothesis stated in the Introduction, participants did not compose written letters faster than they composed letters with most versions of the listening typewriter. Participants generally composed letters faster with connected speech than with isolated word speech, and this difference was accounted for mainly by the pauses required with isolated word speech. Quality of the letters were generally the same with all letters, except that letters composed with a first time final strategy were of somewhat higher quality than those composed with a draft strategy. The participants were careless proofediting, regardless of composing method. There were only a few changes in each letter during proofediting except in those letters which contained words that were not recognized during composition. Years of experience at dictating did not lead to significantly faster composition with the listening typewriter, in part perhaps because the experienced dictators sometimes reported being frustrated by being slowed down by listening typewriters.

APPENDIX: INSTRUCTIONS FOR USING A LISTENING TYPEWRITER

I. How do I start?
SAY "START" AND BEGIN TALKING

II. How do I change what I said?
ERASE and DICTATE
Say: "Nuts 3" to erase last three words on the screen
Re-dictate

III. How do I punctuate?
USE PUNCTUATION KEYWORDS

Apostrophe	Quotation Mark
Hyphen	Period
Question Mark	Number Sign
Comma	Right Parentheses
Percent Sign	Semicolon
Left Parentheses	Dollar Sign
Colon	Exclamation Point

IV. What if the word I say is not recognized? ERASE and SPELL THE WORD
Say: "Nuts" to erase that word
Say: "Spellmode" to enter spelling mode
Say: The characters you want, for example, "i" "n" "k" for "ink"
(You do not need to pause between letters when you spell.)
Say: "Endspellmode" to leave spell mode

V. What if the sound I say is shown by the wrong spelling?
(for example, "sell" rather than "cell") ERASE and SAY THE WORD AGAIN
Say: "Nuts" to erase that word
Say: The same sound again

VI. How do I capitalize?
USE CAPIT AND SAY THE WORD
Say: "Capit" to capitalize the next word
Say: The word you wish capitalized or
Say: "Capall" to capitalize the entire word

VII. How do I format?
USE FORMATTING KEYWORDS

New Paragraph	Begin a new paragraph
Newline n	Begin a new line n lines down
Indent n	Indent n spaces from the left
Space n	Leave n spaces (plus normal spacing)

VIII. What if I want numbers?
USE NUMBER MODE
Say: "Nummode" to enter number mode
Say: The number you want, for example, "1" "." "9" "5" for "1.95"
Say: "Endnummode" to leave the number mode

IX. What if I want to review part of my letter not shown on the screen?
SAY "SCROLL-TOWARD-BEGINNING" or "SCROLL-TOWARD-END"

REFERENCES

[1]   Beek, B., F. Cupples, J. Nelson, J. Woodard, and R. Vonusa. "Trends and Application of Automatic Speech Technology." In S. Harris, ed. *Proceedings of Symposium on Voice-Interactive Systems: Applications and Payoffs.* Dallas, Tx., 1980, pp. 63-72.

[2]   Doddington, G.R., and T.B. Schalk. "Speech Recognition: Turning Theory to Practice." *IEEE Spectrum,* Vol. 18, No. 9 (September 1981), pp. 26-32.

[3]   Gould, J.D. "An Experimental Study of Writing, Dictating, and Speaking." In J. Requin, ed. *Attention and Performance VII.* Hillsdale, N.J.: Lawrence Erlbaum Associates, 1978, pp. 299-319.

[4]   _____. "How Experts Dictate." *Journal of Experimental Psychology: Human Perception and Performance,* Vol. 4, No. 4 (1978), pp. 648-61.

[5]   _____. "Experiments on Composing Letters: Some Facts, Some Myths, and Some Observations." In I. Gregg and I. Steinberg, eds. *Cognitive Processes in Writing.* Hillsdale, N.J.: Erlbaum and Associates, 1980, pp. 98-127.

[6]   _____. "Writing and Speaking Letters and Messages." *International Journal Man-Machine Studies,* Vol. 16 (1982), pp. 147-71.

[7]   _____. "Composing Letters with Computer-Based Text Editors." *Human Factors,* Vol. 23 (1981), pp. 593-606.

[8]   _____, and S.J. Boles. *Human Factors Challenges in Creating a Principal Support Office System—The Speech Filing System Approach.* IBM Research Report, RC-9788, 1982.

[9]   Harris, S., ed. *Proceedings of Symposium on Voice-Interactive Systems: Applications and Payoffs.* Dallas, Tx., 1980.

[10]   Kato, Y. "NEC Connected Speech Recognition System." Unpublished manuscript, 1980.

[11]   Kucera, H., and W.N. Francis. *Computational Analysis of Present-Day American English.* Providence, R.I.: Brown University Press, 1967.

[12]   Moshier, S.L., R.R. Osborn, J.M. Baker, and J.K. Baker. "Dialog Systems Automatic Speech Recognition Capabilities—Present and Future." In S. Harris, ed. *Proceedings of Symposium on Voice-Interactive Systems: Applications and Payoffs.* Dallas, Tx., 1980, pp. 163-87.

[13]   Poock, G.K. *A Longitudinal Study of Computer Voice Recognition Performance and Vocabulary Size.* Naval Postgraduate School Report, NPS55-81-013, Monterey, Calif. 93940, 1981.

[14]   Robinson, A.L. "More People Are Talking to Computers as Speech Recognition Enters the Real World." *Science,* Vol. 203, 1979, pp. 634-38.

[15]   Thomas, J.C., and J.D. Gould. *A Psychological Study of Query-By-Example.* IBM Research Report, RC-5124, 1974.

27

Editors' Note
Heckbert: "Ray Tracing Jell-O Brand Gelatin"

Insight: We all need a good giggle sometimes. This is the best one of the decade.

In our book *Peopleware,* we mentioned a lunch-time conversation at our office on the topic of what is funny, and what isn't. For instance, we concluded that chickens are funny, but horses aren't. Mr. Heckbert has hit upon several things that are screamingly funny: Jell-O®, hairy mathematics, and the format of most journal articles.*

Our hats are off to the ACM for publishing this beauty in their flagship journal. We are sure that there were some people out there who were very unhappy about the use of the pages in the *Communications of the ACM.* Ignore 'em if they can't take a joke.

---

*Jell-O is a registered trademark of General Foods.

27

Ray Tracing Jell-O Brand Gelatin
by Paul S. Heckbert

Ray tracing has established itself in recent years as the most general image-synthesis algorithm. [10] Researchers have investigated ray-surface intersection calculations for a number of surface primitives. These have included checkerboards [Whitted 80]; chrome balls [Whitted 80]; glass balls [Whitted 80]; robot arms [Barr 82]; blue abstract things [Hanrahan 82]; more glass balls [Watterberg 83]; mandrills [Watterberg 83]; more mandrills [Sweeney 83]; green fractal hills [Kajiya 83]; more glass balls [SEDIC 83]; aquatic blobby things [Kaw 83]; more chrome balls [Heckbert 83]; pool balls [Porter 84]; more glass balls [Kajiya 86].

Unfortunately, *nobody* has ray traced any food. So far, the most realistic foods were Blinn's classic orange and strawberry images, but these were created with a scanline algorithm [2]. The *Dessert Realism Project* at Pixar is addressing this problem. This article presents new technology for ray tracing a restricted class of dessert foods, in particular Jell-O®–brand gelatin. We believe this method may have application to other brands of gelatin and, perhaps, pudding as well.

This article is divided into three parts: methods for modeling static Jell-O, simulation of Jell-O motion using impressive mathematics, and ray-Jell-O intersection calculations.

JELL-O SHAPE

To model static Jell-O, we employ a new synthesis technique wherein attributes are added one at a time using abstract object-oriented classes we call *ingredients*. Ingredient attributes are combined during a preprocessing pass to accumulate the desired set of material properties (consistency, taste, torsional strength, flame resistance, refractive index, etc.). We use the RLS orthogonal basis (raspberry, lime, and strawberry, from which any type of Jell-O can be synthesized [9]).

Ingredients are propagated through a large 3-D lattice using vectorized pipeline SIMD parallel processing in a systolic array architecture that we call the *Jell-O Engine*. Furthermore, we can compute several lattice points simultaneously. Boundary conditions are imposed along free-form surfaces to control Jell-O shape, and the ingredients are mixed using *relaxation* and *annealing* lattice algorithms until the matrix is chilled and *ready-to-eat*.

JELL-O DYNAMICS

Previous researchers have observed that, under certain conditions, Jell-O *wiggles* [8]. We have been able to simulate these unique and complex Jell-O dynamics using spatial deformations [1] and other hairy mathematics. From previous research with rendering systems, we have learned that a good dose of gratuitous partial differential equations is needed to meet the paper quota for impressive formulas.

Therefore, we solve the Schrödinger wave equation for the Jell-O field $\mathbf{J}$:

$$\nabla^2\mathbf{J} + \frac{2m}{\hbar}\,(E - V)\mathbf{J} = 0.$$

Transforming to a spherical coordinate system [7],

$$\nabla\mathbf{J} = \xi_x\frac{\delta\mathbf{J}}{\delta r} + \xi_y\frac{1}{r}\frac{\delta\mathbf{J}}{\delta\theta} + \xi_z\frac{1}{r\sin\theta}\frac{\delta\mathbf{J}}{\delta\phi}$$

$$\nabla^2\mathbf{J} = \frac{1}{r^2}\frac{\delta}{\delta r}\left(r^2\frac{\delta\mathbf{J}}{\delta r}\right) + \frac{1}{r^2\sin\theta}\frac{\delta}{\delta\theta}\left(\sin\theta\frac{\delta\mathbf{J}}{\delta\theta}\right)$$
$$+ \frac{1}{r^2\sin^2\theta}\frac{\delta^2\mathbf{J}}{\delta\phi^2}.$$

Fuller has given a concise and lucid explanation of the derivation from here:

The "begetted" eightness as the system-limit number of the nuclear uniqueness of self-regenerative symmetrical growth may well account for the fundamental octave of unique interpermutative integer effects identified as plus one, plus two, plus three, plus four, as the interpermuted effects of the integers one, two, three, and four, respectively; and as minus four, minus three, minus two, minus one, characterizing the integers five, six, seven, and eight, respectively [3].

In other words, to a first approximation:

$\mathbf{J} = 0.$
The Jell-O® Equation

RAY-JELL-O INTERSECTION CALCULATION

The ray-Jell-O intersection calculations fortunately require the solution of integral equations and the simulation of Markov chains [6], so they cannot be computed efficiently. In fact, we have proved that their solution is linear-time reducible to the traveling-salesman problem, where n is the number of Jell-O molecules, so we can be sure that ray tracing Jell-O will be practical only on a supercomputer. [5]

IMPLEMENTATION

A preliminary implementation has been completed on a VAX 11/780 running the UNIX® operating system. To create a picture using the full Jell-O Engine simulation, we estimate that 1 CPU eon of CRAY time and a lot of hard work would be required. We made several simplifying approximations, however, since the article is due today. As a first approximation, we have modeled a gelatin cube governed by the first-order Jell-O equation with judiciously selected surface properties; that is, color = (0, 255, 0).

Work is underway on a complete Jell-O Engine implementation in Lisp *flavors*. We will shortly begin computing a 100-by-100 image of a bowl of lime Jell-O using a roomful of Amigas. [4] The picture should be ready in time for SIGGRAPH with hours to spare.

CONCLUSIONS

Jell-O goes well with a number of other familiar objects, including mandrills, glass balls, and teapots. The composition and animation possibilities are limited only by your imagination (personal communication by Lance Williams, 1980). The Dessert Foods Division is generalizing the methods described here to other brands of gelatin. Further research areas include the development of algorithms for ray tracing puddings and other dessert foods. Another outstanding problem is the suspension of fruit in Jell-O, in particular, fresh pineapple and kiwifruit.

Jell-O is:

- visually appealing
- futuristic
- hydrodynamically captivating
- tasty
- goes well with other objects

REFERENCES

[1]   Barr, A.H. "Ray Tracing Deformed Surfaces." *SIGGRAPH 86 Proceedings,* Vol. 20, No. 4 (August 1986), pp. 287-96.

[2]   Blinn, J.F. "Computer Display of Curved Surfaces." Ph.D thesis. Computer Science Dept., University of Utah, Salt Lake City, 1978.

[3]   Fuller, R.B. *Synergetics.* New York: Macmillan, 1975, p. 125.

[4]   Graham, E. "Graphic Scene Simulations," *Amiga World* (May-June 1987), pp. 18-95.

[5]   Haeberli, P., and P. Heckbert. "A Jell-O Calculus." *ACM Transactions on Graphics* (special issue on ray tracing moist surfaces). Submitted 1872. To be published.

[6]   Kajiya, J.T. "The Rendering Equation." *SIGGRAPH 86 Proceedings,* Vol. 20, No. 4 (August 1986), pp. 143-50.

[7]   Plastock, R.A., and G. Kalley. *Schaum's Outline of Computer Graphics.* New York: McGraw-Hill, 1986.

[8]   Sales, S. *The Soupy Sales Show,* 1966.

[9]   Weller, T. *Science Made Stupid.* Boston: Houghton Mifflin, 1985.

[10]   Whitted, T. "An Improved Illumination Model for Shaded Display," *Communications of the ACM,* Vol. 23, No. 6 (June 1980), pp. 343-49.

28

Editors' Note
Curtis: "Fifteen Years of Psychology in Software Engineering: Individual Differences and Cognitive Science"

Insight: Cognitive science provides some clues about how an expert programmer got to be just that, and what an expert does that elevates his performance far above the norm.

Curtis gives a succinct introduction to the important work of cognitive science in the area of software development. He touches on the impact of cognitive science on all matters of daily work: the effect of response time on performance, the behavior of expert programmers and how CASE tools could assist, the "chunking" of information, and the construction of reusable software components.

If you are intrigued by this overview, you might want to explore further in the area, guided by the paper's excellent reference section. By the way, Bill Curtis is also a provocative and entertaining speaker. Don't miss any opportunity to hear him.

28

Fifteen Years of Psychology in Software Engineering: Individual Differences and Cognitive Science
by Bill Curtis

PARADIGMS IN SEARCH OF A FIELD

Since the 1950s psychologists have studied the behavioral aspects of software engineering. However, the results of their research have never been organized into a subfield of either software engineering or psychology. This failure results from the difficulty of integrating theory and data from the mixture of paradigms borrowed from psychology. The behavioral studies performed by computer scientists have been criticized by Brooks (1980) and Sheil (1981) for a lack of experimental rigor. Although they occasionally scoured the fine print to uncover something about each study to condemn, the gist of their remarks is well taken.

Every psychological study portrays a paradigm, a model of what the investigator believes is really important in human behavior. When the choice of paradigms is unconscious, investigators are often faced with defending their hypotheses with data which do not address the argument. The motley body of psychological studies on programming has been guided by numerous psychological paradigms, among them individual differences, human factors, cognitive science, group behavior, and organizational behavior. These paradigms represent different ways of

looking at human beings, and differ in the aspects of human behavior they explain. Due to the limited space in the conference proceedings, only contributions from the individual differences and cognitive science areas will be reviewed. See Curtis (1981a,b) for reviews of research from other psychological paradigms.

Individual Differences

In the beginning was the need to hire the best person for the job. Programmers had always differed from each other in large ways, especially in their ability to write programs which optimized the precious resources of the machine. Since programming was a mental activity, it stood to reason that tests of cognitive ability should predict who would make the best programmers. However, measurement was difficult when the phenomena underlying the performance of a skill were unobservable, such as with mental abilities.

To measure mental abilities, a task must be devised which exercises the theoretical mental construct. The critical factors for this approach are:

1) a clear definition of the mental construct,

2) a carefully developed performance scale, and

3) a scientifically sound validation of both the construct and the scale.

The best known of the early tests used to predict programmer performance was the IBM Programmer Aptitude Test (PAT). This test contained three tasks which required job candidates to figure out the next number in a series, figure out analogies represented in figures, and solve arithmetic problems. These tasks were fine measures of mental abilities and could be used to select people for almost any white collar job in the company. Unfortunately, the relationships between this test battery and the job performance of programmers were often quite low (Reinstedt, 1966). Often these low correlations reflected little more than the well-known failure of managerial performance ratings to accurately represent individual performance. Even worse, experience in having taken the test improved subsequent scores (not a desired characteristic for a measure of native intellectual capacity). There were two reasons managers continued using tests of questionable validity:

1) they could shift responsibility for hiring decisions from themselves to the test, and

2) even with their weaknesses the tests were probably better judges of programming potential than were many managers.

Programmer selection testing had already fallen into disfavor by the Garmisch conference. This initial attempt of psychologists to aid software engineering had failed poorly not because the principles and technologies of psychology were not up to the task, but because the psychologists involved took the easy road out. Psychologists failed to adequately model the mental and behavioral aspects of programming before selecting tests to measure it.

Nevertheless, individual differences in performance among programmers remained a critical problem on programming projects. Sackman, Erickson, and Grant (1968) produced data displaying a 28:1 range in debugging performance. However, their data were confounded by the use of different programming languages. I subsequently reported debugging data collected with my colleagues at GE (Curtis, 1981c) which displayed 23:1 differences without confounding factors. Boehm (1981) reported that differences in personnel and team capability was the most significant factor affecting programming productivity in his multi-year cost estimating study at TRW.

Recent efforts to develop more appropriate tests measuring individual differences among programmers have met with greater success. Wolfe (1971) developed a series of tests for assessing programming aptitude which require candidates to manipulate numbers according to an intricate set of procedures that are not unlike some assembler tasks. A validation study of one of these tests appears in DeNelsky and McKee (1974). The Wolfe tests for programming aptitude primarily assess an individual's ability to follow detailed procedural instructions. However, this skill is only one of those required of entry level programmers.

Ray Berger began with a thorough job analysis of programming jobs and subsequently produced a series of tests for assessing different levels of skill and knowledge in programming. His initial aptitude test requires candidates to learn a short procedural language and then use it in solving problems of increasing complexity. This is the only widely marketed test that directly assesses the ability of applicants to learn and use a language. This skill is especially important when hiring entry level programmers who will be placed in a training program. Studies of the Berger Aptitude for Programming Test (B-APT) have obtained some of the highest validities to date, although these studies have not been reported in the archival literature.

The bottom line after two decades of work on programmer selection is that the individual differences model has never been applied to programming as effectively as it should have been. Programmer selection research has rarely considered more than a few mental abilities. The full set of individual characteristics which affect programming performance has never been modelled and studied in the same set of data. Figure 1 presents some of the characteristics that would need to be considered in a model of individual programming performance. Most programmer selection tests only assess factors listed on the left side of Fig. 1.

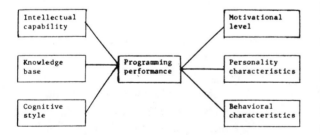

Figure 1. Factors affecting individual programming performance.

Couger and Zawacki (1980) took the individual differences model further than

most psychologists had in studying programmers. They identified how differences in the motivational structure of programmers interacted with the kinds of jobs they were assigned. They found that programmers had higher needs for personal growth and personal development than those in any other job category measured. However, programmers had lower needs for social interaction than people in most other types of jobs. This result should not be interpreted to imply that programmers are antisocial, rather that they get their greatest source of satisfaction from their job and their own professional development.

Couger and Zawacki used the Hackman and Oldham (1975) model of job characteristics to analyze programming jobs on the dimensions which have the greatest impact of the motivational structure of programmers. A summary of this analytic model is presented in Fig. 2. The Hackman-Oldman model postulates that various characteristics of the job have substantial impact on the psychological state of the individuals performing the job. These job characteristics define its motivating potential. It is the job's motivating potential interacting with the primary motivations of the individual which will result in a level of performance, satisfaction, turnover, etc.

Since programmers have shown such high levels of need for personal growth, it is important that their jobs be structured to provide high levels of the five job dimensions. Programmers who do not have the characteristic strong growth need may be more suited for programming jobs with less motivating potential. This model makes a sophisticated use of the individual differences approach by considering the match between personal characteristics and the surrounding environment.

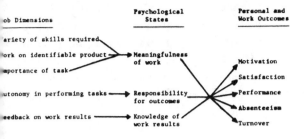

Figure 2. Hackman-Oldman model of a job's motivating potential.

Until the many sources of variation among individuals have been compared in the same set of data, it will not be possible to determine precisely which of the potential sources is the most important predictor of success in training programs or on the job. Further, as Weinberg (1971) suggested over a decade ago, it is unclear that we have assessed all of the important mental abilities related to programming. He specifically pointed toward a failure to assess the ability to consider alternate causal explanations of erroneous operation during debugging. More recently, Green (1977) has shown that the type of task involved in debugging is separate from the type involved in writing code.

It would appear from work in cognitive science (to be discussed later) that the most important determinant of individual differences in programming is the knowledge base possessed by a programmer. As will be described in the section on cognitive science, the performance of someone tackling a complicated programming task is related to the richness of their knowledge about the problem area. Thus, while the individual differences paradigm provides a method for predicting perfor-

mance differences among programmers, it fails to offer an explanation of why these differences occur or how to reduce them. Although the individual differences paradigm attempts to assess the mental structure of a human being, it rarely captures the dynamic growth or interaction among these structures. Its limitation is that it presents a static model of human beings. A better model will be needed to explain how individual differences occur.

The following points summarize the almost three decades of research which have investigated the individual differences among programmers.

- It took two decades to realize that programmers had more than one dimension.

- Managers rely on aptitude tests like a drowning sailor grasping for floating debris.

- A test is no better than the job analysis and validation study which supports it.

- Good tests are currently available, but they should only constitute part of the selection process.

- Advances in individual difference models will come from a better understanding of the programmer knowledge base.

Cognitive Science

The paradigm of cognitive science seeks to understand how knowledge is developed, represented in memory, and used. The interaction of cognitive science and computer science has led to the emergence of artificial intelligence, the attempt to make computers process information in ways similar to those used by humans.

There are several different levels at which researchers have modelled cognitive processes in programming. The differences in the models presented here are primarily in the levels of explanation. Cognitive theories of programming have not been elaborated to the extent that they present alternative explanations of programmer performance. In fact, on the surface many of the theories are interesting applications of psychological principles to programming, but they have not been sufficiently elaborated for consistent practical application at a technical level. Nevertheless, the models presented here are promising approaches to understanding how programmers develop programs.

Most cognitive models of programming begin with the distinction between short and long term memory. Short term memory is a limited capacity workspace which holds and processes those items of information currently under our attention. The capacity of short term memory was originally characterized by Miller (1956) as holding 7 ± 2 items. An item is a single piece of information, although there is no requirement that it be an elementary piece resulting from the decomposition of a larger body of information.

Currently, many cognitive theorists portray short term memory as allocating the scarce resources of the cognitive processor, rather than as possessing a limited number of mental slots for information. Nevertheless, this limited capacity information buffer provides one of the greatest limitations to our ability to develop large scale computer systems. That is, we simply cannot think of enough things simultaneously to keep track of the interwoven pieces of a large system.

A process called "chunking" expands the capacity of our short term mental workspace. In chunking, several items with similar or related attributes are bound together conceptually to form a unique item. For instance, through experience and training programmers are able to build increasingly larger chunks based on solution patterns which emerge frequently in solving problems. The lines of code in the program listing:

```
      SUM = 0
      DO 10 I = 1, N
      SUM = SUM + X(I)
10    CONTINUE
```

would be fused by an experienced programmer into the chunk "calculate the sum of array X." The programmer can now think about working with an array sum, a single entity, rather than the six unique operators and seven unique operands in the four program statements above. When it is necessary to deal with the procedural implementation, the programmer can call these four statements from long term memory as underlying the chunk "array sum."

Much of a programmer's maturation involves observing more patterns and building larger chunks. The scope of the concepts that programmers have been able to build into chunks provides one indication of their programming ability. The particular elements chunked together have important implications for educating programmers. Educational materials and exercises should be presented in a way which maximize the likelihood of building useful chunks.

Long term memory is usually treated as having limitless capacity for storing information. An important concern with long term memory is how the information stored there is interrelated and indexed such that:

1) items in short term memory can quickly cue the recall of appropriate chunks of information from long term memory,

2) items in short term memory can be linked into and transferred quickly to long term memory for retention, and

3) information retrieved from long term memory can cue the retrieval of additional chunks of information when appropriate.

The effects of both experience and education are on the knowledge base they construct in long term memory. The construction of this base is not merely one of accumulating facts, but of organizing them into a rich network of semantic material.

Shneiderman and Mayer (1979) have characterized the structure of knowledge in long term memory into a syntactic/semantic model. In their model, syntactic and semantic knowledge are organized separately in memory. Semantic knowledge concerns general programming concepts or relationships in the applications domain which are independent of the programming language in which they will be executed. Syntactic knowledge involves the procedural idiosyncrasies of a given programming language.

An important implication of the Shneiderman and Mayer model is that the development of programming skill requires the integration of knowledge from several different knowledge domains (Brooks, 1983). For instance, the programming of an on-board aircraft guidance system may require knowledge of:

1) aeronautical engineering

2) radar and sensors technology

3) mathematical algorithms

4) the design of the on-board processor

5) the development machine and tools

6) a high level programming language

7) an assembly language

Each of these is a separate field of knowledge, some of which require years of training and experience to master. Thus, programming skill is specific to the application being considered. One can be a talented avionics programmer, and still be a novice at programming simultaneous multi-user business databases.

Several efforts have been made to model the structure of programming knowledge at a level deeper than that of Shneiderman and Mayer. Brooks (1977) used Newell and Simon's (1972) production system approach to model the rules a programmer would use in writing the code for a program. These rules are of the type, "If the following conditions are satisfied, then produce the following action." Based on analysis of a verbal protocol, Brooks identified 73 rules which were needed to model the coding process of a single, and relatively simple, problem solution. Brooks estimated that the number of production rules needed to model the performance of an expert programmer was in the tens to hundreds of thousands.

Atwood, Turner, Ramsey, and Hooper (1979) modelled a programmer's understanding of a program using Kintsch's (1974) model of text comprehension. Their approach treats a program as a text base composed of propositions. Comprehension occurs as elementary or micro-propositions are fused into macro-propositions which summarize their meaning or content. This process is similar to chunking. The result of this process is a hierarchy of macro-propositions built from the micro-propositions at the bottom of the tree. A micro-proposition is a simple statement composed of a relational operator and one or more arguments (operands).

Atwood et al. (1979) demonstrated that a program design could be broken into a hierarchical structure of propositions. They observed that after studying the design, more experienced programmers were able to recall propositions at a greater depth in the hierarchy than novices. The more experienced programmers had more elaborate structures in long term memory for use in encoding such designs. Thus, they were able to retain propositions at greater depth because:

1) the higher level macro-propositions in the design did not represent new information, and thus could be referenced by existing knowledge structures, and

2) the propositions representing new information could be linked into the existing knowledge structures of experienced programmers and shifted into long term memory.

This propositional hierarchy is one representation of how knowledge is structured in long term memory. To understand how these knowledge structures develop, cognitive scientists have studied differences between expert and novice programmers.

Expert-novice differences

The study of expert-novice differences in programming has generated information on how the programming knowledge base is developed. Both Adelson (1981) and Weiser and Shertz (1983) demonstrated that novices comprehend a program based on its surface structure, that is, the particular applications area of the program such as banking, or avionics. Experts, however, analyze a program based on its deep structure, the solution or algorithmic structure of the program. Similarly, McKeithan, Reitman, Rueter, and Hirtle (1981) observed that experts are able to remember language commands based on their position in the structure of the language. Novices, not having an adequate mental representation of the language structure, often use mnemonic tricks to remember command names.

Results of the expert-novice differences research in programming agree with the results of similar research on other subject areas (e.g., thermodynamics, physics, and chess) conducted by Herbert Simon and his associates at Carnegie-Mellon. They have determined that experts are not necessarily better at operational thinking than novices. Rather, experts are better at encoding new information than novices. The broader knowledge base of experts guides them to quickly cue in on the most important aspects of new information, analyze them, and relate them to appropriate schema in long term memory.

Developing technical skill is not merely a matter of learning a long list of facts. Rather, developing technical skill is an effort to learn the underlying structure of the knowledge required for the task. McKeithan et al. found that the knowledge structures developed by experts were more similar to each other than were those of intermediates or novices. Thus, programmers tend to gravitate toward a similar understanding of the language structure with experience. The development of this structure enhances the ability of experienced programmers to assimilate new information.

Soloway and his colleagues at Yale (Soloway, Bonar, and Ehrlich, 1983; Soloway, Ehrlich, and Bonar, 1981) have modelled the programming knowledge base as a collection of plans or templates. These plans represent the algorithmic or computational structures programmers use in conceiving the solution to a problem. These plans become more efficient and elaborate as programmers gain in experience. Soloway et al. (1983) demonstrated that programmers can work more effectively when the language they use supports the structure of the templates in their knowledge base.

In a psychological study of the program design process, Jeffries, Turner, Polson, and Atwood (1981) noted that programmers with greater experience decomposed a problem more richly into minimally interacting parts. The design knowledge of novices did not appear sufficient to provide for a full decomposition. In particular, more experienced programmers spent greater time evaluating the problem structure prior to beginning the design process. Observations similar to these were also made by Nichols (1981).

Jeffries et al. hypothesized that there is the equivalent of a mental design executive. This executive attempts to recursively decompose the problem statement and relate the components emerging from the decomposition to patterns in the programming knowledge base in long term memory. The shallowness of the novices' decomposition reflects the shallowness of the knowledge base against which they attempt to compare pieces of the problem statement. The richer knowledge base of experts allows them a fuller decomposition of the problem statement. The criterion used by experts for terminating the decomposition process for a particular aspect of the problem is when it has been decomposed to a level for which the programmer can retrieve a solution template.

Design problem solving

Most problem solving research has been performed on well defined problems with finite solution states. In problems such as the Towers of Hanoi, there is an optimal path to the solution. The path to a successful solution in chess is not so clearly defined. Nevertheless, in chess there are a finite number of moves which can be chosen at any time and a well defined solution state. In a semantically rich domain such as programming, neither are the options from which one can choose limited nor is there a clearly defined solution state. Therefore, studying problem solving in programming is a qualitatively different task than most of those used in problem solving research.

Carroll, Thomas, and Malhotra (1980) argued that solving unstructured problems could not be explained with existing theory. They began their investigations of the design process by studying how analysts and clients interacted in establishing the requirements for a system. Carroll, Thomas, and Malhotra (1979) observed that client/analyst requirements sessions were broken into cycles which represented the decomposition of the problem. However, these cycles did not decompose the problem in a top-down fashion as recommended by structured programming practices. Rather, these cycles represented a linear or sequential decomposition of the problem in which the subproblem to be attacked in the next cycle was cued by the results of the last cycle. The only a priori structure placed on the content of these client/analyst cycles was determined by the initial goal structure of the client.

The problem in moving from the idea for a system to its final implementation is in transforming a linearly derived sequence of desired components into a hierarchical arrangement of functions or data transformations. Once the requirements have been delineated, they must be organized so that the inherent structure of the problem becomes visible. The next step is to construct a solution structure which matches the problem structure. To the extent that these structures are logically organized and matched, the system will possess a structural integrity which can expedite its implementation.

A series of studies by Carroll and his associates at IBM's Watson Research Center identified several factors which impact the effectiveness of designing a solution. First, they demonstrated differences in problem analysis based on differences in the application attempted. It has been consistently found in problem solving research that people do not transfer solution structures across problem isomorphs. Isomorphs are problems with the same structural characteristics, but whose cover stories (or subject areas) differ. Previous problem solving research has established that there is poor transfer of previously learned problem solutions across isomorphs. The structure of the cover story affects the difficulty people experience in reaching a solution.

Carroll et al. (1980) observed that people had more difficulty solving a problem that involved temporal relations (designing a manufacturing process) than an isomorph which involved spatial relations (arranging an office layout). The difference arose in part because the spatial problem lends itself to graphical representation. However, the temporal isomorph does not present spatial cues and participants had difficulty representing it to themselves. Many retreated to a verbal description of the problem, and several were totally unable to solve it. When a graphical aid was provided for solving the temporal problem, it appeared to make the problem easier to understand. The spatial aid did not make the problem easier to solve, however, since the same number of participants were unable to solve it.

The structuring of the requirements also seems to have an impact on the characteristics of the problem solution. Presenting the requirements in clusters based on their inherent structure assisted participants in designing solutions which better reflected the problem structure and were more stable when new requirements were added (Carroll, Thomas, Miller, and Friedman, 1980). Greater structure in the original problem statement seems to reduce the amount of iteration through design cycles. Thus, a critically important focus of the structured programming movement should be on methods of structuring the statement of requirements. Far less attention has been paid this problem than to areas, such as coding, that have less impact on system integrity and costs.

Hoc (1981) studied the results of designing a program from the data structure versus the results structure. He suggested that a choice of design method is often made prematurely, prior to understanding the relation between the data and results structures and the processing which transformed the former into the latter. He felt that the choice of design method was better made after this problem analysis stage.

The conceptual integrity of the program design is critical to the success of a programming project. No level of management talent can sustain high productivity and quality on a project which fails to achieve it. A most critical area for programming research, then, is requirements and design techniques. The current level of behavioral research on these topics is only a start in what needs to be a major thrust.

The detection of procedural faults

At least part of the process of developing an organized knowledge structure about programming is the abstraction of rules from the myriad patterns and facts that programmers know or can recognize. Whereas an expert programmer may be able to recognize 50,000 patterns, the number of rules which govern the structure of these patterns is substantially less, perhaps 1,000 to 3,000. Brooks (1977) estimated many more rules, but he may have been referring to the recognizable patterns from which these rules are drawn. Rule-based knowledge in programming has been studied most frequently in the detection of procedural faults.

One of the most critical and time consuming tasks in programming is the detection and correction of faults (bugs).

While debugging has been used as an experimental task for studies on specifications or language features, relatively little behavioral research has been directed toward understanding the debugging process.

John Seely Brown and his associates (Brown and Burton, 1978; Brown and Van Lehn, 1980) have laid some theoretical groundwork for modelling the generation of bugs in procedural tasks. They treat bugs not as random occurrences, but as systematic and predictable outcomes of the incomplete or incorrect application of the rules underlying a procedural skill. Their explanation entails four components:

1) the first component is that an individual acquire a formal representation of a procedural skill. Such a representation would be a set of rules which guide the development of procedures for solving a problem.

2) the second component of their model is a set of principles for determining which rules can be deleted from the formal representation to simulate the incomplete or incorrect learning of rules or the forgetting of rules.

3) the third component is a set of repair heuristics used by the individual to patch over gaps in the formal representation. These heuristics generate bugs by creating inappropriate procedures for completing procedural solutions.

4) the final component is a set of mechanisms for screening out some of the heuristics which generate blatantly incorrect procedures.

This type of model is guiding some of the

current work on intelligent debugging aids (Johnson and Soloway, 1984).

Youngs (1974) reported some descriptive data on the types of errors typically made by programmers. His data were similar to several databases collected on large system development projects by the Information Sciences Program at Rome Air Development Center. The most frequent category of faults was logic errors, especially for experienced programmers. Syntactic errors occurred relatively infrequently. This observation reinforces the importance of providing useful control constructs in the programming languages. The results also indicate that novices and professionals make different kinds of errors.

During the early 1970s John Gould and his associates at IBM's Watson Research Center made several studies of program debugging. In the first study, Gould and Drongowski (1974) found that providing debugging aids to programmers did not necessarily make fault detection faster. Programmers adopted debugging strategies based on the types of information they were presented about the program and the problem. This strategy included attempts to localize the section of code likely to contain the error, and employed a hierarchical search in which the most complex sections were left for last. In a further study, Gould (1975) identified that this hierarchical search was for:

1) syntactic faults,

2) grammatical faults not caught by the compiler, and

3) substantive faults.

Sheppard, Curtis, Milliman, and Love

(1979) observed several different search strategies among programmers. Some programmers felt they had to understand the entire program before they could begin searching for the fault. The more effective strategy, however, was to identify that portion of the output which was in error and quickly trace back from the print statement for that variable to locate the area in which the fault was likely to have occurred. This technique is similar to the program slicing strategy studied by Weiser (1982).

One of the most extensive programs of research on fault diagnosis has been conducted by William and Sandra Rouse now at Georgia Tech. They have made an important distinction between perceptual complexity and problem solving complexity (Rouse and Rouse, 1979). They suggest that the latter is more affected by individual differences, especially those related to understanding a problem. Brooke and Duncan (1981) demonstrated that factors which primarily impact perceptual complexity, such as the display format, can affect problem solving effectiveness. Subsequently, Rouse, Rouse, and Pelligrino (1980) have developed a rule-based model of fault diagnosis that agrees at a global level with the actual performance of people on a similar task.

Learning to program

There are two primary ways in which the rules which govern programming can be learned. They can be abstracted from the developing knowledge base as the programmer gains increasing experience. This, of course, is a lengthy process. On the other hand, rules can be taught in organized training programs. Training not only develops the knowledge base more quickly than experiential learning, but it is also likely to be more thorough and accurate. However, experiential learning is often the primary method for acquiring the contextual information used in interpreting the appropriateness of various rules for programming.

Mayer (1976, 1981) described several training techniques grounded in psychological theory and research which can be used successfully in training novice programmers. Mayer (1976) stressed the importance of "advanced organizers" to help structure new material as it is learned. These advanced organizers help build a preliminary model or outline of the new information so that later input can be more easily assimilated into an appropriate knowledge structure. Mayer emphasized that one of the most effective advanced organizers is a concrete model of the machine which is manipulated by instructions coded in a computer language. Mayer argued that students benefit from being forced to elaborate these models in their own words.

DuBoulay, O'Shea, and Monk (1981) extended Mayer's concept of a concrete model of the machine. They discussed a "notional machine" which is a simplified machine whose facilities are only those which are implemented by the available commands in the programming language. They also stressed the importance of a student's gaining visibility into the processes occurring inside the abstract notional machine. They have built several training systems based on this concept.

Coombs, Gibson, and Alty (1982) have identified two learning styles which characterize the different ways novices learn to program: comprehension learning and operational learning. Comprehension learners acquire an overall layout of the information under study, but may not understand the rules which allow them to operate with and on the information. Operational learners grasp the rules for operating on information, but they do not acquire a complete picture of the knowledge domain. Comprehension learners are primarily interested in understanding, while operational learners are primarily interested in doing something. These characterizations represent idealized students, whereas most people will fall on a continuum in between, displaying varying degrees of both styles.

Coombs et al. concluded from their data that operational learners were better able to learn a programming language. Their learning strategy was characterized by attention to the details of the language structures, the abstraction of critical language features, and an orientation towards representing important structural relations in rules. The major learning activity for operational learners was in practice sessions, whereas for comprehension learners this occurred in lectures.

Lemos (1979) investigated the benefits of structured walkthroughs as a classroom learning exercise. This approach seemed to have advantages in allowing novices to compare alternative approaches to the problem and gain immediate feedback on their strategy. Shneiderman (1980) has used a similar feedback mechanism with experienced programmers and found benefits in terms of learning new approaches to a problem.

Conclusions

I have argued that individual differences among project personnel (and this should be even more true in the unstudied area of programming managers) account for the largest source of variation in project performance. In fact, Sheppard, Kruesi, and Curtis (1981) found that half of the variation in the efficiency of extracting information from different documentation formats was attributable to individual differences among the professional programmers involved in the experiment. However, the individual differences paradigm only allows us to characterize and predict these differences, but not explain how they develop and change over time. Cognitive science has provided a representation of knowledge organization and development which presents an explanation of the basis for these differences. Therefore, cognitive science is a paradigm which offers the best opportunity to study and gain control over the largest source of influence of project performance.

Cognitive science presents an opportunity for psychologists to get on the leading edge of programming technology, rather than sweeping up behind the directions already set by computer scientists. As a driving force in artificial intelligence, cognitive science provides a vehicle for analyzing the most appropriate ways to automate more of the programming process in ways that are helpful to those who must develop large systems.

The following points describe some of the important themes emerging from cognitive science research on software engineering:

- Expertise is specific to different knowledge domains. A programmer can be expert in one domain and a novice in another.

- The development of expertise involves building a massive knowledge base of recognizable patterns (perhaps 50,000) and abstracting a set of rules (perhaps 1,000 to 3,000) which govern their behavior.

- Rule-based models of programming need to be expanded far beyond their current use, primarily in fault diagnosis. Rule-based models hold substantial promise for automating programming tasks.

- So little research is being performed on the problem solving process during requirements definition, functional specification, and program design, that this must be a crucial area for improving software engineering practice.

- Rather than teaching isolated commands, educators should liberally model abstract machines for teaching the structure of a programming language.

- Learning styles will play an important role in how quickly, accurately, and thoroughly an individual learns to program.

- Cognitive science is the easiest way for a psychologist to communicate with a computer scientist, but someone with artificial intelligence may have to interpret one to the other.

There will remain behavioral questions with significant impact on the usefulness of new developments in programming technology. Some of these questions involve:

1) techniques for insuring the completeness of a requirements statement,

2) techniques for clustering the requirements to better reveal the inherent structure of the problem,

3) techniques for deciding on the allocation of requirements between hardware and software,

4) techniques for bridging the gap between a statement of requirements and the preliminary program design,

5) techniques for indexing and retrieving reused program modules,

6) techniques for proving the correctness of reused program modules,

7) techniques for coordinating the work of project team members, and

8) techniques for designing and verifying the data flow among modules.

Thus, there will need to be a shift in emphasis in behavioral research away from coding issues toward the concerns enumerated above. If behavioral scientists, and especially psychologists, begin attacking these problems immediately, they can influence the development of new technology in software engineering. Further, the models of programmer performance being developed by cognitive scientists can be useful in developing knowledge-based tools and environments for software engineering.

REFERENCES

Adelson, B. "Problem Solving and the Development of Abstract Categories in Programming Languages." *Memory and Cognition,* Vol. 9, No. 4, 1981, pp. 422-33.

Atwood, M.E., A.A. Turner, H.R. Ramsey, and J.N. Hooper. "An Exploratory Study of the Cognitive Structures Underlying the Comprehension of Software Design Problems." (Technical Report 392). Alexandria, Va.: Army Research Institute, 1979.

Boehm, B.W. *Software Engineering Economics.* Englewood Cliffs, N.J.: Prentice-Hall, 1981.

Brooke, J.B., and K.D. Duncan. "Effects of System Display Format on Performance in a Fault Location Task." *Ergonomics,* Vol. 24, No. 3, 1981, pp. 175-89.

Brooks, R. "Towards a Theory of Cognitive Processes in Computer Programming." *International Journal of Man-Machine Studies,* Vol. 9, 1977, pp. 737-51.

_____ . "Studying Programmer Behavior Experimentally: The Problems of Proper Methodology." *Communications of the ACM,* Vol. 23, No. 4, 1980, pp. 207-13.

_____ . "Towards a Theoretical Model of the Comprehension of Computer Programs." *International Journal of Man-Machine Studies,* Vol. 17, 1983.

Brown, J.S., and R.R. Burton. "Diagnostic Models for Procedural Bugs in Basic Mathematics Skills." *Cognitive Science,* Vol. 2, 1978, pp. 155-92.

Brown, J.S., and K. VanLehn. "Repair Theory: A Generative Theory of Bugs in Procedural Skills." *Cognitive Science,* Vol. 4, 1980, pp. 379-426.

Carroll, J.M., J.C. Thomas, and A. Malhotra. "Clinical-Experimental Analysis of Design Problem Solving." *Design Studies,* Vol. 1, No. 2, 1979, pp. 84-92.

_____ . "Presentation and Representation in Design Problem Solving." *British Journal of Psychology,* Vol. 71, 1980, pp. 143-53.

Carroll, J.M., J.C. Thomas, L.A. Miller, and H.P. Friedman. "Aspects of Solution Structure in Design Problem Solving." *American Journal of Psychology,* Vol. 93, No. 2, 1980, pp. 269-84.

Coombs, M.J., R. Gibson, and J.L. Alty.

"Learning a First Computer Language: Strategies for Making Sense." *International Journal of Man-Machine Studies,* Vol. 16, 1982, pp. 449-86.

Couger, J.D., and R.A. Zawacki. *Motivating and Managing Computer Personnel.* New York: Wiley, 1980.

Curtis, B. *Human Factors in Software Development.* Silver Spring, Md.: IEEE, 1981a.

————. "A Review of Human Factors Research on Programming Languages and Specifications." *Proceedings of Human Factors in Computer Systems.* New York: ACM, 1981b.

————. "Substantiating Programmer Variability." *Proceedings of the IEEE,* Vol. 69, No. 7, 1981c, p. 846.

DeNelsky, G.Y., and M.C. McKee. "Prediction of Computer Programmer Training and Job Performance Using the AABP Test." *Personnel Psychology,* Vol. 27, 1974, pp. 129-37.

DuBoulay, B., T. O'Shea, and J. Monk. "The Black Box Inside the Glass Box: Presenting Computer Concepts to Novices." *International Journal of Man-Machine Studies,* Vol. 14, 1981, pp. 237-49.

Gould, J.D. "Some Psychological Evidence on How People Debug Computer Programs." *International Journal of Man-Machine Studies,* Vol. 7, 1975, pp. 151-82.

————, and P. Drongowski. "An Exploratory Study of Computer Program Debugging." *Human Factors,* Vol. 16, No. 3, 1974, pp. 258-77.

Green, T.R.G. "Conditional Program Statements and Their Comprehensibility to Professional Programmers." *Journal of Occupational Psychology,* Vol. 50, 1977, pp. 93-109.

Hackman, J.R., and G.R. Oldham. "Development of the Job Diagnostic Survey." *Journal of Applied Psychology,* Vol. 60, No. 2, 1975, pp. 159-70.

Hoc, J.M. "Planning and Direction of Problem Solving in Structured Programming:

An Empirical Comparison Between Two Methods." *International Journal of Man-Machine Studies,* 1981, Vol. 15, pp. 363-83.

Jeffries, R., A.A. Turner, P.G. Polson, and M.E. Atwood. "The Processes Involved in Designing Software." In J.R. Anderson, ed. *Cognitive Skills and Their Acquisition.* Hillsdale, N.J.: Erlbaum, 1981, pp. 255-83.

Johnson, W.L., and E. Soloway. "PROUST: Knowledge-Based Program Understanding." *Proceedings of the Seventh International Conference on Software Engineering.* Silver Spring, Md.: IEEE, 1984.

Kintsch, W. *The Representation of Meaning in Memory.* Hillsdale, N.J.: Erlbaum, 1974.

Lemos, R.S. "An Implementation of Structured Walkthroughs in Teaching Cobol Programming." *Communications of the ACM,* Vol. 22, No. 6, 1979, pp. 335-40.

Mayer, R.E. "Some Conditions for Meaningful Learning in Computer Programming: Advance Organizers and Subject Control of Frame Order." *Journal of Educational Psychology,* Vol. 68, 1976, pp. 143-50.

————. "The Psychology of How Novices Learn Computer Programming." *ACM Computing Surveys,* Vol. 13, No. 1, 1981, pp. 121-41.

McKeithen, K.B., J.S. Reitman, H.H. Rueter, and S.C. Hirtle. "Knowledge Organization and Skill Differences in Computer Programmers." *Cognitive Psychology,* Vol. 13, 1981, pp. 307-25.

Miller, G.A. "The Magical Number Seven Plus or Minus Two: Some Limits on Our Capacity to Process Information." *Psychological Review,* Vol. 63, 1956, pp. 81-97.

Newell, A., and H.A. Simon. *Human Problem Solving.* Englewood Cliffs, N.J.: Prentice-Hall, 1972.

Nichols, J.A. "Problem Solving Strategies and Organization of Information in Computer Programming." *Dissertation Abstracts International,* 1981.

Reinstedt, R.N., et al. "Computer Personnel Research Group Programmer Performance Prediction Study." *Proceedings of the Fifth Annual Computer Personnel Research Conference.* New York: ACM, 1966.

Rouse, W.B., and S.H. Rouse. "Measures of Complexity of Fault Diagnosis Tasks." *IEEE Transactions on Systems, Man & Cybernetics,* Vol. 9, No. 11, 1979, pp. 720-27.

_____ , and S.J. Pelligrino. "A Rule-Based Model of Human Problem Solving Performance in Fault Diagnosis Tasks." *IEEE Transactions on Systems, Man & Cybernetics,* Vol. 10, No. 7, 1980, pp. 366-76.

Sackman, H., W.J. Erickson, and E.E. Grant. "Exploratory and Experimental Studies Comparing On-Line and Off-Line Programming Performance." *Communications of the ACM,* Vol. 11, 1968, pp. 3-11.

Sheil, B.A. "The Psychological Study of Programming." *ACM Computing Surveys,* Vol. 13, No. 1, 1981, pp. 101-20.

Sheppard, S.B., B. Curtis, P. Milliman, and T. Love. "Modern Coding Practices and Programmer Performance." *Computer,* Vol. 12, No. 12, 1979, pp. 41-49.

Sheppard, S.B., E. Kruesi, and B. Curtis. "The Effects of Symbology and Spatial Arrangement on the Comprehension of Software Specifications." *Proceedings of the Fifth International Conference on Software Engineering.* Silver Spring, Md.: IEEE Computer Society, 1981, pp. 207-14.

Shneiderman, B. *Software Psychology: Human Factors in Computer and Information Systems.* Cambridge, Mass.: Winthrop, 1980.

_____ , and R.E. Mayer. "Syntactic/Semantic Interactions in Programmer Behavior: A Model and Experimental Results." *International Journal of Computer and Information Sciences,* Vol. 8, 1979, pp. 219-38.

Sime, M.E., T.R.G. Green, and D.J. Guest. "Psychological Evaluation of Two Conditional Constructions Used in Computer Languages." *International Journal of Man-Machine Studies,* Vol. 5, 1973, pp. 105-13.

Soloway, E., J. Bonar, and K. Ehrlich. "Cognitive Strategies and Looping Constructs: An Empirical Study." *Communications of the ACM,* Vol. 26, No. 11, 1983, pp. 853-60.

Soloway, E., K. Ehrlich, and J. Bonar. "Tapping into Tacit Programming Knowledge." *Proceedings of Human Factors in Computer Systems.* New York: ACM, 1982, pp. 52-57.

Weinberg, G.M. *The Psychology of Computer Programming.* New York: Van Nostrand Reinhold, 1971.

Weiser, M. "Programmers Use Slices When Debugging." *Communications of the ACM,* Vol. 25, No. 7, 1982, pp. 446-52.

_____ , and J. Shertz. "A Study of Programming Problem Representation in Novice Programmers." *International Journal of Man-Machine Studies,* Vol. 17, 1983.

Wolfe, J. "Perspectives on Testing for Programmer Aptitude." *Proceedings of the 1971 Annual Conference of the ACM.* New York: ACM, 1971, pp. 268-77.

Youngs, E.A. "Human Errors in Programming." *International Journal of Man-Machine Studies,* Vol. 6, 1974, pp. 361-76.

29

Editors' Note
Guindon, Krasner, and Curtis: "Breakdowns and Processes During the Early Activities of Software Design by Professionals"

Insight: There is a qualitative difference between the way novices and experienced practitioners go about design: The experienced designer makes use of a repertoire of past constructs (the so-called design schema) and adapts the best fitting of these to the present need.

Guindon, Krasner, and Curtis are members of the cognitive psychology group at MCC in Austin, Texas. As this sample of their work indicates, their goal is nothing less than to crawl inside the mind of a software professional at work and figure out what the relevant thought processes are. Their methods are as fascinating as their findings.

29

Breakdowns and Processes During the Early Activities of Software Design by Professionals
by Raymonde Guindon, Herb Krasner, and Bill Curtis

MOTIVATION AND GOALS

The goal of this study is to identify the breakdowns most often experienced by professional software designers and determine the software tools that would alleviate these breakdowns. This chapter will not describe these tools but will concentrate on describing the breakdowns. Breakdowns have been broadly defined as ineffective design activities, undesirable consequences of these ineffective activities, activities that are difficult to perform because they tax the designers' limited cognitive resources, or causes of these ineffective or difficult design activities. These breakdowns are likely to produce design solutions that are incorrect. Our strategy toward the identification of breakdowns has been to

- Study designers with real, extensive, and widely varied software design experience.

- Give the designers a more complex and realistic problem than has been given in other studies of software design, yet not so different that our results cannot be easily compared to them (e.g., Jeffries, Turner, Polson, and Atwood [1]; Adelson and Soloway [2]; Kant and Newell [3]).

- Use the observational technique of

thinking aloud protocol rather than controlled experimental manipulations because of the scarcity of previous empirical work on software design. This initial study is exploratory and we have observed many design behaviors and many breakdowns that will provide a foundation for modeling cognitive activities during software design.

Our study differs from other studies of software design by individuals on two main points. First, we are taking a next step in advancing the empirical study of software design by using a more complex and realistic design problem than used in other software design studies. Second, this study is especially oriented toward identifying the breakdowns occurring during software design by professional designers.

DESCRIPTION OF THE METHODOLOGY

Participants

Thinking aloud protocols were collected from 8 professional programmers and system designers. Three experienced designers were selected for a full protocol analysis from these 8 professionals. P6 had a Ph.D. in Electrical Engineering with more than 10 years of professional experience, mainly in communication systems and hardware architecture. P8 had a Masters in Software Engineering with 5 years of experience, mainly in real time systems. P3 was a Ph.D. Candidate in Computer Science with 3 years of professional experience, mainly in logic programming. These particular designers were selected because they were considered by their peers to be experienced and competent designers, because of the wide variety of their educational backgrounds and years of experience, because their design solutions were considered the best among the eight designers, and because of the wide variety of their design strategies and solutions. We deliberately choose to analyze the widest spectrum of design behaviors in order to gather a wide variety of breakdowns and design strategies.

Problem Statement

The *lift control problem* is currently a standard problem used in the areas of software specification and software requirements modeling research. The goal is to design the logic to move N lifts between M floors given the constraints expressed in the problem statement. The problem statement is given in the Appendix.

Procedure

Thinking aloud reports were collected from participants who were asked to design the logic for the N-lift problem. They were given two hours to produce a design solution that was in such a form and level of detail that it could be handed off to a competent system programmer to imple-

ment. The participants were videotaped and given paper and pencil to work their solution. The notes and diagrams produced by the participants were time-stamped regularly by the experimenter. The transcript of each participant was also time-stamped, and the written notes and diagrams were included in the transcript. The procedure departed from typical verbal protocols in that the experimenter intervened more substantively, often acting as a client and sometimes providing some help when the participants encountered difficulties. There were two reasons for this departure. First, in realistic design situations one or more people are typically available to answer questions or arbitrate issues in the requirements. This communication and negotiation between client and designer is perceived as a critical element in early design. Carroll, Thomas, and Malhotra [4] have provided an analysis of the cyclic nature of these interactions. At least one participant, P6, would frequently want to discuss design issues with the experimenter as this represented his normal mode of designer-client interactions. However, such a veridical feature conflicts with the traditional methods for collecting and analyzing verbal protocols. Second, our objective was to generate as much design behavior as possible in order to observe a broad range of design breakdowns. The participants were selected and the verbal protocols collected by the second author. The videotapes and transcripts were independently analyzed by the first author later.

Protocol Analysis Process

The process of protocol analysis was divided into three major steps:

1. Enumeration of possible cognitive activities that could occur during the session based on previous studies, the problem-solving literature in psychology, and artificial intelligence models of design. The function of these preliminary models is to guide the protocol analysis, though not limit it. New activities or interactions between them are also sought.

2. Segmentation of the protocols into episodes indicating breakdowns or corresponding to cognitive activities during software design.

3. Identification of the relations between the software design activities. Four main types of relations were identified: 1) temporal (e.g., precedence, iteration, interruptions, and resumptions); 2) transition between internal, mental activities and external activities (e.g., from mental to external representation of lifts and floors on paper); 3) transition between activities dealing mainly with the problem domain (e.g., lifts, floors, buttons) and activities dealing mainly with the solution domain (e.g., control structures, data structures); 4) functional composition (e.g., the activity of understanding the requirements was composed of shorter episodes such as disambiguation of the problem statement through mental simulations, the addition of an assumption, or the abstraction of critical statements).

Verbal protocol analysis is essentially an exploratory observational technique particularly suited for research in new domains. The study of cognitive processes during software design is such a domain.

Issues of Validity Generalization

There are three issues that must be addressed in determining the validity of generalizing results from these data to realistic design situations. These issues deal with the task, the sampling of participants, and the external validity of the experimental situation. As stated earlier, the lift problem is a standard exercise in research on software specification techniques. Although it is not as complex a task as, for example, designing a distributed electronic fund transfer system, it is nevertheless a next step in increasing the technical challenge offered by tasks used in empirical studies of design. Thus, as we begin to understand how designers marshal their cognitive resources to solve problems of this complexity, we can move on to tasks of even greater complexity.

The second issue concerns how representative our sample of participants is of the larger population of software designers. There is simply no reliable way to answer this question given the current maturity of the field. That is, there are no population data available against which to compare the variability of our sample. There is no standard type of individual who becomes a software designer. Their educational backgrounds, work experience, job settings, and variability of skills differ radically. Furthermore, there is not even agreement on the relevant variables to measure if we wanted to characterize this population. Another significant problem is that there is no standard job title or description for those who perform software design.

We attempted to get a broad sampling of educational backgrounds, application experiences, and previous working environments in the eight designers selected to participate. Further, we selected three protocols for analysis that represented completely different strategies in attacking the design. We make no claim that these protocols represent the full range of strategies in the larger population of software designers. Rather, we believe that since it is unlikely that a multi-environment population study of software designers will be funded in the foreseeable future, the description of this population must be pieced together from studies like this that describe the problem-solving characteristics of a few designers in great depth.

The third issue concerns the extent to which the conditions under which the data were collected are representative of those under which actual design occurs. Clearly, designing programs of any significance normally takes more than two hours, unless the designer has extensive experience in designing programs of great similarity. Our goal in collecting these data was to gather information on a concentrated problem-solving effort that would provide a broad range of cognitive behaviors and would display an interesting array of breakdowns. We cannot be sure that additional breakdowns would not have been observed had we carried the data collection out over several days or even weeks with a more complex problem. Furthermore, some of the breakdowns may have been exacerbated by the concentrated nature of the two-hour session. However, other studies of software design by individuals have collected verbal protocols over a session of two hours (Jeffries, Turner, Polson, and Atwood [1]; Adelson and Soloway [2]; Kant and Newell [3]). Therefore, we can at least compare

our results to their results legitimately.

Finally, some of the breakdowns and processes we have observed were also reported by Kant and Newell [3] and Adelson and Soloway [2], and more importantly in a study of mechanical engineering design using a ten-hour design session by Ullman, Stauffer, and Dietterich [5]. This overlap between some of our findings and findings in other studies performed in other domains and under different conditions supports the validity and generalizability of our new findings.

GENERAL OBSERVATIONS ON DESIGN BEHAVIOR

The three designers adopted very different strategies during design. A brief characterization of their overall strategies follows.

P6 seems to have the most relevant specialized computer science knowledge to solve the N-lift problem—he has **specialized design schemas** relevant to distributed systems. P6 uses these design schemas to **decompose the problem into simpler subproblems.** He opts for a distributed control solution. He then decomposes the problem into two subproblems, communication between each lift and route scheduling by each lift. However, he clearly has better design schemas for the communication subproblem than for the scheduling subproblem. He successively refines his solution for the communication subproblem while he performs much more exploratory design for the scheduling subproblem. By exploratory design, we mean design with many mental simulations of the problem environment and mental simulations of tentative solutions unguided by a plan. Another aspect of his design activities is that they are **issue-driven:** he identifies some critical features his solution should have, such as *reliability and no single point of failure,* and uses them to **control** the selection of alternative solutions for many of the sub-problems (e.g., selection of a control structure and selection of a communication scheme between lifts). Moreover, P6 also consciously generates many **simplifying assumptions,** which he evaluates for their plausibility, as a **complexity reduction strategy.** So, P6's process is mainly characterized by the use of specialized design schemas, by being issue-driven, and by the generation of simplifying assumptions.

P8 seems to follow more closely than the other participants a **meta-schema for design.** This meta-schema seems to be derived from software engineering practices, especially the Jackson System Development method [6]. P8 explicitly acknowledges the need for **exploring the problem environment** to achieve a good understanding of the requirements before seeking a solution. The problem environment is the set of objects, events, and behaviors in the domain relevant to the computer system being designed (e.g., floors, lifts, buttons, buildings, people waiting, fires). An important part of his design activities is the representation of entities and relations in the problem environment and their mental simulations. However, P8 does not seem to have as relevant specialized design schemas as P6, which may have induced him in exploring the problem environment. Possibly as a consequence of exploring the problem environment, the design process of P8 is partly controlled by recognition of **partial solutions, at different levels of detail or ab-** straction, without having previously decomposed the problem into sub-problems. We call such design process **serendipitous design.** As another aspect of P8's process, he decomposes the problem into handling the requests coming from floors and handling the requests coming from inside the lifts. He also attempts, within this problem decomposition, to solve initially for one lift and then attempts to expand the solution to N lifts. However, he experiences great difficulty in merging the partial solutions from handling requests from floors and requests from lifts and expanding the solution from 1 lift to N lifts. The decomposition of the problem into requests from floors and requests from lifts, and the reduction of the problem from N lifts to 1 lift does not appear to be based on a specialized design schema. Such a design schema would have provided P8 a plan for a well-motivated decomposition of the problem into subproblems and a merging of the partial solutions. So, P8's design process is characterized by the use of a meta-schema for design, by exploration of the problem environment, by serendipitous design, and by difficulty in merging the partial solutions.

P3's design activities appear the least systematic and the most locally governed. They are the least systematic because P3 does not seem to use a meta-schema for design and he does not seem to use specialized design schemas to guide the decomposition of the problem into sub-problems. They are the most locally governed in the sense that he does not exhibit exploration of the problem environment and consideration of alternative solutions to problems. P3 does not, as opposed to P6, consider one or more issues as crucial and select the solution from a set of alternative solutions that best satisfies the issues. His approach seems mostly governed by a **familiar computational paradigm,** logic programming. He produces many cycles of generating a tentative solution, simulating it, debugging it locally, and simulating it again. He has difficulty with mental simulations of the many tentative solutions and with keeping track of the test cases during these simulations. So, P3's design process is characterized by a generate-test-debug strategy and difficulty with mental simulations of tentative solutions.

Likewise, the solutions produced by the designers are quite different. We will discuss mainly the solution architectures and the representation schemes of the solutions.

P6's solution is a communicating ring of independent elevators. He selects distributed control over centralized control. In this scheme, each elevator operates on its own and passes information around the ring to the others, coordinating the schedules of pickups that they had decided on independently. P6's solution is represented as finite state machines. In each elevator there are two communicating finite state machines; one for handling the local processing of the elevator as it decides what stops to make along its route, and the second for communicating with the other elevators independently.

P8 adopts the classic star architecture in which the elevators communicate through a central process. P8 uses abstract data types, data flow diagrams, and pseudocode as representation schemes.

P3 works at developing a global model of system behavior described as a set of logical assertions with initial thoughts of centralized control. P3 represents the behavior of the system by logical assertions written in a Prolog style.

So, experienced designers can exhibit a very wide variety of design strategies, both between and within designers. This variety of design strategies is also accompanied by different types of breakdowns (which will be described in the next section). Finally, design solutions vary widely between designers. These observations highlight the complexity of the design process. These observations also highlight the critical contribution of specialized knowledge to the design process, and as a consequence, the wide individual differences that will be observed between designers' strategies. Finally, these observations indicate that a wide variety of tools and methodologies are needed to best support the variety of design strategies.

SOME OF THE BREAKDOWNS OBSERVED DURING DESIGN

The breakdowns that we are reporting consist of both symptoms and causes of difficulties during the design process. Moreover, these breakdowns are not necessarily independent of each other. We observed two main classes of breakdowns, with a third class being a combination of the other two. The first class consists of **knowledge-related** breakdowns. They are due to 1) lack of specialized knowledge of computational solutions corresponding to characteristics of the application domain, 2) lack of knowledge/experience of the design process itself, or 3) lack of domain knowledge. The second class of breakdowns are due to general **cognitive limitations.** They result from

1) capacity limitations of short-term or working memory, and 2) the unreliable retrieval of relevant information from long-term memory. They are also due to the weakness of our standard tools and methodologies aimed at alleviating cognitive limitations (e.g., checklists). The third class of breakdowns results from a combination of both knowledge deficiencies and cognitive limitations. These latter breakdowns occur because the lack of relevant specialized knowledge induces designers to use weak problem-solving methods, such as generate and test means-end analysis. Unfortunately, weak methods can be very taxing cognitively and they often translate into poor performance because they require search of a large space of possibilities (Laird, Rosenbloom, and Newell [7]). Moreover, the lack of specialized knowledge is also associated with a lack of cognitive knowledge structures supporting memory for the activities during the design process (e.g., supporting memory for postponed subproblems or memory for test cases).

Knowledge-Related Breakdowns

Lack of relevant problem-specific design schemas. The main determinant of performance appears to be the presence or absence of specialized design schemas. Design schemas are mental representations of software design families. Borrowing from a definition given by Rich and Waters [8], a design schema consists of a set of roles embedded in an underlying matrix. The roles of the schema are the parts that vary from one use of the design schema to the next. The matrix of the schema contains both fixed elements of structure (parts that are present in every

occurrence) and constraints. Constraints are used both to check that the parts that fill the roles in a particular occurrence are consistent, and also to compute parts to fill empty roles in a partially specified occurrence. These schemas can be instantiated through refinements and specializations to particular instances of software designs. The design schemas embody the knowledge of alternative solutions to classes of problems. Problem-solving using design schemas proceeds through recognition that the requirements may be an instance of a known design schema followed by propagation of constraints from the explicit and implicit requirements and specialization of the design schema. Examples of design schemas and their specializations are given in the work by Lubars and Harandi [9] and Rich and Waters [8]. The Inventory Control System design schema can be specialized into the Reservable Inventory Control System schema and the Non-Reservable Inventory Control System schema. A Library Inventory Control System schema is a specialization of the Non-Reservable Inventory Control System schema. In the Library Inventory Control System schema the role Check Out Book (an operation) is a specialization of the role Dispense Inventory specified in the Non-Reservable Inventory Control System schema.

Regarding retrievability, a design schema is composed of a description of the conditions under which its solution is relevant. These conditions contain an abstract representation of critical features in the given problem environment. For example, in the N-lift problem the abstract representation could be in terms of many clients who might make simultaneous requests for service to many servers (lifts) at different times and locations. Such a description could be sufficient to retrieve a design schema appropriate for the N-lift problem. Regarding problem decomposition, a design schema also contains a solution plan to guide the decomposition of the problem into subproblems, each subproblem with its own design schema. The design schema as a cognitive structure also supports the storage and retrieval of intermediate solutions and backtracking if necessary, and as a consequence, reduces working memory load during design and increases the probability that partial solutions and postponed subproblems will be retrieved when needed. The design schema also guides the expansion of a reduced solution or the merging of individual solutions to subproblems into a complete solution.

P6, because of his specialized design schemas for distributed and communication systems, could quickly identify the main design issues (i.e., no single point of failure) and knew alternative solutions to be evaluated (e.g., central vs. distributed solutions for control and communication between lifts). He could also quickly retrieve from memory, for example, known solutions for posting messages and for avoiding a race condition. However, for the subproblem of scheduling service and especially its subproblem of choosing a route, for which he seems to lack design schemas, his design process appeared much more exploratory and accompanied with mental simulations.

The following excerpts from the protocols indicate the use of such schematic knowledge. P6 immediately recognizes that in scheduling N lifts the problem of control arises. His design schema for control represents two alternatives, centralized

and distributed, which he immediately retrieves. His knowledge of the alternatives also contains their advantages and disadvantages. He opts for distributed control. He then recognizes the next problem to solve, communication between lifts. He retrieves the possible alternatives and again opts for distributed communication between lifts, where each lift broadcasts which requests it will service to all other lifts. He then recognizes the problem of a race condition and immediately retrieves from his design schemas a solution to the race condition problem, that is, arrange the lift in a ring for sequential polling of the lift requests.

P6—*"I'm going to schedule the elevators. Do we have a central controller? It doesn't say in the problem. We have a central controller or a distributed controller, is that up to me? ...The good news about central control is it's an easier algorithm vs. distributed control. The bad news is that you have a single point of failure... I'll start off by thinking about a distributed control system..."*

P6—*"Let's say all the elevators are sitting down at the bottom floor and there's an up button pressed on floor three. Someone's got to post that request and someone's got to pick it up and mark it that he's responding to it. That implies a centralized place to post the requests and we're back to the single point of failure... Well, you could broadcast a message to all the other elevators that you are servicing number one. Seems like the algorithm is: every elevators (sic) look at all the buttons all the time; he sees an up posted on floor number three; ... one of them grabs it and post a message..."*

P6—*"Now we have to make sure we don't get in a race condition. And we can do that algorithmically usually. You can do some king of ring system by allowing them to scan in sequence and tell one another when they've got scanned so they don't get in a race."*

P3 applies a familiar computational paradigm, logic programming, but seems to lack relevant specialized design schemas. P3 recognizes at the beginning of the session that the lift problem is not a type of problem he is used to solve: *". . .this is different from what I am used to thinking about because we don't just have one lift we can decide algorithmically what to do about. . . ."* As a consequence, P3 adopts central control for its computational simplicity: *". . .Maybe I can assume there's some central processor that can receive signals from all the lifts and decide on things? . . . Well, I think it might be easiest to do it that way."*

Lack of or poor meta-schema for design. The next main determinant of performance appears to be the presence or absence of a meta-schema of software design. A design meta-schema is a schema about the process of design itself and not about a particular class of problems. The meta-schema is used to **control** the design process. A design meta-schema guides the execution of design activities and resource management. A design meta-schema represents design process goals and their alternatives and guides the amount of effort spent in different activities. For example, a design meta-schema will help answer questions such as:

- How much time and money should be spent on the complete design process?

- How much time and money should

be spent on exploring the problem environment?

- How much time and money should be spent exploring alternative solutions for identified subproblems?

- Which subproblem should be attempted to be solved next?

- How many alternative solutions should be considered for the selected subproblem?

P8 has been trained as a software engineer and he seems to be using a meta-schema about design to guide the resources he allocates to various design activities and the amount of exploration done. This meta-schema is based on the design technique developed by Jackson [6]. P8 first explores his mental model of the problem environment using various representation techniques to a much greater extent than P6 and P3 before proceeding to define an initial solution. The *problem environment* is a part of the real world, outside of the designed computer system, with which the computer system interacts. It contains the objects, properties, behaviors, and constraints in the world that are relevant to the design of a solution. In our case, the problem environment of a lift system contains such entities as floors, lifts, floor buttons, lift buttons, people, people waiting, requests for lifts, buildings, lift doors, lift panels, the safety of passengers, etc. The designer produces a mental model of the problem environment, possibly incomplete and inconsistent, based on the requirements and the designer's knowledge about the world. The mental model of the problem environment specifies more information than is contained explicitly in the requirements, and will often be more complete than the requirements or may sometimes be inconsistent with the stated requirements. The purpose of exploring the problem environment is to increase the completeness of the requirements and to discover unstated constraints, properties, behaviors, or objects that may generate constraints on the solution.

The following excerpt exemplifies how P8 uses a meta-schema about design to guide how much time he spends on various design activities and the amount of exploration done. About twenty minutes after the beginning of the session, while P8 is still exploring the problem environment, he shifts to a subproblem at a very low level of detail. He starts exploring the subproblems of handling inputs on an interrupt basis and of scheduling the service to lift requests. He then dramatically shifts back to a high level of abstraction. *"But at this point I feel I might be getting ahead of myself, so I want to think about other basic strategies. For instance, usually when I'm doing a design I try to think about things in a data abstraction way or object-oriented way. So now I'm trying to see if I can think about the objects and the system kind of independently."* About 5 minutes later, one can again see from the protocol how P8 seems to apply conscious strategies of resource allocation: *"...I'm sort of working at a high-level now, but I just have the feeling that if I maybe just tried working at a lower level for a second I might get some ideas...just kind of imagine in my mind how I could actually do this at some deeper* (i.e., more concrete, precise) *level."* Again about 14 minutes later, P8 makes clear that he is applying some strategies to allocate resources to different activities during design: *"...I feel I*

still need to think about the problem. On the other hand, I feel a little bit frustrated because I don't know why things haven't gelled enough yet. And so on the other hand, I'm impatient to sort of have things gelling; but on the other hand, I feel like there's some relationship between lift requests and floor requests that I feel I just haven't really grasped that yet." P8 recognizes that he should explore the problem in greater detail before adopting a solution.

P6 combines exploration of the problem environment and issue-driven design. P6 does not seem to use as sophisticated a meta-schema about design as P8. Nevertheless, about sixteen minutes after the beginning of the session, where he has already explored cursorily the subproblems of posting lift requests and servicing the requests, his use of a meta-schema based on software engineering practices is revealed by his comment: *"I'm just putting down the criteria which I'm basing this algorithm on, and I want to be sure I get the requirements that I'm trying to satisfy before I get the solution...I do not want to fall in the trap of solutions without requirements."*

We hypothesize that the use of a meta-schema for design is particularly useful if the designer lacks more specialized relevant design schemas. The use of a meta-schema about design helps the designer control the amount of effort spent in different activities during design (e.g., exploration for understanding the problem environment, exploration and evaluation of different solutions).

Poor prioritization of issues leading to poor selection from alternative solutions. Tong [10] views design as a dialectic between the designer and what is possible. Design can be conceived as the process of producing an optimized artifact given a set of interrelated or independent constraints, explicit or implicit, imposed by the problem, the medium, and the designer (see also Mostow [11]). Examples of constraints provided by each of these sources are:

—the problem

- a given (perhaps informal) functional specification

- limitations of the available media (e.g., available hardware and software)

- implicit and explicit requirements on performance and usage (e.g., cost, power, speed, space)

- implicit and explicit requirements on the form of the artifact (e.g., maintainability, reliability, reusability, simplicity)

—the design process itself

- time available
- allowable costs
- tools available (e.g., type of workstation, special hardware)
- team work or individual work
- organizational procedures

—the designer

- knowledge of the application domain

- knowledge of the class of system being designed (i.e., special design schemas)

- knowledge or experience of the

design process itself (i.e., meta-schema for design)

- cognitive and motivational attributes

Very good designers seem to know how to prioritize and balance these constraints on the basis of their domain knowledge, knowledge of the type of system to be designed and developed (i.e., design schemas), and their knowledge of the design process itself (i.e., design meta-schema). Following this prioritization, they allocate their time to the various subproblems according to their relation to these priorities. So, this third breakdown is related to management of resources and to the meta-schema of the design process.

Part of this prioritization process is the evaluation of alternative solutions based on a set of selected criteria as described above. These evaluation criteria are called *issues and their alternatives*. For example, P6's main issue is reliability and no single point of failure. He infers this issue from his knowledge of the problem domain and the class of system he is designing. When dealing with the subproblem of control, and its alternatives as centralized vs. distributed, he evaluates the two alternatives and opts for distributed control because of its perceived greater reliability. He does likewise when considering alternatives for communication schemes between lifts. The following excerpt demonstrates his evaluation of alternative solutions on the basis of the inferred issue of no single point of failure.

P6—*'The good news about central control is it's an easier algorithm vs. distributed control. The bad news is you have a single point of failure... You would rather not have a single point of failure because if, you know if all the elevators go down because it goes down... You would not want everything to go down... So, I'll start off thinking about a distributed control system...you got to post that request and then someone's got to pick it up and mark that he's responding to it. That set of words implies a centralized place to post the request and we're back to the single point of failure.... Well, you could broadcast a message to all the other elevators that you are servicing number one. Seems like a simple algorithm..."*

Breakdowns Due to Cognitive Limitations

Difficulty in considering all the stated or inferred constraints in refining a solution. This breakdown represents a failure to integrate known or assumed constraints in the design solution. These failures occurred even though these constraints were explicitly given in the problem statement and the problem statement was available throughout the session to the designers.

In the example below, P3 knows the constraints that all floors must be serviced equally and that direction of travel must be kept. In his design he decides to keep the elevator going in one direction until all outstanding requests in this direction are satisfied.

P3—*"If there are still requests and those requests are higher than we want to go, then we'll keep going up... If an elevator was going up, it keeps going up until all up requests are satisfied...that insures that requests will eventually be met, otherwise there could just be oscillating between floor one and floor two."*

Nevertheless, later, he forgets about his solution on these constraints and evaluates improperly his overall solution. P3 seems to believe that requests to go down while the lift is going up are going to be serviced immediately. As a consequence, the lift would not keep direction of travel, violating a problem constraint.

P3—*"...well this is interesting now, it brings up the questions of what if an elevator is on its way up to a floor to pick up somebody up there and a person snatches it at the floor below and wants it to go down...it's going to be priority driven and that's nasty..."*

A somewhat related breakdown is to disregard certain relevant aspects of the problem—the "rose-colored glasses" syndrome. In the excerpt below, P3 proposes a non-deterministic solution to allocate floor requests to lifts. He also acknowledges that this may jeopardize the requirement that all floors be given equal priority, thereby violating a given constraint. He nevertheless adopts the non-deterministic solution without any more analysis of its consequences.

P3—*"Our processor will look to see what elevators are moving up and down. We'll do this non-deterministically. Maybe that's dangerous for this priority* (all floors given equal priority) *but OK."*

Difficulty in performing complex mental simulations with many steps or with many test cases. Designers find it very difficult to mentally simulate their partial or complete solutions. They find it difficult to simulate the interactions between components of the artifact. They also find it difficult to simulate the behavior of a component if it extends over many steps. We also observed the multiple simulations of the same test case and the failure to simulate a crucial test case during evaluative simulations, leading to incorrect assessment of the correctness of the solution to a given subproblem and hindering progress on other subproblems. To help mental simulations, designers often resorted to diagrams. However, because they were poor medium to represent changes in location and time, they were not sufficient to prevent the breakdowns. The following excerpts show how designers had difficulty even with the simplest simulations.

P8—*". . .it's kind of confusing, there's lifts* (requests) *and there's floors* (requests) *and it says 'all requests for floors within lifts must be serviced eventually with floors being serviced sequentially'* (in the direction of travel). *Apparently that means. . . Let me give a better example. . . I'll have to draw a picture."*

P3—*". . .the way I've written this doesn't capture the continuity of direction. 'Cause this just looks to see some other. We've happened to have reached some floor, this now just picks some other request. Oh, no, that's right, this tries to find a request that's in the same direction."*

P8—*"When an interrupt happens it adds a request to my list and the structure of requests are floor request, a lift request, or the emergency button. . . Let's say the third guy wants to go to the fifth floor. Let's say there's a floor request on the. . . Oh, I missed something here. Floor request has originating floor and direction. . . Could I borrow that pencil?* (to draw a picture).*"*

The next excerpt shows how the mental simulation of the test cases is at the beginning quite systematic and quickly becomes unsystematic and finally incomplete as other concerns attract the attention of the designer.

P3—*". . .Given the fact that somebody in a lift has pushed a 'go to floor' button (that's a floor he wants to go to). First of all, if that lift is at that floor then I can just de-illuminate the button. . ."* Here, he digresses for about one minute. *". . .On the other hand, if he pushes a lift button and he's not at the floor he requested, what I'll do is I'll put that into this global base which means that by the demon watching, the light will go on. And that's all I really have to do other than examine this and decide which way the elevators move. So I'm trying to handle the request right now. . . So really all I'm doing is filtering out requests that can be handled immediately, but OK, let's go with that for a second. . . I'll handle emergencies later."* He digresses for about 30 seconds and than changes topic drastically. He abandons the simulations of the other test cases, those requests that cannot be handled immediately. *"OK. Now comes time to build a mechanism which causes all the stuff to change."*

Breakdowns Due to Lack of Knowledge and Due to Cognitive Limitations

Difficulty in keeping track and returning to aspects of problems whose solution refinements have been postponed. When focusing on one aspect of the problem and postponing the solution refinement of others, the designer must be able to remember to return to the postponed subproblems. If the designer fails to do so, the partial solutions could be incomplete and could not be merged or expanded into a complete solution. This problem is especially acute if the designer does not have specialized design schemas for the given problem, since its structure acts as an aid for the storage and retrieval of intermediate solutions. However, failing to return to a postponed subproblem is not always detrimental. A designer may uncover a new solution or adopt a new strategy that makes useless returning to a postponed subproblem. Nevertheless, this is different than failing to return to a subproblem because one forgets to look at one's mental notes or external notes or because these mental notes or external notes are insufficient.

In the following excerpt, P8 explicitly mentions an aspect of the problem he plans to return to. He forgets to return to it as he concentrates on the decomposition of the problem into requests from floors and requests from lifts and on merging the partial solutions. Note here that postponing that subproblem is appropriate because it is at a lower level of detail than the other subproblems he is handling. However, the postponed subproblem is crucial for the complete solution.

P8—*"It seems like in my interrupt system I don't just want a way of sequentially handling requests. I'm really going to need to be able to scan all outstanding requests because of the service constraints. I think I'll do that next. Capture these constraints in some way."*

Difficulty in expanding or merging partial solutions into a complete solution. The designers in our study had difficulties expanding their solution, from 1 lift to N lifts, or in merging their partial solutions, handling requests from lifts and handling requests from floors. Kant and Newell [3] also observed that the merging of the individual solutions was very difficult in the convex hull problem. Once acceptable solutions have been

reached for some or all of the subproblems, these solutions must be merged together or expanded to compose a solution for the complete problem. This expansion relies on a history of the design process, and general and specialized computer science knowledge. The expansion of partial solutions actually seems difficult for most designers (this was also observed in Kant and Newell [3]). We hypothesize that the expansion of or merging of partial solutions is more difficult than the decomposition of the problem into smaller problems for three reasons:

1. Evaluative simulations for the merged or expanded solutions are more complex, more taxing cognitively than evaluative simulations for the partial solutions to the subproblems. This is because merged or expanded solutions are more complex, they have more solutions components and more interactions between these components than partial or reduced solutions.

2. Certain problem decompositions based on obvious or surface features of the problem environment (e.g., number of lifts—solve for 1 lift and expand to N lifts) may suggest solutions that do not reflect the structure of the original problem and for which no simple solution expansion exists. For example, in the case of the 1-lift problem there are no notions of coordination, communication between lifts, and race condition, which are crucial in the N-lift problem.

3. One view of the progression from design to solution/implementation is of a process of *dispersion.* When a

designer breaks the problem into sub-problems and refines the solution for each subproblem into more implementation-oriented representations, the implementation-oriented concepts blur the structure the original problem was to solve. The solutions to the subproblems are then more difficult to merge because their original correspondence to each other has been altered. This should be more acute for complex problems where the solution of individual subproblems extends over a long period of time.

There is possibly a fourth reason. If a designer does not follow balanced development, the partial solutions will not be at the same level of detail and will be difficult to merge. This could happen for example to P8 who performed serendipitous design. However, it is difficult to precisely define when partial solutions are at the same level of detail and can, as a consequence, be mentally simulated. Therefore, it is difficult from the protocol to identify whether two partial solutions could not be merged because they were not at the same level of detail.

In the following excerpts from P8, each separate segment comes from different times in chronological order in the session and they capture the difficulty of merging the solution for one lift into a solution for N lifts.

". . .I'm basically considering what's happening for one lift. I'm imagining that everything happens independently. That's not a good assumption to make. I guess I'm considering this a global list." He then attempts to solve the scheduling of requests and to perform evaluative simulations for N lifts.

". . .Well the fact that I have N lifts makes it kind of complicated. So I'll just try to consider the case of one lift, try to simplify it. . . I'm going to back up now and try to handle this with one lift."

RELATIONS TO OTHER STUDIES AND OTHER OF OUR FINDINGS

We will now relate some of our breakdowns to other of our findings or to other studies. Adelson and Soloway [12] studied expert designers (about eight years of professional experience) in three contexts: 1) designing an unfamiliar artifact in a familiar domain; 2) designing an unfamiliar artifact in an unfamiliar domain; and 3) designing a familiar artifact in a familiar domain. They also studied two novice designers, with less than two years of experience as designers. If one were trying to compare our designers to those of Adelson and Soloway's study, we could tentatively define: 1) P6, an expert designing an unfamiliar artifact in a familiar technical domain; 2) P8, an expert designing an unfamiliar artifact in an unfamiliar technical domain; and 3) P3, an expert/novice designing an unfamiliar artifact in an unfamiliar technical domain.

The lack of specialized design schemas seems the primary breakdown to alleviate. The reasons are both empirical and logical. P6's design solution was considered superior to P8's and P3's. P6 also exhibited a more balanced systematic design process than P8 and P3. P6 appeared to have more relevant specialized design schemas than P8 and P3. These design schemas are provided by his expertise in a relevant technical domain, i.e., communication systems. Design schemas are assumed to represent a plan to decompose a problem into subproblems. As a consequence we believe that design schemas underlie balanced development. During balanced development, which was described by Adelson and Soloway [2], each solution component is developed at a similar level of detail to permit mental simulations.

Design schemas are also believed to provide a cognitive structure to help store partial solutions and their evaluations and to help remember which subproblem to focus on next. As a consequence, they are believed to support mental note-taking. Mental note-taking was observed by Adelson and Soloway [2] and described as a mechanism supporting balanced development. As a consequence, a lack of specialized design schemas will worsen another breakdown, the difficulty in keeping track and returning to postponed subproblems. This breakdown was rarely observed in P6 but was very frequent in P3.

The lack of relevant specialized design schemas appears to be associated with another breakdown, difficulty in expanding a reduced solution or merging of partial solutions. A design schema provides a plan for a well-motivated decomposition of the problem into subproblems. The partial solutions from such decompositions can be easily merged together to form a complete solution. When a problem is not decomposed on the basis of a design schema, the partial solutions may be difficult to expand or merge together. P6 had very little difficulty merging his partial solutions, while this was particularly difficult for P8.

Finally, we believe that the use of specialized design schemas frees the designers from reliance on weak problem-solving methods such as generate and test

and means-ends analysis. These weak problem-solving methods, especially generate-and-test, can be very taxing cognitively. In fact, P3 had the least relevant specialized design schemas and adopted a "generate-and-test-and-debug" strategy. Not surprisingly, he experienced many difficulties with mental simulations with many steps or many test cases.

The next important breakdown is the lack of meta-schema of the design process which leads to poor allocation of resources and time to the various activities during the design process. We believe that relevant specialized design schemas obviate the need for sophisticated meta-schemas about the design process. Specialized design schemas provide for systematic decomposition of the problem and for solutions to each subproblem. The need to carefully manage resources is less critical in this context. However, when specialized design schemas are lacking, the need to carefully balance exploration of the problem environment, consideration of alternative solutions, and evaluations of selected tentative solutions is critical for the quality of the solution reached. While P8 seemed to have less specialized design schemas relevant to the problem than P6, he appeared to have a sophisticated design meta-schema, which was lacking in P3. P8's solution was considered better than P3's. P8's design meta-schema guided him to explore the problem environment before focusing testing and debugging solutions. We speculate that exploration of the problem environment induced *serendipitous problem-solving activities*. By serendipitous design, we mean a design process controlled by recognition of **partial solutions, at different levels of detail or abstraction,** without having previously decomposed the problem into subproblems. We hypothesize that serendipity in design arises from a form of data-driven processing as opposed to goal-directed processing, such as described by Anderson [13]. This data-driven processing can be triggered by aspects of the problem environment at different levels of detail or abstraction. The concept of serendipity in design is similar to the idea of *opportunistic* problem-solving (Hayes-Roth and Hayes-Roth [14]), though different in some crucial aspects. The main difference is that in serendipitous design the partial solutions are not synergetic, they do not necessarily interact and they do not fulfill more goals than originally anticipated. An important observation to make is that serendipitous design does not follow balanced development. Moreover, P8 did not extensively exhibit mental note-taking. However, we believe that when specialized design schemas are lacking, the presence of a design meta-schema supporting important exploration of the problem environment is advantageous. We speculate that exploration of the problem environment induces serendipitous design, as opposed to balanced development. However, in the absence of specialized design schemas we believe serendipitous design is advantageous. In fact, serendipitous design might be a hallmark of an important type of design, designing new innovative software systems. For such systems are not simply modifications of previously well understood systems, they introduce genuinely new ideas. As a consequence, their design cannot rely on computer science knowledge embodied in specialized design schemas. Moreover, because of real-life constraints designers may of-

ten face the situation of designing systems outside their areas of expertise, that is, for which they lack specialized design schemas. Finally, a certain amount of exploration of the problem environment is always desirable as it permits uncovering critical missing information in the requirements. In all these cases, we need to develop tools and methodologies which permit designers to benefit as much as possible from serendipitous problem-solving, as opposed to discourage it because it does not follow the prescriptive practices from software engineering.

While this is a preliminary study, it is very encouraging to see that similar design processes and breakdowns have been observed in other very different fields. After the completion of this study, we became aware of the work by Ullman, Stauffer, and Dietterich [5] on the mechanical design process. They collected verbal protocols from four professional engineers working on problems related to their areas of expertise. Our designer P8 performed a great deal of serendipitous problem-solving, probably underlied by his extensive exploration of the problem environment. Ullman, Stauffer, and Dietterich labelled these problem-solving activities opportunistic. We believe that the name opportunistic is misleading, as synergy did not appear in the partial solutions reached by the designers. The partial solutions did not satisfy unanticipatedly more goals than they were originally meant to. Interestingly, Adelson and Soloway [12] described some design behaviors which may be related to serendipitous design. The particularly relevant observation is that the **experienced** designer designing a **familiar object** in a **familiar technical domain** departed from balanced development and systematic expansion of his solution when dealing with the aspect of the problem that was unfamiliar to him, the functionality of a particular chip.

Ullman, Stauffer, and Dietterich also observed that not all designers followed balanced development (even though all their designers were experienced). They observed the use of diagrams to prevent breakdowns from difficulty of mental simulations, even though diagrams were only partly successful. They also observed that designers forget to return to postponed subproblems. They also noticed that designers have a tendency to elaborate mainly one main design idea throughout the design session with few considerations of major changes to the basic design.

So, it appears that experienced designers are aware of the power of exploration of the problem environment in uncovering new important information (i.e., as part of their meta-schema about the design process). They use exploration of the problem environment when dealing with unfamiliar information or when progress toward a solution is insufficient using balanced development. This exploration of the problem environment induces problem solving that does not follow balanced development but is more appropriately described as serendipitous.

Similarly, Flower and Hayes and their colleagues have observed rapid shifts between levels of abstraction and detail in the planning and writing of documents and the use of design schemas and of meta-schemas [15]. Finally, Schoenfeld [16] has observed similar behaviors in mathematical problem solving.

CONCLUSIONS

While the study reported in this chapter is an exploratory study, it provides a wealth of observations that enrich our understanding of the software design process by individuals. Our findings were related to previous studies of the design process by individuals and revealed new behaviors and some important new questions about the design process.

Our observations of designers working on the N-lift problem show that designers use a wide variety of design strategies, both between and within designers, in addition to the top-down refinement approach described in software engineering. We also found that our designers were able to work at different levels of abstraction and detail and not just follow a balanced development strategy. We also observed serendipitous problem solving, not reported in previous studies of software design by individuals. We also observed a great emphasis on understanding and elaborating the requirements through mental simulations. We have observed a wide variety of breakdowns, also not reported or emphasized in previous studies: 1) lack of specialized design schemas; 2) lack of a meta-schema about the design process leading to poor allocation of resources to the various design activities; 3) poor prioritization of issues leading to poor selection of alternative solutions; 4) difficulty in considering all the stated or inferred constraints in defining a solution; 5) difficulty in keeping track and returning to subproblems whose solution has been postponed; 6) difficulty in performing mental simulations with many steps or test cases; and 7) difficulty in expanding or merging solutions from individual sub-problems to form a complete solution.

There was also overlap between our findings and the findings of other studies in varied fields (e.g., mechanical engineering and mathematical problem solving). This overlap suggests that we are tapping general problem-solving strategies for design problems. This also suggests that the tools we are designing to alleviate the breakdowns have wider applicability than software design. This overlap also increases confidence about the validity of the findings and their generalizability.

For each breakdown, we have recommended software tools or methodologies to alleviate them (Guindon, Krasner, and Curtis [17]). In further studies, we will test the effectiveness of these tools and methodologies. These further studies will be indirect tests of the hypotheses raised in this study. In addition, they will provide empirical results on the influence of software tools on the design process. We will also explore in greater depth the nature of the application-specific design schemas, their role in design performance, their role in the different expertise exhibited by our designers, their relation to the breakdowns we have observed, and how software tools could be designed to alleviate lack of design schemas.

REFERENCES

[1] Jeffries, R., A.A. Turner, P. Polson, and M.E. Atwood (1981). "The Processes Involved in Designing Software." In J.R. Anderson, ed. *Cognitive Skills and Their Acquisition*. Hillsdale, N.J.: Erlbaum, 1981, pp. 225-83.

[2] Adelson, B., and E. Soloway. *A Cognitive Model of Software Design*. Technical Report No. 342, Department of Computer Science, New Haven, Conn., Yale University, 1985.

[3] Kant, E., and A. Newell. "Problem Solving Techniques for the Design of Algorithms." *Information Processing and Management*, Vol. 28, No. 1, 1984, pp. 97-118.

[4] Carroll, J.M., J.C. Thomas, and A. Malhotra. "Clinical-Experimental Analysis of Design Problem Solving." *Design Studies*, Vol. 1, No. 2, 1979, pp. 84-92.

[5] Ullman, D.G., L.A. Stauffer, and T.G. Dietterich. "Preliminary Results of an Experimental Study of the Mechanical Design Process." *Proceedings of the Workshop on the Study of the Design Process*. Oakland, Calif.: 1987.

[6] Jackson, M. *System Development*. Englewood Cliffs, N.J.: Prentice-Hall, 1983.

[7] Laird, J., P. Rosenbloom, and A. Newell. *Universal Subgoaling and Chunking*. Norwell, Mass.: Kluwer Academic Publishers, 1986.

[8] Rich, C., and R.C. Waters. "Toward a Requirements Apprentice: On the Boundary Between Informal and Formal Specifications." M.I.T. A.I. Memo No. 907, 1986.

[9] Lubars, M.T., and M.T. Harandi. "Knowledge-Based Software Design Using Design Schemas."

Proceedings of the Ninth International Conference on Software Engineering. Monterey, Calif., 1987, pp. 253-62.

[10] Tong, C. "Knowledge-Based Circuit Design." Ph.D. Dissertation, Department of Computer Science, Stanford University, 1984.

[11] Mostow, J. "Toward Better Models of the Design Process." *AI Magazine,* 1985, pp. 44-57.

[12] Adelson, B., and E. Soloway. "The Role of Domain Experience in Software Design." *IEEE Transactions on Software Engineering,* Vol. 11, No. 11, 1985.

[13] Anderson, J.R. *The Architecture of Cognition.* Cambridge, Mass.: Harvard University Press, 1983.

[14] Hayes-Roth, B., and F. Hayes-Roth. "A Cognitive Model of Planning." *Cognitive Science,* Vol. 3. No. 4, 1979, pp. 275-310.

[15] Flower, L., J.R. Hayes, L. Carey, K. Schriver, and J. Stratman. "Detection, Diagnosis, and the Strategies of Revision." *College Composition and Communication,* Vol. 37, No. 1, 1986.

[16] Schoenfeld, A.H. *Mathematical Problem Solving.* New York: Academic Press, 1987.

[17] Guindon, R., H. Krasner, and B. Curtis. "A Model of Cognitive Processes in Software Design: An Analysis of Breakdowns in Early Design Activities by Individuals." MCC Technical Report, in preparation, 1987.

ACKNOWLEDGMENTS

We wish to thank Glenn Bruns, Jeff Conklin, Michael Evangelist, and Colin Potts for very insightful comments and criticisms on an earlier version of this paper.

APPENDIX

Problem Statement

An N-lift (N-elevator) system is to be installed in a building with M floors. The lifts and the control mechanism are supplied by a manufacturer. The internal mechanisms of these are assumed (given) in this problem.

DESIGN THE LOGIC TO MOVE LIFTS BETWEEN FLOORS IN THE BUILDING ACCORDING TO THE FOLLOWING RULES:

1. Each lift has a set of buttons, 1 button for each floor. These illuminate when pressed and cause the lift to visit the corresponding floor. The illumination is canceled when the corresponding floor is visited (i.e., stopped at) by the lift.

2. Each floor has 2 buttons (except ground and top), one to request an up-lift and one to request a down-lift. These buttons illuminate when pressed. The buttons are canceled when a lift visits the floor and is either traveling in the desired direction, or visiting the floor with no requests outstanding. In the latter case, if both floor request buttons are illuminated, only 1 should be canceled. The al-

gorithm used to decide which to service first should minimize the waiting time for both requests.

3. When a lift has no requests to service, it should remain at its final destination with its doors closed and await further requests (or model a "holding" floor).

4. All requests for lifts from floors must be serviced eventually, with all floors given equal priority (can this be proved or demonstrated?).

5. All requests for floors within lifts must be serviced eventually, with floors being serviced sequentially in the direction of travel (can this be proved or demonstrated?).

6. Each lift has an emergency button which, when pressed, causes a warning signal to be sent to the site manager. The lift is then deemed "out of service." Each lift has a mechanism to cancel its "out of service" status.

30

Editors' Note
James and Morrill: "The Real Ada, Countess of Lovelace"

Insight: There was a real-life Ada who gave her name to the DoD's programming language.

The Ada language was named for the world's first programmer, Ada, Countess of Lovelace. She was Lord Byron's daughter and Charles Babbage's mistress and who knows what all else? Read James and Morrill's delicious biographical snippet to find out.

30

The Real Ada, Countess of Lovelace
by Carol L. James and Duncan E. Morrill

It was becoming embarrassing. The Department of Defense had been working for some years on the development of the high-order language to program its embedded computers, but the language still had no official name—only informal designations like DoD-1, which no one in the DoD High Order Language Working Group favored because that implied a language specifically for military purposes and might inhibit its use in universities and other non-military spheres.

According to Air Force Colonel William A. Whitaker, the first HOLWG chairman, many names were proposed, but it was Commander John D. Cooper, the Navy's HOLWG member, who in May 1979 came up with a name that HOLWG (representing various government branches) could approve unanimously: Ada,* in honor of an obscure but talented mathematician—Ada, Countess of Lovelace.

Back in the 1840s, Ada Lovelace had worked with Charles Babbage on his mechanical computer invention, the analytical engine. Babbage's hopes for continued funding from the British government for building his machine were frustrated after a few years, compounding his technical difficulties—the greatest

one being that the engine required parts whose fabrication was beyond the state of the art then and for many decades thereafter—so that the computer never became fully operational. Nonetheless, the Countess of Lovelace worked out most of its theoretical principles, as well as its programming, and has thus been called—with much justification—the first computer programmer.

Evidently inspired by Bertram V. Bowden's 1950s computer book, *Faster Than Thought,* which dealt with the work of Babbage and the countess, HOLWG approved the name "Ada" and received permission from Ada's descendant, the Earl of Lytton, to use it. Colonel Whitaker says the earl, himself a retired lieutenant colonel of the British army, was immediately enthusiastic about the idea and pointed out that the letters "Ada" stood "right in the middle of 'radar.' "

The Ada project is still almost as unfamiliar to most people as the name Ada Lovelace, but its activities and accomplishments are considerable and include the Ada language MIL-STD-1815 (10 Dec 1980), Ada for MIL-STD-1750A instruction-set architecture, Ada-Europe, and AdaTEC of the ACM.

Use of the countess's name seems especially fitting for such ambitious endeavors since any serious study of the historical record shows that hers was not

---

*Ada is a registered trademark of the U.S. Department of Defense (OUSDRE-AJPO).

some idiosyncratic affliction but a comprehensive and integrated faculty encompassing the philosophical and the practical. Her major extant scientific work—notes she appended to her translation into English of the L.F. Menabrea paper on Babbage's analytical engine—attest to her mathematical knowledge and scientific intellect. About three times longer than the Menabrea work itself, the notes display mastery of both the mathematical theory and numerical techniques of Babbage's computing engines. England's scientific leaders of the day—Michael Faraday, Sir John Herschel, Charles Wheatstone, Mary Somerville, and Augustus De Morgan—knew and appreciated her abilities.

Her father was the poet Lord Byron who, while still a bachelor, underwent an experience that was to have profound effects upon his only legitimate child, born Augusta Ada Byron. At 25, he fell in love with his married half sister, Augusta Leigh; and to deny that an incestuous relationship existed between them is to ignore an overwhelming body of evidence, although his paternity of her daughter Elizabeth Medora Leigh, born in 1814, is less certain.

In January 1815, Byron married Annabella Milbanke, a puritanical young woman of good family and an amateur mathematician. Unfortunately, their personalities were incompatible, and a few weeks after Augusta was born (December 10, 1815), the couple separated. Shortly afterward, rumors concerning Byron's previous affair with Augusta destroyed his reputation and social acceptability, forcing him to take up permanent residence on the Continent. However, subsequent letters and much of his poetry show tender concern for the child he never saw again. He died at 36, eight years after her birth.

Lady Byron resolved to bring up her daughter (now called Ada, for obvious reasons) to be as unlike Byron as possible. Setting herself up as a paragon while hinting of unspeakable evil in her husband's character, she encouraged Ada's mathematical talent but discouraged any traits that reminded her of Byron.

When Ada was about 14, she suffered a severe paralytic illness—possibly of psychosomatic origin. Unable to walk for almost three years, she pursued the mathematical studies she loved and became an accomplished musician and linguist. Like most young ladies of her social class, she was taught by tutors—some of whom were preeminent scientists and mathematicians, such as Augustus De Morgan, a family friend.

At 19, Ada married William King (created Lord Lovelace three years later). Her mother became the dominant and domineering figure in the marriage, forming a kind of ruling partnership with Ada's husband—the covert reason being that Ada—whose mercurial Byronic temperament they wished to control—must be kept busy and out of mischief. Together they freed Ada from many of the usual feminine social and family responsibilities so that she would have time to carve out a mathematical and scientific career; but, tragically, the countess's health never allowed her to progress as far as she would have liked.

After the birth of her third child, and about the time her notes on the Menabrea paper were published (when she was 29), she began to suffer both physical and mental breakdown. Because she was subject to frequent digestive and breathing problems, her doctor advised her to use various dangerous combinations of brandy, wine, beer, opium, and morphine, which led to serious personality disorders, including delusions to the effect that her mind—admittedly brilliant—could comprehend the secrets of the universe and make her God's prophet on earth.

After some years, she came to recognize that drugs were disastrous to her equilibrium and managed to shake off the addiction through sheer will power—only to fall victim to a new obsession: horse race gambling. Since highborn ladies did not deal directly with bookmakers, she used a servant and Babbage as go-betweens. Unbeknownst to Babbage at first, she ran into catastrophic debt, pawned family jewels, and became the target of blackmailers who threatened public exposure. Her husband, when he learned of her difficulties, stood by her; but consequent family squabbles among Ada, Lord Lovelace, and Ada's mother brought permanent estrangement on all sides.

To add to her torment, Ada was suffering from internal cancer, to which she succumbed in 1852 at the age of 36. She was buried, at her request, beside Lord Byron in the Byron family vault. If there is one bright spot in the darkness of her last years, it is that she had finally come to understand and accept her own identity, and that of the father she had been taught to despise.

REFERENCES

[1]   Huskey, V.R., and H.D. Huskey. "Lady Lovelace and Charles Babbage." *Annals of the History of Computing,* Vol. 2, No. 4, October 1980.

[2]   James, C.L. "Ada: They Named a Language After Her." *Softalk,* Vol. 2, November 1981.

[3]   Moore, D.L. *Ada, Countess of Lovelace.* New York: Harper & Row, 1977.

[4]   Moseley, M. *Irascible Genius: The Life of Charles Babbage.* Chicago: Henry Regnery Company, 1964.

31

Editors' Note
Knuth: "The Errors of TEX"

Insight: Bugs, the bane of mere mortal programmers, can plague even a Donald Knuth. Keeping rigorous track of defects can shed some light on how to improve.

Donald Knuth is the Turing Award winning professor of computer science at Stanford University. Most of us know Knuth as the author of *The Art of Computer Programming,* certain volumes being mandatory reading in our student days, and now an indispensable resource in our professional careers. Knuth is revered by programmers as a near software deity.

During the past decade, he spent much of his time defining and implementing a software system for typesetting he named TEX. This article presents a diary of part of Knuth's work on TEX for the last ten years. The professor calmly displays his own failings; he lets us look at his bug list, and he describes his strategy for implementing a large complex piece of software.

Yes, he can program better than we can, and yes, he can write a program faster than we can, but by golly, the man makes a few mistakes too. Proving his deific status is earned, Knuth does not shy away from his errors as we mortals do, but uses them to offer insight into the long difficult process of development and refinement of a piece of useful software.

This article also supplies us with one of the most practical error classification schemes we have come across. In addition, it has a lovely discussion of testing. Can you get a mental picture of Professor Knuth when he writes, "I get into the meanest, nastiest frame of mind that I can manage, and I write the nastiest code I can think of. . ."?

31

The Errors of TeX
by Donald E. Knuth

SUMMARY

This paper is a case study of program evolution. The author kept track of all changes made to TeX during a period of ten years, including the changes made when the original program was first debugged in 1978. The log book of these errors, numbering more than 850 items, appears as an appendix to this paper. The errors have been classified into fifteen categories for purposes of analysis, and some of the noteworthy bugs are discussed in detail. The history of the TeX project can teach valuable lessons about the preparation of highly portable software and the maintenance of programs that aspire to high standards of reliability.

KEY WORDS   Errors   Debugging   TeX   Program evolution   Language design   True confessions

INTRODUCTION

I make mistakes. I always have, and I probably always will. But I like to think that I learn something, every time I go astray. In fact, one of my favourite poems consists of the following lines by Piet Hein:[1]

> The road to wisdom? Well, it's plain
> and simple to express:
>> Err
>> and err
>> and err again
>> but less
>> and less
>> and less.

I am writing this paper on 5 May 1987, exactly ten years since I began to work intensively on software systems for typesetting. I have certainly learned a lot during those ten years, judging from the number of mistakes I made; and I would like to share what I have learned with other people who are developing software. The best way to do this, as far as I know, is to present a list of all the errors that were corrected in TeX while it was being developed, and to attempt to analyse those errors.

---

* TeX is a trademark of the American Mathematical Society.

481

When I mentioned my plan for this paper to Paul M. B. Vitányi, he told me about a best-selling book that his grand-uncle had written for civil engineers, devoted entirely to descriptions of foundation work that had proved to be defective. The preface to that book[2] says

> It is natural that engineers should not wish to draw attention to their mistakes, but failures are sometimes due to causes of which there has been no previous experience or of which no information is available. An engineer cannot be blamed for not foreseeing the unknown, and in such cases his reputation would not be harmed if full details of the design and of the phenomena that caused the failure were published for the guidance of others. . . . To be forewarned is to be forearmed.

In my own case I cannot claim that 'unknown' factors lay behind my blunders, since I was totally in control of my programming environment. I can justly be blamed for every mistake I made, and I am certainly not proud of the record. But I see no harm in admitting the horrible truth about my tendency to err, when such details might shed light on the problem of writing large programs. (Besides, I am lucky enough to have a secure job.)

Empirical studies of programming errors, conducted by Endres[3] and by Basili and Perricone,[4] have already led to interesting results and to the conclusion that 'more data must be collected on different projects'. I cannot claim that the data presented below will be as generally applicable as theirs, because all of the programming I shall discuss was done by one person (me). Insightful models of truly large-scale software development and program evolution have been introduced by Belady and Lehman.[5] However, I do have one advantage that the authors of previous studies did not have; namely, the entire program for TeX has been published.[6] Hence I can give fairly precise information about the type and location of each error. The concept of scale cannot easily be communicated by means of numerical data alone; I believe that a detailed list gives important insights that cannot be gained from statistical summaries.

TYPES OF ERROR

Some people undoubtedly think that everything I did on TeX was an error, from start to finish. But I shall consider only a limited class of errors here, based on the log books I kept while I was developing the program. Whenever I made a change, I noted it down for future reference, and it is these changes that I shall discuss in detail. Edited forms of my log books appear in the appendix below.

I guess I could say that this paper is about 'changes', not 'errors', because many of the changes were made in order to introduce new features rather than to correct malfunctions. However, new features are necessary only when a design is deficient (or at least non-optimal). Hence, I will continue to say that each change represents an error, even though I know that no complex system will ever be error-free in this extended sense.

The errors in my log books have each been assigned to one of fifteen general categories for purposes of analysis:

A, an algorithm awry. Here my original method proved to be incorrect or inadequate, so I needed to change the procedure. For example, error no. 212 fixed a problem in which footnotes appeared on a page backwards: the last footnote came out first.

B, a blunder or botch. Here I knew what I ought to do, but I wrote something else that was syntactically correct—sort of a mental typo. For example, in error no. 126 I wrote 'before' when I meant 'after' and vice versa. I was thinking so much of the Big Picture that I did not have enough brainpower left to get the small details right.

C, a clean-up for consistency or clarity. Here I changed the rules of the language to make things easier to remember and/or more logical. Sometimes this was just a surface change to TEX's 'syntactic sugar', as in error no. 16 where I decided that \input would be a better name than \require.

D, a data structure debacle. Here I did not properly update the representation of information to preserve the appropriate invariants. For example, in error no. 105 I failed to return nodes to available memory when they were no longer accessible.

E, an efficiency enhancement. Here I changed the program so that it would run faster; the existing code was correct but slow. For example, in error no. 287 I decided to give TEX the ability to preload fount information, since it took a while to read thirty short files at the beginning of every run.

F, a forgotten function. Here I did not remember to do everything I had intended, when I actually got around to writing a particular part of the code. It was a simple error of omission, rather than commission. For example, in error no. 11 and again in no. 172 I had a loop of the form while p $\neq$ null do, and I forgot to advance the pointer p inside the loop! This seems to be one of my favourite mistakes: I often forget the most obvious things.

G, a generalization or growth of ability. Here I realized that some extension of the existing specifications was desirable. For example, error no. 303 generalized my original primitive command '\ifT $\langle$char$\rangle$' (which tested if a given character was 'T' or not) to the primitive '\if $\langle$char$\rangle\langle$char$\rangle$' (which tested if two given characters were equal). Eventually, in no. 666, I decided to generalize further and allow '\if$\langle$token$\rangle\langle$token$\rangle$'.

I, an interactive improvement. Here I made TEX respond better to the user's needs. Sometimes I saw how to help TEX identify and recover from errors in the documents it was processing. I also kept searching for better ways to communicate the reasons underlying TEX's behaviour, by making diagnostic information available in symbolic form. For example, error no. 54 introduced '...' into the display of context lines so that users could easily tell when information was truncated.

L, a language liability. Here I misused or misunderstood the programming language or system hardware I was working with. For example, in error no. 24 I wanted to reduce a counter modulo 8, so I wrote t := (t − 1) mod 8; this unfortunately made t negative because of the way mod was defined. Sometimes I forgot the precedence of operators, etc.

M, a mismatch between modules. Here I forgot the conventions I had built into a subroutine when I actually got around to using that subroutine. For example, in error no. 64 I had a macro with four parameters (x_0, y_0, x_1, y_1) that define a rectangle; but when I used it, I gave the parameters in different order, (x_0, x_1, y_0, y_1). Such 'interface errors' included cases when a procedure had unwanted side-effects (such as clobbering a global variable) that I failed to take into account. Some mismatches (such as incorrect data types) were caught by the compiler and not entered in my log.

P, a promotion of portability. Here I changed the organization or documentation of the program; this affected only a person who would try to read or modify the code, not a person who tried to run it. For example, in error no. 59, one of my comments about how to set the size of memory had '$\geq$' where I meant to say '$\leq$'. (Most changes of this kind were not recorded in my log; I noted only the noteworthy ones.)

Q, a quest for quality. Here I changed the specifications of what the program should output from given input, when I learned how to improve the typographic appearance of the output. For example, error no. 187 changed TEX's behaviour when typesetting formulae that have an unusually complex superscript; as a result, TEX now produces

$$e^{\frac{1}{1-q_j^2}} \qquad \text{instead of} \qquad e^{\frac{1}{1-q_j^2}} .$$

R, a reinforcement of robustness. Whenever I realized that TEX could loop or crash in the presence of certain erroneous input, I tried to make the code bullet-proof. For example, error no. 200 made sure that a user-supplied character number was between 0 and 127; otherwise parts of TEX's memory could be wiped out.

S, a surprising scenario. Errors of type S were particularly bad bugs that forced me to change my original ideas, because of unforeseen interactions between various parts of the program. For example, error no. 25 was logged when I first discovered a consequence of TEX's convention about blank lines denoting the end of a paragraph: There is often a blank space in TEX's internal data structure just before a paragraph ends, because a space is usually supplied at the end of the line just preceding a blank line. Thus I had to write new code to delete the unwanted space. Whenever such unexpected phenomena showed up, I had to go back to the drawing board and fix the design.

T, a trivial typo. Sometimes I did not type the right thing when I entered the program into the computer, although my original pencil draft was correct. For example, in error no. 48 I had typed '$-$' instead of '$+$'. If a typing mistake was detected by the compiler as a syntax error, I did not log it, because bad syntax can easily be corrected.

Nine of these categories (A, B, D, F, L, M, R, S, T) represent 'bugs'; such errors absolutely had to be corrected. The other six categories (C, E, G, I, P, Q) represent 'enhancements'; I could have refused to consider the existing situation erroneous. As remarked earlier, I am considering all items in the log to be indications of error. But there is a significant difference between errors of these two kinds: I felt guilty when fixing the bugs, but I felt virtuous when making the enhancements.

My classification of errors into fifteen categories is *ad hoc*, but at the moment it is the best way I can think of to make sense out of my experiences. Some of the bug categories refer to simple flaws in the basic mechanics of programming: writing the right thing but typing it wrong (T); thinking the right thing but writing it wrong (B); knowing the right thing but forgetting to think it (F); imperfectly knowing the tools (L) or the specifications (M). Such bugs are easy to fix once they have been identified. Categories A and D represent the next level of difficulty, as we get into technical aspects of what programming is all about. (As Niklaus Wirth has said, Algorithms + Data Structures = Programs.) Category R covers the special situation in which we want a program to survive even when its input is incorrect. Finally, category S accounts for higher-level surprises; these are the subtle bugs that result from complex interactions between different parts of a system. Thus the nine types of bugs have a somewhat logical structure. The remaining six categories—cleanliness (C), efficiency (E), generalization (G), interaction (I), portability (P) and quality (Q)—seem to provide a reasonable way to classify the various kinds of enhancements that were made to TEX during its development.

My classification scheme relies more on essential functionality than on the external form of the program. Thus it is not easy to use my statistics about the number of errors per category to answer questions such as 'How many bugs were due to improper use of goto statements?' Such questions are interesting to teachers of programming, but I no longer think that they are extremely important. If I had indexed my errors by syntactic categories, I would have found that error nos. 45, 91, 119, 155, 231, 352, 354, 419, 523, 581 and 801 could be ascribed to my use or abuse of goto; also no. 512 could be added to this list, since return and goto are analogous. Thus we can conclude from my experience with TEX that goto statements can indeed be harmful. On the other hand we must balance this fact with the realization that bad gotos account for only 1·4 per cent of my errors; we must identify other culprits if we're going to do away with the other 98·6 per cent. Sure enough, several other errors were caused by lapses in my use of other control structures: A case statement got me in trouble in no. 21; a while confused me in no. 29; if–then–else led me astray in nos. 467, 471, 680 and 843. (See also nos. 796 and 845, where efficiency of control was important.) I conclude that *every* feature of a programming language can be harmful, if it is misused.

Some of the errors noted in my log book were much more devastating than others. In certain cases the changes were far-reaching, affecting dozens of different parts of the program; several days of 'hacking' were necessary before such changes had been made and verified. For example, change no. 110 required major surgery to the program, because my original ideas were incapable of handling aligned tables inside of aligned tables. On the other hand, some of my errors were only venial sins, and some of the changes were merely twiddles; for example, no. 87 simply improved the wording of a diagnostic message. Although the log does not give an explicit weighting to the errors, the 'heavy' errors tend to cancel with the 'light' ones, so we can still get a reasonable insight into the stability of the program if we calculate, say, the number of errors logged per year.

CHRONOLOGY

The development of TEX has taken place over a period of ten years, and the lessons I learned can best be understood when they are put into the context of the other things I was doing during that time. Typography has many facets, hence TEX itself was only one of the projects I decided to work on. The two most significant companion systems were METAFONT* (a system for typeface design) and Computer Modern (a family of typefaces defined in terms of the METAFONT language); these programs had to be

---

* METAFONT is a trademark of Addison-Wesley Publishing Company, Inc.

debugged just as TEX did, and their debugging logs show a similar development history. I also needed a dozen or so utility routines to support TEX and METAFONT; the most notable of these are TANGLE and WEAVE, which constitute the WEB system of structured documentation.[7,8]

Beginnings

The genesis of TEX probably took place on 1 February 1977, when I first chanced to see the output of a high-resolution typesetting machine. I was told that this fine typography (the galley proofs of a book by Winston,[9] which our faculty was considering for inclusion in an exam syllabus) was produced by entirely digital methods; yet I could see no difference between the digital type and 'real' type. Therefore I realized that a central aspect of printing had been reduced to bit manipulation. As a computer scientist, I could not resist the challenge of improving print quality by manipulating those bits better. Therefore my diary entry for 8 February says that, already at that time, I began discussing the possibility of new typesetting software with people at Stanford's Artificial Intelligence Lab. By 13 February I had changed my plan to spend a forthcoming sabbatical year in South America; instead of travelling to an exotic place and working on Volume 4 of *The Art of Computer Programming*, I had decided to stay at Stanford and work on digital typography.

I mentioned earlier that the design of TEX was begun on 5 May 1977. A week later, I wrote a draft report containing what I thought was a pretty complete design, and I stayed up until 5 a.m. typing it into the computer. The problem of typesetting seemed quite straightforward, so I soon started thinking about founts instead; I spent the next 45 days writing a program that was destined to evolve into METAFONT. By 28 June, I had 25 lower-case letters in various styles that looked reasonably good to me at the time; and three days later I figured out how to handle the 26th letter, which required some new ideas.[10]

I went back to thinking about TEX on 3 July. Several people had made thoughtful comments on my earlier draft, and I prepared a thoroughly revised language definition after two weeks of further study. (This included two days of working with dictionaries in order to develop an algorithm for hyphenation of English.) The resulting document, I thought, was a reasonably complete specification of a language for typesetting, and I left it in the capable hands of two graduate students who were my research assistants that summer (Frank Liang and Michael Plass). Their job was to implement TEX while I flew off for a visit to China. I returned on 25 August and had just one day to meet with them before leaving on another three-week trip. On 14 September I returned and they presented me with a sheet of paper that had been typeset by their proto-TEX program! They had implemented only about 15 per cent of the language, and they had used data structures that were not general enough or efficient enough to support the remaining 85 per cent; but they had chosen their subset wisely, so that a small test program could run from start to finish. Hence it was easy for me to imagine what a complete system would entail.

Now it was time for Liang and Plass to go back to school, and time for my sabbatical year to begin. I started coding the 'final version of TEX' (or so I thought) on 16 September, and immediately I discovered that their summer work represented a truly heroic achievement. Although I had thought that my specification of TEX was quite complete, I encountered loose ends every 15 minutes or so when I was actually faced with writing the code. I soon realized that if I had been in my students' shoes—having to implement this language when the author was completely unreachable—I would have thrown up my hands in despair; important policy decisions had to be made at every turn.

That was the first big lesson I learned during my work with TEX: *the designer of a new kind of system must participate fully in the implementation*. Even if I had been available for consultation with my students, they would have had to come to me so often with questions that the work would have dragged on forever. I can imagine them having to spend a half hour or so explaining each particular problem to me, and we would have needed literally hundreds of those meetings. Now I knew why other projects I had heard about, in which the language designer had decided not to be the compiler writer, had failed.

By 14 October I had coded all of TEX except for the parts that typeset mathematics, and except for the routines that convert from TEX's internal representation into codes for an output device. At this point I had to leave for three weeks of travel in Europe. This European trip had been planned long before, so it was mostly unrelated to typesetting; but I did have some interesting discussions about curve-drawing with mathematicians I met in Oberwolfach, Germany, and in Oslo, Norway. I also was able to arrange a visit to the headquarters of Monotype Corporation in Redhill, England.

After returning, I spent November finishing the numerals, upper-case letters, and punctuation marks of the first-draft Computer Modern types. I needed to have a complete fount because I had been invited to give a lecture about this work to the American Mathematical Society, and I did not want to have only lower-case examples to show. I prepared the AMS lecture[11] during December and presented it in January, so I did not have a chance to resume the coding of TEX until 14 January. But finally I was able to write the following in my diary on 9 February 1978:

> Finished the TEX programs including all loose ends and got them all compiled without syntax errors (4 a.m.).

TEX was the first fairly large program I had written since 1970; so it was my first non-trivial 'structured program', in the sense that I wrote it while consciously applying the methodology I had learned in the early 1970s from Dijkstra, Hoare, Dahl and others. I found that structured programming greatly increased my confidence in the correctness of the code, while the code still existed only on paper. Therefore I could wait until the whole program was written, before trying to debug any of it. This saved a lot of time, because I did not have to prepare 'dummy' versions of non-existent modules while testing modules that were already written; I could test everything in its final environment. Of course I had a few qualms in January about whether my code from September would really work; but that gave me more of an incentive to finish the whole thing sooner.

Even on 10 February, when TEX had been compiled and was ready to be tested, I did not feel any compelling need to try it immediately. I knew that the program was fairly readable and 'informally proved correct', so I spent the next month making italic, greek, script, symbols and large delimiter founts. My test program for TEX required those founts, so I did not want to start testing until everything was in place. Again, I knew I was saving time by not having to prepare prototypes that would merely simulate the real thing; structured programming gave me the courage to wait until the whole system was ready. I finished the large symbols on 8 March, and I happily penned the following in my diary on 9 March:

> Entered all accumulated corrections to TEX program and compiled it— tomorrow the debugging begins!

My log book for errors in TEX began that next day, 10 March; the debugging process will be discussed below. By 29 March I had decided that TEX was essentially working,

> . . . (except perhaps for error recovery)—it's time to celebrate!

I began tuning up the founts and drafting ideas for a user manual; then I spent a few days at Alphatype Corporation in Illinois, from whom Stanford had decided to purchase a phototypesetter. From 11 April to 11 May I took time off from typography to work on dozens of updates to *Seminumerical Algorithms*, which is Volume 2 of *The Art of Computer Programming*;[12] I wanted to incorporate new research results into that text, which was to be TEX's first big application. Then on 14 May I began to get TEX running again; proof copies of pages iv to 8 of Volume 2 came out of our Xerox Graphics Printer on 15 May.

My work was cut out for me during the next weeks: I became a production user of TEX, typing the manuscript of Volume 2. This proved to be an invaluable experience, as explained below. By the time my sabbatical year ended, on 24 September, I had finished the typing up to page 441 of that 700-page book. Improvements to TEX kept occurring to me all during that time, of course—except during a month-long vacation trip with my family. (Even on vacation I kept seeing founts everywhere and thinking about how to draw such letterforms by computer. I spent one morning sitting by one of the trails in the Grand Canyon designing the algebraic notation for METAFONT; my founts had previously been written in a primitive macro language and compiled directly into machine code, not interpreted.) I also spent three weeks that summer writing the first manual for TEX.

Although my sabbatical year was over, I kept working on typography in odd moments between classes in the autumn; the text of Volume 2 was completed on the morning of 15 November. On 17 November I began writing METAFONT, and my diary entry for 31 December 1978 was this:

> Finished the METAFONT interpreter, just in time to celebrate New Year's eve (11:59 p.m.).

Other people had begun to use TEX in August of 1978, and I was surprised to see how fast the system was propagating. I spent my spare time during the first three months of 1979 thinking about how to make TEX available in Pascal form. (The original program was written in SAIL, a language that was available on only a few computers.) During this period I began to experiment with the typesetting of Pascal programs; I wrote a program called BLAISE that converted Pascal source code into a TEX file for pretty-printing. BLAISE soon developed into a system called DOC for structured documentation, completed on 31 March, 1979; programs in DOC format could be converted either to Pascal or to TEX. Luis Trabb Pardo and Ignacio Zabala subsequently used DOC to prepare a highly portable version of TEX in Pascal, completed in April of 1980.

About this time I learned another big lesson: *writing software is much harder than writing books*. I could not simultaneously teach classes well and finish what needed to be done on typography. So I asked to be excused from teaching in the spring of 1979; my diary for March 22 said,

> Now my obligations are fairly well cleared away and it's back to the stalled research on TEX.

(It turned out that I was able to teach during only 13 of the 21 academic quarters between my sabbatical years in that period. I continued to supervise graduate students, but I gave no classroom lectures during 1983 when the work on TEX and METAFONT was at its peak; I also missed three months in 1982, 1984 and 1985. I really enjoy teaching, but I could not see any way to finish the TEX project without relinquishing almost all of my other duties.)

On 1 April 1979, I returned to METAFONT, which had been written but not debugged. METAFONT began to work on 28 April. Then I began to design software for the Alphatype machine; that took about three months. During the summer I wrote the METAFONT manual, which gave me further experience with TEX. And TEX also received an important stimulus from the American Mathematical Society that summer, when several people (including Barbara Beeton and Michael Spivak) were given the opportunity to spend some time at Stanford developing TEX macros. The AMS people introduced me to several important applications, such as the indexes to *Mathematical Reviews*, which stretched TEX to its limits and led to substantial improvements.

Endings

By 14 August 1979, I felt that TEX was essentially complete and fairly stable. I lectured that evening to about 100 participants of the Western Institute for Computer Science in Santa Cruz, telling about my experiences developing and debugging the program. At that time my log book of errors had accumulated 420 items; little did I know that the final total would be more than twice that! But already I knew that I had learned a lot by keeping the log, and I must have been enthusiastic because I lectured from 7:30 to 9:30 p.m. (The audience was equally enthusiastic—they kept asking me questions until 11:30 p.m. So I resolved to write a paper about the errors of TEX, and at last I am able to do so.)

I devoted the last months of 1979 and the first months of 1980 to Computer Modern, which needed to be rewritten in terms of the new METAFONT. Then I needed to update Volume 2 again—computer science marches inexorably forward—until I had finally finished producing camera-ready copy on our Alphatype. This was the goal I had hoped to achieve during my sabbatical year; I reached it at 2 a.m. on 29 July 1980, about two years late. During the rest of 1980 I wrote papers about what I thought were the most novel ideas in TEX[13] and in METAFONT.[14]

But my research on TEX was by no means finished. About 50 people from all over the U.S.A. met at Stanford on 22 February 1980, and established the TEX User Group (TUG). I asked them if they would mind my cleaning up the language in several upward-incompatible ways, even though this would make the user manual and their existing computer files obsolete; and nobody objected to such changes! Soon TUG grew dramatically, under the able chairmanship of Richard Palais, and it became international. I realized that I could not disappoint all these people by leaving TEX in its current state and returning immediately to work on subsequent volumes of *The Art of Computer Programming*.

I needed to work out a better 'endgame strategy', and it soon became clear what ought to be done: the original versions of TEX and METAFONT should be scrapped, once they had served their purpose of accumulating enough user experience to indicate what such languages ought to be. New versions of TEX and METAFONT should be written, designed to last a long time and to be highly portable between computers and typesetting devices of all kinds. Moreover, these new programs should be published, because TEX was making it possible to improve the state of the art of program documentation. I decided to do my best to produce a stable system and to explain all I knew about it, so that other people could take it over and maintain it if it proved to be important. This way I could return to other pursuits in good conscience, knowing that if my typographic research had any merit it would be carried on by others in whatever ways would prove to be necessary.

So that was my new goal; I thought I could achieve it in one or two more years. The original TEX program was renamed TEX78, and the new one was to be called TEX82.

Classes and miscellaneous chores kept me too busy to do much else during the first half of 1981, but I began to write TEX82 on 22 August. By 9 September I realized that the DOC system needed to be completely revised, so I spent two months replacing it by a much better system called WEB[8]. Since then my programming language of choice has been WEB (which, unlike DOC, was written in its own language). After a month in Europe, I was able to resume writing TEX82 on 1 December 1981. The draft of TEX82 was completed on 29 June 1982; as before, I wrote the entire program before trying to run any of it.

Meanwhile I had other problems to worry about. When my new copy of *Seminumerical Algorithms* arrived in January 1981, I had expected to be filled with joy at the consummation of so much hard work. Instead, I burned with disappointment, as I realized that I still had a great deal to learn about founts. The early Computer Modern typefaces were not at all what I had hoped to achieve, when I first saw them in print. They had looked reasonably good at low resolution, so I had blithely assumed that high resolution would be much better. Not so. My education in typefaces was barely beginning. Later in 1981 I met Richard Southall, a professor of type design who had exactly the expertise I was lacking; so I invited him to visit Stanford. We spent the entire month of April 1982 working about 16 hours a day, revising Computer Modern from A to z.

I debugged TEX82 in the summer of 1982, then began to write the new manual—called *The TEXbook*[15]—in October. The first manual had been written hastily and finished in 21 days, but I wanted *The TEXbook* to meet much higher standards. Therefore I was not able to finish it until a full year later.

It was during this period, October 1982 to October 1983, that TEX became a mature system. I had to rethink every aspect of its design as I rewrote the manual. Fortunately I was aided by a wonderful group of knowledgeable volunteers, who would meet with me for two or three hours every Friday noon and we would discuss the trade-offs of every **important** decision. The diverse backgrounds of these people provided an important counterweight to my one-sided views. Finally, on 9 December 1983, I decided that the first phase of my endgame strategy was complete; I gratefully hosted a coming-of-age party for TEX, with 36 guests of honour, at the Fuki-Sushi restaurant in Palo Alto.

The rest is history. I wrote METAFONT in WEB between December 1983 and July 1984; I wrote *The METAFONTbook* between August 1984 and October 1985, taking off five months (February to July) to rewrite Computer Modern in terms of the new METAFONT. I began another sabbatical year in October 1985, just after the TEX project disbanded. Finally, after adding a few more finishing touches, I was able to celebrate the long-planned completion of my 'endgame' on 21 May 1986, when my publishers sponsored a reception at the Computer Museum in Boston; that was the day I first saw the five hardcover volumes of *Computers & Typesetting*, the books that summarize my nine years of work on TEX, METAFONT and Computer Modern.

Another year has gone by and I would like to report that TEX has proved to be 100 per cent correct. But I cannot, not yet. For I stumbled across a hidden TEX anomaly last January. And I have just been teaching a course about software development based on the internal structure of TEX; students in the class have noticed a few things that should be improved. So I suppose there is still at least one bug lurking there. I plan to hold off publishing this paper until another year or so has gone by, so that I will have more reason to believe that my log book of errors is complete.

CONTENTS OF THE LOG BOOKS

As I said, the appendix to this paper reproduces the entire list of errors that I kept as TEX was evolving. The best way to comprehend how TEX evolved is to peruse this list. The first 519 items refer to the original program TEX78, which was written in SAIL, from the time I began to debug it to the time I stopped maintaining it. The remaining items, numbered 520–849 (as of May 1987), refer to the 'real' program TEX82, which was written in WEB. I did not keep any record of errors removed during the hectic period when TEX82 was being debugged, but items 520 and following include every change that was made to TEX82 after it passed its first test. The differences between TEX78 and TEX82, seen from a user's standpoint, have been listed elsewhere.[16]

I have tried to edit the log entries so that they can be understood in terms of the published listing[6] of TEX82. For example,

15 Add the forgotten case 'set_font:' to eq_destroy.   §275 F

is entry no. 15. My original log entry referred to case '[font]' in 'eqdestroy' using SAIL syntax, but I have changed to Pascal syntax in the edited log. Similarly, the 1978 identifier font eventually became set_font, so I have adopted the published equivalent. TEX82 contains a procedure called eq_destroy in §275 of the program, and this procedure is quite similar to the eqdestroy of TEX78; so I have supplied §275 as a program reference. (It turns out that eq_destroy no longer needs a 'set_font:' subcase, but it did in 1978.) The 'F' after §275 means that this was a bug of type F, a forgotten function.

Changes to a program often spawn other changes later. I have tried to **indicate that** phenomenon in the appendix by prefixing the number of a prior error when it was an important part of the reason for a subsequent error. Thus no. 67 is

25 $\mapsto$ **67** Replace the space at paragraph end by fillglue, not by zero.   §816 B

Error no. 25 was logged when I had been surprised to find a space at the end of TEX's internal representation of a paragraph. I had 'cured' the problem by converting the space from a normal interword space to a space of width zero. But that was not good enough, since it was possible for TEX to try breaking a line at the zero-width space. A better solution was to replace the space by the glue that is always added to fill out the end of a paragraph.

Figure 1 shows a time chart of the first 519 log entries—the errors of TEX78. There is a burst of activity right near the beginning, since I logged the first 237 errors during the three weeks of initial debugging. Thus the main line in Figure 1, which shows the cumulative number of errors as a function of time, is nearly horizontal at the beginning. But it is nearly vertical at the end, since only 13 changes were made during the last year of TEX78's activity.

Another line also appears in Figure 1: it represents the total number of different pages I typeset with TEX78 as I was experimenting with the first version. The dotted line in July 1978 stands for the 200 pages of the first TEX manual, and the dotted line in June 1979 stands for the 100 pages of the first METAFONT manual; the remaining solid lines stand for the 700 pages of Volume 2 and some experiments with DOC.

Figure 1 shows that four different phases can be distinguished in the development of TEX78. First came the debugging phase (Phase 0), already mentioned. Then came a longer period of time (Phase 1) when I typeset several hundred pages of Volume 2 and the first user manual; this experience suggested many amendments to my original design. Then TEX suddenly had more than one user, and different kinds of errors began to show up. *New users find new bugs.* This coming-out phase (Phase 2) included small bursts of changes when I faced new applications—a suite of difficult test cases posed by the American Mathematical Society, then the application to Pascal formatting, then the complex index to *Mathematical Reviews.* Finally there was Phase 3, when changes were made in anticipation of a future TEX82; I wanted several new ideas to be well tested before I programmed the 'ultimate' TEX.

THE INITIAL DEBUGGING STAGE

Let us roll the clock back now and look more closely at the earliest days of TEX78. In some ways this was the most interesting time, because the whole concept of TEX was just beginning to take shape. Figure 2 is a modified version of Figure 1, redrawn with a time warp. There is now exactly one error per time unit, so the 18-day debugging phase has been slowed down to almost half of the total development time; on the other hand, the years 1981–1982 at the bottom go by so fast as to be barely visible.

I mentioned that TEX78 was entirely coded before I first tried to run it on 10 March. My debugging strategy was to walk through the program using the BAIL debugger, a system program by John Reiser that allowed me to execute the statements of my program one at a time; BAIL would also interpret additional SAIL statements that I entered on-line. Whenever I came to a section of program that I had seen before,

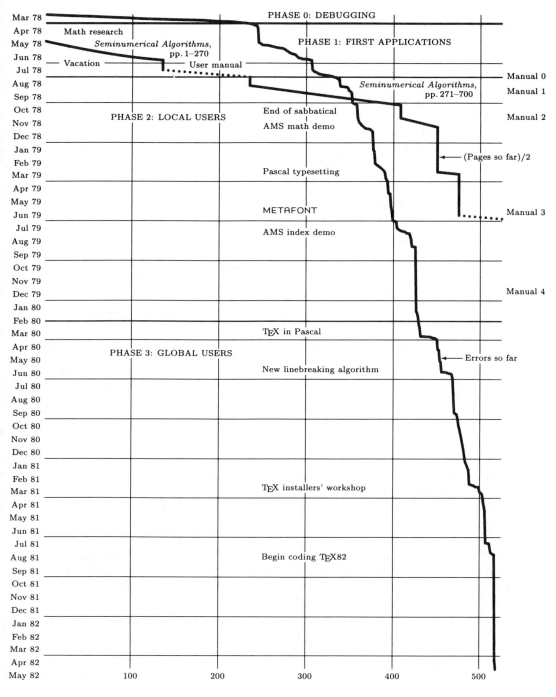

Figure 1. The rise and fall of TEX78

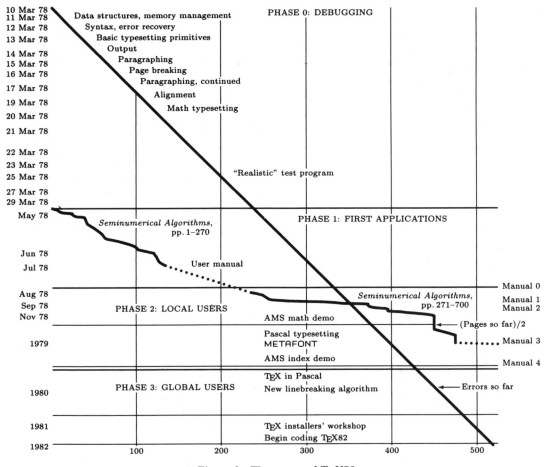

Figure 2. The errors of TₑX78

I could set a break-point and continue at high speed until coming to new material. Watching the program execute itself in this 'dynamic order' has always been insightful for me, after I have desk-checked it in the 'static order' of my original code.

Figure 2 shows that I got through the program initialization the first day; then I was gradually able to check out the routines for basic data management, parsing and error reporting. On the fourth day TₑX began to combine boxes and glue, and there was visible output on the fifth day. During the following three days I tested the algorithms for breaking paragraphs into lines and breaking lines into pages. All this went rather smoothly; I had already logged 101 errors during this first week, but all of the problems were comparatively minor oversights, to be expected in any program of this size.

On the ninth day I tackled alignment of tables, and got a big shock: my original algorithms were quite wrong. I had greatly misunderstood this aspect of TₑX, because I had greatly underestimated the complications of nested alignments. (The log mentions some of the puzzlement and frustration I felt at the time.) I wrestled with alignment for two days before finding a solution.

Then I looked at the last remaining part of TEX, the code for typesetting mathematics; this took another four days. (Well, the 'days' were nights actually; I worked during the night to avoid delays due to time-sharing.) Finally I had seen essentially all of TEX in operation, and I could let it run at full speed instead of relying on single-step mode. I spent six more days helping TEX get through its first test data; finally the test was passed. Whew! The debugging phase was over, 18 days and 237 log-book entries after it began.

I kept track of how long this process took, so that I'd be better able to estimate the duration of future programming projects. Table I gives the figures.

The total debugging time, 132 h, was extremely encouraging to me, because it was much less than the 41 days it had taken me to write the program. Previously I had needed to devote about 70 per cent of program development time to debugging, but now the figure had dropped to about 30 per cent. I considered this to be a tremendous victory for structured programming, since my programming time had also decreased from what it had been with old habits. Later, with the WEB system, I noticed even further gains in productivity.

How big was TEX at the time? I estimated this by counting the number of semicolons (4857) and the number of occurrences of the SAIL reserved words comment (480) and else (223). Since I always put semicolons before end, the total number of statements in the program could be computed as

$$; - \text{comment} + \text{else} = 4857 - 480 + 223 = 4600$$

Thus the debugging strategy I used allowed me to verify about 35 statements per hour.

The fact that I made 237 log entries in 132 h means that I was logging things only about once every 33 min; thus the total time needed to keep the log was negligible. I can definitely recommend the practice to everybody. During most of the debugging time I was clicking away at the keys of my terminal, getting to know exactly what TEX was doing; I needed only a few extra minutes to make the log entries, which helped me to get to know myself.

EARLY TYPESETTING EXPERIENCE

Now that TEX was able to typeset its test program, I could proceed to my main goal, the typesetting of Volume 2. This was a somewhat tedious task—the keyboarding of a

Table I

Day	Time, h	Day	Time, h
10 March 1978	6	19 March 1978	7·5
11 March 1978	7	20 March 1978	10
12 March 1978	8	21 March 1978	8
13 March 1978	7	22 March 1978	6
14 March 1978	8	23 March 1978	7·5
15 March 1978	8	25 March 1978	7
16 March 1978	7	26 March 1978	6
17 March 1978	7	27 March 1978	8
18 March 1978	8	29 March 1978	6

700-page book is not one of life's greatest pleasures—but the regular appearance of nice-looking pages kept me happy. The jagged line in Figure 2 shows my progress in terms of pages typeset versus errors in the TeX log; a similar (even more jagged) line appears in Figure 1, showing pages typeset as a function of time.

The most striking thing about the jagged line in Figure 2 is that it is almost straight. Ideas about how to improve TeX kept occurring to me quite regularly as I typed the manuscript. Between 13 May and 22 June I processed about 250 pages, and added 69 new entries to the log. Those 69 entries included 29 'bugs' and 40 'enhancements'; thus, I thought of a new way to improve TeX at a regular rate of about one enhancement for every six pages typed.

I mentioned earlier my firm conviction that I could not have correctly delegated the coding of TeX to another person; I had to be doing it myself, because writing a new sort of program implies continually revising the specifications. Similarly, I could not have correctly delegated these initial typing experiments to another person. I had to put myself in the rôle of a regular user; there is no substitute for such experience, when a new system is being designed.

But at the time I was not thinking about creating a system that would be used widely; I was designing TeX primarily for my own use. The idea that TeX could or should be generalized to other applications besides *The Art of Computer Programming* dawned on me only gradually, as people kept noticing what I was doing and expressing an interest in it.

John McCarthy observed during this period that TeX was doing a reasonable job with respect to traditional mathematical copy, but he suspected that I would have a tough time typesetting a book about TeX itself. 'That will be the real test', he said, 'because you'll have to shut off many of TeX's automatic features in order to handle problems of self-reference'.

In July I succumbed to John's challenge and prepared a user manual for TeX. Sure enough, this experience helped me identify quite a few weaknesses in the existing design, things that I probably wouldn't have noticed if I had confined my attention to *The Art of Computer Programming* alone. Again I thought of enhancements at the rate of about one for every six or seven pages, as I wrote the manual; but these were not really occasioned by defects in TeX's ability to be self-referential, as John had predicted. The new enhancements came about because the process of manual-writing forced me to think about TeX as a whole, in a new way. The perspective of a teacher/expositor helped me to notice several inconsistencies and shortcomings.

Thus, I came to the conclusion that the designer of a new system must not only be the implementor and the first large-scale user; *the designer should also write the first user manual*. The separation of any of these four components would have hurt TeX significantly. If I had not participated fully in all these activities, literally hundreds of improvements would never have been made, because I would never have thought of them or perceived why they were important.

PHASES 2 AND 3: USERS

But a system cannot be successful if it is too strongly influenced by a single person. Once the initial design is complete and fairly robust, the real test begins as people with many different viewpoints undertake their own experiments. At the beginning of August, I distributed 45 copies of the draft manual to people who had expressed interest in using TEX and who had promised to give me feedback before the 'real' user manual would be issued in September. So TEX had a multitude of users for the first time, and I began to learn about a wide variety of new applications and perceptions.

I continued to typeset the remaining 450 pages of Volume 2, and my personal experiences with those pages continued to suggest regular improvements to TEX until I got up to about page 500. But the final 200 pages were just drudgework, not really inspirational to me in any way as far as TEX was concerned. Nor did I learn much more, except about page layout, when I typed the METAFONT manual some months later. The really important influences on TEX after the first manual was published were the users, first because they made different kinds of mistakes than I had anticipated, and later because they had important suggestions about how to improve TEX's capabilities.

Guy Steele was visiting Stanford that summer; he took a copy of TEX back to MIT with him, and I began to get feedback from two coasts. One of Guy's suggestions, which I staunchly resisted at the time, was to include some sort of mini-programming language in TEX so that users could do numerical calculations. Slowly but surely I began to understand the need for such features, which eventually became a basic part of TEX82. Another early user was Terry Winograd, who pushed TEX's early macro capabilities to their limits. He and Michael Spivak, who began to work with TEX in the summer of 1979, taught me a lot about the peculiar properties of macro expansion. Researchers at Xerox PARC also had a significant influence on TEX at this time; Lyle Ramshaw modified the program to work with Xerox's new founts and new output devices, while Leo Guibas and Doug Wyatt undertook to rewrite TEX in the MESA language.

Figures 1 and 2 indicate that the first TEX user manual was issued in five versions. 'Manual 0' was the preliminary draft, handed out to 45 guinea pigs who agreed to help me test the very first system. 'Manual 1' was a Stanford technical report issued a month later; it was reprinted as 'Manual 2' in November, using the higher-resolution printing devices at Xerox PARC. The American Mathematical Society published a paperback version[17] of Manual 2 in the summer of 1979; that was 'Manual 3'. Then Digital Press published 'Manual 4', which included the METAFONT manual and some background information, in December 1979.[18]

The publishers of manuals 3 and 4 asked readers to mail a reply card if they were interested in forming a TEX User's Group, and more than 100 people answered Yes. So the first TUG meeting, in February 1980, marked the beginning of yet another phase in the life of the SAIL program TEX78. A great influx of new users and new applications made me strive for a more complete language. Hence there was a flurry of activity at the end of March 1980, when I decided to extend TEX in more than a dozen ways. These extensions represented only a fraction of the ideas that had been suggested, but they seemed to provide all the requested functions in a clean way. The time was ripe to make the extensions now or never, because the first versions of TEX in Pascal were due to be released in April.

The last significant batch of changes to TEX78 were made in the summer of 1980, when TEX acquired the ability to typeset paragraphs with arbitrary shapes. Still, the error log shows that I kept adding enhancements regularly as the world-wide use of TEX continued to grow. It turned out that the final bugs corrected in TEX78 were all introduced by recent enhancements; they were not present in the program of 1978.

The most significant pattern to be found among the enhancements made to TEX78 after its earliest days is the 'unbundling' of things that used to be frozen inside the code. At first I had fairly rigid ideas about how much space to put in certain places, about how much penalty to charge for certain line breaks, about how to interpret various characters in the input, and even about where to find certain characters in founts. One by one, starting already at change no. 104, these things became parameters that could be changed by users who had different requirements and/or different preferences.

THE REAL TEX

I had vastly underestimated the complexities and subtleties of typesetting when I had naïvely expected to work out a complete system for myself during a single sabbatical year. By 1980 it became clear that I had acquired almost a moral obligation to advance the art and science of typography in a more substantial way. I realized that I could never be happy with the monster I had created unless I started over and built an entirely new system, using the experience I had gained from TEX78.

I began writing the new system in the summer of 1981, and I decided to call it TEX82 because I knew it would take a year to complete. Once again I could not delegate the job to an associate; I wanted to rethink every detail of TEX, and I wanted to have a thorough taste of 'literate programming' before I dared to inflict such ideas on others.[7] I wanted to produce truly portable software that would have a chance to serve for many years as a reliable component of larger systems. I wanted TEX82 to justify the confidence that people were placing in TEX78, which was getting more praise than it deserved.

Figure 3 shows the development of TEX82, starting at the moment I decided that it was essentially bug-free; this illustration uses the same time-warp strategy as Figure 2.

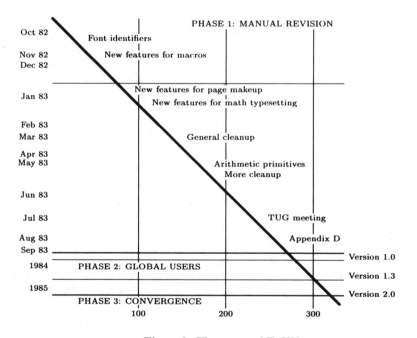

Figure 3. The errors of TEX82

From the beginning there were hundreds of users, so TEX82's Phase 1 was analogous to TEX78's Phase 2. But now there was yet a new dimension: several dozen people were also reading the code and making well-informed comments on how to improve it. Furthermore I had regular meetings with volunteer helpers who represented many different points of view. So I had a golden opportunity to hone the ideas to a new state of perfection.

Two major changes were installed very early in TEX82's history. One was to the way founts are selected in a document (change no. 545), and the other was to the treatment of conditional parts of macros (change no. 564). Both of these changes impinged on many of the fundamental assumptions I had made when writing the code; these were definitely the most traumatic moments in TEX's medical history. I was glad to see that WEB's documentation facilities helped greatly to make such drastic revisions possible.

Phase 1 of TEX82 ended about a year after it began, when I completed writing *The TEXbook*. The log reveals that most of the changes made to TEX during 1983 relate to the chapters of the manual that I was writing at the time. This was the period when TEX really grew up. As I said above, manual writing provides an ideal incentive for system improvements, because you discover and remove glitches that you cannot justify in print. When you are writing a user manual, you also have your last chance to make any enhancements that you have thought about before; if certain enhancements are not made then, you know that you will forever wish you had taken time to add them.

As with TEX78, the error log of enhancements to TEX82 shows a significant trend toward greater user control. More and more things that were originally hardwired in the system became parametric instead of automatic.

Phase 2 of TEX82 began with the paperback publication of *The TEXbook* and ended with the publication of the hardcover edition. During this phase (which lasted from October 1983 to May 1986) I was mostly working on METAFONT and Computer Modern, so TEX changed primarily in ways that would blend better with those systems. The log entries of Phase 2, nos. 790 to 840, also show that a number of ever-more subtle bugs were detected by ever-more sophisticated users during this time. There was also a completely unsubtle bug, no. 808, which somehow had sneaked through all my tests and caused no apparent harm for an amazingly long time.

Now TEX82 is in its third and final phase. It has grown from the original 4600 statements in SAIL to 1376 modules in WEB, representing about 14,000 statements in Pascal. Five volumes describing the complete systems for TEX, METAFONT and Computer Modern have been published. No more changes will be made except to correct any bugs that still might lurk in the code (or perhaps to improve the efficiency or portability, when it is easy to do so while correcting a real bug). I hope TEX82 will remain stable at least until I finish Volume 7 of *The Art of Computer Programming*.

TEST PROGRAMS

Since 1960 I have had extremely good luck with a method of testing that may deserve to be better known: instead of using a normal, large application to test a software system, I generally get best results by writing a test program that no sane user would ever think of writing. My test programs are intended to break the system, to push it to its extreme limits, to pile complication on complication, in ways that the system programmer never consciously anticipated. To prepare such test data, I get into the meanest, nastiest frame of mind that I can manage, and I write the nastiest code I can think of; then I turn around and embed that in even nastier constructions that are almost obscene. The resulting test program is so crazy that I could not possibly explain to anybody else what it is supposed to do; nobody else would care! But such a program proves to be an admirable way to flush the bugs out of software.

In one of my early experiments, I wrote a small compiler for Burroughs Corporation, using an interpretive language specially devised for the occasion. I rigged the interpreter so that it would count how often each instruction was interpreted; then I tested the new system by compiling a large user application. To my surprise, this big test case did not really test much; it left more than half of the frequency counts sitting at zero! Most of my code could have been completely messed up, yet this application would have worked fine. So I wrote a nasty, artificially contrived program as described above, and of course I detected numerous new bugs while doing so. Still, I discovered that 10 per cent of the code had not been exercised by the new test. I looked at the remaining zeros and said, 'Shucks, my source code wasn't nasty enough, it overlooked some special cases I had forgotten about'. It was easy to add a few more statements, until eventually I had constructed a test routine that invoked all but one of the instructions in the compiler. (And I proved that the remaining instruction would *never* be executed in *any* circumstances, so I took it out.)

I used such 'torture tests' to debug three compilers during the 1960s. In each case very few bugs were ever discovered after the tests had been passed, so the methodology was quite effective. But when I debugged TEX78, my test program was quite tame by comparison—except when I was first testing the mathematics routines (20–23 March). I guess I was not trying as hard as usual to make TEX a bullet-proof system, because I was still thinking of myself as TEX's main user. My original test program for TEX78 was written with an 'I hope it works' attitude, rather than 'I bet I can make it fail'. I suppose I would have found several dozen of the bugs that showed up later (such as nos. 240 and 263) if I had stuck to the torture-test methodology. Still, considering my mood at the time, I suppose it was a good idea to have a test program that would look like real typography; I did not know what TEX should do until I could judge the æsthetic quality of its output.

At any rate, my first test program was based on a sampling of material from Volume 2. I went through that book and boiled it down to five pages that illustrated just about every kind of typographical difficulty to be found in the entire volume. (The output of this test program can be seen in another paper,[19] where David Fuchs and I used the same test data to study some algorithms for fount management.)

Years later, when TEX82 was ready to be debugged, I understood pretty clearly what the program was supposed to do, so I could then apply the superior torture-test methodology. My test program was called TRIP; I spent about five days preparing the first draft of TRIP in July 1982. Here, for example, is a relatively tame part of the original TRIP code:

```
\def\gobble#1{}  \floatingpenalty 100
\everypar{A\insert200{\baselineskip400pt\splittopskip\count15pt
  \hbox{\vadjust{\penalty999}}\hbox to -10pt{}}\showthe\pagetotal
  \showthe\pagegoal\advance\count15by1\mark{\the\count15}%
  \splitmaxdepth−1pt\paR\gobble}%abort every paragraph abruptly
```

```
\def\weird#1{\csname\expandafter\gobble\string#1
   \string\csname\endcsname} \message{\the\output\weird\one}
```

(Please do not ask me what it means.) Since then I have probably spent at least 200 hours modifying and maintaining TRIP, but I consider that time well spent, and I think TRIP is one of the most significant products of the TEX project.[20] The reason is that the TRIP test has detected extremely subtle bugs in hundreds of implementations of TEX, bugs that would have been almost impossible to track down in any other way. TEX82, with its TRIP test, has proved to be much more reliable than any of the Pascal compilers it has been compiled with. In fact, I believe it is fair to say that TEX82 has helped to flush out at least one previously unknown compiler bug whenever it has been ported to a new machine or tried on a compiler that has not seen TEX before! These compiler errors were detectable because of the TRIP test. Later I developed a similar test program for METAFONT, called TRAP,[21] and it too has helped to exorcise dozens of compiler bugs.

A single test program cannot detect all possible mistakes. For example, TEX might terminate with a 'fatal error' in several ways, only one of which can happen on any particular run. Furthermore, TRIP runs almost automatically, so it does not test all of TEX's capability for on-line interaction. But TRIP does exercise almost all of TEX's code, and it does so in tricky combinations that tend to fail if any part of TEX is damaged. Therefore it has proved to be a great time-saver: whenever I modify TEX, I simply check that the results of the TRIP test have changed appropriately.

The only difficulty with the TRIP methodology is that I must check the output myself to see if it is correct. Sometimes I need to spend several hours before I have determined the appropriate output; and I am fallible. So TEX might give the wrong answer without my being aware of it. This happened in bug nos. 543 and 722, when I learned to my surprise that TEX had never before done the correct thing with TRIP. A system utility for comparing files suffices now to convince me that incremental changes to TEX or TRIP cause the correct incremental changes to the TRIP test output; but when I began debugging, I needed to verify by hand that thousands of lines of output were accurate.

I should mention that I also believe in the merit of formal and informal correctness proofs. I generally try to prove my programs correct, informally, by stating appropriate invariants in my documentation and checking at my desk that those relations are preserved. But I can make mistakes in proofs and in specifying the conditions for correctness, just as I make mistakes in programming; therefore I do not rely entirely on correctness proofs, nor do I rely entirely on empirical test routines such as TRIP.

LOCATION AND TYPE OF ERRORS

Let me review again the fifteen classes of errors that are listed in my error log:

A — Algorithm	F — Forgotten	P — Portability
B — Blunder	G — Generalization	Q — Quality
C — Cleanup	I — Interaction	R — Robustness
D — Data	L — Language	S — Surprise
E — Efficiency	M — Mismatch	T — Typo

I mentioned before that each of the errors listed in the appendix refers where possible to its approximate location in the program listing of TEX82. It is natural to wonder whether the errors are uniformly interspersed throughout the code, or if certain parts were particularly vulnerable. Figure 4 shows the actual distribution. No part of the program has come through unscathed—or, shall we rather say, unimproved—but some parts have seen significantly more action. The boxes to the left of the vertical lines in Figure 4 represent 'bugs' (A, B, D, F, L, M, R, S, T), whereas the boxes to the right represent 'enhancements' (C, E, G, I, P, Q). The most unstable parts of TEX78 were the parts I understood least when I began to write the code, namely mathematical formatting and alignment. The most unstable parts of TEX82 were the parts that differed most from TEX78 (the conditional instructions and other aspects of macro expansion; also the increased user access to registers and internal quantities used in TEX's decision-making).

I should mention why hyphenation is almost never mentioned in the log of TEX78. Although I said earlier that TEX78 was entirely written before any of it was tested, that is not quite true. The hyphenation algorithm was quite independent of everything else and easily isolated from the code, so I had written and debugged it separately during three days in October 1977. (There is obviously no advantage to testing independent programs simultaneously; that leads only to confusion. But the rest of TEX was highly interdependent, and it could not easily be run when any of the parts

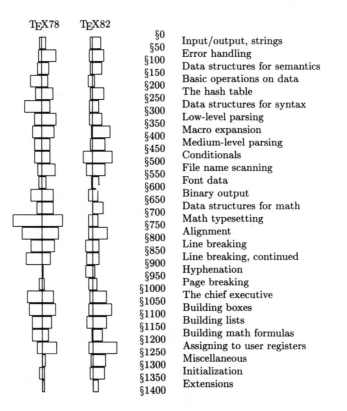

§0	Input/output, strings
§50	Error handling
§100	Data structures for semantics
§150	Basic operations on data
§200	The hash table
§250	Data structures for syntax
§300	Low-level parsing
§350	Macro expansion
§400	Medium-level parsing
§450	Conditionals
§500	File name scanning
§550	Font data
§600	Binary output
§650	Data structures for math
§700	Math typesetting
§750	Alignment
§800	Line breaking
§850	Line breaking, continued
§900	Hyphenation
§950	Page breaking
§1000	The chief executive
§1050	Building boxes
§1100	Building lists
§1150	Building math formulas
§1200	Assigning to user registers
§1250	Miscellaneous
§1300	Initialization
§1350	Extensions
§1400	

Figure 4. Distribution of [bugs | enhancements] by program location

were absent, except for the routines that produced the final output.) The hyphenation algorithm of TEX78 was English-specific; Frank Liang, who had helped me with this part of TEX78, developed a much better approach in his thesis,[22] and I ultimately incorporated his algorithm in TEX82.

Figure 5 shows the accumulated number of errors of each type in TEX78, with bugs at the bottom and enhancements at the top. Initially the log entries are mostly bugs, with occasional enhancements of type I; at the end, however, enhancements C, G and Q predominate. Figure 6 is a similar diagram for TEX82. In the latter case the vast majority of errors are enhancements, and there are no bugs of types M or T. That is because the debugging phase of TEX82 does not appear in the log, not because I learned how to make fewer mistakes.

SOME NOTEWORTHY BUGS

The gestalt of TEX's evolution can best be perceived by scanning through the log book, item by item. But I would like to single out several errors that were particularly instructive or otherwise memorable.

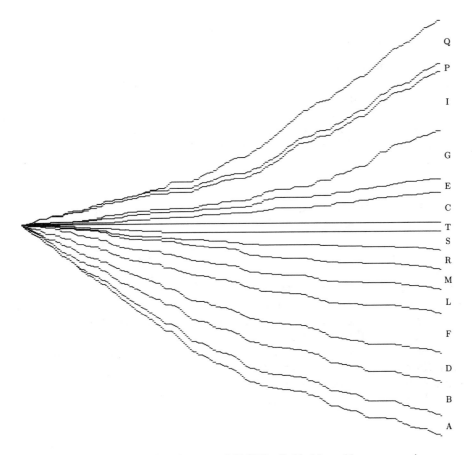

Figure 5. Accumulated errors of TEX78, divided into fifteen categories

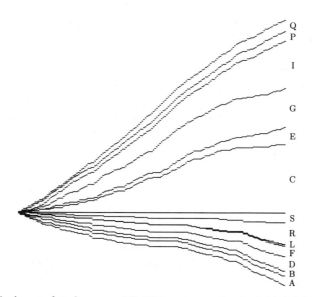

Figure 6. Accumulated errors of TEX82, not counting its initial debugging stage

A, Algorithmic anomalies

I decided from the beginning that the algorithms of TEX would be in the public domain. But if I were to change my mind and charge a fee for my services in inventing them, I would probably request the highest price for a comparatively innocuous-looking group of statements now found in sections 851 and 854 of the program. This precise sequence of logical tests, used to control when a line break is being forced because there is no 'feasible' alternative, has the essential form

```
if α₁ ∨ α₂ then
    if α₃ ∧ α₄ ∧ α₅ ∧ α₆ then σ₁
    else if α₇ then σ₂ else σ₃
else σ₄
```

and most of the appropriate boolean conditions α_i were discovered only with great difficulty. The program now warns any readers who seek to improve TEX to 'think thrice before daring to make any changes here'. Some indications of my struggles with this particular logic appear in error nos. 75, 93 and 506.

TEX's line-breaking algorithm determines the optimum sequence of breaks for each paragraph, in the sense that the total 'demerits' are minimized over all feasible sequences of breaks. The original algorithm was fairly simple, but it continued to evolve as I fiddled with the formula used to calculate demerits. Demerits are based on the 'badness' b of the line (which measures how loose or tight the spacing is) and the 'penalty' p for the break (which may be at a hyphen or within a mathematical formula). A penalty might be negative to indicate a good break. The original formula for demerits in TEX78 was

$$D = \max(b + p, 0)^2$$

error no. 76 replaced this by

$$D = \begin{cases} (1 + b + p)^2, & \text{if } p \geq 0 \\ (1 + b)^2 - p^2, & \text{if } p < 0 \end{cases}$$

The extra constant 1 was used to encourage paragraphs with fewer lines; the subtraction of p^2 when $p < 0$ gave fewer demerits to good breaks. This improved formula was published on page 1128 of the article on line-breaking by Knuth and Plass.[13] The first draft of TEX82 added an obvious generalization to the improved formula by introducing a \linepenalty parameter, l, to replace the constant 1. A further improvement was made in change no. 554, when I realized that better results would be obtained by computing demerits as follows:

$$D = \begin{cases} (l + b)^2 + p^2, & \text{if } p \geq 0 \\ (l + b)^2 - p^2, & \text{if } p < 0 \end{cases}$$

Otherwise, a line with, say, $(b, p) = (50,100)$, followed by a line with $(b, p) = (0,0)$, would be considered inferior to a pair of lines with $(b, p) = (0,100)$ and $(100,0)$, although the second pair of lines would actually look much worse.

B, Blunders

A typical blunder, among the 50 or so errors of class B in the appendix, is illustrated by error nos. 7 and 92. I had declared two symbolic constants in my program, new_line (for one of the three states of TEX's lexical scanner) and next_line (for the sequence of ASCII codes carriage_return and line_feed, needed in SAIL output conventions). Although the meanings were quite dissimilar, the names were quite similar; therefore I confused them in my mind. The compiler did not detect any syntax error, because both were legal in an output statement, so I had to detect and correct the bugs myself. I could have avoided these errors by using a name like cr_lf instead of next_line; but that sounds too jargony. A better alternative would have been new_line_state instead of new_line.

D, Data disasters

My most striking error in data-structure updating was no. 630, which crept in when I made change no. 625. The error needs a bit of background information before I can explain it: using an idea of Luis Trabb Pardo, I was able to save one bit in each node of TEX's main data structures by putting the nodes in which the bit would be 0—the so-called charnodes—into the upper part of the mem array, all other nodes into the lower part. (It was very important to save this bit, because I needed at least 32 additional bits in every charnode.) One of the aspects of change no. 625 was to optimize my data structure for representing mathematical subformulae that consist of a single letter. I could recognize and simplify such a subformula by looking for a list that consisted of precisely two elements, namely a charnode followed by a 'kern node' (for an 'italic correction'). A kern node is identified by (a) not being a charnode, i.e. not having a high memory address, and (b) having the subfield type = 11.

I forgot to test condition (a). But my program still worked in almost every case, because unsuitable lists of length 2 are rare as subformulae, and because the type subfield of a charnode records a fount number. Amazingly, however, within one week of my installing change no. 625, some user happened to create a mathematical list of length 2 in which the second element was a character from fount number 11!

This example demonstrates that I was lucky to have a wide variety of users. Still, such a bug might survive for years before it would cause trouble for anybody.

F, Forgetfulness

As I am writing this paper, I am trying to remember all the points I wanted to explain about TEX's evolution. Probably I will forget something, as I did when I was writing the program for TEX.

Usually a bug of class F was easily noticed when I first looked at the corresponding part of the code, with my walk-through-in-execution-order method of debugging. But I would like to mention two of the F errors that were among the most difficult to find. Both of them occurred in routines that had worked correctly the first few times they were exercised; indeed, these routines had been called hundreds of times, with perfect results, so I no longer suspected that they could be the source of any trouble.

Error no. 91 occurred in the memory allocation subroutine, the first time I ran out of memory. That subroutine had the general form

```
begin ⟨Get ready to search⟩;
repeat ⟨Look at an available slot⟩;
   if ⟨big enough⟩ then goto found;
   ⟨Move to next slot⟩;
until ⟨back at the beginning⟩;
found: ⟨Allocate and return, unless the available list becomes exhausted⟩;
ovfl: ⟨Give an overflow message⟩;
end
```

The bug is obvious: I forgot to say 'goto ovfl' just before the label 'found:'. And it is also obvious why this bug was hard to find: I had lost my suspicions that this subroutine could fail, but when it did fail it allocated one node right in the middle of another. My linked data structure was therefore destroyed, but its defective fields did not cause trouble until several hundred additional operations had been performed by the parts of the program where I was still looking for bugs.

Error no. 203 was even more difficult to find; it lurked in TEX's get_next routine, the subroutine that is executed far more than any other. Whenever TEX is ready to see another token of input, get_next comes into action. Therefore, by the time I had corrected 200 errors, get_next had probably obtained the correct next token more than 100,000 times; I considered it rock-solid reliable.

Since get_next is part of TEX's 'inner loop', I had wanted it to be efficient. Indeed, I learned later that the very first statement of get_next, 'cur_cs ← 0', is performed more often than any other single statement of TEX82. (Empirical tests covering a period of more than a year show that 'cur_cs ← 0' was performed more than 1·4 billion times on Stanford's SUAI computer. The get_avail routine, which is next in importance, was invoked only about 438 million times.) Knowing that get_next was critical, I had tried to avoid performing 'cur_cs ← 0' in my first implementations, in cases where I knew that the value of cur_cs would not be examined by the consumers of get_next's tokens. In fact, I knew that cur_cs would be irrelevant in the vast majority of cases. (But I also knew, and forgot, Hoare's dictum that premature optimization is the root of all evil in programming.)

Well, you can almost guess the rest. When I corrected my serious misunderstanding of alignments, error nos. 108 and 110, I introduced a new case in get_next, and that new case filled my thoughts so much that I forgot to worry about the 'cur_cs ← 0' operation. Still, no harm was done unless cur_cs was actually being looked at; TEX would not fail unless \cr occurred in an alignment having a special sort of template that required back-up in the parser. As before, the effect of this error was buried in a data structure, where it remained hidden until much later. I found the bug only by temporarily inserting new code that continually monitored the integrity of the data structures. (Such code later became a standard diagnostic feature of TEX82; it can be seen for example in section 167.)

L, Language lossage

Some of my errors (nos. 98, 295, 296, 480) were due to the fact that algorithms involving floating-point numbers sometimes fail because of round-off errors. (I have assigned these errors to class L instead of class A, although it was a close call.) TEX82 was designed to be portable so that it gives essentially identical results on all computers; therefore I avoided floating-point calculations in critical parts of the new program.

Two other errors in my log belong unambiguously to class L: in nos. 63 and 827, I failed to insert parentheses into a macro definition. As a result, when I used the macro with text replacement, any frequent user of macros can guess what happened. (Namely, in no. 827, I had declared the macro

$$\text{hi\_mem\_stat\_min} \equiv \text{mem\_top} - 13$$

and used it in the statement

$$\text{dyn\_used} \leftarrow \text{mem\_top} + 1 - \text{hi\_mem\_stat\_min};$$

this gave a minus where I wanted a plus.)

M, Mismatches

When I write a program I tend to forget the exact specifications of its subroutines. One of my frequent flubs is to blur the distinction between an object and a pointer to that object. In TEX82, for example, I noticed when I got to error no. 79 that I had called vpackage (p, ...) where p pointed to the first node of a vlist, whereas in the declaration of vpackage I had assumed parameters of the form (h, ...) where h points to a list header; thus link(h), not h itself, was assumed to point to the first list item. The compiler did not catch the error because both h and link(h) were of type pointer.

While fixing this bug it occurred to me that vpackage was an oft-used subroutine and that I might have made the same mistake more than once. So I looked closely at each of the 26 places I had called vpackage, and the results proved that I was remarkably inconsistent: I had specified a list head 14 times, and a direct pointer 12 times! (Fortunately there was not a 13–13 split; that would have been unlucky.)

This error reminded me that I should always check the entire program whenever I notice a mistake; *failures tend to recur*. In fact, several errors of TEX82 (nos. 803, 813, 815, 837) were first noticed when I was debugging similar portions of METAFONT.

R, Robustness

Most of the changes of type R were introduced to keep TEX from crashing when users supply input that does not obey the rules. But some of the Rs in the log are intended to keep TEX alive even when other parts of TEX are failing, because of my programming errors or because somebody else is trying to produce a new modification of TEX.

Thus, for example, in nos. 99 and 123, I redesigned two of my procedures so that they would produce a symbolic printout of given data structures in memory even when those data structures were malformed. I made it possible to obtain meaningful output from arbitrary bit configurations in memory, so that while debugging TEX I could interactively look at garbage and guess how it might have arisen.

One of the most recent changes to TEX, no. 846, has the same flavour: the parameter to show_node_list was redeclared to be of type integer instead of type pointer, because buggy calls on show_node_list might not supply a valid pointer.

S, Surprises

The most serious errors were those due to my global misunderstandings of how the system fits together. The final error in TEX78 was of type S, and I suppose the final error of TEX82 will be yet another surprise.

Let me mention just two of these. The first is extremely embarrasing, but it makes a good story. TEX produces DVI files as output, where DVI stands for DeVice Independent. The DVI language is like a machine language, consisting of 8-bit instruction codes followed in certain cases by arguments to the instructions. Two of the simplest instructions of DVI language are push (code 141) and pop (code 142). It turns out that TEX might output push followed immediately by pop in various circumstances, and this needlessly clutters up the DVI file; so I decided to optimize things a bit by checking to see whether the final byte in my output buffer was push before TEX would output a pop. If so, I could cancel both instructions. This technique even made it possible to detect and cancel long redundant sequences such as push push pop push push pop pop pop. Naturally, I checked to see that the buffer had not been entirely cancelled out when I tested for such an optimization. (I was not 100 per cent stupid.) But I failed to realize that the byte just preceding pop might just happen to be 141 (the binary code for push) when it was the final operand byte of some *other* instruction. Ouch!

The other S bug I want to discuss is truly an example of global misunderstanding, because it arose in connection with my misperceptions about \global definitions in TEX documents. Users can define control sequences such as \abc inside a TEX 'group', which is essentially a 'block' in the sense of Algol scope rules. At the end of a group, local definitions are rescinded and control sequences revert to the meanings they had at the beginning of the group. In my first implementation of TEX78 I went even further: If \abc was defined inside a group but not before the group had begun, I actually removed \abc from the hash table when the group ended.

There is one exception, however, to TEX's local scope rules (and it is usually the exceptions that lead to surprises). Users can state that a definition is \global; this means that the new definition will survive at the end of the current group, unless it has been globally redefined again. Therefore my implementation removed control sequences from the hash table at group endings only when they had not been globally defined.

That caused bug no. 422, which was identical to one of the first serious bugs I had ever encountered when learning to program in the 1950s: deletions from an 'open' hash table might make other keys inaccessible, unless the deletions occur in FIFO order, or unless the deletion algorithm takes special precautions to relocate keys in the table. (See my book *Sorting and Searching*,[22] pp. 526–527, where I say—in italics—'*The obvious way to delete records from a scatter table doesn't work.*') Alas, I had deleted the control-sequence records in the 'obvious way' in TEX78, not realizing that global definitions destroyed the FIFO order.

To fix bug no. 422, I could not patch the definition procedure by using Algorithm 6.4R from my book,[22] because the organization of TEX did not allow for relocation of keys. So I needed to change the hash table algorithm from linear probing to chaining, which supports arbitrary deletions. This change was not as painful as it might have been at this late date (August 1979), because I had needed an excuse anyway to overcome my initial hash table design. In order to keep the original implementation simple, I had decided to require that control sequence names be essentially unique when restricted to their first six letters. Such a restriction was quite reasonable when I was to be the only user of TEX; but it was becoming intolerable when the number of users began to grow into the thousands. Therefore change no. 422 not only altered the hash discipline, it also changed the entire representation mechanism so that identifiers of arbitrary length could be accommodated.

And that was not the end of the story. Another year and a half went by before I realized (in no. 493) that TEX allows declarations like

```
\def\abc{...}
\global\def\xyz{...\abc...}
```

within a group. In such cases I could not eliminate \abc from the hash table at the end of the group, because a reference to \abc still survived within \xyz. I finally decided not to delete *anything* from the hash table (although I did provide a mechanism to prevent unwanted keys from ever getting in; see nos. 294 and 769).

How did such serious bugs remain undetected for so long? They lay dormant because normal usage of TEX does not require complicated interactions between local and global definitions in groups. Most formatting is simpler than this; even complex books such as *The Art of Computer Programming* and the TEX manual itself do not need such generality. But if I had used the TRIP test methodology in the early days, I would have found and corrected the local/global problems right at the start. This experience suggests that all software systems be subjected to the meanest, nastiest torture tests imaginable; otherwise they will almost certainly continue to exhibit bugs for years after they have begun to produce satisfactory results in large applications.

T, Typographical trivia

The typographical errors of TEX were not especially significant, but I will mention two of them (nos. 69 and 86), where my original SAIL code looked like this:

```
glueshrink(q)← glueshrink(q)← glueshrink(t);
x← x← width(q).
```

SAIL was written for the extended ASCII character set that once was widely used at Stanford, MIT, CMU and a few other places; one of the important characters was '←', for Algol's ':='. The language allowed multiple assignment, hence both of these statements were syntactically correct (although rather silly).

A language designer straddles a narrow line between restrictiveness and permissiveness. If almost every sequence of characters is syntactically correct, the inevitable typographical errors will almost never be detected. But if almost no sequences of characters are syntactically correct, typing becomes a real pain.

In TEX78 I made a terrible decision (no. 402) to allow users to type a letter such as 'A' whenever TEX was expecting to see a number; the meaning was to use the ASCII code of A (97) as the number. This extended the language for certain hacker-type applications; but it caused all sorts of grief to ordinary users, because their typographical errors were being treated as perfectly meaningful TEX input, and they could not figure out what was going wrong. (I compounded the error in no. 507; see also no. 511. This is a sorry part of the record.) TEX82 resolved the problem by using a special character to introduce ASCII constants.

SOME NOTEWORTHY ENHANCEMENTS

Let us turn now to the other six kinds of errors in the log.

C, Clean-ups

The stickiest issue in TEX has always been the treatment of blank spaces. Users tend to insert spaces in their computer files so that the files look nice, but document processors must also treat spaces as objects that appear in the final output. Therefore, when you see documents nowadays that have been prepared by systems other than TEX, you often find cases where double spaces appear incorrectly between words; and when you see documents prepared with TEX, you run into cases where a necessary space between words has disappeared. I kept searching for rules that would be simple enough to be easily learned, yet natural enough that they could be applied almost unconsciously. I finally concluded that no such rules existed, and I opted for the best compromise I could find.

Several of the log entries refer to the question of optional spaces after a macro definition. In no. 133, I decided to ignore a space that appears there; this was prompted by experiences recorded in my comments following nos. 115 and 119. But no. 133 caused a timing problem in no. 560, because the macro definition had not been fully processed when TEX wanted to check for the optional space; if the user invoked the macro immediately, instead of putting a space there, TEX was not ready to respond. Finally in no. 606 I came to the conclusion that TEX users will best be able to keep their sanity if I do not ignore spaces after definitions; then dozens of similar-appearing cases all have consistent rules.

(See also no. 220, for space after $$; nos. 361, 708, 720 and 723, for space after constants; no. 440, for space after active characters; and no. 632, for space after '\\'.)

G, Generalizations

TEX continued to grow new capabilities as people would present me with new applications. When I could not handle the new problem nicely with the existing TEX, I would usually end up changing the system. (But I kept the changes minimal, because I always wanted to finish and get on with other things. More about that later.)

Such generalizations were often built incrementally on the shoulders of their predecessors. For example, the original TEX78 had \output and \mark and macro definitions, which scanned and remembered lists of tokens, but there was no good way to assign a list of tokens to a 'token list variable' without causing macro expansion. Then TEX82 added a feature called \everypar, which Arthur Keller had long been lobbying for. One day I noticed that I could solve a user's problem in a tricky way by temporarily using \everypar to store a list of tokens. This was quite different from the intended use of \everypar, of course; so I introduced a new primitive operation called \tokens for such purposes (no. 559). Later, \everypar spawned several descendants called \everymath and \everydisplay (no. 568), \everyhbox and \everyvbox (no. 649), \everyjob (no. 657), \everycr (no. 688). I eventually found applications where \tokens was not enough by itself and I needed to borrow one of the \every features temporarily to do some non-standard hackery. So I finally replaced \tokens by an array of 256 registers called \toks (no. 713), analogous to TEX's existing arrays of registers for integers, dimensions, boxes and glue. TEX82 also acquired the ability to make assignments between different kinds of token_list variables (no. 746). In such ways I tried to keep the design 'orthogonal' as the language grew.

Of course every language designer likes to keep a language simple by applying Occam's razor. I was pleased to discover early in 1977 that simple primitive operations involving boxes, glue and penalties could account for many of the fundamental operations of typesetting. This was a real unification of basic principles, and it turned out to be even better when I realized that the concepts of ordinary line-breaking applied also to tasks that seemed much harder.[13] But I also fooled myself into thinking that TEX had fewer primitives than it really did, by 'overloading' operations that were essentially independent and calling them single features.

For example, my original design of TEX78 would break paragraphs into lines by ignoring all lines whose badness exceeded 200. Later (no. 104) I made this threshold value user-settable by introducing a new primitive called \jpar. Setting \jpar=2 was something like setting \tolerance=200 in TEX82; but I also included a peculiar new convention: if \jpar was odd, the paragraphs would be set with ragged right margins, otherwise they would be justified to the full width!

Thus, in my attempt to minimize primitives, I had loaded two independent ideas onto a single parameter. I had also packed half a dozen different kinds of diagnostic output into a single number called \tracing (see no. 199), whose binary digits were examined individually when TEX was deciding whether to trace parts of its operations.

Then I began to see the need for more user-settable numbers, and I shuddered to think at the resultant multiplicity of new primitives. So I replaced both \jpar and

\tracing by a *single* primitive called \chpar (no. 244); one could now say, for example, \chpar1=2 instead of \jpar=2. This change gave me the courage to add new parameters for hyphen penalties, etc., and I even added a new parameter to control the raggedness of right margins (no. 334). Now the parity of \jpar was irrelevant; henceforth, the right margins could be either straight or ragged, or they could be produced using some smoothly varying compromise between those extremes—'one third of the way to full raggedness.'

My decision to introduce \chpar in TEX78 was not too bad, because TEX is a macro language and I could immediately define \jpar and \tracing as abbreviations for \chpar1 and \chpar2. But still, those arbitrary numerical codes were inelegant. TEX82 now has fifty different primitive operations that denote integer-valued parameters, each with standard (but user-changeable) names. The old \jpar has become \tolerance and \pretolerance. The old \tracing has been unbundled into \tracingparagraphs, \tracingpages, \tracingmacros, and half a dozen more, with separate parameters such as \showboxdepth to govern the amount of display.

I, Interactions

About 15 per cent of the errors in the TEX log have been classified type I. The main issue in such cases is to help users identify and recover from errors in their source programs, and this is always problematical because there are so many ways to make mistakes. 'When your error is due to misunderstanding rather than mistyping, . . . TEX can only explain what looks wrong from its own viewpoint; such an explanation is bound to be mysterious unless you understand the machine's attitude'.[15] Which you don't.

Still, I kept trying to make TEX respond more productively, and every such change was logged as an 'error' in my original design. The most memorable error of this type was probably no. 213, when I first realized how nice it would be if I could insert a token or two that TEX could read immediately, instead of aborting a run and starting from scratch. (This was soon followed by no. 242, when deletion of tokens was also allowed in response to an error message.) I would never have thought of these improvements if I had not participated in the implementation and testing of TEX, and I have often wished for similar features in the compilers I have used since. This one feature must have saved me hundreds of hours as a TEX user during recent years.

Another improvement in interaction did not occur to me until several months and several hundred pages of output later. Error no. 338 records the blessed day when I gave TEX the ability to track 'runaways', parts of the program that were being processed in the wrong mode because of missing right delimiters. (Further refinements to that change were logged as entry nos. 344, 426 and 793.) Without such provisions, errors that TEX could not have detected until long after their appearance would have been much harder to track down.

There was another significant improvement in interaction that never made it into my error log, because I included it in the original TEX82 without ever putting it into TEX78. This is the short_display procedure, for showing the contents of 'overfull boxes' and such things in an abbreviated form easily understood by novice users. The short_display idea was invented by Ralph Stromquist, who installed it in his early version of TEX at the University of Wisconsin.

P, Portability

The first changes of type P were simply enhancements to the comments in my SAIL program, but the advent of WEB made it possible for TEX to become truly independent of the machine and operating system it was being run on.

Change no. 633 is perhaps the most instructive class-P modification: I decided to guarantee compatibility between DEC-like systems (which break the source file into lines according to the appearance of ASCII carriage_return characters) and IBM-like systems (which have fixed-length source lines reminiscent of 80-column cards),* in the following way: whenever TEX reads a line of input, on any system, it automatically removes all blank spaces that appear at the right end. The presence or absence of such blanks therefore cannot influence the behaviour of TEX in any way. An ASCII file whose lines are at most 80 characters long (as defined by carriage returns, with or without blanks in front of those carriage returns) can be converted to a file of 80-character records that will produce identical results with TEX, simply by padding each line with blanks.

Change no. 791 carried no. 633 to its logical conclusion.

Q, Quality

From the beginning, I wanted TEX to produce documents of the highest possible typographical quality. The time had come when computer-produced output no longer needed to settle for being only 'pretty good'; I wanted to equal or exceed the quality of the best books ever printed by photographic methods.

As Kernighan and Cherry have said, 'The main difficulty is in finding the right numbers to use for esthetically pleasing positioning. . . . Much of this time has gone into two things—fine-tuning (what is the most esthetically pleasing space to use between the numerator and denominator of a fraction?), and changing things found deficient by our users (shouldn't a tilde be a delimiter?)'.[23]

I too had trouble with numerators and denominators: change no. 229 increased the amount of space surrounding the bar line in displayed fractions, and I should have made a similar change to fractions in text. (Page 68 of the new Volume 2 turned out to be extremely ugly because of badly spaced fractions.) TEX82 was able to improve the situation because of my experiences with TEX78, but even today I must take special precautions in my TEX documents to get certain square roots to look right.

THE EVOLUTION PROCESS AS A WHOLE

Looking now at the entire log of errors, I am struck by the fact that my attitude during those years was clearly far from ideal: my overriding goal was always to finish, to finish, to get this long-overdue project done so that I could resume work on other long-overdue projects. I never wanted to spend extra time studying alternatives for the best possible typesetting language; only rarely was I in a mood to consider any changes

---

*Paradoxically, DEC has also introduced the VMS operating system, which has fixed-length lines that can include troublesome carriage-returns. But that is another story.

to TEX whatsoever. I wanted TEX to produce the highest quality, sure, but I wanted to achieve that with the minimum amount of work on my part.

At the end of almost every day between 29 March 1978 and 29 March 1980, I felt that TEX78 was a complete system, containing no bugs and needing no further enhancements. At the end of almost every day since 9 September 1982, I have felt that TEX82 was a complete system, containing no bugs and needing no further enhancements. Each of the subsequent steps in the evolution of TEX has been viewed not as an evolutionary step towards a vague distant goal, but rather as the final evolutionary step towards the finally reached goal! Yet, over time, TEX has changed dramatically as a result of many such 'final steps'.

Was this horizon-limiting attitude harmful, or was it somehow a blessing in disguise? I am pleased to see that TEX actually kept getting simpler as it kept growing, because the new features blended with the old ones. I was constantly bombarded by ideas for extensions, and I was constantly turning a deaf ear to everything that did not fit well with TEX as I conceived it at the time. Thus TEX converged, rather than diverged, to its final form. By acting as an extremely conservative filter, and by believing that the system was always complete, I was perhaps able to save TEX from the 'creeping featurism'[24] that destroys systems whose users are allowed to introduce a patchwork of loosely connected ideas.

If I had time to spend another ten years developing a system with the same aims as TEX—if I were to start all over again from scratch, without any considerations of compatibility with existing systems—I could no doubt come up with something that is marginally better. But at the moment I cannot think of any big improvements. The best such system I can envision today would still look very much like TEX82; so I think this particular case study in program evolution has proved to be successful.

Of course I do not mean to imply that all problems of typography have been solved. Far from it! There still are countless important issues to be studied, relating especially to the many classes of documents that go far beyond what I ever intended TEX to handle.

CONCLUSIONS

My purpose in this paper has been to describe what I think are the most significant aspects of the experiences I had while developing TEX, basing this on a study of more than 800 errors that I noted down in log books over the years. I have tried to interpret many specific facts and observations in a sufficiently general way that readers may understand how to apply similar concepts to other software developments.

In Volume 1 of *The Art of Computer Programming*,[25] I wrote:

> Debugging is an art that needs much further study . . . The most effective debugging techniques seem to be those which are designed and built into the program itself . . . Another good debugging practice is to keep a record of every mistake that is made. Even though this will probably be quite embarrassing, such information is invaluable to anyone doing research on the debugging problem, and it will also help you learn how to reduce the number of future errors.

Well, I hope that my error log in the appendix below, especially the first 237 items (which relate specifically to debugging), will be useful somehow to people who study the debugging process.

But if you ask whether keeping such a log has helped me learn how to reduce the number of future errors, my answer has to be no. I kept a similar log for errors in METAFONT, and there was no perceivable reduction. I continue to make the same kinds of mistakes.

What have I really learned, then? I think I have learned, primarily, to have a better sense of balance and proportion. I now understand the complexities of a medium-size software system, and the ways in which it can be expected to evolve. I now understand that there are so many kinds of errors, we cannot stamp them out by systematically eliminating everything that might be 'considered harmful'. I now understand enough about my propensity to err that I can accept it as an act of life; I can now be convinced more easily of my fallacy when I have made a mistake. Indeed, I now strive energetically to find faults in my own work, even though it would be much easier to look for assurances that everything is OK. I now look forward to making (and correcting) hundreds of future errors as I write Volume 4 of *The Art of Computer Programming*.

ADDENDUM: FIFTEEN MONTHS MORE

As I mentioned above, I began to write this paper in May 1987, but I decided to wait before publication until more time had gone by. Then I could present a 'complete' and 'final' record of TEX's errors.

Now it is September 1988, and I have decided to bring this paper to a possibly premature conclusion, because I am scheduled to present it at a conference.[26] TEX still has not shown encouraging signs of becoming quiescent; indeed, sixteen more entries have entered the error log since May 1987, including three as recent as June 1988. Therefore it still is not the right moment to manufacture TEX on a chip!

All errors known to me as of 1 September 1988, are now included in the appendix to this paper; the total has now reached 865.* I plan to publish a brief note ten years from now, bringing the list to its absolutely final form.

I have been paying a reward to everyone who discovers new bugs in TEX, and doubling the amount every year. Last December I made two payments of $40.96 each, and my chequebook has been hit for five $81.92 payments in recent months. I am desperately hoping that this incentive to discover the final bugs will produce them before I am unable to pay the promised amount. (Surely in 1998 I won't be writing cheques for $83,886.08?)

As I expected, half of the most recent errors have fallen into the surprise (S) category—even though surprises, by definition, are unexpected. But one of the others (error no. 854) was perhaps the most surprising of all, because it was the result of a terrible algorithm by a person who certainly should have known better (me). I wanted to multiply the two's-complement fixed-point number

$$A = -16 + a_1 \times 2^{-4} + a_2 \times 2^{-12} + a_3 \times 2^{-20}, \qquad 0 \le a_i < 256$$

---

*Errors 866 and 867 were added after this paper was first submitted.

by the positive quantity $Z/2^{16}$, where Z is an integer, $2^{26} \leq Z < 2^{27}$, obtaining an answer of the form $P/2^{16}$ where P is an integer, $|P| < 2^{31}$; all intermediate quantities in the calculation were required to be less than 2^{31} in absolute value. My program did this by computing

$$C \leftarrow 16 * Z;$$
$$Z \leftarrow Z \text{ div } 16;$$
$$P \leftarrow ((a_3 * Z) \text{ div } 256 + a_2 * Z) \text{ div } 256 + a_1 * Z - C;$$

I should rather have computed

$$Z \leftarrow Z \text{ div } 16;$$
$$P \leftarrow ((a_3 * Z) \text{ div } 256 + a_2 * Z) \text{ div } 256 + (a_1 - 256) * Z$$

(Consider, for example, the case $Z = 2^{26} + 15$ and $a_1 = a_2 = a_3 = 255$, so that $A = -2^{-20}$. The first method gives $P = -304$; the second method gives the correct answer, $P = -64$.)

Let me close by discussing one more recent error, no. 864. This change yields only a slight gain in efficiency, so I need not have made it; but it was easy to correct one more statement while I was fixing no. 863. It is an instructive example of how a design methodology based on invariants might not lead to the best algorithm unless we think a bit harder about what is going on.

Here is the idea: each run of TEX determines a threshold value θ above which the (one-word) charnodes will reside, below which all other (variable-size) nodes will be stored. Actually there are two values, θ_0 and θ_1; memory positions between θ_0 and θ_1 are empty. (In the program, θ_0 is actually called lo_mem_max, and θ_1 is called hi_mem_min.) TEX changes θ_0 and θ_1 conservatively as it runs, so that they will converge to values appropriate to particular applications. The boundary value θ was originally fixed at compile time; this transition to 'late binding' was change no. 819.

When TEX needs more space for charnodes, it usually sets $\theta_1 \leftarrow \theta_1 - 1$; when TEX needs more space for variable-size nodes, it usually sets $\theta_0 \leftarrow \theta_0 + 1000$. But we need to have $\theta_0 < \theta_1$. Therefore, instead of setting $\theta_0 \leftarrow \theta_0 + 1000$, my original code said

if $\theta_1 - \theta_0 > 1000$ then $\theta_0 \leftarrow \theta_0 + 1000$
else if $\theta_1 - \theta_0 > 2$ then $\theta_0 \leftarrow (\theta_0 + \theta_1 + 2)$ div 2
else ⟨Report memory overflow⟩.

(The variable θ_0 had to increase by at least 2.) Chris Thompson of Cambridge University pointed out that this strategy, although preserving the necessary invariants, is discontinuous. If $\theta_1 - \theta_0 = 1001$, the algorithm gobbles up all the discretionary space that is left. Therefore change no. 864 substituted better logic:

if $\theta_1 - \theta_0 \geq 1998$ then $\theta_0 \leftarrow \theta_0 + 1000$
else if $\theta_1 - \theta_2 > 2$ then $\theta_0 \leftarrow \theta_0 + 1 + (\theta_1 - \theta_0)$ div 2
else ⟨Report memory overflow⟩.

The new version also avoids problems on certain computers when θ_0 and θ_1 are negative; that was error no. 863. (Of course, when TEX is this close to running out of memory, it probably will not survive much longer anyway. I am grasping at straws. But I might as well grasp intelligently.)

ACKNOWLEDGEMENTS

I have already mentioned that the TEX project has had hundreds of volunteers who helped to guide me through all these developments. Their names can be found in the rosters of the TEX Users Group; I couldn't possibly list them all here. Luis Trabb Pardo and David R. Fuchs were my 'right-hand men' for TEX78 and TEX82, respectively. The project received generous financial backing from several independent sources, notably the System Development Foundation, the U.S. National Science Foundation, and the Office of Naval Research. The material on which this report has been based is now housed in the Stanford University Archives; I wish to thank the archivist, Roxanne L. Nilan, for her friendly co-operation. The preparation of this paper has been supported by U.S. National Science Foundation grant CCR-86-10181. Thanks are due to the referee who helped me to remove errors not from TEX but from this paper. And above all, I want to thank my wife, Jill, for ten years of exceptional tolerance; software development is much more demanding than the other things I usually do. Jill also helped me to design the format for the appendix that follows.

APPENDIX: THE COMPLETE ERROR LOG

Each entry is numbered and cross-referenced (where possible) to other entries and to the TEX program, as explained in the text above. Sometimes I have given credit to the person who detected the error or suggested the change, but (alas) I did not always remember to note such information down. Here are the initials of people who made so many contributions that I have abbreviated their names in the log entries:

ARK	Arthur Keller
CET	Chris Thompson
DRF	David Fuchs
FY	Frank Yellin
HWT	Howard Trickey
JS	Jim Sterken
LL	Leslie Lamport
MDS	Mike Spivak

10 Mar 1978

1 Rename a few external variables to make their first six letters unique.   L

2 Initialize *escape_char* to −1, not 0 [it will be set to the first character input].   §240 D

3 Fix bug: The test '*id* < *'200*' was supposed to distinguish one-letter identifiers from longer (packed) ones, but negative values of *id* also pass this test.   §356 L

4 Fix bug: I wrote '**while** $\alpha \wedge (\beta \vee \gamma)$' when I meant '**while** $(\alpha \wedge \beta) \vee \gamma$'.   §259 B

5 Initialize the input routines in INITEX [at this time a short, separate program not under user control], in case errors occur.   §1337 R

6 Don't initialize *mem* in INITEX, it wastes time.   §164 E

7 Change '*new_line*' [which denotes a lexical scanning state] to '*next_line*' [which denotes *carriage_return* and *line_feed*] in print commands.   B

8 Include additional test '*mem*[*p*] ≠ 0 ∧' in *check_mem*.   §168 F

9 Fix inconsistency between the *eq_level* conventions of *macro_def* and *eq_define*. §277 M

• *About six hours of debugging time today.*

• *INITEX appears to work, and the test routine got through start_input, chcode [the test TEX78 command for assigning a cat_code], get_next, and back_input the first time.*

11 Mar 1978

10 Insert space before '(' on terminal when opening a new file.   §537 I

11 Put '*p* ← *link*(*p*)' into the loop of *show_token_list*, so that it doesn't loop forever.   §292 F

12 Shift the last item found by *scan_toks* into the *info* field. [With SAIL all packing of fields was done by arithmetic operations, not by the compiler.]   §474 L

12 ↦ **13** Fix the previous bugfix: I shifted by the wrong amount.   §474 B

14 Add a feature that prints a warning when the end of a file page occurs within a macro definition or call. [System dependent.]   §336 I

• *Unintended bugs in my test routine [a format intended eventually to typeset The Art of Computer Programming] helped check out the error recovery mechanisms. For example, I had '*\lft{#}*' instead of '*\lft{##}*' inside a macro, and three cases of improper { and } nesting.*

15 Add the forgotten case '*set_font:*' to *eq_destroy*.   §275 F

16 Change \require to \input.   §376 C

17 Add code for the case *cur_cmd* = 0 [later known as the case '*t* ≥ *cs_token_flag*'] when scanning a tokenlist.   §357 F

• *That's the first "big" error I've spotted so far.*

18 Introduce a 'd' option in the error routine, to facilitate debugging.   §84 I

19 Assign a floating-point constant *ignore_depth* to *prev_depth*, instead of assigning the integer constant *flag* [since *prev_depth* is type *real* in TEX78].   §215 L

20 Improve the readability and spacing of *show_node_list* output.   §182, 187 I

21 Set the variable *v* before using the **case** construction in *show_node_list*, because there's one case where *v* didn't receive a value [as part of the field unpacking]. §182 F

• *About seven hours today.*

12 Mar 1978

• *One hour to enter yesterday's corrections and recompile.*

• *At this point TEX correctly located further unintended syntax errors in* acphdr *[the test file].*

22 Insert *debug_help* into *succumb*, giving a chance to look at memory before the system dies.   §93 I

23 Use *eq_destroy* wherever necessary in *unsave*.   §283 D

24 Change '$t \leftarrow (t-1) \bmod 8$' to '$t \leftarrow (t-1) \text{ land } 7$' in *id_name*, since **SAIL** has $-1 \bmod 8 = -1$. [At this time, *id_name* is a routine that unpacks control sequence names, according to a scheme that will become obsolete after change #422.]   L

25 Remove the space that appears at end of paragraph. (I hadn't anticipated that.)   §816 S

26 Throw away unwanted *line_feed* after getting a *carriage_return* in response to *in_chr_w* [a system routine for input from the terminal].   §83 L

27 Delete spurious call to *flush_list* in *end_token_list*.   §324 B

- *Why did I make such a silly mistake?*

28 Fix bug in *get_x_token*: I forgot to say '*macro_call*' (which is the main point of that routine)!   §380 F

- *While tracking that bug down, I found out incidentally that kerning is okay.*
- *Also TEX correctly caught an error* Op *for* Opt.

29 Fix bug in *scan_spec* (**while** instead of **repeat**).   §404 L

30 Make the table entries for \hfill and \hskip consistent with the program conventions.   §1058 M

31 Disable unforeseen coercion: When *scan_spec* put *hsize* on *save_stack*, the value changed from *real* to *integer*.   §645 L

32 Use '*' instead of '-1.0' for running dimensions of rules in *show_node_list*.   §176 I

33 Clear *mem*[*head*] to null in *push_nest* [in TEX82, this will be done by *get_avail*]. §216 D

- *A vrule link got clobbered because I forgot to do this.*

34 Translate ASCII control codes to special form when displaying them.   §48,68 I

- *Ligatures work, but* show_node_list *showed them funny.*

35 Remember to clear parameters off *save_stack* in *package* routine.   §1086 F

- *About eight hours today.*

13 Mar 1978

36 Introduce a new variable *hang_first* [later the sign of *hang_after*].   §849 D

$36 \mapsto$ **37** Simplify the new code, realizing that if *hang_indent* $= 0$ then *hang_first* is irrelevant.   §848 E

- *Time sharing is very slow today, so I'm mostly reading technical reports while waiting* **three hours** *for compiler, editor, and loading routine.*
- *I'm not counting this as debugging time!*
- *(Came back in the evening.)*

38 Spruce up the comments in the *line_break* routine, which appears to be almost working.   §813 P

39 Rethink the setting of *best_line*; it's 1 too high in many cases. [The final line of a paragraph was handled in a treacherous way.]   §874 D

40 Compute proper initialization for *prev_depth* when beginning an \hbox with a paragraph inside. [This refers to a special 'paragraph box' construction, used when an hbox of specified size becomes overfull; TEX78 doesn't have the concept of internal vertical mode.]   §1083 D

41 Also initialize *tail* in that case.   §1083 D

42 Also put the result of line-breaking into the correct list.   M

43 Fix a typo in the *free_node* routine ('*link*' not '*llink*'); by strange chance it had been harmless until today.   §130 T

44 Fix bug: *post_line_break* forgot to set *adjust_tail*.   §889 F

45 Update *act_width* properly when looking for end of word while line breaking. §866 D

46 Repair the "tricky" part of *get_node*: I used the *info* field when I meant to say *llink*.   §127 B

- *Now the* \corners *macro of* acphdr *works!* [See \setcornerrules *in The* TEXbook, *page 417.*]

47 Reset *contrib_tail* properly in *build_page*.   §995 D

48 Fix typo (- for +) in computation of *page_total*.   §1004 T

49 Change the page-breaking logic: TEX reached *fire_up* with *best_page_break* = *null* in one case, since the badness was too bad.   §1005 S

50 Perform the operation *delete_token_ref* (*top_mark*) only when *top_mark* ≠ 0.   §1012 M

51 Make *scan_toks* omit the initial { of an \output routine.   §473 F

52 Insert a comma to make memory usage statistics look better.   §639 I

- *About seven good hours of debugging today.*
- *Tomorrow will be first-output day (I hope).*

14 Mar 1978

- *(Came in evening after sleeping most of day, to get computer at better time.)*
- *(Some day we will have personal computers and will live more normally.)*
- *8:30pm, began to enter corrections to yesterday's problems.*

53 Issue an error message for non-character in filename or in font name.   §771 I

54 Display '...' for omitted stuff in *show_context* routine.   §643 I

55 Watch out for the SAIL syntax '$\alpha + \beta$ lsh γ'; it doesn't shift $\alpha + \beta$ left (only β).   §464 L

- *That error was very hard to track down; it created a spurious link field and sent hash*[0] = \beta *to the scanner!*
- *I could have found this bug an hour sooner if I had looked at the correct stack entries for* name *and* token_type.

56 Show the correct page number when tracing pages before output is shipped.   §638 D

57 Remember to nullify a box after using it.   §1079 F

58 Issue an error message if \box255 isn't consumed by the output routine.   §1015 I

- *I'm having trouble with the* BAIL *debugger; it makes an illegal memory reference and dies, when single-stepping past the entry to recursive procedures* hlist_out *and* vlist_out. *So I have to reload and be careful to go thru these procedures at high speed.*

59 Fix bug in comment (memory parameter description said ≥ not ≤).   §11 P

60 Fix typo in definition of rule output (said x, y not $x0, y0$). [This part of the code went away when DVI files were introduced.]   B

61 Correct the embarrassing bug in shellsort, where I said '≤ *str*[*k*]' not '≤ *t*'. [The first TEX had to sort all output by vertical position on page.]   B

62 Make *start_input* set up *job_name* in the form needed by *shipout*; it uses obsolete conventions.   §532, 537 M

63 Insert (and) into the SAIL macro definition of *new_string*. [This macro was for pre-DVI output.]   L

64 Unscramble the parameters of *out_rule*: The declaration was ($x0, y0, x1, y1$) while the call was ($x0, x1, y0, y1$).   M

- *4:30am, TEX's first page is successfully output!*
- *(It was '\titlepage\setcpage1\corners\eject\end'.)*

15 Mar 1978

- *10:30pm. Today I'm instrumenting the line-breaking routine and putting it through a bunch of tests.*
- *(The inserted instrumentation had bugs that won't be mentioned here.)*

65 Don't abort the job when *eq_destroy* redefines a TEX control sequence.   §275 C

- *The first word of a paragraph won't be hyphenated ... so be it!*

66 Fix the typo in *line_break* that spoils the test for 'letters in the same font'.   §896 T

- *The effect of that typo was to suppress all hyphenation attempts.*

25 ↦ **67** Replace the space at paragraph end by fillglue, not by zero.   §816 B

68 Pack the hyphen character properly into its node.   §582 L

69 Fix a typo ('⊢' for '+') in the computation of *break_width*.   §838 T

70 Change the `\end` maneuver; the present code doesn't end the job, since I forgot that *back_input* uses *cur_tok*.   §1054 M

71 Add a parameter to *try_break*, since the width is different at a discretionary hyphen. [This problem will be solved differently in TEX82, when discretionaries become much more general.]   §840 A

72 Bypass kern nodes in pre-hyphenation.   §896 F

73 Supply code for the forgotten case '< "a"' in pre-hyphenation. [This case was later generalized to a test of *lc_code*.]   §897 F

74 Change *mem*[*q*] to *prev_break*(*q*) in the reverse-linking loop.   §878 B

• *(Such blunders. Am I getting feeble-minded?)*

75 Introduce special logic for *eject_penalty*; I was wrong to think that forced ejection was exactly like an infinitely negative penalty.   §851 A

76 Use $(1 + b)^2 - p^2$ when computing demerits with $p < 0$.   §859 A

• *6:30am. The line-breaking algorithm appears to be working fine and efficiently. On small measures (about 20 characters per line), it gives overfull boxes instead of spaced out ones. Surprising but satisfactory.*

16 Mar 1978

• *9pm. The plan for tonight is to test page breaking and more paragraphing.*

77 Insert '`\topskip`' glue at beginning of page.   §1001 G

78 Add '`\pausing`' feature.   §363 I

79 Fix discrepancy: In *make_accent* I called *vpackage* with a pointer to the first list item, but *vpackage* itself assumes that the parameter is a pointer to that pointer. [The *vpackage* of TEX82 will be different.]   §668 M

• *I checked for other lapses like that. Result: 14 calls OK, 12 NG.*

80 Create a new temporary list head location, *hold_head*, since there's a case where *vpackage* is improperly called with parameter *temp_head*. [At this time *vpackage* uses *temp_head* to make a list of all insertions found.]   §1014 M

• *11:30pm. The machine is tied up again.*

81 Write code to handle charnodes in vlists; I forgot that I'd decided to allow them. [Later I prohibited them again!]   §669 F

82 Combine the page lists before pruning off glue in *fire_up*; otherwise the pruning doesn't go far enough.   §1017 F

25 ↦ **83** Fix typo where line-breaking starts: '*fill_glue*' should be '*new_glue*(*fill_glue*)'.   §816 B

84 Add `/q` to `xspool` command (cosmetic change). [This changes a system command that causes TEX output to be printed on the Xerox Graphics Printer (XGP), the progenitor of future laser printers; the `/q` option says that the queue of printing requests should be displayed on the user's terminal.]   §642 I

85 Don't write a form feed after the last page of output.   §642 E

• *To fix this, I reorganized ship_out, and it became simpler.*

86 Correct a typo ('⊢' for '+') in the *vlist_node* case within *hlist_out*. [The output routines were quite different at this time, because output went directly to the XGP.]   §622 T

87 Change the message '`completed page`' to '`Completed for page`'.   §638 I

48 ↦ **88** Fix yet another typo in the computation of *page_total*: My original code said *stretch*(*p*) instead of *stretch*(*q*) (terrible).   §1004 B

89 Document the dirty trick about *bot_mark*'s reference count. [That trick is, fortunately, no longer useful.]   §1016 P

90 Rethink the algorithm for contributing an insertion: The original code tests for a page break after incrementing the totals but before the *contrib_list* is updated. [TEX78 handles insertions in a hardwired manner that will be greatly generalized in TEX82.]   A

91 Fix *get_node* again: After the variable memory overflows, control falls through
to *found* instead of going to the *overflow* call.   §125 F
- *I spent several hours tracking down that data structure bug!*

92 Change *new_line* to *next_line* in yet another print command (see #7).   B

75 ↦ **93** Amend the line-breaking algorithm: \break in paragraph doesn't work with
really bad breaks.   §851 A
- *A problem to be diagnosed tomorrow: Each time I run the test program, the
amount of memory in use grows by 13 cells not returned.*
- *Seven hours tonight.*

17 Mar 1978

94 Introduce *dead_cycles* to keep \end active until *ship_out* occurs.   §1054 G

95 Don't call *line_break* with an empty list.   §1096 E

96 Take proper account of the (infinite) fillglue when computing the width of a
paragraph line preceding a display.   §1146 S

97 Add a new parameter to *hpack* so that *line_break* won't be called at the wrong
time. [This is for the soon-to-be-obsolete feature described in #40.]   M

98 Give a warning message if there's an \hfill in the middle of a paragraph;
fillglue upsets the line breaker, because floating-point calculations don't have
sufficient accuracy.   §869 L
- *I spent an hour looking for another bug in TEX, but the following one was in
METAFONT: The xgp_height data in fonts had been supplied wrong.*
- *It took two hours to recompile 32 fonts with proto-METAFONT.*

99 Make *show_node_list* and *show_token_list* more robust in the presence of software bugs.   §182 R

97 ↦ **100** Do not remove nodes with *eject_penalty*, when the new parameter to *hpack* is
true.   D

97 ↦ **101** Put a fast exit into *hpack*; e.g., at glue nodes, test 'if *paragraphing* ∧ ⟨current
width is large⟩'.   E
- *2am. I have to go to bed "early" tonight.*

18 Mar 1978

- *3:30pm. (Saturday)*

102 Add a parameter to *check_mem* (to suppress display unless needed).   §167 I

103 Introduce a user-settable parameter \maxdepth, and pass it as a parameter to
vpackage.   §668 G
- *I realized the need for \maxdepth while fixing insertions (see #90).*

104 Introduce a user-settable parameter for *line_break*: The constant 2.0 in my
original algorithm becomes \jpar [later \tolerance], to be set like \tracing.   §828 G

105 Reclaim the *eject_penalty* nodes removed during line-breaking.   §879 D
- *(Those were the 13 extra nodes reported on Thursday.)*
- *The init_align procedure worked right the first time!*
- *Also init_row, init_col. But then...*

106 Rethink the command codes: *endv* in a token list has too high a code for the
assumptions of *get_next*.   §207 S

107 Add a *prev_cmd* variable for processing delimited macro parameters; the original algorithm loses track of braces. [The rules will change slightly in TEX82,
and *rbrace_ptr* will take on a similar function.]   §400 A

108 Make the *get_next* routine intercept & and \cr tokens.   §342 S
- *I'd thought I could just put & and \cr into big_switch [i.e., in the stomach of
TEX, not the eyes]; that was a great big mistake.*

109 Make more error checks on *endv*; e.g., it must not occur in a macro definition
or call.   §780 R

$108 \mapsto$ **110** No, rethink alignments again; the new program still fails!   §768 S

- *For the first time I can glimpse the hairiness of alignment in general (e.g., '\halign{\u#\v&...}' when \u and \v are defined to include &'s and possible alignments themselves).*
- *I think there's a "simple" solution, by considering only whether an alignment is currently active [in §342].*
- *11:30pm. Went to bed.*

19 Mar 1978

- *Woke up with "better" idea on how to handle & and \cr.*
- *(Namely, to consider a special kind of \def whose parameters don't interrupt on &'s and \cr's.)*
- *But replaced this by a much better idea (to introduce align_state).*
- *11pm. Began to use computer. Performed major surgery (inserting align_state and updating the associated routines and documentation).*

111 Pop the alignment stacks in *fin_align*.   §800 D

$110 \mapsto$ **112** Fix a (newly inserted) typo in *show_context*.   §314 T

$110 \mapsto$ **113** Set *align_state* false when a live & or \cr is found. [Originally *align_state* was of type *boolean*.]   §789 D

114 Insert \cr when '}' occurs prematurely in an alignment.   §1132 I

115 Remember to record *glue_stretch* when packaging an unset node.   §796 M

- *I had a mistake in* acphdr *definition of* \quoteformat; *also extra spaces.*
- *My first test programs, used before today, were contrived to test macro expansion, line-breaking, and page layout.*
- *Next I'm using a test program based on Volume 2.*

116 Make carriage-return, space, and tab equivalent for macro matching.   §348 C

117 Omit the reference count node when displaying a mark.   §176 F

118 Correct a silly slip: I wrote '*type_displacement*' instead of '*value_displacement*' when packing data in a penalty node.   §158 B

119 Don't go to *build_page* after seeing \noindent; TEX isn't ready for that. [In the original program, this was an instance of a bad **goto**.]   §1091 M

- *I had undesired spaces coming thru the scanner in my macro definitions of* \tenpoint *[see The TEXbook, page 414].*
- *4am. TEX now knows enough to typeset page 1 of Volume 2!*
- *Also it did its first "math formula" (namely 'X') without crucial error.*
- *(Except that the italic correction was missing for some reason.)*

120 Remember to decrement *cur_level* in *fin_align*. [The routines will eventually become more general and use *unsave* here.]   §800 D

121 Remember to increment *cur_level* in error corrections by *handle_right_brace*. [A better procedure will be adopted later.]   §1069 D

122 Fix a typo: ('{' instead of '}') in error message for *mmode + math_shift*.   §1065 T

$99 \mapsto$ **123** Make *show_noad_list* more robust and more like the new *show_node_list*. [The routines will be combined in TEX82.]   §690 R

124 Fix a typo in *char_box*: should say *font_info_real*. [In TEX78 a single array is used for both *real* and *integer*; in TEX82 things will be *scaled*.]   §554 L

125 Fix typos in the definitions of *default_rule_thickness* and *big_op_spacing*; they shouldn't start at *mathex*(7).   §701 B

126 Reverse the *before* and *after* conventions in math nodes.   §1196 B

- *I had them backwards; this turned hyphenation on just before math, and off just after it!*
- *Seven and a half hours debugging today. Got through the test program a little more. But TEX blew up on '$Y+1$'; tomorrow I hope to find out why.*

20 Mar 1978

- *8pm. I decided to work next on a super-hairy formula.*

127 Change '\ascii' to '\cc' (character code). [This name will change again later, to '\char'.]   §265 C

128 Don't bother to store a penalty node at the beginning of $$ when the paragraph-so-far fits on a single line, since such a penalty has already been stored. [These conventions will change later, and the \predisplaypenalty will always be stored.]   §1203 E

129 Avoid reference to *tail* in *build_page*, if *nest_ptr* > 0.   §995 S

130 Correct a silly slip in *math_comp* (the exact opposite of what I did in #118). §1158 B

131 Rectify my mental lapse in *make_fraction*; I said *nucleus* instead of *thickness*. §743 B

132 Mask off the math class when scanning delimiters.   §1160 F

133 Allow an optional space after \def{...}. [This decision will be retracted later.] §473 C

- *My test example is so complicated it causes the semantic stacks to overflow!*

134 Don't test for no pages output by looking at the channel status.   §642 L

135 Fix typo in definition of \mathop (*open_noad* not *op_noad*).   §1156 T

136 Rewrite *fin_mlist*, because '\left(...\above...\right)' doesn't parse correctly; the \left goes into the numerator, the \right into the denominator. §1184 A

137 Correct the use of *depth_threshold* in *print_subsidiary_data*: Simple fields get shown while others look empty.   §692 B

78 ↦ **138** Return the carriage before showing the first line of a new file when pausing. §538 I

139 Fix bug: The call *show_noad_list*(mem[..]) should be *show_noad_list*(..), in the *incompleat_noad* case of *show_activities*.   §219 M

- *3am. The whole messy formula has been parsed correctly into a tree.*
- *The easy part is done, now comes the harder part.*

140 Don't shift single characters down in *make_op*.   §749 F

141 Make *clean_box* return a box (as its name implies), not an hlist.   §720 D

- *Font info still isn't quite right, it has the wrong value of quad.*

142 Retain the italic correction when doing *rebox*; can make *glue_set* ≠ 0 a flag for this. [A better solution will be adopted later.]   §715 A

143 Fix the bug that makes *rebox* bomb out: *value*(p) should be *value*(mem[p]).   §715 B

- *6am; ten hours today. TEX didn't do $\pi\over2$ correctly, but was close.*
- *I found that the rebox problem (#142) went away when I fixed the clean_box problem (#141); but I will leave the extra stuff about glue_set ≠ 0 in the program anyway, just for weird cases.*

144 Omit extra levels of boxing when possible in *clean_box*.   §721 E

- *(To do this, I need to face the rebox problem anyway.)*

21 Mar 1978

- *10pm. The computer is rather heavily loaded tonight.*

145 Don't forget *thickness* when making a square-root sign (see #131). [The rule thickness will later be derived from the character height.]   §737 F

146 Define *p* local to the *make_fraction* routine.   §743 L

- *Unwittingly using the global p was a disaster.*

147 Don't show the amount of *glue_set* when it's zero.   §186 I

142 ↦ **148** Make *glue_set* nonzero in the result of *var_delimiter*.   §706 D

149 Fix bug: The *math_glue* function didn't return any result.   §716 F

150 Fix typo in *char_box* (*c* not *w*); this caused a subscripted *P* to come out the same width as an unsubscripted *P*. [Later changes in the rules will move this computation to §755.]   §709 T

144 ↦ **151** Revise *clean_box* to do operations that are needed often because of the *rebox* change.   §720 P

152 Use the new *clean_box* to avoid a bug in \sqrt{\raise...}.   §737 D

153 Change the definition of \not so that it's a relation (which will butt against the following relation). [All math symbols and Greek letters are defined in **INITEX** at this time, not in a changeable format definition.]   Q

154 Give error message '`Large delimiter must be in mathex font`', instead of calling *confusion*, since the error can occur. [This particular error is impossible in TEX82.]   §706   I

155 Change the use of p in *var_delimiter*; it isn't always set when I say **goto** *found*. §706   F

  • *Another font problem now surfaced: The mathex meta-font didn't compute TEX info in a machine-independent way. (It took two hours to correct this.)*

156 Don't forget to set *type(b)* in all relevant cases of *var_delimiter*.   §708   D

157 Use the correct sign convention for *shift_amount* in *hpackage*.   §653   B

158 Always kern by *delta* when there's no superscript.   §755   F

159 Declare *space_table* to be $[0..6, 0..6]$ not $[0..7, 0..7]$; otherwise its entries are preloaded into the wrong positions. [The *space_table* in TEX78 is 7×7; it will become 8×8 in TEX82, represented as a string called *math_spacing*.]   §764   M

160 Use a negative value, not zero, to represent a null delimiter. [Actually zero will come back again later.]   §685   C

127 ↦ **161** Change \cc to \char.   §265   C

162 Don't use tricky subtraction on packed data when changing q to an *ord_noad* in *mlist_to_hlist*; subtraction isn't always safe.   §729   L

163 Fix two typos in the *space_table* (∗ for 0).   §764   B

164 Initialize *cur_size* everywhere (I forgot it in two places).   §703   F

165 Reset *op_noad* before resetting *bin_noad*.   §728   A

166 Treat *display_style* + *cramped* the same as *display_style* inside *make_op*.   §749   F

167 Shift the character correctly in the non-\displaystyle case of *make_op*.   §749   B

  • *Still another font problem: The italic corrections are wrong because the corresponding array was declared real in proto-METAFONT (and italic corrections were used in nonstandard way in mathex).*

168 Use *depth* instead of *height* in *var_delimiter*. [Later, both were used.]   §714   B

169 Skew the accents according to the font *slant*. [Soon retracted.]   §741   Q

  • *At this point I think nearly all the math routines have been exercised.*

  • *Tomorrow they should work!*

  • *Eight hours debugging today.*

22 Mar 1978

  • *(Wednesday, but actually Thursday: I began at midnight because I was proofreading a paper.)*

  • *I checked out the font access tables, slowly (i.e., all the \mathcode and special-character name entries were catalogued).*

169 ↦ **170** Do **not** consider slants after all in the math accent routine, since slanted math letters are put differently into fonts.   §741   Q

171 Don't use q for two different things simultaneously in *make_math_accent*.   §738   B

172 Fix bug in *compact_list* (I forgot to advance the loop variable). [This procedure became unnecessary in TEX82.]   F

173 Avoid conflict between *var_delimiter* and *mlist_to_hlist*, which want to use *temp_head* simultaneously.   §713   M

174 Fix bad typo in *overbar* routine (b for p).   §705   T

  • *Finally TEX got to after_math after dealing with that hairy formula...*

175 Fix another bad typo: p for b this time.   §1199   T

176 Insert more parentheses (twice) because of '`lsh`' precedence in **SAIL**.   §1199   L

36 ↦ **177** Use the new hanging-indentation conventions when formatting displayed equations.   §1199   M

178 Recompute penalties so that break is allowed after *punct_noads*.   §761   Q

179 Center the large delimiters vertically.   §749 F

180 Round all rule sizes (up) before drawing them.   §589 Q

181 Provide more space over x in $\sqrt{x}$, and more space atop vincula.   §705, 737 Q

182 Make large delimiters large enough to cover formula height (important for subscripts, superscripts).   §762 Q

183 Insert /ntn=33 on XGP prompt message so that complex math won't blow the device driver. [See #84.]   I

161 ↦ **184** Update the comment about the meaning of \char, since it can be used in math mode.   §208 P

- *Six hours today.*

23 Mar 1978

- *11pm, Maundy Thursday.*

104 ↦ **185** Make \tracing and \jpar follow block structure.   §283 C

- *It took me two hours to enter yesterday's corrections, because the changes were so numerous.*

186 Fix bad call on *begin_token_list* when marks are to be scanned.   §396 M

- *Now the formula looks like it should, modulo problems in fonts.*

187 Prevent an exponent from going below baseline + xheight/4.   §758 Q

188 Change *quad* to *math_quad* when finishing a display (several places).   §1199 B

189 Don't use *append_to_vlist* when putting an \eqno box on a separate line, because the page shouldn't break at glue there. [Later, the *append* will be used but preceded by an infinite penalty.]   §1205 A

190 Increase the input *stack_size*; TEX may need to back up a lot.   §11 S

191 Don't assume that p always points to a glue node when a page is broken. §1017 A

192 Use *epsilon* in *scan_spec* (I had used a different small constant). [This was a kludge to avoid the extra parameter later called *exactly* or *additional*.] §645 A

193 Introduce a new procedure *scan_positive_length*, to prevent negative or zero lengths in *scan_rule_spec*. [This restrictive rule will be "overruled" later.] §463 R

194 Fix ridiculous bug in the leaders routine of *vlist_out*: I had the initialization **inside** the loop!   §635 B

195 Eliminate confusion between the two temp variables named h; one is *real* and the other is *integer*.   §629 L

196 Include forgotten case (*leader_node*) in *hlist_out*. [Type *leader_node* will be absorbed into *glue_node* in TEX82.]   §622 F

197 Don't forget to compute *x0* in variable horizontal rules.   §624 F

- *Seven and a half hours today.*
- *TEX seems to be ready to tackle my test file based on Volume 2.*

198 Calculate *y00* in horizontal rules as an integer number of pixels from the baseline, so that the baseline doesn't jump.   §589 S

25 Mar 1978

- *2am Saturday. (Might as well drop Friday.)*

185 ↦ **199** Make *def_code* consistent with the new \tracing conventions. [Many tracing options are packed into a single parameter called \tracing.]   §1233 D

185 ↦ **200** Don't allow users to change nonexistent things like \catcode1000.   §1232 R

110 ↦ **201** Reset *align_state* at beginning of *init_align*.   §774 F

202 Don't forget *scan_left_brace* after \noalign.   §785 F

110 ↦ **203** Set *cur_cs* ← 0 in *get_next*, after \cr causes a switch to the $\langle v_j \rangle$ template.   §342 F

- *Ouch, that was a big bad bug, which took me three hours to find (since I thought TEX's low-level scanning mechanism was working).*

- *Note to myself: I **knew** it would be cleaner to define get_next so that it sets cur_cs to zero every time it begins [i.e., in §341, where this change will in fact be made in TeX82]. But I had avoided this on grounds of efficiency in the inner loop. Well, now I have earned this tiny bit of efficiency.*

204 Prohibit the first word of an unavailable node from becoming negative. [The storage allocator of TeX78 uses a negative value to signify a node that is available, just as '*link = max_halfword*' will signal availability in TeX82.]   §124 D

- *That was another bad one, it's not my night.*
- *At least I'm developing more subtle diagnostic techniques.*

205 Remember to un-negate the top *save_stack* entry when *handle_right_brace* finishes an *insert_group*. [This routine was completely revised in TeX82.]   §1100 M

185 ↦ 206 Initialize \jpar [i.e., \tolerance].   §240 F

207 Correct the display of insertion nodes by *show_node_list*.   §188 B

208 Prevent *show_token_list* from generating really long strings when in a loop.   §292 R

209 Increase the reference count of *bot_mark* when *vpackage* finds it. [This was later the job of *fire_up*.]   §1016 D

210 Remember that the tokenlist for a mark ends with a }.   §1101 M

211 Don't let *vpackage* lose the top insert. (It fails when the very first item is a \topinsert.)   §1014 D

212 And when that stupid code is corrected, make it handle insertions first-in-first-out.   §1018 A

- *Seven hours today.*

26 Mar 1978

- *Easter Sunday, will work till sunrise.*

213 Add an 'i' feature to the *error* recovery routine.   §87 I

214 Include a prompt.   §87 I

215 Ignore space after \noalign{...}.   §1133 C

- *Otherwise, things are going well tonight; I'm finding more bugs in my test program than in TeX.*
- *The 'i' feature is proving to be very helpful.*
- *I increased the size of mem (now lo_mem_max = 3500, mem_max = 10000).*
- *In fact I just needed to increase it again (now lo_mem_max = 4500, mem_max = 11000).*

216 Make INITEX output *mem_top* for consistency checking.   §1307 R

217 Calculate the size of delimiters by considering the enclosed formula's distance from the axis, not from the baseline.   §762 A

- *I'm having trouble with a SAIL compiler bug; I must rearrange the program, more or less at random, until it compiles correctly. I hope the bug isn't more severe than it appears.*

210 ↦ 218 Don't put a new group on *save_stack* if a null mark is expanded. [TeX82 will remove the '}' from the mark text.]   §386 D

- *I had to redo the typewriter-style font since its width tables were wrong.*
- *And I increased low-memory size again to 5500, then 6500.*
- *Finally the entire test program was TeXed. Happy Easter! Six hours today.*

27 Mar 1978

- *Beginning at 2:30am.*

219 Move \vcenter processing to the first pass of *mlist_to_hlist*; otherwise the height, depth, subscripts, etc., are way off.   §733 A

220 Omit space after closing $$.   §1200 C

- *Spacing is wrong in the formula $Y_1 + \cdots + Y_k$; I have to rethink the use of three dots.*

221 Make conditional thin space available to user as \≤. [Later will retract this.]   §226 G

222 Introduce \dispaskip and \dispbskip [later called \abovedisplayshortskip
and \belowdisplayshortskip].   §226 Q

- *Reminder: I need to test line-breaking with embedded math formulas.*

223 Make sure that *interaction ≠ error_stop_mode* in the 'Whoa' error [*fatal_error*].   §93 I

224 Fix a big mistake in the *style_node* routine (which points to a glue spec, not
to glue itself); somehow this didn't cause trouble yesterday. [In TEX78, style
nodes double as placeholders for math glue like thin spaces.]   §732 B

225 Make \fntfam obey group structure. [TEX78's \fntfam operation is a combination of TEX82's \textfont, \scriptfont, and \scriptscriptfont.]   §1234 C

- *At this point the test routine for Volume 2 works perfectly.*
- *But I will change the page width in order to check harder cases.*

178 ↦ **226** Disable automatic line breaks after punctuation in math (e.g., consider $f(x,y)$). §761 Q

227 Represent italic corrections as boxes, not glue, so that they won't be broken.
[The \kern command doesn't exist yet.]   §1113 S

- *Eight hours today.*

228 Fix a bug that just clobbered the memory: Call *free_avail*, not *free_node*, in
the *ins_node* case of *vpackage*. [This logic will change completely in TEX82.] §1019 B

29 Mar 1978

- *(Wednesday) Again beginning at 2:30am.*

229 Put still more space above and below fraction lines in displayed formulas.   §746 Q

189 ↦ **230** Install an infinite penalty feature, which positively suppresses breaks; use it in
displayed formulas whose \eqno doesn't fit.   §1205 G

231 Call *build_page* after finishing a display; and don't go to the \noindent routine
because of the next remark.   §1200 F

232 Put \parskip glue just before a paragraph, not just after (since it interferes
with a penalty after).   §1091 S

- *Although the test program gives correct output, it generates 46 locations of
variable-size memory and 280 of one-word memory that are not freed.*

233 Recycle the ulists and vlists in *fin_align*.   §801 F

25 ↦ **234** Fix bug when deleting space at end of paragraph: *delete_glue_ref(cur_node)*
not *delete_glue_ref(value(cur_node))*.   §816 M

- *There's also a more mysterious type of uncollected garbage, a fraction_noad
corresponding to $p\choose$, an incompleat_noad not completed.*
- *Couldn't find that one, so I recompiled with #233 and #234 corrected.*
- *Now it gains just 10 locations of variable-size memory and 7 of the other kind.*

235 Extend *search_mem* to search *eqtb* also.   §255 I

143 ↦ **236** Fix bug in *rebox* when *list_ptr(b) = 0*.   §715 D

- *The seven one-word nodes were generated by this bug; rebox put them onto a
linked list starting with mem[0], growing at the far end!*

237 Remember to complete each *incompleat_noad*.   §1184 D

- *This solved the other mystery. I had never noticed that my test output was
actually wrong: $p\choose k$ came out as 'k'.*
- *After these corrections, the test routine worked... I feel that TEX is now pretty
well debugged (except perhaps for error recovery)—it's time to celebrate!*

1 Apr 1978

238 Don't quit after file lookup fails.   §530 I

2 Apr 1978

239 Add TEX_font_area, so that it's easier to change the default library area associated with a device.   §514 P

3 Apr 1978

240 Insert parentheses again, to cope with the precedence of **lsh** when packing data. (See #55 and #176.)   §1114 L

- *I had never tried hmode + discretionary before!*

241 Remember that *back_error* requires *cur_tok* to be set. (Problem can arise during error recovery on parameter #*n* with *n* out of range.)   §476 M

4 Apr 1978

242 Add a deletion feature to the *error* routine.   §88 I

5 Apr 1978

243 Reset *space_factor* after \/ [this was later rescinded] and after math in text.   §1196 Q

10 Apr 1978

104 ↦ **244** Replace **\jpar** and **\tracing** by a new primitive **\chpar** for parameters. It allows a user to change those quantities as well as the penalties for hyphens, relations, binary ops, widows.   §209 G

14 May 1978

- *Beginning to typeset a real book (Volume 2, second edition), not just a test.*

245 Make math in text end with spacing as if it were followed by punctuation. [This rule will soon be rescinded.]   §760 Q

246 Insert **\times** into the hash table; I left it out by mistake. [It will eventually move into **plain.tex**.]   F

247 Change the names of Scandinavian accents from **\o**, **\oslash**, **\Oslash** to **\a**, **\o**, **\O**. [This will also move to **plain**.]   C

17 May 1978

248 Fix a silly bug that hasn't been tweaked until today: '**\halign to size**' [obsolete in TEX82] used *vsize* instead of *hsize*.   §645 B

19 May 1978

249 Add a **\topbaseline** feature [later called **\topskip**].   §1001 G

245 ↦ **250** Subtract the math spacing change of May 14.   §760 Q

251 Skip past blanks in the *scan_math* procedure. [This blank-skipping will eventually go into *scan_left_brace*.]   §403 A

252 Introduce a *missing_brace* routine [later generalized] to improve error recovery in *mmode + math_shift*, when the top of *save_stack* isn't a *math_shift_group*.   §1065 I

253 Adjust the math spacing between closing parentheses and Ord, Op, Open, Punct.   §764 Q

254 Make the underline go further under.   §735 Q

96 ↦ **255** Compute the proper natural width when a displayed equation follows a paragraph whose fillglue has been deleted by *line_break*.   §1146 S

20 May 1978

256 Fix the spurious value of *prev_depth* inside alignments.   §775 A

257 Consider (and defeat) the following scenario: The u and v lists are built in *init_align* using *temp_head*; then while scanning '**\tabskip 2pt\rt{...}**' the macro **\rt** is expanded, clobbering *temp_head*.   §779 S

- *That bug was more subtle than usual.*

258 Add the parameter *num3*, so that the positioning of **\atop** can be different from that for fractions.   §700 Q

259 Add new parameters *delim1* and *delim2*, so that **\comb** can use fixed size delimiters, not computed as with **\left**.   §748 Q

22 May 1978

221 ↦ **260** Change \≤ to \≥ and introduce \≦ as the negative of \≥. [Later obsolete.]   §226 C

261 Fix the display of negative penalty nodes; *show_node_list* is confused when a negative value has been packed into the middle of a word.   §194 L

  • *Memory overflow just occurred with lo_mem_max = 7500 and mem_max = 16384. So I have to go to 15-bit pointers. (A problem on 32-bit machines?)*

23 May 1978

262 Add a new parameter *big_op_spacing5*, for extra space above and below limits of big displayed operators.   §751 Q

263 Initialize *incompleat_noad* in `$$\halign{...}$$`.   §775 F

  • *That was another heretofore-untested operation. How much of the code has not yet been exercised?*

238 ↦ **264** Close the file when doing lookup-failure recovery.   §27 F

265 Improve the error recovery for '`Extra &`'.   §792 I

266 The top piece must be calculated mod 128 in *var_delimiter*, to guarantee a valid subscript range. [Obsolete in TEX82.]   §546 R

252 ↦ **267** Fix a blunder in new *missing_brace* code.   §1065 B

262 ↦ **268** Fix a blunder in new code for limits on display operators.   §751 B

26 May 1978

269 Don't insert a new penalty after an explicit penalty in math mode.   §767 Q

  • *The hash table overflowed; I ought to make it much bigger.*

110 ↦ **270** Avoid possible bad memory references in alignment when there is erroneous input after `\cr`. [Instead of *extra_info*, the value of *cur_align* in TEX78 is negated, because we need only distinguish `\cr` from `&`.]   §789 R

271 Make the dimension parameters like `\hsize` all global, so that they can be set in the `\output` routine.   §279 S

  • *This led to major simplifications, also to major surgery.*

  • *[But it was a kludgy decision, overruled in TEX82.]*

94 ↦ **272** Don't forget to set the type of the new null box in the `\end` routine.   §1054 D

27 May 1978

  • *The data overflowed memory again, both low and high, doing Section 3.3.2.*

184 ↦ **273** Mask off extra bits of `\char` in math mode, to avoid bad memory references.   §1151 R

274 Zero out the negative `\medmuskip` in script styles.   §732 B

29 May 1978

275 Be prepared to handle an undefined control sequence during *get_x_token*. (Can fix this by brute force, using *get_token* instead of *get_next*.)   §380 S

276 Correct the superscript shift when a single character is raised.   §758 D

184 ↦ **277** Mask off all but 7 bits in `\char` routine, to avoid space-factor index out of range.   §435 R

  • *More memory capacity overflows.*

22 ↦ **278** Fix TEX's overflow stop so that I don't have to wait for loading of the `BAIL` debug routines. [System dependent.]   §93 E

279 Remember to adjust the page number when a file page ends in mid-macro. [System dependent.]   §306 F

5 Jun 1978

280 Make sure that the arguments of positioning commands don't overflow their field size.   §610 R

281 Report the excess amount when giving an overfull box warning.   §666, 677 I

7 Jun 1978

282 Use ≥ instead of > as termination criterion in *var_delimiter*.   §714 Q

283 Disallow `\eject` in math mode. [In TEX78, `\eject` is distinct from `\break`; in horizontal mode it includes TEX82's '`\vadjust{\break}`'.]   §1102 R

284 Don't put too much clearance above \sqrt in text style.   §737 Q

9 Jun 1978

110 ↦ **285** Make *align_state* an integer variable, not *boolean*, so that \eqalign can be
within another \eqalign.   §309 G

286 A \mark should expand its input.   §1101 C

10 Jun 1978

287 Provide for preloading of fonts.   §1320 E

288 Close the output file before switching to edit the input file with the 'e' option.   §84 L

289 Return adjustments found by *hpack* to free storage if they're not used. [Later,
hpack will detach them only when they're used.]   §655 E

290 Strive for consistency between *make_under* and *make_over*.   §735 Q

18 Jun 1978

236 ↦ **291** Fix a serious error in *rebox* ('*b*' instead of '*list_ptr(b)*').   §715 B

• *Strange that such a bug would now surface for the first time!*

292 Remove \deg from INITEX, since macros suffice.   C

293 Add an extra hyphenation penalty for two hyphenated lines in a row.   §859 Q

19 Jun 1978

294 Introduce the '*no_new_control_sequence*' switch. Among other things, this will
prevent an undefined control sequence following *scan_math* from clobbering
the save stack.   §259 S

20 Jun 1978

295 Change the badness test '*glue* ≤ 0.0' to '*glue* ≤ 0.0001'. [TEX82 will avoid such
problems by calculating badness without floating point arithmetic.]   §99 L

296 Force *badness* to be at most 10^{19}.   §108 R

297 Add *end_template* for better error recovery in alignments.   §375 I

287 ↦ **298** Make INITEX more like the real TEX; my simple scheme for font preloading was
no good because it left thousands of 'dead' words in memory.   §8 E

299 Economize disk space by using internal arrays in load modules that aren't being
reinitialized. [System dependent.]   E

300 Move the declaration of *mem* to the semantics module, so that the object code
will be more efficient. [System dependent. The code of TEX78 was divided
into separately compiled modules for syntax, semantics, output, extensions,
and general organization.]   E

21 Jun 1978

• *Today I'm working on the user manual.*

301 Disallow \input except in vertical mode. [I will change this in TEX82, treating
\input as a case of expansion.]   §378 C

302 Add error recovery for *endv* and *par_end* occurring in math mode.   §1047 I

303 Generalize \ifT to \if T.   §506 G

22 Jun 1978

304 Preload the \bullet [later done by plain.tex].   F

256 ↦ **305** Get the correct *prev_depth* at the beginning of an alignment.   §775 D

306 Change \eject so that it ejects only once.   §1000 C

14 Jul 1978

307 Look in standard area if a file isn't found in the user's area.   §537 I

308 Echo all online inputs in the transcript file.   §71 I

19 Jul 1978

309 Equalize spacing when only one of numerator/denominator is big.   §745 Q

310 Prevent subscript from getting too high above baseline.   §757 Q

311 Avoid infinite loop when stack overflows: *push_input* should say 'if *input_ptr* $\geq$ *stack_size* $\wedge$ *interaction* $=$ *error_stop_mode*'.   §321 R

22 Jul 1978

312 Make \quad meaningful outside math mode. (All fonts must be generated again!)   §558 C

313 Show the nesting level at the end of *show_activities*. [But I decided not to do this in TEX82.]   §218 I

314 Put in \> [namely, \mskip\medmuskip; TEX78 already has \≳, for conditional \thinmuskip, as well as the negative amounts \<, \≲]. Change the name of vector accent from \> to \b. [Math spacing operators will become much more general in TEX82.]   §716 C

25 Jul 1978

94 ↦ **315** Give the correct \hsize and \vsize to the null boxes created at \end.   §1054 Q

94 ↦ **316** And don't "append" them. [Later this was changed, so that it would work better with generalized output routines.]   §1054 A

297 ↦ **317** Remove the control sequence \endv, since error recovery is now better.   §375 I

318 Define another mode of tracing: It says 'OK' and stops after \showlists.   §1298 I

244 ↦ **319** Give better defaults to parameters. [Later done by plain.tex.]   §209 Q

320 Allow more bits in the packed representation of \showboxdepth.   §238 I

321 Scan past delimiters and/or dimensions when recovering from ambiguous fractions.   §1183 I

322 Reduce accent numbers modulo 128 or 512, depending on the mode.   §1165 R

323 Include a warning, '(\end occurred on level ...)'.   §1335 I

28 Jul 1978

• *(I'm writing Chapter 27 of the manual: 'Recovery From Errors'.)*

324 Improve the error message in *scan_digit*. [This procedure will change its name to *scan_eight_bit_int*, when the number of registers increases from 10 to 256.]   §433 I

325 Don't report overfull boxes if they're less than .1 point over.   §666, 677 I

326 Give the user extra chances to define the font, if *read_font_info* is unsuccessful. §560 I

327 Change default recovery for bad parameter number from #1 to ##, since #1 won't always work and since ## is probably intended.   §479 I

328 Omit the "Negative?" message on things like *scan_char_num*.   §435 I

329 Improve error recovery when a large delimiter isn't in family 3. [Obsolete.]   I

330 Give a more appropriate error message when the input is '$\right'.   §1192 I

• *Currently TEX says 'Missing $'!*

331 Call *back_input* before the error message in *back_error*, not afterwards.   §327 I

1 Aug 1978

332 Give an appropriate warning when there's no input file and the user types 'e'. §84 I

333 Increase the system pushdownlist size so that the manual will compile. [Procedures *hlist_out* and *vlist_out* can recurse deeply.]   L

• *Yesterday I distributed 45 preliminary copies of the manual; today I took out the "debugging hooks" and put TEX up as a system program.*

2 Aug 1978

• *I'm typing Volume 2 again (currently in Section 4.2.2). Culture shock!*

334 Introduce a \ragged parameter, to indicate a degree of raggedness. [Previously, ragged-right setting was performed when the \tolerance/100 was odd! Eventually a better approach, with \rightskip and such things, will be discovered.]   §886 G

335 Omit the 'widow penalty' in one-line paragraphs.   §890 Q

5 Aug 1978

336 Generalize \pageno to \count⟨digit⟩.   §236 G

285 ↦ **337** Update *align_state* when recovering from 'Missing {' and 'Extra }' errors.
                                                                      §1069, 1127 D

338 Show "runaway" tokens, making it easier to pinpoint an error.   §306 I

22 Aug 1978

339 Add \predisplaypenalty.   §1203 G

340 Clarify error messages; they should indicate when something has been inserted,
    etc.   §1064 I

23 Aug 1978

114 ↦ **341** Substitute 'Extra }' for the losing 'Missing \cr' error message.   §1069 I

213 ↦ **342** Go past online insertions in *show_context*.   §311 I

343 Exact no penalty for breaking one line before a display.   §1145 Q

338 ↦ **344** Check for runaways at end of file.   §362 I

345 Give error message when a macro argument begins with }.   §395 I

24 Aug 1978

213 ↦ **346** Remove extra line-feed in *show_context* after printing insertions. [System de-
    pendent.]   §318 L

25 Aug 1978

347 Leave no glue at top of page, even after \eject.   §997 Q

27 Aug 1978

348 Adopt Guy Steele's new version of the TEX source files. [He has recently
    made a copy and modified it by introducing compile-time switches for MIT
    conventions as an alternative to SUAI. This is the first time that TEX is being
    ported to another site; additional switches for PARC, TENEX, TOPS10, and
    TOPS20 will be added later, using the Steele style.]   P

1 Sep 1978

349 Don't pass over leader nodes in the *try_break* background computation. [At
    this time, leaders have not yet been unified with glue.]   §837 Q

82 ↦ **350** Prune away all penalties at the top of a page.   §997 Q

4 Sep 1978

338 ↦ **351** Include '\' in error message about a runaway argument.   §306 I

8 Sep 1978

    • *I just remade all the fonts, with increased ligature field size.*

350 ↦ **352** Insert a necessary **goto** statement in the first branch of the new penalty routine
    within *build_page*.   §997 B

30 Sep 1978

338 ↦ **353** Make the token list for runaway arguments meaningful outside of *macro_call*.
    (I just had a runaway argument ending with '\lcm', which turned out to be
    the control sequence in hashtable location 0.)   §371 M

354 Avoid infinite loop when recovering from $$ in restricted horizontal mode.   §1138 R

355 Fix two hyphenation bugs related to -ages, -ers. [A completely new algorithm
    for hyphenation will go into TEX82.]   L

356 Add -est to hyphenation routine; also disable puz-zled and rat-tled, etc.   Q

4 Oct 1978

357 Add new primitive \vtop.   §1087 G

358 Treat implicit kerns properly after discretionary hyphens have been inserted.   §914 Q

4 Nov 1978

359 Forget the half quad originally required at left and right when centering displayed equations without equation numbers.   §1202 Q

11 Nov 1978

360 Don't let the postamble come out empty. [This could occur if no fonts were selected.]   §642 R

15 Nov 1978

361 Allow optional space after digit in *scan_int* routine.   §444 C

17 Nov 1978

362 Make the *check_mem* procedure slightly more robust.   §167 R

20 Nov 1978

363 Make the \par in a \def match the \par that comes automatically with a blank line. (Suggested by Terry Winograd.)   §351 C

364 Add new parameter \mathsurround for spacing before and after math in text. §1196 G

365 Extend \advance to allow increase by other than unity. [At this time it applies only to the ten \count registers, and it is called \advcount.]   §1238 G

25 Nov 1978

366 Add a new primitive: \unskip.   §1105 G

367 Add new primitives \uppercase and \lowercase.   §1288 G

28 Nov 1978

338 ↦ **368** Don't let \mark and *macro_call* interfere with each other's *scanner_status*.   §306 M

369 Omit extra } after *show_node_list* shows a \mark, since the right brace is already there. (See #210.)   §176 M

370 Add a new primitive suggested by Terry Winograd: \xdef.   §1218 G

29 Nov 1978

371 Delete a space following \else{...} also in the false case. [TEX78 uses braces, not \fi, for conditionals.]   S

320 ↦ **372** Make \tracing set \showboxbreadth as advertised.   §198 D

373 Account properly for kerns in width calculations of *line_break*.   §866 F

364 ↦ **374** Delete a *math_node* at the beginning of a line.   §148 Q

339 ↦ **375** Guarantee that \predisplaypenalty=10000 will suppress page breaking before a display.   §1005 A

6 Dec 1978

376 Change the file opening statement to allow lines up to 150 characters long. [System dependent.]   L

16 Jan 1979

365 ↦ **377** Initialize *negative* properly in the \advance routine with a \count as argument. §440 F

20 Jan 1979

378 Try to keep complex, buggy preambles of alignments from crashing the program.   §789 R

17 Feb 1979

376 ↦ **379** Give more detailed information when warning about a long line being broken. [System dependent; the buffer size in TEX78 is very limited.]   I

380 Declare *p* local to *try_break*, for the "rare" case code. [My original program included the following comment: "This case can arise only in weird circumstances due to changing line lengths, and the code may in fact never be executed." Later Michael Plass will discover that variable line lengths require an entirely different algorithm, using *last_special_line*.]   §847 L

334 ↦ **381** Don't omit the raggedness correction when the last line of paragraph has to shrink. [Obsolete in TEX82.]   F

22 Feb 1979

363 ↦ **382** Don't forget to return from *get_x_token* after finding \par.   §351 F

383 Add a new parameter: \lineskiplimit.   §679 Q

384 Change the syntactic sugar: '\hbox par' replaces '\hjust to ...{overfull}'. [This vastly improves on the old idea (see #40), but there still is no internal vertical mode.]   C

385 Introduce new names \hbox and \vbox for \hjust and \vjust.   §1071 C

386 Add a new condition: \ifpos. [It will later be generalized to \ifnum and \ifdim.]   §513 G

387 Add vu and \varunit. [TEX82 will eventually allow arbitrary internal dimensions as units of measure.]   §453 G

312 ↦ **388** Add an em unit.   §455 G

389 Legalize \hbox spread ⟨negative dimension⟩ [since *scan_spec* no longer uses the sign as a flag].   §645 C

10 Mar 1979

370 ↦ **390** Make *scan_toks* expand \count during \xdef. [This will change later when \the and \number are introduced.]   §367 C

23 Mar 1979

391 Put only 100000 pt stretch at the end of a paragraph instead of 10000000000 pt. [In TEX78, "infinite" glue is actually finite but large; in the language of TEX82 we would say that \parfillskip, which is not yet user-settable, is being changed to be like \hfil instead of like \hfill.]   §816 Q

392 Treat the last line of a paragraph more consistently with the other lines (e.g., when \hfil appears in mid-paragraph), by effectively inserting *inf_penalty* at the end.   §816 Q

31 Mar 1979

393 Ensure that penalty nodes aren't wiped out, in weird cases where breaks occur at penalties that normally disappear.   §879 S

27 Apr 1979

394 Correct the page number count when files begin with an empty page. [System dependent.]   A

395 Allow the *math_code* table to be changeable via \chcode. [In TEX82, \chcode will split into \mathcode and \catcode.]   §1232 G

332 ↦ **396** Don't accept 'e' after an error message if not inputting from a file.   §84 I

29 May 1979

397 Don't call *end_file_reading* if you haven't already invoked *begin_file_reading*; this could happen when trying to recover from an error in *start_input*.   §537 F

7 Jun 1979

306 ↦ **398** Be sure to eject two pages, when \eject comes just at the time another break is preferable (e.g., when the page has just become too full).   §1005 A

27 Jun 1979

354 ↦ **399** Don't say 'You can't do that in math mode' when the user says '$$' in restricted horizontal mode!   §1138 I

30 Jun 1979

400 Add wd, dp, ht dimension units.   §455 G

307 ↦ **401** Don't try the system area for file names whose area is explicitly indicated.   §537 I

1 Jul 1979

402 Allow letters as (ASCII) numbers [without the ' marker introduced later].   §442 G

2 Jul 1979

403 Fix a \gdef bug: If the control sequence was never defined before [this later became the *restore_zero* option], don't remove it at group end.   §282 F

16 Jul 1979

320 ↦ **404** Update *show_noad_list* to be like *show_node_list*. [The two routines, originally separate, will be merged in TEX82.]   §238 I

18 Jul 1979

405 Extend capacity from 32 fonts to 64 fonts if desired.   §134 G
406 Add new *extra_space* parameter to all text fonts (requested by Frances Yao).   §558 Q
407 Make each *node_noad* print properly in *show_noad_list*.   §183 F
408 Make \jpar allow any break if it is 1000000 or more. [In TEX82, a \tolerance of 10000 or more allows any break.]   §851 Q

23 Jul 1979

409 Introduce new primitives \hfil, vfil, \hfilneg, \vfilneg.   §1058 E
410 Add \ifmmode.   §501 G
411 Add \firstmark.   §1012, 1016 G
412 Allow break at leaders (horizontal mode only).   §149 C

25 Jul 1979

213 ↦ **413** Revise *error* so that online insertions work properly after end-of-file errors.   §336 I
411 ↦ **414** Change 'if *first_mark* ≠ 0' to 'if *first_mark* ≥ 0' [because −1 is used to indicate 'not yet given a value'].   §1012 B

28 Jul 1979

370 ↦ **415** Stop \xdef from expanding control sequences after \def's. [This decision will be rescinded later, after several more years of experience with macro expansion will suggest better ways to cure the problem.]   §366 C
416 Change symbolic printout for control symbols. [System dependent.]   §49 I
308 ↦ **417** Avoid linefeeds in the transcript file. [System dependent.]   L
370 ↦ **418** Expand topmark, etc., in \xdef.   §366 C

4 Aug 1979

413 ↦ **419** Fix an error introduced recently: \par was suddenly omitted at end of page. [System dependent.]   B

11 Aug 1979

420 Change error messages that use SAIL characters not in standard ASCII.   §360 P

28 Aug 1979

411 ↦ **421** Move the command '*first_mark* ← −1' from *vpackage* to *fire_up*.   §1012 D
403 ↦ **422** Correct a serious \gdef bug: Control sequences don't obey a last-in-first-out discipline, so TEX loses things from the hash table when deleting a control sequence.   §259 S
- *To fix this, I either need to restrict TEX (so that \gdef can be used inside a group only for control sequences already defined on the outer level) or need to change the hash table algorithm. Although all applications of TEX known to me will agree to the former restriction, I've chosen the latter alternative, because it gives me a chance to improve the language: Control sequences of arbitrary length will now be recognized.*

423 Make sure that *unsave* cannot call *eq_destroy* with a value from the upper part of *eqtb*.   §282 D

- *I noticed this long-standing bug while fixing #422. It had very low probability of causing damage (e.g., it required a certain field of a floating-point number to have a certain value), but it would have been devastating on the day it first showed up!*

29 Aug 1979

424 Call *eq_destroy* when a control sequence is \gdef'ed after being \def'ed. §283 F

418 ↦ **425** Treat the first token consistently when \topmark and its cousins are expanded in *scan_toks*. §477 F

- *Now I've checked things pretty carefully and I think TEX is "fully debugged."*

25 Jan 1980

338 ↦ **426** Display runaway alignment preambles. §306 I

427 Introduce active characters (one-stroke control sequences). [I don't yet go all the way: The meanings of 'x' and '\x' have to be identical.] §344 G

7 Feb 1980

314 ↦ **428** Fix a glaring omission: Op space \> was never implemented in math mode! §716 F

25 Feb 1980

429 Add a new dimension 'ex' (for units of xheight). §455 G

3 Mar 1980

427 ↦ **430** Allow the control sequence \: to be redefined [it was the 'select font' operator]; this allows the character : to be active. [Obsolete.] C

23 Mar 1980

- *An extend-TEX-for-the-eighties party:*

431 Add a new \copy feature. §204 G

432 Add a new \unbox feature. §1110 G

433 Add a new \open feature [later \openout]. §1351 G

434 Add a new \send feature [later \write]. §1352. G

435 Add a new \leqno feature, requested by MDS. §1204 G

436 Add a new \ifdimen feature [later \ifdim]. §513 G

437 Make \⟨space⟩ in vertical mode begin a paragraph. §1090 C

438 Add a new \font feature [replacing the silly previous convention that a font must be defined when it is first selected]. §1256 G

439 Add new \parval and \codeval features [later \the ⟨whatever⟩]. §413 G

427 ↦ **440** Don't let active characters gobble the following space. §344 C

208 ↦ **441** Add a new parameter to govern amount of token list dumped. [Obsolete.] §295 G

442 Add a new \linebreak feature [later replaced by \break]. §831 G

25 Mar 1980

- *(Still working on the above, also thought of more.)*

443 Add a new \mskip feature. §716 G

444 Add a new \newname feature (soon changed to \let). §1221 G

430 ↦ **445** Allow any control sequence to be redefined. §275 G

446 Send the output to the user's current file area, even when input comes from elsewhere. §532 I

27 Mar 1980

447 Compute the xheight for accents in math mode from family 1, not family 3. [Obsolete.] Q

28 Mar 1980

448 Increase minimum clearance between subscript and superscript. §759 Q

29 Mar 1980

222 ↦ **449** When a display follows a display, the second should have the 'shortskip' glue. §1146 Q

4 Apr 1980

445 ↦ **450** Look at current token meanings when trying to recognize `\tabskip` in alignment preambles.   §782 A

23 Apr 1980

451 Estimate the length of printed output, for the new priority feature on our XGP device driver. [System dependent.]   I

434 ↦ **452** Break long `\send` lines into pieces so that the file can be read in again. [System dependent.]   C

19 May 1980

182 ↦ **453** Don't make `\left` and `\right` delimiters too large; they need to be only 90% of the enclosed size. [This eventually became `\delimiterfactor`.]   §762 Q

21 May 1980

454 Add a new `\pagebreak` feature [later `\vadjust{\break}`].   §655 G

13 Jun 1980

- *Today I'm beginning to overhaul the line-breaking routine, and I'll also install miscellaneous goodies.*

455 Allow a radical sign to be in different font positions.   §737 G

456 Clear empty tokenlists off input stacks to allow deeper recursions (suggested by Jim Boyce's macros for chess positions).   §325 E

457 Make `\spaceskip` and `\parfillskip` changeable.   §1228 G

458 Add a new parameter `\rfudge` (per request of Zippel) [later `\mag`].   §288 G

459 Add a new parameter `\loose` [later `\looseness`]; now parameters are allowed to take negative values.   §875 G

460 Remove the variable *just_par*. [Obsolete; it was the *real* equivalent of an *integer*].   E

14 Jun 1980

461 Install new line-breaking routines, including `\parshape`. (These major changes are introduced as Michael Plass and I write our article.)   §813 Q

462 Add a new parameter `\exhyf` [later `\exhyphenpenalty`].   §870 G

16 Jun 1980

444 ↦ **463** Change conventions in *eqtb* so that glue is distinguishable from other equivalents.   §275 S

444 ↦ **464** Don't expand `\b` in `\xdef{\d\b{...}}` after `\let\d=\def`. [Obsolete.]   A

444 ↦ **465** Avoid creating dead storage when doing *unsave* in certain regions.   §275 D

17 Jun 1980

466 Allow negative dimensions in rules.   §138 C

19 Jun 1980

463 ↦ **467** Make the new test for glue at the outer level of *show_eqtb*.   §252 B

27 Jun 1980

453 ↦ **468** Don't let `\left` and `\right` become too small for big matrices. [This eventually became `\delimitershortfall`.]   §762 Q

3 Aug 1980

469 Don't move extra-wide, numbered equations flush left unless they begin with glue.   §1202 Q

15 Sep 1980

461 ↦ **470** Say '$\geq fz$' instead of '$> fz$' in the pre-hyphenation routine; I'd forgotten my definition of *fz* [a variable used to test for a sequence of lowercase letters in the same font].   §897 M

395 ↦ **471** Check the range of the index in `\chcode` before saving the old value.   §1232 R

18 Sep 1980

457 ↦ **472** Don't forget to increase the reference count to \parfillskip, or it will mysteriously vanish.   §816 D

19 Sep 1980

412 ↦ **473** Make leaders break like glue in both horizontal and vertical modes.   §149 C

364 ↦ **474** Make \mathsurround break properly at left and right end of lines.   §879 Q

13 Oct 1980

461 ↦ **475** Remove spurious overfull boxes generated when the looseness criterion fails. [Obsolete.]   I

461 ↦ **476** Redesign the iteration for looseness; breakpoints were not chosen optimally. §875 A

461 ↦ **477** Avoid storing a lot of breakpoints when they are dominated by others.   §836 E

366 ↦ **478** Don't say '*cur_node*' when you mean '*mem*[*cur_node*]'.   §1105 B

461 ↦ **479** Prefer the oldest break to the youngest break when two break nodes have the same total demerits.   §836 Q

461 ↦ **480** Don't make badness too big for floating-point calculations, when forced to make an overfull box. [Obsolete.]   L

10 Dec 1980

481 Make it impossible to get unmatched '}' in a delimited macro argument.   §392 R

482 Add new \topsep and \botsep features. [These are TEX78's way to put space at the edge of inserts, replaced in TEX82 by the \skip register corresponding to an \insert class.]   §1009 G

6 Jan 1981

483 Install new routines for reading the font metrics, using Ramshaw's TFM files instead of TFX files.   §539 P

484 Abort after reporting 100 errors, if not pausing on errors.   §82 I

485 Add new \spacefactor and \specskip and \skip primitives. [At this time we write '\specskip3=10pt' and '\skip3' for what will become '\skip3=10pt' and '\hskip\skip3' in TEX82.]   §1060 G

366 ↦ **486** \unskip is now allowed in internal vertical mode.   §1105 G

26 Jan 1981

482 ↦ **487** Don't say '*mem*[*q*]' when you mean '*q*'. (See #143 and #478.)   §1009 B

27 Feb 1981

417 ↦ **488** Put some linefeeds back into the transcript file, in order to prevent overprinting in listings. [System dependent.]   I

489 Add a new \dpenalty feature [later \postdisplaypenalty].   §1205 G

490 Add the dimension cc for European users.   §458 G

491 Make *scan_keyword* match uppercase letters as alternatives to lowercase ones (suggested by Barbara Beeton's experiments with \uppercase).   §407 C

492 Add nonstop mode so that overnight batch processing is possible.   §73 I

2 Mar 1981

422 ↦ **493** Fix a still more serious \gdef bug: The generality of \gdef almost makes it a crime to forget **any** control sequence names, ever! (The previous bug was only the tip of an iceberg.)   §259 S

494 Issue warning message at the end of a file page if nesting level isn't zero. [System dependent.]   I

5 Mar 1981

495 Keep track of maximum memory usage, for statistical reporting. [Obsolete.]   §125 I

350 ↦ **496** Prune away glue and penalties at top of page after marks, sends, inserts.   §1000 Q

497 Allow \mark in horizontal mode. [Later it will be \vadjust{\mark...}.]   §655 G

498 Allow optional space before a required left brace, e.g., \if AA {...}. [See #251.]   §403 C

499 Issue an incomplete \if error, to help catch a bad \if.   §336 I

17 Mar 1981

494 ↦ **500** Omit the warning message at end of a file page unless the nesting level has changed on that page. [System dependent.]   I

310 ↦ **501** Fix the spacing when there is a very tall subscript with a superscript.   §759 Q

20 Mar 1981

371 ↦ **502** Make space-eating after \else fully consistent between the true and false cases. [Obsolete.]   S

24 Mar 1981

496 ↦ **503** Change *glue_spec_size* to *ins_spec_size* in *vpackage* [where insertions are done]. [Obsolete.]   B

5 Apr 1981

501 ↦ **504** Fix a typo ('+' instead of '-') in the new subscript code; this shifted certain subscripts down instead of up.   §759 B

18 Apr 1981

505 Make leaders with rules of specified size act like variable rules.   §626, 635 G

29 Apr 1981

461 ↦ **506** Don't consider *badness* > *threshold* at a line \break except in an emergency.   §854 A

13 Jul 1981

402 ↦ **507** Allow other characters as numbers.   §442 C

294 ↦ **508** Avoid dead storage if a *no_new_control_sequence* error occurs. [Obsolete.]   §259 R

509 Add a new \ifx feature.   §507 G

510 Add new features \xleaders and \cleaders.   §626, 635 G

14 Jul 1981

507 ↦ **511** Amend the new code for constants; the '.' in '.5' is thought to mean ´056!   §442 S

507 ↦ **512** And fix an egregious blunder in that code: New commands at the end of a procedure are ignored when earlier statements exit via **return**.   §442 L

4 Aug 1981

513 Accept alphabetic codes for all online error recovery options, instead of insisting on control codes like line feed or form feed. [The original error-recovery codes were suggested by the conventions of the SAIL compiler.]   §84 P

514 Add a new \thebox feature [later \lastbox].   §1079 G

7 Aug 1981

515 Add fil, fill, and filll as units for glue stretching or shrinking.   §454 G

516 Suppress the overfull box error when shrinkage amount is negative.   §664 I

9 Aug 1981

517 Let unset boxes inherit the size of their parent in alignments.   §810 Q

12 Apr 1982

518 Make INITEX dump out the *font_dsize* array needed by the new DVI output module.   §1322 F

1 May 1982

151 ↦ **519** Fix *clean_box* so that *mlist_to_hlist* cannot make $link(q) = 0$ and $type(q) = glue\_node$.   §720 S

- *[That was the historic final change to T$_E$X78. All subsequent entries in this log refer to T$_E$X82.]*

28 Sep 1982

- *Here are the first changes made to the preliminary listing of TEX82 that was published by the TEX project earlier this month.*

520 Insert the missing cases *letter* and *other_char* after *x_token* looks ahead.   §1036 F

521 Change '\pause' to '\pausing'.   §236 C

522 Reset *overfull_rule* when determining tabskip glue.   §804 D

523 Fix the logic for scanning \ifcase [in obsolete syntax—everything is still done with braces since '\fi' doesn't exist yet].   §509 A

30 Sep 1982

524 Change "0.0" to "?.?" (suggested by DRF).   §186 I

2 Oct 1982

525 Use conditional thin spacing next to 'Inner' noads.   §764 Q

526 Make thick spaces conditional.   §766 Q

4 Oct 1982

527 Increase *trie_size* from 7000 to 8000, because of Frank Liang's improved (but longer) hyphenation patterns.   §11 P

6 Oct 1982

528 Change the string lengths to match the new *TEX_format_default*.   §520 F

- *Version 0 of TEX is being released today!*

8 Oct 1982

529 Fix a blunder: I decreased *h* mod a quarterword when it should have been decreased mod *trie_op_hash_size* (HWT).   §944 B

9 Oct 1982

530 Fix a typo ('!' not '&') in the WEB documentation.   §524 P

531 Remember to call *initialize* if a different format was preloaded (Max Díaz).   §1337 F

- *Version 0.1 incorporates the above changes.*

12 Oct 1982

532 Add the '\immediate' feature, by popular request.   §1375 G

- *Version 0.2 incorporates this (somewhat extensive) change.*

13 Oct 1982

533 Introduce new WEB macros so that *glue_ratio* is more easily changed.   §109 P

- *I began writing The TEXbook today: edited the old preface and searched in the library for quotations.*

14 Oct 1982

534 Change the type of *hd* to *eight_bits*; it's not a *quarterword* (HWT).   §649 B

535 Revise the optimization of DVI commands: It's not always safe to eliminate *pop* when the preceding byte is *push*, since DVI commands have variable length! (Embarrassing oversight caught by DRF.)   §601 S

15 Oct 1982

536 Test '*prev_depth* > *ignore_depth*', not '≠'.   §679 C

- *Version 0.3 incorporates the above changes.*

16 Oct 1982

537 Omit definition of *align_size*; it's never used (Bill Scherlis).   §11 P

538 Inhibit error messages when packaging box 255.   §1017 I

21 Oct 1982

539 Subtract *width*(*q*) from *page_goal*, don't add it to *page_so_far*[1].   §1009 A

- *The comment in §982 is correct, and so was my first draft of this code; but when desk checking the program some months after writing it, I introduced this bug, believing that I was making the algorithm more elegant or something.*

- *Version 0.4 incorporates the above changes.*

22 Oct 1982

540 Increase the amount of lower (variable-size) memory from 12000 to 13000, since the TₑX program listing now needs about 11500. [At this time there still is a fixed boundary between upper and lower memory.]   §12 P

541 Add a new parameter \boxmaxdepth.   §1086 G

- *Version 0.5 incorporates the above changes.*

26 Oct 1982

542 Fix an off-by-one error caught by Gabi Kuper and HWT. (I forgot ' + 1').   §1317 B

543 Fix the spacing of displayed control sequences: *print_cs* should base its decision on $cat\_code(p - single\_base)$, not $cat\_code(p)$.   §262 B

- *The TRIP test detected this bug, but I didn't notice.*

27 Oct 1982

544 Set *math_type* before saying $fetch(nucleus(q))$, since fetching can have a side effect.   §752 S

28 Oct 1982

545 Install a major change: Fonts now have identifiers instead of code letters. Eliminate the '\:' primitive, and give corresponding new features to '\the'.   §209 G

- *Actually I began making these changes on October 26, but I needed two days to debug them and to put Humpty Dumpty together again.*
- *At this time I'm also drafting macros for typesetting The TₑXbook.*
- *The above changes have been incorporated into Version 0.6.*

30 Oct 1982

- *After years of searching, I've finally found a definitive definition of the printer's point; and (unfortunately) my previous conjecture was wrong. The truth is that* 83 pc = 35 cm, *exactly; so I am changing TₑX to conform.*

546 Revise unit definitions for the 'real' printer's point.   §458, 617 C

- *Version 0.7 incorporates the above.*

1 Nov 1982

- *Oops! Retract error #546, and retract TₑX Version 0.7; the source of my information about points was flaky after all. My original suppositions were correct, as confirmed by NBS Circular 570.*

4 Nov 1982

547 Revise the definition of dd, conforming to the definitive value shown me by Chuck Bigelow.   §458 C

545 ↦ **548** Introduce "frozen" copies of font identifiers, to be returned by \the\font, so that font manipulation is more robust.   §1257 R

5 Nov 1982

549 Reset *looseness* and paragraph shape when beginning a \vbox.   §1083 D

6 Nov 1982

550 De-update *align_state* when braces are in constants.   §442 D

551 Improve error recovery for bad alignments.   §1127 I

- *Today I wrapped up Chapters 4 and 5.*

8 Nov 1982

552 Give more power to \let: the right-hand side needn't be a control sequence.   §1221 G

553 Amend *show_context* to say '($base\_ptr = input\_ptr$) ∨ '; otherwise undefined control sequences can be invisible in unusual cases (John Hobby).   §312 I

554 Compute demerits more suitably by adding a penalty squared, instead of adding penalties before squaring.   §859 A

- *Previously a slightly loose hyphenated line followed by a decent line was considered worse than a decent hyphenated line followed by a quite loose line.*

10 Nov 1982

555 Save a bit of buffer space by declaring *pool_file* only in INITEX.   §50   E

11 Nov 1982

556 Introduce a new context indicator to clarify TEX's scanning state: A special type called *backed_up* is distinguished from other kinds of *inserted* lists; it is called 'recently read' or 'to be read again', while others are called 'inserted'. §314   I

557 Append a comment, '**treated as zero**', to the missing-number message.   §446   I

558 Ignore the settings of \hfuzz or \vfuzz if \hbadness or \vbadness is less than 100.   §666, 677   I

13 Nov 1982

- *Major surgery on the program is planned for today, because of new ideas suggested by correspondence with MDS and other macro writers.*

559 Introduce a new \tokens register; this will be useful and easy to add, since TEX already can handle \everypar and \output.   §1227   G

560 Change *get_x_token* to *get_token* when scanning an optional space; then a construction like \def\foo{...}\foo won't complain that \foo is undefined.   §443   C

- *This change was retracted when it was being debugged, because it could cause* endv *to abort the job. Then it was re-established again when I found that* endv *needed to be more robust anyway. [But it was eventually rescinded again.]*

561 Make \span mean 'expand' in a preamble.   §782   G

562 Use three separate **if** tests instead of '∧' in the inner loop of *get_next*, to gain efficiency.   §342   E

563 Introduce *get_r_token* so that assignments have uniform error messages and so that frozen equivalents cannot be changed.   §1215   R

- *I gave a few variables more mnemonic names as I made these changes.*

564 Move conditional statements from the semantics ('stomach') part of TEX to the syntax ('mouth') part, by introducing '\fi'. Also introduce \csname and \endcsname.   §372, 489–500   C

- *This makes macros much more predictable and logical, but it is by far the most drastic change ever made to TEX. The program began to come back to life only after three days of solid hacking.*
- *Several other things were cleaned up as part of this change because it is now more natural to handle them differently. For example, a null control sequence has now become more logical.*
- *The result of all this is called Version 0.8.*

18 Nov 1982

- *Today I resumed writing Chapter 8. Tomorrow I'm 2^{14} days old!*

21 Nov 1982

565 Declare *c* as a local variable for hyphenation (DRF).   §912   F

566 Omit the "first pass" and try hyphenations immediately, if \pretolerance is negative (suggested by DRF).   §863   E

567 Don't ship out incredibly huge pages; they might foul up DVI files.   §641   R

2 Dec 1982

568 Add new features \everymath and \everydisplay.   §1139, 1145   G

569 Add a new feature \futurelet.   §1221   G

- *The changes above have been incorporated into Version 0.9 of TeX.*

7 Dec 1982

570 Add a new `\endinput` primitive (suggested by FY).   §362, 378 G

8 Dec 1982

571 Try *off_save*, if `\par` occurs in restricted horizontal mode. (This avoids embarrassment if TeX says 'type a command or say `\end`', then when you type `\end` it says you can't!) [However, I soon retracted this change.]   §1094 I

21 Dec 1982

572 Redefine `\relax` so that its *chr* field exceeds 127. (This facilitates the test for end in *scan_file_name*.)   §265 A

566 ↦ **573** Call *begin_diagnostic* when omitting the first pass of line breaking.   §863 F

574 Fix the logic of glue scanning: In `\hskip-1pt plus2pt` the minus should apply only to the 1pt.   §461 A

23 Dec 1982

575 Renumber the decimal codes in paragraph statistics for loose and tight lines; they were ordered backwards.   §817 I

576 Treat a paragraph that ends with leaders like a paragraph that ends with glue. §816 C

577 Allow commas as alternates to radix points, for Europeans.   §438 C

578 Change `\hangindent` to a normal dimension parameter. [It had been a combination of `\hangindent` and `\hangafter`, with special syntax.]   §247 C

579 Make `\prevgraf` accessible to users.   §422, 1244 G

580 Split `\clubpenalty` off from `\widowpenalty`.   §890 G

- *I'm typing Chapter 14 while making these changes.*

24 Dec 1982

581 Use *back_input* instead of **goto** *reswitch* when inserting `\par`, because `\par` may have changed.   §1095 S

25 Dec 1982

- *It's 10pm after a very Merry Christmas!*

582 Don't prompt for a new file name if `\openin` doesn't find a file.   §1275 I

583 Add a new `\jobname` primitive.   §472 G

584 Give the user a way to delete the dollar sign, when TeX decides to insert one. §1047 I

585 Allow optional equals after `\parshape`, and implement `\the\parshape`.   §423, 1248 C

26 Dec 1982

586 Add an *if_line_field* to the condition stack entries, so that more informative error messages can be given.   §489 I

549 ↦ **587** Introduce a *normal_paragraph* procedure, since initialization is needed also within `\insert`, `\vadjust`, `\valign`, `\output`.   §1070 D

27 Dec 1982

588 Give users access to `\pagetotal` and `\pagegoal`. (Analogous to #679 and #585, but simpler.)   §1245 G

589 Introduce `\tracingpages`, allowing users to see page-optimization calculations. Also split `\tracingparagraphs` off from `\tracingstats`.   §987, 1005, 1011 I

- *The changes above have been incorporated into Version 0.91 of TeX.*

31 Dec 1982

590 Break the *build_page* procedure into two parts, by extracting the section now called *fire_up*. [This is necessary because some Pascal compilers, notably for IBM mainframes, cannot deal with large procedures.]   §1012 P

564 ↦ **591** Make `\ifodd1\else` legal by introducing *if_code*.   §489 S

592 Improve alignments when columns don't occur: Don't append null boxes for columns missing before `\cr`, and zero out the tabskip glue after nonpresent columns.   §802 Q

593 Make the error message about overfull alignment more intelligible.   §801, 804   I

- *The changes above have been incorporated into Version 0.92 of TEX82, which was the last version of 1982, completed at 11:59pm on December 31.*

3 Jan 1983

- *Today I'm beginning to write Chapter 15, and planning the \output routine of plain.tex.*

594 Change the logic of *its_all_over*; use *max_dead_cycles* instead of the fixed constant 100.   §1054   C

595 Don't forget to *pop_nest* when an insert is empty. Also disallow optional space after \insert *n* {...}.   §1100   F

4 Jan 1983

541 ↦ **596** Use the \boxmaxdepth that's declared inside a \vbox when packaging it.   §1086   C

597 Rename \groupbegin and \groupend as \begingroup and \endgroup.   §265   C

598 Make \deadcycles accessible to users.   §1246   G

599 Base the split insertions on natural height plus depth, not on *delta*.   §1010   Q

- *The changes above have been incorporated into Version 0.93.*

6 Jan 1983

600 Add *push_math* to handle a case where I forgot to clear *incompleat_noad*. (This long-standing bug was unearthed today by Phyllis Winkler.)   §1136   D

588 ↦ **601** Add \pageshrink, etc., too.   §1245   G

602 Introduce new parameters \floatingpenalty, \insertpenalties. Also adopt a new internal representation of insertion nodes, so that \floatingpenalty, \splittopskip and \splitmaxdepth can be stored with each insertion. §140, 1008   G

7 Jan 1983

603 Improve the rules for entering *new_line*, in particular when the end-of-line character is active.   §343   Q

9 Jan 1983

604 Distinguish between implicit and explicit kerns.   §155, 896   Q

605 Change the name \ignorespace to \ignorespaces.   §265   C

560 ↦ **606** Don't omit a blank space after \def, \message, \mark, etc.; the previous hodgepodge of rules is impossible to learn.   §473   C

- *The above changes appear in Version 0.94.*

12 Jan 1983

- *Beginning to write the chapters on math today.*

607 Add a new feature: active characters in math mode.   §1151   G

15 Jan 1983

608 Fix a surprise bug: '$1-$' treated the - as binary.   §729   A

609 Initialize *space_factor* inside discretionaries.   §1117   D

16 Jan 1983

610 Fix an incredibly embarrassing bug: I forgot to update *spotless* in the *error* routine!   F

- *While fixing this, I decided to change spotless to a more general history variable, as suggested by IBMers who want a return code.*   §76, 82, 1335

611 Replace two calls of *confusion* by attempts at error recovery, in places where 'This can't happen' could actually happen.   §1027, 1372   I

18 Jan 1983

612 Introduce the *normalize_selector* routine to protect against startup anomalies when the transcript file isn't open. Also make *open_log_file* terminate in some cases.   §92, 535   R

$591 \mapsto$ **613** Insert `\relax`, not a blank space, to cure infinite loop like `\ifeof\fi` (LL).   §510 R

614 Change the old `\limitswitch` to `\limits`, `\nolimits`, and `\displaylimits`.
Incidentally, this fixes a bug in the former positioning of integral signs. §682, 749 G

615 Give a `\char` in math mode its inherited `\mathcode`.   §1151 C

$525 \mapsto$ **616** Make underline, overline, radical, vcenter, accent noads and `{...}` all revert
to type Ord instead of type Inner. Introduce a new primitive `\mathinner`.
(This fixes the spacing, which got worse in some ways after change #525.) §761 Q

- *I'm working on Appendix G today.*

19 Jan 1983

617 Introduce a `\mathchoice` primitive.   §1174 G

618 Move `\input` from the stomach to the eyes.   §378 C

619 Introduce `\chardef`, analogous to `\mathchardef`.   §1036, 1224 C

620 Change `\unbox` to `\unhbox` and `\unvbox`; also add `\unhcopy`.   §1110 G

621 Consider `\spacefactor`, `\pagetotal`, etc., as part of *prefixed_command*, even
though they are always global.   §1211 C

20 Jan 1983

622 Switch modes when `\hrule` occurs in horizontal mode or `\vrule` in vertical.
§1090, 1094 C

623 Add a new `\globaldefs` feature.   §1211 G

21 Jan 1983

624 Optimize the code, in places where it's important (based on frequency counts
of TEX usage accumulated during the past week): Introduce *fast_get_avail*
and *fast_store_new_token*; reduce procedure-call overhead in *begin_token_list*,
end_token_list, *back_input*, *flush_node_list*; change some tests from 'if $a \wedge b$'
to 'if a then if b'.   §122, 371 E

22 Jan 1983

625 Save space in math lists: Don't insert penalties within restricted horizontal
mode; simplify trivial boxes.   §721, 1196 E

626 Fix a surprising oversight in the *rebox* routine: Ensure that b isn't a vbox.   §715 S

$545 \mapsto$ **627** Make `\nullfont` a primitive, so that *cur_font* always has a value. (This is
a dramatic improvement to TEX78, where a missing font was a fatal error
called 'Whoa'!)   §552 C

24 Jan 1983

$586 \mapsto$ **628** List all incomplete `\if`'s when the job ends.   §1335 I

29 Jan 1983

629 Change initialization of *align_state* so that `\halign\bgroup` works.   §777 C

30 Jan 1983

$625 \mapsto$ **630** Be sure to test '*is_char_node(q)*' when checking for a trivial box.   §721 D

- *By extraordinary coincidence, this bug was caught when somebody used font
  number 11 (= kern_node) in the second character of a list of length 2!*

631 Improve format for stats at end of run, as suggested by DRF.   §1334 I

- *The changes above have been incorporated into Version 0.95.*

632 Don't ignore the space after a control symbol (except '\ ').   §354 C

633 Remove all trailing spaces at the right of input lines, so that there's perfect
compatibility with IBM systems that extend short lines with spaces.   §31 P

3 Feb 1983

634 Assume that a *math_accent* was intended, after giving an error message in the
case *mmode* + *accent*.   §1165 I

635 Add new primitives `\iftrue` and `\iffalse`.   §488 G

6 Feb 1983

636 Improve the accuracy of fixed-point arithmetic when calculating sizes for `\left` and `\right`. (I had started by dividing *delimiter_factor*, not *delta1*, by 500.) §762 A

12 Feb 1983

637 Change the name `\delimiterlimit` to `\delimitershortfall`.   §248 C

638 Make `\abovewithdelims..` equivalent to `\above`; change the order of operands so that delimiters precede the dimension.   §1182 C

607 ↦ **639** Remove the kludgy math codes introduced earlier; make `\fam` a normal integer parameter and allow `\mathcode` to equal 2^{15} §1233 C

640 Don't let `\spacefactor` become 2^{15} or more.   §1233, 1243 R

• *I finished drafting Chapter 17 today.*

14 Feb 1983

639 ↦ **641** Replace octal output (*print_octal*) by hexadecimal (*print_hex*) so that math codes are clearer.   §67 I

619 ↦ **642** Don't forget *char_given* in the *math_accent* routine.   §1124 F

17 Feb 1983

643 Switch modes when `\halign` occurs in horizontal mode, or `\valign` in vertical mode.   §1090, 1094 C

18 Feb 1983

644 Add a new feature `\tracingrestores`. This requires a new procedure called *show_eqtb*, whose code can be interspersed with the *eqtb* definitions.   §252 I

25 Feb 1983

622 ↦ **645** Suggest using `\leaders` when the user tries a horizontal rule in restricted horizontal mode.   §1095 I

27 Feb 1983

646 Specify the range of source lines, when giving warning messages for underfull or overfull boxes in alignments.   §662, 675 I

• *Why did it take me all day to type the middle part of Chapter 18?*

4 Mar 1983

647 Introduce a new feature `\xcr` (suggested by LL). [Changed later to '`\crcr`'.]   §785 G

631 ↦ **648** Subtract out TEX's own string requirements from the stats.   §1334 I

6 Mar 1983

649 Add new features `\everyhbox` and `\everyvbox`.   §1083, 1167 G

9 Mar 1983

650 Avoid accessing *math_quad* when the symbol fonts aren't known to be present. §1199 R

533 ↦ **651** Introduce *float* and *unfloat* macros to aid portability (HWT).   §109 P

652 Introduce new names `\abovedisplayskip` and `\belowdisplayskip` for the old `\dispskip`; also `\abovedisplayshortskip` and `\belowdisplayshortskip` for the old `\dispaskip` and `\dispbskip`.   §226 C

10 Mar 1983

653 Unbundle `\romannumeral` from `\number` (suggested by FY).   §468 C

12 Mar 1983

654 Ignore leading spaces in *scan_keyword*.   §407 C

14 Mar 1983

631 ↦ **655** Use *write* and *write_ln* directly when printing stats.   §1334 E

16 Mar 1983

602 ↦ **656** Refine the page-break cost function (introducing '*deplorable*', which is not quite '*awful_bad*'), after suggestion by LL.   §974, 1005 Q

- *The changes above have been incorporated into Version 0.96.*

18 Mar 1983

657 Add a new feature \everyjob suggested by FY.   §1030 G

19 Mar 1983

658 Don't treat left braces specially when showing macros.   §294 I

659 Ignore blanks that would otherwise become undelimited arguments.   §393 C

21 Mar 1983

660 Make \lastskip handle *mu_glue* as well as ordinary glue.   §424 F

561 ↦ **661** Expand only one level in a preamble \span.   §782 C

22 Mar 1983

662 Let a single # suffice in \tokens, \message, etc. (The previous rule, in which ## was always required as in macros, was a loser especially in \write where you had to say ####!)   §477 C

663 Require the keyword 'to' in \read. (This will avoid the common error of an incomplete constant when no space appears before the \cs.) Also allow terminal I/O as a default when a stream number is out of range. §482, 1225, 1370 C

26 Mar 1983

664 Replace \ifeven⟨countnumber⟩ by \ifodd⟨number⟩, for better consistency of language.   §504 C

564 ↦ **665** Introduce the *change_if_limit*, to overcome a big surprise bug relating to \if\if aabc\fi.   §497 S

- *Such examples show that* cur_if *might not be current, in my original implementation.*

28 Mar 1983

666 Tolerate non-characters as arguments to \if and \ifcat.   §506 G

667 Change 'absent' to 'void', a better word.   §487 C

668 Clear the *shift_amount* in \lastbox, since I don't want to figure out what it means in all cases.   §1081 C

29 Mar 1983

669 Wake up the terminal before giving an error message. (This means a special *print_err* procedure is introduced.) (Suggested by DRF.)   §34, 73 I

1 Apr 1983

- *Today I finished Chapter 21 (boxes) and began to draft Chapter 22 (alignments).*

670 Allow periodic preambles in alignments.   §793 G

671 Make \leaders line up according to the smallest enclosing box. §627, 636 C

672 Allow hyphenation after whatsits (e.g., after items for an index).   §896 Q

2 Apr 1983

673 Call *build_page* when \par occurs in vertical mode.   §1094 Q

674 Clear *aux* in *init_row*, for tidyness.   §786 C

4 Apr 1983

675 Let digits switch families in math mode.   §232 C

7 Apr 1983

602 ↦ **676** Refine the test for not splitting an insertion.   §1008 Q

8 Apr 1983

647 ↦ **677** Rename \xcr as \crcr, at LL's request.   §780 C

9 Apr 1983

- *Took a day off and had a chance to help print a sample page on a 150-year-old letterpress in Murphys, California.*

11 Apr 1983

678 Recover more sensibly after a runaway preamble.   §339   I

12 Apr 1983

679 Make \read span several input lines, if necessary to get balanced braces.   §482   C

14 Apr 1983

680 Fix a subtle bug found by JS: §882 can make q a *char_node*, so we need to test 'if $\neg is\_char\_node(q)$'. [Actually I discovered much later that the real bug was to omit '**else**' at this point.]   §881   S

15 Apr 1983

681 Make \uppercase and \lowercase apply to all characters, regardless of category.   §1289   C

- *7:30am. After working all night, I completed a draft of the manual thru Chapter 22, for distribution to volunteer readers.*
- *5pm. The changes above have been incorporated into Version 0.97.*

17 Apr 1983

682 Change '*small_number*' to '0 . . 65' in the hyphenation routine (DRF).   §901   R
683 Flush patterns in the input when the user tries \patterns outside of INITEX (suggested by DRF).   §1252   I

- *Tomorrow I fly to England, where I'll lecture and write a paper about 'Literate Programming' [Comp. J. **27** (1984), 97–111].*

14 May 1983

663 ↦ 684 Improve the behavior of \read from terminal (suggested by Todd Allen at Yale). [I'd forgotten to implement the extended stream numbers in #663. Also, the prompt is now omitted if $n < 0$.]   §484   I

18 May 1983

685 Restrict \write n to the transcript file only, if $n < 0$.   §1350   I
686 Unify the syntax for registers and internal quantities. (Remove primitives called '\insthe' and '\minusthe'; rename *scan_the* to *scan_something_internal*, and change its interface accordingly; clean up command codes generally.)   §209, 413   C
687 Introduce new parameters \hoffset, \voffset.   §617   G

24 May 1983

688 Introduce a new parameter \everycr (suggested by MDS).   §774, 799   G

- *Many macro writers and preliminary-manual readers have been requesting new features; I'll try to keep the language as concise and consistent as possible.*

25 May 1983

689 Introduce \countdef, \dimendef, etc. (suggested by DRF long ago, easy now in view of #686).   §1224   G
690 Introduce \advance, \multiply, \divide (suggested by FY).   §1240   G
691 Introduce \hyphenchar; this requires a new command *assign_font_int*, plus minor changes to about 15 modules.   §915   G
692 Introduce \skewchar (easy because of #691).   §741   G
693 Introduce \noexpand. (I had difficulty thinking of how to implement this one!)   §358, 369   G
694 Introduce \meaning.   §296   G
695 Remove 'dm' and 'vu'; allow the more general '.5\hsize'.   §455   G
696 Change '\texinfo f n' to '\fontdimen n f'.   §578   C

27 May 1983

697 Add a new feature \afterassignment (suggested by ARK).   §1269 G

698 Adjust the timing so that commands like '\chardef\xx=5\xx' behave sensibly. §1224 C

28 May 1983

699 Ignore '\relax' as if it were a space, in math mode and in a few other places where \relax would otherwise be erroneous.   §404 C

700 Improve \mathaccent spacing with respect to subscripts and superscripts (suggested by HWT).   §742 Q

30 May 1983

594 ↦ **701** Terminate a job only when $dead\_cycles = 0$.   §1054 C

- *The changes above constitute Version 0.98.*

3 Jun 1983

- *I finished the draft of Chapter 23 (output routines) today.*

702 Allow \mark and \insert and \vadjust in restricted horizontal mode, and also in math mode. (This is a comparatively big change, triggered by the fact that \mark in a display presently causes TeX to crash with 'This can't happen'!) The global variable *adjust_tail* is introduced.   §796, 888, 1085 G

6 Jun 1983

695 ↦ **703** Replace (and generalize) the previous uses of ht, wd, and dp in dimensions by introducing the new control sequences \ht, \wd, and \dp.   §1247 G

704 Display sub-parts of noads with the symbols ^ and _ instead of (and [.   §696 I

694 ↦ **705** Allow A..F in hex constants to be *other_char* as well as *letter*.   §445 C

7 Jun 1983

654 ↦ **706** Remove an instance of ⟨Scan optional space⟩, since it's now redundant. §457 E

707 Legalize \mkern\thinmuskip and \mkern5\thinmuskip.   §456 C

708 Clean up the treatment of optional spaces in numerical specifications.   §455 C

- *A construction like 2.5\space\space\dimen0 was previously valid after 'plus' or 'minus' only!*
- *I'm obviously working on Chapter 24 today.*

545 ↦ **709** Allow '\font' as a ⟨font identifier⟩ for the current font.   §577 C

623 ↦ **710** Don't make \gdef global when $global\_defs < 0$.   §1218 C

711 Produce *zero_glue* as the outcome of \advance\spaceskip by-\spaceskip.   §1229 E

712 Make \show do something appropriate for every possible token.   §1294 I

559 ↦ **713** Replace the (single) \tokens parameter by an array of 256 token registers. §230 G

714 Allow \indent in math mode; also make \valign in math mode produce the 'Missing $' error.   §1046, 1093 C

715 Remove redundant code: There's no need to check *cur_group* or call *off_save* when starting alignments or equation numbers in displays.   §1130, 1142 E

8 Jun 1983

716 Disallow \openout-1 and \closeout-1.   §1350 C

717 Disallow \lastbox in math mode.   §1080 C

9 Jun 1983

718 Call *back_error*, not *error*, when \leaders aren't followed by proper glue. §1078 I

719 Initialize for a possible paragraph, after \noalign in a \valign.   §785 D

10 Jun 1983

720 Expand the optional space after an ASCII constant.   §442 C

12 Jun 1983

721 Set *space_factor* ← 1000 after a rule or a constructed accent.   §1056, 1123 C

14 Jun 1983

722 Correct a serious blunder: Set $disc\_width \leftarrow 0$ before testing if s is null (caught by JS).   §870 D

- *This is a real bug that existed since the beginning! It showed up on page 37 of the Version 0 TRIP manual, but I didn't notice the problem.*

708 ↦ **723** Make optional spaces after ⟨dimen⟩ like those after ⟨number⟩.   §448 C

568 ↦ **724** Insert *every_display* before calling *build_page*.   §1145 C

648 ↦ **725** Report TEX's capacity on overflow errors in a way that's fully consistent with other statistical reports.   §42 I

17 Jun 1983

726 Make all \tracing decisions on the basis of $\geq$ versus $<$, not $\neq$ versus $=$.   §581 C

- *Today I finished the draft of Chapter 27 (the last chapter)!*
- *The changes above were released as Version 0.99 on June 19, 1983.*

20 Jun 1983

727 Set \catcode'\%=14 in INITEX.   §232 C

587 ↦ **728** Call *normal_paragraph* when \par occurs in vertical mode.   §1094 C

- *Once again I'm retiring about 8am and awaking about 4pm.*

21 Jun 1983

558 ↦ **729** Don't append an overfull rule solely because of \hbadness.   §666 C

730 Don't allow the glue-ratio of shrinking to be less than -1.   §810, 811 R

22 Jun 1983

653 ↦ **731** Declare the parameter to *print_roman_int* to be of type *integer*, instead of *nonnegative_integer* (found by Debby Clark).   §69 B

690 ↦ **732** Make the keyword 'by' optional (suggested by LL).   §1236 C

24 Jun 1983

733 Say 'preloaded' when announcing *format_ident*.   §1328 I

25 Jun 1983

734 Add extra boxes and glue to the output of alignment. [This thwarts possible attempts at trickery by which system-dependent glue set values computed by \span could have gotten into TEX's registers by things like \valign and \vsplit. It also has the advantage of perfect accuracy in alignment of vertical rules.]   §809 R

735 Make leaders affect the height or width of the enclosing boxes.   §656, 671 C

- *Today I'm mainly installing a much-improved format for change files in WEB programs (suggested by DRF).*

28 Jun 1983

736 Permit \unskip in vertical mode when we know that it does nothing.   §1106 C

1 Jul 1983

700 ↦ **737** Avoid redundant boxes when things like '{\bf A}' occur in math.   §1186 E

738 Add a 'scaled' feature to \font input.   §1258 G

700 ↦ **739** Remember to correct *delta* when an accented box changes.   §742 D

2 Jul 1983

740 Introduce *bypass_eoln*, to remove anomalous behavior on input files of length 1. (Suggested by DRF after the problem was discovered by LL).   §31 R

4 Jul 1983

741 Allow codes like ^^b as well as ^^B.   §352, 355 G

742 Introduce new parameters \escapechar, \endlinechar, \defaulthyphenchar, and \defaultskewchar, to make TeX less dependent on the character set. (This affects many modules, since a lot of error messages must be broken up so that they use *print_esc*.)   G

7 Jul 1983

743 Use a system-dependent function *erstat* when opening or closing files (suggested by DRF).   §27   P

11 Jul 1983

- *The computer is back up after more than 50 hours down time (due to air conditioning failure).*

744 Show total glue in the output of \tracingpages.   §985   I
745 Guard against insertion into an hbox.   §993   R
746 Legalize the assignment ⟨tokenvar⟩=⟨tokenvar⟩.   §1227   C
747 Introduce a new parameter \errhelp.   §1283   I
623 ↦ **748** Don't forget to check *global_defs* when \tabskip is changed.   §782   F

12 Jul 1983

749 Allow an \outer macro to appear after \string, \noexpand, and \meaning (Todd Allen).   §369, 471   C
750 Make '\the' an expandable control sequence (i.e., move it from the stomach to the throat); this cleans up several annoying glitches.   §367   C
751 Allow \unhbox and \unhcopy in math mode if the box is void.   §1110   C

13 Jul 1983

- *I lectured for four hours at the TUG meeting today after very little sleep!*

16 Jul 1983

- *The following were suggested by TUG meeting discussions.*

752 Round the value of *default_rule* more properly: It should be 26215.   §463   L
700 ↦ **753** Fix \mathaccent again; it's still not right! The final height should be the maximum of the height of accented letter without superscript and the height of unaccented letter with superscript.   §742   Q
754 Add a new feature \newlinechar.   §59   G
755 Allow boxes and rules in discretionaries (suggested by somebody from Hewlett-Packard).   §1121   G
756 Show all token expansions, not just macros, when \tracingcommands.   §367   I
757 Allow \char in a \hyphenation list.   §935   C
758 Introduce a new feature \aftergroup; it can be implemented with *save_stack*.   §326   G
759 Run the running dimensions to alignment boundaries (suggested by ARK).   §806   C

17 Jul 1983

760 Zero out *hyf* values at the edges, so that weird pattern data cannot lead to Pascal range checks.   §965   R
761 Decrease the hc codes for hyphenation, so that code 127 cannot possibly be matched.   §937, 962   R
672 ↦ **762** Allow whatsits after hyphenatable words.   §899   C
604 ↦ **763** Represent an italic correction as an explicit kern.   §1113   C

18 Jul 1983

764 Allow lowercase letters in file names.   §519   C
765 Change the message 'No output file' to: 'No pages of output'.   §642   I
766 Confirm that a quiet mode is being entered, when error interaction ends with Q, R, or S (suggested by ARK).   §86   I

- *Version 0.999 was finally installed today; a new program listing has been printed.*

- *From now on, I plan to keep all section numbers unchanged.*
- *I'm done writing Appendix H; beginning to revise Chapter 20.*

25 Jul 1983

663 ↦ **767** Allow space after 'to' in the \read command (FY).   §1215 C
- *To bed at 1pm today.*

27 Jul 1983

665 ↦ **768** Stack the current type of \if; this precaution is necessary in general (FY).   §498 S
- *To bed at 2pm today.*

29 Jul 1983

769 Avoid putting a control sequence in the hash table when it occurs after \ifx. (Requested by Math Reviews people.)   §507 E
- *Finished a version of The TeXbook lacking only Appendices D, E, and I, for distribution to interested readers.*
- *To bed at 10:30pm, planning to arise regularly at 6am for a change.*

31 Jul 1983

766 ↦ **770** Call *update_terminal* when going quiet (HWT).   §86 I

1 Aug 1983

771 Don't put an empty line at the end of an \input file! (This simplifies the rules and the program, and also gets around a bug that occurred at the end of files with *end_line_char* < 0.)   §362 C
- *The changes above went into Version 0.9999, which was widely distributed.*

16 Aug 1983

665 ↦ **772** Rectify a ridiculous gaffe: I initialized q every time the loop of *change_if_limit* was performed! (Found by FY.)   §497 B
648 ↦ **773** Distinguish 'string' from 'strings' when reporting statistics.   §1334 I
774 Introduce lx, to correct a bug in \xleader computations (found by FY).   §627 A

20 Aug 1983

775 Don't forget to apply \/ to ligatures!   §1113 F
- *Today I began to read all previous issues of TUGboat, in preparation for Appendix D.*

27 Aug 1983

776 Add debugging hack number 16, to help catch subtle data structure bugs.   §1339 I
777 Remove redundant setting and resetting of *name_in_progress*.   §531 E
778 Suppress \input during a font size spec; otherwise *cur_name* is clobbered (found by MDS).   §1258 S
779 Introduce new conditionals \ifhbox and \ifvbox.   §505 G

29 Aug 1983

750 ↦ **780** Test for an empty list, if emptiness will mess up the data structure. (Found by Todd Allen.)   §478 D
781 Use *fast_for_new_token* for efficiency.   §466 E
782 Say 'has only' instead of 'has'.   §579 I
- *These changes yield Version 0.99999, used only at Stanford.*

30 Aug 1983

783 Make funny blank spaces showable.   §298 C

31 Aug 1983

754 ↦ **784** Make \newlinechar affect *print_char*, not just *print*.   §58 C

4 Sep 1983

785 Add new features \lastkern, \lastpenalty, \unkern, \unpenalty. §424, 996, 1105 G

- *OK, Appendix D is finished!!*
- *The above changes have been installed in Version 0.999999.*

17 Sep 1983

548 ↦ **786** Don't bother making duplicate font identifiers; that was overkill, not really needed. §1258 P

- *Will this be the historic last change to TEX?*

18 Sep 1983

787 Correct a minor inconsistency, 'display' not 'displayed'. §211 I

20 Sep 1983

604 ↦ **788** Treat the kerns inserted for accents as explicit kerns. §1125 C

26 Sep 1983

789 Change 'log' to 'transcript' in several messages. §535, 1335 I

- *The index was finished today; I mailed the entire TEXbook East for final proofreading before publication.*

1 Oct 1983

790 Prevent uninitialized trie positions in case of overflow (found by Bernd Schulze). §944 D

7 Oct 1983

- *Henceforth our weekly 'TEX lunch' meetings will be called 'METAFONT lunch'.*
- *DRF begins to produce The TEXbook on our APS phototypesetter.*

14 Oct 1983

633 ↦ **791** Ignore spaces at the ends of lines also in TEX.POOL (found by DRF). §52 P

792 Initialize the *history* variable at *start_here* (DRF). §1332 D

18 Oct 1983

793 Extend *runaway* to catch runaway text (suggested by FY). §306 I

794 Reset *cur_cs* after *back_input*, not after scanning the '=' (found by FY). §1226 D

24 Oct 1983

638 ↦ **795** Change the error recovery for bad delimiters, in accordance with the changed syntax. (Found by Barry Smith.) §1183 I

9 Nov 1983

796 Optimize the code a bit more, based on empirical frequency data gathered during September and October: In §45, use the fact that the result is almost always true. In §380, delete '**while** *true* **do**' since many compilers implement that badly. Rewrite §852 to avoid calling *badness* in the most common case. §45, 380, 852 E

3 Dec 1983

797 Don't forget to call **error** after the message has been given (noticed by Gabi Kuper). §500 F

- *Version 1.0 released today incorporates all of the above.*

9 Dec 1983

- *Dinner party with 36 guests to celebrate TEX's coming of age.*

2 Feb 1984

786 ↦ **798** Reinstall \font precautions that I thought were unnecessary. I overlooked many problematic possibilities, like '{\font\a=x \global\a} \the\font' and '\font\a=x \font\b=x \let\b=\undefined \the\a', etc. (Found by Mike Urban.) The new remedy involves removal of the *font_ident* array and putting the identifiers into a frozen part of the hash table; so there's a sprinkling of

corrections in lots of modules. But basically the change is quite conservative, so it shouldn't spawn any new bugs (it says here).   §222, 267, 1257   S

9 Feb 1984

799 Remove the possibility of double interrupt, in a scenario found by Clint Cuzzo.   §1031   S

12 Feb 1984

800 Improve spacing in a formula like `$(A,<)$`.   §764   Q

13 Feb 1984

801 Avoid a bad **goto**, as diagnosed by Clint Cuzzo and George O'Connor. (Must not go directly to *switch*.)   §346   A

802 Conserve string pool space by not storing file name in two guises (suggested by DRF).   §537   E

26 Feb 1984

803 Make scaled output look cleaner by printing fewer decimals whenever this involves no loss of accuracy. (Suggested by METAFONT development.)   §103   I

2 Mar 1984

804 Maintain 17-digit accuracy, not 16; now constants like '`.00000762939453126pt`' will round correctly.   §452   R

16 Mar 1984

805 Plug a loophole that permitted recursion in *get_next*, by disallowing deletions in *check_outer_validity*.   §336   R

24 Mar 1984

806 Open the terminal before trying to wake it up, when the program starts bad. §1332   I

27 Mar 1984

807 Check that $k < 63$, to avoid the `\patterns{xxx...xxxdxxxdxxx}` anomaly found by Jacques Désarménien.   §962   R

11 Apr 1984

808 Supply code for the missing case *adjust_node* in *copy_node_list*.   §206   F

- *Yoicks, how could serious bugs like that have escaped detection?*

11 Jun 1984

627 ↦ **809** Initialize *char_base*, etc., for *null_font*. (Found by Nick Briggs.)   §552   D

810 Clear the *buffer* array initially (Briggs).   §331   R

21 Jun 1984

811 Look ahead for ligature or kern after a `\chardef`'d item (Désarménien).   §1036   C

4 Jul 1984

812 Make the quarterword constraint explicit with a new '*bad*' case (19).   §111   R

7 Jul 1984

813 Optimize *firm_up_the_line* slightly, to be consistent with the METAFONT program.   §363   E

8 Jul 1984

814 Give additional diagnostics when `\tracingmacros>1`.   §323   I

- *The changes above were incorporated in Version 1.1, released July 9, 1984.*

27 Jul 1984

815 Say '`see the transcript file`' after handling offline `\show` commands. (Suggested by METAFONT.)   §1298   I

20 Oct 1984

816 Allow '0' in response to error prompts.   §84   I

- *Those two changes led to Version 1.2.*

25 Nov 1984

817 Don't forget to check for *null* before looking at subfields of a node. (This was "dirty Pascal," with two quarterword 0's read as a halfword.)   §846 R

818 Ditto in another place!   §939 R

819 Remove the fixed-at-compile-time partition between lower and upper memory.
§116, 125, 162 E

- *This major change in memory management completes Version 1.3, which was published in preliminary looseleaf form as 'TEX: The Program'.*

20 Dec 1984

820 Keep the *node_size* field from overflowing if the lower part of memory is too large.   §125 R

- *That was another bug in existence from the beginning!*

5 Jan 1985

821 Improve the missing-format-file error (DRF).   §524 I

7 Jan 1985

822 Update the terminal right away so that the welcoming message will appear as soon as possible (DRF).   §61 I

23 Jan 1985

823 Convey more uncertainty in the help message at times of *confusion*.   §95 I

824 Improve the *history* logic in the *warning_issued* case.   §245 I

18 Feb 1985

810 ↦ **825** Stick to standard Pascal: Don't use *first* in a **for** loop. [Some procedures "threaten" it globally, according to British Standard 6192, section 6.8.3.9.] (Pointed out by CET.)   §331 P

11 Apr 1985

826 Prevent nonexistent characters from being output by unusual combinations of ligatures and hyphenation.   §915 S

15 Apr 1985

819 ↦ **827** Compute memory usage correctly in INITEX; the previous number was wrong because of a WEB text macro without parentheses (DRF).   §164 L

16 Apr 1985

828 Speed up *flush_list* by not calling *free_avail* (DRF).   §123 E

17 Apr 1985

788 ↦ **829** Introduce a special kind of kern for accent positioning; it must not disappear after a line break.   §837, 879, 1125 A

18 Apr 1985

755 ↦ **830** Prevent \lastbox and \unkern from removing discretionary replacements.
§1081, 1105 R

- *That completes Version 1.4.*

26 Apr 1985

831 Don't try TEX_area if a nonstandard file area has been specified (DRF).   §537 C

- *That was #401 in TEX78; I never learn!*

30 Apr 1985

754 ↦ **832** Eliminate the limitation on \write length; the reason for it has disappeared (Nancy Tuma).   §1370 C

8 May 1985

819 ↦ **833** Allocate two words for the head of the *active* list (CET).   §162 D

11 May 1985

834 Change *wterm* to *wterm_ln* after a bad beginning (Bill Gropp).   §1332 I

806 ↦ **835** Don't open the terminal twice (CET).   §1332 E

22 May 1985

836 Test for *batch_mode* after trying to open the transcript file, not before (DRF). §92 R

837 Be prepared for string pool overflow while reading the command line! (This
bug was first found in METAFONT, when it could occur more easily.)   §525 R

7 Aug 1985

838 Fix a bug in `\edef\foo{\iffalse\fi\the\toks0}`: TEX should stay in the
loop when expanding non-`\the`. (Found by Dan Brotsky.)   §478 A

- *The above changes were incorporated in Version 1.5.*

27 Nov 1985

764 ↦ **839** Make 'plain' a lowercase name, for consistency with the manual.   §521 C

669 ↦ **840** Wake up the terminal for `\show` commands.   §1294, 1297 I

- *The above changes were incorporated in Version 2.0, which was published as
Volume B of the Computers & Typesetting series.*

15 Dec 1986

841 Punctuate the Poirot help message more carefully.   §1283 I

28 Jan 1987

842 Make sure that *max_in_open* doesn't exceed 127 (DRF).   §14 R

680 ↦ **843** Don't allow a `\kern` to be clobbered at the end of a pre-break list when a
discretionary break is taken. (A missing '**else**' was the source of the error,
diagnosed incorrectly before.)   §881 D

844 Take account of discarded nodes when computing the background width after
a discretionary.   §840 D

- *That was the first really serious bug detected for more than 17 months! I found
it while experimenting with right-to-left extensions.*
- *Version 2.1 was released on January 26, 1987.*

5 Feb 1987

845 Remove cases in *shorthand_def* that cannot occur (found by Pat Monardo).   §1224 E

14 Apr 1987

846 Improve robustness of data structure display when debugging (Ronaldo Amá).
§174, 182 R

21 Apr 1987

847 Make the storage allocation algorithm more elegant and efficient.   §127 E

22 Apr 1987

742 ↦ **848** Calculate the empty-line condition properly when *end_line_char* is absent.   §360 A

- *The previous three changes were found while I was teaching a class based on
Volume B; they led to Version 2.2.*

28 Apr 1987

849 Avoid closing a file when TEX knows that it isn't open (JS).   §560 E

3 Aug 1987

850 Clean up unfinished output if it's necessary to *jump_out* (Klaus Gunterman). §642 S

- *That makes Version 2.3; subsequent version numbers won't be logged here.*

19 Aug 1987

851 Indent rules properly in cases like
`\hangindent=1pt$$\halign{...\cr\noalign{\hrule}}$$`.   §806 A

D. E. KNUTH

20 Aug 1987

852 Introduce *co_backup* because of cases like `\hskip 0pt plus 1fil\ifdim` (Alan Guth).   §366 S

9 Nov 1987

853 Change the calculation for number of leader boxes, so that it won't be too sensitive to roundoff error near exact multiples (M. F. Bridgland).   §626 S

17 Nov 1987

854 Replace my stupid algorithm for fixed-point multiplication of negatives (W. G. Sullivan).   §572 A

12 Dec 1987

855 Fix a typo in the initialization of hyphenation tables (Peter Breitenlohner).   §952 B
  • *That error was almost completely harmless, thus undetectable, except if some* `\lccode` *is 1 and no* `\patterns` *are given.*

23 Dec 1987

564 ↦ **856** Be more cautious when "relaxing" a previously undefined `\csname`; you might be inside a group (CET).   §372 S

20 Apr 1988

857 Make sure *temp_head* is well-formed whenever it can be printed in a "runaway" message: Consider constructions like `\outer\def\a0{}\a\a` (Silvio Levy).   §391 S

24 Apr 1988

858 Avoid conflicting use of the string pool in constructions like `\def\\#1{}\input a\\b` (Robert Messer).   §260 S

10 May 1988

859 Amend the `\patterns` data structure when *trie_min* = 0 (Breitenlohner).   §951,953 R

25 May 1988

860 Guarantee that *trie_pointer* cannot be out of range.   §923 R
861 Avoid additional bugs like #858 in constructions like `\input a\romannumeral1`, etc.   §464,465,470 S
862 Prevent similar string pool confusion that could occur during the processing of `**\input\romannumeral6`.   §525 R

19 Jun 1988

819 ↦ **863** Prevent a negative dividend from rounding upward, causing a loop (CET).   §126 S
819 ↦ **864** Adopt a smoother allocation strategy when memory is nearly gone (CET).   §126 E

20 Jun 1988

852 ↦ **865** Initialize *cur_order*, now that it's being backed up (Tsunetoshi Hayashi).   §439 D

6 Nov 1988

612 ↦ **866** Disable *fatal_error* in *prompt_input*, so that *open_log_file* can use it safely (Tim Morgan).   §71 S
836 ↦ **867** Force terminal output whenever *open_log_file* fails.   §535 S
  • *We're now up to Version 2.94; I sincerely hope all bugs have been found.*

REFERENCES

1. Piet Hein, *Grooks*, MIT Press, 1966.
2. C. Széchy, *Foundation Failures*, Concrete Publications, London, 1961.
3. A. Endres, 'An analysis of errors and their causes in system programs', *Proc. Int. Conf. Software Eng.*, 1975, pp. 327–336.
4. Victor R. Basili and Barry T. Perricone, 'Software errors and complexity: an empirical investigation', *Communications of the ACM,* **27**, 42–52 (1984).
5. L. A. Belady and M. M. Lehman, 'A model of large program development', *IBM Systems J.,* **15**, 225–252 (1976).
6. Donald E. Knuth, *TEX: The Program*, Addison-Wesley, 1986.
7. Donald E. Knuth, 'Literate programming', *The Computer Journal,* **27**, 97–111 (1984).
8. Donald E. Knuth, 'The WEB system of structured documentation', *Stanford Computer Science Report STAN-CS-980*, September 1983.
9. Patrick Winston, *Artificial Intelligence: An MIT Perspective*, MIT Press, 1979.
10. Donald E. Knuth, 'The letter S', *The Mathematical Intelligencer,* **2**, 114–122 (1980).
11. Donald E. Knuth, 'Mathematical typography', *Bulletin of the American Mathematical Society* (new series) **1**, 337–372 (1979).
12. Donald E. Knuth, *Seminumerical Algorithms*, second edition, Addison-Wesley, 1981.
13. Donald E. Knuth and Michael F. Plass, 'Breaking paragraphs into lines', *Software—Practice and Experience,* **11**, 1119–1184 (1981).
14. Donald E. Knuth, 'The concept of a meta-font', *Visible Language,* **16**, 3–27 (1982).
15. Donald E. Knuth, *The TEXbook*, Addison-Wesley, 1984.
16. Barbara Beeton (ed), *TEX and METAFONT: Errata and Changes, 09 September 1983*, distributed with *TUGboat,* **4** (1983).
17. Donald E. Knuth, *TEX, a System for Technical Text*, American Mathematical Society, 1979.
18. Donald E. Knuth, *TEX and METAFONT: New Directions in Typesetting*, Digital Press, 1979.
19. David R. Fuchs and Donald E. Knuth, 'Optimal prepaging and font caching', *ACM Transactions on Programming Languages and Systems,* **7**, 62–79 (1985).
20. Donald E. Knuth, 'A torture test for TEX', *Stanford Computer Science Report STAN-CS-1027*, November 1984.
21. Donald E. Knuth, 'A torture test for METAFONT', *Stanford Computer Science Report STAN-CS-1095*, January 1986.
22. Donald E. Knuth, *Sorting and Searching*, Addison-Wesley, 1973.
23. Brian W. Kernighan and Lorinda L. Cherry, 'A system for typesetting mathematics', *Communications of the ACM,* **18**, 151–157 (1975).
24. Guy L. Steele Jr., Donald R. Woods, Raphael A. Finkel, Mark R. Crispin, Richard M. Stallman and Geoffrey S. Goodfellow, *Hacker's Dictionary: A Guide to the World of Wizards,* Harper and Row, 1983.
25. Donald E. Knuth, *Fundamental Algorithms*, Addison-Wesley, 1968.
26. Reinhard Budde, Christiane Floyd, Reinhard Keil-Slawik and Heinz Züllighoven, (eds) *Software Development and Reality Construction*, in preparation.

Author Index

Subject Index